Catalogue of Marathi and Gujarati Printed Books in the Library of the British Museum

J. F. Blumhardt

Alpha Editions

This edition published in 2020

ISBN : 9789354032493

Design and Setting By
Alpha Editions
email - alphaedis@gmail.com

THIS Catalogue has been compiled by Mr. J. F. Blumhardt, formerly of the Bengal Uncovenanted Civil Service, in continuation of the series of Catalogues of books in North Indian vernacular languages in the British Museum Library, upon which Mr. Blumhardt has now been engaged for several years. It is believed to be the first Library Catalogue ever made of Marathi and Gujarati books. The principles on which it has been drawn up are fully explained in the Preface.

R. GARNETT,
KEEPER OF PRINTED BOOKS.

BRITISH MUSEUM,
Feb. 24, 1892.

PREFACE.

THE present Catalogue has been prepared on the same plan as that adopted in the compiler's "Catalogue of Bengali Printed Books." The same principles of orthography have been adhered to, *i.e.* pure Sanskrit words ('*tatsamas*') are spelt according to the system of transliteration generally adopted in the preparation of Oriental Catalogues for the Library of the British Museum, whilst forms of Sanskrit words, modified on Prakrit principles ('*tadbhavas*'), are expressed as they are written and pronounced, but still subject to a definite and uniform method of transliteration. Analogous principles are applied to words of Persian or Arabic origin.

It is satisfactory to observe that Marathi authors themselves have recognized the necessity of adopting a systematic method of spelling their names. Where an English title-page is given, the author has generally followed the regular Sanskrit form of spelling, except perhaps in the omission of a final unexpressed inherent 'a.'

Marathi names are composed generally of the personal name, followed by the father's name, and by a name denoting lineage, profession, place of residence or of birth, which is generally regarded in the light of an English surname. Wherever the full name has not been given by the author, it has been supplied if possible. Gujarati authors are so extremely lax and irregular in spelling their names, even in the native character, that to adopt their own forms would inevitably result in endless confusion, and it is therefore necessary to follow a systematic and fixed principle of spelling for cataloguing purposes.*

The same difficulty, though in a lesser degree, has presented itself in the case of Parsi names. A systematic orthography has been adopted, by which an attempt is made to represent, as far as possible, the original Pehlevi forms, but without unduly interfering with the established usage of the Parsis of Gujarat. Thus, for instance, both "Minuchehrjī" and "Mancherjī," "Peshotan" and "Pestanjī," are to be found amongst the names of Parsi authors in the Catalogue, in accordance with the forms adopted by the men themselves.

For the spelling of Indian geographical names, the system adopted in the second edition of Hunter's "Gazetteer" has been followed.

J. F. BLUMHARDT.

LONDON, *Feb.* 18, 1892.

---

* The following are one or two instances of such inconsistency out of many that might be given, "Ranachhodabhái Udayarám" and "Runchodebhái Ooderam;" यशोविजय, जसोविजय and जसघोजय; जरतोसतो, जरतोश्तो, जरथुशतो and जरथोशतो; शामल भट and सामळ भट्ट.

ADDENDA ET CORRIGENDA.

MARATHI CATALOGUE.

Col. 20, line 8 to 10, *Delete* and *substitute* [Another copy of the work immediately following, but containing a revised edition of the Gospels of St. Matthew and St. Mark.]

" 38, " 12 } *for* 14140. f. 25. *read* 14080. d. 18.
" 105, " 15 }

" 45, " 16, *for* Christianity *read* Chemistry.

" 70, " 31, *for* 14139 c. 16. *read* 14139. c. 29.

" 85, " 30, *for* Pt. ii. *read* Pt. i.-ix. *Insert etc.* after the date, *delete* pagination and note, and *alter* press-mark to 14139. f. 31.

" 93, " 36 } *for* Patteṉ *read* Patreṉ.
" 166, " 22, 23 }

" 95, " 29, *for* Vol. i. *etc. read* 11 vol., *alter* date to 1878-88, and *delete* note.

" 115, " 18, *for* Vol. i. *etc. read* Vol. i. pt. 1, 2., *delete* note, and *etc.* after date.

" 141, " 25, *for* Pt. i. *read* 2 pt., and *alter* dato to 1885-90.

ADDENDA ET CORRIGENDA.

GUJARATI CATALOGUE.

Col. 3, line 11 and 38, *for* Kāwusjī *read* Kāvasjī.

,, 4, ,, 40, *for* Mīnūchirjī Kāwusjī Shāpurjī *read* Mancherjī Kāvasjī.

,, 9, ,, 9, *for* Noshīrwānjī Shahriyārjī *read* Nasarvānjī Shehriyārjī.

,, 16, ,, 42, *for* Hormuzjī *read* Hormasjī.

,, 16, ,, 43, *for* Naurozjī *read* Navarojī.

,, 19, ,, 6, *for* 22 *read* 17.

,, 93, ,, 39, *for* 1885, *etc.*, *read* 1885-87, and *delete* 6.

,, 93, ,, 43, *insert* Vol. i-ii., *alter* date to 1888-89, and *delete* note.

,, 102, ,, 10, *insert* 3 vol., *alter* date to 1885-87, and *delete* note.

,, 103, ,, 5, *insert* Vol. i.-ii., and *alter* date to 1885-87.

,, 133, ,, 34, *insert* Vol. i. before the pagination.

TABLE OF TRANSLITERATION.

NAGARI AND GUJARATI ALPHABETS.

Nag.	Guj.		Nag.	Guj.		Nag.	Guj.		Nag.	Guj.	
अ	અ	a	क	ક	ka	ठ	ઠ	ṭha	ब	બ	ba
आ	આ	ā	ख	ખ	kha	ड	ડ	ḍa	भ	ભ	bha
इ	ઈ	i	ग	ગ	ga	ढ	ઢ	ḍha	म	મ	ma
ई		ī	घ	ઘ	gha	ण	ણ	ṇa	य	ય	ya
उ	ઊ	u	ङ	*	ṅa	त	ત	ta	र	ર	ra
ऊ		ū	च	ચ	cha	थ	થ	tha	ल	લ	la
ऋ		ṛi	छ	છ	chha	द	દ	da	व	વ	va
ए	એ	e	ज	જ	ja	ध	ધ	dha	श	શ	ṣa
ऐ	ઐ	ai	झ झ	ઝ	jha	न	ન	na	ष		sha
ओ	ઓ	o	ञ	*	ña	प	પ	pa	स	સ	sa
औ	ઔ	au	ट	ટ	ṭa	फ	ફ	pha	ह	હ	ha
									ळ	ળ	ḷa

* Represented by the nasal symbol °.

The Sanskrit signs ं, ः and ँ represented by ṃ, ḥ and ṉ, respectively.

PERSIAN, ARABIC AND HINDUSTANI ALPHABETS.

ب	b	د	d	ص	ṡ	گ	g
پ	p	ڈ [1]	ḍ	ض	ẓ	ل	l
ت	t	ذ	z̲	ط	ṫ	م	m
ٹ [1]	ṭ	ر	r	ظ	z̤	ن	n
ث	s̤	ڑ [1]	ṛ	ع	‘	و	w, (v[2])
ج	j	ز	z	غ	g̲h̲	ه	h
چ	ch	ژ	zh	ف	f	ي	y
ح	ḣ	س	s	ق	k̇		
خ	k̲h̲	ش	sh	ک	k		

[1] Peculiar to Hindustani only. [2] When corresponding to the Sanskrit व.

Hamzah in the middle of a word ’.

CATALOGUE

OF

MARATHI BOOKS.

AARON SAMSON. *See* Āshṭamkar (A. S.)

ABHIMANYU. अथ अभिमन्यु विवाह. [Abhimanyu vivāha. A poem on the marriage of Abhimanyu to Uttara, daughter of Rājā Virāṭa.] pp. 51, *lith.* मुंबई १७७० [*Bombay*, 1848.] 12°. **14140. a. 1(3.)**

ADBHUTA CHAMATKĀRA. अद्भुत चमत्कार संग्रह. [Adbhuta chamatkāra saṅgraha. A collection of amusing tales and anecdotes.] Pt. I. pp. 80, *lith.* मुंबई १८७८ [*Bombay*, 1878.] 12°. **14139. f. 13.**

ADDRESS. ज्या बायकांस लेंकरें आहेत त्यांस सुबोध. Address to mothers. [Jyā bāykāṉs leṉkreṉ ahet tyāṉs subodha. A Christian tract.] pp. 25. [*Bombay*,] 1841. 12°.

No. 34 of the American Mission Series.

14137. a. 2(3.)

ĀDINĀTHA. अथ श्री नाथलीलामृत प्रारंभः [Nāthalīlāmṛita. A legendary poem in 28 chapters on the lives and miracles of famous Nātha saints.] 28 pt. मुंबई १८८५ [*Bombay*, 1885.] *obl.* 8°.

14140. c. 36.

ÆSOP. *Begin:* प्रपंच्या माजि जें शास्त्र लोपस्यां मनुष्य सृष्टीचें श्रेष्ठपण [Bālabodhamuktāvalī. A translation of Æsop's Fables into Marathi, interspersed with Sanskrit verse, by Sakhkhaṇa Paṇḍita.] ff. 196. तंजापुरी १७२८ [*Tanjore*, 1806.] 8°. **14139. g. 7.**

—— Murat,hee translation of Æsop's Fables. [By Sadāṣiva Kāṣīnātha Chhatre.] इसपनीति कथा. pp. xiv. 357. *lith.* *Bombay*, 1837. 8°. **14139. g. 3.**

—— [Another edition.] pp. x. 355. पुणे १८४१ [*Poona*, 1841.] 8°. **14139. g. 9.**

ÆSOP. Æsop's Fables translated into Marathi by . . . Sadáshiva Káshináth Chhatre; corrected, revised, and enlarged by Major T. Candy. Third edition. pp. vi. viii. 310. *Bombay*, 1856. 8°.

14139. g. 4.

—— Æsop's Fables, selected from the third edition of the Maráthí translation of Sadáshiva Káshináth Chhatre. Revised and enlarged by Major T. Candy. Second edition. pp. ix. 95. *Bombay*, 1861. 12°. **14139. f. 7.**

—— Æsop's Fables, originally translated into Maráṭhí by Sadáshiva Káshináth Chhatre. Revised from the first edition [with illustrations.] (इसापकृत कल्पित गोष्टी.) pp. ix. 218. iii. *Bombay*, 1877. 8°.

14139. g. 13.

AFRICAN GIRL. Story of an African girl, cast out by her parents. काफर देशाची मुलगी इची गोष्ट. [Kāphar deṣāchī mulgī.] pp. 7. [*Bombay*? 1845?] 24°. **14137. a. 1(2.)**

AHALYĀBĀĪ TARKHADKAR. *See* Dādobā Pāṇḍuraṅga Tarkhadkar. A Hindu gentleman's reflections respecting the works of Swedenborg . . . Translated . . . from the original in English by Ahlyábái Tarkhadkar. [1881.] 12°. **14137. a. 10.**

AITIHĀSIKA GOSHṬĪ. ऐतिहासिक गोष्टी [Aitihāsika goshṭī. Stories from Indian history, and information on various useful subjects.] Pt. 1 and 3. ठाणे नासिक, १८७७-८० [*Thana, Nasik*, 1877–80.] 12°. 8°

Wanting pt. 2.

14139. f. 11(2) and e. 12.

AITIHĀSIKA NĀṬAKAMĀLĀ. ऐतिहासिक नाटकमाला. [Aitihāsika nāṭakamālā. A series of historical dramas.] Pt. I. अलीबाग [*Alibagh*, 1880.] 8°
14140. f. 11(1).

ĀKHANḌĀŚRAMA. *See* ŚAṄKARA ĀCHĀRYA. अथ श्री लघुवाक्यवृत्ति प्रारंभ: [Laghuvākyavṛitti. With a Marathi commentary by Ā.] [1883.] 12°.
14048. b. 15.

ALANDĪ. The pilgrimage to Alandi. अळंदीची यात्रा. [Aḷandīchī yātrā. A description of the festival held there, and dialogues between a Christian and a Hindu on idolatry.] Seventh edition. pp. 31. *Bombay*, 1877. 16°.
Bombay Tract and Book Society. Marathi 16*mo series.*
14139. d. 5(2.)

ALEXANDER, *the Great, King of Macedon. Life.* *See* VINĀYAKA KONḌADEVA OK. The life of Alexander the Great.

AMĀNAT 'ALĪ. *See* VĀSUDEVA NĀRĀYAṆA ḌONGRE. संगीत इंद्रसभा नाटक. [Saṅgīta Indrasabhā nāṭaka. A dramatised version of A. 'A.'s Indrasabhā.] [1883.] 8°. **14140. f. 11(2.)**

AMARU. श्रीमच्छंकराचार्यविरचित अमरुशतक. [Amaruśataka. A Sanskrit poem, wrongly attributed to Śaṅkara Āchārya, with a translation in Marathi by Gaṇeśa Lele Tryambakakar.] pp. viii. 78. पुणें १८८१ [*Poona*, 1881.] 16°. **14076. a. 12(3.)**

AMĪR CHAND. दामाजीची रसद. [Dāmājīchī rasad. A tale in verse, taken from the Hindustani of A. Ch.] ff. 19, *lith.* मुंबई [*Bombay*, 1856?] *obl.* 12°.
14140. a. 6(1.)

AMṚITARĀVA ĀBĀJĪ KARṆĪK. *See* PURĀṆAS.—Mārkaṇḍeyapurāṇa.—*Devīmāhātmya.* सप्तशति आर्या [Saptaśati āryā. The Devīmāhātmya, translated into verse by A. Ā. K.] [1880.] 8°.
14137. d. 13.

AMṚITARĀYA. अमृतराय कृत शुकचरित्र [Śukacharitra. A poem on the story of the saint Śuka, and the nymph Rambhā.] pp. 40, *lith.* मुंबई १९८१ [*Bombay*, 1860.] 12°. **14140. a. 4(2.)**

—— अमृतरायकृत शुक-चरित्र [Another edition. Followed by miscellaneous poems by the same author.] *See* PERIODICAL PUBLICATIONS. — *Poona.* काव्येतिहास-संग्रह [Kāvyetihāsa saṅgraha.] Vol. VI. Nos. 2–5. [1878, *etc.*] 8°. **14072. d. 37.**

ĀNANDARĀVA CHĀMPĀJĪ. A dictionary, English, Marathi, Gujarati and Sanskrit ... by Ánandráv Chápájí. Pt. 1, 2. [A.-Beet.] [*Bombay*, 1885.] 4°.
No more published. **760. k. 9.**

ĀNANDARĀVA RĀMACHANDRA MĀNKAR. A manual of English sentences with Marathi equivalents. Pt. I. *Bombay*, 1885. 12°.
14140. g. 38.

ĀNANDATANAYA. मार्कंडेय आख्यान [Mārkaṇḍeya ākhyāna. A poem on the life of the sage Mārkaṇḍeya.] ff. 14, *lith.* मुंबई १९१८ [*Bombay*, 1856.] *obl.* 12°. **14140. a. 6(6.)**

—— आनन्दतनयकृत ताटकावध (कंदुकाख्यान, बालचरित, पुतनावध) [Tāṭakāvadha, Kandukākhyāna, Bālacharita and Putanāvadha. Four poems on mythological subjects.] *See* PERIODICAL PUBLICATIONS.—*Poona.* काव्येतिहास-संग्रह [Kāvyetihāsa saṅgraha.] Vol. II.–VI. [1878, *etc.*] 8°. **14072. d. 37.**

ANANTA, *Kavi.* श्री अहीमही आख्यान श्लोक प्रारंभ: [Ahīmahī ākhyāna. A mythological tale in verse.] pp. 21, *lith.* मुंबई १९८५ [*Bombay*, 1863.] 12°. **14140. a. 4(8.)**

—— [Another edition.] *See* PERIODICAL PUBLICATIONS. — *Poona.* काव्येतिहास-संग्रह [Kāvyetihāsa saṅgraha.] Vol. IX. No. 7. [1878, *etc.*] 8°.
14072. d. 37.

—— अनंतकविकृत गोपीगीत (सीतास्वयंवर) [Gopīgīta, Sītāsvayaṃvara and other poems.] *See* PERIODICAL PUBLICATIONS.—*Poona.* काव्येतिहास-संग्रह [Kāvyetihāsa saṅgraha.] Vol. VIII. Nos. 8 and 9. [1878, *etc.*] 8°. **14072. d. 37.**

ANANTA BHAṬṬA, *the Poet.* अनंतभट्टकृत चंपूभारत [Champūbhārata. Sanskrit text, with paraphrases in Sanskrit and Marathi.] *See* PERIODICAL PUBLICATIONS.—*Dharwar.* काव्यनाटकादर्श. [Kāvyanāṭakādarṣa.] Pt. 1. [1882, *etc.*] 8°. **14076. d. 35.**

ANANTACHATURDAŚĪPŪJĀ. अथानंतचतुर्दशी व्रतांगमकथानंतपूजाप्रा ० [Description of a ceremony called Anantachaturdaśīpūjā, in Sanskrit, with the Anantavratakathā, or text of the legend taken from one of the Purāṇas, with a Marathi commentary.] ff. 20, *lith.* [*Bombay*, 1860?] *obl.* 4°. **14016. d. 10.**

ANANTADĪKSHITA JOSĪ CHIPḶŪṆKAR. Sudarshana charitra. A drama [in seven acts, on the story of Sudarṣana, king of Ayodhya] based on the Dewi Bhagawata, and other miscellaneous poems, by Ananta Dixita Joshi Chiplunkara. (सुदर्शनचरित्र नाटक) pp. iv. 240. iii. *Bombay*, 1881. 12°. **14140. a. 27.**

ANANTA MĀDHAVARĀVA MORE. आपल्या निकृष्टावस्थेचीं कारणें व त्यांची सुधारणा. [Āplyā nikṛishṭāvasthechīṇ kāraṇeṇ. A pamphlet on the amelioration of the social condition of Hindu society.] pp. 11. मुंबई १८७७ [*Bombay*, 1877.] 12°. **14139. c. 17(1.)**

ANANTA NĀRĀYAṆA PAṆḌITA. बालविवाह दुःखदर्शन प्रहसन. [Bālavivāha duḥkhadarṣana prahasana. A farce showing the evil results of early marriages.] pp. 38. पुणें १८८५ [*Poona*, 1885.] 16°. **14140. e. 4(2.)**

ANANTA PHANDĪ. अनंतफंदीकृत लावण्या [Lāvaṇī songs.] *See* RĀVAJĪ ṢRĪDHARA GONDHAḶEKAR. रामजोशि ... सुरस लावण्या [Surasa lāvaṇyā.] pp. 129–140. [1878.] 8°. **14140. c. 25.**

ANANTA RĀMAKṚISHṆA KASAḶĪKAR. *See* PURĀṆAS.—*Ṣivapurāṇa.* शिवतत्त्वप्रकाश [Ṣivatattvaprakāṣa. Translated by A. R. K.] [1880.] 8°. **14016. d. 39.**

ANANTA ṢĀSTRĪ TAḶEKAR. Sanskrit-Marāthī Vocabulary. संस्कृतप्राकृतशब्दकोश. [Saṃskṛita-prākṛitaṣabdakoṣa. Founded upon the Amarakoṣa, compiled by A. Ṣ. T. under the direction of T. Candy, and revised by Raghunātha Ṣāstrī Taḷekar.] pp. ii. 15, 480, *lith.* पुणें १८५३ [*Poona*, 1853.] 8°. **14090. d. 5.**

ANANTASUTA. अथ चेंडूफळी प्रारभः [Chenḍūphaḷī. An account in verse of Kṛishṇa's sports with his companions with bat and ball.] ff. 10, *lith.* पुणें [*Poona*, 1875 ?] 16°. **14140. a. 9(9.)**

ANANTAVRATAKATHĀ. *See* ANANTACHATURDAṢĪPŪJĀ. अथानंतचतुर्दशी व्रतांगसकथानंतपूजाप्रा ° [Description of a ceremony called Anantachaturdaṣīpūjā, together with the Anantavratakathā, with a Marathi commentary.] [1860 ?] *obl.* 4°. **14016. d. 10.**

AṄKAGAṆITA. Ankgunit, ... अंकगणित प्रथमभाग. [The elements of simple arithmetic.] Pt. I. pp. 78. मुंबई १८६५ [*Bombay*, 1865.] 8°. **14139. b. 7(1.)**

AṄKALIPI. अंकलीपि. [Aṅkalīpi, or Numerical exercises, and tables of English and Indian weights and measures. Tenth edition.] pp. 24. मुंबई १८६८ [*Bombay*, 1868.] 12°. **14140 g. 2(4.)**

—— Ankalipi, or Ujalni. Compiled for the Educational Department, Hyderabad Assigned Districts. pp. 22, *lith.* *Poona*, 1877. 16°.
In the Modi character. **14140. g. 9(4.)**

AṆṆĀ BHIMVRĀVA. *See* INDIA.—*Civil Service.* Codes of the Financial Department. The ... Civil Pension Code ... translated ... by Anna Bhivrao. 1877. 8°. **14137. g. 10.**

AṆṆĀ MOREṢVARA KUṆṬE. स्त्रीरोगविज्ञान [Strīrogavijñāna. A work on the diseases of women and their treatment. Compiled from English and Sanskrit medical works.] pp. ii. xvi. 98. मुंबई १८८१ [*Bombay*, 1881.] 8°. **14137. h. 12.**

AṆṆĀPĀ ĀPĀ VĀḌAKAR. श्रीपालचरित्र. [Ṣrīpālacharitra, or the story of king Ṣrīpāla. A Jain legend, translated into Marathi verse, from the original Māgadhī, by A. Ā. V., assisted by Nāgeṣa Raghunātha Dīkshita.] pp. ii. 71. मुंबई १८८३ [*Bombay*, 1883.] 8°. **14137. d. 6.**

ANUBHAVALAHARĪ. अनुभवलहरी. [Anubhavalaharī. Verses on Vedanta philosophy.] ff. 20, *lith.* [*Bombay?* 1857 ?] *obl.* 12°. **14140. a. 6(7.)**

ĀRATYĀ. आरत्यांची वही [Āratyā. Songs in praise of different deities, sung when worshipping them.] Pt. I. and II. *Lith.* मुंबई १७७० [*Bombay*, 1848.] 32°. **14137. c. 3(1.)**

—— आरत्या भाग २ प्रारंभ (भाग ३) [Another edition.] Pt. II. and III. *Lith.* मुंबई १७८५ [*Bombay*, 1863.] 32°.
Wanting Pt. I. **14137. c. 4.**

—— [Another collection of āratīs, differing from the preceding.] Pt. I. and II. *Lith.* मुंबई १७८६ [*Bombay*, 1864.] 12°. **14140. a. 11(2.)**

—— [Another edition of the preceding.] 3 pt. *Lith.* मुंबई १७९९ [*Bombay*, 1877.] 12°. **14140. a. 12(7.)**

—— अथ सुरस आरत्या प्रारंभ [A selection of āratīs.] pp. 13, *lith.* पुणें १८७८ [*Poona*, 1878.] 12°. **14140. a. 12(11.)**

ARJUNA. **अर्जुन गर्वपरिहार** [Arjuna garvaparihāra. A poem on an episode in the history of Arjuna.] ff. 8, *lith.* **मुंबई १७७८** [*Bombay*, 1856.] *obl.* 12°.
14140. a. 6(2.)

ĀSHTAMKAR (AARON SAMSON). **काळकर्मणूक अथवा वाळखेळ** [Kāḷakarmaṇūka.] (The book of amusement [containing riddles, conundrums, and amusing anecdotes.] Part II. Prepared and published by Aaron Samson.) pp. 72. *Bombay*, 1879. 16°.
Wanting Part I. **14139. a. 32(1.)**

ĀSVALĀYANA. **सार्थ आश्वलायनगृह्यसूत्र** [Gṛihyasūtra of Ā., with a translation, glossary and preface in Marathi by Lokahitavādī, i.e. Gopālarāva Hari.] pp. vii. 56, 151, 17, 3. **मुंबई १८८०** [*Bombay*, 1880.] 8°.
14010. e. 31.

AṢVINĪ. **अश्विनी आख्यान** [Aṣvinī ākhyāna. A poem on the story of Aṣvinī.] ff. 30, *lith.* **मुंबई १७७९** [*Bombay*, 1857.] *obl.* 12°. **14140. a. 6(8.)**

BĀBĀJĪ RAGHUNĀTHA MARĀṬHE. Life of Babajee. **बाबाजीची बखर.** [Bābājīchī bakhar. An account of his conversion to Christianity.] pp. 76. *Bombay*, 1844. 12°. **14137. a. 2(1.)**

BĀBĀJĪ VIṬHṬHALA KUḶAKARṆĪ MĀLVAṆKAR. **तारकादर्श** [Tārakādarṣa. Astronomical charts with directions for their use.] pp. 28. **रत्नागिरी १८८६** [*Ratnagiri*, 1886.] 4°. **14139. b. 17.**

BĀBĀ PADMANJĪ. *See* BIBLE.—*New Testament.* Annotated New Testament in Marathi ... Edited by B. P. [1877.] 8°. **3068. dd. 20.**

—— Examination of the claims of Deism. **निःशास्त्रवाद परीक्षा.** [Niḥṣāstravāda parīkshā.] pp. xxiii. 164. *Bombay*, 1858. 12°.
14137. a. 5(1.)

BACON (FRANCIS), *Viscount St. Albans. Life. See* GOVINDA NĀRĀYAṆA KĀṆE. An account of the life and writings of Lord Bacon.

BAITĀL PACHĪSĪ. **वेताळपंचविशी** *etc.* [Baitāl pachīsī, or Twenty-five tales of a demon, translated from the Hindi by Sadāṣiva Kāṣinātha Chhatre.] pp. 94, *lith.* **मुंबई १८६२** [*Bombay*, 1862.] 8°.
14140. c. 6.

—— [Another edition.] pp. 159. **मुंबई १८६२** [*Bombay*, 1862.] 12°. **14139. f. 10.**

BAITĀL PACHĪSĪ. [Another edition.] pp. 90, *lith.* **पुणे १८७५** [*Poona*, 1875.] 8°. **14139. g. 6(3.)**

—— [Another edition.] pp. 190, *lith.* **पुणे १८८०** [*Poona*, 1880.] 12°. **14139. f. 29.**

BĀJĀBĀ BĀḶĀJĪ NENE. *See* COWPER (W.), *the Poet.* The William Cowper's diverting history of John Gilpin, translated into Marathee arya metre by Bajaba Balajee Nene. 1867. 8°. **14140. b. 5.**

—— **हिडिंबवध.** [Hiḍimbavadha. A poem on the destruction of the demon Hiḍimba by Bhīma.] pp. 14. iii., *lith.* **पुणे १८७५** [*Poona*, 1875.] 12°.
14140. a. 10(11.)

BĀJĀBĀ RĀMACHANDRA PRADHĀNA. *See* MĀDHAVARĀVA.

BAKER (F. P.) **लिपिधारा** Lipidhárá. [A Marathi and Modi writing book], compiled expressly for the use of accepted candidates for the Bombay Civil Service. pp. 57, *lith.* *London* [1868 ?] 8°.
14140. h. 13(1.)

BAKHTYĀR. **बखत्यारनामा अथवा बखत्यार नामक राजपुत्र आणि दाहा वजीर यांचा कथा** [Bakhtyār-nāma. A Persian romance, translated by Nārāyaṇa Keṣava from the English of Sir William Ouseley.] pp. 127, iv., *lith.* **मुंबई १८५५** [*Bombay*, 1855.] 8°.
14139. g. 6(1.)

BĀḶA GAṄGĀDHARA ṢĀSTRĪ JĀMBHEKAR. *See* ELPHINSTONE (*Hon.* M.) Introduction to the history of India, abridged ... by Ball Gungadher Shastree. 1852. 8°. **14139. e. 4.**

—— *See* MURRAY (L.) Abridgment of Murray's English grammar, with a Maráthí translation, ...Revised by Ball Gungadher Shastree. 1837. 8°.
14140. h. 2.

—— *See* VINĀYAKA ṢĀSTRĪ DIVEKAR and GOVINDA VIṬHṬHALA MAHĀJAN **शब्दसिद्धिनिबंध** [Ṣabdasiddhinibandha. Compiled with the assistance of B. G. Ṣ. J.] [1859.] 12°. **14140. g. 8(1.)**

—— History of British India; abridged from English works, by ... Ball Gungadhur Shastree Jambhekur; revised and prepared for the press by ... T. Candy. **हिंदुस्थानांतील इंग्लिशांच्या राज्याचा इतिहास.** Second edition. pp. xxvi. 274. **मुंबई १८५४** [*Bombay*, 1854.] 8°. **14139. e. 5.**

BĀLA GANGĀDHARA ŚĀSTRĪ JĀMBHEKAR. Library of useful knowledge. Mathematical geography, to which is added an essay on the system of Bhaskeracharya. Translated into the Muratheo language by Ball Gungadhur Shastree. (भूगोलशास्त्र गणितभाग.) pp. 121. मुंबई [*Bombay*,] 1836. 8°. **14139. b. 3.**

BĀḶĀJĪ BHIKĀJĪ PINGE. मराठी पहिलें मोडी पुस्तक. [Marāṭhī pahileṇ Moḍī pustaka.] First Marathi Modi reader for schools in the Central Provinces. pp. 40, *lith.* *Bombay*, 1877. 12°. **14140. g. 31(1.)**

—— Modi Second Book ... मोडी दुसरें पुस्तक. [Moḍī dusreṇ pustaka.] pp. 102, *lith.* *Nágpúr*, 1877. 12°. **14140. g. 31(2.)**

—— Second edition. pp. 102, *lith.* *Nágpúr*, 1880. 12°. **14140. g. 25(3.)**

BĀḶĀJĪ PRABHĀKARA MODAK. Elementary treatise on Physics experimental and applied. (सृष्टिशास्त्र) [Srishṭiśāstra.] Vol. I. Second edition, revised and enlarged with numerous additions and illustrations. pp. xiv. xxi. 517, 100. *Bombay*, 1881. 12°. **14139. a. 38.**

BĀḶĀJĪ SUNDARAJĪ. *See* MAHĀBHĀRATA.—*Bhagavadgītā*. श्री गीता भावचंद्रिका. [Bhāvachandrikā. A prose translation of the Bhagavadgītā, by B. S.] [1851.] 12°. **14137. d. 4.**

BĀḶĀJĪ VIŚVANĀTHA, *Peshwa*. [*Administration*.] *See* RĀVAJĪ HARI ĀṬHVALE. बाळाजी विश्वनाथ पेशवे यांचें नाटक [Bāḷājī Viśvanātha nāṭaka. An historical drama on the administration of B.V.] [1882.] 8°. **14140. f. 12.**

BĀḶAKṚISHṆA ĀTMĀRĀMA GUPTE. Agricultural Chemistry and Geology compiled from standard English works on the subject by Bálkrishṇa Átmárám Gupté. (कृषिकर्मांतर्गत रसायनशास्त्र व भूगर्भशास्त्र) [Krishikarmāntargata rasāyanaśāstra.] pp. iv. iii. xi. 269. *Bombay*, 1879. 12°. **14139. a. 44.**

BĀḶAKṚISHṆA BĀBĀJĪ KARKARE and **GOPĀLA BĀḶAKṚISHṆA VAIDYA.** त्र्यंबकवर्णन [Tryambaka varṇana. A description of the sacred city of Tryambaka, and its temples.] pp. ii. 52. मुंबई १८८५ [*Bombay*, 1885.] 12°. **14139. d. 23.**

BĀḶAKṚISHṆA DINKAR VAIDYA KALYĀNKAR. रोगी व वैद्य. [Rogī va vaidya, or The doctor and his patient. A tale intended to illustrate the evil effects of using quack medicines. Revised, with a preface by Gaṇeṣa Krishṇa Garde.] pp. ii. iv. vi. 117. पुणें [*Poona*, 1880.] 12°. **14137. ff. 4.**

BĀḶAKṚISHṆA LAKSHMAṆA BĀPAṬ. *See* NĀRĀYAṆA HARI. मोडी बालबोध तिसरें बुकांतील शब्दार्थ [Moḍī Bālabodha tisreṇ bukāntīl śabdārtha. A glossary to the "Berar Third Book" of B. L. B.] [1880.] 12°. **14140. g. 29(3.)**

—— Berar Third Book. Prepared for the Educational Department, Hydrabad Assigned Districts, by Balkrishna Luxman Bapat. (वऱ्हाडांतील शाळांच्या उपयोगाकरितां तिसरें पुस्तक.) Third edition. pp. ii. 120. *Poona*, 1877. 12°. **14140. g. 27(3.)**

BĀḶAKṚISHṆA LELE. सुलोचनासतीनाटक. [Sulochanāsatī nāṭaka. A drama in prose and verse.] pp. 76, *lith.* पुणें १८७० [*Poona*, 1870.] 8°. **14140. f. 4.**

BĀḶAKṚISHṆA MALHĀR BĪDKAR. Ratnakośa, or a complete vocabulary of all words occurring in the Marathi series of the Educational Department from Books I.–IV. Compiled by Balkrishna Malhár Bídkar. (रत्नकोश) pp. iv. iv. 366. *Bombay*, 1869. 12°. **14140. g. 17.**

BĀḶAKṚISHṆA MALHĀR HAṂSA. प्रख्यात महाराष्ट्रपंडित ... व कवि वामनपंडित ह्याचें चरित्र, ग्रंथ व काव्यसंबंधी गुणदोष *etc.* [A biography of the poet Vāmana, with a critical examination of his writings, and a comparison between them and the works of Moro panta.] pp. ii. 126. मुंबई १८८४ [*Bombay*, 1884.] 12°. **14139. d. 24.**

BĀḶĀMANGEṢA. *See* BELL (A.) *of Edinburgh*. प्रश्न सोडविण्याचें साधन. [Praśna soḍaviṇyācheṇ sādhana. Bell's "Key to the Elements of plane geometry," translated by B.] [1862.] 12°. **14139. a. 20.**

BĀḶA ŚĀSTRĪ. Bál Shástrí's Outlines of grammar. बालव्याकरण [Bālavyākaraṇa. Twelfth edition.] pp. 24. मुंबई १८६० [*Bombay*, 1860.] 12°. **14140. g. 2(2.)**

BĀḶA ŚĀSTRĪ GHAGVE. A dictionary of the Marathi language, compiled by Bal Shastree Ghugwe, Gungadhur Shastree Phurke, Sukha Ram Joshee, Dajee Shastree Sheokl, and Pursheo Ram Punt Gorbole. (महाराष्ट्र भाषेचा कोश) 2 vol. *lith.* *Bombay*, 1829. 4°.

A note is attached to the fly-leaf stating that this Dictionary was compiled by Captain J. T. Molesworth with the assistance of Lieuts. G. and T. Candy, and the Pandits named in the title-page. **14140. i. 1.**

BAḶAVANTA HARI JOSĪ BORGĀNVAKAR. इतिहासरूप दर्शिका. [Itihāsarūpa darṣikā. A brief chronological account of the principal events in the history of India, England, Persia, Greece, Rome, and Arabia, up to the year 1857.] pp. ii. 78. पुणे १८६७ [*Poona*, 1867.] 12°. **14140. g. 2 (3.)**

BAḶAVANTA KHANḌERĀVA PESHVE. मल्हारी चरित्र अथवा जेजुरी इतिहास. [Malhārī charitra. The story of Malhārī, i.e. Khaṇḍerāva, or Khaṇḍobā, the god of Jejurī, founded chiefly on the Mallāri-māhātmya, a portion of the Adhyātmarāmāyaṇa, a section of the Brahmāṇḍapurāṇa.] pp. ii. 119. पुणे १९९९ [*Poona*, 1877.] 12°. **14139. f. 11 (3.)**

BAḶAVANTA KHAṆḌOJĪ PĀRAKH. ज्ञानेश्वर महाराजांचें चरित्र [Jñānesvara Mahārājāñchen charitra. A life of the poet Jñānadeva.] pp. iv. 220. मुंबई १८८६ [*Bombay*, 1886.] 12°. **14139. d. 25.**

BAḶAVANTA RĀMACHANDRA SAHASRABUDDHE. *See* Blanford (H. T.) The rudiments of physical geography ... Translated into Marathi by Rao Saheb Balvant Ramchandra Sahasrabuddhe. 1881. 12°. **14139. a. 40.**

BAḶAVANTARĀVA KAMALĀKAR. *See* Kālidāsa, *pseud.* श्री पुष्पबाणविलास [Pushpavāṇavilāsa. With a translation into verse by B. K.] [1881.] 16°. **14072. b.**

BAḶAVANTA VĀSUDEVA JOGḶEKAR. सातारा जिल्ह्याचें वर्णन. [Sātārā jilhyāchen varṇana. A description of the district of Satara.] pp. 46. मुंबई १८७७ [*Bombay*, 1877.] 12°. **14139. d. 15 (2.)**

BĀḶA YAJÑEṢVARA GURJAR. हिंगलाजदेवीचें स्तोत्र. [Hiṅgalāja devīchen stotra. A hymn of praise to the goddess Hiṅgalāja.] pp. 10. मुंबई १८७४ [*Bombay*, 1874.] 12°. **14140. a. 10 (6.)**

BAL GUNGADHUR SHASTREE JAMBHEKUR. *See* Bāḷa Gaṅgādhara Ṣāstrī Jāmbhekar.

BALKRISHNA LUXMAN BAPAT. *See* Bāḷakrishṇa Lakshmaṇa Bāpaṭ.

BALLĀḶA DĀDO. अंगदशिष्टाईचे श्लोक [Aṅgadaṣishṭāī. A poem on the embassy of the monkey Aṅgada from Rāma to Rāvaṇa for the giving up of Sītā. Fifth edition.] pp. 22, *lith.* मुंबई १९८२ [*Bombay*, 1860.] 12°. **14140. a. 1 (9.)**

—— [Another edition. With a sequel, entitled Pt. 2.] pp. 13, 23, *lith.* मुंबई १९८४ [*Bombay*, 1862.] 12°. **14140. a. 5 (2.)**

BALLĀḶA DĀDO. [Another edition.] pp. 13, *lith.* पुणे १९९९ [*Poona*, 1877.] 12°. **14140. a. 13(6.)**

BALL GUNGADHER SHASTREE. *See* Bāḷa Gaṅgādhara Ṣāstrī Jāmbhekar.

BAL SHASTREE GHUGWE. *See* Bāḷa Ṣāstrī Ghagve.

BÁL SHÁSTRI. *See* Bāḷa Ṣāstrī.

BĀṆA. Párvatípariṇaya nátaka, translated [with the Sanskrit text] from Sanskṛit into Maráṭhí by Parashurám Bullál Godbole, Poona, 1869. Revised by Vishṇu Parashurám Shástrí Paṇḍit ..... Dakshiṇá Prize book Series. No. 5. (पार्वतीपरिणय नाटक) pp. 3, 155, 2. *Sansk.* and *Mar.* *Bombay*, 1872. 12°. **14079. a. 7.**

—— संस्कृत कवि बाणभट्ट. [Saṃskṛitakavi Bāṇa Bhaṭṭa. An essay on the Sanskrit poet Bāṇa, his life and writings, with quotations from his works.] pp. 32. पुणे १८७७ [*Poona*, 1877.] 8°. **14137. d. 5(2.)**

BĀPŪ GOKHALE. [*Life.*] *See* Ṣaṅkara Tukārāma Ṣāligrām. बापू गोखले यांचें चरित्र [Bāpū Gokhale yāñchen charitra.]

BĀPŪ PURUSHOTTAMA JOṢĪ ṬOṆKEKAR. Geography of India in Maráthí, by Bápu Purushotam Joshi Tonkekar. (हिंदुस्थानाचा भूगोल.) [Hindusthānāchā bhūgola.] pp. 80. *Bombay*, 1867. 12°. **14139. d. 18.**

BĀPŪ ṢĀSTRĪ MOGHE. *See* Kāṣīnātha Upādhyāya. श्री धर्मसिंधु. [Dharmasindhusāra. With a translation by B. Ṣ. M.] [1874.] 8°. **14033. b. 28.**

—— *See* Manu. श्री मनुस्मृति. [Manusmṛiti. With a translation by B. Ṣ. M.] [1877.] 8°. **14038. d. 19.**

—— वैद्यकसंग्रह [Vaidyakasaṃgraha. A treatise on medicine.] pp. xx. 403. मुंबई १८७५ [*Bombay*, 1875.] 8°. **14137. h. 8.**

BARODA, *Native State of.* *See* Paraṣurāma Ghanaṣyāma Rege. बेलिफ्स गायड [Bailiff's guide for the use of officials of the Civil Courts of the Baroda State.] [1877.] 12°. **14137. f. 2.**

BARODA, *Native State of.* बडोदेसरकारची तैनाती फौज. [Badode Sarkārchī tainātī phauj. A pamphlet condemning the action of the Government of India with regard to the Gaikwar of Baroda's Contingent of 3000 horse.] pp. ii. xiv. 53. पुणें १८८१ [*Poona*, 1881.] 8°. **14139. c. 18 (3.)**

BASVALIṄGA. गजगौरीव्रत [Gajagaurīvrata, and other poems.] *See* PERIODICAL PUBLICATIONS.—*Poona.* काव्येतिहास संग्रह [Kāvyetihāsa saṅgraha.] Vol. VIII. Nos. 5–12. [1878, *etc.*] 8°. **14072. d. 37.**

BELL (ANDREW), *of Edinburgh.* *See* EUCLID. Elements of plane geometry [according to Euclid, Bks. I.–VI., by A. B.], translated into Maráthí, *etc.* 1867. 8°. **14139. a. 16.**

—— प्रश्न सोडविण्याचें साधन [Prasna sodaviṇyāchen sādhana. Bell's "Key to the Elements of plane geometry," containing solutions of all the exercises in that work on Bks. I. to IV. and Bk. VI. of Euclid. Translated by Bāḷāmaṅgeṣa.] मुंबई १८६२ [*Bombay*, 1862.] 12°. **14139. a. 20.**

BELLAIRS (H. S. K.) European fairy stories, translated from English into Marathi. (युरोपांतील वनदेवतांच्या गोष्टी) [Yuropāntīl vanadevatāṅchyā goshṭī.] pp. 134. *Bombay*, 1868. 12°. **14139. f. 9.**

BENISCH (ABRAHAM). *See* PETHAHIAH ben JACOB, *of Ratisbon.* Travells [*sic*] of Rabbi Petachia ... [Translated from the English of A.B.] [1877.] 12°. **14137. a. 8 (1.)**

BENJAMIN (SIMEON). Kavyadosha vivechana. An exposition of faults in the Marathi poems taught in Government schools. ... काव्यदोषविवेचन *etc.* मुंबई १८८३ [*Bombay*, 1883.] 12°. **14140. a. 35.**

BERAR FIRST BOOK. Berar First Book. Prepared for the Educational Department, Hydrabad Assigned District. (वऱ्हाडांतील शाळांच्या उपयोगाकरितां पहिलें पुस्तक) Fifth edition. pp. 30. *Poona*, 1878. 12°.
In Devanagari and Modi characters. **14140. g. 27 (1.)**

BERAR SECOND BOOK. Berar Second Book. Prepared for the Educational Department, Hydrabad Assigned Districts. (दुसरें पुस्तक) Fourth edition. pp. ii. 96. *Poona*, 1877. 12°.
In Devanagari and Modi characters. **14140. g. 27 (2.)**

BERQUIN (ARNAUD). Marat'ha translation [by Sadāṣiva Kāṣinātha Chhatre] of Berquin's Children's Friend. Vol. I. बाळमित्र (Vol. II. by Lieutenant T. Gaisford.) pp. 403, 364, *lith.* मुंबई १८२८–३३ [*Bombay*, 1828–33.] 8°. **14137. b. 2.**

—— Maráthí translation of Berquin's Children's friend, Vol. I. by ... Sadáshiva Káshináth Chhatre. Revised and corrected by Major T. Candy. Second edition. pp. 420, *lith.* *Poona*, 1854. 8°. **14137. b. 14.**

—— Bálmitra, Vol. I. Translated from the English translation of Berquin's Ami dés enfâns [*sic*], by Sadáshiva Káshináth Chhatreh. Reprint of the original work newly revised by Náráyen Vishwanáth Shástrí. pp. 247. *Bombay*, 1859. 8°. **14137. b. 7.**

BHAIRAVA JYOTIRVID. प्रश्नभैरव. [Praṣnabhairava. A Sanskrit astrological work in verse, with a Marathi translation by Lakshmaṇa Gopāla Dīkshita Sātārkar.] pp. viii. 44, *lith.* पुणें १८८१ [*Poona*, 1881.] 8°.
The work is described as Pt. I., but no more seems to have been published. **14053. cc. 40.**

BHĀLACHANDRA KṚISHṆA BHĀṬAVAḌEKAR. आर्यवैद्यक व पाश्चिमात्य वैद्यक [Ārya vaidyaka va pāṣchimātya vaidyaka. A lecture on the Aryan and Western systems of medicine.] pp. 43. *See* BOMBAY.—*Hindu Union Club.* हेमंत व्याख्यानमाला [Hemanta vyākhyānamālā.] Vol. III. No. 7. [1886, *etc.*] 8°. **14139. c. 26.**

—— Public health, or the first principles of popular hygiene, by Bhálchandra Krishna Bhátawdékar. [With an extract in English from an address delivered by Sir Richard Temple at the Grant Medical College on the 5th March 1879, and a Marathi translation of the same.] (सार्वजनिक आरोग्य) [Sārvajanika ārogya.] pp. ii. iii. xiii. xviii. 138. *Bombay*, 1879. 12°. **14137. ff. 3.**

BHĀLCHANDRA KRISHNA BHÁTAWÉDKAR. *See* BHĀLACHANDRA KṚISHṆA BHĀṬAVAḌEKAR.

BHĀRATĪ VIṢVANĀTHA. अथ नाभिकपुराण प्रारंभः [Nābhikapurāṇa. A supposititious Purāṇa in 14 chapters on the origin and duties of the barber caste.] *Lith.* मुंबई १९०० [*Bombay*, 1877.] *obl.* 8°. **14137. d. 14.**

BHĀRGAVA BĀBĀ. *See* BRAHMENDRA SVĀMĪ.

BHARTṚIHARI. अथ भर्तृहरीकृत नीतिशतक प्रारंभः [Nītiṣataka. Sanskrit text with a commentary in Marathi.] pp. 58, *lith.* मुंबई १७८० [*Bombay*, 1858.] 8°. **14070. b. 3.**

—— अथ भर्तृहरीकृत शृंगारशतक प्रारंभः [Sṛingāra-ṣataka. Sanskrit text, with a commentary in Marathi.] pp. 38. मुंबई १७८४ [*Bombay*, 1862.] 8°. **14070. c. 20.**

—— अथ भर्तृहरीकृत वैराग्यशतक प्रारंभः [Vairāgya-ṣataka. Sanskrit text, with a commentary in Marathi.] pp. 64, *lith.* मुंबई १७८० [*Bombay*, 1858.] 8°. **14070. b. 4.**

BHĀSHĀMAÑJARĪ. अथ भाषामंजरी संस्कृत व प्राकृत [Bhāshāmañjarī. An easy story in Sanskrit, literally translated word for word into Marathi in parallel columns.] pp. 55, *lith.* मुंबई १७९६ [*Bombay*, 1874.] 12°. **14085. b. 16.**

—— [Another edition.] pp. 55, *lith.* मुंबई १८०३ [*Bombay*, 1881.] 16°. **14140. g. 29(6.)**

BHĀSKARA ĀCHĀRYA. *See* BĀḶA GAṄGĀDHARA ṢĀSTRĪ JĀMBHEKAR. Library of useful knowledge. Mathematical geography, to which is added an essay on the system of Bhaskeracharya. 1836. 8°. **14139. b. 3.**

—— *See* JANĀRDANA BĀḶĀJĪ MOḌAK. Bhaskara Áchárya and his astronomical system. [Consisting of extracts from Bh. Ā.'s Siddhāntaṣiromaṇi, with an interpretation in Marathi.] 1877. 8°. **14053 b. 9(1.)**

BHĀSKARA DĀMODARA. *See* PARASURĀMA PANTA GOḌBOLE. Selections from the Maráthí poets .... to which is added a paper on Marathi versification, and biographical and critical notices of the principal Marathi poets, by Ráo Sáhob Bháskar Dámodar. 1860. 8°. **14140. b. 2.**

—— Maráthí First Book, Part First (Part Second), for the use of Government schools in the Bombay presidency, by Rao Saheb Bhaskar Damodar (लहान मुलांकरितां पहिलें पुस्तक.) Second edition. *Bombay*, 1860. 16°. **14140. g. 9(1.)**

—— Maráṭhí First Book ... Recast and revised by the Maráṭhí translator, E[ducational] D[epartment.] Second edition. pp. 48. *Bombay*, 1870. 12°. **14140. g. 18(1.)**

BHĀSKARA SAKHĀRĀMA. *See* PERSIAN TALES. The Thousand and one days, translated by Bhaskar Sakharam. 1863. 8°. **14139 g. 5.**

BHAṬṬOJĪDĪKSHITA. *See* KRISHṆA ṢĀSTRĪ BHĀṬAVAḌEKAR. Subanta-prakâsha, or the declensions of Sanskrit nouns ... [Founded on Bh.'s] Siddhantakaumudî. 1867. 8°. **14140. h. 11.**

—— सिद्धान्तकौमुदी महाराष्ट्रानुवादसहिता [Siddhāntakaumudī. Sanskrit text, with a Marathi version by Rāmachandra Bhikājī Guñjīkar.] *See* RĀMACHANDRA BHIKĀJĪ GUÑJĪKAR.] कौमुदीमहोत्साह: [Kaumudīmahotsāha.] [1877, *etc.*] 8°. **14093. c.**

BHĀŪ DĪKSHITA SĀTĀRKAR. कृष्णाकुमारी [Krishṇakumārī. A tale in verse.] pp. 119. १८८० [*Akola*, 1880.] 16°. **14140. a. 5(5.)**

BHĀŪ GOVINDA SĀPKAR. *See* INDIA.—*Legislative Council.* The Code of Civil Procedure (Act No. X. of 1877), with explanatory notes, abstracts of important decisions by the High Courts in India. .... [Compiled by Bh. G. S.] [1877.] 8°. **14137. g. 6.**

—— उपयुक्त चमत्कार संग्रह [Upayukta chamatkāra saṅgraha. A treatise on chess, native games, conjuring tricks and the like.] Pt. I. and VII. पुणें १८८० [*Poona*, 1880.] 12°. *Wanting pt. II.-VI.* **14139. a. 32(2.)**

BHĀŪ SĀHEB. भाऊ साहेबांची बखर [Bhāū Sāhebāṇchī bakhar. An account of the Maratha campaigns during the time of Sadāṣiva Rāva, called Bhāū Sāheb, from A.D. 1753 to 1761.] *See* PERIODICAL PUBLICATIONS.—*Poona.* काव्येतिहास-संग्रह [Kāvyetihāsa saṅgraha.] Vol. I. and II. [1878, *etc.*] 8°. **14072. d. 37.**

—— भाऊ साहेबांची बखर ... The chronicle of Bháu Sáheb ... Edited by K. N. Sane with critical and explanatory notes. [Second edition]. pp. ii. 132. *Poona*, 1886. 8°. **14139. e. 22.**

BHAVABHŪTI. Utarrámcharitra. A drama in seven acts [by Bh. in prose and verse.] Translated from Sanscrit into Maráthí by Parshurámpant Godbole. (उत्तररामचरित्र नाटक) pp. vi. 164. *Bombay*, 1859. 8°. **14140. f. 21.**

—— Second edition. pp. vii. 160. *Bombay*, 1881. 12°. **14140. f. 13.**

BHAVĀNARĀVA PĀVAGĪ. आमची कुटुंबव्यवस्था. [Āmchī kuṭumba-vyavasthā. A lecture on the obligations of Hindus towards their relations.] pp. 10. *See* BOMBAY.—*Hindu Union Club.* हेमंत व्याख्यानमाला. [Hemanta vyākhyānamālā.] Vol. II. No. 7. [1886, *etc.*] 8°. **14139. c. 26.**

BHAVĀNĪ ASHṬAKA. भवानी अष्टक [Bhavānī ashṭaka. Eight stanzas in praise of the goddess Bhavānī.] ff. 3, *lith.* मुंबई १७७८ [*Bombay*, 1856.] *obl.* 12°. **14140. a. 6(3.)**

BHICAJEE AMROOT. *See* BHIKĀJĪ AMṚITA.

BHIKĀJĪ AMṚITA. A treatise on human anatomy; compiled from the English by Bhicajee Amroot. (मानुष शारीर शास्त्र) [Mānusha ṣārīra ṣāstra.] pp. vi. ii. xiv. ii. 401. vii. vi. xx. *Bombay*, 1863. 8°. **14137. h. 4.**

—— A treatise on human physiology, compiled from the English by Bhicajee Amroot. (मानुष इंद्रियविज्ञान शास्त्र) [Mānusha indriyavijñāna ṣāstra.] pp. ii. vi. 459. *Bombay*, 1865. 8°. **14137. h. 3.**

BHIKĀJĪ ṢĀSTRĪ MOGHE. *See* YĀJÑAVALKYA. याज्ञवल्क्यस्मृति मिताक्षरव्यवहाराध्याय *etc.* [The Vyavahārādhyāya of Yājñavalkya's Smṛiti, with Vijñāneṣvara's Mitākshara, and a Marathi translation of both by Bh. Ṣ. M.] [1879.] 8°. **14038. d. 25.**

BHIKSHUKA. भिक्षुक [Bhikshuka. An essay on the subject of mendicant Brahmans, suggested by a discussion at a meeting of the Bombay Ārya Samāj held on the 12th August 1877.] pp. 18, 13. ठाणे १८७७ [*Thana*, 1877.] 12°. **14139. f. 12(3.)**

BHĪMĀCHĀRYA JHAḶKĪKAR. *See* VIṢVANĀTHA PAÑCHĀNANA BHAṬṬĀCHĀRYA TARKĀLAṄKĀRA. Nyāya bhārati or the translation of Nyāya siddhānta muktâvali … by Bh. Jh. 1882–84. 8°. **14048. d. 49.**

—— मध्वमत. [Madhva-mata. A lecture on the Madhva Brahmans and their tenets.] pp. 15. *See* BOMBAY.—*Hindu Union Club.* हेमंत व्याख्यानमाला [Hemanta vyākhyānamālā.] Vol. II. No. 6. [1886, *etc.*] 8°. **14139. c. 26.**

BHĪMA RĀJĀ. *See* BOMBAY, *City of.—Pathare Reform Association.* Marriage of Hindu widows …. With an epitome of the history of Bim Raja, the founder of the race of Pathare Prabhus. [1863.] 8°. **14139. e. 11.**

BHOJARĀJA PAṆḌITA. भोजराजकृत चंपूरामायण [Champūrāmāyaṇa. Sanskrit text, with paraphrases in Sanskrit and in Marathi.] *See* PERIODICAL PUBLICATIONS.—*Dharwar.* काव्यनाटकादर्श [Kāvyanāṭakādarṣa.] Pt. I. [1882, *etc.*] 8°. **14076. d. 35.**

BHŪPĀḶYĀ. भूपाळ्या [Bhūpāḷyā. Morning hymns to different deities, in the Bhūpāḷī measure.] pp. 32. मुंबई १७८० [*Bombay*, 1858.] 12°. **14140. a. 1(8.)**

—— [Another edition.] pp. 32. मुंबई १७८५ [*Bombay*, 1863.] 12°. **14140. a. 10(3.)**

BIBLE. The Holy Bible, containing the Old and New Testaments, translated from the originals into the Mahratta language by the Serampore missionaries. Vol. 1–3. *Serampore* [1812–21]. 8°.

Containing only the books from Genesis to Song of Solomon. Vol. 1 has no English title-page; Vol. 2 is without any title-page; Vol. 3 has 2 title-pages, one in English, the other in Marathi. **1108. e. 16–18.**

—— [Another copy.] Vol. 1. **218. i. 9.**

—— [Another copy.] Vol. 1. **842. c. 7.**

—— पवित्र शास्त्र ह्मणजे जुना व नवा करार … The Holy Bible in the Maráthí language. pp. 1196. *Bombay*, 1857. 12°. **3068. bb. 18.**

APPENDIX.

—— *See* PURĀṆAS.—*Matsyapurāṇa.* मत्स्यपुराण आणि इब्री शास्त्र … A comparison of … ancient events as found in the Mutsya Pooran and the Hebrew Scriptures. 1845. 24°. **14137. a. 1(5.)**

—— Scripture narratives. 2 pt. मुंबई [*Bombay*,] 1835–37. 8°.

Nos. 47 and 48 of the Bombay Tract and Book Society's Series. **544(7.)**

SELECTIONS.

—— Child's Text book. शास्त्रवचनमाला [Ṣāstravachanamālā.] pp. 36. मुंबई १७९५ [*Bombay*, 1875.] 32°. **14137. a. 3(2.)**

OLD TESTAMENT.

—— *Genesis.* पहिलें पुस्तक [The Book of Genesis, translated by J. Dixon and the American missionaries.] pp. 110. मुंबई १७६८ [*Bombay*, 1846.] 8°. **3070. bb. 11.**

OLD TESTAMENT [*continued*].

—— *Exodus.* दुसरें पुस्तक [The Book of Exodus, translated by J. Dixon and the American missionaries] pp. 88. मुंबई १८४६ [*Bombay*, 1846.] 8°. **3070. bb. 12.**

—— *Deuteronomy.* पांचवें पुस्तक ह्यणजे नेमप्रकरण Deuteronomy. [Translated by J. Dixon and the American missionaries.] pp. 80. [*Bombay*,] 1846. 8°. **3070. bb. 13.**

—— *Samuel.* शमुवेलाचें पहिलें (-दुसरें) पुस्तक [The Books of Samuel, translated by J. Dixon and the American missionaries.] 2 pt. pp. 74, 75. मुंबई १८४६ [*Bombay*, 1846–42.] 8°. **3070. bb. 15.**

—— *Esther.* [*Polyglott.*] מגלת אסתר एस्तेरचे पुस्तक [The Book of Esther, followed by the hymn of Purim.] pp. 20. 20. *Heb.* and *Marathi.* मुंबई १८८६ [*Bombay*, 1886.] 8°. **3166. e. 24.**

—— *Job.* इयोबाचें पुस्तक. *See* below: *Miscellaneous Parts.* पुरातन परमपवित्र लेखांतले काव्यग्रंथ. The Poetical Books of the Old Testament, *etc.* 1839. 8°. **3068. d. 7.**

—— *Psalms.* गीतें. The Psalms of David. In Murathee metre. Part I. Edited by the Rev. C. P. Farrar. pp. 84, *lith.* नाशिक [*Nasik*,] 1836. 8°.

As far as Psalm lv. *inclusive.*

3070. bb. 14.

—— —— गीतांचें पुस्तक. *See* below: *Miscellaneous Parts.* पुरातन परमपवित्र लेखांतले काव्यग्रंथ. The Poetical Books of the Old Testament, *etc.* 1839. 8°. **3068. d. 7.**

—— *Proverbs.* दृष्टांतवचनांचें पुस्तक. *See* below: *Miscellaneous Parts.* पुरातन परमपवित्र लेखांतले काव्यग्रंथ. The Poetical Books of the Old Testament, *etc.* 1839. 8°. **3068. d. 7.**

—— *Ecclesiastes.* उपदेशक. *See* below: *Miscellaneous Parts.* पुरातन परमपवित्र लेखांतले काव्यग्रंथ. The Poetical Books of the Old Testament, *etc.* 1839. 8°. **3068. d. 7.**

—— *Song of Solomon.* शेलोमोचें गीत. *See* below: *Miscellaneous Parts.* पुरातन परमपवित्र लेखांतले काव्यग्रंथ. The Poetical Books of the Old Testament, *etc.* 1839. 8°. **3068. d. 7.**

OLD TESTAMENT [*continued*].

—— *Miscellaneous Parts.* पुरातन परमपवित्र लेखांतले काव्यग्रंथ. The Poetical Books of the Old Testament. Translated by J. B. Dickson; assisted by Dajee Shastree Shookl. pp. 291. *Bombay*, 1839. 8°. **3068. d. 7.**

NEW TESTAMENT.

—— *Begin:* मात्योकडून सवर्तमान [The New Testament, translated by the Serampur missionaries.] 20 pt. [*Serampur*, 1821?] 8°.

Without title-page. The Gospel of St. John is wanting. Each part has a separate pagination, and was apparently issued separately.

1110. f. 9.

—— The New Testament, translated from the original Greek, into the Mahratta language, by the American missionaries in Bombay. *Bombay*, 1826. 8°.

Each book has a separate pagination.

1004. g. 10.

—— आमचा प्रभु आणि तारणारा जो येशू ख्रीस्त याविषयीं हा नवा करार ... The New Testament ... translated from the original Greek into Maráthi. *Printed for the Ahmednugger Mission; Bombay*, 1851. 8°. *Printed in parts*, 1847–51. **3068. c. 11.**

—— आमचा प्रभु आणि तारणारा येशू ख्रीस्त याविषयीं हा नवा करार ... The New Testament in the Maráthi language. pp. 452. *Bombay*, 1857. 12°. **3068. b. 21.**

—— [Another edition.] pp. 650. *London*, 1864. 8°. **3068. cc. 29.**

—— Annotated New Testament in Marathi. Acts to Revelation. नव्या करारावर टीका ... Edited by Baba Padmanji. pp. iv. 855. मुंबई १८७७ [*Bombay*, 1877.] 8°. **3068. dd. 20.**

—— *Gospels. Begin:* मंगळ समाचार । [The Four Gospels, translated by the Serampur missionaries.] pp. 331. [*Serampur*, 1811?] 12°. *Without title-page.* **1108. b. 16.**

—— *Matthew.* आमचा प्रभु व तारणारा जो येशु ख्रीस्त याविषईं मात्योचें शुभवर्तमान. [The Gospel of Matthew in the Modi character.] pp. 132. [*Bombay*, 1848?] 8°. **3068. cc. 5.**

—— *Mark.* The Gospel of Mark. मार्कसाने केलेलें शुभवर्तमान. pp. 67. मुंबई १८६६ [*Bombay*, 1866.] 12°. **3068. aa. 2.**

NEW TESTAMENT [*continued*].

—— *Luke.* Commentary on the Gospel according to Luke [including the text]. By the Rev. R. G. Wilder. लूकानें केलेलें शुभवर्त्तमान या वरील टीका. pp. 192. *Bombay,* 1875. 8°.
3061. dd. 1.

—— *John, Gospel of.* The Gospel of John. योहानान केलेलें शुभवर्त्तमान. pp. 81. मुंबई १८७७ [*Bombay,* 1877.] 12°.
3068. aa. 17.

—— —— The Gospel according to St. John in English and Maráthí, the Maráthí expressed in Roman characters. [By J. M. Mitchell.] pp. 163. *Bombay,* 1861. 8°.
3068. dd. 16.

—— *Acts.* प्रेषितांचीं कृत्यें. Acts of the Apostles. [In Modi characters.] pp. 150. मुंबई १८४८ [*Bombay,* 1847–48.] 12°.
3068. b. 3.

—— —— Acts of the Apostles. प्रेषितांचीं कृत्यें pp. 102. मुंबई १८७७ [*Bombay,* 1877.] 12°.
3068. aa. 16.

BINGLEY (WILLIAM) *Rev.* The voyages of Captain Cook. Translated from the original of the Rev. William Bingley [i.e. from the concluding chapters of "Biographical conversations on the most eminent voyagers of different nations"] by Ganesh Sadáshiw Shástree Lele (कप्तान कुक साहेब त्याचे जलपर्यटनाचा वृत्तांत.) pp. 163. *Poona,* 1853. 8°.
14139. d. 3(2.)

BLANFORD (HENRY FRANCIS). The rudiments of physical geography; for Indian schools. ... Translated into Marathi by Rao Saheb Balvant Ramchandra Sahasrabuddhe, *etc.* (भूतल विषयक विद्येचीं मूलतत्वें.) [Bhūtala vishayaka vidyechīṉ mūlatattveṉ.] pp. vi. 167. *Bombay,* 1881. 12°.
14139. a. 40.

BODHAKATHĀ. Bod,hkutha. बोधकथा. [An instructive reading-book for schools. Third edition.] pp. 68. मुंबई १८३८ [*Bombay,* 1868.] 12°.
14140. g. 3(3.)

BODHALA. बोधल्याचे अभंग. [Bodhalyāche abhaṅga. A poem on the legend of King Bodhala, a devout worshipper of Pāṇḍuraṅga.] *See* SAKHU. अथ सखूचें चरित्र प्रारंभः [Sakhūcheṉ charitra.] pp. 9–13. [1875.] 12°.
14140. a. 10(12.)

BOMBAY, *City of.—Hindu Union Club.* हेमंत व्याख्यानमाला. [Hemanta vyākhyānamālā. A series of lectures on social, religious and other topics, delivered during the cold season under the auspices of the Hindu Union Club.] Vol. I.–III. मुंबई १८८६ [*Bombay,* 1886, etc.] 8°.
In progress. **14139. c. 26.**

—— *Pathare Reform Association.* Marriage of Hindu widows, advocated by the Pathare Reform Association of Bombay; with an epitome of the history of Bim Raja, the founder of the race of Pathare Prabhus. *Mar.* and *Engl.* [*Bombay,* 1863 ?] 8°.
14139. e. 11.

—— *Presidency of.—Court of Ṣadr Dīwānī 'Adālat.* मुंबईंतील सदा दिवाणी अदालतींत मुकद्दमे फैसल झाले *etc.* [Decisions in cases tried by the Bombay Ṣadr Dīwānī 'Adālat from A.D. 1840 to 1848. Translated by Henry Newton.] pp. xi. 163. मुंबई १८५२ [*Bombay,* 1852.] 8°.
14137. g. 2.

—— *Government Schools.* School dialogues for the use of Government schools in the Bombay Presidency. (संभाषणाचीं सोपीं वाक्यें) [Sambhāshaṇāchīṉ sopīṉ vākyeṉ.] Seventh edition. pp. 31. *Engl.* and *Mar.* *Bombay,* 1860. 12°. **14140. g. 11.**

BRAHMACHĀRĪ. *See* VISHṆU BHIKĀJĪ GOKHALE, called BRAHMACHĀRĪ.

BRAHMANS. On the second marriage of the widows of Brahmans. [A treatise in four parts advocating female education, and widow-marriage.] ब्राह्मणजातीच्या विधवा कन्येचे पुनर्विवाहाविषयीं प्रकरण. [Brāhmaṇa jātīchyā vidhavā vishayīṉ prakaraṇa.] ff. 19, 4, 4, 3. १८४१ [*Bombay?,* 1841.] *obl.* 12°.
14139. c. 4.

BRĀHMA SAMĀJ.—*Ahmadabad Prārthanā Samāj.* ईश्वर नित्योपासना *etc.* [Īṣvaranityopāsanā. Daily prayers for the use of the Ahmadabad Prārthanā Samāj, in Sanskrit, with a Marathi translation.] ff. 4. अमदावाद १८८२ [*Ahmadabad,* 1882.] *obl.* 16°.
14028. a.

—— *Poona Prārthanā Samāj.* पुणें प्रार्थनासमाजाचे नियम. [Puṇeṉ Prārthanā Samājāche niyama. The rules and objects of the Poona Prārthanā Samāj.] pp. 11. पुणें १८८० [*Poona,* 1880.] 12°.
14137. c. 1(2).

BRAHMENDRA SVĀMĪ. **धावडशी येथील ब्रह्मेंद्रस्वामी उर्फ भार्गवबावा यांचें चरित्र.** [Brahmendra Svāmī yāṉcheṉ charitra, or The life of Br. Sv.] *See* PERIODICAL PUBLICATIONS.—*Poona.* **काव्येतिहास-संग्रह** [Kāvyetihāsa saṅgraha.] Vol. IV. Nos. 1–7. [1878, *etc.*] 8°. **14072. d. 37.**

BROUGHAM (HENRY) *Baron Brougham and Vaux.* **उपयोगि ज्ञानाचा पुस्तक समूह** [Upayogi jñānāchā pustaka samūha.] Library of useful knowledge. Preliminary treatise on the objects, advantages and pleasures of science. Translated from the English original [of Lord Brougham] into the Maratha language by .. G. R. Jervis, pp. 169. *Bombay,* 1829. 8°. **14139. b. 2.**

BROWN (CHARLES PHILIP). *See* RĀMACHANDRA RĀVA, *Panganūrī.* Memoirs of Hyder and Tippoo . . . Translated into English and illustrated with annotations by C. P. B. 1849. 8°. **14139. e. 26.**

BRUCE (HENRY J.) Illustrated primary arithmetic. **लहान मुलांकरितां गणित.** [Lahān mulāṉkaritāṉ gaṇita.] pp. 52. **सातारा १८८१** [*Satara,* 1881.] 8°. **14139. a. 35.**

BUDDHABĀVANĪ. **अथ बुद्धबावनी प्रारंभ.** [Buddhabāvanī. A philosophical poem.] ff. 7, *lith.* [*Bombay*? 1864?] *obl.* 16°. **14140. a. 9(4.)**

CANDY (THOMAS). *See* ÆSOP. Æsop's Fables translated into Marathi ... Corrected, revised, and enlarged by T. C. Third edition. 1856. 8°. **14139. g. 4.**

—— —— 1861. 12°. **14139. f. 7.**

—— *See* ANANTA ŚĀSTRĪ TAḶEKAR. Sanscrit-Maràthì Vocabulary [compiled under the direction of T. C.] [1853.] 8°. **14090. d. 5.**

—— *See* BĀḶA GAṄGĀDHARA ŚĀSTRĪ JĀMBHEKAR. History of British India .... Revised ... by T. C. [1854.] 8°. **14139. e. 5.**

—— *See* BERQUIN (A.) Maráthí translation of Berquin's Children's Friend ... Revised and corrected by T. C. 1854. 8°. **14137. b. 14.**

—— *See* ELPHINSTONE (*Hon.* M.) Introduction to the history of India .... A new edition, edited by T. C. 1852. 8°. **14139. e. 4.**

CANDY (THOMAS). *See* ESDAILE (D. A.) Murathee translation [by T. C.] of the Principles of Morality. 1848. 12°. **14139. c. 3(1.)**

—— *See* MACCULLOCH (J. M.) *D.D.* Wáchan Páth Málá .... Being a series of translations from English into Maráthí, by Major T. C. 1857. 8°. **14140. h. 5.**

—— *See* PARAŚURĀMA PANTA GOḌBOLE. **संक्षिप्त भूगोल वर्णन** [Saṃkshipta bhūgolavarṇana. An abridged version of T. C.'s "Manual of Geography."] [1866.] 8°. **14139. a. 17.**

—— A general account of India. (**हिंदुस्थानाचें वर्णन.**) [Hindusthānācheṉ varṇana.] Second edition. pp. 156. ii. *Bombay,* 1860. 12°. **14139. d. 4.**

—— A manual of geography for schools and young persons. (**भूगोलाचें वर्णन.**) [Bhūgolācheṉ varṇana.] 2 vol. *Bombay,* 1863–65. 8°. **14139. a. 11.**

CAPON (DAVID). *See* DUFF (J. G.) History of the Marathas, translated ... by Captain D. C. 1830. 4°. **14142. b. 1.**

—— —— 1846. 8°. **14139. e. 3.**

—— —— 1857. 12°. **14139. d. 11.**

CHAMBERS (WILLIAM) and (ROBERT) *Publishers.* *See* KRISHṆA ŚĀSTRĪ GOḌBOLE. A treatise on astronomy, prepared from Chambers' work on that science, *etc.* 1862. 8°. **14139. a. 14.**

CHĀṆAKYA. **श्रीवृद्धचाणाक्य प्रारंभः** [Vṛiddhachāṇakya. The larger edition of Ch.'s Rājanītisamuchchaya, in 341 verses. Sanskrit text, with a Marathi commentary, called Subodhinī.] pp. 180, *lith.* **मुंबई १९८० ** [*Bombay,* 1858.] 8°. **14076. b. 3.**

—— **अथ वृद्धचाणाक्य प्रारंभः** [Another edition of the preceding text and commentary, numbering 342 verses.] pp. 86, *lith.* **मुंबई १९८२** [*Bombay,* 1860.] 8°. **14076. b. 5.**

—— [Another edition.] pp. 66. **पुणें १८८०** [*Poona,* 1880.] 8°. **14076. d. 32.**

—— [Another edition.] pp. 72, *lith.* **पुणें १८८०** [*Poona,* 1880.] 8°. **14076. d. 30.**

CHĀṄGADEVA. चांगदेवाचे अभंग प्रारंभ [Abhangas.] *See* JÑĀNADEVA. श्री ज्ञानदेवाचा गाथा [Jñānadevāchā gāthā.] [1877.] 8°. **14140. c. 23.**

CHARAKA. *See* PĀṆḌURAṄGA GOPĀLA MANTRĪ. भारतवर्षीय वनौषधिसंग्रह *etc.* [Bhāratavarshīya vanaushadhisaṅgraha. A work on the medicinal properties of Indian plants, showing their uses according to the Sanskrit works of Ch.] [1886.] 8°. **14137. h. 14.**

CHINTĀMAṆA ANANTA LIMAYE. A treatise on practical hygiene, by Chintaman Anant Limaye .... आरोग्य रक्षक विद्या. [Ārogyarakshakavidyā.] pp. iv. iii. 113. vii. *Poona*, 1880. 8°. **14137. h. 11.**

CHINTĀMAṆI. चिंतामणि विरचित सीतास्वयंवर [Sītāsvayaṃvara. A poem on the marriage of Sītā to Rāma.] *See* PERIODICAL PUBLICATIONS.—*Poona.* काव्येतिहास संग्रह [Kāvyetihāsa saṅgraha.] Vol. VI. No. 5–10. [1878, *etc.*] 8°. **14072. d. 37.**

CHINTĀMAṆI NĀGĀMVAKAR. *See* ṢĀRṄGADHARA. संस्कृत शार्ङ्गधरवैद्यकग्रंथ. [Vaidyakagrantha. With Ch. N.'s Marathi commentary.] [1854.] 4°. **14043. d. 4.**

—— —— [1877.] 8°. **14043. d. 28.**

CHOLERA. The Cholera. [A Christian tract in form of a dialogue.] ... जरीमरीविषयीं. [Jarīmarī vishayīṇ.] pp. 32. [*Bombay?*, 1845?]. 24°. **14137. a. 1(3.)**

CHOVĪSANĀVA. अथ चोवीसनावांचे अभंग [Chovīsanavāṇche abhaṅga. Verses in praise of Vishṇu, under twenty-four different names. Second edition.] pp. 16, *lith.* मुंबई १७८६ [*Bombay*, 1864.] 12°. **14140. a. 4(12.)**

CHRISTIAN. *Begin:* एका दिवसीं कोणीएक ख्रिस्ती. [A missionary tract, containing a conversation between a Christian, a Hindu, and a Muhammadan.] pp. 12. [*Bombay?*, 1845?] 24°. **14137. a. 1(8.)**

CHRISTIAN DOCTRINE. Cathechismo da doutrina Cristam. (Cristanchi sastrazza cathexismo.) pp. 143. *Portug.* and *Marathi.* *Roma*, 1778. 12°.

The Marathi translation is in the Roman character.

3505. bb. 21.

CHRISTIANITY. Evidences of Christianity, briefly stated. हिंदुलोकांस कळविण्यासाठीं काढलेलीं ख्रिस्ती धर्माच्या सत्यतेचीं प्रमाणें. [Khristī dharmāchyā pramāṇeṇ.] pp. vi. 124. १८५० *Bombay*, [1850.] 16°.

No. 47 *of the Bombay Tract and Book Society's Series.*

14137. a. 4(1.)

COOK (JAMES) *the Circumnavigator.* *Voyages.* *See* BINGLEY (W.) *Rev.* The voyages of Capt. Cook.

COPERNICUS (NICOLAUS). *See* RĀMACHANDRA SŪBĀJĪ BĀPŪ. A comparison of the Pooranic, Sidhantic, and Copernican systems, *etc.* 1836. 8°. **14139. a. 1.**

COWPER (WILLIAM) *the Poet.* The William Cowper's diverting history of John Gilpin. Translated into Marathee arya metre by Bajaba Balajee Nene. (गिलपीन - चरित्र) pp. 28. *Engl.* and *Mar.* *Kurrachee*, 1867. 8°. **14140. b. 5.**

CRISHNAJI GUNESH DONGRE. *See* KṚISHṆAJĪ GAṆEṢA DONGRE.

CULLIAN SITARAM CHITRAY. *See* KALYĀṆA SĪTĀRĀMA CHITRE.

CUNINGHAM (JAMES MACNABB). A sanitary primer for Indian schools. ... Translated by Mr. Venayak Rao. (स्वच्छता की पहिली पुस्तक) [Svachchhatā kī pahilī pustaka.] pp. 40. *Bombay*, 1880. 12°. **14137. ff. 2(2.)**

CYRUS, surnamed *the Great, King of Persia.* *Life.* *See* ROLLIN (C.) The life of Cyrus.

DĀDOBĀ PĀṆḌURAṄGA TARKHAḌKAR. A Hindu gentleman's reflections respecting the works of Swedenborg and the doctrines of the New Jerusalem Church. Translated into Marathí from the original in English [by D. P. T.] by Miss Ahlyábái Tarkhadkar, assisted by her brother N. D. Tarkhadkar. (स्वीदनबोर्गे ह्यांच्या मता विषयीं एका हिंदु गृहस्थाचे विचार.) pp. iii. 135. *Bombay*, [1881.] 12°. **14137. a. 10.**

—— मराठी भाषेचें व्याकरण [Marāṭhī bhāshecheṇ vyākaraṇa.] (A Murat,hee grammar comprehending the principles and rules of the language, by Dadoba Pandurung Turkhudkur.) pp. ix. 194. *Bombay*, 1836. 8°. **14140. h. 1.**

—— A grammar of the Marát,hí language for the use of students, by Dadoba Pandurang. (महाराष्ट्र भाषेचें व्याकरण). Third edition. pp. xiii. 352. iv. *Bombay*, 1857. 12°. **14140. g. 6.**

DĀDOBĀ PĀṆḌURAṄGA TARKHAḌKAR. Fourth edition. pp. ix. xxiii. 352. *Bombay*, 1866. 12°.
14140. g. 16.

—— A grammar of the Marát,hí language for the use of senior students by .. Dadoba Pandurang. Seventh edition, revised, improved, and enlarged. pp. xv. 396. *Bombay*, 1879. **14140. g. 33.**

—— Rudimentary English grammar in the Marat,hi language, by Dadoba Pandurung ..... इंग्लिश व्याकरणाची मूळपीठिका [Ingliṣ vyākaraṇāchī mūlapīṭhikā.] Second edition. pp. 102. पुणें १८६३ [*Poona*, 1863]. 12°. **14140. g. 14.**

—— A rudimentary Maráthí grammar, for the use of junior students in the Maráṭhí schools, by Dadoba Pandurang. (मराठी लघु व्याकरण) [Marāṭhī laghu vyākaraṇa.] Fourth edition. pp. 63. *Bombay*, 1868. 12°. **14140. g. 3(2.)**

—— Tenth edition. pp. 67. *Bombay*, 1877. 12°.
14140. g. 12(3.)

—— Vidhavásrumárjanam, or Wiping the widow's tears, being an essay in Sanscrit on the remarriage of Hindu widows ... To which is added a translation in Marathi (विधवाश्रुमार्जनाभिधायकोऽयम् निबंधः) pp. 27, 18. *Bombay*, 1857. 8°.
14038. b. 5.

DAJEE SHASTREE SHEOKL. *See* DĀJĪ ṢĀSTRĪ ṢUKLA.

DĀJĪ NĪLAKAṆṬHA NAGARKAR. *See* HADDON (J.) *M.A.* Elements of Algebra, translated into Maráthí.... by Dájí Nílcanth Naggarkar. 1865. 8°.
14139. a. 15.

DĀJĪ ṢĀSTRĪ ṢUKLA. *See* BĀLA ṢĀSTRĪ GHAGVE. A dictionary of the Maratha language, compiled by ... Dajee Shastree Sheokl, *etc.* 1829. 4°.
14140. i. 1.

—— *See* BIBLE.—*Miscellaneous Parts.* पुरातन परमपवित्र लेखांतले काव्यग्रंथ. The Poetical Books of the Old Testament. Translated by J. B. Dickson; assisted by Dajee Shastree Shookl. 1839. 8°.
3068. d. 7.

DĀMODARA EKANĀTHA PĀṬSAKAR. सीमंतिनी नाटक. [Sīmantinī nāṭaka. A drama in prose and verse, founded on an episode of Ṣrīdhara's Ṣivalīlāmṛita.] pp. ii. ii. 112. मुंबई १८८१ [*Bombay*, 1881.] 12°. **14140. a. 8(2.)**

DĀMODARA GAṆEṢA JOṢĪ. *See* RĀVAJĪ ṢRĪDHARA GONDHAḶEKAR. कीर्तनतरंगिणी. [Kīrtana-taraṅgiṇī. Pt. I. on various mythological stories, composed by D. G. J.] [1885, *etc.*] 8°. **14140. c. 37.**

DĀMODARA HARI CHITḶE. वत्सलाहरणनाटक [Vatsalāharaṇa nāṭaka. The abduction of Vatsalā. A drama in prose and verse. Third edition.] pp. 69, *lith.* पुणें १८८० [*Poona*, 1880.] 16°.
14140. e. 1(3.)

DĀMODARA PANTA. दामोदरकविकृत श्रीकृष्णलीला आख्यान (बाळक्रीडा) [Kṛishṇalīlā ākhyāna, and Bālakrīḍā. Two dramatic sketches, each in three acts, on the sports of Kṛishṇa and the milkmaids.] pp. 171, *lith.* मुंबई १७८२ [*Bombay*, 1860.] 12°.
14140. e. 1(1.)

DĀMODARA VISHṆU SAPRE. नारायणबलि अर्थात् नारायण राव पेशवे यांचे अपघाताने हत्या. [Nārāyaṇabali. Verses on the assassination of Nārāyaṇa Rāva, Peshwa, and on other subjects.] pp. iii. 70. पटना १८७६ [*Patna*, 1879.] 8°. **14140. b. 9(3.)**

DANIELLS (S.) and **SAMUEL** (R.) *See* PETHAHIAH ben JACOB, *of Ratisbon.* Travells [*sic*] of Rabbi Petachia *etc.* [Translated by S. D. and R. S.] [1877.] 12°. **14137. a. 8(1.)**

DAṢĀVATĀRA. अथ दशावताराचे श्लोक [Daṣāvatārāche ṣloka. Verses on the ten incarnations of Vishṇu.] *See* GAJAGAURĪ. अथ गजगौरी आख्यान प्रारंभ. [Gajagaurī ākhyāna.] pp. 20–22. [1860?] 12°.
14140. a. 4(3.)

DATTĀRĀMA MOREṢVARA MANVĀCHĀRYA. शबरी ललीत नाटक [Ṣabarī lalita nāṭaka. A drama on the story of King Rāma and the Bhil woman Ṣabarī.] pp. vii. viii. 129. मुंबई १८८६ [*Bombay*, 1886.] 8°.

The dialogue here and there, and some of the songs, are in Hindi. **14140. f. 28.**

DATTĀTRAYA MOREṢVARA MANVĀCHĀRYA. *See* DATTĀRĀMA MOREṢVARA MANVĀCHĀRYA.

DATTĀTRAYA VĀSUDEVA JOGḶEKAR. The Bhámá willása [a dramatised version of the story of Kṛishṇa and Rukmiṇī] prepared for the public amusement by Dattátraya Wássudeo Joglaykar. (भामाविलास नाटक.) pp. 84. *Bombay*, 1877. 12°.
14140. e. 1(2.)

DATTĀTRAYA VĀSUDEVA JOGḶEKAR. **चित्रसेनगंधर्व नाटक** [Chitrasenagandharva nāṭaka. A drama on the story of Chitrasena, leader of the Gandharvas. With illustrations.] pp. 46, *lith.* **मुंबई १८६७** [*Bombay*, 1867.] 8°. **14140. f. 1(1.)**

—— **सौरिविक्रम नाटक** [Sauri Vikrama nāṭaka. A drama in five acts, based on the Ṣanimāhātmya of Mahīpati, containing a legend of King Vikramāditya falling under the curse of the god Ṣani.] pp. viii. 178. **मुंबई १८८१** [*Bombay*, 1881.] 12°. **14140. a. 28.**

—— **शृंगारसुंदर ... चमत्कारिक गोष्टींचा संग्रह** [Sṛingārasundara. Tales of domestic life.] Pt. I., pp. ii. 300, *lith.* **मुंबई १८७९** [*Bombay*, 1879.] 8°. **14139. g. 18.**

DATTO VINĀYAKA GOKHALE. **संगतिविपाक नाटक** [Saṅgativipāka nāṭaka. A drama in six acts on the fruits of evil companionship.] pp. v. 164. **मुंबई १८८६** [*Bombay*, 1886.] 12°. **14140. e. 6.**

DAVID HAEEM. *See* Hāīm (D.)

DAVYS (George) *Bishop of Peterborough.* A plain and short history of England for children, in letters from a father to his son ... Translated ... into Marathee by Hari Keshavaji. (**इंग्लंडाचा वृत्तांत**) [Inglāṇḍāchā vṛittānta.] Third edition. pp. ii. 136. *Bombay*, 1867. 12°. **14139. e. 9.**

DE MORGAN (Augustus). De Morgan's Elements of Algebra: translated into the Marathi language by Colonel George Ritso Jervis, ... assisted by Vishnoo Soonder Chutray, Gungadhur Shastri Phudkay, and Govind Gungadhur Phudkay. (**बीजगणित मूळपीठिका**) [Bījagaṇita mūḷapīṭhikā.] pp. 386. *Bombay*, 1848. 8°. **14139. b. 5.**

DEVACHANDA MĀṆAKACHANDA. *See* Māṇatuṅgāchārya. **सार्थ भक्तामर स्तोत्र** [Bhaktāmara-stotra. With a Marathi paraphrase by D. M.] [1883.] 16°. **14100. a.**

DEVANĀTHA. **देवनाथकृत कृष्णजन्म** [Krishṇajanma. A poem on the birth of Kṛishṇa.] *See* Periodical Publications.—*Poona.* **काव्येतिहास-संग्रह** [Kāvyetihāsa saṅgraha.] Vol. VIII. No. 12. [1878, *etc.*] 8°. **14072. d. 37.**

DEVANĀTHA. **देवनाथकृत श्रावण आख्यान** [Ṣrāvaṇa ākhyāna. A poem on the life of the sage Ṣrāvaṇa.] *See* Periodical Publications.—*Poona.* **काव्येतिहास-संग्रह** [Kāvyetihāsa saṅgraha.] Vol. II. Nos. 2 and 3. [1878, *etc.*] 4°. **14072. d. 37.**

DEVĪDĀSA. **अथ करुणामृतस्तोत्र प्रारंभः** [Karuṇāmṛitastotra. Devotional songs.] ff. 23. **मुंबई १७७०** [*Bombay*, 1848.] *obl.* 16°. **14140. a. 2(1.)**

—— [Another edition.] ff. 15, *lith.* **मुंबई १७८१** [*Bombay*, 1859.] *obl.* 16°. **14140. a. 9(1.)**

—— **अथ व्यंकटेशस्तोत्रप्रारंभ ॥** [Vyaṅkaṭeṣastotra. A hymn of praise to Vyaṅkaṭeṣa, a god worshipped in the Carnatic, as an incarnation of Kṛishṇa.] ff. 14. **१७८०** [*Bombay?* 1858.] *obl.* 16°. **14140. a. 2(2.)**

—— [Another edition.] ff. 10, *lith.* **मुंबई १७९९** [*Bombay*, 1877.] *obl.* 12°. **14137. c. 11(2.)**

—— [Another edition.] ff. 10, *lith.* **पुणें १७९९** [*Poona*, 1877.] *obl.* 12°. **14140. a. 9(10.)**

DHĀṆVE. **अथ धांवे प्रारंभः** [Dhāṇve. Invocations, and hymns addressed to several gods and goddesses.] pp. 24, *lith.* **मुंबई १७८४** [*Bombay*, 1862.] 12°. **14140. a. 13(2.)**

DHOṆḌO BĀḶAKṚISHṆA SAHASRABUDDHE. The life and poems of Ekanath, the great saint, poet and philosopher of Paiṭhan. (**पैठण येथील प्रसिद्ध ... श्री एकनाथ महाराज यांचें चरित्र** *etc.*) [Ekanātha Mahārāja yāṇcheṇ charitra.] pp. ii. 198. vi. [*Bombay*,] 1883. 12°. **14139. d. 29.**

DHUḶĀKSHARA. **धुळाक्षर प्रारंभः** [Dhuḷākshara. A primer in Devanagari and Modi characters, with arithmetical tables.] pp. 39, *lith.* [*Bombay?*, 1860?] *obl.* 12°. **14140. g. 13(1.)**

—— [Another edition.] pp. 43, *lith.* **मुंबई** [*Bombay*, 1864?] *obl.* 12°. **14140. g. 13(2.)**

—— [Another edition.] pp. 30, *lith.* **बेळगांव १७९९** [*Belgaum*, 1877.] 12°. **14140. g. 7(3.)**

—— [Another edition.] pp. 24, *lith.* **पुणें १८८१** [*Poona*, 1881.] 12°. **14140. g. 7(5.)**

DIALOGUES. Dialogues on Geography and Astronomy . . . translated into the Marathee language. (**भूगोल आणि खगोलइत्यादि विषयक संवाद**) [Bhūgola āṇi khagola vishayaka saṃvāda.] pp. 250. *Poona*, 1832. **14139. a. 3.**

DICKSON (JOHN BATHURST). *See* BIBLE.—*Miscellaneous Parts.* पुरातन परमपवित्र लेखांतले काव्यग्रंथ. The Poetical Books of the Old Testament. Translated by J. B. D., *etc.* 1839. 8°. **3068. d. 7.**

DIXON (JOHN) *Rev., Missionary at Nasik.* *See* BIBLE.—Old Testament.—*Genesis.* पहिलें पुस्तक [The Book of Genesis, translated by J. D.] [1846.] 8°. **3070. bb. 11.**

—— —— *Exodus.* दुसरें पुस्तक. [The Book of Exodus, translated by J. D.] [1846.] 8°. **3070. bb. 12.**

—— —— *Deuteronomy.* पांचवें पुस्तक ह्मणजे नेमप्रकरण. Deuteronomy. [Translated by J. D.] 1846. 8°. **3070. bb. 13.**

—— —— *Samuel.* शमुवेलाचें पहिलें (-दुसरें) पुस्तक. [The Books of Samuel, translated by J. D.] [1846.] 8°. **3070. bb. 15.**

—— *See* LITURGIES.—ENGLAND, *Church of.—Common Prayer.* इंग्लीश ख्रिस्ती मंडलीची भजनपद्धति. The Book of Common Prayer ... Translated ... by J. D. **3406. cc. 25.**

DOG. The faithful dog, and his basket. विश्वासु कुत्रा, आणि त्याची टोपली [Viṣvāsu kuttā āṇi tyāchī ṭoplī.] Illustrated in silhouette. pp. 14. सातारा १८७८ [*Satara*, 1878.] 8°. **14139. g. 14.**

DREW (WILLIAM HENRY). A geometrical treatise on conic sections, with notes, being the translation of the treatise of W. H. D. by Náráyáṇa Sádáśiva Kuḷakarṇi. (क्षेत्र शङ्कुच्छेद) [Kshaitra saṅkuchchheda.] pp. 262. *Bombay*, 1879. 8°. **14139. a. 36.**

DUFF (JAMES GRANT). *See* ESDAILE (D. A.) Catechism of the geography and history of Maháráshtra. Translated ... [from D. A. Esdaile's English epitome of J. G. D.'s "History of the Mahrattas."] 1869. 12°. **14139. d. 5.**

—— History of the Marat,has, translated from the English original of Captain Grant Duff, by Captain D. Capon. (मराठ्यांची बखर) [Marāṭhyāṇchī bakhar.] pp. iv. xxix. 427. iv. *Bombay*, 1830. 4°. **14142. b. 1.**

—— Second edition. Vol. I. pp. 319, *lith. Poona*, 1846. 8°. **14139. e. 3.**

DUFF. History of the Maráthás. Translated .... by D. Capon. Corrected ... by Keshava Sakhárám Shástrí. Fourth edition. 2 vol. *Bombay*, 1857. 12°. **14139. d. 11.**

DURGĀSTOTRA. दुर्गास्तोत्र ॥ [Durgāstotra. A hymn of praise to Durgā. Third edition.] ff. 4, *lith.* मुंबई १७६८ [*Bombay*, 1846 ?] *obl.* 32°. **14137. c. 2(1.)**

DVĀRAKĀNĀTHA NĀRĀYAṆA RAṆADIVE. The S'ikshâkâ or The tutor. A tale by Dwárkánáth Náráyan Raṇadive. Vol. I. (शिक्षक.) pp. ii. 181. *Bombay*, 1883. 12°. **14139. f. 27**

DVĀRAKĀNĀTHA RĀGHOBĀ TARKHAḌKAR. Anglo-Marâṭhî translation series ... By Dwárkánáth Rághobá Tarkhadkar. (भाषांतरपाठमाला) [Bhāshāntara pāṭhamālā.] Bk. I. II. *Bombay*, 1886–81. 12°.

Bk. I. is in 2 parts, of which pt. 1 is of the 5th and pt. 2 of the 4th edition. Bk. II. is of the 2nd edition.

14140. h. 23.

DWÁRKÁNÁTH. *See* DVĀRAKĀNĀTHA.

EKĀKSHARĪ ṢLOKA. एकाक्षरी श्लोक [Ekāksharī ṣloka. A hymn of praise to Vishṇu. Third edition.] pp. 12. मुंबई १७७० [*Bombay*, 1848.] 12°. **14140. a. 1(5.)**

EKANĀTHA. *Life.* *See* DHONḌO BĀḶAKRISHṆA SAHASRABUDDHE. The life and poems of Ekanath.

—— *See* PURĀṆAS.—*Bhāgavatapurāṇa.* अथ श्रीभागवत एकनाथकृत प्रारभ्यते. [Sanskrit text, with E.'s Marathi commentary.] [1881.] *obl.* 4°. **14018. d. 16.**

—— अथ आनंदलहरी [Ānandalaharī. A philosophical poem.] ff. 14, *lith.* पुणें १८८३ [*Poona*, 1883.] *obl.* 12°. **14137. c. 11(3.)**

—— एकनाथकृत अर्जदास्त वगैरे प्रारंभ. [Arjadāsta and other short poems.] pp. 23, *lith.* पुणें १८८२ [*Poona*, 1882.] 12°. **14140. a. 11(8.)**

—— एकनाथकृत अर्जदास्त प्रारंभः [Another edition of the preceding, with the addition of several other of E.'s poems.] pp. 48, *lith.* मुंबई १८८४ [*Bombay*, 1884.] 12°. **14140. a. 30(2.)**

EKANĀTHA. अथ श्रीएकनाथी भागवतप्रारंभः [Ekanāthī Bhāgavata. A commentary in the Ovī metre in thirty-one chapters, on the eleventh book of the Bhāgavatapurāṇa.] *Lith.* पुणें १८८१ [*Poona*, 1881.] **14140. d. 19.**

—— अथ एकनाथकृत गारुड वगैरे प्रारंभ. [Gāruḍa, and other short poems.] pp. 15, *lith.* पुणें १८८२ [*Poona*, 1882.] 12°. **14140. a. 30(1.)**

—— अथहस्तामलक प्रारंभः [Hastāmalaka. A work on Vedanta philosophy, on the nature of the soul, in the form of a dialogue between Ṣaṅkara Āchārya and his disciple Hastāmalaka.] ff. 62, *lith.* मुंबई १८०४ [*Bombay*, 1882.] *obl.* 12°. **14140. a. 31.**

—— अथ श्री रुक्मिणीस्वयंवर प्रारंभ ॥ [Rukmiṇīsvayaṃvara. A poem in 18 chapters on the marriage of Rukmiṇī to Kṛishṇa; founded chiefly on the tenth chapter of the Bhāgavatapurāṇa. Second edition.] *Lith.* १७८२ [*Bombay*, 1860.] *obl.* 8°. **14140. f. 6.**

—— [Another edition.] *Lith.* मुंबई १७८३ [*Bombay*, 1861.] *obl.* 8°. **14140. b. 7.**

—— [Another edition.] *Lith.* पुणें १७८४ [*Poona*, 1862.] *obl.* 8°. **14140. b. 4.**

—— [Another edition.] ff. 154, *lith.* पुणें १८८१ [*Poona*, 1881.] *obl.* 12°. **14140. a. 26.**

—— अथ श्रीएकनाथचरित्रप्रारंभः [Ekanāthacharitra. A poem, in 31 adhyāyas, on the life of Ekanātha and miracles ascribed to him.] *Lith.* पुणें १८८३ [*Poona*, 1883.] *obl.* 8°. **14139. e. 24.**

EKANĀTHA AṆṆĀJĪ JOṢĪ. "शिवाजी महाराज यांस दादोजी कोंडदेवकृत उपदेश" [Ṣivājī mahārāja yāṉs .... upadeṣa. A poem on the advice given by Dādojī Koṇḍadeva to Ṣivājī on his determination to deliver his country from the Muhammadan rule.] pp. 32. मुंबई १८७७ [*Bombay*, 1877.] 12°. **14140. a. 19(2.)**

EKANĀTHA GAṆEṢA BHĀṆḌĀRE. कामकंदला नाटक [Kāmakandalā nāṭaka, or The adventures of King Kāmasena. A drama in five acts.] pp. 228. viii. ठाणें १८८१ [*Thana*, 1881.] 12°. **14140. a. 29.**

ELPHINSTONE (*Hon.* MOUNTSTUART). The history of India, the Hindu and Mahomedan periods ... Translated into Maráthí by Vishvanáth Náráyan Mandlik. (हिंदुस्थानाचा इतिहास) [Hindusthānāchā itihāsa.] 3 vol. *Bombay*, 1861-62. 8°.

Vol. III., entitled "Introduction," contains a translation of the first 3 books of the original. **14139. e. 10.**

ELPHINSTONE. Introduction to the history of India, abridged from the work of the Hon. Mountstuart Elphinstone, by ... Ball Gungadher Shastree. A new edition, edited by Major Candy. (हिंदुस्थानाचा इतिहास). pp. 197. viii., *lith.* *Poona*, 1852. 8°. **14139. e. 4.**

—— [Second edition.] pp. 205. viii., *lith.* *Poona*, 1855. 8°. **14139. e. 2.**

ENGLAND. History of England [to the year A.D. 1820] translated ... into the Marathee language. (इंग्लंड देशाची बखर). 2 vol. *Poona*, 1832-34. 8°. **14139. d. 1.**

—— —— Third edition. Corrected for the press by Keshava Sakhárám Shástrí. 2 vol. *Bombay*, 1857. 8°. **14139. d. 9.**

ENGLISH AND MARATHI FIRST BOOK. English and Marathi First Book. Revised edition. pp. 72. *Bombay*, 1881. 16°. **14140. g. 30(3.)**

ENGLISH GRAMMAR. Principles of English grammar and idiomatic sentences, in English and Maráthí. इंग्लिश व्याकरण आणि भाषण सांप्रदायिक वाक्यं. pp. xi. 284. *Bombay*, 1851. 12°. **14140. h. 3.**

ENQUIRY. Inquiry concerning the want of rain. पावसाविषयीं विचार [Pāvasā vishayīṉ vichāra. A Christian tract.] pp. 8. [*Bombay*? 1845?] 24°. **14137. a. 1(4.)**

—— मोठा विचार [Moṭhā vichāra.] Great inquiry. [A Christian tract.] Eighth edition. pp. 16. *Bombay*, [1845?] 12°.

No. 8 of the "Bombay Tract and Book Society's Series." **14137. a. 2(5.)**

EPHEMERIDES. शके १७८८ क्षयनामसंवत्सरे ॥ [Pañchāṅga. An almanac for the year A.D. 1866.] *Sansk.* and *Mar.* ff. 18, *lith.* मुंबई [*Bombay*, 1866.] *obl.* 8°. **14096. a. 1.**

ESDAILE (D. A.) Catechism of the geography and history of Maháráshtra. Translated into Máráthí [by Kuṣābā Limaye from D. A. E.'s English epitome of J. D. Duff's "History of the Mahrattas."] (महाराष्ट्र देशाचें वर्णन) [Mahārāshṭra deṣācheṉ varṇana.] Twelfth edition. pp. 72. *Bombay*, 1869. 12°. **14139. d. 5.**

—— Murathee translation [by T. Candy] of the Principles of morality [of D. A. E.] (नीतिज्ञानाची परिभाषा.) [Nītijñānāchī paribhāshā.] pp. 64. पुणें १८४८ [*Poona*, 1848.] 12°. **14139. c. 3(1.)**

ESHWARACHANDRA VIDYÁSÁGAR. *See* Īśvarachandra Vidyāsāgara.

ESMARCH (Friedrich). First Aid to the Injured. Translated into Marathi (by Mr. Ramchandra Raghoba Dharadhar) from the English translation ... by H.R.H. Princess Christian [of Professor Esmarch's German work]. (इजेवर प्रथम उपाय०) [Ijevar prathama upāya.] pp. 54. *Education Society's Press; Bombay,* 1883. 8°.
14137. h. 13.

EUCLID. Elements of plane geometry [according to Euclid, Bks. I–VI, by Andrew Bell] translated into Maráthí by Náná Shástrí Ápte. (युक्लिडचे सरळरेखा गणिताचीं मूलतत्वें). Fourth edition. pp. 252. *Bombay,* 1867. 8°. **14139. a. 16.**

FAIRBANK ( ) *Mrs.* Incidents from the life of Mrs. F. ... फरबेंक मडम साहेब ह्यांच्या गोष्टी. Pt. I. pp. 24. *Ahmednagar,* 1878. 16°. **14139. d. 16(1.)**

FAMILY FRIEND. The Family Friend [consisting of dialogues on domestic matters, intended chiefly for the families of native Christians.] कुटुंबाचा मित्र. [Kuṭumbāchā mitra.] pp. vii. 195. *Bombay,* 1877. 12°.
One of the "American Mission Prize Series."
14139. c. 16.

FARRAR ( ) *Mrs.* चमत्कारिक गोष्टी. [Chamatkārika goshṭī.] The Ayah and Lady. Modified and translated by Mrs. Farrar. pp. 94. १८३५. *Nasik* [1835.] 8°.
No. 32 of the Bombay Tract and Book Society's Series.
14137. b. 5(5.)

FARRAR (Charles Pinhorn). *See* Bible.—Old Testament.—*Psalms.* गीतं The Psalms of David. In Murathee metre. Part I. Edited by the Rev. C. P. F. 1836. 8°. **3070. bb. 14.**

——— ईश्वराचें पवित्रत्व व न्यायत्व यांचें प्रदर्शन. [Īśvarācheṇ pavitratva.] On the holiness and justice of God. pp. 22. नाशिक १८३५ [*Nasik,* 1835.] 8°.
No. 33 of the Bombay Tract and Book Society's Series.
14137. b. 5(6.)

FIRST BOOK. लेंकराची पहिली पोथी. [Leṇkrāchī pahilī pothī.] First book for children. 45th edition. pp. 44. *Bombay,* 1875. 16°.
One of the Bombay Tract and School Book Society's Series.
14140. g. 9(3.)

——— 47th edition. pp. 44. *Bombay,* 1877. 16°.
14140. g. 30(1.)

FORMS. भजनांची पद्धति. [Bhajanānchī paddhati.] Forms of worship. 6th edition. pp. 22. [*Bombay,*] 1841. 12°.
No. 35 of the "American Mission Series."
14137. a. 2(4.)

GAISFORD (Thomas) *Captain, Bombay Artillery. See* Berquin (A.) Marat'ha translation of Berquin's Children's Friend. (Vol. 2 by T. G.) [1833.] 8°. **14137. b. 2.**

GAJAGAURĪ. अथ गजगौरी आख्यान प्रारंभ. [Gajagaurī ākhyāna. A poem on the worship of the image of Pārvatī, placed on an elephant, followed by Daśāvatārāche śloka, or verses on the ten incarnations of Vishṇu.] pp. 22, *lith.* मुंबई [*Bombay,* 1860 ?] 12°. **14140. a. 4(3.)**

GAJĀNANA BHĀŪ VAIJYA. A complete system of short-hand for Marathi [based on Pitman's system] by Gajanan Bhau Vaijya. (लघुलेखनपद्धति) [Laghulekhanapaddhati.] pp. x. 66. *Bombay,* 1881. 12°. **14139. a. 42.**

GAṆAPATA MAHĀDEVA AIREKAR. *See* Howard (E. J.) The English primer by E. J. Howard. With translation and pronunciation ... by Ganpat Mahadew Airekar. 1868. 8°. **12984. f. 5.**

GAṆAPATARĀVA HARIHARA PAṬAVARDHANA. गणेशपुराण आर्या. [Gaṇeśapurāṇa āryā. A poem in the ārya metre, giving the substance of the Gaṇeśapurāṇa.] pp. ix. 107. ii. *lith.* पुणें १७९९ [*Poona,* 1877.] 8°. **14137. c. 10.**

GAṆAPATARĀVA SĀTĀRKAR. *See* Hemādrī. हेमाद्रीकृत लेखनकल्पतरु [Lekhanakalpataru. With a commentary and additional matter by G. S.] [1853.] 12°. **14140. g. 5.**

GAṆAPATI. संकटनाशन श्लोक ॥ गणपतीचे ॥ [Saṅkaṭanāśana. Invocations to the god Gaṇapati, or Gaṇeśa, for the purpose of averting evils. Second edition.] pp. 5. मुंबई १७७५ [*Bombay,* 1855.] 16°.
14140. a. 3(2.)

GAṆEŚA BAḶAVANTA LIMAYE. Kavitádarsha, or The mirror of poetry [containing a syntactical construction, and explanation of selected poems from the writings of well known Marathi poets; with marginal notes]. कवितादर्श pp. iv. 244. पुणे १८७७ [*Poona,* 1877.] 8°. **14140. b. 11.**

GAṆEṢA HARI BHIḌE. Marathi English Primer, by Ganesh Hari Bhide. pp. vi. 108. *Bombay,* 1889. 8°. **14140. g. 43.**

GAṆEṢA KRISHṆA ĀPṬE. सृष्टिज्ञान भाग पहिला. [Srishṭijñāna. An elementary work on physical science, in verse.] Pt. I. pp. iii. 22. पुणें १९९९ [*Poona,* 1877.] 16°. **14139. a. 33(1.)**

GAṆEṢA KRISHṆA GARDE. *See* BĀLAKRISHṆA DINKAR VAIDYA KALYĀṄKAR. रोगी व वैद्य [Rogī va vaidya. Revised, with a preface, by G. K. G.] [1880.] 12°. **14137. ff. 4.**

GAṆEṢA LAKSHMAṆA ḌHORE. संक्षिप्त भूगोलविद्या. [Saṃkshipta bhūgolavidyā. An elementary manual of geography.] pp. 68. पुणें १९९९ [*Poona,* 1877.] 12°. **14139. d. 31(2.)**

GAṆEṢA MAHĀDEVA LIMAYE. वेणु. [Veṇu. A tale of social life and manners.] pp. 250. पुणें १८८६ [*Poona,* 1886.] 12°. **14139. f. 26.**

GAṆEṢA MOREṢVARA SOVANĪ. तुर्क व रशियन लोकांचे लढाईचा इतिहास. [Turk va Raṣiyan lokāṇche laḍhāīchā itihāsa. An account of the Turco-Russian war of 1877–78, compiled from various English works by G. M. S. assisted by Ṣivarāma Gaṇapatarāva Bābras.] pp. ii. 137. पुणें १८८० [*Poona,* 1880.] 8°. **14139. e. 20.**

GAṆEṢA RĀMACHANDRA KILOSKAR. सरकारचे कर. [Sarkārche kar. A lecture on the Government revenues derived from India.] pp. 8. *See* BOMBAY, *City of.—Hindu Union Club.* हेमंत व्याख्यानमाला [Hemanta vyākhyānamālā.] Vol. II. No. 1. [1886, *etc.*] 8°. **14139. c. 26.**

GAṆEṢA SADĀṢIVA ṢĀSTRĪ LELE. *See* BINGLEY (W.) *Rev.* The voyages of Capt. Cook. Translated ... by Ganesh Sadáshiw Shástree Lele. 1853. 8°. **14139. d. 3.**

GAṆEṢA ṢĀSTRĪ ABHYAṄKAR. तत्वविचार. [Tattvavichāra. An enquiry into idol-worship.] pp. 12. मुंबई १८७५ [*Bombay,* 1875.] 12°. **14137. a. 7(1.)**

GAṆEṢA ṢĀSTRĪ LELE TRYAMBAKAKAR. *See* AMARU. श्रीमच्छंकराचार्य विरचित अमरुशतक [Amaruṣataka. Edited with a translation by G. Ṣ. L. T.] [1881.] 16°. **14076. a. 12(3.)**

GAṆEṢA ṢĀSTRĪ LELE TRYAMBAKAKAR. *See* KĀLIDĀSA. Málavikágnimitra : .... Translated from the original Sanskrit ... by Ganesh Shástrí Lele. 1867. 12°. **14140. e. 9.**

—— *See* PUSHPADANTA. महिम्नस्तोत्र *etc.* [Mahimnaḥ stotra. With a verse translation by G. Ṣ. L. T.] [1875.] 8°. **14033. a. 6.**

—— *See* RĀMABHADRA DĪKSHITA. जानकीपरिणय नाटक समांकी. [Jānakīpariṇaya nāṭaka. Translated by G. Ṣ. L. T.] [1865.] 12°. **14140. f. 26.**

—— —— [1866.] 8°. **14140. f. 25.**

GAṆEṢA VINĀYAKA KĀNIṬKAR. मनोरंजक दमयंती. [Manorañjaka Damayantī. The story of Nala and Damayantī in prose, taken from the Mahābhārata]. pp. 82. मुंबई १८७७ [*Bombay,* 1877.] 8°. **14139. g. 15.**

GAṆEṢA VISHṆU GADRE. *See* MOROPANTA. केकासार *etc.* [Kekāsāra. The Kekāvalī with paraphrase, explanations and glossary, by G. V. G.] [1883.] 12°. **14140. a. 19(3.)**

GANESH HARI BHIDE. *See* GAṆEṢA HARI BHIḌE.

GANESH SHÁSTRÍ LELE. *See* GAṆEṢA ṢĀSTRĪ LELE TRYAMBAKAKAR.

GAṄGĀDHARA, *Author of a work on the Hindu religion. See* GAṄGĀDHARA ṢĀSTRĪ PHAḌKE.

GAṄGĀDHARA, *Kavi.* गंगाधरकृत रसकल्लोल [Rasakallola. Erotic verses.] *See* PERIODICAL PUBLICATIONS.—*Poona.* काव्येतिहास संग्रह [Kāvyetihāsa saṅgraha.] Vol. VIII. Nos. 10 and 11. [1878, *etc.*] 8°. **14072. d. 37.**

GAṄGĀDHARA BĀLAKRISHṆA GADRE. प्रार्थनासमाज. ... उपासनांच्या व भजनाच्या वेळीं गावयाचीं पद्यें. [Upāsanāṇchyā ... veḷīṇ gāvayāchīṇ padyeṇ. Hymns sung at the services of the Prārthanā Samāj.] pp. 14. मुंबई १८८४ [*Bombay,* 1884.] 12°. **14137. a. 11.**

GAṄGĀDHARA DĪKSHITA. आरत्यापंचक प्रारंभ: [Āratyāpañchaka. Five āratīs, or hymns of praise to the gods.] pp. 9, *lith.* मुंबई १८६० [*Bombay,* 1860.] 12°. **14140. a. 4(4.)**

GANGĀDHARA GOPĀLA PATKĪ. *See* SARASVATI GANGĀDHARA. अथ श्रीगुरुचरित्र प्रारंभः ॥ [Gurucharitra. Edited by G. G. P., with an introductory chapter, containing a summary of each chapter of the poem.] [1875.] *obl.* 8°. **14137. e. 8.**

GANGĀDHARA GOVINDA SĀPKAR. Marathi Proverbs. मराठी प्रचारांतील म्हणी. [Marāṭhī prachārāntīla mhaṇī.] Second edition, pp. 72. १८८५ [*Poona,* 1885.] 12°. **14139. c. 22.**

—— तोंडचे हिशेब. [Toṇḍache hiseb. Exercises in mental arithmetic. Fifth edition.] pp. 36. मुंबई १८६७ [*Bombay,* 1867.] 16°. **14140. g. 9(2.)**

GANGĀDHARA RĀMACHANDRA TILAKA. [Gungadhur's rudiments of [Marathi] grammar लघुव्याकरण [Laghuvyākaraṇa. Second edition.] pp. 78, *lith.* १८५९ [*Poona?* 1859.] 12°. **14140. g. 7(1.)**

GANGĀDHARA SĀSTRĪ PHADKE. *See* BĀLA SĀSTRĪ GHAGVE. A dictionary of the Maratha language, compiled by Gungadhur Shastree Phurke, *etc.* 1829. 4°. **14140. i. 1.**

—— *See* DE MORGAN (A.) De Morgan's elements of Algebra: translated into the Marathi language by Colonel George Ritso Jervis, assisted by ... Gungadhur Shastri Phudkay. 1848. 8°. **14139. b. 5.**

—— *Begin:* हिंदुधर्मतत्वस्य प्रस्तावना अध्यायःप्रथमः [Hindudharmatattva. A treatise in twelve chapters, on Hindu religious observances, and teaching of the Vedas.] pp. 176. [*Bombay,* 1858.] 12°. *With no title-page.* **14137. c. 13.**

—— महाराष्ट्र भाषेचें व्याकरण. [Mahārashṭra bhāshecheṇ vyākaraṇa. A grammar of the Marathi language. Second edition.] pp. 165. मुंबई १८३८ [*Bombay,* 1838.] 12°. **14140. g. 4.**

GANGĀDHARA VITHṬHALA MOGRE. आर्य मातृविलाप. [Ārya mātṛivilāpa. The lament of a Hindu mother over her apostate son. A poem.] pp. 25. बांबे १८७७ [*Bombay,* 1877.] 16°. **14140. a. 5(4.)**

GĀṆĪN. कुलिन स्त्रियां साठीं गाणीं. [Kulina striyāṇ sāṭhīṇ gāṇīṇ. A collection of songs, mostly mythological, sung by women.] 3 pt. पुणें १८८३ [*Poona,* 1883.] 12°. **14140. a. 32.**

GARBHAKĀṆḌA. अथ गर्भकांड गर्भावळी प्रारंभः [Garbhakāṇḍa. A treatise in verse on procreation and parturition.] ff. 10, *lith.* मुंबई १९८५ [*Bombay,* 1863.] *obl.* 16°. **14140. a. 9(3.)**

GARUḌA. गरुडाख्यान. [Garuḍākhyāna. Verses describing the exploits of the god Garuḍa.] ff. 10, *lith.* [*Bombay?* 1857 ?] *obl.* 12°. **14140. a. 6(4.)**

GĀRUḌA. गारुड्याचा तमाशा आणि इंद्रजाल विद्येचे अद्भुत चमत्कार. [Gāruḍyāchā tamāshā. An explanation of certain tricks of native jugglers.] Pt. I. pp. 42. मुंबई १८८५ [*Bombay,* 1885.] 12°. **14139. a. 32(3.)**

GAURĪSAṄKARA SĀSTRĪ. यात्राकल्पलता [Yātrākalpalatā. An account of the pilgrimages made in the North and South Carnatic by Raghunātharāva Viṭhṭhala, commonly known as Aṇṇā Sāheb, the Chief of Vinchur, between A.D. 1881 and 1884.] pp. ii. iv. 128. पुणें १८८४ [*Poona,* 1884.] 12°. **14137. d. 17.**

GĀYANAPRAKĀRA. गायनप्रकार. [Gāyanaprakāra. Songs by various poets in the pada and lāvaṇī metres.] pp. 46, *lith.* मुंबई १९८५ [*Bombay,* 1863.] 12°. **14139. c. 11(9.)**

—— [Another edition.] pp. 54, *lith.* मुंबई १९८६ [*Bombay,* 1864.] 12°. **14140. a. 11(3.)**

GEIKIE (ARCHIBALD). Science primers in Marāṭhī. Physical geography. Translated from the original work of A. G. ... by Kâshinâth Bâlkrishna Marâthé. (अनेक विद्या विषयक बालशिक्षाग्रंथमाला ग्रंथ ४ भूवर्णन.) pp. iv. 104. *Bombay,* 1880. 16°. **14139. d. 32.**

GOOD BOYS. Good boys, or Examine yourselves. चांगले मुलगे किंवा तुम्ही आपली परीक्षा करा. [Chāṅgle mulge.] pp. 34. मुंबई १८३८ [*Bombay,* 1838.] 12°. *One of the Bombay Tract and Book Society's Series.* **14137. b. 5.**

GOPĀLA BĀLAKRISHṆA VAIDYA. *See* BĀLAKRISHṆA BĀBĀJĪ KARKARE and GOPĀLA BĀLAKRISHṆA VAIDYA. त्र्यंबकवर्णन [Tryambaka varṇana.] [1885.] 12°. **14139. d. 23.**

GOPĀLADĀSA. चिकित्सासार. [Chikitsāsāra. A Sanskrit work on medicine by G., accompanied by a Marathi translation. Third edition.] ff. 239, *lith.* पुणें १८८१ [*Poona,* 1881.] 8°. **14043. e. 7.**

GOPĀLA GOVINDA DĀBAK. त्रिवेणी प्रमाथ. अथवा असतीसंग दुष्परिणाम नाटक. [Triveṇī Pramātha. A tale showing the evil effects of a profligate life.] pp. iii. 309. ठाणें १८८१ [*Thana*, 1881.] 8°. **14140. f. 17.**

GOPĀLA HARI DEṢMUKH. प्राचीन आर्यविद्या व रीति. [Prāchīna āryavidyā va rīti. The ancient Aryans, their literature and religion.] pp. 14. अलीबाग १९९९ [*Alibagh*, 1877.] 8°. **14139. e. 5(2.)**

GOPĀLARĀVA HARI. *See* LOKAHITAVĀDĪ, *pseud.*

GOPĀLA ṢĀSTRĪ GHĀṆṬE. विग्रहकोश. [Vigrahakoṣa. A Sanskrit-Marathi dictionary.] pp. 723. xxxiv. *lith.* मुंबई १९८९ [*Bombay*, 1867.] 8°. **14093. d. 6.**

GOPĀLA ṢIVARĀMA VAIDYA. A treatise on surgery, compiled from English works by Gopál Shivarám Vaidya. (शस्त्रवैद्यक.) [Ṣastravaidyaka.] pp. ii. ii. xxi. 632. xi. xiii. *Bombay*, 1869. 8°. **14137. h. 6.**

GOPĀLA YAJÑEṢVARA BHIḌE. जमाखर्चाची माहिती. [Jamākharchāchī māhitī. An explanation of the native plan of book-keeping, with specimens of various methods adopted. Third edition.] pp. 18, 12, 7, 4, 1. रत्नागिरी १८९९ [*Ratnagiri*, 1877.] 8°. **14139. b. 7(3.)**

GOPÁL SHIVARÁM VAIDYA. *See* GOPĀLA ṢIVARĀMA VAIDYA.

GOPĪNĀTHA SADĀṢIVAJĪ HĀṬE. परमेश्वराच्या आराधनेचें पुस्तक. [Parameṣvarāchyā ārādhanecheṇ pustaka. Brahmist hymns and prayers.] pp. 27. मुंबई १९९५ [*Bombay*, 1874.] 8°. **14137. b. 9(1.)**

GOVINDA GAṄGĀDHARA PHAḌKE. *See* DE MORGAN (A.) De Morgan's elements of Algebra: translated into the Marathi language by Colonel George Ritso Jervis, assisted by ... Govind Gungadhur Phudkay. 1848. 8°. **14139. b. 5.**

GOVINDA MOROBĀ KĀRLEKAR. बहुरूपी संतखेळ आणि भजनी भारूड संग्रह. [Bahurūpī santakheḷ. A collection of obscure and epigrammatic songs on Vedanta philosophy, by popular Marathi poets and saints.] pp. viii. 142. मुंबई १८८६ [*Bombay*, 1886.] 12°. **14140. a. 33.**

GOVINDA NĀRĀYAṆA. Bombay past and present: An historical sketch in Marathi, with maps and glossary. (मुंबईचें वर्णन) [Mumbaīcheṇ varṇana.] pp. viii. iii. 401. *Bombay*, 1863. 8°. **14139. e. 13.**

—— Description of trees. (वृक्षवर्णन) [Vrikshavarṇana.] pp. v. 108. *Bombay*, 1857. 12°. **14139. a. 8.**

—— Drama on a practical subject. व्यवहारोपयोगी नाटक. [Vyavahāropayogī nāṭaka.] pp. 32. मुंबई १८५९ [*Bombay*, 1859.] 12°. **14140. a. 8(1.)**

—— The observance of truth, with special reference to the administration of justice, and the advancement of the best interests of society. (सत्यनिरूपण) [Satyanirūpaṇa.] Third edition. pp. ii. 89. *Bombay*, 1877. 12°. **14139. c. 3(2.)**

—— Vegetable Substances, corn, pulse, roots, tubers, fruits, etc. etc. etc., used for the food of man. (उद्भिद्जन्यपदार्थ) [Udbhidjanyapadārtha]. pp. 216. *Bombay*, 1856. 12°. **14139. a. 9.**

GOVINDA NĀRĀYAṆA KĀṆE. An account of the life and writings of Lord Bacon, founder of the inductive philosophy ... लार्ड बेकन याचें चरित्र व त्यानें केलेल्या ग्रंथांचें वर्णन. मुंबई १८८० [*Bombay*, 1880.] 12°. **14139. d. 22.**

GOVINDA NĀRĀYAṆA KSHĪRASĀGARA. सन्मार्गदीपिका. [Sanmārgadīpikā. A translation by G. N. Ksh. of the English "Social and moral duties."] pp. 55. मुंबई १८७७ [*Bombay*, 1877.] 8°. **14139. c. 18(1.)**

GOVINDA RĀMAKṚISHṆA PHAṆSALKAR. Shabda sangraha. (शब्दसंग्रह भाग पहिला.) [A vocabulary of difficult words occurring in the Marathi First, Second, and Third Books.] 2 pt. १८७७ [*Bombay*, 1877.] 12°.
Pt. I is of the 4th and pt. II of the 11th edition.
14140. g. 42.

GOVINDARĀVA BHIKĀJĪ PAṬAVARDHAN. *See* PURĀṆAS. काशीप्रताप *etc.* [Kāṣīpratāpa. Compiled by G. Bh. P.] 1880. 4°. **14028. e. 34(3.)**

—— *See* SA'DĪ. गुलिस्तां. (The "Gulistan" ... translated ... with a life of the poet by Govindrao Bhikaji Patwardhan, *etc.*) [1884]. 8°. **14139. g. 19.**

GOVINDA RĀVAJĪ MĀṆḌE. *See* MAC CUDDEN (T.) The Oriental eras .... Translated into the Marathee language by Govind Raojee Mundey .... from the English of T. McCudden. 1860. 4°. **14142. b. 3.**

GOVINDA ṢAṄKARA ṢĀSTRĪ BĀPAṬ. *See* SAINT PIERRE (J. H. B. DE). Paul and Virginia. ... Translated into Marathi by Govind Shankar Shástri Bápat. 1875. 12°. **14139. f. 17.**

—— History of Hari and Trimbaka. [A tale] by Govind Shankar Shástrí Bápat. (**हरि आणि त्रिंबक**). pp. viii. 219. *Bombay*, 1875. 12°. **14139. f. 18.**

—— Nitimandira, or Mansion of morality, by Govind Shankar Shástri Bápata. [A collection of moral precepts and stories, taken from the Manusmṛiti, Viduranīti, and Hitopadeṣa.] (**नीतिमन्दिर.**) pp. ii. 200. *Bombay*, 1879. 12°. **14139. c. 15.**

—— Panchatantrasára or Fables of Vishnu Sharmá. Adapted from Panchatantra and moralized by Govind Shankar Shástrí Bápat. (**पञ्चतन्त्रसार.**) pp. ii. 131. *Bombay*, 1881. 12°. **14139. f. 30.**

—— Vyutpattipradîpa, or a Manual of etymology of the Marâthî language. By Govind Shankar Shâstrî Bâpat. (**व्युत्पत्तिप्रदीप**). pp. iii. 86. *Bombay*, 1885. 12°. **14140. g. 39.**

—— Second edition, revised and enlarged. pp. iv. 116. *Bombay*, 1886. 12°. **14140. g. 40.**

GOVINDĀSHṬAKA. **गोविंदाष्टक** [Govindāshṭaka. Eight stanzas in praise of Kṛishṇa.] ff. 3, *lith.* **मुंबई १७७८** [*Bombay*, 1856.] *obl.* 12°. **14140. a. 6(5.)**

GOVINDA VĀSUDEVA KĀNIṬKAR. *See* VIṬHṬHALA BĀPŪJĪ KARMARKAR. The Himalayas ... A Sanskrit prize poem ... Translated into Marathi verse by Govind Wasudev Canitkar. [1875.] 8°. **14076. c. 46.**

GOVINDA VIṬHṬHALA MĀHĀJAN. *See* VINĀYAKA ṢĀSTRĪ DIVEKAR and GOVINDA VIṬHṬHALA MĀHĀJAN. **शब्दसिद्धिनिबंध** [Ṣabdasiddhinibandha.] [1859.] 12°. **14140. g. 8(1.)**

GOVIND SHANKAR SHÁSTRI BÁPAT. *See* GOVINDA ṢAṄKARA ṢĀSTRĪ BĀPAṬ.

GOVIND WASUDEV CANITKAR. *See* GOVINDA VĀSUDEVA KĀNIṬKAR.

GRANT (*Sir* ALEXANDER) *Bart.* Catalogue of native publications in the Bombay Presidency up to 31st December 1864. Prepared under orders of Government by Sir A. Grant, Bart. Second edition, with numerous additions and corrections. pp. 35. 239. *Bombay*, 1867. 8°.
The continuation is by J. B. Peile. **752. e. 14.**

GREEN (HENRY) *Superintendent of Government Schools in Gujarat.* *See* HARI KESAVAJĪ. Elements of political economy .... Compiled under the superintendence of H. G. 1854. 8°. **14139. c. 7.**

—— A collection of English phrases ... with their Marathi equivalents by Sadáshiva Vishwanáth Háté. Revised by Mahádeo Govind Ranade. pp. iv. 259. *Bombay*, 1868. 8°. **12906. cc. 6.**

GUNGADHUR. *See* GAṄGĀDHARA RĀMACHANDRA ṬILAKA.

HADDON (JAMES) *M.A.* Elements of Algebra ... Translated into Maráthí .... by Dájí Nílcanth Naggarkar. Revised and corrected by Krishna Shástrí Godbole. (**बीजगणिताचीं मूलतत्वें**) [Bījagaṇitāchīṇ ·mulatattveṇ.] Third edition. pp. 228. *Bombay*, 1865. 8°. **14139. a. 15.**

HAIDAR SHĀH, *Nawab of Mysore.* *Memoir.* *See* Rāmachandra Rāva, *Panganūrī.* Memoirs of Hyder and Tippoo, *etc.* **14139. e. 26.**

HĀĪM (DAVID). *See* TAḶKAR (H. J.) **हिंदुस्थानांत आल्यापासून बेने इस्राएल लोकांचा इतिहास** [Bene Israel lokāṇchā itihāsa. Compiled with the assistance of D. H.] [1874.] 12°. **14139. d. 14.**

—— Rásakrídá, a Marathi drama [on the festival of the circular dance of Kṛishṇa], by David Haeem .... **कृष्णखंडांतील नाटकरूपी रासक्रीडा.** pp. 52. **मुंबई १८७४** [*Bombay*, 1874.] 16°. **14139. d. 20.**

HAMSARĀJA SVĀMĪ. *See* ṢAṄKARA ĀCHĀRYA. **अथ वाक्यवृत्तीप्रारंभा** [Vākyavṛitti. A Vedantic work in verse in the form of a commentary in the 18 aphorisms of Ṣaṅkara Āchārya.] [1880.] *obl.* 8°. **14048. d. 36.**

HARIDĀSA. **विक्रमचरित्रप्रारंभः** [Vikramacharitra. An account of the life of King Vikramāditya, in verse, in eighteen chapters.] *lith.* **मुंबई १७८५** [*Bombay*, 1863.] *obl.* 8°.

Fol. 4 of Adhyāya 2 is erroneously repeated, and fol. 7 of Adhyāya 7 omitted in pagination.

14137. e. 6.

—— Vickram Charitra ... Translated from the Prakrit [*i.e.* Marathi] poem of Hurridass into ... English ... by Ragoba Moroba. pp. viii. 285. *Bombay*, 1855. 8°. **14137. d. 12.**

HARI KEṢAVAJĪ. *See* Davys (G.) *Bishop of Peterborough.* A plain and short history of England for children ... Translated ... into Marathee by Hari Keshavaji. 1867. 12°. **14139. e. 9.**

—— Conversations on Christianity, translated from English into Maratheo; with a glossary of difficult terms, by Hurree Keshoujee. (**रसायनशास्त्र विषयक संवाद**) [Rasāyanaṣāstra.] pp. xii. 478. vi. *Bombay*, 1837. 4°. **14139. b. 4.**

—— Elements of political economy. An imitation of, and partly translated from, Mrs. Marcet's Conversations, comprising also a paraphrase into popular Marathi dialogue of many of the most important portions of Mill's Principles. Compiled under the superintendence of ... H. Green ... by Hari Keshowaji .... and Vishwanáth Náráyan Mandlik. (**देशव्यवहार व्यवस्था**) [Deṣavyavahāra vyavasthā.] pp. 280. *Bombay*, 1854. 8°.

14139. c. 7.

HARIKRISHṆA DĀMLE. *See* Swift (J.) *Dean of St. Patrick's.* Gulliver's Travels. Part I. The voyage to Liliput .... [Translated by H. D.] [1880.] 12°. **14139. f. 23.**

HARI NĀRĀYAṆA LIMAYE. **मराठी साहाव्याइयत्तेचा गणित विषय.** [Marāṭhī sāhāvyā iyattechā gaṇita vishaya. A mathematical course of study in arithmetic and geometry for advanced pupils.] pp. 242, *lith.* **रत्नागिरी १८८१** [*Ratnagiri*, 1881.] 8°.

14139. b. 15.

HARI RAGHUNĀTHA GĀḌGĪḶ. **विंचूरकर घराण्याचा इतिहास.** [Vinchūrkar gharāṇyāchā itihāsa. A biographical account of the family of the Chief of Vinchurkar, a jaghirdar in the Nasik District in the Deccan. Compiled, from old manuscripts, family records and other sources, by H. R. G.] **पुणे १८८३** [*Poona*, 1883.] 8°. **14139. e. 21.**

HARIRĀJA. *See* Mudgala Āchārya. **रामार्याचे श्लोकबद्ध भाषांतर** [Rāmāryā. A Sanskrit poem, translated by H.] [1878, *etc.*] 8°. **14072. d. 37.**

HARI SAKHĀRĀMA. The Ready Reckoner. Arranged ... for the use of Railway Station Masters and Goods Clerks, showing at a glance the value of any number of rates from 1 to 100 Rupees per 100 maunds ..... by Hurry Succaram. pp. 56. *Engl. Bombay*, 1878. 12°. **14139. a. 27(4.)**

HARIṢCHANDRA. **अथ हरिश्चंद्राख्यान प्रारंभः** [Hariṣchandrākhyāna, or The story of king Hariṣchandra in verse.] ff. 18, *lith.* **मुंबई** [*Bombay*, 1866?] *obl.* 8°. **14139. g. 11(2.)**

HARSHADEVA. **श्रीहर्षदेवकृतित्वेन प्रसिद्ध नागानंद नाटक** *etc.* [Nāgānanda nāṭaka. A Sanskrit drama in five acts, with a Marathi translation. Edited, with a Marathi preface by Krishṇa Ṣāstrī Chiplūṇkar.] pp. ii. 190. 16. **मुंबई १७८७** [*Bombay*, 1865.] 12°. **14080. c. 28.**

HAUG (Martin). A lecture and notices on the Vedas ... Traslated [*sic*] by a Svadesh Hitechhu. **वेदांविषयीं** [Vedāṇvishayīṇ.] pp. 32. **मुंबई १७८५** [*Bombay*, 1863.] 8°. **14137. d. 5(1.)**

—— The origin of Brahmanism, and second lecture on the Vedas ... Translated by a Swadesha Hitechhu. **डाक्तर मार्तिन होग .... यांच्या ब्राह्मणवर्णाचें मूळ** [Brāhmaṇavarṇāchen mūḷa.] pp. 48. **मुंबई १७८५** [*Bombay*, 1864.] 12°. **14139. c. 6(2.)**

HAVELOCK (William Henry). *See* Napier (F.) *Baron Napier.* Translation into Marathi by W. H. H. ... of a lecture on architecture in India, *etc.* 1871. 8°. **14139. a. 23.**

HEART BOOK. The Heart Book. [Translated from the English.] **हृदयदर्पण. मनुष्याचें अंतःकरण हें देवाचें देवालय** [Hṛidayadarpaṇa.] Second edition. pp. 86. *Bombay*, 1864. 12°.

One of the Bombay Tract and Book Society's Series.

14137. a. 6.

HELENA AUGUSTA VICTORIA, *Princess Christian of Schleswig-Holstein.* *See* Esmarch (F.) First Aid to the Injured. Translated ... from the English translation ... by Princess Christian. 1888. 8°. **14137. h. 13.**

HEMĀḌAPANTA. **हेमाडपंतकृत नीति** [Hemāḍapantakrita nīti. A treatise on ethics.] pp. 12. [*Poona*, 1884.] 32°. **14139. c. 28.**

HEMĀDRĪ. हेमाद्रीकृत लेखनकल्पतरु [Lekhanakalpataru. A treatise in verse on the art of letter-writing. With a commentary and additional matter by Gaṇapatarāva Sātārkar.] pp. v. 160. viii. मुंबई १७७४ [*Bombay*, 1853.] 12°.
14140. g. 5.

HINDU. Játibhed viveksár, or Reflections on the institution of caste, by a Hindu. (जातिभेद विवेकसार.) Second edition. pp. 170. *Bombay*, 1865. 8°.
14139. c. 13(1.)

HINDU UNION CLUB. *See* BOMBAY, *City of.*—*Hindu Union Club.*

HINDUS. अविचार पश्चात्ताप व प्रायश्चित्त यांविषयीं गोष्ट. [Avichāra, paṣchāttāpa va prāyaṣchitta.] Folly of Hindoos in matters regarding their salvation and necessity of repentance ... Reprinted from the Dnyanodaya. pp. 28. मुंबई १८४५ [*Bombay*, 1845.] 24°. **14137. a. 1(6.)**

HITOPADEṢA. *See* GOVINDAṢAṄKARA ṢĀSTRĪ BĀPAṬ. Nitimandira, *etc.* [A collection of moral precepts and stories, taken from the Hitopadeṣa.] 1879. 12°.
14139. c. 15.

—— Hitopadeśa, being the Sanskrit text, with a vocabulary in Sanskrit, English, and Murathi, together with a partial [English] translation. pp. vii. 296. *Bombay*, 1859. 8°. **14072. c. 19.**

—— हितोपदेश । [Hitopadeṣa, translated into Marathi.] pp. 248. श्रीरामपुर १८१५ [*Serampur*, 1815.] 8°. **14139. g. 2.**

HOLKAR, *Family of.* होळकरांची कैफियत [Holkarāṇchī kaiphiyat. The chronicles of the Holkar family of Indore, Malhār Rāva and his successors.] *See* PERIODICAL PUBLICATIONS.—*Poona.* काव्येतिहाससंग्रह [Kāvyetihāsa saṅgraha.] Vol. VIII.-IX. [1878, *etc.*] 8°. **14072. d. 37.**

HOMER. श्री सांबसदाशिव. मूळ ग्रीक कवि होमर यांच्या "इलियड" .... मराठी भाषेत आर्याबद्ध भाषांतर. अध्याय १ ला [Sāmbasadāṣiva. Homer's Iliad, Bk. I., translated into ārya verse, from the English version of A. Pope.] pp. 60. [*Poona?*, 1870?]. 12°.
14140. a. 12(5.)

HONĀJĪ BĀḶA. लावण्या होनाजी बाळाच्या [Lāvaṇī songs.] *See* RĀVAJĪ ṢRĪDHARA GONDHAḶEKAR. रामजोशि ... सुरस लावण्या [Surasa lāvaṇyā.] pp. 93–118. [1878.] 8°. **14140. c. 25.**

HOWARD (EDWARD IRVING). *See* VĀSUDEVA MOREṢVARA POTADĀR and NĀRĀYAṆA MOREṢVARA KARANDĪKAR. हावडकृत इंग्रजी पहिल्या पुस्तकांतील ... शब्दसंग्रह [Ṣabdasaṅgraha. A vocabulary of English words occurring in E. I. H.'s "English Primer."] [1877.] 12°. **14140. g. 29(1.)**

—— A collection of words and phrases, with the grammar, pronunciation, derivation and English and Marathi meanings of words, and English and Marathi explanations of phrases, occurring in [E. I. Howard's English] Departmental Third Book. New issue. (हावर्डकृत इंग्लिश तिसरें पुस्तक.) pp. 118. *Bombay*, 1877. 8°. **14140. i. 7.**

—— The English primer by E. I. H. With translation and pronunciation into Marathi, Hindustani, and Persian. Translated by Ganpat Mahadew Airekar. pp. xxii. 45. *Bombay*, 1868. 8°.
12984. f. 5.

HURREE KESHOUJEE. *See* HARI KEṢAVAJĪ.

HURRIDASS. *See* HARIDĀSA.

HURRY SUCCARAM. *See* HARI SAKHĀRĀMA.

HYDER, *Nawab of Mysore.* *See* HAIDAR SHĀH, *Nawab of Mysore.*

IDOLS. मूर्त्तींचा उच्छेद The idols destroyed. [Mūrtoṇchā uchchheda. Anecdotes of converts from idolatry to Christianity.] pp. 32. *Bombay*, 1850. 32°.
No. 4 of the Bombay Tract and Book Society's Series.
14137. a. 3(1.)

'INĀYAT ALLĀH. बाहारदानीष अथवा फारसी भाषेंतील सुरस व चमत्कारिक गोष्टी [Bahār i dānish, or Persian tales, by 'I. A., translated by Nāro Āpājī Godbole.] Pt. I. pp. 157. पुणें १८६५ [*Poona*, 1865.] 12°.
14139. f. 12(1.)

INDIA.—*Civil Service.* Codes of the Financial Department. The whole of the Civil Pension Code, except Forms B, C, D, and E in Appendix A, Appendix F, and supplements A, B, C, and D; and Chapters II. and VI. and supplement F of the Civil Leave Code; and Chapters VI., VII., and IX. of the Acting Allowance Code. Translated ... from the second "Authorized Edition" of 1874, by Anna Bhivrao. (सिविल् पेन्शन कोद.) pp. ii. 240. ii. *Ratnagiri*, 1877. 8°. **14137. g. 10.**

INDIA.—*Legislative Council.* कोड आफ् सीवल प्रोसिजर. दिवाणी काम चालविण्याचा कायदा सन १८७७ चा कायदा १० वा. [The Code of Civil Procedure, or Act X. of 1877. Edited by Rāvajī Śrīdhara Gondhaḷekar, assisted by Nīlakaṇṭha Purushottama Joṣī Chaulkar.] pp. xvi. 222. 148. iv. पुणें १८७७ [*Poona*, 1877.] 8°. **14137. g. 7.**

—— The Code of Civil Procedure, with explanatory notes, abstracts of important decisions by the High Courts in India. दिवाणी काम चालविण्याचे रीति विषयींचा कायदा ह्मणजे सन १८७७ चा अक्ट १० वा. [Compiled by Bhāū Govinda Sāpkar, assisted by Nārāyaṇa Bāpujī Kānīṭkar.] pp. ii. iv. xxiv. 228. 140. पुणें १८७७ [*Poona*, 1877.] 8°. **14137. g. 6.**

—— [Another edition. With notes and rulings of the High Courts in India, and orders of the High Court of Bombay. Compiled by Trimbakarāva Nārāyaṇa Rājmāchīkar, assisted by Śivārāma Hari Sāṭhe.] pp. iv. vi. xxxii. 284. 138. पुणें १८७७ [*Poona*, 1877.] 8°. **14137. g. 8.**

—— Act No. XV. of 1877, or The Indian Limitation Act. With schedules, and explanatory notes. फिर्यादी करण्याच्या मुदती ठरविण्याविषयीं व इतर कारणांविषयीं आक्ट. *etc.* [Compiled by Rāmachandra Keṣava Limaye.] pp. iv. 20. 50. 27. ii. पुणें १८७७ [*Poona*, 1877.] 8°. **14137. g. 4.**

—— हिंदुस्थानचा मुदतीविषयीं आक्ट, *etc.* [Another edition. Edited by Rāvajī Śrīdhara Gondhaḷekar, assisted by Nīlakaṇṭha Purushottama Joṣī Chaulkar.] pp. ii. 51. पुणें १८७७ [*Poona*, 1877.] 8°. **14137. g. 5(2.)**

INQUIRY. *See* Enquiry.

ĪŚVARACHANDRA VIDYĀSĀGARA. Marriage of widows, written in Bengali and English, by Eshwarachandra Vidyáságar, and translated into Maráthi by Vishnu Parashurám Shástri Pandit. (विधवाविवाह) [Vidhavāvivāha.] pp. vi. iii. iii. 159. *Bombay*, 1865. 12°. **14139. c. 11(2.)**

JAGANNĀTHA LAKSHMAṆA MĀNKAR. *See* Krishṇajī Ananta. The life and exploits of Shivaji. Translated into English ... by Jagannath Lakshuman Mankar. 1884. 8°. **14139. e. 25.**

JAGANNĀTHA PAṆḌITARĀJA. गंगालहरी टीकेसहित [Gaṅgālaharī. A hymn in praise of the goddess Gaṅgā. Sanskrit text, with a Marathi paraphrase by Vāmana Paṇḍita.] pp. 28, *lith.* पुणें १८७९ [*Poona*, 1879.] 8°. **14033. a.**

JAGANNĀTHA PAṆḌITARĀJA. गंगामृतप्रसाद [Gaṅgāmṛitaprasāda. The Sanskrit text of the Gaṅgālaharī, with a prose translation by Kāṣīnātha Ṣāstrī.] pp. ii. 40. मुंबई १८७७ [*Bombay*, 1877.] 8°. **14028. c. 40.**

JAGANNĀTHA ṢĀSTRĪ KRAMAVANTA. *See* Pasley (*Sir* C. W.) Marat,ha version of a course of practical geometry ... Translated ... [with the aid of J. Ṣ. K.] 1826. 4°. **14139. b. 1.**

JANĀBĀĪ. अथ स्थालिपाक अभंग प्रारंभ [Sthālīpāka. Invocation of Kṛishṇa by Draupadī when the sage Durvāsa asked the Pāṇḍavas for food. Followed by the Ayodhyākāṇḍa of Moropanta's Mantrarāmāyaṇa.] pp. 14, *lith.* [*Poona*, 1863.] 12°. **14140. a. 12(1.)**

JANĀRDANA BĀḶĀJĪ MOḌAK. *See* Lagadha. वेदांग ज्योतिष *etc.* (The Vedang jyotisha translated into Marathi by J. B. M.) 1885. 12°. **14053. b. 11(2.)**

—— Bháskara Áchárya and his astronomical system. [Consisting chiefly of extracts from Bhāskara's Siddhāntaṣiromaṇi, with an interpretation in Marathi.] (भास्कराचार्य व तत्कृत ज्योतिष *etc.*) pp. iii. ii. 83. *Ratnagiri*, 1877. 8°. **14053. b. 9(1.)**

—— महाभारत [Mahābhārata. A critical lecture on the Sanskrit epic poem.] pp. 41. *See* Bombay, *City of.—Hindu Union Club.* हेमंत व्याख्यानमाला. [Hemanta vyākhyānamālā.] Vol. II. No. 5. [1886, *etc.*] 8°. **14139. c. 26.**

JANĀRDANA BĀḶĀJĪ MOḌAK and **KĀṢĪNĀTHA NĀRĀYAṆA SĀNE.** *See* Periodical Publications.—*Poona.* काव्येतिहास-संग्रह [Kāvyetihāsa saṅgraha. A monthly serial, edited by J. B. M. and K. N. S.] [1878, *etc.*] 8°. **14072. d. 37.**

JANĀRDANA BHĀSKARA KRAMAVANTA. *See* Ṣukadeva. ज्योतिषसार. [Jyotishasāra. Sanskrit text, with a Marathi commentary by J. Bh. K.] [1858.] 4°. **14053. d. 4.**

—— —— [1863.] 4°. **14053. d. 7.**

—— —— [1881.] 8°. **14053. cc. 23.**

JANĀRDANA HARI ĀṬHALYE. *See* Mūrkhaṣataka. मूर्खशतक *etc.* (With their translation into Maráthi by Janárdan Hurry Áthalye). 1877. 8°. **14076. b. 15(2.)**

JANĀRDANA HARI ĀṬHALYE. *See* NĪLAKAṆṬHA DĪKSHITA. Kalividambana ... The original Sanskrit piece with a Marathi translation ... by Janárdan Hurry Áthalye. 1878. 12°. **14076. a. 12(2.)**

—— बालवैद्य [Bālavaidya. A treatise on parturition, and the treatment of diseases peculiar to children. Founded on an English work entitled "A domestic guide to mothers in India."] pp. 121. रत्नागिरी १८६१ [*Ratnagiri*, 1861.] 8°. **14137. h. 1.**

—— शब्दसिद्धिनिबंध. [Ṣabdasiddhinibandha. A manual of Marathi etymology, by J. H. Ā., assisted by Vināyaka Ṣāstrī Āgāṣī. Second edition.] pp. 104. मुंबई १८६८ [*Bombay*, 1868.] 12°. **14140. g. 8(2.)**

—— A manual of Marathi etymology, by Janárdan Hari Athlye, and Vináyak Shástri Ágashe. Sixth edition, pp. 88. *Bombay*, 1875. 12°. **14140. g. 26.**

—— Seventh edition. pp. 88. *Bombay*, 1880. 12°. **14140. g. 37.**

JANĀRDANA MAHĀDEVA GURJAR. *See* SARASVATI GAṄGĀDHARA. अथ श्रीगुरुचरित्र प्रारंभः ॥ [Gurucharitra. Edited by J. M. G., with an introductory chapter, containing a summary of each chapter of the poem.] [1875.] *obl.* 8°. **14137. e. 8.**

—— *See* YĀJÑAVALKYA. याज्ञवल्क्यस्मृतिः *etc.* [The Vyavahārādhyāya of Yājñavalkya's Smṛiti and Mitākshara. Text and translation by Bhikājī Ṣāstrī Moghe, edited by J. M. G.] [1879.] 8°. **14038. d. 25.**

JANĀRDANA RĀMACHANDRAJĪ. Biographical sketches of eminent Hindu authors; being memoirs of the lives of both prose and poetical writers, ancient and modern, who have flourished in different provinces of India. Compiled from various Sanscrit, Marathi, and English works by Janárdan Rámchandrají. (कविचरित्र.) [Kavicharitra.] pp. vii. 245. xv. *Bombay*, 1860. 8°. **14139. e. 6.**

JANĀRDANA SAKHĀRĀMA GĀDGIL. *See* TUKĀRĀMA. A complete collection of the poems of Tukárámа .... Vol. I. to which is prefixed a life of the poet in English by Janárdan Sakhárám Gádgil. 1869. 8°. **14140. c. 14.**

JANĪ. *See* JANĀBĀĪ.

JĀTIBHEDA. जातिभेद [Jātibheda. An essay on Hindu caste distinctions.] pp. 26. ठाणें १८७७ [*Thana*, 1877.] 12°. **14139. c. 17(2.)**

JAYADEVA. भावदीपिका. म्हणजे गीतगोविंदाची समश्लोकी प्राकृतटीका ... मूलसंस्कृतासहित [Gītagovinda. Sanskrit text, with Lakshmaṇa Govindabhāū Ashṭaputre's Marathi commentary, called Bhāvadīpikā or Padabhāvānukāriṇī.] pp. iv. 77, *lith.*, with 24 pages of plates. पुणें १८६० [*Poona*, 1860.] 4°. **14072. d. 1.**

—— Prasannrághava. A drama in seven acts, translated from Sanscrit into Maráthí by Shivarám Shástrí Pálande. (प्रसन्नराघव नाटक) pp. ii. 161. *Bombay*, 1859. 12°. **14140. f. 22.**

JERVIS (GEORGE RITSO). *See* BROUGHAM (H.) *Baron Brougham and Vaux.* उपयोगि ज्ञानाचा पुस्तक ... Treatise on the objects, advantages and pleasures of science. Translated from the English ... by G. R. J. 1829. 8°. **14139. b. 2.**

—— *See* DE MORGAN (A.) De Morgan's Elements of Algebra: translated into the Marathi language by G. R. J. 1848. 8°. **14139. b. 5.**

—— *See* PASLEY (*Sir* C. W.) Marat,ha version of a course of practical geometry .... Translated by Captain George Jervis. 1826. 4°. **14139. b. 1.**

JEWS. इस्राएलास हितोपदेश. [Isrāelās hitopadeṣa. Advice to the Jews. A Christian tract.] pp. 62. [*Bombay*, 1845?]. 12°. **14137. a. 2(2.)**

JÑĀNADEVA. [*Life.*] *See* BALAVANTA KHAṆḌOJĪ PĀRAKH. ज्ञानेश्वर महाराजांचें चरित्र [Jñāneṣvara Mahārājāñcheṇ charitra.]

—— *See* MAHĀBHĀRATA.—*Bhagavadgītā.* अथ ज्ञानेश्वरी प्रारंभः ॥ [Bhagavadgītā. Sanskrit text, with Jñānadeva's commentary called Jñāneṣvarī.] [1874.] *obl.* 4°. **14065. f. 1.**

—— —— [1877.] *obl.* 4°. **14060. f. 12.**

—— *See* MAHĀBHĀRATA.—*Uttaragītā.* अथ ज्ञानेश्वरकृतटीका सहित उत्तरगीता प्रारंभः॥ [Uttaragītā. Sanskrit text, with a preface and translation in Marathi by Jñānadeva.] [1881.] *obl.* 8° **14065. b. 13.**

—— [*Life.*] *See* RAGHUNĀTHABOVĀ BHIṄGĀRKAR. श्री ज्ञानदेव चरित्र [Jñānadeva charitra.]

JÑĀNADEVA. श्री ज्ञानदेवाचा गाथा [Jñānadevāchā gāthā. A collection of poems by Jñānadeva. Followed by abhangas attributed to his two brothers Nivrittinātha and Sopānadeva, also to his sister Muktābāī, and to his disciple Chāngadeva.] pp. xviii. xii. 235. 97, *lith.* पुणें १९९९ [*Poona*, 1877.] 8°. **14140. c. 23.**

—— ज्ञानदेवकृत अभंग प्रारंभ [Abhangas.] *See* MUKTĀBĀĪ. अथ मुक्ताबाईकृत ताटीचे अभंग प्रारंभः [Tāṭīche abhanga.] [1863.] 12°. **14140. a. 10(5.)**

—— अनुभवामृत पदबोधिनी [Anubhavāmṛita padabodhinī. A Vedantic work in ten chapters; with a running commentary by Nirañjana Raghunātha. Edited by Kāśīnātha Mahādeva Thatte.] 10 pt. *lith.* पुणें १८८२ [*Poona*, 1882.] 8°. **14140. c. 30.**

—— श्रीभगवद्गीता [Bhagavadgītā, translated by Jñānadeva.] *See* MAHĀBHĀRATA.—*Selections.* अथ पंचरत्नगीता प्रारंभ [Pañcharatna.] [1857.] *obl.* 16°. **14137. c. 8.**

—— ज्ञानदेवकृतहरिपाठ अभंग [Haripāṭha. Abhangas in praise of Vishṇu. Fifth edition.] pp. 15, *lith.* मुंबई १९८३ [*Bombay*, 1861.] 12°. **14140. a. 1(11.)**

—— [Another edition.] pp. 14, *lith.* मुंबई १९८५ [*Bombay*, 1863.] 12°. **14140. a 10(4.)**

—— [Another edition.] pp. 28. पुणें १८८५ [*Poona*, 1885.] 16°. **14140. a. 36.**

—— अथ ज्ञानदेवकृत ताटीचे अभंग [Tāṭīche abhanga.] *See* TUKĀRĀMA. अथ तुकारामाचे अभंग प्रारंभः [Tukārāmāche abhanga.] pp. 76–85. [1860.] 12°. **14140. a. 4(6.)**

—— अथ विष्णुनमन प्रारंभ ॥ [Vishṇunamana stotra. A translation of the Sanskrit Vishṇusahasranāma.] *See* MAHĀBHĀRATA.—*Selections.* अथ पंचरत्नगीता प्रारंभ [Pañcharatna.] [1857.] *obl.* 16°. **14137. c. 8.**

JÑĀNEŚVARA. *See* JÑĀNADEVA.

JÑĀNOBĀ. *See* JÑĀNADEVA.

JOŚI (P. B.) Victoria-mahotsava, or Verses in commemoration of the Jubilee of Her Majesty's reign by P. B. Joshi. pp. 4, 5. *Mar.* and *Engl.* *Bombay*, 1887. 12°. **14140. a.**

K. (S. M.) *See* S. M. K.

KABĪR. पदें कबिराचीं प्रारंभः भाग १ [Paden. Miscellaneous short poems.] Pt. I. pp. 16. मुंबई १८७२ [*Bombay*, 1872.] 16°. **14140. a. 11(5.)**

—— कबीरादि प्रेमळ भक्तांनीं केलेलीं उत्कृष्ट पदें प्रारंभ [Kabīrādi premaḷa bhaktāṇnīṇ kelelīṇ utkṛishṭa padeṇ. Devotional songs by Kabīr and other poets.] pp. 29, *lith.* पुणें १८८३ [*Poona*, 1883.] 12°. **14140. a 11(7.)**

—— सुरस पदें कबिराचीं वगैरे. [Surasa padeṇ. An enlarged edition of Kabīr's poems.] pp. 29, *lith.* पुणें १८७७ [*Poona*, 1877.] 12°. **14140. a. 12(8.)**

KĀLIDĀSA.

MĀLAVIKĀGNIMITRA.

—— Málavikágnimitra: a drama in five acts, translated from the original Sanskrit of Kálidás by Ganesh Shástrí Lele. Revised and edited by Shankar P. Pandit. (मालविकाग्निमित्र.) pp. xix. 127. *Bombay*, 1867. 12°. **14140. e. 9.**

ŚAKUNTALĀ.

—— कालिदासकृत अभिज्ञानशकुंतला नाटक. सभोकी (Shakuntalá or Shakuntalá recognized by the Ring. A Sanskrit drama ... with a translation into Maráthí [by Krishṇa Śāstrī Rājvāḍe] and illustrations.) ff. 4 and pp. iv. vi. i. 266 and nine plates. *Bombay*, 1869. 4°. **14079. e. 10.**

—— कालिदासकृत शकुंतला नाटक *etc.* [Śakuntalā nāṭaka. Sanskrit text, with paraphrases in Sanskrit and Marathi.] *See* PERIODICAL PUBLICATIONS. —*Dharwar.* काव्यनाटकादर्श [Kāvyanāṭakādarśa.] [1882, *etc.*] 8°. **14076. d. 35.**

—— शाकुंतल नाटक. [Translated by Paraśurāma Panta Godbole.] pp. 269, *lith.* पुणें १९८३ [*Poona*, 1861.] 8°. **14140. f. 3.**

—— कालिदासाचें अभिज्ञान शकुंतला नाटक [Translated by Mahādeva Chimṇājī Āpṭe.] *See* MAHĀDEVA CHIMṆĀJĪ ĀPṬE. मौंजेच्या चार घटका [Maunjechyā chār ghaṭakā.] Pt. I. [1881.] 8°. **14140. f. 16.**

VIKRAMORVAŚĪ.

—— विक्रमोर्वशी नाटक. [Vikramorvaśī nāṭaka. Translated into prose and verse, with a preface, and epitome of the plot, by Krishṇa Śāstrī Rājvāḍe.] pp. vii. 174. पुणें १९९६ [*Poona*, 1874.] 8°. **14140. f. 8.**

KĀLIDĀSA, *pseud.* **श्री पुष्पबाणविलास.** [Pushpavāṇavilāsa. Sanskrit text, with a Marathi verse translation by Baḷavantarāva Kamalākar.] pp. 16. १८८१ [*Poona,* 1881.] 16°. **14072. b.**

KALIYUGA. **कलियुग** [Kaliyuga, or The iron age. An address delivered at the Bombay Ārya Samāj on the 29th July, 1877.] pp. 15. **मुंबई** १८७७ [*Bombay,* 1877.] 8°. **14137. b. 9(2.)**

KALYĀṆA SĪTĀRĀMA CHITRE. A manual for the use of the candidates for Magistrates and Police examinations, by Cullian Sitaram Chitray. (**प्रश्नोत्तर संग्रह.**) [Praṣnottara saṅgraha.] pp. ii. iii. 260. vii. *Bombay,* 1877. 8°. **14137. g. 9.**

KAMALĀKARA BHAṬṬA, *Son of Rāmakṛishṇa Bhaṭṭa.* **शूद्रकमलाकर अथवा शूद्रधर्मतत्त्वप्रकाश** *etc.* [Ṣūdrakamalākara. Sanskrit text, with a Marathi translation by Vāmana Ṣāstrī Islāmpūrkar.] pp. viii. 293. **मुंबई** १८०२ [*Bombay,* 1880.] 8°. **14033. bb. 2.**

KĀNHOBĀ RAṆCHHOḌDĀS KĪRTIKAR. **अश्रु त्यांची उत्पत्ति आणि योजना.** [Aṣru, tyāṇchī utpatti āṇe yojanā. A lecture on tears, their origin and modes of secretion.] pp. 10. *See* BOMBAY, *City of.—Hindu Union Club.* **हेमंत व्याख्यानमाला.** [Hemanta vyākhyānamālā.] Vol. II. No. 8. [1886, *etc.*] 8°. **14139. c. 26.**

KARMAVIPĀKA. **कर्मविपाक प्रारंभः** [Karmavipāka. A treatise on the rewards and punishments of actions performed in previous births.] pp. 33. [*Bombay ?* 1860 ?] 12°. **14139. c. 10(1.)**

KĀṢĪNĀTHA BAHIRAVA LIMAYE. **कवितार्थदीपिका** [Kavitārthadīpikā. An explanation of the poetical selections contained in the "Marathi Fourth Book." Third edition.] pp. 108. **पुणें** १८७५ [*Poona,* 1875.] 12°. **14140. g. 8(3.)**

—— [Fifth edition.] pp. 101. **मुंबई** १८७७ [*Bombay,* 1877.] 12°. **14140. g. 7(4.)**

KĀṢĪNĀTHA BĀḶAKṚISHṆA MARĀṬHE. *See* GEIKIE (A.) Science primers in Marathi. Physical geography. Translated .... by Kâshinâth Bâlkrishna Marâṭhé. 1880. 16°. **14139. d. 32.**

—— *See* LOCKYER (J. N.) Science primers in Marâṭhi. Astronomy. Translated ... by Kâshinâth Bâlkrishna Marâṭhé. 1880. 16°. **14139. a. 41.**

KĀṢĪNĀTHA MAHĀDEVA THATTE. *See* JÑĀNADEVA. **अनुभवामृत पदबोधिनी.** [Anubhavāmṛita padabodhinī. Edited by K. M. Th.] [1882.] 8°. **14140. c. 30.**

—— **कारागीर लोकांचे कामाविषयीं तिमाही पुस्तक** [Kārāgīr lokāṇche kāmāvishayīṇ. A work, issued in tri-monthly parts, containing information on various arts and sciences.] Pt. I. pp. 24. **पुणें** १८७८ [*Poona,* 1878.] 8°. **14139. b. 9.**

—— **सवाई माधवराव पेशवे यांचें नाटक.** [Savāī Mādhava Rāva Peshwe yāṇcheṇ nāṭaka. A drama, in prose and verse, on the chief events in the life of the Peshwa Mādhava Rāva I.] pp. 80, *lith.* **पुणें** [*Poona,* 1884.] 8°. **14140. f. 2(5.)**

—— **शेतकीविषयीं तिमाही पुस्तक.** [Ṣetakīvishayīṇ. A treatise on agriculture.] Vol. I. No. 1. **पुणें** १८७८ [*Poona,* 1878.] 8°. **14139. b. 8.**

—— **उपयुक्त ज्ञानसार.** [Upayukta jñānasāra. A treatise on agriculture, drawing, and engineering.] Vol. I. No. 1–3. **पुणें** १८७७ [*Poona,* 1877, *etc.*] 8°. **14139. b. 14.**

KĀṢĪNĀTHA NĀRĀYAṆA SĀNE. *See* BHĀU SĀHEB. **भाऊ साहेबांची बखर** ... The chronicle of Bháu Sáheb ... Edited by K. N. Sane, with critical and explanatory notes. 1886. 8°. **14139. e. 22.**

—— *See* PERIODICAL PUBLICATIONS.—*Poona.* **काव्येतिहास-संग्रह** [Kāvyetihāsa saṅgraha. A monthly serial, edited by Janārdana Bāḷājī Modak and K. N. S.] [1878, *etc.*] 8°. **14072. d. 37.**

—— *See* RAGHUNĀTHA NĀRĀYAṆA. **राजव्यवहारकोश** [Rājavyavahārakoṣa. Edited, with a preface and alphabetical index, by K. N. S.] [1881.] 12°. **14140. h. 27.**

KĀṢĪNĀTHA PĀṆḌURAṄGA PARAB. *See* RĀMACHANDRA BHIKĀJĪ GUÑGĪKAR. **कौमुदीमहोत्साहः** [Kaumudīmahotsāha. Edited by Rāmachandra Bhikājī Guñjīkar and K. P. P.] [1877–79.] 8°. **14093. c.**

KĀṢĪNĀTHA ṢĀSTRĪ. *See* JAGANNĀTHA PAṆḌITARĀJA. **गंगामृतप्रसाद** [Gaṅgāmṛitaprasāda. The Sanskrit text of the Gaṅgālaharī, with a prose translation by K. Ṣ.] [1877.] 8°. **14028. c. 40.**

KĀṢĪNĀTHA TRIMBAK KHARE. पढ़े इंडियन न्याशनल कांग्रेस (हिंदुस्थानांतील तिसरी राष्ट्रीयसभा) [Hindusthānāntīl tisrī rāshṭrīya-sabha. An account of the Third National Congress, held at Madras in December 1887.] pp. 16. *See* BOMBAY, *City of.—Hindu Union Club.* हेमंत व्याख्यानमाला [Hemanta vyākhyānamāla.] Vol. III. No. 2. [1886, *etc.*] 8°.
14139. c. 26.

—— हिंदुस्थान देशाच्या व्यावहारिक स्थितीविषयीं काहीं विचार. [Hindusthān deṣāchyā sthitivishayīṇ vichāra. A lecture on the present condition of India.] pp. 11. *See* BOMBAY, *City of.—Hindu Union Club.* हेमंत व्याख्यानमाला. [Hemanta vyākhyānamālā.] Vol. I. No. 5. [1886, *etc.*] 8°.
14139. c. 26.

KĀṢĪNĀTHA TRIMBAK TELANG, *C. I. E.* शास्त्र व रूढि यांच्या बलाबलाविषयीं विचार [Ṣāstra va rūḍhi yāṇchyā balābalāvishayīṇ vichāra. Two lectures on the Sastras and prevailing customs, and a report of discussions thereon.] *See* BOMBAY, *City of.—Hindu Union Club.* हेमंत व्याख्यानमाला [Hemanta vyākhyānamālā.] Vol. I. Nos. 2–4. [1886, *etc.*] 8°.
14139. c. 26.

KĀṢĪNĀTHA UPĀDHYĀYA. श्री धर्मसिंधु, *etc.* [Dharmasindhusāra. A Sanskrit work by K. U. on religious duties, and an appendix by Vāsudeva, called Ekādaṣīnirṇaya, accompanied by a Marathi translation by Bāpū Ṣāstrī Moghe.] pp. 796. xvi. vi. मुंबई १७९६ [*Bombay,* 1874.] 8°.
14033. b. 28.

KĀṢĪRĀVA RĀJEṢVARA GUPTA. नागपूरकर भोंसल्याची बखर [Nāgpūrkar Bhoṇsalyāṇchī bakhar. The Chronicles of the Bhoṇsalas of Nagpur. Edited with notes by Vāmana Dājī Ok.] *See* PERIODICAL PUBLICATIONS.—*Poona.* काव्येतिहास-संग्रह [Kāvyetihāsa saṅgraha.] Vol. VI.–VIII. [1878, *etc.*] 8°.
14072. d. 37.

KERO LAKSHMAṆA CHHATRE. *See* NĀRO RAGHUNĀTHA MOHOḶKAR. केरोकृत संकगणित यांतील प्रश्नसमुदाय ... पृथक्करण [A solution of exercises contained in K. L. Chh.'s "Treatise on arithmetic."] [1877.] 12°. **14139. a. 27(1.)**

—— *See* VISHṆU VĀSUDEVA SĀṬHYE GONDHAḶEKAR. त्रैराशिक समूह [Trairāṣika samūha. Pt. II. containing 130 exercises from K. L. Chh.'s "Treatise on Arithmetic."] [1877.] 8°.
14139. b. 11.

KERO LAKSHMAṆA CHHATRE. ग्रहसाधनाचीं कोष्टकें [Grahasādhanachīṇ koshṭakeṇ. Astronomical and planetary tables, compiled from English sources.] pp. iv. ix. 331. मुंबई १७८२ [*Bombay,* 1860.] 8°.
14139. a. 13.

—— A treatise on arithmetic for beginners, arranged and chiefly designed for the use of Government Vernacular Schools, by Keru Laxuman Chhatre (संकगणित) [Aṅkagaṇita.] Second edition. pp. 122. *Bombay,* 1863. 12°.
14139. a. 21.

—— Third edition. pp. xi. 228. 33. ii. *Bombay,* 1864. 12°. **14130. a. 18.**

—— Fifth edition. pp. xi. 228. 26. *Bombay,* 1868. 12°. **14139. a. 19.**

—— Eighth edition. pp. xi. 243. 27. *Bombay,* 1874. 12°. **14139. a. 25.**

—— Eleventh edition. pp. xi. 200. 26. *Bombay,* 1881. 12°. **14139. a. 39.**

KERU LAXUMAN CHHATRE. *See* KERO LAKSHMAṆA CHHATRE.

KEṢAVACHANDRA SENA. आदिशास्त्र व ईश्वरज्ञान [Ādiṣāstra va Īṣvarajñāna. A Brahmist discourse by K. S. translated into Marathi.] मुंबई १९०६ [*Bombay,* 1879.] 16°. **14137. a. 12.**

KEṢAVA SADĀṢIVA RISBŪḌ. पद्यात्मक स्वदेश कल्याणचंद्रिका. कीर्तनपर कथा भाग चार *etc.* [Svadeṣa kalyāṇachandrikā. A poem, in four parts, on the best means for promoting national prosperity.] pp. vii. 58. iii. पुणें १७९७ [*Poona,* 1875.] 8°.
14140. b. 10.

KEṢAVA SAKHĀRĀMA ṢĀSTRĪ. *See* DUFF (J. G.) History of the Maráthás. Translated .... by D. Capon. Corrected for the press by Keshava Sakhárám Shástri. 1857. 12°. **14139. d. 11.**

—— *See* ENGLAND. History of England ... translated into Marathi. Corrected for the press by Keshava Sakhárám Shástri. 1857. 8°.
14139. d. 9.

—— अथ आत्मानुभव प्रारंभः ॥ [Ātmānubhava. A work on Vedanta philosophy in sixteen chapters. Sanskrit text, with a commentary in Marathi.] ff. 151. [*Bombay,* 1868?] *obl.* 12°. **14048. b. 9.**

KIṄKARA, *Kavi.* सुदामचरित्र [Sudāma-charitra, Draupadī vastraharaṇa, and Ṣuka Rambhā saṃvāda. Poems.] *See* PERIODICAL PUBLICATIONS.—*Poona.* काव्येतिहास-संग्रह [Kāvyetihāsa saṅgraha.] Vol. VIII. Nos. 3–5. [1878, *etc.*] 8°.
14072. d. 37.

KṚISHṆAJĪ ANANTA, *Sabhāsad.* शिवछत्रपतीचें चरित्र. [Ṣivachhatrapatīcheṇ charitra. The life of Ṣivājī, published with numerous notes from a manuscript by K. A.] *See* PERIODICAL PUBLICATIONS.—*Poona.* काव्येतिहास-संग्रह [Kāvyetihāsa saṅgraha.] Vol. III. [1878, *etc.*] 8°. **14072. d. 37.**

—— The life and exploits of Shivaji. Translated into English ... by Jagannath Lakshuman Mankar. pp. xii. 113. *Alibag*, 1884. 8°.
14139. e. 25.

KṚISHṆĀJĪ BALLĀLA ṬHĀKURA. बोधपर पदें. [Bodhapar padeṇ. A collection of verses in the pada metre by old Marathi poets. Compiled by K. B. Th.] 4 pt., *lith.* मंबई १८८४ [*Bombay*, 1884.] 12°. **14140. a. 11(9.)**

KṚISHṆAJĪ GAṆEṢA DONGRE. The help to old mustering carkoons etc., as well as to English beginners as mustering carkoons in the Public Work Department, by Crishnaji Gunesh Dongre. (मस्तरिंग कारकुनांस मदत, *etc.*) pp. vi. 60, *lith. Ahmednagar*, 1884. 8°. **14140. h. 25.**

KṚISHṆAJĪ VINĀYAKA SOHANĪ. पेशव्यांची बखर. [Peshwyāṇchī bakhar, or Chronicles of the Peshwas from Bālājī Viṣvanātha to Bājīrāva Raghunātha, A.D. 1713 to 1818. With critical and explanatory notes.] *See* PERIODICAL PUBLICATIONS.—*Poona.* काव्येतिहास-संग्रह [Kāvyetihāsa saṅgraha.] Vol. I. and II. [1878, *etc.*] 8°.
14072. d. 37.

KṚISHṆAMIṢRA. प्रबोधचंद्रोदय नाटक [Prabodhachandrodaya nāṭaka. A Sanskrit drama by K., translated by Sadāṣiva Bājābā Ṣāstrī Amrāpurkar and Rāvajī Bāpujī Ṣāstrī Bāpaṭ.] pp. iv. 86. iv. 67, *lith.* मुंबई १९१३ [*Bombay*, 1885.] 8°.
14140. f. 19.

KṚISHṆA RAGHUNĀTHAJĪ. Agamprakash. आगमप्रकाश *etc.* [A treatise on mystic religion. With numerous extracts from the Tantras, and translations by Viṭhṭhala Ṣāstrī Tarlekar.] pp. ii. 253. *Bombay*, 1884. 8°. **14137. d. 3.**

KṚISHṆARĀVA BĀ[ḶĀJĪ ?] BULEL. आपल्या राहण्याच्या रीति आणि आरोग्यशास्त्र [Āplyā rāhaṇyāchyā rīti āṇi ārogyaṣāstra. A lecture on native modes of living and principles of sanitation.] pp. 23. *See* BOMBAY, *City of.—Hindu Union Club.* हेमंत व्याख्यानमाला [Hemanta vyākhyānamālā.] Vol. III. No. 3. [1886, *etc.*] 8°. **14139. c. 26.**

KṚISHṆARĀVA BHĀSKARAJĪ REḶE. सुबोधमालिनी [Subodhamālinī. Advice on social and domestic duties.] pp. 108. मुंबई १८०१ [*Bombay*, 1880]. 12°.
14139. c. 23.

KṚISHṆA ṢĀSTRĪ BHĀṬAVAḌEKAR. *See* LOLIMBARĀJA. वैद्यजीवन [Vaidyajīvana. With a Marathi commentary by K. Ṣ. Bh.] [1861.] 4°.
14043. d. 7.

—— वैद्यावतंस [Vaidyāvataṃsa. With a Marathi commentary by K. Ṣ. Bh.] [1860.] 8°.
14043. c. 2.

—— *See* MĀDHAVA, *Son of Indukara.* Madhavanidana ... Translated into Marathi by Krishna Shastri Bhatuvadekar. 1862. 4°. **14043. d. 8.**

—— *See* MOREṢVARA, *Son of Māṇika Bhaṭṭa.* वैद्यामृत [Vaidyāmṛita. With a Marathi commentary by K. Ṣ. Bh.] [1862.] 4°.
14043. d. 9.

—— *See* RAGHUNĀTHA ṢĀSTRĪ DĀNTYE and KṚISHṆA ṢĀSTRĪ BHĀṬAVAḌEKAR. वैद्यसारसंग्रह [Vaidyasārasaṅgraha.] [1865.] 8°. **14139. c. 1.**

—— *See* TRYAMBAKA. त्र्यंबकी [Tryambakī. With a prose version by K. Ṣ. Bh.] [1863.] 8°.
14137. h. 9.

—— *See* VOPADEVA. बोपदेवशतक [Ṣataṣlokī. With a Marathi paraphrase by K. Ṣ. Bh.] [1860.] 4°.
14043. d. 6.

—— Subanta-prakâsha, or the declensions of Sanskrit nouns... [Founded on Bhaṭṭojīdīkshita's] Siddhânta Kaumudî. (सुबंतप्रकाश). pp. iv. 127. *Bombay*, 1867. 8°. **14140. h. 11.**

KṚISHṆA ṢĀSTRĪ CHIPḶŪṆKAR. *See* HARSHADEVA. श्रीहर्षदेवकृतित्वेन प्रसिद्ध नागानंद नाटक *etc.* [Nāgānanda nāṭaka. Edited by K. Ṣ. Ch.] [1865.] 12°.
14080. c. 28.

—— *See* MILL (J. S.) Arth Shástra Paribháshá, or The Principles of Political Economy, from the work of John Stuart Mill, by Krishna Shástrí Chiplonkar. 1855. 8°. **14140. h. 4.**

KRISHṆA ṢĀSTRĪ CHIPḶŪṆKAR. *See* PEILE (J. B.) Catalogue of native publications in the Bombay Presidency ... Prepared ... by J. B. Peile [assisted by K. Ṣ. Ch.] 1869. 8°. **752. e. 15.**

—— *See* PERSIAN TALES. The Thousand and one days, translated by Bhaskar Sakharam, ... corrected and revised by Krishna Shastri Chiplonker. 1863. 8°. **14139. g. 5**

—— *See* ROLLIN (C.) The life of Socrates, translated ... by Krishna Shastree Chiplonker. 1852. 8°. **14139. d. 3.**

—— —— 1875. 12°. **14139. d. 18.**

—— *See* VINĀYAKA NĀRĀYAṆA BHĀGAVATA. Murad the unlucky and Saladin the lucky; ... Revised by Krishna Shástri Chiplonkar. 1862. 12°. **14139. f. 6.**

—— *See* VIṢĀKHADATTA. Mudrárákshasa .... Revised by Kṛishṇa Shástri Chiplonkar. 1867. 8°. **14140. f. 23.**

—— Anekawidya mulatatwa sangraha, or Lessons on the elementary principles of several sciences. Prepared from English works by Krishna Shástri Chiplonkar (**अनेकविद्या मूलतत्व संग्रह.**) pp. ii. ii. 302. *Bombay,* 1861. 8°. **14139. a. 24.**

—— An elementary grammar of the Sanskrit language, for the use of the Marathi students of the Poona College. Compiled and prepared by Krishna Shastrí Chiploonkur. (**संस्कृत भाषेचें .. लहान व्याकरणाचें पुस्तक**) [Saṃskṛita bhāsheche͟n lahān pustaka.] pp. 56. *Bombay,* 1859. 8°. **14140. h. 6.**

—— Second edition. pp. 82. *Poona,* 1864. 8°. **14140. g. 15.**

KRISHṆA ṢĀSTRĪ GOḌBOLE. *See* HADDON (J.) *M.A.* Elements of Algebra ... Revised and corrected by Krishna Shástri Godbole. 1865. 8°. **14139. a. 15.**

—— A new grammar of the Maráthi language, and its analogy with Sanskrit and Prákrit, with an appendix containing an abridged grammar and vocabulary of Prákrit. (**मराठी भाषेचें नवीन व्याकरण**) [Marāṭhī bhāsheche͟n navīna vyākaraṇa.] pp. xv. 271. *Bombay,* 1867. 12°. **14140. h. 12.**

—— A treatise on astronomy, prepared from Chambers' work on that science. (**ज्योतिःशास्त्र**) [Jyotiḥṣāstra.] pp. viii. 154. *Bombay,* 1862. 8°. **14139. a. 14.**

KRISHṆA ṢĀSTRĪ GOḌBOLE. Treatment of children. [A lecture delivered at the Bombay Ārya Samāj.] **बालसंगोपन ह्या विषयावर व्याख्यान.** pp. 50. **मुंबई १८८०** [*Bombay,* 1880.] 12°. **14137. ff.**

KRISHṆA ṢĀSTRĪ GURJAR. *See* MOROPANTA. **अथ मयूरकृत मंत्ररामायण आर्याप्रारंभः** [Mantrarāmāyaṇa āryā. Edited by K. Ṣ. G.] [1860.] *obl.* 8°. **14137. e. 3(1.)**

KRISHṆA ṢĀSTRĪ RĀJVĀḌE. *See* KĀLIDĀSA. **कालिदासकृत अभिज्ञानशकुंतला नाटक.** (Shakuntalá ... With a translation into Marathi [by K. Ṣ. R.].) 1869. 4°. **14079. e. 10.**

—— —— **विक्रमोर्वशी नाटक.** [Vikramorvaṣī nāṭaka. Translated, with a preface and epitome of the plot, by K. Ṣ. R.] [1874.] 8°. **14140. f. 8.**

—— *See* VIṢĀKHADATTA. Mudrárákshasa ... Translated into Maráṭhí [prose and verse] from the original Sanskrit ... by Krishna Shástri Rájváde. 1867. 8°. **14140. f. 23.**

—— Alankár-wiweka, or The figures of speech. Compiled from the Sanscrit, by Krishna Shástri Rájwáde. (**अलंकारविवेक.**) pp. vi. 151, *lith. Poona,* 1853. 8°. **14139. a. 5.**

—— **उत्सवप्रकाश** [Utsavaprakāṣa. Miscellaneous poems.] pp. ii. 91. **पुणें १७९६** [*Poona,* 1874.] 8°. **14140. f. 7(2.)**

KRISHNA SHASTREE CHIPLONKER. *See* KṚISHṆA ṢĀSTRĪ CHIPḶŪṆKAR.

KSHATRIYAVAMṢA. **श्री क्षत्रिय वंशोद्गममाला** *etc.* [Kshatriyavaṃṣodgamamālā. An account of the origin of the Kshatriya caste.] pp. 80, *lith.* **मुंबई १७७७** [*Bombay,* 1855.] 8°. **14139. c. 5(1.)**

KSHĪRASĀGARA (G. N.) *See* GOVINDA NĀRĀYAṆA KSHĪRASĀGARA.

KULLŪKA BHAṬṬA. *See* MANU. **श्री मनुस्मृति** *etc.* [Manusmṛiti. With a translation founded upon K. Bh.'s commentary.] [1877.] 8°. **14038. d. 19.**

KURŪḶKAR (ABRAHAM DANIEL). Kirat. A Marathi novel in two volumes, depicting human nature in all its shades and colours .... Vol. 1. (**किरात**) pp. iii. 169. *Bombay,* 1880. 12°. **14139. f. 24.**

KUṢĀBĀ LIMAYE. *See* ESDAILE (D. A.) Catechism of the geography and history of Mahárāshtra. Translated into Márāthí [by K. L.]. 1869. 12°. **14139. d. 5.**

KUVARAJĪ. अथ कुवरजी महाराज यांचें चरित्र प्रारंभः [Kuvarajī Mahārāja yāñchen charitra. Verses on supernatural powers ascribed to the saint K.] ff. 16. धळें १८७७ [*Dhulia,* 1877.] 12°. **14140. a. 9(12.)**

LAGADHA. वेदांग ज्योतिष मूळ ग्रंथ व त्याचें मराठी भाषांतर. (The Vedang jyotisha translated into Marathi by Janardan Balaji Modak.) pp. ii. 28. *Thana,* 1885. 12°. **14053. b. 11(2.)**

LAGNAYANTRA. लग्नयंत्र [Lagnayantra. An astronomical chart.] १७९९ [*Poona,* 1877.] 4°. **14142. b. 2.**

LAKSHMAṆA GAṄGĀJĪ TOḌĀVĀR. दिवाळीची लूट सोडा पैशाची मुठ [Divāḷīchī lūṭ. Various receipts for making Indian fireworks.] pp. 20. मुंबई १८७५ [*Bombay,* 1875.] 32°. **14140. g. 1(2.)**

LAKSHMAṆA GOPĀLA DĪKSHITA SĀTĀRKAR. *See* BHAIRAVA JYOTIRVID. प्रश्नभैरव, *etc.* [Praṣnabhairava. With a Marathi translation by L. G. D. S.] [1881.] 8°. **14053. cc. 40.**

LAKSHMAṆA GOVINDABHĀŪ ASHṬAPUTRE. *See* JAYADEVA. भावदीपिका *etc.* [Gītagovinda. With a Marathi commentary by L. G. A. called Bhāvadīpikā or Padabhāvānukāriṇī.] [1860.] 4°. **14072. d. 1.**

LAKSHMAṆA MOREṢVARA ṢĀSTRĪ HALBE. Muktamálá. A novel composed .... by Laxman Moreshvar Shástri Halbe. (मुक्तमाला). Second edition. pp. xi. 226. *Bombay,* 1866. 12°. **14139. f. 8.**

—— Fourth edition. pp. xi. 231. *Bombay,* 1874. 12°. **14139. f. 16.**

—— Fifth edition. pp. xi. 231. *Bombay,* 1880. 12°. **14139. f. 28.**

—— Ratnaprabhá. A Maráthí original novel composed by Laxman Moreshvar Shástrí Halbe. (रत्नप्रभा). Second edition. pp. xii. 182. *Bombay,* 1878. 12°. **14139. f. 14.**

LAKSHMAṆA ṢAṄKARA ABHYAṄKAR. सीतास्वयंवर नाटक [Sītāsvayaṃvara nāṭaka. A drama on the destruction of Rāvaṇa, and the rescue of Sītā.] pp. 50, *lith.* मुंबई १८६७ [*Bombay,* 1867.] 8°. **14140. f. 1(2.)**

LAKSHMĪ. लक्ष्मी अष्टक [Lakshmī ashṭaka. Verses in praise of the goddess Lakshmī.] pp. 8. मुंबई १७७० [*Bombay,* 1848.] 32°. **14137. c. 3(2.)**

—— [Another edition.] ff. 3, *lith.* मुंबई १७८५ [*Bombay,* 1863.] *obl.* 16°. **14137. c. 2(6.)**

LAVA KUṢA. लव कुशाची बखर [Lava Kuṣāchī bakhar, or The story of Lava and Kuṣa, twin sons of Rāma.] pp. 23, *lith.* पुणें १८७५ [*Poona,* 1875.] 16°.
In the Modi character. **14139. f. 15(1.)**

—— [Another edition.] pp. 23, *lith.* पुणें [*Poona,* 1877 ?]. 16°. **14140. g. 24(2.)**

LAXMAN MORESHVAR SHÁSTRÍ HALBE. *See* LAKSHMAṆA MOREṢVARA ṢĀSTRĪ HALBE.

LEKHANADĪPIKĀ. लेखनदीपिका [Lekhanadīpikā. An elementary treatise on etymology, and spelling.] pp. 21. मुंबई १८७५ [*Bombay,* 1875.] 12°. **14140. g. 7(2.)**

LEKHANAPADDHATĪ. लेखनपद्धती [Lekhanapaddhatī. A letter-writer, with a translation of Indian postal rules.] pp. 40. [*Bombay* ? 1860 ?]. 8°. **14140. i. 9.**

LESSONS. Easy lessons in reading, with an English and Maráthí vocabulary. pp. vi. 141. 170. *Bombay,* 1851. 8°. **760. d. 28.**

—— Easy lessons in [Marathi] grammar. Part. II. व्याकरणसंबंधी सोपे धडे .... Second edition. pp. 32. *Bombay,* 1877. 16°.
Wanting Pt. I. **14140. g. 32.**

LĪLĀVATĪ. Lilavati. (A tale) by the author of "Minorabai," "Mirabai," "Vairagi" *etc.* (लीलावती). pp. 12. *Bombay,* 1875. 12°. **14139. f. 15(2.)**

LITURGIES.—ENGLAND, *Church of.—Common Prayer.* इंग्लीश खिस्ती मंडलीची भजनपद्धति. The Book of Common Prayer ... Translated into Maráthí by the Rev. J. Dixon. pp. 711. *Bombay,* 1835. 8°. **3406. cc. 25.**

—— Missa de Angelis, a Plain-chant Service for the Holy Communion. पवित्र भागीपणाच्या विधीसाठीं राग. [Pavitra Bhāgīpaṇāchyā vidhisāṭhīṇ rāga.] pp. 15. *Bombay,* 1886. 8°. **14137. b. 14.**

LOCKYER (JOSEPH NORMAN). Science primers in Marâthi. Astronomy. Translated from the original work of J. N. L. by Kâshinâth Bâlkrishna Marâthé. (ज्योतिःशास्त्र) [Jyotiḥṣāstra.] pp. iv. 140. *Bombay,* 1880. 16°. **14139. a. 41.**

LOKAHITAVĀDĪ *pseud.* [i.e. GOPĀLARĀVA HARI.] *See* ĀSVALĀYANA. सार्थ आश्वलायनगृह्यसूत्र [Grihyasūtra. With a translation and preface in Marathi by L.] [1880.] 8°. **14010. c. 31.**

LOLIMBARĀJA. वैद्यजीवन [Vaidyajīvana. Sanskrit text, with a Marathi commentary by Krishṇa Sāstrī Bhāṭavaḍekar. Fourth edition.] pp. xiv. 71, *lith.* मुंबई १८६१ [*Bombay*, 1861.] 4°. **14043. d. 7.**

—— वैद्यावतंस [Vaidyāvataṃsa. Sanskrit text, with a Marathi commentary by Krishṇa Sāstrī Bhāṭavaḍekar.] pp. iv. 26, *lith.* मुंबई १८६० [*Bombay*, 1860.] 8°. **14043. c. 2.**

LORD'S PRAYER. Exposition of the Lord's Prayer. येशू ख्रिस्ताने जी प्रार्थना आपल्या शिष्यांस सांगितली तिजवर टीका. pp. 45. [*Bombay*, 1838 ?] 8°.
No. 51 of the Bombay Tract and Book Society's Series.
14137. b. 5(9.)

—— Third edition. pp. 40. *Bombay*, 1841. 12°.
No. 24 of the "Bombay Tract and Book Society's Series."
14137. a. 2(9.)

MAC CUDDEN (THOMAS). The Oriental eras; being a compilation of the different eras in use among Hindoos, Mahomedans, Arabians, Christians, and Parsees, with chronological notices of important events connected with India and the East. Translated into the Marathee language by Govind Raojee Mandey ... from the English original of Thomas Mc Cudden. (हिंदुस्थानाची शकावळी) [Hindusthānāchī ṣakāvaḷī.] pp. ii. 82. *Bombay*, 1860. 4°. **14142. b. 3.**

MAC CULLOCH (JOHN MURRAY) *D.D.* Wáchan páth málá. Vernacular reader. No. 1. Being a series of translations (of most of the prose pieces in McCulloch's "Series of Lessons," and of some of the prose pieces of his "Third Reading Book") ... by Major T. Candy. (वाचनपाठमाळा) Third edition. pp. 292, *lith.* *Poona*, 1857. 8°. **14140. h. 5.**

MĀDHAVA, *Son of Indukara.* Madhavanidana. A Sanskrit treatise on pathology. Translated into Marathi by Krishna Shastri Bhatavadekar [under the name of Mādhavārthaprakāṣikā]. pp. 6. 20. 460, *lith.* *Bombay*, 1862. 8°. **14043. d. 8.**

MĀDHAVA CHANDROBĀ. *See* MOROPANTA. मोरोपंतकृत सभापर्व (वनपर्व *etc.*) आर्या [The Mahābhārata paraphrased in āryā verse. Edited, with foot-notes, by M. Ch.] [1860–64.] 8°. **14140. c. 10.**

—— *See* SARVASAṄGRAHA. सर्वसंग्रह [Sarvasaṅgraha. Edited, with notes, by M. Ch.] [1862, 63.] 8°. **14137. e. 4.**

—— *See* TUKĀRĀMA. तुकारामकृत अभंग [Tukārāmakrita abhaṅga. Philosophical and other poems. Revised and edited by M. Ch.] [1862.] 8°. **14140. c. 3.**

—— *See* VĀMANA PAṆḌITA. वामनपंडितकृत श्लोक [Vāmana Paṇḍitakṛita ṣloka. Edited by M. Ch.] [1860–63.] 8°. **14140. c. 15.**

—— A Dictionary in Sanscrit and Marathi. (शब्दरत्नाकर किंवा संस्कृत व प्राकृत शब्दकोश) pp. ii. 679. 14. *Bombay*, 1870. 4°. **14090. f. 14.**

MĀDHAVA RĀVA I., *Peshwa.* *See* KĀṢĪNĀTHA MAHĀDEVA THATTE. सवाई माधवराव पेशवे यांचें नाटक [Savāī Mādhava Rāva Peshwe yāṇcheṇ nāṭaka. A drama on the chief events in the life of the Peshwa Mādhava Rāva I.] [1884.] 8°. **14140. f. 2(5.)**

—— *See* VINĀYAKA JANĀRDANA KĪRTANE. नाटक थोरले माधवराव पेशवे यांजवर [Nāṭaka thorle Mādhava Rāva yāṇjvar. A drama on the administration of the Peshwa Mādhava Rāva I.] [1864.] 12°. **14140. a. 15.**

MĀDHAVA RĀVA II., *Peshwa.* खरड्याच्या स्वारीची बखर [Kharaḍyāchyā svārīchī bakhar, or The Chronicles of M. R.] *See* PERIODICAL PUBLICATIONS.—*Poona.* काव्येतिहास-संग्रह [Kāvyetihāsa saṅgraha.] Vol. VIII. Nos. 1–4. [1878, *etc.*] 8°. **14072. d. 37.**

MĀDHAVARĀVA, called **BAJĀBĀ RĀMACHANDRA PRADHĀNA.** Daivaseni, or a story of the king of Jayapur. A poem. (दैवसेनी) pp. ii. iii. 63. *Bombay*, 1867. 12°. **14140. a. 14.**

MĀDHAVARĀVA MOREṢVARA KUNTE. *See* PERIODICAL PUBLICATIONS.—*Poona.* The Ṣaddarshanachintanikâ. [Compiled and edited by M. M. K.] 1877, *etc.* 8°. **14048. d.**

MAHĀBHĀRATA.

SELECTIONS.

—— अथ पंचरत्नगीता प्रारंभ [Pañcharatna. Five theological tracts, taken from the Mahābhārata, and translated from the Sanskrit, viz. (1.) Bhagavadgītā, and (2.) Vishṇunamanastotra, both translated by Jñānadeva; (3.) Bhīshmastavarāja; (4.) Anusmṛiti, and (5.) Gajendramoksha.] मुंबई १७७९ [*Bombay*, 1857.] *obl.* 16°. **14137. c. 8.**

—— अथ प्राकृत पंचरत्नप्रा॰ [Another edition.] *Lith.* मुंबई १७८४ [*Bombay*, 1862.] *obl.* 16°. **14137. c. 6.**

—— अथ अर्जुनगीता प्रारंभोयं [Another edition, under the title Arjunagītā.] ff. 110, *lith.* पुणें १८८० [*Poona*, 1880.] *obl.* 16°. **14137. c. 7.**

PORTIONS.

BHAGAVADGĪTĀ.

—— *See* NESBIT (R.) भगवद्गीतेचें सार (Analysis of the Bhagawat Gítá.) [1840.] 8°. **14137. b. 5(2.)**

—— *See* UDDHAVA CHIDGHANA. उद्धव चिद्घनकृत भगवद्गीता [A metrical version of the Bhagavadgītā.] [1878, *etc.*] 8°. **14072. d. 37.**

—— अथ भाषाविवृतिसहित गीताप्रारंभः [Bhagavadgītā. Sanskrit text, with a Marathi commentary by Raghunātha Ṣāstrī.] ff. 276, *lith.* पुणें १७८२ [*Poona*, 1860.] *Fol.* **14065. e. 5.**

—— अथ श्रीगीतार्थबोधिनी प्रारंभः [Sanskrit text, with metrical paraphrases in Marathi by Vāmana Paṇḍita and Mukteṣvara, and in Hindi by Tulasīdāsa. The whole edited under the title of Gītārthabodhinī.] मुंबई १७८३ [*Bombay*, 1861.] 8°. **14065. d. 15.**

—— अथ ज्ञानेश्वरी प्रारंभः ॥ [Sanskrit text, with Jñāneṣvarī, a Marathi poem, in 18 cantos, by Jñānadeva, enlarging upon the same. Revised, and provided with a vocabulary of difficult words, by Ṣaṅkara, son of Gaṇeṣa.] १७९६ [*Bombay*, 1874.] *obl.* 4°. **14065. f. 1.**

—— अथ श्रीपरिभाषे सहित ज्ञानेश्वरी प्रारंभः [Another edition of the text, with the Jñāneṣvarī and a glossary of difficult words at the end of each adhyāya. Edited, with a Marathi preface by Rāvajī Ṣrīdhara Gondhaḷekar.] 18 pt., *lith.* पुणे १७९९ [*Poona*, 1877.] *obl.* 4°. **14060. f. 12.**

PORTIONS [BHAGAVADGĪTĀ].

—— श्री गीता भावचंद्रिका श्रीकृष्णार्जुन संवाद [Bhāvachandrikā. A prose translation of the Bhagavadgītā by Bāḷajī Sundarajī, assisted by Rāmachandra Ṣāstrī Muḍle.] pp. 106. मुंबई १७७३ [*Bombay*, 1851.] 12°. **14137. d. 4.**

HARIṢCHANDRĀKHYĀNA.

—— *See* MUKTEṢVARA. अथ हरिश्चंद्राख्यान प्रारंभः [Hariṣchandrākhyāna. Founded on an episode from the Vanaparva of the Mahābhārata.] [1861.] *obl.* 8°. **14139. g. 11(1.)**

NALOPĀKHYĀNA.

—— *See* GAṆEṢA VINĀYAKA KĀNIṬKAR. मनोरंजक दमयंती [Manorañjaka Damayantī. The story of Nala and Damayantī, founded on an episode in the Mahābhārata.] [1877.] 8°. **14139. g. 15.**

—— *See* MOROPANTA. मोरोपंतकृत ... नलाख्यान आर्या [Nalākhyāna āryā. The story of Nala and Damayantī, in verse.] [1862.] 8°. **14140. c. 10(1.)**

—— नलाख्यानाची बखर [Nalākhyānāchī bakhar, or The story of King Nala.] ff. 30, *lith.* मुंबई १७७९ [*Bombay*, 1857.] *obl.* 16°.

In the Modi character.

14140. a. 6(13.)

SABHĀPARVA.

—— *See* MUKTEṢVARA. सर्वसंग्रह ... सभापर्व [Sabhāparva. A paraphrase in verse.] [1863.] 8°. **14140. c. 7.**

ṢAKUNTALOPĀKHYĀNA.

—— *See* MOROPANTA. अथ शकुंतलाख्यान [Ṣakuntalākhyāna. The story of Ṣakuntalā in verse.] [1857.] *obl.* 12°. **14140. a. 6(9.)**

SĀVITRYUPĀKHYĀNA.

—— *See* ṢRĪDHARA. सावित्री आख्यान [Sāvitrī ākhyāna. The story of Sāvitrī, taken from the Mahābhārata.] [1857.] *obl.* 12°. **14140. a. 6(11.)**

UTTARAGĪTĀ.

—— अथ श्रीज्ञानेश्वरकृत टीकासहित उत्तरगीता प्रारंभः ॥ [Uttaragītā. Sanskrit text, with a preface and Marathi translation by Jñānadeva.] ff. 63, *lith.* पुणें १८८१ [*Poona*, 1881.] *obl.* 16°. **14065. b. 13.**

VANAPARVA.

—— *See* MUKTEṢVARA. श्री मुक्तेश्वर कृत महाभारत-वनपर्व [An annotated edition.] [1878, *etc.*] 8°. **14072. d. 37.**

PORTIONS.

VIDURANĪTI.

—— *See* GOVINDAṢANKARA ṢĀSTRĪ BĀPAṬ. Nitimandira. [A collection of moral precepts and stories taken from the Viduranīti.] 1879. 12°. **14139. c. 15.**

—— Vídoor néetée. महाराष्ट्र विदुर नीति. [Advice on polity and ethics given by Vidura to his cousin Dhṛitarāshṭra. Translated from the Udyogaparva of the Mahābhārata.] pp. 95, *lith.* *Bombay*, १८३४ [1834.] 8°. **14137. d. 1(1.)**

—— विदुरनीति *etc.* [Another edition.] pp. 118, *lith.* १७७१ [*Bombay ?*, 1849.] 12°. **14140. a. 4(1.)**

—— Vidoorneetee. विदुरनीति. [Followed by Nāradanīti.] Third edition. pp. 132. मुंबई १७८० [*Bombay*, 1858.] 12°. **14137. c. 9.**

—— विदुरनीति. [Another edition.] pp. 101, *lith.* मुंबई १७८४ [*Bombay*, 1862.] 12°. **14137. c. 12.**

—— [Another edition.] pp. 86, *lith.* पुणें १७९९ [*Poona*, 1877.] 12°. **14137. c. 15.**

APPENDIX.

—— *See* JANĀRDANA BĀḶĀJĪ MODAK. महाभारत [Mahābhārata. A critical lecture on the Sanskrit poem.] [1886, *etc.*] 8°. **14139. c. 26.**

—— *See* MOROPANTA. मोरोपंतकृत सभापर्व (वनपर्व *etc.*) आर्या [The Mahābhārata, paraphrased in āryā verse.] [1860–64.] 8°. **14140. c. 10.**

—— *See* VĀMANA PANḌITA. अजामिळ आख्यान [Ajāmiḷākhyāna. Founded on the Śāntiparva of the Mahābhārata.] [1849.] 16°. **14140. a. 3(1.)**

MAHĀDEVA BĀḶAKṚISHṆA CHITḶE. Manorama nataka, a tragi-comedy [in five acts, on Hindu social manners and customs]. (मनोरमा नाटक). Second edition. pp. v. vi. 230. *Poona*, 1877. 12°. **14140. e. 5.**

MAHĀDEVA CHIMṆĀJĪ ĀPṬE. मौजेच्या चार घटका. भाग पहिला. कालिदासाचें अभिज्ञान शकुंतल नाटक. [Manjechyā chār ghaṭakā, or Four hours of entertainment. Part I. containing a translation of the Ṣakuntalā of Kālidāsa.] pp. xi. 202. मुंबई [*Bombay*, 1881.] 8°.

In progress. **14140. f. 16.**

MAHĀDEVA GOVINDA RĀNAḌE. *See* GREEN (H.) *Superintendent of Government Schools in Gujarat.* A collection of English phrases ... with their Marathi equivalents... Revised by Mahádeo Govind Ranade. 1868. 8°. **12906. cc. 6.**

MAHĀDEVA GOVINDA ṢĀSTRĪ. First Book of Maráthí poetry. Translated from the First Book of English poetry... by Mahadeo Govind Shastree. (प्राकृत कवितेचें पहिलें पुस्तक) [Prākṛita kavitechen̤ pahilen̤ pustaka.] pp. vi. 102. iv. *lith.* पुणें १८६० [*Poona*, 1860.] 16°. **14140. a. 5(1.)**

MAHĀDEVA GOVINDA ṢĀSTRĪ KOLHAṬKAR. *See* SHAKSPERE (W.) Othello,...translated into Maráthí by Ráv Sáheb Mahádev Govind Shástrí Kolhatkar. 1867. 12°. **14140. e. 10.**

MAHĀDEVA ṢĀSTRĪ PURĀṆIKA. *See* SULLIVAN (R.) *LL.D.* Bhugol Khagol .... Translated from Professor Sullivan's Geography, generalized, by Mahádeva Shástrí Puránik. 1880. 12°. **14139. a. 45.**

MAHĀDEVA VINĀYAKA KEḶKAR. प्रमिलार्जुन नाटक. [Pramilārjuna nāṭaka. A drama on the fabled story of Pramilā and Arjuna.] Second edition. pp. 47, *lith.* मालवण १८०४ [*Malvan*, 1882.] 8°. **14140. f. 2(3.)**

MAHĀDEVA VIṬHṬHALA RĀHĀḶKAR. A friend of teachers and pupils, or A manual of education, by Mahadeva Vithal Rahalkar .... Revised by the Maráṭhí translator, E[ducational] D[epartment.] (शिक्षक व विद्यार्थी त्यांचा मित्र) [Ṣikshaka va vidyārthī tyān̤chā mitra.] pp. 110. *Bombay*, 1877. 12°. **14139. c. 16.**

MAHĪPATI. अथ भक्तलीलामृत प्रारंभः [Bhaktalīlāmṛita. A poem in 51 chapters containing accounts of the lives and miracles of Vaishṇava saints and poets.] *Lith.* मुंबई १७८६ [*Bombay*, 1864.] *obl.* 4°. **14140. d. 13.**

—— अथ भक्तिविजय प्रारंभः [Bhaktivijaya. A poem in 57 chapters, on the lives of Vaishṇava saints.] *Lith.* मुंबई १७८२ [*Bombay*, 1860.] *obl.* 4°.

Chapter 34 appears to be wanting. **14140. d. 4.**

—— पांडुरंगस्तोत्रप्रारंभ ॥ [Pāṇḍuraṅgastotra. A hymn of praise to Pāṇḍuraṅga.] ff. 16. १७७८ [*Bombay ?*, 1856.] *obl.* 16°. **14140. a. 7(1.)**

—— [Another edition.] ff. 14, *lith.* पुणें [*Poona*, 1866 ?] *obl.* 12°. **14137. c. 11(1.)**

—— [Another edition.] ff. 14, *lith.* पुणें १७९९ [*Poona*, 1877.] *obl.* 12°. **14140. a. 9(13.)**

MAHĪPATI. अथ शनिमाहात्म्य प्रारंभ ॥ [Ṣanimāhātmya. A hymn of praise to Saturn, translated from the Sanskrit.] ff. 27. मुंबई १८६१ [*Bombay*, 1861.] *obl.* 8°. **14137. d. 10(2.)**

—— [Another edition.] ff. 19, *lith.* १८६६ [*Bombay*?, 1864.] *obl.* 8°. **14140. c. 11(1.)**

—— [Another edition. Followed by Navagrahastotra, a Sanskrit hymn addressed to nine planets, ascribed to Vyāsa. Fourth edition.] ff. 30, *lith.* पुणें १९९६ [*Poona*, 1874.] *obl.* 12°. **14140. a. 9(7.)**

—— [Another edition.] ff. 31. मुंबई १८७७ [*Bombay*, 1877.] *obl.* 8°. **14137. d. 16.**

—— *See* Dattātraya Vāsudeva Joglekar. सौरिविक्रमनाटक. [Sauri Vikrama nāṭaka. A drama based on the Ṣanimāhātmya of M.] [1881.] 12°. **14140. a. 28.**

—— अथ श्री संतळीलामृत प्रारंभः ॥ [Santalilāmṛita. A work in 35 chapters and in verse containing legendary accounts of Vaishṇava saints.] मुंबई १८८५ [*Bombay*, 1885.] *obl.* 8°. **14140. c. 35.**

—— अथ तुकारामचरित्र प्रारंभः [Tukārāma charitra. A poem in 17 chapters on the life of the poet Tukārāma.] *lith.* मुंबई १९८५ [*Bombay*, 1863.] *obl.* 8°. **14140. d. 6.**

—— [Another edition.] मुंबई १९९७ [*Bombay*, 1875.] *obl.* 8°. **14140. c. 11(2.)**

MAINĀNĀTHA. अथ आगमनिगम ग्रंथः प्रारंभः [Āgamanigama grantha. A metaphysical treatise in verse in 10 chapters.] मुंबई १८८५ [*Bombay*, 1885.] *obl.* 8°. **14137. d. 15.**

MALHĀR RĀMARĀVA CHITṆĪS. श्रीमंत छत्रपती थाकटे रामराजे व थाकटे शाहू महाराज यांचीं चरित्रें चतुरसिंग राजे यांच्या हकीकती सुद्धां [An account of the lives of Rāmarāja, and Shāhū II. Rajas of Satara. With a short notice of Raja Chatura Simha.] *See* Periodical Publications.—*Poona*. काव्येतिहास-संग्रह [Kāvyetihāsa saṅgraha.] Vol. VI. Nos. 10–12, and Vol. VII. Nos. 1–8. [1878, *etc.*] 8°. **14072 d. 37.**

—— श्रीमंत छत्रपति संभाजी महाराज व थोरले राजाराम महाराज यांचीं चरित्रें [Srīmanta chhatrapati Sambhāji Mahārāja va thorle Rājārāma Mahārāja yāṉchīṉ charitreṉ. An account of the lives of Sambhāji, and of Rājārāma his brother, Rajas of Satara.] *See* Periodical Publications.—*Poona*. काव्येतिहास-संग्रह [Kāvyetihāsa saṅgraha.] Vol. IV.–VI. [1878.] 8°. *Imperfect; wanting pp.* 1–8. **14072. d. 37.**

MALHĀR RĀMARĀVA CHITṆĪS. थोरले शाहू महाराज यांचें चरित्र [Thorle Shāhū Mahārāja yāṉcheṉ charitra. The life of Shāhū I. Raja of Satara.] *See* Periodical Publications.—*Poona*. काव्येतिहास-संग्रह [Kāvyetihāsa saṅgraha.] Vol. V. [1878, *etc.*] 8°. **14072. d. 37.**

MALHĀR RĀVA, *Gaikwar of Baroda*. *See* Nārāyana Bāpujī Kāniṭkar. Malharrao Maharaj, ex Gaikwar of Baroda, a historical drama, *etc.* 1875. 12°. **14140. a. 20.**

MĀLU NARAHARI. अथ श्रीभक्तिसार नवनाथ ग्रंथप्रारंभः [Bhaktisāra, also called Navanātha grantha. A work in verse, in 40 chapters, containing legendary accounts of the miraculous deeds of nine saints of the Nātha sect.] *lith.* पुणें १८८४ [*Poona*, 1884.] *obl.* 8°. **14140. c. 33.**

MANAṢCHANDRABODHA. अथ मनश्चंद्रबोध प्रारंभः [Manaṣchandrabodha. A metaphysical treatise in verse.] ff. 56, *lith.* मुंबई १९९९ [*Bombay*, 1855.] *obl.* 12°. **14140. d. 1.**

—— [Another edition.] ff. 85, *lith.* मुंबई १९९७ [*Bombay*, 1873.] *obl.* 12°. **14137. c. 14.**

MĀNATUṄGĀCHĀRYA. सार्थ भक्तामर स्तोत्र [Bhaktāmara-stotra. A Jain hymn in 48 Sanskrit verses, with a Marathi paraphrase by Devachanda Māṇakachanda.] pp. iii. 30. पुणें १८८३ [*Poona*, 1883.] 16°. **14100. a.**

MAṄGĪṢA. राधाविलास [Rādhāvilāsa, or The lament of Rādhā. A poem.] *See* Periodical Publications.—*Poona*. काव्येतिहास-संग्रह [Kāvyetihāsa saṅgraha.] Vol. VIII. Nos. 2 and 3. [1878, *etc.*] 8°. **14072. d. 37.**

MANU. *See* Govindaṣaṅkara Ṣāstrī Bāpaṭ. Nitimandira. [A collection of moral precepts and stories, taken from the Manusmṛiti and other works.] 1879. 12°. **14139 c. 15.**

—— श्री मनुस्मृति प्राकृत भाषान्तर सहित । [Manusmṛiti. Sanskrit text, with a Marathi translation, founded upon Kullūka's commentary, by Bāpū Ṣāstrī Moghe.] pp. iv. xxxiv. 430. मुंबई १८७७ [*Bombay*, 1877.] 8°. **14038. d. 19.**

MARATHI ANTHOLOGY. अनेक-कवि-कृत-कविता. [Aneka kavikṛita kavitā. A collection of poems by various Marathi poets.] *See* Periodical Publications.—*Poona*. काव्येतिहास-संग्रह. [Kāvyetihāsa saṅgraha.] Vol. II, *etc.* [*Poona*, 1878, *etc.*] 8°. **14072. d. 37.**

MARATHI FIFTH BOOK. Marathi Fifth Book, for the use of Government schools in the Bombay presidency. By the Maráthí translator and his assistants (पांचवें पुस्तक) [Pānchaveṉ pustaka.] pp. iv. 312. iv. *Bombay*, 1860. 8°. **14140. h. 7.**

—— Fourth edition. pp. iii. 285. *Bombay*, 1866. 8°. **14140. h. 10.**

—— Recast and revised ... First edition. pp. vii. 348. *Bombay*, 1870. 8°. **14140. h. 16.**

MARATHI FIRST BOOK. Marathi First Book. Part I. Simple letters and vowel combinations. (Part II. Compound letters, and reading lessons.) मुलांकरितां पहिलें पुस्तक. pp. 24. *Bombay*, 1875. 12°. **14140. g. 2(5.)**

—— Second edition. pp. 24. *Bombay*, 1877. 12°. **14140. g. 19(3.)**

MARATHI FOURTH BOOK. Máráthí Fourth Book, for the use of Government schools in the Bombay presidency. By the Maráthí translator and his assistants. (चौथें पुस्तक) [Chautheṉ pustaka.] Third edition. pp. iv. 192. *Bombay*, 1861. 8°. **14140. h. 9.**

—— Recast and revised ... Second edition. pp. ix. 324. *Bombay*, 1870. 12°. **14140. g. 21.**

—— Fourth edition. pp. ix. 324. *Bombay*, 1874. 12°. **14140. g. 22.**

—— Fifth edition. pp. ix. 324. *Bombay*, 1877. 12° **14140. g. 28.**

MARATHI PRIMER. Maráthí Primer, or the art of learning to read soon. वाचनविद्या, किंवा लवकर वाचतां येण्याची युक्ति [Vāchanavidyā.] pp. iv. 38. मुंबई १८७५ [*Bombay*, 1875.] 12°. **14140. g. 2(6.)**

MARATHI SECOND BOOK. Maráthí Second Book, for the use of Government schools in the Bombay presidency. By the Maráthí translator and his assistants. (दुसरें पुस्तक) [Dusreṉ pustaka.] Fourth edition. pp. 72. *Bombay*, 1860. 12°. **14140. g. 12(1.)**

—— Recast and revised ... Second edition. pp. vii. 76. *Bombay*, 1871. 12°. **14140. g. 18(2.)**

MARATHI SIXTH BOOK. Maráthí Sixth Book, for the use of Government schools in the Bombay presidency. By the Maráthí translator and his assistants. (सहावें पुस्तक) [Sahāveṉ pustaka.] pp. 339. *Bombay*, 1861. 8°. **14140. h. 8.**

MARATHI SIXTH BOOK. Fourth edition. pp. 371. *Bombay*, 1869. 8°. **14140. h. 15.**

—— Recast and revised ... Second edition. pp. viii. 458. *Bombay*, 1875. 8°. **14140. h. 18.**

MARATHI SPELLING BOOK. बाराखड्या Maratha spelling book. [Bārākhaḍyā.] *Bombay*, 1845. 32°. **14140. g. 1(1.)**

MARATHI THIRD BOOK. Maráthí Third Book, for the use of Government schools in the Bombay presidency. By the Maráthí translator and his assistants. (तिसरें पुस्तक) [Tisreṉ pustaka.] Third edition. pp. 111. *Bombay*, 1860. 12°. **14140. g. 10.**

—— Recast and revised ... Second edition. pp. viii. 135. *Bombay*, 1870. 12°. **14140. g. 20.**

—— Fifth edition. pp. viii. 235. *Bombay*, 1875. 12°. **14140. g. 23.**

—— Maráthi Third Book for the use of schools. मुलांकरितां तिसरें पुस्तक. Sixth edition. pp. vi. 128. *Bombay*, 1877. 16°.
Published by the Christian Vernacular Education Society. **14140. g. 30(2.)**

MARCET (JANE). *See* HARI KEṢAVAJĪ. Elements of political economy. An imitation of, and partly translated from, J. M.'s Conversations. 1854. 8°. **14139. c. 7.**

MARKS. Marks of the true religion. खऱ्या धर्माचीं चिन्हें [Kharyā dharmāchīṉ chihneṉ. A Christian tract.] Seventh edition. pp. 30. *Bombay*, 1877. 16°.
One of the Bombay Tract and Book Society Marathi 18 mo. Series. **14137. a. 4(4.)**

MĀRUTĪJANMA. अथ मारुतीजन्मप्रारंभः [Mārutījanma. Verses on the birth of the monkey-chief Hanumān.] ff. 6, *lith.* मुंबई १७९७ [*Bombay*, 1875.] *obl.* 12°. **14140. a. 9(8.)**

MASLAHUDDIN SHAIK SADI. *See* SAʿDĪ.

MAXIMS. Moral maxims. नवीन लघु हितोपदेश. [Navīna laghu hitopadeṣa.] Third edition. pp. 23. मुंबई १८५६ [*Bombay*, 1856.] 12°. **14140. g. 3(1.)**

MAYŪRA. *See* MOROPANTA.

MILL (JOHN STUART). *See* HARI KEṢAVAJI. Elements of political economy ... comprising also a paraphrase into popular Marathi dialogue of many of the most important portions of Mill's Principles. 1854. 8°. **14139. c. 7.**

MILL (John Stuart). Arth Shástra Paribháshá; or The Principles of Political Economy, from the work of J. S. M. by Krishna Shástrí Chiplonkar. (अर्थशास्त्रपरिभाषा) pp. 295, *lith.* *Poona*, 1855. 8°. **14140. h. 4.**

MISSIONARIES. येशू ख्रीस्ताचा धर्म शिकविणार्यांची गोष्ट. Account of missionaries. pp. 34. [*Bombay*, 1838?]. 8°.

One of the Bombay Tract and Book Society's Series. **14137. b. 5(10.)**

MITCHELL (John Murray) *LL.D.* *See* Bible.—New Testament.—*John, Gospel of.* The Gospel according to St. John in English and Maráthí, the Maráthí expressed in Roman characters. [By J. M. M.] 1861. 8°. **3068. dd. 16.**

MORA BHAṬṬA DĀṆḌEKAR. An exposure of the Hindu religion, in reply to M. Bh. D., to which is prefixed a translation of the Bhatta's tract, by ... J. Wilson. (Translation of the verification of the Hindu religion, Shri Hindu-dharma-st,hapana.) pp. 159. *English.* *Bombay*, 1832. 8°. **4506. cc. 3.**

MOREṢVARA, *Son of Dhuṇḍi.* धुंडिकुमार मोरेश्वरकृत चंद्रावळी-आख्यान [Chandrāvalī ākhyāna. The story of Chandrāvalī, sister to Rādhā, and one of Kṛishṇa's favourite female companions.] *See* Periodical Publications.—*Poona.* काव्येतिहास-संग्रह [Kāvyetihāsa saṅgraha.] Vol. VI. No. 10. [1878, *etc.*] 8°. **14072. d. 37.**

MOREṢVARA, *Son of Māṇika Bhaṭṭa.* वैद्यामृत । [Vaidyāmṛita. A treatise on therapeutics, Sanskrit text, with a Marathi commentary by Kṛishṇa Ṣāstrī Bhāṭavaḍekar. Fourth edition.] pp. x. 62, *lith.* १८८२ [*Bombay*, 1862.] 4°. **14043. d. 9.**

MOREṢVARA GOPĀLA DEṢMUKH. विवाहकालाविषयीं शारीरशास्त्राचें मत [Vivāha-kālāvishayīṇ ṣārīra-ṣāstrācheṇ mata. A lecture on the physical laws regarding a suitable age for marriage.] pp. 11. *See* Bombay, *City of.*—*Hindu Union Club.* हेमंत व्याख्यानमाला. [Hemanta vyākhyānamālā.] Vol. II. No. 9. [1886, *etc.*] 8°. **14139. c. 26.**

MOROPANTA. अथ दशमस्कंधाच्या आर्या प्रारंभ ॥ [Daṣama skandhāchyā āryā. A poem in 110 verses in the āryā metre, founded on the tenth chapter of the Bhāgavatapurāṇa, containing a life of Kṛishṇa, the first letters of each line of each verse forming an acrostic on the words "Namo Bhāgavate Vāsudevāya."] pp. 111. मुंबई १७७० [*Bombay*, 1848.] 8°. **14140. c. 1.**

MOROPANTA. हरिश्चंद्रोपाख्यान [Hariṣchandropākhyāna. The story of king Hariṣchandra, in verse, taken from the Mārkaṇḍeyapurāṇa.] pp. 42. पुणें १७८१ [*Poona*, 1859.] 8°. **14137. d. 1(2.)**

—— केकासार .... मयूरकविकृत केकावलि, शब्दकोश *etc.* [Kekāsāra. The Kekāvalī of M. with paraphrase, explanations and glossary by Gaṇeṣa Vishṇu Gadre.] pp. 94, *lith.* १८८३ [*Bombay*, 1883.] 12°. **14140. a. 19(3.)**

—— मोरोपंत कृत केकावलि प्रारंभ [Kekāvalī. A Vaishṇava poem.] pp. 37, *lith.* मुंबई १७९३ [*Bombay*, 1876.] 12°. **14140. a. 10(14.)**

—— मोरोपंतकृत सभापर्व (वनपर्व, विराटपर्व *etc.*) आर्या [The Mahābhārata paraphrased in āryā verse. Edited, with notes, by Mādhava Chandrobā, with the assistance of Paraṣurāma Panta Goḍbole.] मुंबई १७८२-८६ [*Bombay*, 1860–64.] 8°.

Each book is published separately, some of them forming parts of a series entitled Sarvasaṅgraha. Wanting the first and last books, also pp. 1–16, 41–64, and 73–80 of Virāṭaparva. The latter part of the Ṣalyaparva is called Gadāparva. Sauptikaparva is here reckoned as a portion of the Gadāparva. **14140. c. 10.**

—— अथ मयूरकृत मंत्ररामायण आर्या प्रारंभः [Mantrarāmāyaṇa āryā. A paraphrase of the Rāmāyaṇa in acrostic āryā metre. Edited, with foot-notes explaining difficult words, by Kṛishṇa Ṣāstrī Gurjar.] ff. 74, *lith.* १७८० [*Bombay?* 1860.] *obl.* 8°. **14137. e. 3(1.)**

—— अथ मंत्ररामायण अयोध्याकांड मयूरकृत [The Ayodhyākāṇḍa of M.'s Mantrarāmāyaṇa.] *See* Janābāī. अथ स्थालिपाक अभंग प्रारंभ [Sthālīpāka.] pp. 8–14. [1863.] 12°. **14140. a. 12(1.)**

—— मोरोपंतकृत प्रकरणें [Moropantakṛita prakaraṇeṇ. A collection of miscellaneous poems by M.] *See* Periodical Publications.—*Poona.* काव्येतिहास-संग्रह [Kāvyetihāsa saṅgraha.] Vol. II, *etc.* [*Poona*, 1878, *etc.*] 8°.

In progress. **14072. d. 37.**

—— मोरोपंतकृत वनपर्वांतील नलाख्यान आर्या [Nalākhyāna. The story of Nala and Damayantī in āryā verse, founded on the Vanaparva of the Mahābhārata.] pp. 32. मुंबई १७८४ [*Bombay*, 1862.] 8°. **14140. c. 9(1.)**

MOROPANTA. अथ शकुंतलाख्यान आर्या मयूरकृत प्रारंभः [Ṣakuntalākhyāna. The story of Ṣakuntalā in āryā verse, founded on the Ādiparva of the Mahābhārata.] ff. 12. मुंबई १९१९ [*Bombay*, 1857.] *obl.* 12°. **14140. a. 6(9.)**

—— आर्या सुभद्राहरणाच्या [Subhadrāharaṇa. A poem in āryā verse on the abduction of Subhadrā.] *See* RUKMIṆĪ. आर्या रुक्मिणीस्वयंवरच्या [Rukmiṇī svayaṃvara.] pp. 9–16. [1860?] 12°. **14140. a. 1(10.)**

—— मोरोपंतकृत वामनचरित्र [Vāmanacharitra. The life of the poet Vāmana in verse.] *See* PERIODICAL PUBLICATIONS.—*Poona.* काव्येतिहास-संग्रह [Kāvyetihāsa saṅgraha.] Vol. IX. Nos. 2 and 3. [1878, *etc.*] 8°. **14072. d. 37.**

MORRIS (HENRY) *of the Madras Civil Service. See* VISHṆU YEṢAVANTA DURVE. मारिसकृत हिंदुस्थानच्या इतिहासांतील .... संक्षिप्त माहिती. [A short account of remarkable battles, taken from H. M.'s History of India.] [1877.] 8°. **14139. e. 16(1.)**

—— The History of India, by H. M., translated into Marathi by several translation exhibitioners. Revised by Ravji Shastri Godbole. हिंदुस्तानाचा इतिहास [Hindustānāchā itihāsa.] Eighth edition. pp. 205. *Bombay*, 1880. 12°. **14139. e. 21.**

MORRIS (R.) *of the Government Educational Department.* Marathi songs for children, with music. (मुलांकरितां मराठी गाणें) [Mulāṇkaritāṇ Marāṭhī gāṇeṇ]. pp. 26. *Engl.* and *Mar. Bombay*, 1880. 12°. **14140. a. 11(6.)**

MORTIMER (FAVELL LEE) *Mrs.* Line upon line. Part II. [Translated from the English of Mrs. F. L. M.] ओळीवर ओळ [Oḷīvar oḷ.] pp. v. 204. *Bombay*, 1879. 12°. **14137. a. 9.**

MUDGALA ĀCHĀRYA. रामार्यांचें श्लोकबद्ध भाषांतर [Rāmāryā. A Sanskrit poem of 108 stanzas, also called Āryāṣataka, in praise of Rāma, translated into verse by Harirāja.] *See* PERIODICAL PUBLICATIONS. — *Poona.* काव्येतिहास-संग्रह [Kāvyetihāsa saṅgraha.] Vol. VIII. Nos. 7 and 8. [1878, *etc.*] 8°. **14072. d. 37.**

—— मुद्गलाचार्य आर्यांचें श्लोकबद्ध महाराष्ट्र भाषांतर [An anonymous translation of eighty stanzas only of the Rāmāryā.] *See* PERIODICAL PUBLICATIONS.—*Poona.* काव्येतिहास-संग्रह [Kāvyetihāsa saṅgraha.] Vol. IX. No. 5. [1878, *etc.*] 8°. **14072. d. 37.**

MUIR (JOHN) *D.C.L.* ईश्वरोक्तशास्त्रधारा संस्कृत महाराष्ट्रदेशीय प्राकृतेति भाषाद्वयेन प्रणीता ... The Course of Divine Revelation, in Sanskrit and Marathi, *etc.* pp. 105. [*Bombay*,] 1852. 8°. **14006. d. 2.**

—— मतपरीक्षा ... [Mataparīkshā.] Examination of religions ... Translated from the Sanscrit [of J. M.] into Marathi. 2 pt. *Bombay*, 1856–58. 12°. **14137. b. 6.**

MUKTĀ BĀĪ. मुक्ताबाईचे अभंग प्रारंभ [Abhaṅgas.] *See* JÑĀNADEVA. श्री ज्ञानदेवाचा गाथा [Jñānadevāchā gāthā.] [1877.] 8°. **14140. c. 23.**

—— अथ मुक्ताबाईकृत ताटीचे अभंग प्रारंभः [Tāṭīche abhaṅga. Followed by a few abhaṅgas of Jñānadeva and Tukārāma.] pp. 31, *lith.* मुंबई १९८५ [*Bombay*, 1863.] 12°. **14140. a. 10(5.)**

MUKTEṢVARA. *See* MAHĀBHĀRATA.—*Bhagavadgītā.* अथ श्रीगीतार्थबोधिनी प्रारंभः [Bhagavadgītā. With a metrical paraphrase by M.] [1861.] 8°. **14065. d. 15.**

—— अथहरिश्चंद्राख्यान प्रारंभः [Hariṣchandrākhyāna. The story of king Hariṣchandra, founded on an episode from the Vanaparva of the Mahābhārata.] ff. 24, *lith.* मुंबई १९८३ [*Bombay*, 1861.] *obl.* 8°. **14139. g. 11(1.)**

—— रंभाशुक-संवाद [Rambhā Ṣuka saṃvāda. A philosophical poem in the form of a dialogue between the nymph Rambhā and the saint Ṣuka. Also Murkhāṇchīṇ lakshaṇeṇ, or The characteristics of a fool; and Ṣatamukha Rāvaṇa vadha, or The destruction of the hundred-headed demon Rāvaṇa by Rāma.] *See* PERIODICAL PUBLICATIONS.—*Poona.* काव्येतिहास-संग्रह [Kāvyetihāsa saṅgraha.] Vols. V. and VI. [1878, *etc.*] 8°. **14072. d. 37.**

—— सर्वसंग्रह मुक्तेश्वर सभापर्व ओव्या [Sabhāparva. A paraphrase in verse in the Ovī metre of the Sabhāparva of the Mahābhārata. Revised by Paraṣurāma Panta Godbole.] pp. 248, *lith.* मुंबई १९८४ [*Bombay*, 1863.] 8°.

Part of a series entitled "Sarvasaṅgraha."

14140. c. 7.

—— श्री मुक्तेश्वर कृत महाभारत — वनपर्व [The Vanaparva of the Mahābhārata. An annotated edition of M.'s verse paraphrase.] *See* PERIODICAL PUBLICATIONS. — *Poona.* काव्येतिहास-संग्रह [Kāvyetihāsa saṅgraha.] Vol. I. and II. [1878, *etc.*] 8°. **14072. d. 37.**

MUKUNDARĀJA. अथ पवनविजय प्रारंभः [Pavana-vijaya. A tantric treatise in verse, translated from the Sanskrit by M.] ff. 30, *lith.* पुणें १७९९ [*Poona*, 1877.] *obl.* 12°. **14140. a. 9(14.)**

—— अथ विवेकसिंधु प्रारंभः [Vivekasindhu. A treatise in verse on Vedanta philosophy. Edited, with a preface and glossary, by Rāvajī Ṣrīdhara Gondhaḷekar.] 2 pt. *lith.* पुणें १७९७ [*Poona*, 1875.] *obl.* 8°. **14140. c. 17.**

MŪḶASTAMBHA. अथ मूळस्तंभ प्रारंभः [Mūḷastambha. A poem, in seven chapters, containing an account of the creation of the universe as emanating from the god Ṣiva.] ff. 26, *lith.* मुंबई १७८२ [*Bombay*, 1860.] *obl.* 8°. **14137. d. 9(1.)**

—— [Another edition.] ff. 30, *lith.* मुंबई १७८४ [*Bombay*, 1862.] *obl.* 8°. **14137. d. 10(3.)**

MŪRKHAṢATAKA. मूर्खशतक. The hundred characteristics of fools. (With their translation into Maráthí by Janárdan Hurry Áthalye). pp. ii. 9. (*Ratnagiri*, 1877.) 8°. **14076. b. 15(2.)**

MURRAY (Hugh). A Maráṭhí version of Murray's History of British India ... Part the first, (Part the second) by Narsingh Vináyak Shástri Ok. (Part the third by Vishnu Parashurám Shástrí.) हिंदुस्थानाचा इतिहास [Hindusthānāchā itihāsa.] *Bombay*, 1859–61. 8° and 12°. **14139. e. 8.**

MURRAY (Lindley). Abridgment of Murray's English grammar, with a Maráthí translation ... by Rághobá Janárdhan, and revised by Ball Gungadher Shastree. (मरेयाच्या इंग्रेजी व्याकरणाचा संक्षेप) [Ingrejī vyākaraṇāchā saṃkshepa.] pp. 230. *Bombay*, 1837. 8°. **14140. h. 2.**

MUSLIḤ al-DĪN SAʻDĪ. *See* Saʻdī.

NĀGEṢA RAGHUNĀTHA DĪKSHITA. *See* Annāpā Āpā Vāḍkar. श्रीपालचरित्र [Ṣrīpālacharitra. Translated with the assistance of N. R. D.] [1883.] 8°. **14137. d. 6.**

NĀGEṢARĀVA VINĀYAKA BĀPAṬ. A historical romance. Chhatrapati Sambhaji Maharaj . . . Period 1680–1689. Compiled from various historical English works and old Marathi bakhars and legends, by Nageshrao Vinayak Bapat. (छत्रपति संभाजी महाराज *etc.*) pp. ii. 252. *Bombay*, 1884. 12°. **14139. d. 30.**

NĀGPŪR. नागपूरकर भोंसल्यांच्या संबंधाचे कागदपत्र [Nāgpūrkar Bhoṇsalyāṇchyā sambandhāche kāgadpatra. A collection of papers and documents relating to the Bhoṇsalas of Nagpur, with critical notes.] *See* Periodical Publications. — *Poona.* काव्येतिहास-संग्रह [Kāvyetihāsa saṅgraha.] Vol. III.–IX. No. 9. [1878, *etc.*] 8°.
In progress. **14072. d. 37.**

—— नागपूरकर भोंसल्यांची वंशावळ [Nāgpūrkar Bhoṇsalyāṇchī vaṃṣāvaḷa. The genealogy of the Bhoṇsalas of Nagpur.] *See* Periodical Publications.—*Poona.* काव्येतिहास-संग्रह [Kāvyetihāsa saṅgraha.] Vol. IX. No. 4. [1878, *etc.*] 8°. **14072. d. 37.**

NAKUḶA. अथ नकूळकृत शालिहोत्रटीका [Ṣālihotraṭīkā. A treatise on the veterinary art in two parts. Pt. I. Aṣvaparīkshā, on the selection and general treatment of horses, in verse. Pt. II. Aushadhaprakāra, or 58 recipes for the cure of diseases, in prose. Founded on a Sanskrit work by Rāmanātha.] pp. 126, *lith.* मुंबई १७८५ [*Bombay*, 1863.] 12°. **14137. ff. 1.**

—— अथ अश्वपरीक्षा सटीक [Aṣvaparīkshā. Extracts from the first part of N.'s Ṣālihotra, with explanatory notes by Nāro Āpājī Goḍbole. Second edition.] pp. 31, *lith.* पुणें १७८९ [*Poona*, 1867.] 12°. **14137. ff. 6.**

NĀMADEVA. अभंग बाळक्रीडेचे ॥ [Abhaṅga bāḷakrīḍeche. A poem in the abhaṅga metre on the childhood of Kṛishṇa. Third edition.] pp. 85. मुंबई १७८४ [*Bombay*, 1862.] 8°. **14140. b. 8.**

—— शिवरात्री माहात्म्याचे अभंग [Ṣivarātrī māhātmyāche abhaṅga. A poem, in the abhaṅga metre, on the origin of the institution of the Ṣivarātrī festival. Third edition.] pp. 44. मुंबई १७६९ [*Bombay*, 1847.] 12°. **14140. a. 1(1.)**

—— अथ नामदेवकृत तीर्थावळीचे अभंगप्रारंभ [Tīrthāvaḷīche abhaṅga. Verses on pilgrimages.] pp. 40, *lith.* पुणें १७८२ [*Poona*, 1862.] 8°. **14140. f. 7(1.)**

NĀNĀ KOḶEKAR also called **SANMATIDĀSA.** भजनसद्बोध मालिका [Bhajana sadbodha mālikā. Jain hymns, chiefly in the abhaṅga metre.] pp. iv. 62. सोलापुर [*Solapur*, 1884.] 8°. **14140. a. 34.**

NĀNĀ ṢĀSTRĪ ĀPṬE. *See* Euclid. Elements of plane geometry .... translated into Maráthí by Náná Shástrí Ápte. 1867. 8°. **14139. a. 16.**

NAPIER (Francis) *Baron Napier.* Translation into Marathi [with an English preface] by W. H. Havelock ... of a lecture on architecture in India delivered at Madras by His Excellency Lord Napier. **(हिंदुस्थानांतील शिल्पशास्त्र)** [Hindusthānāntīl ṣilpaṣāstra.] pp. vi. 31. *Poona*, 1871. 8°.
14139. a. 23.

NĀRADANĪTI. **नारदनीति प्रारंभः** [Nāradanīti. Advice on ethics and polity given by the sage Nārada to king Yudhishṭhira, on the occasion of his performing the horse-sacrifice.] *See* Mahābhārata.—*Viduranīti.* Vidoorneetee. pp. 113–132. [1858.] 12°.
14137. c. 9.

NARAHARI. **दानव्रत** [Dānavrata. A poem.] *See* Periodical Publications.—*Poona.* **काव्येतिहास-संग्रह** [Kāvyetihāsa saṅgraha.] Vol. VIII. Nos. 4 and 5. [1878, *etc.*] 8°.
14072. d. 37.

NARASIṂHA VINĀYAKA ṢĀSTRĪ OK. *See* Murray (H.) A Maráṭhí version of Murray's History of British India ... Part the first, (Part the second) by Narsingh Vináyak Shástrí Ok. 1859–61. 12°.
14139. e. 8.

NĀRĀYAṆA, *the Poet.* *See* Rāmadāsa Svāmī, *Son of Sūryopanta.*

NĀRĀYAṆA BĀḶAKṚISHṆA GODBOLE and **VISHṆU PĀṆḌURAṄGA ṢAHĀNE.** Chronological Tables, containing corresponding dates of the Christian, Hindu, Mahomedan and Parsi eras, from A.D. 1852 to 1880. pp. 88. *Engl.* and *Mar. Bombay*, 1880. 8°.
14139. a. 34.

NĀRĀYAṆA BĀPUJĪ KĀNIṬKAR. *See* India.—*Legislative Council.* The Code of Civil Procedure . . . with explanatory notes, *etc.* [Compiled with the assistance of N. B. K.] [1877.] 8°.
14137. g. 6.

——— Malharrao Maharaj, ex Gaikwar of Baroda. A historical drama, in seven acts [on the charge made against him of attempting to poison Col. Phayre, the British Resident in 1875.] **(मल्हारराव महाराज नाटक)** pp. iii. 176. *Bombay*, 1875. 12°.
14140. a. 20.

——— **तरुणीशिक्षण नाटिका.** [Taruṇī ṣikshaṇa nāṭikā. A drama in four acts, directed against the modern high class system of female education.] pp. xiv. ii. 110. **पुणें १८८६** [*Poona*, 1886.] 12°.
14140. f. 10.

NĀRĀYAṆA BHĀĪ DĀṆḌEKAR. Váchanmálá. Being a collection of petitions, depositions, reports and other official papers in the Modi or current Maráthí characters, for the use of candidates for Her Majesty's Indian Civil Service. Compiled ... by Ráo Sáheb Náráyan Bhái Dándekar. **(वाचनमाला.)** pp. 152, *lith.* *Poona*, 1867. 4°.
14140. i. 5.

——— Key to Váchanmálá; with an introduction, containing remarks on the current Marathi character and on the forms used in petitions and in official correspondence; drawn up ... by Rao Saheb Náráyan Bhái Dándekar. pp. viii. xiv. 85. *Poona*, 1868. 4°.
14140. i. 6.

NĀRĀYAṆA BHĀSKARA RĀNAḌE and **NĀRĀYAṆA VĀMANA ṬIḶAKA CHIKHALGĀNVKAR.** **हिंदुलोकांच्या लग्नकार्यांत सरकार नको** [Hindu lokāṇchyā lagnakāryāṇt Sarkār nako. A tract on infant-marriages, showing that the evil custom will gradually be abolished, without the intervention of Government legislation.] pp. 12. **१८८६** [*Bombay*, 1886.] 12°.
14139. c. 27.

NĀRĀYAṆA BHAṬṬA called **MṚIGARĀJALAKSHMAṆA.** Venísanhárnátak, a drama in six acts. Translated from Sanscrit into Marathi [prose and verse] by Parashurampunt Godbole. **(वेणीसंहार-नाटक.)** Second edition. pp. iv. 156. *Bombay*, 1861. 8°.
14140. f. 20.

——— Third edition. pp. 166. *Bombay*, 1881. 12°.
14140. f. 15.

NĀRĀYAṆA DĀDOBĀ TARKHAḌKAR. *See* Dādobā Pāṇḍuraṅga Tarkhaḍkar. A Hindu gentleman's reflections respecting the works of Swedenborg ... Translated into Marathi ... by Miss Ahlyábái Tarkhadkar, assisted by her brother N. D. T. [1881.] 12°.
14137. a. 10.

NĀRĀYAṆA DĀJĪ. A treatise on materia medica, and therapeutics; compiled from the English. **(औषधिविद्या)** [Aushadhividyā.] pp. xxiii. ii. 469. *Bombay*, 1865. 8°.
14137. h. 5.

NĀRĀYAṆA HARI. **मोडी बालबोध तिसरे बुकांतील शब्दार्थ** [Moḍī Bālabodha tisre bukāntil ṣabdārtha. A glossary to the "Berar Third Book" of Bāḷakṛishṇa Lakshmaṇa Bāpaṭ.] pp. 39. **मुंबई १८८०** [*Bombay*, 1880.] 12°.
14140. g. 29(3.)

NĀRĀYAṆA KEṢAVA. *See* BAKHTYĀR. बखत्यार-नामा *etc.* [Bakhtyār-nāma. Translated by N. K.] [1855.] 8°. **14139. g. 6(1.)**

NĀRĀYAṆA KEṢAVA VAIDYA. Sangita gata-bhartriká rodan or The lamentations of Hindu widows ... A work in Marathi verse ... and a brief resume of the subjects treated in the first part ... in English, *etc.* (संगीत. गतभर्तृकारोदन आणि तन्निवारणार्थ यथान्याय शास्त्रोक्त साधन.) Second edition. pp. 16; vi. 56. iv. [*Bombay,* 1884.] 12°. **14139. c. 20.**

NĀRĀYAṆA MOREṢVARA KARANDĪKAR. *See* VĀSUDEVA MOREṢVARA POTADĀR and NĀRĀYAṆA MOREṢVARA KARANDĪKAR. हावडकृत इंग्रजी पहिल्या पुस्तकांतील ... शब्दसंग्रह [Ṣabdasaṅgraha.] [1877.] 12°. **14140. g. 29(1.)**

NĀRĀYAṆA RĀMACHANDRA SOHANĪ. उपयुक्तकथासंग्रह [Upayuktakathā saṅgraha. A collection of poems, religious and mythological, being chiefly translations from the Sanskrit; together with hymns in praise of various deities, and a chapter on auguries and interpretation of dreams. Second edition.] pp. 310. मुंबई १८७५ [*Bombay,* 1875.] 8°. **14140. c. 27.**

—— [Third edition.] pp. 304. मुंबई १८७७ [*Bombay,* 1877.] 8°. **14140. c. 24.**

NĀRĀYAṆA RĀVA, *Peshwa.* *See* DĀMODARA VISHṆU SAPRE. नारायणबलि [Nārāyaṇabali. Verses on the assassination of N. R.] [1879.] 8°. **14140. b. 9(3.)**

—— [*Life.*] *See* PĀṆḌURAṄGA. नारायणराव पेशवे यांचे चरित्र [Nārāyaṇa Rāva Peshwe yāṇchen charitra.]

—— नारायणराव यांची बखर [Nārāyaṇa Rāva yāṇchī bakhar. A poem on the life of N. R.] pp. 27. पुणें १८५४ [*Poona,* 1854.] 12°. **14139. d. 8.**

—— श्रीमंत नारायणराव पेशवे यांची बखर [An account of the life of N. R.] *See* PERIODICAL PUBLICATIONS.—*Poona.* काव्येतिहास-संग्रह [Kāvyetihāsa saṅgraha.] Vol. VIII. and IX. [1878, *etc.*] 8°. **14072. d. 37.**

NĀRĀYAṆA RĀVA, *of Satara.* *See* WILSON (J.) *D.D., F.R.S., etc.* दुसरें हिंदूधर्म प्रसिद्धीकरण ... A second exposure of the Hindu religion; in reply to Náráyaṇa Ráo of Satárá. 1835. 8°. **14137. b. 5(12.)**

NĀRĀYAṆARĀVA BHĀGAVATA. मोर एल. एल. बी. प्रहसन. अथवा अप्रबुद्धतरुणक्रिया त्यांचें परिणाम. [Mora L. L. B. A farce condemning the manners and airs of graduates of the Bombay University. Second edition.] pp. 35. मुंबई १८८४ [*Bombay,* 1884.] 8°. **14140. f. 11(3.)**

NĀRĀYAṆA SADĀṢIVA KULAKARṆĪ. *See* DREW (W. H.) A geometrical treatise on conic sections ... being the translation of the treatise of ... W. H. Drew ... by N. S. K. 1879. 8°. **14139. a. 36.**

NĀRĀYAṆA VĀMANA ṬILAKA CHIKHALGĀNVKAR. *See* NĀRĀYAṆA BHĀSKARA RĀNAḌE and NĀRĀYAṆA VĀMANA ṬILAKA CHIKHALGĀNVKAR. हिंदुलोकांच्या लग्नकार्यांत सरकार नको [Hindu lokāṇchyā lagnakāryāṇt Sarkār nako.] [1886.] 12°. **14139. c. 27.**

NĀRĀYAṆA VISHṆU BĀPAṬ. संस्कृतविद्येचें पुनरुज्जीवन [Saṃskrita vidyecheṇ punarujjīvana. A lecture on the revival of Sanskrit literature.] pp. 26. *See* BOMBAY, *City of.—Hindu Union Club.* हेमंत व्याख्यानमाला [Hemanta vyākhyānamālā.] Vol. III. No. 4. [1886, *etc.*] 8°. **14139. c. 26.**

—— उन्नति म्हणजे काय व तिची आवश्यकता [Unnati mhaṇaje kāy. A lecture on the benefits of civilization.] pp. 13. *See* BOMBAY, *City of.—Hindu Union Club.* हेमंत व्याख्यानमाला [Hemanta vyākhyānamālā.] Vol. I. No. 1. [1886, *etc.*] 8°. **14139. c. 26.**

NĀRĀYAṆA VISHṆU JOṢĪ. मुलींचा खेळ [Mulīnchā kheḷ. Games and other amusements for girls. Second edition.] pp. iv. 66. मुंबई १८७७ [*Bombay,* 1877.] 12°. **14140. g. 2(7.)**

NĀRĀYAṆA VIṢVANĀTHA ṢĀSTRĪ. *See* BERQUIN (A.) Bálmitra, Vol. I. .... Reprint of the original work newly revised by Náráyen Vishwanáth Shástrí. 1859. 8°. **14137. b. 7.**

NĀRĀYAṆA VIṬHṬHALA VAIDYA PURANDARE PUNṬĀMBEKAR. उत्तरकोंकणांतील प्राचीन गङ्गातीरस्थ शुक्लयजुर्वेदीय ब्राह्मण, अथवा देशस्थ शुक्लयजुर्वेदीय ब्राह्मण ह्यांची खरी माहिती [Uttara Koṇkaṇāntīl prāchīna Gaṅgātīrastha Ṣukla Yajurvedīya Brāhmaṇa. A work on the Brahmans of the Ṣukla Yajur Veda sect, generally known as Palshes, who came from the banks of the Ganges and have settled in North Konkan, with proofs in support of their claims to be considered as Brahmans.] pp. x. 400. मुंबई १८८४ [*Bombay,* 1884.] 8°. **14139 e 14**

NĀRĀYAṆA YAJÑEṢVARA BHIḌE. लघु पूर्णांक [Laghu pūrṇāṅka. A small treatise on simple arithmetic. Second edition.] pp. 90. रत्नागिरी १८७७ [*Ratnagiri*, 1877.] 12°. **14139. a. 27(2.)**

NÁRÁYEN VISHWANÁTH SHÁSTRÍ. *See* NĀRĀYAṆA VIṢVANĀTHA ṢĀSTRĪ.

NĀRO ĀPĀJĪ GOḌBOLE. *See* 'INĀYAT ALLĀH. बाहारदानीष [Bahār i dānish. Translated by N. Ā. G.] [1865.] 12°. **14139. f. 12(1.)**

—— *See* NAKULA. अथ अश्वपरीक्षा सटीक [Aṣvaparīkshā. With explanatory notes by N. Ā. G.] [1867.] 12°. **14137. ff. 6.**

—— अर्जुनाची बखर [Arjunāchī bakhar. The story of Arjuna.] pp. 29, *lith.* पुणें १८७७ [*Poona*, 1877.] 16°.
In the Modi character. **14139. f. 20(1.)**

—— वालि वानराची बखर [Bāli vānarāchī bakhar. The story of the monkey-king Bāli.] pp. 13, *lith.* पुणें १८७७ [*Poona*, 1877.] 16°.
In the Modi character. **14139. f. 20(2.)**

—— भीमसेनाची बखर [Bhīmasenāchī bakhar. The story of Bhīma.] pp. 21, *lith.* पुणें १८७७ [*Poona*, 1877.] 16°.
In the Modi character. **14139. f. 20(4.)**

—— चमत्कारिक गोष्टी भोज, कालिदास वगैरे याच्या. भाग २ *etc.* [Chamatkārika goshṭī. Tales of king Bhoja, and Kālidāsa, and other anecdotes.] Pt. II. pp. 159. पुणें १८६५ [*Poona*, 1865.] 12°.
Wanting Pt. I. **14139. f. 12(2.)**

—— चंद्रहास राज्याची बखर [Chandrahāsa rājyāchī bakhar. The story of king Chandrahāsa.] pp. 17, *lith.* पुणें १८७७ [*Poona*, 1877.] 16°.
In the Modi character. **14139. f. 20(5.)**

—— च्यवन भार्गवाची बखर [Chyavanabhārgavāchī bakhar. The story of the sage Chyavana, son of Bhṛigu.] pp. 7, *lith.* पुणें १८७७ [*Poona*, 1877.] 16°.
In the Modi character. **14139. f. 20(6.)**

—— लहान मुलांकरितां गमतीचें पहिलें पुस्तक ह्यांत मनोरंजक उखाणे व कोडीं (कूटें) अर्थ सहीत *etc.* [Gamatīcheṉ pahileṉ pustaka. A book of riddles and conundrums for children.] pp. 64. पुणें १८७५ [*Poona*, 1875.] 12°. **14139. a. 22.**

NĀRO ĀPĀJĪ GOḌBOLE. कंस राज्याची बखर [Kaṃsa rājyāchī bakhar. The story of Kaṃsa.] pp. 5, *lith.* पुणें १८७७ [*Poona*, 1877.] 16°.
In the Modi character. **14139. f. 20(7.)**

—— कर्ण राज्याची बखर [Karṇa rājyāchī bakhar. The story of Karṇa.] pp. 32, *lith.* पुणें १८७७ [*Poona*, 1877.] 16°.
In the Modi character. **14139. f. 20(8.)**

—— कीचकाची बखर [Kīchakāchī bakhar. The story of Kīchaka.] pp. 21, *lith.* पुणें १८७७ [*Poona*, 1877.] 16°.
In the Modi character. **14139. f. 20(9.)**

—— कोष्टकें [Koshṭakeṉ. Tables of English and Indian weights and measures. Fourth edition.] pp. 14. पुणें १८७७ [*Poona*, 1877.] 32°. **14140. g. 1(3.)**

—— कृष्णाची बखर [Kṛishṇāchī bakhar. An account of the life of Kṛishṇa]. pp. 47, *lith.* पुणें १८७७ [*Poona*, 1877.] 16°.
In the Modi character. **14139. f. 20(10.)**

—— नकुलाची बखर [Nakulāchī bakhar. The story of the Pāṇḍava prince Nakula.] pp. 5, *lith.* पुणें १८७७ [*Poona*, 1877.] 16°.
In the Modi character. **14139. f. 20(3.)**

—— राम राज्याची बखर [Rāma rājyāchī bakhar. The story of Rāma.] pp. 45, *lith.* पुणें १८७७ [*Poona*, 1877.] 16°.
In the Modi character. **14139. f. 20(11.)**

—— रावण राज्याची बखर [Rāvaṇa rājyāchī bakhar. The story of the demon-king Rāvaṇa.] pp. 47, *lith.* पुणें १८७७ [*Poona*, 1877.] 16°.
In the Modi character. **14139. f. 20(12.)**

—— सहदेवमताचें ज्योतिषरत्न [Sahadevamatācheṉ jyotisharatna. A work on popular astrology. Fourth edition.] pp. iv. 48, *lith.* पुणें १९९९ [*Poona* 1877.] 8°. **14139. b. 13.**

—— सावित्रीची बखर [Sāvitrīchī bakhar. The story of Sāvitrī.] pp. 13, *lith.* पुणें १८७७ [*Poona*, 1877.] 16°.
In the Modi character. **14139. f. 20(13.)**

NĀRO ĀPĀJĪ GODBOLE. त्रीशंकु राज्याची बखर [Triśaṅku rājyāchī bakhar. The story of king Triśaṅku.] pp. 13, *lith.* पुणें १८७७ [*Poona*, 1877.] 16°.
In the Modi character.
14139. f. 20(14.)

—— बृहन्नलाची बखर [Vṛihannalāchī bakhar. The Mahābhārata story of Arjuna at the court of king Virāṭa, under the assumed name of Vṛihannala.] pp. 13, *lith.* पुणें १८७७ [*Poona*, 1877.] 16°.
In the Modi character.
14139. f. 20(15.)

NĀRO BHĀSKARA KHERA. मनोरंजक [Manorañjaka. Verses on asceticism.] pp. 20. पुणें १८७५ [*Poona*, 1875.] 12°. **14140. a. 13(8.)**

—— श्रीहरसिद्धीदेवी [Śriharasiddhīdevī. Verses on asceticism.] pp. 18, *lith.* पुणें [*Poona*, 1875?]. 12°. **14140. a. 13(7.)**

NĀRO RAGHUNĀTHA MOHOḶKAR. हिशेबाचें पहिलें पुस्तक [Hiśebāṅcheṉ pahileṉ pustaka. Elementary arithmetic for schools.] Pt I. pp. iv. 40. पुणें १८७७ [*Poona*, 1877.] 12°. **14140. g. 12(2.)**

—— Hisheba ratnamálá, or Indeterminate equations हिशेब रत्नमाला किंवा कुट्टक गणित. pp. iv. iv. 166. ii. पुणें १८८० [*Poona*, 1880.] 8°. **14139. b. 16.**

—— केरोकृत अंकगणित यांतील प्रश्नसमुदाय ... पृथक्करण [A solution of exercises contained in Kero Lakshmaṇa Chhatre's "Treatise on arithmetic." Fourth edition.] pp. iv. 137, *lith.* पुणें १८७७ [*Poona*, 1877.] 12°. **14139. a. 27(1.)**

—— उपयुक्त अंकलिपी गणिताच्या मूळतत्वा सहीत. अथवा उजळणी [Upayukta aṅkalipī. An elementary arithmetic for schools.] pp. 28, *lith.* पुणें १८७८ [*Poona*, 1878.] 12°. **14139. a. 7(3.)**

—— उपयुक्त अक्षरलिपि आणि अंकलिपि *etc.* [Upayukta aksharalipī aṇi aṅkalipī. Another edition of the preceding, with an additional part containing the alphabet in Devanagari and Modi characters.] 4 pt. pp. ii. 36, *lith.* पुणें १८८० [*Poona*, 1880.] 12°. **14139. a. 27(6.)**

NĀRO SADĀŚIVA RISBUḌ SANGAMNERKAR. Manjughosha. A novel composed in the Marathi language. (मंजुघोषा कल्पित कादंबरी) Third edition. pp. vi. 167. *Poona*, 1875. 12°. **14139. g. 12.**

NARSINGH VINÁYAK SHÁSTRÍ OK. *See* NARASIṂHA VINĀYAKA ŚĀSTRĪ OK.

NESBIT (ROBERT). भगवद्गीतेचें सार [Bhagavadgītecheṉ sāra.] (Analysis of the Bhagawat Gítá.) Second edition. pp. 118. मुंबई १८४० [*Bombay*, 1840.] 8°.
With title-page of the first edition, dated 1832. *No.* 20 *of the Bombay Tract and Book Society's Series.*
14137. b. 5(2.)

NEWTON (HENRY) *Assistant Judge.* *See* BOMBAY, *Presidency of.* — *Court of Ṣadr Dīwānī 'Adālat.* मुंबईंतील सदर दिवाणी अदालतींत मुकदमे फैसल झाले. [Decisions in cases tried by the Bombay Ṣadr Dīwānī 'Adālat. Translated by H. N.] [1852.] 8°. **14137. g. 2.**

NĪLAKAṆṬHA DĪKSHITA. Kalividambana, a description of the Iron Age. The original Sanskrit piece with a Marathi translation ... by Janárdan Hurry Áthalye. (कलिविडंबन) pp. 33. *Ratnagiri*, 1878. 12°. **14076. a. 12(2.)**

NĪLAKAṆṬHA GORE (NEHEMIAH). ख्रिस्तीधर्म ईश्वरदत्त आहे यास कांहीं प्रमाण आहे काय? [Khristīdharma Iśvaradatta āhe, or Is Christianity a Divine revelation? An attack on Hinduism and a defence of Christianity.] pp. xvi. xiv. 148. 23. *Poona*, [1883.] 8°. **14137. b. 11.**

—— प्रार्थनासमाजाचा धर्म स्वबुद्धिकल्पित असल्यानें मनुष्यांच्या उपयोगी पडणार नाहीं [Prārthanā Samājāchā dharma svabuddhikalpita, *etc.* A tract condemning the tenets of the Prārthanā Samāj, and advocating the claims of Christianity.] pp. 11. पुणें [*Poona*, 1884.] 12°. **14137. a. 13.**

NĪLAKAṆṬHA MĪMĀṂSAKABHAṬṬA, *Son of Śaṅkara.* *See* VIJÑĀNEŚVARA. Marathe translation of the ... Wyawahar Mayukh [of N. M.] *etc.* [1884.] 4°. **14137. g. 1.**

—— —— 1862. 8°. **14137. g. 3.**

—— *See* VIŚVANĀTHA NĀRĀYAṆA MAṆḌALIK, *C.S.I.* हिन्दुधर्म शास्त्र [Hindudharma śāstra. Containing a translation of N. M.'s Vyavahāramayūkha.] [1883.] 8°. **14137. g. 11.**

NĪLAKAṆṬHA PURUSHOTTAMA JOŚĪ CHAULKAR. *See* INDIA. — *Legislative Council.* कोड आफ् सीवल प्रोसिजर. [The Code of Civil Procedure. Edited by N. P. J. Ch.] [1877.] 8°. **14137. g. 7.**

NĪLAKANṬHA PURUSHOTTAMA JOSĪ CHAULKAR. *See* INDIA.—*Legislative Council.* हिंदुस्थानचा मुदती विषयीं आक्ट. [The Indian Limitation Act. Edited by N. P. J. Ch.] [1877.] 8°. **14137. g. 5(2).**

NILOBĀ RĀYA. श्रीनिळोबारायकृत अभंगांचा गाथा [Abhangāchā gāthā. A collection of philosophical poems by N. R. a disciple of Tukārāma, preceded by a poem in praise of Tukārāma, and followed by another poem, entitled Chāngadeva charitra, also by N. R. Edited by Vināyaka Viṭhṭhala Rānaḍe.] pp. xxx. 24, 294, 30, *lith.* पुणें १८०५ [*Poona*, 1883.] 8°. **14140. c. 38.**

NIRAÑJANA RAGHUNĀTHA. *See* JÑĀNADEVA. अनुभवामृत पदबोधिनी [Anubhavāmṛita padabodhinī. The Anubhavāmṛita, with a running commentary by N. R.] [1882.] 8°. **14140. c. 30.**

NĪTIKATHĀ. नीतिकथा [Nītikathā. A reading book for children. Third edition.] pp. 67. मुंबई १८३८ [*Bombay*, 1838.] 12°. **14139. f. 1.**

NĪTIPAR KAVITĀ. नीतिपर कविता [Nītipar kavitā. Moral poems. Second edition.] pp. 28. मुंबई १९८२ [*Bombay*, 1860.] 12°. **14140. a. 4(5.)**

NIVṚITTINĀTHA. अथ निवृत्तिनाथाचे अभंग प्रारंभ [Abhangas.] *See* JÑĀNADEVA. श्री ज्ञानदेवाचा गाथा [Jñānadevāchā gāthā.] [1877.] 8°. **14140. c. 23.**

OUSELEY (*Sir* WILLIAM). *See* BAKHTYĀR. बखत्यारनामा *etc.* [Bakhtyār-nāmah. Translated from the English of Sir W. O.] [1855.] 8°. **14139. g. 6(1.)**

PĀḌAVAHĪ. पाडवही [Pāḍavahī. Tables of wages, in a month of 30 days, from 4 annas to 2000 rupees *per mensem.*] pp. 31. मुंबई १७७९ [*Bombay*, 1857.] 12°. **14139. a. 7(1.)**

PADEṆ. पदें भाग १ (भाग २) [Padeṇ. A collection of hymns in the pada metre.] 2 pt. *lith.* मुंबई १७८४-८५ [*Bombay*, 1862-63.] 12°. **14140. a. 4(10.)**

PĀL. श्री पालीची कारिका प्रारंभः [Pālīchī kārikā. Superstitions connected with the falling of a lizard on various parts of the body.] *Sansk.* and *Mar.* pp. 31, *lith.* मुंबई १७८७ [*Bombay*, 1865.] 8°. **14053. b. 6.**

PĀḶṆE. पाळणे ॥ [Pāḷṇe. Cradle songs addressed to various gods. Fourth edition.] pp. 30, *lith.* मुंबई १७७७ [*Bombay*, 1855.] 16°. **14140. a. 3(3.)**

PĀḶṆE. [Another edition, with additional songs.] pp. 23, *lith.* मुंबई १७८५ [*Bombay*, 1863.] 12°. **14140. a. 4(11.)**

—— [Another edition of the preceding.] pp. 21, *lith.* पुणें १७९९ [*Poona*, 1877.] 12°. **14140. a. 10(17.)**

PAÑCHATANTRA. *See* GOVINDAŚAṄKARA ŚĀSTRĪ BĀPAṬ. Panchatantrasára, or Fables of Vishnusharmá. Adapted from Panchatantra ... and moralized. 1881. 12°. **14139. f. 30.**

—— पंचोपाख्यान [Pañchopākhyāna, or Pañchatantra. Moral tales and fables, translated from the Sanskrit.] pp. 138. [*Bombay?*, 1848?] 8°.
Wanting title-page. **14139. g. 8.**

—— पंचतंत्रप्रभृतिनीतिशास्त्रोद्धृत नित्रलाभाद्यवयवेनान्वित पंचोपाख्यान. [Third edition.] मुंबई १७८० [*Bombay*, 1858.] 12°.
Each of the five books has a separate pagination. **14139. f. 3.**

PĀṆḌURAṄGA. पांडुरंगकृत नारायणराव पेशवे यांचें चरित्र [Nārāyaṇa Rāva Peshwe yāncheṇ charitra, or The life of the Peshwa Nārāyaṇa Rāva in verse.] *See* PERIODICAL PUBLICATIONS.—*Poona.* काव्येतिहाससंग्रह [Kāvyetihāsa sangraha.] Vol. VI. [1878, *etc.*] 8°. **14072. d. 37.**

PĀṆḌURAṄGA ĀBĀJĪ MOYE. *See* RĀVAJĪ ŚRĪDHARA GONDHALEKAR. कीर्तनतरंगिणी [Kīrtana-taranginī. Pt. II. on the birth and life of Krishṇa, by P. Ā. M.] [1885, *etc.*] 8°. **14140. c. 37.**

PĀṆḌURAṄGA GOPĀLA MANTRĪ. भारतवर्षीय वनौषधिसंग्रह व त्यांचें गुणानुदर्शन [Bhāratavarshīya vanaushadhisangraha. A work on the medicinal properties of Indian plants, showing their uses according to the present system of medical science, and also according to the Sanskrit works of Suśruta and Charaka.] मुंबई १८८६ [*Bombay*, 1886.] 8°.
Each portion of the work has a separate pagination. **14137. h. 14.**

PĀṆḌURAṄGA GOVINDA ŚĀSTRĪ PARAKHĪ. मित्रचंद्र [Mitrachandra. A tale.] pp. iv. iii. 254. पुणें १८८० [*Poona*, 1880.] 8°. **15139. g. 16.**

PĀṆḌURAṄGA MOREŚVARA POTADĀR. हिंदुस्थानच्या इतिहासांतील ... संक्षिप्त माहिती. [Hindusthānāchyā itihāsāntīl ... saṃkshipta māhitī. A manual of Indian history for the use of schools.] pp. 48. मुंबई १८८१ [*Bombay*, 1881.] 16°. **14140. g. 8(4.)**

PĀṆḌURAṄGA VEṄKAṬEŚA CHINTĀMAṆIPEṬKAR. Gangavarnana. An original Marathi poem [on the Ganges, and places of interest along its course]. (गंगावर्णना) pp. vi. 79. *Belgaum*, 1874. 12°. **14140. a. 12(6.)**

PANIPAT. पानपतची लढाई [Pānapatchī laḍhāī. An account of the battle of Panipat, with a brief sketch of the events in Indian history anterior to it, with reference to the downfall of the Mahratta power.] pp. vii. 33, 77, xxiv. १९९९ [*Bombay?*, 1877.] 12°. **14139. d. 19.**

PĀRADHĪ. पारधी आख्यान [Pāradhī ākhyāna. The huntsman and the devotee. With other short poems.] pp. 16, *lith.* [*Bombay?*, 1860 ?] 12°. **14140. a. 10(2.)**

PARAŚURĀMA, *Kavi.* परशरामकृत लावण्या [Lāvaṇī songs.] *See* Rāvajī Śrīdhara Gondhaḷekar. रामजोशि ... सुरस लावण्या [Surasa lāvaṇyā.] pp. 60–93. [1878.] 8°. **14140. c. 25.**

PARAŚURĀMA BALLĀLA GODBOLE. *See* Paraśurāma Panta Godbole.

PARAŚURĀMA GHANAŚYĀMA REGE. बेलिफस् गायड् अथवा बजावणीच्या उपयोगाचे पुस्तक. [The Bailiff's guide for the use of persons executing processes of the Civil Courts.] pp. iii. iv. 51. मुंबई १८७७ [*Bombay*, 1877.] 12°. **14137. f. 2.**

—— The Bailiff's Guide, *etc.* [Second edition.] pp. iv. vii. 82, 20, xii. मुंबई १८८१ [*Bombay*, 1881.] 12°. **14137. f. 3.**

PARAŚURĀMA PANTA GODBOLE. *See* Bāla Śāstrī Ghagve. A dictionary of the Maratha language, compiled by Bal Shastree Ghugwe ... and Pursheo Ram Punt Gorbole. 1829. 4°. **14140. i. 1.**

—— *See* Bāṇa. Párvatípariṇaya náṭaka. Translated [with the text] from Sanskrit into Maráṭhí by Parashwrám Bullál Godbole, *etc.* 1872. 12°. **14079. a. 7.**

—— *See* Bhavabhūti. Utarrámcharitra .... Translated from Sanscrit into Maráthí by Parshurámpant Godbole. 1859. 8°. **14140. f. 21.**

—— —— 1881. 12°. **14140. f. 13.**

—— *See* Kālidāsa. शाकुंतलनाटक [Śakuntalā nāṭaka. Translated by P. P. G.] [1861.] 8°. **14140. f. 3.**

PARAŚURĀMA PANTA GODBOLE. *See* Moropanta. मोरोपंतकृत सभापर्व (वनपर्व *etc.*) आर्या [Mahābhārata, paraphrased in āryā verse. Edited by Mādhava Chandrobā with the assistance of P. P. G.] [1860–64.] 8°. **14140. c. 10.**

—— *See* Mukteśvara. सर्वसंग्रह ... सभापर्व *etc.* [Sabhāparva. Revised by P. P. G.] [1863.] 8°. **14140. c. 7.**

—— *See* Nārāyaṇa Bhaṭṭa called Mṛigarājalakshmaṇa. Venísanhárnátak, a drama ... translated from Sanscrit into Marathi [prose and verse] by Parashurampunt Godbole. 1861. 8°. **14140. f. 20.**

—— —— 1881. 8°. **14140. f. 15.**

—— *See* Rāmadāsa Svāmī, *Son of Sūryopanta.* रामदासकृत अभंग [Rāmadāsakṛita abhaṅga. Revised by P. P. G.] [1861.] 8°. **14140. c. 31.**

—— *See* Śūdraka. Mrichchhakatika ..... Translated from Sanskrit into Maráṭhi by Parashurám Pant Gódbóle. 1881. 8°. **14140. f. 14.**

—— *See* Vāmana Paṇḍita. वामन पंडितकृत श्लोक [Vāmana Paṇḍitakṛita śloka. Edited with the assistance of P. P. G.] [1860.] 8°. **14140. c. 15.**

—— पाठावलिः संस्कृत भाषेचें प्रथम पुस्तक [Pāṭhāvali. An elementary Sanskrit grammar in Marathi.] pp. 62. पुणें १७८५ [*Poona*, 1863.] 8°. **14140. h. 14.**

—— Plane Trigonometry with tables of logarithms &c. ... by Purashoo Ram Punt Godbolay. (सरळरेघ त्रिकोणमिति.) [Saraḷaregha trikoṇamiti.] pp. 59. *Poonah*, 1845. 8°.

The tables of logarithms have no pagination. **14139. a. 2.**

—— संक्षिप्त भूगोल वर्णन [Saṃkshipta bhūgolavarṇana. An abridged version of T. Candy's "Manual of Geography." Second edition.] pp. iv. 100. मुंबई १८६६ [*Bombay*, 1866.] 8°. **14139. a. 17.**

—— Selections from the Maráthí poets by Parashurám Pant Godboley. (नवनीत) [Navanīta.] Third edition. pp. v. 355. xxxiii. *Bombay*, 1859. 8°. **14140. b. 1.**

PARAṢURĀMA PANTA GOḌBOLE. Selections from the Maráthí poets by Parashurám Pant Godboley... to which are added a paper on Marathi versification, and biographical and critical notices of the principal Marathi poets, by Rao Sáheb Bháskar Dámodar. Third edition. pp. v. lxxii. 355. xxxiii. *Bombay*, 1860. 8°. **14140. b. 2.**

—— Selections from the Maráṭhí poets by ... Parshurám Pant Godbole. New edition, revised and annotated by Shríkrishna Shástrí Talekar and Ráwjí Shástrí Godbole. pp. ii. vi. 373. xlii. *Bombay*, 1878. 8°. **14140. b. 12.**

—— **नवनीत भाग २ कवितासार संग्रह** [Selections from the Navanīta of P. P. G.] pp. ii. 126. **पुणें १८६३** [*Poona*, 1863.] 8°. **14140. b. 3.**

—— **वृत्तदर्पण** [Vṛittadarpaṇa. A short treatise on prosody. Third edition.] pp. 44. **मुंबई १८६७** [*Bombay*, 1867.] 8°. **14139. a. 10.**

—— Maraṭhi vṛittadarpaṇa, or Mirror of Prosody by Parashurám Ballál Godbole. Seventh edition. pp. 48. *Bombay*, 1877. 8°. **14140. h. 17.**

PARIMĀṆAMĀLĀ. **परिमाणमाला** [Parimāṇamālā. Tables of English and Indian weights and measures.] pp. 40. **मुंबई १८७४** [*Bombay*, 1874.] 12°. **14139. a. 7(2.)**

PARSHURÁMPANT GODBOLE. *See* PARAṢURĀMA PANTA GOḌBOLE.

PASLEY (*Sir* CHARLES WILLIAM). Marat,ha version of a course of practical geometry, compiled by Lieutenant Colonel Pasley ... Translated by Captain George Jervis ... [with the aid of Jagannātha Ṣāstrī Kramavanta.] (**भूमिति**) [Bhūmiti.] pp. x. 173. *Bombay*, 1826. 4°. **14139. b. 1.**

PATHARE REFORM ASSOCIATION. *See* BOMBAY, *City of.—Pathare Reform Association.*

PATTEṈ. **पत्रें यादी वगैरे** [Patteṉ yādī waghairah. A collection of hitherto unpublished letters, biographical notes and the like.] *See* PERIODICAL PUBLICATIONS.—*Poona.* **काव्येतिहास-संग्रह** [Kāvyetihāsa saṅgraha.] Vol. I.–IX. [1878, *etc.*] 8°. *In progress.* **14072. d. 37.**

PEET (JOHN). *See* SAKHĀRĀMA ARJUNA. The principles and practice of medicine ... [founded chiefly on J. P.'s "Practice of medicine."] 1869. 8°. **14137. h. 7.**

PEILE (*Sir* JAMES BRAITHWAITE). Catalogue of native publications in the Bombay Presidency from 1st January 1865 to 30th June 1867, and of some works omitted in the previous catalogue [by Sir A. Grant]. Prepared under orders of Government by J. B. P. [assisted by Kṛishṇa Ṣāstrī Chipḷūṇkar]. pp. 120. *Bombay*, 1869. 8°.

Continued in the form of quarterly lists prepared under the provisions of Act XXV. of 1867. **752. e. 15.**

PERIODICAL PUBLICATIONS.

AHMADNAGAR.

—— **ज्ञानोदय** ... The Dnyanodaya. [A Christian magazine, partly in English and partly in Marathi.] Vols. I.–IIII. and XI.–XIII. *Ahmednuggur, Bombay*, 1842–54. 8°.

Vols. I.–III. were published in monthly parts at Ahmadnagar; Vol. XI.–XIII. in bi-monthly parts at Bombay. Wanting Nos. 21, 23 *and* 24 *of Vol. XII. and No.* 20 *of Vol. XIII.* **14137. b. 1.**

ALIBAGH.

—— **अबलामित्र.** Abalamitra. [A monthly magazine for women, conducted with the view to the advancement of female education.] Vol. I. Nos. 6–12; Vol. II. No. 1; Vol. III. Nos. 6–8. **अलीबाग १८७७** [*Alibagh*, 1877–79.] 8°. **14139. c. 19.**

—— **सद्धर्मदीप** [Saddharmadīpa. A monthly Hindu literary journal.] Vol. IV. Nos. 1–5. **अलीबाग १८०३** [*Alibagh*, 1882.] 8°. **14139. c. 25.**

BOMBAY.

—— **दंभहारक** [Dambhahāraka] or Exposer of hypocrisy. [An anti-Christian literary and critical magazine.] Vol. IX. Nos. 9–12. **मुंबई १८७७** [*Bombay*, 1877.] 8°. **14137. b. 10.**

—— **ज्ञानोदय** ... The Dnyanodaya. [A bimonthly Christian magazine in English and Marathi.] *See* above: AHMADNAGAR. **14137. b. 1.**

—— **ज्ञानादर्श** [Jñānādarṣa. A monthly literary magazine.] Vol. I. Nos. 1–5. **मुंबई १८८६** [*Bombay*, 1886.] 8°. **14142. a. 5.**

—— Ṣaddarshana-Chintanikâ, or Studies in Indian Philosophy. *See* below: POONA. **14048. d.**

PERIODICAL PUBLICATIONS [Bombay, *continued*].

—— **विविधज्ञान विस्तार.** Vividhajñanavistâra. A monthly magazine of Marathi literature, *etc.* Vol. IX. Nos. 5–10, 12; Vol. X. No. I; Vol. XIII. No. 1. मुंबई १८७७ [*Bombay*, 1877–81.] 8°. **14142. a. 2.**

Dharwar.

—— **काव्यनाटकादर्श.** [Kāvyanāṭakādarṣa. A serial for the publication of Sanskrit works, chiefly poetical, with commentaries in Sanskrit and Marathi. धारवाड १८८२ [*Dharwar*, 1882, *etc.*] 8°.
In progress. **14076. d. 35.**

Poona.

—— **आर्यमित्र. मासिकपुस्तक.** [Āryamitra. A monthly literary periodical.] Vols. I. and II. पुणें १८८४ [*Poona*, 1884–85.] 8°. **14142. a. 1.**

—— **वऱ्हाड शालापत्रक.** Berar School-paper. [Barhāḍ ṣālāpatraka. A monthly educational publication for schools.] Vol. I. Nos. 2–10. पुणे १८७७ [*Poona*, 1877.] 12°. **14140. h. 21.**

—— **इंजीनियरिंग विषयावर (शिल्पविद्येवर)** *etc.* [Engineering. A monthly magazine.] Vol. II. Nos. 1–5. पुणें १८७७ [*Poona*, 1877.] 8°. **14139. b. 10.**

—— **काव्येतिहास-संग्रह** [Kāvyetihāsa saṅgraha. A monthly serial for the publication of old Marathi chronicles, and of Marathi and Sanskrit poetry. Edited with copious notes, critical and explanatory, by Janārdana Bāḷājī Moḍak and Kāṣīnātha Nārāyaṇa Sāne.] Vol. I, *etc.* पुणें १८७८ [*Poona*, 1878, *etc.*] 8°.
In progress. **14072. d. 37.**

—— **निबंधमाला** [Nibandhamālā. A monthly review of current literature.] Nos. 40, 41, 42, 44, 46. पुणें १८७७ [*Poona*, 1877.] 8°. **14140. h. 20.**

—— The Saddarshana-Chintanikâ, or Studies in Indian Philosophy. A monthly publication stating and explaining the aphorisms of the six schools of Indian Philosophy, with their translation into Marathi and English. (**षड्दर्शनचिंतनिका**) [Compiled and edited by Mādhavarāva Moreṣvara Kunte.] Vol. I–III.; Vol. IV. Nos. 1–4; Vol. V. No. 8–Vol. VI. No. 2. *Poona, Bombay*, 1877–82. 8°.
Vols. 1 and 2 published at Poona. Vol. 3, etc. at Bombay.
14048. d.

PERIODICAL PUBLICATIONS [Poona, *continued*].

—— **संगीतमीमांसक** (The Sangît mîmânsak, a monthly magazine of music comprising Sanskrit works on music, songs, musical traditions, plans and descriptions [in Marathi] of the several ... instruments [with correspondence in Marathi.]) Vol. I, *etc.* पुणें १८८६ [*Poona*, 1886, *etc.*] 8°.
In progress. **14053. cc. 45.**

—— **सर्वसंग्रह मासिक पुस्तक** [Sarvasaṅgraha. A monthly literary magazine, containing for the most part selections from the works of celebrated Marathi poets. Edited, with commentaries and notes, by Rāvajī Ṣrīdhara Gondhaḷekar.] *Lith.* पुणें १८७७ [*Poona*, 1877.] 8°.
Imperfect; containing portions only of Vols. I.–III.
14142. a. 3.

PERSIAN TALES. The Thousand and one days [being selections from the well known Persian Tales], translated by Bhaskar Sakharam, ...; corrected and revised by Krishna Shastri Chiplonker. (**आरबी गोष्टी.**) [Ārabī goshṭī.] pp. viii. 346. *Bombay*, 1863. 8°. **14139. g. 5.**

PESHWAS. श्रीमंत पंत प्रधान यांची शकावली [Srīmanta Pantapradhāna yānchī ṣakāvalī. Historical events in the lives of the Peshwas, chronologically arranged.] *See* Periodical Publications.—*Poona.* **काव्येतिहास-संग्रह** [Kāvyetihāsa saṅgraha.] Vol. VI. Nos. 1–7. [1878, *etc.*] 8°.
14072. d. 37.

PETHAHIAH ben JACOB, *of Ratisbon.* Travells [*sic*] of Rabbi Petachia. **रिब्बी पेथाह्या याचे प्रवास.** [Ribbī Pethāhyā yāche pravāsa. Translated by S. Daniells, and R. Samuel, from the English version by A. Benisch.] pp. 32. ठाणें १८७७ [*Thana*, 1877.] 12°. **14137. a. 8(1.)**

PHELPS (A.) *Capt. See* Vishṇu Bhikājī Gokhale, called Brahmachārī. An essay in Marathi on beneficent government ... Translated [into English] ... by A. P. 1869. 12°. **14137. f. 1.**

PITMAN (Isaac). *See* Gajānabhāū Vaijya. A complete system of shorthand for Marathi [based on Pitman's system] 1881. 12°. **14139. a. 42.**

POLANO (H.) *See* Talmud.—*Appendix.* **तलमुद** [Selections from the Talmud, translated from the English of H. P.] [1886.] 8°. **14137. b. 13.**

POONA. Discussions in Poonah [on the Christian religion.] संभाषणें [Sambhāshaṇeṉ.] Third edition. pp. 42. मुंबई १८३८ [*Bombay,* 1838.] 8°.
No. 9 of the Bombay Tract and Book Society's Series.
14137. b. 5(3.)

POPE (ALEXANDER) *the Poet. See* HOMER. श्री सांबसदाशिव. [Sāmbasadāṣiva. Homer's Iliad, Bk. I., translated into āryā verse, from the English of A. P.] [1870?] 12. **14140. a. 12(5.)**

PORTUGAL.—*Colonies.—East Indies.* Condiçoes da renda dos dizimos. [An order of the Government of Goa, dated the 10th September 1870, regarding the collection of duties on certain excisable articles of commerce.] pp. 34. *Port.* and *Mar.* [*Goa,* 1870?] 8°. **14137. g. 5(1.)**

PRAHASANASAṄGRAHA. प्रहसनसंग्रह. डाक्तर व वैद्य प्रहसन. [Prahasanasaṅgraha. A collection of farces. No. 1. Ḍāktar va vaidya, or The doctor and his patient; a brochure on the conduct of graduates of the Grant Medical College.] pp. 24. [*Bombay,* 1880.] 8°. **14140. f. 2(2.)**

PRAṢNABHAIRAVA. प्रश्नभैरव भाग १ ला [Praṣnabhairava. Elementary astrological rules in Sanskrit verse, with a commentary in Marathi.] pp. vii. 47, *lith.* पुणें १८७५ [*Poona,* 1875.] 8°. **14053. cc. 5(1.)**

PRAṢNOTTARARATNAMĀLIKĀ अथ प्रश्नोत्तररत्नमालिका प्रारंभः ॥ [Praṣnottararatnamālikā. A philosophical catechism on the duties of life, Sanskrit text with a paraphrase in Marathi.] ff. 11, *lith.* मुंबई १७८२ [*Bombay,* 1860.] *obl.* 8°. **14076. a. 4.**

PRATĀPĀDITYA, *Raja.* [*Life.*] *See* VAIJANĀTHA ṢARMĀ. राजाप्रतापादित्यचें चरीत्र. [Rājā Pratāpādityacheṉ charitra.]

PRATĀPA SIṂHA, *Raja of Jaipur.* श्री अमृतसागर वैद्यक ग्रंथ [Amṛitasāgara. A work on medicine, originally compiled by P. S. from various native sources, in the Marwari dialect, and now translated into Marathi.] Third edition. pp. 579. मुंबई १७८६ [*Bombay,* 1864.] 8°. **14137. h. 2.**

PRATĀPA SIṂHA SĀTĀRKAR, *Mahārājā.* *See* SHĀHŪ III. *Raja of Satara.*

PUBLIC HEALTH. Public health. The worth of fresh air. आरोग्यरक्षण. स्वच्छ हवेची योग्यता. [Ārogyarakshaṇa.] pp. ii. 44. मुंबई १८७५ [*Bombay,* 1875.] 12°. **14137. ff. 2(1.)**

PURĀṆAS.

PURĀṆAS. अथ एकादशीमाहात्म्य प्रारंभ ॥ [Ekādaṣīmāhātmya. A translation by Vishṇudāsa of selections from various Purāṇas on the celebration of the eleventh day of each half moon.] ff. 12. मुंबई १७८३ [*Bombay,* 1861.] *obl.* 8°. **14137. d. 10(1.)**

—— [Another edition.] ff. 10, *lith.* मुंबई १७८६ [*Bombay,* 1864.] *obl.* 8°. **14137. d. 9(2.)**

—— [Another edition.] ff. 14, *lith.* पुणें १८७७ [*Poona,* 1877.] *obl.* 12°. **14140. a. 9(11.)**

—— काशीप्रताप. [Kāṣīpratāpa. Extracts from various Purāṇas, compiled and explained by a Marathi paraphrase by Govindarāva Bhikājī Paṭavardhana.] रत्नगिरि १८८० [*Ratnagiri,* 1880.] 4°. **14028. c. 34(3.)**

—— समूल पुराणार्थप्रकाश [Samūla-purāṇārtha-prakāṣa. A serial for the publication of the text of Puranic and Epic works, with a Marathi translation.] मुंबई १८०६ [*Bombay,* 1884, *etc.*] 8°. **14016. d. 42.**

BHĀGAVATAPURĀṆA.

—— *See* EKANĀTHA. अथ श्री एकनाथी भागवत प्रारंभः [Ekanāthī Bhāgavata. A commentary on the eleventh book of the Bhāgavatapurāṇa.] [1881.] *obl.* 4°. **14140. d. 19.**

—— —— अथ श्री रुक्मिणीस्वयंवर प्रारंभ ॥ [Rukmiṇī-svayaṃvara. A poem, founded on the tenth chapter of the Bhāgavatapurāṇa.] [1860.] *obl.* 8°. **14140. f. 6.**

—— अथ श्रीभगवत एकनाथकृत प्रारंभ्यते [The eleventh book of the Bhāgavatapurāṇa in Sanskrit, with a commentary in Marathi verse by Ekanātha.] *Lith.* पुणें १८८१ [*Poona,* 1881.] *obl.* 4°. **14018. d. 16.**

—— *See* MOROPANTA. अथ दशमस्कंधाच्या आर्या प्रारंभ ॥ [Daṣamaskandhāchyā āryā. A poem, founded on the tenth chapter of the Bhāgavatapurāṇa.] 1848. 8°. **14140. c. 1.**

—— *See* ṢRĪDHARA. अथ श्रीहरिविजयग्रंथ प्रारंभः [Harivijaya. A poem, founded on the Bhāgavatapurāṇa.] [1880.] *obl.* 4°. **14140. d. 17.**

—— *Brahmastuti.* वामनकृत ब्रह्मस्तुतिची टीका ॥ [Brahmastuti. Sanskrit text, with a commentary in Marathi by Vāmana Paṇḍita.] 3 pt. मुंबई १७६४ [*Bombay,* 1842.] *obl.* 8°. **14016. c. 4.**

PURĀṆAS. BHĀGAVATAPURĀṆA (*continued*).

—— *Gopīgītā.* गापीगीता [Gopīgītā. The thirty-first canto of the tenth book of the Bhāgavatapurāṇa; Sanskrit text, with a Marathi commentary.] pp. 16. मुंबई १७७६ [*Bombay*, 1854.] 8°. **14016. a. 2.**

BHAVISHYOTTARAPURĀṆA.

—— *Somavatīpūjā.* अथ श्रीसोमवतीपूजाप्रा॰ [Somavatīpūjā. A ritual for the observance of Monday, when it falls on the day of the full moon. Sanskrit text, with a Marathi version.] ff. 18, *lith.* पुणें १८८० [*Poona*, 1880.] *obl.* 8°. **14016. d.**

BRAHMĀṆḌAPURĀṆA.

—— *Mallārimāhātmya.* See BALAVANTA KHANDERĀVA PESHVE. मल्हारी चरित्र अथवा जेजुरी इतिहास. [Malhārī charitra. Founded chiefly on the Mallārimāhātmya, a portion of the Adhyātmarāmāyaṇa, a section of the Brahmāṇḍapurāṇa.] [1877.] 12°. **14139. f. 11(3.)**

—— श्री मल्लारिमहात्म्य प्रारंभः [Mallārimāhātmya. A poem in praise of the god Mallāri, or Khaṇḍerāva of Jejuri, translated from the Sanskrit.] ff. 118, *lith.* १७८१ [*Bombay?* 1859.] *obl.* 12°. **14140. a. 9(2.)**

—— *Vyaṅkaṭagirimāhātmya.* अथ मारुतीजन्म प्रारंभः [Mārutījanma, also called Hanumantajanma. Verses on the birth of Hanumān; translated from the Vyaṅkaṭagiri māhātmya, a section of the Brahmāṇḍapurāṇa.] ff. 14. मुंबई १७८३ [*Bombay*, 1861.] *obl.* 32°. **14137. c. 2(3.)**

DEVĪBHĀGAVATAPURĀṆA.

—— See ANANTADĪKSHITA JOṢĪ CHIPLŪṆKAR. Sudarshana Charitra. A drama based on the Dewi Bhagawata, *etc.* 1881. 12°. **14139. a. 40.**

GAṆEṢAPURĀṆA.

—— See GAṆAPATARĀVA HARIHARA PAṬAVARDHANA. गणेशपुराण आर्या [Gaṇeṣapurāṇa āryā. A poem, containing the substance of the Gaṇeṣapurāṇa.] [1877.] 8°. **14137. e. 10.**

—— अथ गणेशप्रताप प्रारंभः [Gaṇeṣapratāpa. A poem in praise of Gaṇeṣa, purporting to be a translation of the Gaṇeṣapurāṇa, in two parts, viz. Upāsanakhaṇḍa, and Krīḍākhaṇḍa, containing 22 and 34 chapters respectively.] *Lith.* मुंबई १७७९ [*Bombay*, 1857.] *obl.* 4°. **14137. e. 1.**

PURĀṆAS (*continued*).

MĀRKAṆḌEYAPURĀṆA.

—— साथे मार्कंडेयपुरा॰ [Mārkaṇḍeyapurāṇa. Sanskrit text, with a Marathi prose translation.] पुणें [*Poona*, 1876, *etc.*] *obl.* 4°.

In progress. Wanting Pt. 1–8 of Vol. I.

14018. c. 25.

—— *Devīmāhātmya.* अथ सप्तशती प्रारंभः ॥ [Saptaṣatī, or Devīmāhātmya. A section of the Mārkaṇḍeyapurāṇa, translated into verse.] ff. 125, *lith.* १७६९ [*Bombay?* 1847.] *obl.* 12°. **14137. c. 1.**

—— सप्तशति आर्या [Saptaṣati āryā. The Devīmāhātmya, translated into āryā verse by Amṛitarāva Ābājī Karṇīk.] pp. ii. 62. viii. मुंबई १८०२ [*Bombay*, 1880.] 8°. **14137. a. 13.**

—— *Hariṣchandropākhyāna.* See MOROPANTA. हरिश्चंद्रोपाख्यान. [Hariṣchandropākhyāna. An episode from the Mārkaṇḍeyapurāṇa.] [1859.] 8°. **14137. d. 1(2.)**

MATSYAPURĀṆA.

—— मत्स्यपुराण आणि इब्री शास्त्र ... [Matsyapurāṇa āṇi Ibrī Ṣāstra *etc.*] A compari son of the accounts of some ancient events as found in the Mutsya Pooran and the Hebrew Scriptures ... Reprinted from the Dnyanodaya. pp. 43. *Bombay*, 1845. 24°. **14137. a. 1(5.)**

—— *Prayāgamāhātmya.* अथ प्रयाग माहात्म्य प्रारंभः ॥ [Prayāgamāhātmya. A poem in ten chapters, in praise of the holy city of Allahabad, being a translation of a section of the Matsyapurāṇa.] कराची १७८९ [*Karachi*, 1867.] *obl.* 8°. **14137. e. 7(1.)**

PADMAPURĀṆA.

—— *Kapilagītā.* अथ कपिलगीता प्रारंभः [Kapilagītā. A Sanskrit poem in five chapters, professing to have been delivered by the sage Kapila, and to form part of the Padmapurāṇa, accompanied by a Marathi commentary, by Ṭikārāma, called Paramānandalaharī.] *Lith.* धुळ १८०२ [*Dhulia*, 1880.] *obl.* 8°. **14016. d. 33(2.)**

—— *Pāṇḍuraṅgamāhātmya.* See ṢRĪDHARA. श्रीपंढरीमाहात्म्य प्रारंभ. [Paṇḍharīmāhātmya. A poem founded on the Pāṇḍuraṅgamāhātmya.] [1889.] *obl.* 12°. **14137. c. 16(2.)**

PURĀṆAS. Padmapurāṇa (*continued*).

—— *Rāmāśvamedha.* अथ श्रीरामाश्वमेध प्रारंभः ॥ [Rāmāṣvamedha. The Aṣvamedha, or horse sacrifice of Rāma, a poem in seventy chapters, translated from the Pātālakhaṇḍa, or fourth book of the Padmapurāṇa.] *Lith.* मुंबई १९९९ [*Bombay*, 1877.] *obl.* 4°. **14140. d. 15.**

—— *Śivagītā.* अथ सटीक श्रीशिवगीता प्रारंभः ॥ [Ṣivagītā, supposed to be a portion of the Padmapurāṇa, Sanskrit text, with a Marathi commentary.] ff. 80, *lith.* मुंबई १९१८ [*Bombay*, 1856.] 4°. **14016. d. 5.**

Ṣivapurāṇa.

—— अथ मूळस्तंभ प्रारंभः [Mūḷastambha. A compendium of the Ṣivapurāṇa, in Marathi verse of the Ovī metre, in nineteen chapters.] *Lith.* मुंबई १९९६ [*Bombay*, 1874.] *obl.* 8°. **14137. e. 7(2.)**

—— शिवतत्त्वप्रकाश [Ṣivatattvaprakāṣa. A free translation of the Ṣivapurāṇa, by Ananta Rāmakrishṇa Kaṣaḷīkar.] Pt. I. pp. ii. ii. 60. *Sansk.* and *Mar.* मुंबई १८०२ [*Bombay*, 1880.] 8°.

Apparently no more published.

14016. d. 39.

Skandapurāṇa.

—— *Gokarṇamāhātmya.* श्री गोकर्णमाहात्म्य प्रारंभः ॥ [Gokarṇamāhātmya. A poem in 64 chapters in praise of Gokarṇa, a sacred place of pilgrimage. Translated by Viṭhṭhala Kṛishṇājī Kāyakiṇikar from the Gokarṇakhaṇḍa, a section of the Skandapurāṇa.] मुंबई १९९७ [*Bombay*, 1875.] *obl.* 8°. **14137. e. 9.**

—— *Kāṣīkhaṇḍa.* अथ काशीखंड प्रारंभः [Kāṣīkhaṇḍa. A section of the Skandapurāṇa, in 80 chapters, translated from the Sanskrit.] *Lith.* मुंबई १८५६ [*Bombay*, 1859.] *obl.* 8°. **14137. e. 2.**

—— *Satyanārāyaṇavratakathā.* अथ श्रीसत्यनारायणपूजा सटीक कथाप्रारंभः [Satyanārāyaṇapūjā, or Satyanārāyaṇavratakathā. Sanskrit text, with a Marathi translation.] ff. 24. पुणं १८८० [*Poona*, 1880.] *obl.* 8°. **14033. b. 43(3).**

—— *Tulaṣīmāhātmya.* See Viṭhṭhala Dāsa. अथ तळसीमाहात्म्य प्रारंभ [Tulaṣīmāhātmya. A poem founded on a section of the Skandapurāṇa.] [1862.] *obl.* 8°. **14137. d. 10(4.)**

PURĀṆAS. Skandapurāṇa (*continued*).

—— *Vaṭasāvitrīkathā.* अथ वटसावित्री पूजासहित सार्थकथाप्रा° [Vaṭasāvitrīkathā. An extract from the Skandapurāṇa in Sanskrit and Marathi.] ff. 18, *lith.* पुणं १८५४ [*Poona*, 1875.] 8°. **14016. d. 25.**

PURASHOO RAM PUNT GODBOLAY. *See* Paraṣurāma Panta Godbole.

PURSHEO RAM PUNT GORBOLE. *See* Paraṣurāma Panta Godbole.

PUSHPADANTA. महिम्न स्तोत्र. [Mahimnaḥ stotra. Sanskrit text, with a double translation in Marathi verse, by Gaṇeṣa Lele Tryambakakar, applying the text to Ṣiva as well as to Vishṇu.] pp. iii. 22. मुंबई १९६७ [*Bombay*, 1875.] 8°. **14033. a. 6.**

RĀDHĀNĀTHA. Account of Radhanath, a native Christian in Bengal. राधानाथाची गोष्ट. pp. 37. १८४४ *Bombay*, [1844.] 24°. **14137. a. 1(7.)**

RĀGHOBĀ JANĀRDANA. *See* Murray (L.) Abridgment of Murray's English grammar, with a Maráthí translation .... by Rághobá Janárdhan. 1837. 8°. **14140. h. 2.**

RĀGHOBĀ MOROBĀ. *See* Haridāsa. Vickram Charitra . . . translated . . by Ragoba Moroba. 1855. 8° **14137. d. 12.**

RAGHUNĀTHA ĀCHĀRYA. अथ लघुबोधः प्रारभ्यते ॥ [Laghubodha. Philosophical verses.] ff. 8, *lith.* १९८४ [*Bombay*, 1862.] *obl.* 16°. **14140. a. 7(3.)**

RAGHUNĀTHA BHĀSKARA GODBOLE. *See* Rāmadāsa Svāmī, *Son of Sūryopanta.* अथ श्रीदासबोध प्रारंभः [Dāsabodha. Revised, and containing a glossary of difficult words, by R. Bh. G.] [1875.] *obl.* 4°. **14137. e. 2.**

—— An ancient historical dictionary of Bharat Varsha or Greatest India. Compiled by Raghunath Bhaskar Godbole. (भारत वर्षीय प्राचीन ऐतिहासिक कोश.) [Bhāratavarshīya prāchīna aitihāsika koṣa.] pp. ii. ii. 707. *Bombay*, 1876. 8°. **14139. e. 15.**

—— हिंदुस्थानाचा अर्वाचीन कोश. [Hindusthānāchā arvachīna koṣa. An encyclopædia of Indian history, geography and biography.] pp. viii. 546, 41. पुणें १८८१ [*Poona*, 1881.] 8°. **14139. e. 23.**

RAGHUNĀTHA BHĀSKARA GODBOLE. A new Dictionary of the Maráthí language, compiled by Raghunáth Bháskar Godbole. (मराठी भाषेचा नवीन कोश.) Marāṭhī bhāshechā navīna koṣa.] pp. v. 632. *Bombay*, 1870. **14140. g. 19.**

RAGHUNĀTHABOVĀ BHIṄGĀRKAR. श्री ज्ञानदेव चरित्र [Jñānadeva charitra. A life of the poet Jñānadeva.] pp. iii. 243. iv. १८८६ [*Poona*, 1886.] 8°. **14139. e. 18.**

RAGHUNĀTHA NĀRĀYAṆA. श्री रघुनाथपंडित विरचित राजव्यवहार कोश. [Rājavyavahāra koṣa. A vocabulary in Sanskrit ṣlokas of Arabic, Persian and Urdu words, introduced into the Marathi language. Compiled by order of Ṣivājī about 1675 A.D. Edited, with preface, various readiugs, and alphabetical index, by Kāṣīnātha Nārāyaṇa Sāne.] pp. vii. 50. पुणें १८०२ [*Poona*, 1881.] 12°. **14140. h. 27.**

RAGHUNĀTHA ṢAṄKARA ṢĀSTRĪ ABHYAṄKAR. हरिश्चंद्र सत्वदर्शन नाटक. [Hariṣchandra satvadarṣana nāṭaka. A drama, in three acts, on the story of king Hariṣchandra. Third edition.] pp. 104, *lith.* पुणें १८७७ [*Poona*, 1877.] 8°. **14140. f. 2(1.)**

RAGHUNĀTHA ṢĀSTRĪ DĀNTYE and **KṚISHṆA ṢĀSTRĪ BHĀṬAVAḌEKAR.** वैद्यसारसंग्रह. [Vaidyasārasaṅgraha. A treatise on medicine. Third edition.] pp. xviii. 248, *lith.* मुंबई १७८७ [*Bombay*, 1865.] 8°. **14139. c. 1.**

RAGHUNĀTHA ṢĀSTRĪ PARVATE. *See* MAHĀBHĀRATA.—*Bhagavadgītā.* अथ भाषाविवृत्ति सहित गीता प्रारंभः [Bhagavadgītā. With a Marathi commentary by R. Ṣ. P.] [1860.] *fol.* **14065. e. 5.**

RAGHUNĀTHA ṢĀSTRĪ TAḶEKAR. *See* ANANTA ṢĀSTRĪ TAḶEKAR. Sanscrit-Maráthì Vocabulary. [Revised by R. Ṣ. T.] [1853.] 8°. **14090. d. 5.**

RAGHUNĀTHA VIṬHṬHALA ṢĀSTRĪ DĀNTYE. *See* VIJÑĀNEṢVARA. Marathe translation of the Wyawahar Adhyaya of the Mitakshara, and of the Dayabhaga of the Wyawahar Mayukh, executed by Raghunath Wittal Shastree Dantay. [1844.] 4°. **14137. g. 1.**

—— —— 1862. 8°. **14137. g. 3.**

RAGHUNĀTHA YĀDAVA. पाणिपतची बखर [Pāṇipatchī bakhar. An account of the overthrow of the Maratha power at Panipat A.D. 1761.] *See* PERIODICAL PUBLICATIONS.—*Poona.* काव्येतिहाससंग्रह [Kāvyetihāsa saṅgraha.] Vol. VII. and VIII. [1878, *etc.*] 8°. **14072. d. 37.**

RAGHUNĀTHA YĀDAVA CHITRAGUPTA. रघुनाथ यादव चित्रगुप्तकृत शिव पराक्रम वर्णन [Ṣiva parākrama varṇana. A poem on the greatness of Ṣiva.] *See* PERIODICAL PUBLICATIONS.—*Poona.* काव्येतिहाससंग्रह [Kāvyetihāsa saṅgraha.] Vol. IX. Nos. 8, 9. [1878, *etc.*] 8°. **14072. d. 37.**

RĀJĀRĀMA, *Raja of Satara.* [*Life.*] *See* MALHĀR RĀMARĀVA CHIṬNĪS. थोरले राजाराम यांचें चरित्र प्रकरण [Thorle Rājārāma yāṉcheṉ charitra.]

RĀJĀRĀMA RĀMAKṚISHṆA BHĀGAVATA. *See* RĀMACHANDRA BHIKĀJĪ GUÑJĪKAR. भ्रम-निरास [Bhrama-nirāsa. A reply to R. R. Bh.'s Jaṣās taseṉ.] [1885.] 12°. **14137. d. 7.**

—— जशास तसें पुरवणी [Jaṣās taseṉ purvaṇī. A controversial treatise on the status of various castes of Maratha Brahmans, being a reply to the Bhramanirāsa of Rāmachandra Bhikājī Guñjīkar; the latter work being a rejoinder to the author's attack on the Sarasvatīmaṇḍala, which also was entitled Jaṣās taseṉ.] pp. 31. मुंबई १८८५ [*Bombay*, 1885.] 12°. **14137. c. 17(3.)**

RĀJĀRĀMA ṢĀSTRĪ BODAS. ईश्वर स्मरणपूर्वक स्वपरसंतोषजनक लोकवर्तन [Īṣvara smaraṇapūrvaka svaparasantosha-janaka lokavartana. A lecture on religious and social duties.] pp. 14. *See* BOMBAY, *City of.—Hindu Union Club.* हेमंत व्याख्यानमाला [Hemanta vyākhyānamālā.] Vol. III. No. 5. [1886, *etc.*] 8°. **14139. c. 26.**

RĀJPURKAR (JOSEPH EZEKIEL). השער הראשון אל לשון הקודש (Hebrew primer. इब्री पहिलें पुस्तक.) [Ibrī pahileṉ pustaka.] pp. 36. मुंबई १८८१ [*Bombay*, 1881.] 12°. **14137. a. 8(2.)**

—— מראה אמונת ישראל The true aspect of Judaism; being discourses on the thirteen articles of the Jewish faith, delivered at the old synagogue, Bombay; with an introductory lecture on a general view of Judaism. (इस्राएली धर्माचें खरें स्वरूप) [Isrāelī dharmācheṉ khareṉ svarūpa.] pp. xviii. 88. *Bombay*, 1879. 8°. **14137. b. 8.**

RAMĀBĀĪ SARASVATĪ, *Paṇḍitā.* पंडिता रमाबाई यांचा इंग्लंडचा प्रवास. [Paṇḍitā Ramābāī yāṇchā Iṅglandchā pravāsa. An account of Ramābāī's journey to England, and her impressions of English life and manners. Published from letters to a friend in Bombay.] Pt. I. pp. 47. मुंबई [*Bombay*, 1883.] 12°. **14139. d. 16(2.)**

RĀMABHADRA DĪKSHITA. जानकीपरिणय नाटक समांकी [Jānakīpariṇaya. A Sanskrit drama on the marriage of Sītā, in seven acts, by R. D. Translated into Marathi by Gaṇeśa Śāstrī Lele.] pp. ii. 240. मुंबई १८६५ [*Bombay*, 1865.] 12°. **14140. f. 26.**

—— [Second edition.] pp. 479, xx. मुंबई १८६६ [*Bombay*, 1866.] 8°. **14140. f. 25.**

RĀMACHANDRA AMṚITA DUGAL. जागतीजोत, किंवा शेतपोतरीतभात व्यांविषयीं बात. [Jāgatījota. Lessons, in the form of questions and answers, on natural history, and on other useful subjects.] pp. 66. पुणें १८५२ [*Poona*, 1852.] 8°. **14139. a. 4.**

—— [Another edition.] pp. 99. पुणें १८५७ [*Poona*, 1857.] 12°. **14139. a. 6.**

RĀMACHANDRA BAḌAVE. मयूरकविस्तुति [Mayūrakavi stuti. A poem in praise of the poet Moropanta.] *See* PERIODICAL PUBLICATIONS.—*Poona.* काव्येतिहास-संग्रह [Kāvyetihāsa saṅgraha.] Vol. IX. No. 4. [1878, *etc.*] 8°. **14072. d. 37.**

RĀMACHANDRA BHIKĀJĪ GOKHALE. Sulochaná and Mádhava. A romance composed by Rámchandra Bhikájí Gokle (सुलोचना आणि माधव.) pp. ii. 135. *Bombay*, 1865. 8°. **14139. g. 10.**

RĀMACHANDRA BHIKĀJĪ GUÑJĪKAR. *See* RĀJĀRĀMA RĀMAKṚISHṆA BHĀGAVATA. जशास तसें [Jaśās taseṇ. A controversial treatise on Maratha Brahmans, being a reply to the Bhrama-nirāsa of R. Bh. G.] [1885.] 8°. **14137. c. 17(3.)**

—— भ्रम-निरास [Bhramanirāsa. A reply to objections raised by Rājārāma Rāmakṛishṇa Bhāgavata, in his Jaśās taseṇ, to the author's Sarasvatīmaṇḍala, or description of Māratha Brahmans.] pp. v. iv. 180. मुंबई १८८५ [*Bombay*, 1885.] 12°. **14137. d. 7.**

—— कौमुदीमहोत्साहः [Kaumudīmahotsāha. A collection of Sanskrit grammatical texts, consisting of Pāṇinī and his chief commentators, and accompanied in some cases by Marathi versions. Edited by R. Bh. G. and Kāśīnātha Pāṇḍuraṅga Parab.] Pt. I–VI. मुम्बय्याम् १९६६ [*Bombay*, 1877–79.] 8°.

No more published. **14093. c.**

RĀMACHANDRA BHIKĀJĪ GUÑJĪKAR. सरस्वतीमंडल अथवा महाराष्ट्र देशांतील ब्राह्मणजातींचें वर्णन .... Sarasvatîmandala, or A description of the Marâtha Brâhmans by Rámchandra Bhikájí Gunjíkar. pp. ii. 188. 50. मुंबई [*Bombay*,] 1884. 12°. **14139. c. 21.**

—— विद्यावृद्धीच्या कामीं आमची अनास्था [Vidyāvṛiddhīchyā kāmīṇ āmchī anāsthā. A lecture on the importance of education.] pp. 16. *See* BOMBAY, *City of.*—*Hindu Union Club.* हेमंत व्याख्यानमाला. [Hemanta vyākhyānamāla.] Vol. II. No. 3. [1886, *etc.*] 8°. **14139. c. 26.**

RĀMACHANDRA GOVINDA TAḶVARKAR. ब्रिटिश पार्लमेंट सभेनें हिंदुस्थान संबंधीं केलेले कायदे [A lecture on the action taken by the Parliament of England in the affairs of India.] pp. 29. *See* BOMBAY, *City of.*—*Hindu Union Club.* हेमंत व्याख्यानमाला [Hemanta vyākhyānamālā.] Vol. III. No. 6. [1886, *etc.*] 8°. **14139. c. 26.**

RĀMACHANDRA KEŚAVA LIMAYE. *See* INDIA.—*Legislative Council.* Act No. XV. of 1887, or The Indian Limitation Act. With schedules, and explanatory notes .... [Compiled by R. K. L.] [1877.] 8°. **14137. g. 4.**

RĀMACHANDRA NĀRĀYAṆA NENE. *See* TALMUD.—*Appendix.* तलमुद [Selections from the Talmud, translated by R. N. N. from the English of H. Polano.] [1886.] 8°. **14137. b. 13.**

RĀMACHANDRA RĀGHOBĀ DHARĀDHARA. *See* ESMARCH (F.) First aid to the Injured. Translated ... (by Mr. Ramchandra Raghoba Dharadhar). 1883. 8°. **14137. h. 13.**

RĀMACHANDRA RĀVA, *Panganūrī.* Memoirs of Hyder and Tippoo, rulers of Seringapatam, written in the Mahratta language, by Ram Chandra Rao "Punganuri" ... Translated into English, and illustrated with annotations, by C. P. Brown. MS. CORRECTIONS. pp. 52. *Madras*, 1849. 8°. **14139. e. 26.**

RĀMACHANDRA SAKHĀRĀMA GUPTE. सूपशास्त्र. स्वयंपाक शास्त्र. [Sūpaṣāstra, or Indian cookery. A revised edition, with a preface by Rāvajī Ṣrīdhara Gondhaḷekar.] pp. iii. vi. 112. पुणे १८६७ [*Poona*, 1867.] 8°. **14139. b. 12.**

RĀMACHANDRA ṢĀSTRĪ MUDLE.—*See* MAHĀBHĀRATA.—*Bhagavadgītā.* श्री गीता भावचंद्रिका *etc.* [Bhāvachandrikā. A prose translation of the Bhagavadgītā by Bāḷajī Sundarajī, assisted by R. Ṣ. M.] [1851.] 12°. **14137. d. 4.**

RĀMACHANDRA SŪBAJĪ BĀPŪ. A comparison of the Pooranic, Sidhantic, and Copernican systems of the world; by Soobajee Bapoo. (सिद्धांतशिरोमणिप्रकाश). [Siddhāntaṣiromaṇi prakāṣa.] pp. 129. *Bombay*, 1836. 8°. **14139. a. 1.**

RĀMACHANDRA VISHṆU SAHASRABUDDHE. भूगोल विद्या [Bhūgolavidyā. An elementary geography of Asia.] Pt I. pp. ii. 54. पुणें [*Poona*, 1875?] 12°. **14139. a. 33(2.)**

—— [Another edition.] 2 pt. pp. vi. 84, iv. 46. पुणें १८८० [*Poona*, 1880.] 12°. **14139. d. 31(4.)**

RĀMADĀSA SVĀMĪ, *of Haidarabad.* अथ पंचीकरणप्रारंभ [Pañchīkaraṇa. Verses on the Vedanta system of philosophy, from the Sanskrit original of R. Sv.] ff. 15, *lith.* पुणें १८७७ [*Poona*, 1877.] *obl.* 12°. **14140. a. 9(15.)**

RĀMADĀSA SVĀMĪ, *Son of Sūryopanta.* अथ दासबोध प्रथमदशक प्रारंभः [Dāsabodha. A philosophical poem in twenty chapters.] *Lith.*. मुंबई १८६६ [*Bombay*, 1864.] *obl.* 4°. **14140. d. 12.**

—— [Another edition. Revised and containing a glossary of difficult words, by Raghunātha Bhāskara Goḍbole.] *Lith.* पुणें १८७५ [*Poona*, 1875.] *obl.* 4°. **14140. d. 14.**

—— [Another edition.] *Lith.* पुणें १७९९ [*Poona*, 1877.] *obl.* 4°. **14140. d. 16.**

—— रामदासकृत मनाचे श्लोक ॥ [Manāche ṣloka. Verses on moral rectitude.] pp. 36, *lith.* मुंबई १९८१ [*Bombay*, 1859.] 8°. **14140. f. 9.**

—— [Another edition.] pp. 32, *lith.* मुंबई १९८४ [*Bombay*, 1862.] 8°. **14140. b. 9(1.)**

—— [Another edition.] pp. 54, *lith.* मुंबई १९८६ [*Bombay*, 1864.] 12°. **14140. a. 10(9.)**

RĀMADĀSA SVĀMĪ, *Son of Sūryopanta.* मारुतीस्तोत्र ॥ [Mārutī-stotra, and Karuṇāmṛita bhīmāshṭaka. Invocations of Hanumān as spells for averting evils. Third edition.] ff. 11, *lith.* मुंबई १९७७ [*Bombay*, 1855.] *obl.* 32°. **14137. c. 2(2.)**

—— [Another edition. Together with Hanumān dvādaṣa nāma, or Twelve names of Hanumān.] ff. 6, *lith.* मुंबई १९८५ [*Bombay*, 1863.] *obl.* 16°. **14137. c. 10.**

—— रामदासकृत अभंग भाग १. [Rāmadāsakṛita abhaṅga. A collection of poems and hymns in the abhaṅga metre. Revised by Paraṣurāma Panta Goḍbole.] Pt. I. pp. 154. मुंबइ १९८३ [*Bombay*, 1861.] 8° **14140. c. 31.**

—— श्री राममंत्र श्लोक [Rāmamantra ṣloka. Verses on the attainment of true happiness.] pp. 14, *lith.* मुंबई १९७६ [*Bombay*, 1854.] 12°. **14140. a. 1(6.)**

—— [Another edition.] pp. 13, *lith.* पुणें १८७० [*Poona*, 1870.] 12°. **14140. a. 4(13.)**

—— [Another edition.] pp. 13, *lith.* पुणें १८७८ [*Poona*, 1878.] 12°. **14140. a. 12(13.)**

—— श्रीरामदासस्वामिकृत सुंदरकांड (युद्धकांड, किष्किंधा कांड, भीमरूपि-स्तोत्रें) [A paraphrase in verse of the Sundarakāṇḍa, Yuddhakāṇḍa, and Kishkindhyākāṇḍa of the Rāmāyaṇa; with short poems and an account of the life of the poet.] *See* PERIODICAL PUBLICATIONS. — *Poona.* काव्येतिहास-संग्रह [Kāvyetihāsa saṅgraha.] Vol. V.–VIII. [1878, *etc.*] 8°. **14037. d. 37.**

RĀMAJĪ DHĀYĀJĪ. Lulit Sungurh or Drama. ललितसंग्रह. [A description of some of the principal characters in the Hindu theatre. With illustrations. Second edition.] pp. 87. ii. मुंबई १८७५ [*Bombay*, 1875.] 12°. **14140. e. 11.**

RĀMAJĪ GAṆOJĪ CHAUGULE. Narayen Bodh, or moral advices to Narayen, the son of Ramjee Gunnojee. Composed by him with a view of serving as instructive examples for children in hopes of leading them to good course and noble behaviour. In two parts. (नारायणबोध.) Part I. pp. iv. ii. 460. मुंबई [*Bombay*], 1860. 8°.
Wanting Pt. II. **14139. c. 14.**

RĀMAJĪ GAṆOJĪ CHAUGULE. रसायन शास्त्र अथवा हुन्नरनिधी *etc.* (Rasayan Shastra, or Hoonnur Needhee, which contains description, production, property of natural objects and matters together with complete receipts of good many useful things to be prepared for trades and commerce, by Ramjee Gunnojee Chogley, with aid of many books, and his friends, in 3 volumes.) Vol. II. pp. xxxvi. 708, *lith.* [*Bombay?*], 1859. 8°.
Wanting Vols. I. and III. **14139. b. 6.**

——— Stree Churitra, or Female narration, comprising their course of life, behaviour and undertaking in four parts, with moral reprimands, checking obscenity to secure chastity. Part III. Compiled ... by Ramjee Gunnojee ... स्त्रीचरित्र *etc.* pp. vi. 424. मुंबई १८६२ [*Bombay*, 1862.] 8°.
14139. c. 2.

RĀMA JOṢĪ. रामजोशि [A collection of 66 Lāvaṇī songs by R. J.] *See* ṢAṄKARA TUKĀRĀMA ṢĀLIGRĀMA. लावण्या भाग २ रा [Lāvaṇyā.] Pt. II. [1877.] 8°. **14140. c. 9(2.)**

——— रामजोशीकृत लावण्या [Another edition.] *See* RĀVAJĪ SRĪDHARA GONDHAḶEKAR. रामजोशि ... सुरस लावण्या [Surasa lāvaṇyā.] pp. 1–45. [1878.] 8°.
14140. c. 25.

——— रामजोशीकृत लावण्या. [Another edition, with eight additional songs.] pp. ii. 100, *lith.* १८८१ [*Poona*, 1881.] 12°. **14140. a. 12(14.)**

RĀMAKRISHṆA HARI BHĀGAVATA. क्षमास्तोत्र आणि कायाजीव संवाद [Kshamāstotra, and Kāyājīvasaṃvāda. Two poems.] pp. 10. १७९६ [*Bombay?*, 1874.] 12°. **14140. a. 19(1.)**

RĀMĀNANDA. अथ दीपरत्नाकर प्रारंभः [Dīparatnākara. A treatise in verse, in fourteen chapters, on Vedanta philosophy.] मुंबई १८८५ [*Bombay*, 1885.] *obl.* 8°. **14140. c. 34.**

RĀMANĀTHA. *See* NAKŪḶA. अथ नकूळकृत शालिहोत्रटीका *etc.* [Ṣalihotraṭīkā. Founded on a Sanskrit work by R.] [1863.] 12°. **14137. ff. 1.**

RĀMARĀJA, *Raja of Satara.* [*Life.*] *See* MALHĀR RĀMARĀVA CHITṆĪS. श्रीमंत छत्रपती धाकटे रामराजे *etc.* [An account of the lives of Rāmarāja and Shāhū II.] [1878, *etc.*] 8°.
14072. d. 37.

RĀMA ṢĀSTRĪ. पांडवांची बखर. [Pāṇḍavāṇchī bakhar, or The story of the wars between the Pāṇḍavas and Kauravas.] pp. 17, *lith.* पुणे १८६९ [*Poona*, 1869.] 8°.
In Modi characters. **14139. g. 6(2.)**

RAMBHĀ ṢUKA. रंभाशुकसंवाद [Rambhā Ṣuka saṃvāda. A Sanskrit poem, in the form of a dialogue, in which the nymph Rambhā endeavours by her blandishments to entice the sage Ṣukāchārya, but fails; she extolling the pleasures of love, and he the excellency of virtue and philosophy. With a Marathi prose translation.] pp. 29, *lith.* १८७७ [*Poona*, 1877.] 16°.
14140. a. 12(9.)

——— [Second edition.] १८८० [*Poona*, 1880.] 16°.
14140. a. 10(18.)

RAMJEE GUNNOJEE. *See* RĀMAJĪ GAṆOJĪ CHAUGULE.

RAṄGO SAKHĀRĀMA LĀḶE KIKVĪKAR. वैद्यप्रकाश. (Viydya-prakash, or A handbook of native medicine, by Rungo Succaram Lâle Kikwikar.) pp. xi. 283. *Bombay*, 1876. 8°. **14137. h. 10.**

RAO BAHADUR DADOBA PANDURANG. *See* DĀDOBĀ PĀṆḌURAṄGA TARKHAḌKAR.

RAO SÁHEB BHÁSKAR DÁMODAR. *See* BHĀSKARA DĀMODARA.

RÁO SÁHEB NÁRÁYAN BHÁI DÁNDEKAR. *See* NĀRĀYAṆA BHĀĪ DĀṆḌEKAR.

RAO SAHIB SĪTARAM V. PATAVARDHAN. *See* SĪTĀRĀMA VIṢVANĀTHA PAṬAVARDHANA.

RĀVAJĪ BĀPUJĪ ṢĀSTRĪ BĀPAṬ. *See* KRISHṆAMIṢRA. प्रबोधचंद्रोदय नाटक. [Prabodhachandrodaya naṭaka. Translated by R. B. Ṣ. B.] [1851.] 8°.
14140. f. 19.

RĀVAJĪ HARI ĀṬHVALE. आंग्रे घराण्याचा इतिहास. [Āṅgre gharāṇyāchā itihāsa. An account of the Angria Chieftains of the Kolaba State.] pp. 43. iii. अलीबाग १८८४ [*Alibagh*, 1884.] 8°. **14139. e. 17.**

——— बाळाजी विश्वनाथ पेशवे यांचें नाटक [Bāḷājī Viṣvanātha nāṭaka. A historical drama on the administration of the Peshwa Bāḷājī Viṣvanātha.] pp. 77. अलिबाग १८८२ [*Alibagh*, 1882.] 8°.
14140. f. 12.

RĀVAJĪ HARI ĀTHVALE. ब्रह्मद्वेष [Brahmadvesha. An essay advocating the cause of Brahmans; recommending them to the favourable notice of Government officials and the public.] pp. 20. अलीबाग १८८४ [*Alibagh*, 1884.] 12°. **14137. c. 17(2.)**

—— मराठी कवितान्वयार्थ संग्रह [Marāṭhī Kavitānvayārtha saṅgraha. A prose rendering of selections from the writings of Marathi poets.] pp. 58. अलीबाग १८७७ [*Alibagh*, 1877.] 8°. **14140. c. 19.**

—— पाकशास्त्र - भाग १ ला. [Pākaṣāstra, or Indian cookery book.] Pt. I. pp. ii. 74. अलीबाग १८८० [*Alibagh*, 1880.] 12°. **14139. a. 46.**

RĀVAJĪ ṢĀSTRĪ GODBOLE. *See* MORRIS (H.) *of the Madras Civil Service.* The History of India ... translated into Marathi ..., revised by Ravji Shastri Godbole. 1880. 12°. **14139. e. 21.**

—— *See* PARAṢURĀMA PANTA GOḌBOLE. Selections from the Maráṭhí poets .... New edition, revised and annotated by .... Ráwjí Shástrí Godbole. 1878. 8°. **14140. b. 12.**

RĀVAJĪ ṢRĪDHARA GONDHAḶEKAR. *See* INDIA.—*Legislative Council.* कोड आफ् सीवल प्रोसिजर *etc.* [The Code of Civil Procedure. Edited by R. Ṣ. G.] [1877.] 8°. **14137. g. 7.**

—— —— हिंदुस्थानचा मुदतीविषयीं आक्ट *etc.* [The Indian Limitation Act. Edited by R. Ṣ. G.] [1877.] 8°. **14137. g. 5(2.)**

—— *See* MAHĀBHĀRATA.—*Bhagavadgītā.* अथ श्रीपरिभाषे सहित ज्ञानेश्वरी प्रारंभः [Jñāneṣvarī. Edited by R. Ṣ. G.] [1877.] *obl.* 4°. **14060. f. 12.**

—— *See* MUKUNDARĀJA. अथ विवेकसिंधु प्रारंभः [Vivekasindhu. Edited, with a preface and glossary, by R. Ṣ. G.] [1875.] *obl.* 8°. **14140. c. 17.**

—— *See* PERIODICAL PUBLICATIONS.—*Poona.* सर्वसंग्रह मासिक पुस्तक [Sarvasaṅgraha. A monthly literary magazine. Edited, with commentaries and notes, by R. Ṣ. G.] [1877.] 8°. **14142. a. 3.**

—— *See* RĀMACHANDRA SAKHĀRĀMA GUPTE. सूपशास्त्र. [Sūpaṣāstra. A revised edition, with a preface by R. Ṣ. G.] [1867.] 8°. **14139. b. 12.**

RĀVAJĪ ṢRĪDHARA GONDHAḶEKAR. *See* ṢAṄKARA ĀCHĀRYA. अथ वाक्यवृत्ती प्रारंभा [Vākyavṛitti. Edited by R. Ṣ. G.] [1880.] *obl.* 8°. **14048. d. 36.**

—— *See* ṢRĪDHARA. अथ शिवलीलामृत प्रारंभः [Ṣivalīlāmṛita. Revised, and containing a glossary of difficult words, by R. Ṣ. G.] [1875.] *obl.* 8°. **14140. c. 13(3.)**

—— कीर्तनतरंगिणी [Kīrtana-taraṅgiṇī. A collection of Kīrtanas, edited by R. Ṣ. G. Pt. I. on various mythological stories, by Dāmodara Gaṇeṣa Joṣī. Pt. II. on the birth and life of Krishṇa, by Pāṇḍuraṅga Ābājī Moye, and Vāmana Ekanātha Ṣāstrī Kemkar. Pt. III. also on mythological subjects, by the latter author only.] पुणें १८८५ [*Poona*, 1885, *etc.*] 8°.
In progress. Pt. I. is of the 4th, and Pt. II. and III. of the 2nd edition. **14140. c. 37.**

—— रामजोशि, अनंतफंदी, परशराम, होनाजीबाळ सगनभाऊ व दुसरे अनेक कवि यांच्या सुरस लावण्या. [Surasa lāvaṇyā. Miscellaneous lāvaṇī songs by Rāma Joṣī, Ananta Phandī, Paraṣurāma, Honājī Bāḷa, Sagan Bhāū, and other poets. Edited by R. Ṣ. G.] Pt. I. pp. iv. 140. *lith.* पुणें १८७८ [*Poona*, 1878.] 8°. **14140. c. 25.**

RÁV SÁHEB MAHÁDEV GOVIND SHÁSTRI KOLHATKAR. *See* MAHĀDEVA GOVINDA ṢĀSTRĪ KOLHAṬKAR.

REPENTANCE. On repentance. पश्चात्तापाची गोष्ट [Paṣchattāpāchī goshṭa.] pp. 28. [*Bombay*, 1838?] 8°.
No. 49 of the Bombay Tract and Book Society's Series. **14137. b. 5(8.)**

REVIVAL HYMNS. Revival hymns, in Marathi. धर्मोत्तेजक गीतें. [Dharmottejaka gīteṇ.] मुंबई १८७५ [*Bombay*, 1875.] 12°. **14137. a. 5(2.)**

ROLLIN (CHARLES). The life of Cyrus, translated from Rollin by Vishnu Moreshwar Bhide. (खुसरू राजाचा इतिहास.) [Khusrū rājāchā itihāsa.] pp. 180. *Poona*, 1852. 8°. **14139. d. 3(3.)**

—— The life of Socrates, translated from Rollin by Krishna Shastree Chiplonker. (साक्रेटीस त्याचें चरित्र.) [Sākreṭīs tyācheṇ charitra.] pp. 130, *lith. Poona*, 1852. 8°. **14139. d. 3(1.)**

—— A life of Socrates. Translated ... by Krishna Shástrí Chiplunkar. Fourth edition. pp. ii. ii. 106. *Bombay*, 1875. 12°. **14139. d. 18.**

RUKMIṆĪ. आर्या रुक्मिणीस्वयंवराच्या [Rukmiṇī svayaṃvara. An anonymous poem in āryā verse on the marriage of Rukmiṇī to Krishṇa. Followed by Subhadrāharaṇa, a poem by Moropanta on the abduction of Subhadrā.] pp. 16. [*Bombay*, 1860 ?] 12°. **14140. a. 29(10.)**

RUNGO SUCCARAM LÂLE KIKVIKAR. *See* RAṄGO SAKHĀRĀMA LĀḶE KIKVĪKAR.

S. M. K. *See* RĀMACHANDRA BHIKĀJĪ GUÑJĪKAR.

SADÁSHEW WISHWANÁTH. *See* SADĀṢIVA VIṢVANĀTHA.

SADĀṢIVA, *Kavi.* अथ उमाविलास प्रारं॰ [Umāvilāsa. A poem on the sports of Ṣiva and his consort Pārvatī.] pp. 13, *lith.* पुणें १८७९ [*Poona*, 1887.] 12°. **14140. a. 12(10.)**

—— [Another edition.] pp. 13, *lith.* पुणें १८७८ [*Poona*, 1878.] 12°. **14140. a. 4(14.)**

—— सदाशिव कविकृत उमाविलास [Another edition.] *See* PERIODICAL PUBLICATIONS.—*Poona.* काव्येतिहास-संग्रह [Kāvyetihāsa saṅgraha.] Vol. IX. Nos. 4 and 5. [1878, *etc.*] 8°. **14072. d. 37.**

SADĀṢIVA BAJĀBĀ ṢĀSTRĪ AMRĀPURKAR. *See* KRISHṆAMISRA. प्रबोधचंद्रोदय नाटक. [Prabodhachandrodaya nāṭaka. Translated by S. B. Ṣ. A.] [1851.] 8°. **14140. f. 19.**

SADĀṢIVA BAJYĀBĀ ṢĀSTRĪ. कोकणस्थ ब्राह्मणांची गोत्रमालिका [Konkaṇastha Brāhmaṇāṇchī gotramālikā. A treatise on the family names of the fourteen tribes of Konkani Brahmans. Fourth edition.] pp. 32, *lith.* पुणें [*Poona*, 1880.] 12°. **14137. c. 17.**

SADĀṢIVA KĀṢĪNĀTHA CHHATRE. See ÆSOP. Murat,hee translation of Esop's Fables [by S. K. Chh.] 1837. 8°. **14139. g. 3.**

—— —— 1856. 8°. **14139. g. 4.**

—— —— 1861. 12°. **14139. f. 7.**

—— —— 1877. 8°. **14139. g. 13.**

—— *See* BAITĀL-PACHĪSĪ. वेताळपंचविशी [Baitāl-Pachīsī. Translated by S. K. Chh.] [1862.] 8°. **14140. c. 6.**

—— —— [1862.] 12°. **14139. f. 10.**

—— —— [1880.] 12°. **14139. f. 29.**

SADĀṢIVA KĀṢĪNĀTHA CHHATRE. *See* BERQUIN (A.) Marat'ha translation [by S. K. Chh.] of Berquin's Children's Friend. Vol. I. बाळमित्र. [1828.] 8°. **14137. b. 2.**

—— —— 1854. 8°. **14137. b. 14.**

—— —— 1859. 8°. **14137. b. 7.**

SADĀṢIVA VIṢVANĀTHA. Select proverbs of all nations : four thousand and upwards alphabetically arranged and translated, into Maráthi couplets by Sadáshew Wishwanáth. (सर्वदेशांतील निवडक म्हणी) [Sarvadeṣāntīl nivaḍak mhaṇī.] pp. 465. *Eng.* and *Mar.* *Bombay*, 1858. 8°. **14139. c. 8.**

SADĀṢIVA VIṢVANĀTHA HĀṬE. *See* GREEN (H.) *Superintendent of Government Schools in Gujarat.* A collection of English phrases ... with their Marathi equivalents by Sadáshiva Vishwanáth Háté, *etc.* 1868. 8°. **12906. cc. 6.**

SADĀṢIVA VIṬHṬHALA PĀLKAR. मराठी दुसरे पुस्तकांतील शब्दार्थ. [Marāṭhī dusre pustakāntīl ṣabdārtha. A glossary of difficult words in the Marathi Second Book. Second edition.] pp. 31, *lith.* रत्नागिरी १८८० [*Ratnagiri*, 1880.] 12°. **14140. g. 29(4.)**

SA'DĪ. गुलिस्तां. (The "Gulistan," or Rose-garden, by Maslahuddin Shaik Sadi of Shiraz. Translated from the original ... with a life of the poet by Govindrao Bhikaji Patwardhan.) pp. xvii. 236, viii. *lith.* १८८४ [*Baroda*, *Ratnagiri*, printed 1884.] 8°. **14139. g. 19.**

SAGAN BHĀŪ. सगन भाऊच्या लावण्या [Lāvaṇī songs.] *See* RĀVAJĪ ṢRĪDHARA GONDHALEKAR. रामजोशि ... सुरस लावण्या [Surasa lāvaṇyā.] pp. 118–128. [1878.] 8°. **14140. c. 25.**

SAINT PIERRE (JACQUES HENRI BERNARDIN DE). Paul and Virginia. A tale translated into Marathi by Govind Shankar Shástri Bápat. (पाल आणि व्हर्जिनिया) pp. vi. 132. *Bombay*, 1875. 12°. **14139. f. 15.**

SAKHĀRĀMA ARJUNA. The principles and practice of medicine .. (वैद्यतत्व) [Vaidyatattva. Founded chiefly on J. Peet's "Practice of medicine."] pp. xx. 723. liii. *Bombay*, 1869. 8°. **14137. h. 7.**

SAKHĀRĀMA ARJUNA. विवाहविज्ञान [Vivāhavijñāna. A lecture on Hindu marriages, with special reference to the evils of early marriages, and the desirability of legalizing widow-marriages.] pp. 23. मुंबई १८७७ [*Bombay*, 1877.] 12°.
14139. c. 13(2.)

SAKHĀRĀMA BĀḶAKṚISHṆA SARNĀIK. जरासंधवध नाटक [Jarāsandhavadha nāṭaka. A drama on the Mahābhārata story of the slaying of Jarāsandha by Bhīma.] pp. 38, *lith.* पुणें १८७९ [*Poona*, 1879.] 8°. **14140. f. 1(5.)**

—— कालियमर्दन नाटक [Kāliyamardana nāṭaka. A drama on the mythological story of the defeat of the serpent-king Kāliya, by Krishṇa.] pp. 31. *lith.* पुणें १८७९ [*Poona*, 1879.] 8°. **14140. f. 1(4.)**

—— काव्येंदुशेखर [Kāvyenduṣekhara. A collection of old Marathi poems, compiled by S. B. S.] Vol. I. *etc.* *Lith.* पुणें १८८६ [*Poona*, 1886, *etc.*] 8°. *In progress.* **14142. a. 4.**

SAKHĀRĀMA BĀPŪṢEṬ DĀṆḌEKAR. Elementary physical geography. सृष्टिज्ञानपरिभाषा [Sṛishṭijñānaparibhāshā. Sixth edition.] pp. 96. मुंबई १८७६ [*Bombay*, 1876.] 12°. **14139. d. 31(1.)**

SAKHĀRĀMA JOṢĪ. *See* BĀḶA ṢĀSTRĪ GHAGVE. A dictionary of the Maratha language, compiled by Sukha Ram Joshee, *etc.* 1829. 4°.
14140. i. 1.

SAKHĀRĀMA SONĀR. यशवंतराव महाराज यांचा पवाडा [Yaṣavanta Rāva yāñchā pavāḍā. A poem describing some miraculous actions ascribed to Yaṣavanta Rāva, a pensioned Mamlatdar.] pp. 8, *lith.* धुळें १८७७ [*Dhulia*, 1877.] 12°.
14140. a. 10(15.)

SAKHĀRĀMATANAYA. सखारामतनयकृत रुक्मिणीस्वयंवर [Rukmiṇī svayaṃvara. A poem on the marriage of Krishṇa and Rukmiṇī.] *See* PERIODICAL PUBLICATIONS.—*Poona.* काव्येतिहास-संग्रह [Kāvyetihāsa saṅgraha.] Vol. IX. No. 4. [1878, *etc.*] 8°. **14072. d. 37.**

SAKHKHANA PAṆḌITA. *See* ÆSOP. *Begin:* प्रपंच्यां माजि जें शास्त्र *etc.* [Bālabodhamuktāvalī. A translation of Æsop's Fables by S. P.] [1806.] 8°.
14139. g. 7.

SAKHU. अथ सखूचें चरित्र प्रारंभः [Sakhūcheṇ charitra, or The story of the saint Sakhu, in verse. Followed by Bodhalyāche abhaṅga, a poem on the story of King Bodhala, a devout worshipper of Pāṇḍuraṅga.] pp. 13. पुणें १८७५ [*Poona*, 1875.] 12°.
14140. a. 10(12.)

SAMBHĀJĪ, *Raja of Satara.* [*Life.*] *See* MALHĀR RĀMARĀVA CHITṆĪS. संभाजी राजे यांचें चरित्र [Sambhājī Rāje yāñcheṇ charitra.] .

SAMSĀRACHOPAḌĪ. मराठी संसारचोपडी [Saṃsārachopaḍī. A manual of useful information, containing a primer, elements of arithmetic, interest tables, letter-writer, and an English-Marathi spelling book. Second edition.] pp. iii. 70, 40, 13, *lith.* मुंबई १७८५ [*Bombay*, 1863.] 8°.
14140. i. 4.

—— [Another edition.] pp. 128, 16, *lith.* मुंबई १७९९ [*Bombay*, 1877.] 8°. **14140. i. 8.**

SĀMUDRIKA. अथ सामुद्रिक प्रारंभ [Sāmudrika. A treatise on fortune-telling. Sanskrit text, with a preface and translation in Marathi.] pp. 40, *lith.* १८८२ [*Poona*, 1882.] 16°. **14053. b. 18(2.)**

SAMUEL (R.) *See* PETHAHIAH ben JACOB, *of Ratisbon.* Travells [*sic*] of Rabbi Petachia .... [Translated by S. Daniells, and R. S.] [1877.] 12°.
14137. a. 8(1.)

SANE (K. N.) *See* KĀṢINĀTHA NĀRĀYAṆA SĀNE.

ṢAṄKARA, *Son of Gaṇeṣa.* *See* MAHĀBHĀRATA.—*Bhagavadgītā.* अथ ज्ञानेश्वरी प्रारंभः ॥ [Bhagavadgītā, with the Jñāneṣvarī. Revised, with a glossary by Ṣ.] [1874.] *obl.* 4°. **14065. f. 1.**

ṢAṄKARA ĀCHĀRYA. अथ अपरोक्षानुभूति प्रारंभः ॥ [Aparokshānubhūti. A treatise on Vedanta philosophy in verse. Sanskrit text, with a Marathi metrical translation, called Samaṣlokī, by Vāmana Paṇḍita.] ff. 20, *lith.* मुंबई १७७८ [*Bombay*, 1856.] *obl.* 8°. **14048. c. 27.**

—— प्रारंभ चर्पटपंजरी [Charpaṭapañjarī. A Sanskrit poem, in sixteen slokas, in praise of Vishṇu, with translations into Gujarati, Hindi and Marathi.] pp. 14, *lith.* मुंबई १७८१ [*Bombay*, 1859.] 8°.
14076. a. 3.

—— शंकराचार्यकृत हस्तामलकग्रंथाचें शिवरामकृत महाराष्ट्र भाषांतर [Hastāmalaka. A philosophical treatise ascribed to Ṣ. Ā. translated into verse by Ṣivarāma.] *See* PERIODICAL PUBLICATIONS.—*Poona.* काव्येतिहास-संग्रह [Kāvyetihāsa saṅgraha.] Vol. IX. No. 5. [1878, *etc.*] 8°. **14072. d. 37.**

ṢAṄKARA ĀCHĀRYA. अथ श्री लघुवाक्यवृत्ति प्रारंभः [Laghuvākyavṛitti. A Vedantic work in eighteen stanzas. Sanskrit text with a Sanskrit commentary, and Marathi commentaries by Ṣivarāma Svāmī and Ākhaṇḍāṣrama Yati.] pp. 25, *lith.* पुणें १८८३ [*Poona,* 1883.] 12°. **14048. b. 15.**

—— अथ वाक्यवृत्ती प्रारंभा [Vākyavṛitti. A Vedantic work in verse by Haṃsarāja Svāmī, in the form of a commentary on the eighteen aphorisms of Ṣ. Ā. Edited, with a preface, by Rāvajī Ṣrīdhara Gondhaḷekar.] ff. x. 213, *lith.* पुणें १८८० [*Poona,* 1880.] *obl.* 8°. **14048. d. 36.**

ṢAṄKARA JOṢĪ VYAVAHĀRE. *See* VIJÑĀNEṢVARA. Maráṭhí translation of the Wyawahárádhyáya of the Mitákshara, and of the Dáyabhág of the Wyawahar Mayukh; ... Revised and corrected by Shankar Joshí Wyawaháre. 1862. 8°. **14137. g. 3.**

ṢAṄKARA PĀṆḌURAṄGA PAṆḌITA. *See* KĀLIDĀSA. Málavikágnimitra: ... Revised and edited by Shankar P. Pandit. 1867. 12°. **14140. e. 9.**

—— *See* TUKĀRĀMA. A complete collection of the poems of Tukáráma ... Edited by Vishṇu Parashurám Shástrí ... under the supervision of Sankar Páṇḍurang Paṇḍit. 1869. 8°. **14140. c. 14.**

—— *See* VEDAS.—*Ṛigveda.* The Vedārthayatna ... A Maráṭhí and an English translation of the Ṛigveda [by Ṣ. P. P.] 1876, *etc.* 8°. **14007. c. 11.**

—— *See* VIṢĀKHADATTA. Mudrárákshasa: a drama ... Edited by Shankar P. Pandit. 1867. 8°. **14140. f. 23.**

ṢAṄKARA ṢĀSTRĪ GOKHALE. Vyavahâradarpaṇa, or Mirror of practical knowledge. (Husbandry, Bágáita—Part II.) Prepared by Shankara Shâstrî Gokhale. Revised by Vishṇu Parashurám Shástrí Paṇḍit. (व्यवहारदर्पण. शेतकी, बागाईत *etc.*) pp. vi. iii. 137. *Bombay,* 1876. 12°. **14139. a. 26.**

ṢAṄKARA TUKĀRĀMA ṢĀLIGRĀM. बापू गोखले यांचें चरित्र [Bāpū Gokhale yāṇcheṇ charitra. The life of Bāpū Gokhale, a famous general under the last Peshwa, Bāji Rāva II.] pp. xxi. 102. पुणें १८७७ [*Poona,* 1877.] 8°. **14139. c. 18(2.)**

ṢAṄKARA TUKĀRĀMA ṢĀLIGRĀM. लावण्या भाग २ रा राम जोशि [Lāvaṇyā. A collection of lāvaṇī poems by celebrated Marathi poets. Part II. containing the songs of Rāma Joṣī, with a biographical sketch of the life of the poet.] pp. xxi. 45, *lith.* पुणें १८७७ [*Poona,* 1877.] 8°.
Wanting pt. I. which contains the poems of Ananta Phandi.
14140. c. 9(2.)

SANMATIDĀSA. *See* NĀNĀ KOḶEKAR, also called SANMATIDĀSA.

SARASVATI GAṄGĀDHARA. अथ श्रीगुरुचरित्र प्रारंभः [Gurucharitra. A poem in 53 chapters, containing various mythological stories, accounts of miracles ascribed to saints, and popular legends.] *Lith.* पुणें १७८४ [*Poona,* 1862.] *obl.* 8°. **14137. e. 5.**

—— [Another edition. Edited by Janārdana Mahādeva Gurjar, and Gaṅgādhara Gopāla Patkī, with an introductory chapter containing a summary of each chapter of the poem.] मुंबई १७९७ [*Bombay,* 1875.] *obl.* 8°. **14137. e. 8.**

—— [Another edition.] ff. 362. अलिबाग १८०२ [*Alibagh,* 1881.] *obl.* 12°. **14140. a. 23.**

—— [Another edition.] *Lith.* मुंबई १८८२ [*Poona,* 1882.] *obl.* 8°. **14140. c. 29.**

ṢĀRṄGADHARA, *Son of Dāmodara.* संस्कृत शार्ङ्गधर वैद्यकग्रंथ याचे मराठी भाषांतर [Ṣārṅgadharasaṃhitā. A Sanskrit work on therapeutics, with Chintāmaṇi's Marathi commentary.] pp. xv. 170, x. 196, xii. 133. मुंबई १८५४ [*Bombay,* 1854.] 4°. **14043. d. 4.**

—— [Another edition.] pp. xii. 176, x. 218, xii. 158, *lith.* पुणें १८७७ [*Poona,* 1877.] 4°. **14043. d. 28.**

SARVASAṄGRAHA. सर्वसंग्रह [Sarvasaṅgraha. A Marathi anthology, containing selections from the works of celebrated poets. Edited, with notes, by Mādhava Chandrobā.] *Lith.* मुंबई १७८४-८५ [*Bombay,* 1862-63.] 8°.
Imperfect; consisting of pt. II. and III. and fragmentary portions of other parts. **14137. e. 4.**

SAVĀĪ. सवाई [Savāī. Didactic verses.] ff. 6, *lith.* मुंबई १७७९ [*Bombay,* 1857.] *obl.* 12°. **14140. a. 6(10.)**

SHĀHJĪ PRATĀPA SIṂHA, *Mahārājā.* *See* SHĀHŪ III., *Raja of Satara.*

SHĀHŪ I., *Raja of Satara.* [*Life.*] *See* MALHĀR RĀMARĀVA CHIṬṆĪS. **थोरले शाहू महाराज यांचें चरित्र** [Thorle Shāhū Mahārāja yāṉcheṉ charitra.]

SHĀHŪ II., *Raja of Satara.* [*Life.*] *See* MALHĀR RĀMARĀVA CHIṬṆĪS. **श्रीमंत छत्रपती धाकटे रामराजे** *etc.* [An account of the lives of Rāmarājā and Shāhū II.]

SHĀHŪ III., *Raja of Satara.* **ब्रम्हस्मृती ॥ महाराष्ट्र आणि हिंदी भाषेंत** [Brahmasmṛiti. A collection of Brahmist prayers and hymns, and rules for daily duties and worship. Partly in Marathi, and partly in Hindi.] pp. 263. **पुणें १८८३** [*Poona*, 1883.] 8°. **14137. b. 12.**

SHAKSPERE (WILLIAM). Commedy [*sic*] of errors. **कामेडी आफ एरर्स अथवा भ्रांतिकृत चमत्कार** [Bhrāntikṛita chamatkāra.] pp. 74. **अकोला १८७८** [*Akola*, 1878.] 8°. **14140. f. 18(2.)**

—— Othello, a drama by Shakespeare, translated into Maráthí by Ráv Sáheb Mahádev Govind Shástrí Kolhatkar. (**यथेच्छो**). pp. iii. 220. iv. *Bombay*, 1867. 12°. **14140. e. 10.**

SHANKARA SHÂSTRÎ GOKHALE. *See* ṢAṄKARA ṢĀSTRĪ GOKHALE.

SHANKAR JOSHÍ WYAWAHARE. *See* ṢAṄKARA JOṢĪ VYAVAHĀRE.

SHANKAR P. PANDIT. *See* ṢAṄKARA PĀṆḌURAṄGA PAṆḌITA.

SHIVAJI. *See* ṢIVĀJĪ, *Raja of Satara.*

SHIVARÁM SHÁSTRÍ PÁLANDE. *See* ṢIVARĀMA ṢĀSTRĪ PĀḶANDE.

SHRIKRISHNA SHASTRI TALEKAR. *See* ṢRĪKṚISHṆA ṢĀSTRĪ TAḶEKAR.

SIMEON BENJAMIN. *See* BENJAMIN (S.)

SĪTĀRĀMA BALLĀLA MAHĀJAN. **मल्लविद्या प्रकाशक** [Mallavidyā prakāṣaka. A treatise on the native mode of wrestling. Second edition.] pp. viii. 110. **पुणें १८८५** [*Poona*, 1885.] 12°. **14139. a. 32(4.)**

SĪTĀRĀMA NARAHARA ḌHAVḶE. **बाल शिवाजी नाटक** [Bāla Ṣivājī nāṭaka. A drama on the boyhood of Ṣivājī.] pp. 60, ii. **रत्नागिरी १८८४** [*Ratnagiri*, 1884.] 8°. **14140. f. 2(4.)**

SĪTĀRĀMA PANTA. **विधवाविवाह संहारसार** [Vidhavāvivāha saṃhārasāra. A treatise on widow-marriage. Sanskrit text, with a Marathi commentary.] pp. 27, *lith.* **रत्नागिरि १८६९** [*Ratnagiri*, 1869.] 8°. **14039. b. 8.**

SĪTĀRĀMA RĀMACHANDRA GAIKVĀḌ. **विजापुर वर्णन.** [Bijāpur-varṇana. A description, historical and topographical, of the city of Bijapur.] **पुणें १८८४** [*Poona*, 1884.] 12°. **14139. d. 27.**

—— **पुणें शहर.** [Puṇeṉ shahr. A descriptive account of the city of Poona.] 2 pt. **पुणें १८८६** [*Poona*, 1886.] 12°. **14139. d. 26.**

SĪTĀRĀMA RĀVAJĪ JUNNARKAR. Purram, Dhurma, Tutwa, or Principle of best Religion [according to the tenets of Vedanta philosophy.] **परमधर्मतत्व** pp. v. iii. 117. **मुंबई १८६२** [*Bombay*, 1862.] 12°. **14139. c. 10(2.)**

SĪTĀRĀMA VIṢVANĀTHA PAṬAVARDHANA. Description of the Púna Collectorate, by Rao Sahib Sitaram Vishvanath Patavardhan. (**पुणें जिल्हाचें वर्णन**) pp. 32. *Bombay*, 1875. 12°. **14139. d. 15(1.)**

—— Marathi Modi First Book. Compiled by Rao Sahib Sitaram Vishvanath Patavardhan. (**मोडीचें पहिलें पुस्तक.**) [Moḍīcheṉ pahileṉ pustaka.] pp. 106, *lith. Bombay*, 1875. 12°. **14140. g. 25(1.)**

—— Second edition. pp. 106, *lith. Bombay* 1877. 12°. **14140. g. 25(2.)**

—— [Third edition.] pp. 55, *lith.* **मुंबई १८८०** [*Bombay*, 1880.] 8°. **14140. h. 22(1.)**

—— [Fourth edition.] pp. 68, *lith.* **मुंबई १८८२** [*Bombay*, 1882.] 8°. **14140. h. 13(3.)**

—— Modi Second Book by Rao Sahib Sitaram V. Patavardhan ... **मोडी दुसें पुस्तक.** [Moḍī dusreṉ pustaka.] Second edition. pp. 106, *lith.* **मुंबई १८८०** [*Bombay*, 1880.] 8°. **14140. h. 22(2.)**

—— Modi Third Reading-book (**मोडी तिसें पुस्तक.**) [Moḍī tisreṉ pustaka.] pp. viii. 208, *lith. Bombay*, 1880. 8°. **14140. h. 24.**

ṢIVĀJĪ, *Raja of Satara.* [*Life.*] *See* KṚISHṆAJĪ ANANTA. **शिवछत्रपतीचें चरित्र.** [Ṣivachhatrapatīcheṉ charitra.]

—— *Life.* *See* KRISHṆAJĪ ANANTA. The life and exploits of Shivaji. Translated into English.

ṢIVĀJĪ, *Son of Sambhājī.* See SHĀHŪ I., *Raja of Satara.*

ṢIVARĀMA GAṆAPATARĀVA BĀBRAS. *See* GĀṆESA MOREṢVARA SOVANĪ तुर्क व रशियन लोकांचे लढाईचा इतिहास. [Turk va Raṣiyan lokāñche laḍhāīchā itihāsa. An account of the Turco-Russian war of 1877-78. Compiled with the assistance of Ṣ. G. B.] [1880.] 8°. **14139. e. 20.**

ṢIVARĀMA HARĪ SĀṬHE. *See* INDIA.—*Legislative Council.* दिवाणी काम चालविण्याचे रीतीविषयींचा कायदा. [The Code of Civil Procedure. Compiled with the assistance of Ṣ. H. S.] [1877.] 8°. **14137. g. 8.**

ṢIVARĀMA ṢĀSTRĪ PĀḶANDE. *See* JAYADEVA. Prasannrághava. A drama ... translated from Sanskrit into Maráthí, by Shivarám Shástrí Pálande. 1859. 12°. **14140. f. 22.**

ṢIVARĀMA SVĀMĪ. *See* ṢAṄKARA ĀCHĀRYA. शंकराचार्यकृत हस्तामलकग्रंथाचें ... भाषांतर [Hastāmalaka. Translated into verse by Ṣ. Sv.] [1878. *etc.*] 8°. **14072. d. 37.**

—— अथ श्री लघुवाक्यवृत्ति प्रारंभः [Laghuvākyavṛitti. With a Marathi commentary by Ṣ. Sv.] [1883.] 12°. **14048. b. 15.**

SOCRATES, *the Philosopher. Life.* *See* ROLLIN (C.) The life of Socrates translated ... by Krishna Shastree Chiplonker.

SOKAR BĀPŪJĪ TRILOKEKAR. हरिश्चंद्र नाटक. [Hariṣchandra nāṭaka. A drama on the story of king Hariṣchandra.] pp. ii. 85. viii. मुंबई १८८० [*Bombay*, 1880.] 12°. **14140. a. 25.**

SOḶĀ SOMVĀR. अथ सोळा सोमवार कथा प्रारंभ [Soḷā somvār kathā. Verses on the celebration of religious rites to Ṣiva and Pārvatī, on sixteen Mondays in the year.] ff. 14, *lith.* मुंबई १९८२ [*Bombay*, 1861.] *obl.* 16°. **14140. a. 7.**

—— [Another edition.] ff. 10, *lith.* मुंबई १९८७ [*Bombay*, 1865.] *obl.* 16°. **14137. c. 11(4.)**

—— [Another edition.] ff. 7, *lith.* पुणें १८९९ [*Poona*, 1877.] *obl.* 12°. **14140. a. 9(16.)**

SOOBAJEE BAPOO. *See* RĀMACHANDRA SŪBAJĪ BĀPŪ.

SOPĀNADEVA. श्री सोपानदेवाचे अभंग प्रारंभ [Abhangas.] *See* JÑĀNADEVA. श्री ज्ञानदेवाचा गाथा [Jñānadevāchā gāthā.] [1877.] 8°. **14140. c. 23.**

SPHUṬA ĀRYĀ. अथ स्फुट आर्या व श्लोक प्रारंभः [Sphuṭa āryā va ṣloka. Miscellaneous verses, and hymns of praise to different deities.] pp. 23, *lith.* मुंबई १९८६ [*Bombay*, 1864.] 12°. **14140. a. 13(5.)**

SPHUṬA JYOTISHA. अथ ज्योतिषग्रंथ प्रारंभः [Sphuṭa jyotisha. [An astrological fortune teller. Sanskrit text, with a Marathi commentary. Fourth edition.] pp. 54, *lith.* मुंबई १८५६ [*Bombay*, 1859.] 8°. **14054. b. 2.**

—— [Another edition.] pp. 47, *lith.* मुंबई १९८७ [*Bombay*, 1864.] 12°. **14053. a. 2.**

ṢRĪDATTA. श्रीदत्तबोध [Ṣrīdattabodha. A commentary on Ṣrīdatta's philosophical poems.] pp. ii. 138. ii. पुणें १९९७ [*Poona*, 1875.] 8°. **14140. c. 16.**

ṢRĪDHARA. अथ बभ्रुवाहन आख्यान प्रारंभः [Babhruvāhana ākhyāna. A poem on the exploits of Babhruvāhana, son of Arjuna. Taken from the seventh chapter of the Āṣvamedhikaparva of the Pāṇḍavapratāpa.] ff. 10, *lith.* मुंबई १९८४ [*Bombay*, 1862.] *obl.* 8°.

Fol. 4 is erroneously repeated in pagination.

14140. b. 6(2.)

—— [Another edition.] ff. 10, *lith.* मुंबई [*Bombay*, 1864.] *obl.* 8°. **14140. c. 13(1.)**

—— [Another edition.] ff. 10, *lith.* १९९७ [*Bombay*, 1875.] *obl.* 8°. **14140. c. 5(3.)**

—— [Another edition.] ff. 8, *lith.* मुंबई १९९८ [*Bombay*, 1877.] *obl.* 8°. **14140. c. 20.**

—— अथहरिविजय प्रारंभः [Harivijaya. A poem in 36 chapters, on the life and exploits of Vishṇu, in his incarnation as Kṛishṇa.] *Lith.* मुंबई १९८३ [*Bombay*, 1861.] *obl. fol.* **14140. d. 5.**

—— [Another edition.] *Lith.* पुणें १९८७ [*Poona*, 1865.] *obl.* 4°. **14140. d. 10(1.)**

—— [Revised edition, with notes.] मुंबई १८८० [*Bombay*, 1880.] *obl.* 4°. **14140. d. 17.**

—— [Another edition.] *Lith.* पुणें १८८१ [*Poona*, 1881.] *obl.* 4°. **14140. d. 18.**

—— अथ श्रीकृष्णजन्माध्याय प्रारंभः [Kṛishṇajauma. A poem on the birth of Kṛishṇa, being the third chapter of Ṣrīdhara's Harivijaya.] ff. 13, *lith.* मुंबई १९८४ [*Bombay*, 1862.] *obl.* 8°.

14140. b. 6(3.)

ṢRĪDHARA. [Kṛishṇajanma. Another edition.] ff. 6, *lith.* [*Bombay ?*, 1865.] *obl.* 4°. **14140. d. 8.**

—— अथ श्रीकृष्णजयंती प्रारंभः ॥ [Another edition, under the title Kṛishṇajayantī.] ff. 11, *lith.* मुंबई १८७७ [*Bombay*, 1877.] *obl.* 8°. **14140. c. 18.**

—— अथ पांडवप्रताप प्रारंभः [Pāṇḍavapratāpa. A poem, in 64 chapters, on the Mahābhārata account of the wars between the Pāṇdavas and Kauravas.] *Lith.* [*Bombay*, 1860 ?] *obl.* 4°. **14140. d. 2.**

—— [Another edition.] *Lith.* मुंबई १८८५ [*Bombay*, 1863.] *obl. fol.* **14140. d. 9.**

—— [Another edition.] *Lith.* मुबई १८८५ [*Bombay*, 1863.] *obl.* 4°. **14140. d. 7.**

—— अथ पांडुरंगमाहात्म्य प्रारंभः [Pāṇḍuraṅgamāhātmya. A poem, in 10 chapters, in praise of the god Pāṇḍuraṅga, or Viṭhobā of Pandharpur.] *Lith.* मुंबई १८८३ [*Bombay*, 1861.] *obl.* 8°. **14140. b. 6(1.)**

—— [Another edition.] *Lith.* पुणें [*Poona*, 1870 ?] *obl.* 12°.
Imperfect; wanting ff. 12–15. **14137. c. 16(1.)**

—— श्रीपंढरीमाहात्म्य प्रारंभ [Paṇḍharīmāhātmya. Another edition, under a different title.] ff. 62, *lith.* पुणें १८८० [*Poona*, 1880.] *obl.* 12°. **14137. c. 16(2.)**

—— अथ पांडुरंगमाहात्म्य प्रारंभः [Another edition.] [*Bombay*, 1881.] *obl.* 12°. **14140. a. 24.**

—— अथ श्रीरामविजय प्रारंभः [Rāmavijaya. A poem, in 40 chapters, on the life and exploits of Rāma. With illustrations.] *Lith.* मुंबई १८८२ [*Bombay*, 1860.] *obl. fol.* **14137. ff. 3.**

—— [Another edition.] *Lith.* मुंबई १८८६ [*Bombay*, 1864.] *obl.* 4°. **14140. d. 11.**

—— अथ लहूकुशाख्यान प्रारंभः [Lahūkuśākhyāna. The story of Lava and Kuṣa, sons of Rāma, being chapters 37 to 39 of Śrīdhara's Rāmavijaya.] ff. 31, *lith.* मुंबई १८८४ [*Bombay*, 1862.] *obl.* 8°. **14140. b. 6(4.)**

—— [Another edition.] ff. 26, *lith.* मुंबई [*Bombay*, 1864.] *obl.* 8°. **14140. c. 5(2.)**

—— अथ लवकुशाख्यान प्रारंभः ॥ [Another edition.] ff. 28. १९०७ [*Bombay*, 1875.] *obl.* 8°. **14140. c. 13(2.)**

—— अथ लहूकुशाख्यान प्रारंभः [Another edition.] ff. 24, *lith.* मुं० १९०० [*Bombay*, 1877.] *obl.* 8°. **14140. c. 21.**

ṢRĪDHARA. सावित्री आख्यान [Sāvitrī ākhyāna. A poem on the Mahābhārata story of Sāvitrī.] ff. 20. मुंबई १९१९ [*Bombay*, 1857.] *obl.* 12°. **14140. a. 6(11.)**

—— अथ शिवलीलामृत प्रारंभः ॥ [Ṣivalīlāmṛita. A poem, in 14 chapters, on Ṣiva and Ṣiva-worship.] *Lith.* मुंबई १८८३ [*Bombay*, 1861.] *obl.* 8°. **14137. d. 11.**

—— [Another edition.] *Lith.* पुणे १८८४ [*Poona*, 1862.] *obl.* 8°. **14140. c. 5(1.)**

—— [Another edition.] *Lith.* मुबई १८९७ [*Bombay*, 1875.] *obl.* 8°. **14137. e. 3(2.)**

—— [Another edition. Revised, and containing a glossary of difficult words, by Rāvajī Ṣrīdhara Gondhaḷekar.] *Lith.* पुणे १९०७ [*Poona*, 1875.] *obl.* 8°. **14140. c. 13(3.)**

—— [Another edition.] मुंबई १८७७ [*Bombay*, 1877.] *obl.* 8°. **14140. c. 26.**

—— [Another edition.] *Lith.* मुंबई १९०० [*Bombay*, 1877.] *obl.* 8°. **14140. c. 22.**

—— *See* DĀMODARA EKANĀTHA PĀṬASKAR. सीमंतिनी नाटक. [Sīmantinī nāṭaka. A drama, founded on an episode of Ṣrīdhara's Ṣivalīlāmṛita.] [1881.] 12°. **14140. a. 8(2.)**

ṢRĪKṚISHṆA RAGHUNĀTHA ṢĀSTRĪ TAḶEKAR. A Sanscrit grammar, compiled in Marathi, for the use of Sanscrit students in Government High Schools and Colleges, by Shrikrishna Raghunáth Shástri Taḷekar. (संस्कृत व्याकरण) [Saṃskṛita vyākaraṇa.] pp. iii. iv. iii. 463, ix. xiv. *Bombay*, 1866. 8°. **14140. i. 3.**

ṢRĪKṚISHṆA ṢĀSTRĪ TAḶEKAR. *See* PARAṢURĀMA PANTA GODBOLE. Selections from the Maráṭhí poets .... New edition, revised and annotated by Shrikrishna Shástri Taḷekar. 1878. 8°. **14140. b. 12.**

ṢṚIṄGĀRIKA SPHUṬAṢLOKA. शृंगारिक स्फुट श्लोक [Ṣṛiṅgārika sphuṭaṣloka. Erotic verses.] pp. 21, *lith.* मुंबई १९८५ [*Bombay*, 1863.] 12°. **14140. a. 13(3.)**

ṢRĪPATI RAGHUNĀTHABOVĀ BHIṄGĀRKAR. *See* RAGHUNĀTHABOVĀ BHIṄGĀRKAR.

STAPLEY (L. A.) Part I. of a series of graduated translation exercises, English-Marathi, Marathi-English, with rules and remarks, *etc.* *Bombay*, 1874. 8°. **12906. g. 21.**

STEVENSON (JOHN) *D.D., of the Scotch Mission, Bombay.* Historical sketch of the different systems of speculative philosophy .... काल्पनीक विज्ञानाविषयींचें संक्षेपेंकरून कथन [Kālpanika vijñānavishayeṇ.] pp. 57. *Engl.* and *Mar.* १८५२ *Bombay*, [1852.] 12°.
One of the Bombay Tract and Book Society's Series.
14139. c. 6(1.)

—— The principles of English grammar ... इंग्लिश भाषेचा व्याकरणाची मूळपीठिका मराठी भाषेंत लिहिली, *etc.* Second edition. pp. 127, *lith.* *Bombay*, 1833. 8°. **14140. i. 2.**

STORIES. Instructive stories for children. मुलांसाठीं बोधाच्या गोष्टी [Mulāṇsāṭhīṇ bodhāchyā goshṭī.] Fifth edition. pp. 60. मुंबई १८४९ [*Bombay*, 1849.] 12°.
No. 25 of the Bombay Tract and Book Society's Series.
14140. g. 2(1.)

—— Moral stories. सदाचरणाच्या गोष्टी [Sadācharaṇāchyā goshṭī.] pp. 98. मुंबई १८३५ [*Bombay*, 1835.] 8°.
No. 31 of the Bombay Tract and Book Society's Series.
14137. b. 5(4.)

STRĪVIDYĀ. स्त्रीविद्या वैचित्र्यदर्शन प्रहसन [Strīvidyā vaichitryadarṣana prahasana. A farce, on the subject of female education. Second edition.] pp. 39. मुंबई १८८४ [*Bombay*, 1884.] 8°.
14140. f. 27.

SUBODHA PADEṆ. सुबोध पदें. भाग २ रा [Subodha padeṇ. Didactic poems.] Pt. II. pp. 45, *lith.* मुंबई १७९९ [*Bombay*, 1877.] 12°.
Wanting Pt. I. **14140. a. 21.**

SUDĀMA. सुदामचरित्र [Sudāma charitra. A poem on the story of Sudāma, a poor Brahman, who was raised to wealth by Kṛishṇa. Second edition.] pp. 31. मुंबई १७६९ [*Bombay*, 1847.] 16°.
14140. a. 1(2.)

—— [Another edition.] pp. 29, *lith.* मुंबई १७८४ [*Bombay*, 1862.] 12°. **14140. a. 4(7.)**

SUDARṢANA ṢAṢĪKALĀ. मनोरंजक सुदर्शन शशीकला [Sudarṣana Ṣaṣīkalā. A drama in three acts.] pp. 136. मुंबई १७९९ [*Bombay*, 1877.] 8°.
14140. f. 5.

ṢŪDRAKA. Mrichchhakatika. A drama in ten acts, translated from Sanskrit [of Ṣūdraka] into Maráṭhi by Parashurám Pant Gódbóle. (मृच्छकटिक नाटक) Second edition. pp. ix. 241. *Bombay*, 1881. 8°. **14140. f. 14.**

ṢUKADEVA. ज्योतिषसार ॥ हा ग्रंथ संस्कृत ग्रंथावरून जनार्दन भास्करभट्ट क्रमवंत यांणी महाराष्ट्र भाषेत ... नजर केला असे [Jyotishasāra. A treatise on astrology. Sanskrit text, with a commentary in Marathi by Janārdana Bhāskara Kramavanta] p. i. 8, 142, 82, *lith.* मुंबई १७८० [*Bombay*, 1858.] 4°. **14053. d. 4.**

—— [Another edition.] pp. viii. 186, *lith.* मुंबई १७८५ [*Bombay*, 1863.] 4°. **14053. d. 7.**

—— ज्योतिषरत्न [Jyotisharatna. A reprint of the preceding, with another title-page.]
14053. d. 8.

—— [Another edition.] pp. x. 110, 68, *lith.* पुणें १८८१ [*Poona*, 1881.] 8°. **14053. cc. 23.**

ṢUKASAPTATI. शुकबाहात्तरी [Ṣukabāhāttarī. A Marathi version of the Sanskrit Ṣukasaptati, or Tales of a parrot. Second edition.] pp. ii. 144. मुंबई १७७७ [*Bombay*, 1855.] 12°. **14139. f. 2.**

—— [Another edition.] pp. 118. पुणें १८६१ [*Poona*, 1861.] 8°. **14139. f. 5.**

SUKHA RAM JOSHEE. *See* SAKHARĀMA JOṢĪ.

ṢUKRA. श्री शुक्रनीति प्राकृत समश्लोकी सह *etc.* [Ṣukranīti. An anonymous collection of Sanskrit verses in four adhyāyas on various topics, extracted from the Nītiṣāstra ascribed to Ṣ., accompanied by a Marathi translation, entitled Samaṣlokī, by Vāsudevātmaja.] pp. i. ii. 307. अलीबाग [*Alibagh*, 1875 ?] 8°. **14076. d. 24.**

SULLIVAN (ROBERT) *LL.D.* Bhugol Khagol. An introduction to the study of Mathematical and Physical Geography; and an introduction to Astronomy: translated from Professor Sullivan's Geography, generalized, by Mahádeva Shástri Puránik. (भूगोल खगोल) Third edition. pp. viii. 185. *Bombay*, 1880. 12°. **14139. a. 45.**

SUSRUTA. *See* PĀṆḌURAṄGA GOPĀLA MANTRĪ. भारतवर्षीय वनौषधिसंग्रह *etc.* [Bhāratavarshīya vanaushadhisaṅgraha. A work on the medicinal properties of Indian plants, showing their uses according to the Sanskrit works of Susruta.] [1886.] 8°. **14137. h. 14.**

SVADEṢA HITECHCHHU. *See* HAUG (M.) A lecture and notices on the Vedas ... Translated by a Svadesh Hitechhu. [1863.] 8°.
14137. d. 5(1.)

—— The origin of Brahmanism and second lecture on the Vedas by Dr. Martin Haug ... Translated by a Swadesha Hitechhu. [1864.] 12°.
14139. c. 6(2.)

—— Remarks on the marriage of the Bráhmána girl, by a Swadesh Hitechhu ... ब्राम्हणकन्या विवाह विचार. pp. 28. मुंबई १७८५ [*Bombay*, 1864.] 12°.
14139. c. 11(1.)

SVADHARMA HITECHCHHU. *See* VEDAS.—Ṛigveda.—*Purushasūkta.* A commentary on Purushsúkta by Swadharma Hitechhu, *etc.* [1864.] 8°.
14010. b. 2.

SVĀDHYĀYA. स्वाध्याय अथवा प्राचीन आर्यविद्यांचा क्रम, विचार आणि परीक्षण [Svādhyāya. A treatise on the study of the Vedas, and a brief review of Sanskrit literature.] pp. xiv. ii. 326. नासिक १८०१ [*Nasik*, 1880.] 8°.
14137. d. 8.

SVAPNĀDHYĀYA. स्वप्नाध्याय [Svapnādhyāya. Sanskrit verses on the interpretation of dreams, with a Marathi translation.] pp. 23, *lith.* पुणें १८७८ [*Poona*, 1878.] 8°.
14053. b. 18(1.)

SWADESHA HITECHHU. *See* SVADEṢA HITECHCHHU.

SWEDBERG, afterwards SWEDENBORG (EMANUEL). *See* DĀDOBĀ PĀṆḌURAṄGA TARKHAḌKAR. A Hindu gentleman's reflections respecting the works of Swedenborg and the doctrines of the New Jerusalem Church, *etc.* [1881.] 12°. **14137. a. 10.**

SWIFT (JONATHAN) *Dean of St. Patrick's.* Gulliver's Travels. Part I. The voyage to Liliput. गलिव्हर याचा वृत्तांत. [Translated by Harikṛishṇa Dāmle.] pp. ii. 89. पुणें १८८० [*Poona*, 1880.] 12°.
14139. f. 23.

ṢYĀMĀ, *Kavi.* श्यामाकविकृत स्यमन्तकोपाख्यान [Syamantakopākhyānā. A poem on the jewel worn by Kṛishṇa on his wrist.] *See* PERIODICAL PUBLICATIONS.—*Poona.* काव्येतिहास-संग्रह [Kāvyetihāsa saṅgraha.] Vol. IX. No. 6. [1878, *etc.*] 8°.
14072. d. 37.

TALKAR (HĀĪM JOSEPH). हिंदुस्थानांत आल्यापासून बेने इस्राएल लोकांचा इतिहास [Bene Isrāel lokāṉchā itihāsa. An account of the Beni Israelites, and their appearance in India. Compiled by H. J. T. assisted by David Hāīm.] pp. ii. 73. xi. मुंबई १८७४ [*Bombay*, 1874.] 12°. **14139. d. 14.**

TALMUD.—*Appendix.* तलमुद. [Selections from the Talmud, translated by Rāmachandra Nārāyaṇa Nene from the English of H. Polano.] pp. viii. 431, vii. मुंबई १८८६ [*Bombay*, 1886.] 8°.
14137. b. 13.

TĀRĀBĀĪ ṢINDE. स्त्रीपुरुषतुलना [Strīpurushatulanā. A refutation of the popular oriental belief that woman is by nature more depraved and vicious than man.] pp. iii. 49. पुणें १८८२ [*Poona*, 1882.] 8°. **14139. c. 24.**

TARKHADKAR (N. D.) *See* NĀRĀYAṆA DĀDOBĀ TARKHAḌKAR.

TEMPLE (*Sir* RICHARD) *Bart., Governor of Bombay.* *See* BHĀLACHANDRA KṚISHṆA BHĀṬAVAḌEKAR. Public health .... [With an extract from an address delivered by Sir R. T. at the Grant Medical College.] 1879. 12°. **14137. ff. 3.**

TEN COMMANDMENTS. देवाच्या दाहा आज्ञा [Devāchyā dāhā ājñā.] Exposition of the Ten Commandments. Ninth edition. pp. 14. *Bombay*, 1841. 12°.
No. 3 of the Bombay Tract and Book Society's Series.
14137. a. 2(6.)

ṬHĀṆĀ. साष्टी उर्फ ठाण्याची बखर [Sāshṭī urf Ṭhāṇyāchī bakhar. The chronicles of the district of Ṭhāṇā.] *See* PERIODICAL PUBLICATIONS.—*Poona.* काव्येतिहास संग्रह [Kāvyetihāsa saṅgraha.] Vol. III. Nos. 2–6. [1878, *etc.*] 8°.
14072. d. 37.

ṬIKĀRĀMA. *See* PURĀṆAS.—Padmapurāṇa.—*Kapilagītā.* अथ कपिलगीता प्रारंभः [Kapilagītā. Accompanied by a Marathi commentary by Ṭ., called Paramānandalaharī.] [1880.] *obl.* 8°.
14016. d. 33(2.)

TĪN RĀJAKANYĀ. तीन राजकन्यांची गोष्ट [Tīn rājakanyāṉchī goshṭa, or The story of the three princesses. A tale illustrating the evils of keeping women too strictly in confinement.] pp. 52. मुंबई १८८५ [*Bombay*, 1885.] 8°.
14139. g. 17.

ṬĪPŪ SULṬĀN, *Nawab of Mysore.* *Memoir.* *See* RĀMACHANDRA RĀVA, *Panganūrī.* Memoirs of Hyder and Tippoo, *etc.*

TRANSMIGRATION. अनेकजन्मनिर्णय [Anekajanma-nirṇaya.] On Transmigration. Second edition. pp. 20. *Bombay*, 1877. 18°.

One of the Bombay Tract and Book Society's Series.

14137. a. 4(5.)

TRIMBAKARĀVA NĀRĀYAṆA RĀJMĀCHĪKAR. *See* INDIA.—*Legislative Council.* दिवाणी काम चालविण्याचे रीतीविषयींचा कायदा *etc.* [The Code of Civil Procedure, or Act No. X. of 1877. Compiled by T. N. R.] [1877.] 8°. **14137. g. 8.**

TRIMBAKA SAKHĀRĀMA ṢIRVALKAR. किमिया अथवा रसायन प्रयोग [Kimiyā. A short treatise on chemistry.] pp. 36. मुंबई १८८० [*Bombay*, 1880.] 16°. **14139. a. 33.**

—— A manual of small pox and vaccination by Trimbak Sakharam Shirvalkar. (मसूरिका व गोस्तनरोग संस्कार) [Masūrikā va gostanaroga saṃskāra.] pp. iii. iv. ii. 123. *Bombay*, 1879. 16°. **14137. ff. 5.**

TRYAMBAKA. त्र्यंबकी [Tryambakī. A treatise on medicine, in old Marathi verse. With a prose version by Kṛishṇa Ṣāstrī Bhāṭavaḍekar. Fourth edition.] pp. ii. ii. 36, *lith.* मुंबई १८६३ [*Bombay*, 1863.] 8°. **14137. h. 9.**

TUKĀRĀMA. [*Life.*] *See* MAHĪPATI. अथ श्रीतुकारामचरित्र प्रारंभः [Tukārāmacharitra.]

—— A complete collection of the poems of Tukáráma .... Edited by Vishṇu Parashurám Shástrí Paṇḍit, under the supervision of Śankar Páṇḍurang Paṇḍit, in two volumes .... to which is prefixed a life of the poet in English by Janárdan Sakhárám Gádgil. (With a complete index to the poems and a glossary of difficult words.) (तुकारामबाबाच्या अभंगांची गाथा *etc.*) 2 vol. *Bombay*, 1869–73. 8°. **14140. c. 14.**

—— तुकारामबाबाची गाथा [Tukārāma bābāchī gāthā. The poetical works of Tukārāma. Second edition.] pp. 1142. मुंबई १८०३ [*Bombay*, 1884.] 8°.

The pagination of the two volumes is continuous.

14140. c. 28.

—— अथ तुकारामाचे अभंग प्रारंभः [A collection of 173 abhaṅgas by Tukārāma. Followed by Tāṭīche abhaṅga of Jñānadeva. Fourth edition.] pp. 85, *lith.* पुणें १८६० [*Poona*, 1860.] 12°.

Wanting pp. 32–47. **14140. a. 4(6.)**

TUKĀRĀMA. [Fifth edition.] pp. 55, *lith.* पुणें १८६२ [*Poona*, 1862.] 8°. **14140. b. 9(2.)**

—— तुकारामकृत अभंग [A collection of 1305 of Tukārāma's abhaṅgas. Edited by Mādhava Chandrobā.] pp. 320. मुंबई १७८४ [*Bombay*, 1862.] 8°. **14140. c. 3.**

—— तुकारामकृत अभंग प्रारंभ [A collection of 56 abhaṅgas.] *See* MUKTĀBĀĪ. अथ मुक्ताबाईकृत ताटीचे अभंग प्रारंभः [Tāṭīche abhaṅga.] [1863.] 12°. **14140. a. 10(5.)**

—— तुकारामकृत बाळक्रीडेचे अभंग [Bāḷakrīḍeche abhaṅga. Abhaṅgas on the sports of the youthful Kṛishṇa.] pp. 53. मुंबई १७८१ [*Bombay*, 1859.] 8°. **14140. c. 2.**

—— तुकारामकृत ब्रम्हज्ञानपर अभंग [Brahmajñānapar abhaṅga. Religious poems on the true perception of Brahma.] pp. 34, *lith.* मुंबई १७९६ [*Bombay*, 1874.] 12°. **14140. a. 10(8.)**

—— अभंग एकादशीमहात्माचे [Ekādaṣīmāhātmāche abhaṅga. Verses on the celebration of the eleventh day of each half moon.] pp. 48, *lith.* मुंबई १७७० [*Bombay*, 1848.] 12°. **14140. a. 1(4.)**

—— अथ करुणापर अभंग [Karuṇāpar abhaṅga. Devotional songs. Second edition.] pp. 37, *lith.* पुणें १७९१ [*Poona*, 1871.] 12°. **14140. a. 11(4.)**

—— श्री तुकारामकृत नासिकेताख्यान प्रारंभ [Nāsiketākhyāna. The story of the saint Nāsiketa, and the revelations made to him by Yama of the bliss and torments of a future life. A poem, in 21 chapters.] मुंबई १८०४ [*Bombay*, 1883.] *obl.* 8°. **14140. c. 32.**

—— तुकारामकृत नित्यपाठाचे अभंग [Nityapāṭhāche abhaṅga. Devotional songs intended for daily use.] pp. 9, *lith.* मुंबई १७९६ [*Bombay*, 1874.] 12°. **14140. a. 10(7.)**

—— तुकारामकृत पत्रिकेचे अभंग [Patrikeche abhaṅga. Miscellaneous poems.] pp. 32, *lith.* १७८४ [*Bombay?*, 1862.] 12°. **14140. a. 12(2.)**

—— तुकारामाचे स्फुट अभंग [Sphuṭa abhaṅga. Pt. 1. A collection of 70 separate abhaṅgas.] pp. 32, *lith.* मुंबई १७८१ [*Bombay*, 1859.] 12°. **14140. a. 11(1.)**

TUKĀRĀMA. अथ तुकाराम स्वर्गारोहणाचे अभंग प्रारंभः [Tukārāma svargārohaṇāche abhaṅga. Verses said to have been composed by the poet Tukārāma as he was about to ascend into heaven. Second edition.] pp. 6, *lith.* पुणें १८७८ [*Poona*, 1878.] 12°. **14140. a. 12(12.)**

—— अथ तुकारामवैकुंठाचे अभंग प्रारंभः [Vaikuṇṭhāche abhaṅga. Verses on the paradise of Vishṇu.] pp. 8, *lith.* मुंबई १७८५ [*Bombay*, 1863.] 12°. **14140. a. 13(4.)**

—— अथ वस्त्रहरणाचे अभंग प्रारंभः [Vastraharaṇāche abhaṅga, also called Draupadī vastraharaṇa. A poem on the insult offered to Draupadī by Duryodhana.] pp. 9, *lith.* मुंबई १७८६ [*Bombay*, 1864.] 12°. **14140. a. 12(3.)**

TUKĀRĀMA NATHUJĪ. Vishnupunt. रे. विष्णु भास्कर करमरकर यांचें चरित्र [Vishṇu Bhāskara Karmarkar yāṇcheṇ charitra. A short account of the life of Vishṇu Bhāskara Karmarkar, a Brahman convert, and Pastor of the American Mission at Ahmadnagar.] pp. viii. 96. १८८४ *Satara*, [1884.] 12°. **14139. d. 28.**

UDDHĀRAMAHIMĀ. उद्धारमहिमा [Uddhāramahimā. Verses on the Christian method of salvation. Second edition.] pp. 21. *Bombay*, 1875. 16°. **14137. a. 14.**

UDDHAVA CHIDGHANA. ध्रुवाख्यान-प्रारंभः [Dhruvākhyāna. A poem on the legend of Dhruva, the polar star. Followed by a few abhaṅgas by Tukārāma.] pp. 13, *lith.* मुंबई १७८६ [*Bombay*, 1861.] 12°. **14114. a. 13(1.)**

—— [Another edition.] pp. 15. मुंबई [*Bombay*, 1870?] 16°. **14140. a. 5(3.)**

—— उद्धव चिद्घनकृत भगवद्गीता. [A metrical version of the Bhagavadgītā. Also Nāganātha charitra, Śuka Rambhā saṃvāda, and Mrityuñjaya charitra.] *See* PERIODICAL PUBLICATIONS.—*Poona.* काव्येतिहास-संग्रह [Kāvyetihāsa saṅgraha.] Vol. IV.-VI. and VIII. Nos. 9, 10. [1878, *etc.*] 8°. **14072. d. 37.**

UJAḶṆĪ. लहानमुलांकरितां उजळणीचें पाहिलें पुस्तक [Ujaḷṇīcheṇ pahileṇ pustaka. Marathi primer, containing the alphabet, multiplication and other useful tables.] pp. 24, *lith.* पुणें १८७७ [*Poona*, 1877.] 12°. **14140. g. 29.**

UNITED STATES OF AMERICA.—*Methodist Episcopal Church.* The shorter catechism [of the Methodist Episcopal Church.] लघु प्रश्नोत्तरावळी [Laghu praśnottarāvalī.] pp. 44. मुंबई १८७७ [*Bombay*, 1877.] 16°. **14137. a. 4(3.)**

VAIJANĀTHA ŚARMĀ. राजाप्रतापादित्याचें चरीत्र [Rājā Pratāpādityācheṇ charitra. The life of Raja Pratāpāditya.] pp. 128. श्रीरामपुर १८१६ [*Serampur*, 1816.] 12°. **14139. e. 1.**

VAKĀSURA. वकासुराची बखर [Vakāsurāchī bakhar. The story of the demon Vaka who was defeated by Krishṇa.] ff. 10, *lith.* मुंबई १९१८ [*Bombay*, 1856.] *obl.* 16°.

In the Modi character.

14140. a. 6(12.)

VĀLMĪKI. *See* MOROPANTA. अथ मयूरकृत मंत्ररामायण आर्या प्रारंभः [Mantrarāmāyaṇa āryā. A paraphrase of the Rāmāyaṇa in acrostic āryā metre.] [1860.] *obl.* 8°. **14137. e. 3(1.)**

—— *See* RĀMADĀSA SVĀMĪ. श्रीरामदासस्वामिकृत युद्धकांड. [A paraphrase in verse of the Yuddhakāṇḍa, Sundarakāṇḍa and Kishkindhyākāṇḍa of the Rāmāyaṇa.] [1878, *etc.*] 8°. **14072. d. 37.**

—— अथ महाराष्ट्र टीकासहिताद्भुतरामायणारंभः [Adbhutarāmāyaṇa, attributed to Vālmīki. Sanskrit text, with a Marathi translation.] *See* PURĀṆAS. समूलपुराणार्थप्रकाश ° Pt. 1-12. [1884, *etc.*] 8°. **14016. d. 42.**

VĀMANA, *the Poet.* *See* VĀMANA PAṆḌITA.

VĀMANA ĀBĀJĪ MOḌAK. बालविवाहाच्या संबंधानें हिताहित विचार [Bālavivāhāchyā sambandhāneṇ hitāhita vichāra. A lecture on child-marriage.] pp. 16. *See* BOMBAY, *City of.—Hindu Union Club.* हेमंत व्याख्यानमाला [Hemanta vyākhyānamālā.] Vol. II. No. 2. [1886, *etc.*] 8°. **14139. c. 26.**

VĀMANA ĀTMĀRĀMA BHĀṆḌĀRĪ. संगीत कामकंदला नाटक [Saṅgīta Kāmakandalā nāṭaka. A drama in five acts, founded on the 20th tale of the Singhāsan Battīsī, or Stories of king Vikramāditya.] pp. ii. 118. मुंबई १८८५ [*Bombay*, 1885.] 12°. **14140. e. 3.**

VĀMANA DĀJĪ OK. *See* KĀŚIRĀVA RĀJEŚVARA GUPTA. नागपूरकर भोसल्याची बखर [Nāgpūrkar Bhoṇsalyāchī bakhar. Edited with notes by V. D. O.] [1878, *etc.*] 8°. **14072. d. 37.**

VĀMANA DHOṆḌADEVA KARVE. Satarwadya [or instructions on the Indian guitar] by Waman Dhonddew Karway (सतारवाद्य) pp. 35. *Alibag,* 1879. 12°. **14130. a. 31.**

VĀMANA EKANĀTHA ṢĀSTRĪ KEMKAR. *See* RĀVAJĪ ṢRĪDHARA GONDHAḶEKAR. कीर्तनतरंगिणी [Kīrtana-taraṅgiṇī. Pt. II. and III. by V. E. Ṣ. K.] [1885, *etc.*] 8°. **14140. c. 37.**

—— शिशुपालवधनाटक [Ṣiṣupālavadha nāṭaka. A drama on the slaughter of Ṣiṣupāla by Krishṇa.] pp. 118, *lith.* पुणें १८८१ [*Poona,* 1881.] 8°. **14140. f. 1(6.)**

VĀMANA GAṆEṢA JOṢĪ KEḶṢĪKAR. संगीत बलिसत्वदर्शन [Saṅgīta Balisatva-darṣana, also called Vāmanacharitra nāṭaka. A drama in eleven scenes on the story of Vāmana, the fifth incarnation of Vishṇu, and the demon Bali.] pp. 64. [*Ratnagiri,* 1884.] 12°. **14140. e. 4(1.)**

VĀMANA GOPĀLA KEḶKAR. कालिदास चातुर्यनाटक [Kālidāsa chāturya nāṭaka. A drama in three acts on the life of the poet Kālidāsa.] pp. 40. मालवण १८७८ [*Malwa,* 1877.] 8°. **14140. f. 1(3.)**

VĀMANA PAṆḌITA. [*Life.*] *See* BĀLAKṚISHṆA MALHĀR HAṂSA. प्रख्यात महापंडित ... व कवि वामनपंडित *etc.* [Prakhyāta Vāmana Paṇḍita.]

—— *See* JAGANNĀTHA PAṆḌITARĀJA. गंगालहरी [Gaṅgālaharī. With V. P.'s Marathi paraphrase.] 1879. 8°. **14033. a.**

—— *See* MAHĀBHĀRATA.—*Bhagavadgītā.* अथ श्रीगीतार्थबोधिनीप्रारंभः [Bhagavadgītā. With metrical paraphrases by V. P.] [1861.] 8°. **14065. d. 15.**

—— [*Life.*] *See* MOROPANTA. मोरोपंतकृत वामनचरित्र [Vāmanacharitra.]

—— *See* PURĀṆAS.—Bhāgavatapurāṇa.—*Brahmastuti.* वामनकृत ब्रह्मस्तुतिची टीका ॥ [Brahmastuti. With a commentary by V. P.] [1842.] 8°. **14016. c. 4.**

—— *See* ṢAṄKARA ĀCHĀRYA. अथ अपरोक्षानुभूति प्रारंभः ॥ [Aparokshānubhūti. With a metrical translation, called Samaṣlokī, by V. P.] [1856.] 8°. **14048. c. 27.**

VĀMANA PAṆḌITA. वामन पंडितकृत श्लोक [Vāmana Paṇḍitakṛita ṣloka. The poetical works of V. P. Edited by Mādhava Chandrobā, assisted by Paraṣurāma Panta Godbole.] 3 pt. pp. 472. मुंबई १७८२–८५ [*Bombay,* 1860–63.] 8°.

Pt. I., containing poems on the life of Kṛishṇa, has a distinct title, Kṛishṇacharitra. **14140. c. 15.**

—— वामनपंडित-कृत प्रकरणें [Vāmana Paṇḍitakṛita prakaraṇeṇ. A collection of miscellaneous poems by V. P. With a life of the poet, and critical and explanatory notes.] *See* PERIODICAL PUBLICATIONS.—*Poona.* काव्येतिहास-संग्रह [Kāvyetihāsa saṅgraha.] Vol. I.–III. [*Poona,* 1878, *etc.*] 8°. **14072. d. 37.**

—— वामन पंडितकृत जयद्रथवध [Jayadratha-vadha and Saṅkalita Rāmāyaṇa. Two poems by V. P.] *See* PERIODICAL PUBLICATIONS.—*Poona.* काव्येतिहास संग्रह [Kāvyetihāsa saṅgraha.] Vol. VI. No. 11. [1878, *etc.*.] 8°. **14072. d. 37.**

—— अजामिळ आख्यान [Ajāmiḷākhyāna. A poem on the story of the Brahman Ajāmiḷa, taken from the Ṣāntiparva of the Mahābhārata.] pp. 13. मुंबई १७७१ [*Bombay,* 1849.] 16°. **14140. a. 3(1.)**

—— [Another edition.] pp. 15. मुंबई १७९६ [*Bombay,* 1874.] 16°. **14140. a. 10(10.)**

—— वामनकृत भरतभाव [Bharatabhāva. A poem on the affection shown by Bharata to his brother Rāma, when the latter was exiled from Ayodhyā.] pp. 28, *lith.* मुंबई १७८१ [*Bombay,* 1859.] 12°. **14140. a. 10(1.)**

—— श्री गजेंद्रमोक्ष [Gajendramoksha. An episode of the Mahābhāratā in verse.] pp. 8, *lith.* मुंबई १७७० [*Bombay,* 1848.] 32°. **14137. c. 3(3.)**

—— अथ सीतास्वयंवर प्रारंभः [Sītāsvayaṃvara. A poem on the marriage of Sītā to Rāma.] pp. 29, *lith.* मुंबई १७८६ [*Bombay,* 1864.] 12°. **14140. a. 12(4.)**

—— शिवस्तुती [Ṣivastuti. A hymn of praise to Ṣiva. Second edition.] pp. 13. मुंबई १७७७ [*Bombay,* 1855.] 16°. **14137. c. 3(4.)**

—— [Another edition.] ff. 7. मुंबई १७८४ [*Bombay,* 1862.] *obl.* 16°. **14137. c. 2(5.)**

—— [Another edition.] pp. 6, *lith.* १८७८ [*Poona,* 1878.] 12°. **14140. a. 10(16.)**

VĀMANA PAṆḌITA. अथ सूर्यस्तुती प्रारंभ [Sūryastuti. A hymn of praise to the Sun.] ff. 3, *lith.* मुंबई १७८५ [*Bombay*, 1863.] *obl.* 16°. **14137. c. 2(7.)**

VĀMANA ŚĀSTRĪ ISLĀMPŪRKAR. *See* KAMALĀKAR BHAṬṬA, *Son of* RĀMAKṚISHṆA BHAṬṬA. शूद्रकमलाकर *etc.* [Śūdrakamalākara. With a Marathi version by V. Ś. I.] [1880.] 8°. **14033. bb. 2.**

VASTĀD MURĀRBĀ GONVEKAR. संगीत संजीवनी [Saṅgīta sañjīvanī. A treatise on Indian vocal music.] pp. vi. 136. पुणें १८८७ [*Poona*, 1887.] 12°. **14139. a. 37.**

VĀSUDEVA, *Kavi.* अथ कैकेयीचे श्लोक आणि श्री पांडुरंगाचे श्लोक प्रारंभः [Kaikeyīcheśloka. A poem on the exile of Rāma through the instrumentality of his step-mother Kaikeyī.] pp. 6, *lith.* मुंबई १७९७ [*Bombay*, 1875.] 12°. **14140. a. 10(13.)**

VĀSUDEVA BĀḶAKṚISHṆA LOṬLĪKAR. जमाखर्चाची पद्धति [Jamākharchāchī paddhati. A treatise on the native method of book-keeping, in the form of questions and answers, with specimens of the different methods adopted.] ff. 4, 9, 4. रत्नागिरी १८७५ [*Ratnagiri*, 1875.] *obl.* 8°. **14140. g. 34.**

—— Jamákharcháchí paddhati, or Catechism on native account. Second edition. ff. 5, 9, 5. रत्नागिरी १८७६ [*Ratnagiri*, 1876.] *obl.* 8°. **14140. g. 35.**

—— Jamákharcháchí paddhati, or The native method of book-keeping, containing a series of questions and answers ... Third edition. ff. 8, 8, 5. रत्नागिरी १८७७ [*Ratnagiri*, 1877.] *obl.* 8°. **14140. g. 36.**

—— The native method of book-keeping, containing a series of questions and answers ... Fourth edition. pp. 50. मुंबई १८८० [*Bombay*, 1880.] 8°. **14140. h. 13(2.)**

VĀSUDEVA CHINTĀMAṆA BĀPAṬ. भद्रायुसत्वदर्शन नाटक [Bhadrāyusatvadarśana nāṭaka. A drama in five acts, treating chiefly on mythological subjects.] pp. 151, *lith.* मुंबई १७९९ [*Bombay*, 1877.] 8°. **14140. f. 18(1.)**

VĀSUDEVA GOPĀLA BHĀṆḌĀRKAR. स्त्रियांची खरी योग्यता [Striyāṇchī kharī yogyatā. A lecture on the real worth of women.] pp. 18. *See* BOMBAY, *City of.—Hindu Union Club.* हेमंत व्याख्यानमाला [Hemanta vyākhyānamālā.] Vol. III. No. 1. [1886, *etc.*] 8°. **14139. c. 26.**

VĀSUDEVA MOREŚVARA POTADĀR. आरती संग्रह [Āratī saṅgraha. A collection of 259 āratīs, or hymns of praise to Hindu deities. Compiled from various sources by V. M. P.] pp. 160. मुंबई १७९९ [*Bombay*, 1877.] 8°. **14140. b. 13.**

—— [Second edition, revised and enlarged.] pp. 257. मुंबई १८८० [*Bombay*, 1880.] 12°. **14140. a. 22.**

—— मोडी वचनसार [Moḍī vachanasāra. A reader and letter-writer in the Modi character.] 2 pt. *Lith.* मुंबई १७९९ [*Bombay*, 1877.] 12°.

Pt. I. is of the third edition.

14140. g. 24(3.)

—— [Another edition.] 2 pt. *Lith.* मुंबई १८८० [*Bombay*, 1880.] 12°.

Pt. I. is of the sixth, and pt. II. of the fourth edition.

14140. g. 25(4.)

—— [Another edition.] 3 pt. *Lith.* मुंबई १८८१-८२ [*Bombay*, 1881-82.] 8°. **14140. h. 26.**

—— [Another edition.] 3 pt. *Lith.* मुंबई १८८१-८५ [*Bombay*, 1881–85.] 8°.

Pt. I. is of the fifth, pt. II. of the third, and pt. III. of the fourth edition. **14140. h. 19.**

VĀSUDEVA MOREŚVARA POTADĀR and NĀRĀYAṆA MOREŚVARA KARANDĪKAR. हावडकृत इंग्रजी पहिल्या पुस्तकांतील मराठींत उच्चारार्थे सहित शब्दसंग्रह [Śabdasaṅgraha. A vocabulary of English words occurring in E. J. Howard's "English Primer," with their pronunciation and Marathi equivalents.] pp. 24. मुंबई १८७७ [*Bombay*, 1877.] 12°. **14140. g. 29(1.)**

VĀSUDEVA NĀRĀYAṆA ḌONGRE. संगीत इंद्रसभा नाटक [Saṅgīta Indrasabhā nāṭaka. A dramatical version of the Indrasabhā, a Hindustani fairy tale by Amānat.] pp. 41. मुंबई १८८३ [*Bombay*, 1883.] 8°. **14140. f. 11(2.)**

VĀSUDEVĀTMAJA. *See* ŚUKRA. श्री शुक्रनीति प्राकृत समश्लोकी सह [Śukranīti. With a Marathi translation in verse by V., entitled Samaślokī.] [1875?] 8°. **14076. d. 24.**

VĀSUDEVA VĀMANA ŚĀSTRĪ KHARE. गुणोत्कर्ष नाटक [Guṇotkarsha nāṭaka. A historical drama, in five acts, of the time of Śivājī.] pp. iv. 114. पुणें १८८५ [*Poona*, 1885.] 12°. **14140. e. 2.**

VĀSUDEVA VĀMANA ṢĀSTRĪ KHARE. [Guṇotkarsha nāṭaka. Second edition.] pp. 114. १८८६ [*Bombay*, 1886.] 12°. **14140. e. 8.**

VEDAS. Rigveda. त्रिविद्या त्रिगुणात्मिका १ भाग (The Threefold Science. The Jyotish udhyayu of the Vedu, or astronomical treatise appended to the sacred writing of the Hindoos.) [Containing Sūktas 1-35 of the first Maṇḍala of the Ṛigveda, with a paraphrase in Marathi.] pp. 68, 56, iii. i. *Bombay*, 1833. 4°. **14007. c. 1.**

—— The Vedârthayatna, or an attempt to interpret the Vedas. A Marâṭhī and an English translation of the Ṛigveda [by Ṣaṅkara Pāṇḍuraṅga Paṇḍita] with the original Saṁhitâ and Pada texts in Sanskṛit. (वेदार्थयत्न *etc.*) Vol. I.–IV.; Vol. V. pt. 1–9. *Bombay*, 1876–82. 8°.
Apparently no more published.
14007. c. 11.

—— *Purushasūkta.* A commentary [in Marathi] on Purushsúkta [Rigveda x. 90] by Swadharma Hitechhu. पुरुषसूक्तव्याख्या *etc.* [With the original Sanskrit text.] pp. i. 13. मुंबई १८६४ [*Bombay*, 1864.] 8°. *Title taken from the wrapper.*
14010. b. 2.

VESHADHĀRĪ PAÑJĀBĪ. वेषधारी पंजाबी [Veshadhārī Pañjābī. A tale of a Panjabi merchant and his vicious brother.] pp. 281, xi. मुंबई १८८६ [*Bombay*, 1886.] 12°. **14139. f. 25.**

VIJÑĀNEṢVARA. *See* Yājñavalkya. याज्ञवल्क्यस्मृति मिताक्षर व्यवहाराध्याय *etc.* [The Vyavahārādhyāya of Yājñavalkya's Smṛiti with V.'s Mitākshara, and a Marathi translation of both.] [1879.] 8°.
14038. d. 25.

—— Marathe translation of the Wyawahar adhyaya of the Mitakshara [of Vijñāneṣvara] and of the Dayabhaga of the Wyawahar Mayukh [of Nīlakaṇṭha Mīmāṃsakabhaṭṭa] executed by Raghunath Wittal Shastree Dantay [with a glossary of difficult terms]. मिताक्षरा व्यवहाराध्याय व मयूख दायभाग *etc.* १८४४ [*Bombay*, 1844.] 4°.
14137. g. 1.

—— Maráṭhi translation of the Wyawahárádhyáya of the Mitákshará... Revised and corrected by Shankar Joshí Wyawaháre. Second edition. pp. ii. lvi. 400, 83, xxii. *Bombay*, 1862. 8°.
14137. g. 3.

VIKRAMĀDITYA, *King of Ujjayinī.* *See* Vāmana Ātmārāma Bhaṇḍārī. संगीत कामकंदला नाटक [Saṅgīta Kāmakandalā nāṭaka. A drama, founded on the 20th tale of the Singhāsan Battīsī.] [1885.] 12°. **14140. e. 3.**

—— सिंहासन बत्तीसी [Singhāsan Battīsī, or The tales of king Vikramāditya, translated from the Hindi.] pp. 183. श्रीरामपुर १८१४ [*Serampur*, 1814.] 8°. **14139. g. 1.**

—— [Another edition.] pp. 144. मुंबई १९१८ [*Bombay*, 1855.] 12°. **14139. f. 4.**

—— [Another edition.] pp. 120. मुंबई १९८५ [*Bombay*, 1863.] 12°. **14139. f. 11(1.)**

—— [Another edition, in the Modi character.] pp. 97, *lith.* पुणें १८८१ [*Poona*, 1881.] 12°.
14139. f. 11(4.)

VINĀYAKA GOVINDA LIMAYE. Kavitartha mala, or rendering into prose verses in the Marathi Third Book, with annotations thereon. (कवितार्थमाला) Second edition. pp. 28. *Bombay*, 1881. 12°. **14140. g. 29(7.)**

—— उपयुक्त अक्षरलिपी व अंकलिपी [Upayukta aksharalipi va aṅkalipi. The alphabet, in Devanagari and Modi characters, with multiplication and other tables.] pp. 29, *lith.* रत्नागिरी १८८० [*Ratnagiri*, 1880.] 12°. **14139. a. 27(5.)**

—— [Third edition.] pp. 29, *lith.* रत्नागिरी १८८१ [*Ratnagiri*, 1881.] 12°. **14140. g. 7(6.)**

VINĀYAKA JANĀRDANA KĪRTANE. Jayapál. A drama, in five acts [on native social life]. (जयपाळ) pp. iii. 94. *Bombay*, 1865. 12°.
14140. f. 24.

—— नाटक थोरले माधवराव पेशवे यांजवर [Nāṭaka thorle Mādhava Rāva yāṇjvar. A drama, in four acts, on the administration of the Peshwa Mādhava Rāva I. Second edition.] pp. 57. मुंबई १८६४ [*Bombay*, 1864.] 12°. **14140. a. 15.**

VINĀYAKA KOṆḌADEVA OK. हिंदुस्थानाचा संक्षिप्त इतिहास [Hindusthānāchā saṃkshipta itihāsa. An abridged history of India.] pp. ii. 118. मुंबई १८६८ [*Bombay*, 1868.] 12°.
14139. d. 6.

VINĀYAKA KONDADEVA OK. A short history of India by Vináyak K. Oke. Fourth edition. pp. vi. 201. *Bombay*, 1875. 12°. **14139. d. 21.**

—— The life of Alexander the Great. Compiled from English works by Vinayak Konddeo Oke. (शिकंदर बादशाहाचें चरित्र) [Śikandar bādshāhcheṇ charitra.] pp. x. 287. *Bombay*, 1875. 12°. **14139. d. 17.**

—— The life of the Duke of Wellington. Compiled from English works by Vináyak Konddeo Oke. (ड्यूक आफ् वेलिंग्टन ह्याचें चरित्र) pp. viii. 126. *Bombay*, 1876. 12°. **14139. d. 13.**

—— Mahanmaṇimálá, or Readings in biography by Vináyak Kondadeo Oke. (महन्मणिमाला) pp. 162. *Bombay*, 1880. 8°. **14139. e. 19.**

VINĀYAKA NĀRĀYAṆA BHĀGAVATA. Murad the unlucky and Salaudin the lucky; a story translated from an English work by Vináyak Náráyan Bhágwat ... Revised by Krishna Shástri Chiplonkar. (दुर्दैवी मुराद व दैववान् सलाउदीन) [Durdaivī Murād va daivavān Salāudīn.] pp. iii. 94. *Poona*, 1862. 12°. **14139. f. 6.**

VINĀYAKA RĀVA. *See* CUNINGHAM (J. M.) A sanitary primer ... translated by Mr. Venayak Rao. 1880. 12°. **14137. ff. 2(2.)**

VINĀYAKA ŚĀSTRĪ ĀGĀŚĪ. *See* JANĀRDANA HARI ĀṬHALYE. शब्दसिद्धिनिबंध [Śabdasiddhinibandha. A manual of Marathi etymology by Janārdana Hari Āṭhalye, assisted by V. Ś. Ā.] [1868.] 12°. **14140. g. 8(2.)**

VINĀYAKA ŚĀSTRĪ DIVEKAR and GOVINDA VIṬHṬHALA MAHĀJAN. शब्दसिद्धिनिबंध [Śabdasiddhinibandha. A treatise on Marathi etymology and Sanskrit roots, by V. Ś. D. and G. V. M., assisted by Bāḷa Gaṅgādhara Jāmbhekar. Second edition.] pp. xiv. 84. मुंबई १८५९ [*Bombay*, 1859.] 12°. **14140. g. 8(1.)**

VINĀYAKA VIṬHṬHALA RĀNAḌE. *See* NILOBĀ RĀYA. श्रीनिळोबारायकृत अभंगाचा गाथा [Abhaṅgāchā gāthā. Edited by V. V. R.] [1883.] 8°. **14140. c. 38.**

VINĀYAKA YAŚAVANTA BERḌE. Moral maxims in verse. पद्यात्मक लघुहितोपदेश [Padyātmaka laghuhitopadeśa.] By Vinayeck Eshwant Berday. pp. iv. 49. मुंबई १९१० [*Bombay*, 1858.] 16°. **14140. a. 3(4.)**

VINAYECK ESHWANT BERDAY. *See* VINĀYAKA YAŚAVANTA BERḌE.

VIŚĀKHADATTA. Mudrárákshasa: a drama in seven acts, translated into Maráṭhí [prose and verse] from the original Sanskrit of Visákhadatta by Krishṇa Shástrí Rájváde. Revised by Krishṇa Shástrí Chiplonkar ... and edited by Shankar P. Pandit. (मुद्राराक्षस.) pp. v. 144. *Bombay*, 1867. 8°. **14140. f. 23.**

VISHNOO SOONDER CHUTRAY. *See* VISHṆU SUNDARA CHHATRE.

VISHNUBAWA BRAHMACHARI. *See* VISHṆU BHIKĀJĪ GOKHALE, called BRAHMACHĀRĪ.

VISHṆU BHAGAVĀN LIMAYE. मराठीक्रमिक तीन पुस्तकांतील कवितांचे अन्वय व अर्थ. [A key to the construction and meanings of the poetical parts of the Marathi First, Second, and Third Books. Second edition.] pp. 52, *lith.* रत्नागिरी [*Ratnagiri*, 1880.] 12°. **14140. g. 29(5.)**

VISHṆU BHĀSKARA KARMARKAR. [*Life.*] *See* TUKĀRĀMA NĀTHUJĪ. Vishnupunt. रे. विष्णु भास्कर करमरकर यांचें चरित्र [Vishṇu Bhāskara Karmarkar yāñcheṇ charitra.]

VISHṆU BHIKĀJĪ GOKHALE, called BRAHMACHĀRĪ. भावार्थसिंधु [Bhāvārthasindhu. A poem in five chapters on the principles of Vedānta philosophy.] pp. 56, *lith.* मुंबई १७७८ [*Bombay*, 1856.] 8°. **14137. d. 2.**

—— [Another edition.] pp. 58, *lith.* सातारा १७७८ [*Satara*, 1856.] 8°. **14140. e. 7.**

—— An essay in Marathi on beneficent government by Vishnubawa Brahmachari. Translated [into English] ... by Captain A. Phelps. pp. 31. *Bombay*, 1869. 12°. **14137. f. 1.**

VISHṆU CHIMṆĀJĪ KARVE. A treatise on telegraphy, in theory, history, and practice, for the use of native signallers. (विद्युन्मार्ग) [Vidyunmārga.] pp. ii. ii. iii. iii. 36, iv. *Bombay*, 1876. 12°. **14139. a. 30.**

—— A treatise on the locomotive, in theory, history, and practice ... for the use of Marathi speaking employes in the Railway Department. (लोह मार्ग) [Lohamārga.] pp. ii. ii. vi. iv. 144, 45, xvi. *Bombay*, 1880. 12°. **14139. a. 43.**

VISHṆUDĀSA. *See* PURĀṆAS. अथ एकादशीमाहात्म्य प्रारंभ ॥ [Ekādaṣīmāhātmya. Translated by V.] [1861.] *obl.* 8°. **14137. d. 10(1.)**

—— —— [1864.] *obl.* 8°. **14137. d. 9(2.)**

—— —— [1877.] *obl.* 12°. **14140. a. 9(11.)**

—— अथ चक्रविभु प्रारंभ [Chakravibhu. A poem on the wars between the Pāṇḍavas and Kauravas, and the death of Jayadratha.] ff. 10. मुंबई १७८१ [*Bombay*, 1859.] *obl.* 16°. **14140. a. 2(3.)**

—— [Another edition.] ff. 10, *lith.* मुंबई १७८७ [*Bombay*, 1865.] *obl.* 16°. **14140. a. 9(5.)**

—— विष्णुदास कृत रासक्रिडा [Rāsakrīḍā. Songs on the Rāsa, or circular dance of Krishṇa.] pp. 24. मुंबई [*Bombay*, 1875 ?]. 16°. **14140. a. 3(5.)**

—— *Begin:* श्रीगणेशाय नमः ॥ गणेशगौरीचानंदन ॥ [Tulasī ākhyāna. A poem in praise of the tulasī, or sacred basil. Third edition.] ff. 15, *lith.* मुंबई १७८० [*Bombay*, 1858.] *obl.* 16°. **14137. c. 5.**

—— [Another edition.] ff. 15, *lith.* मुंबई १७८४ [*Bombay*, 1862.] *obl.* 16°. **14137. c. 2(4.)**

VISHṆU DINKAR VAIDYA KALYĀṄKAR. कहाण्या [Kahāṇyā. Short tales on Hindu religious observances, in colloquial Marathi peculiar to Brahman ladies.] Pt. I. मुंबई १८८५ [*Bombay*, 1885.] 12°. **14139. f. 21.**

VISHṆU JANĀRDANA PAṬAVARDHANA. A prize novel styled Hambírrao and Putalábái, or the rebellion of 1857. (कादंबरी १८५७ सालचे बंडाची धामधूम किंवा हंबीरराव आणि पुतळाबाई यांचें चरित्र) pp. ii. v. 192. *Bombay*, 1875. 12°. **14139. f. 19.**

VISHṆU KṚISHṆA CHIPLŪṆKAR. इतिहासावरील निबंध [Itihāsāvarīl nibandha. An essay on the study of history.] pp. 63. पुणें १८८४ [*Poona*, 1884.] 12°. **14139. e. 16(2.)**

VISHṆU MOREṢVARA BHIDE. *See* ROLLIN (C.) The life of Cyrus, translated ... by Vishnu Moreshwar Bhide. 1852. 8°. **14139. d. 3.**

VISHṆU MOREṢVARA THATTE. मोडी वचनपद्धति [Moḍī vachanapaddhati. A Modi primer. Third edition.] pp. 32, *lith.* पुणें १८७५ [*Poona*, 1875.] 16°. **14140. g. 24(1.)**

VISHṆU PĀṆḌURAṄGA ṢAHĀṆE. *See* NĀRĀYAṆA BĀḶAKṚISHṆA GOḌBOLE and VISHṆU PĀṆḌURAṄGA ṢAHĀṆE. Chronological Tables, *etc.* 1880. 8°. **14139. a. 34.**

VISHṆU PARAṢURĀMA ṢĀSTRĪ OK. *See* MURRAY (H.) A Maráṭhí version of Murray's History of British India ... (Part the third by Vishnu Parashurám Shástrí.) 1859–61. 8°. **14139. e. 8.**

VISHṆU PARAṢURĀMA ṢĀSTRĪ PAṆḌITA. *See* BĀṆA. Párvatípariṇaya ... Revised by Vishṇu Parashurám Shástrí Paṇḍit, *etc.* 1872. 12°. **14079. a. 7.**

—— *See* ĪṢVARACHANDRA VIDYĀSĀGARA. Marriage of widows ... by Eshwarachandra Vidyáságar. Translated ... by Vishnu Parashurám Shástrí Pandit. 1865. 12°. **14139. c. 11(2.)**

—— *See* ṢAṄKARA ṢĀSTRĪ GOKHALE. Vyavahâradarpana .... (Husbandry, Bágáita. Part II.) .... Revised by Vishṇu Parashurám Shástrí Paṇḍit. 1876. 12°. **14139. a. 26.**

—— *See* TUKĀRĀMA. A complete collection of the poems of Tukáráma .... Edited by Vishṇu Parashurám Shástrí Paṇḍit. 1869. 8°. **14140. c. 14.**

—— आयुष्यवर्तन क्रमाविषयीं श्रुतिस्मृतींच्या आज्ञा [Āyushya vartana kramāvishayīṇ ṣrutismṛitīṇchyā ājñā. A lecture on the teachings of the Vedas concerning caste distinctions.] pp. 28. मुंबई १८७५ [*Bombay*, 1875.] 12°. **14139. c. 6(3.)**

—— A dictionary of Sanscrit roots in Sanscrit and Maráṭhí. With a list of common roots and an appendix, *etc.* (संस्कृत आणि महाराष्ट्र धातुकोश) pp. iv. iii. iii. 206, 59. *Bombay*, 1865. 8°. **14092. b. 7.**

VISHṆUṢARMAN. [For editions of the Pañchatantra, ascribed to Vishṇuṣarman.] *See* PAÑCHATANTRA.

VISHṆU ṢĀSTRĪ. नीतिदर्पण [Nītidarpaṇa. Moral tales.] pp. 113. पुणें १८४३ [*Poona*, 1843.] 8°. **14139. c. 9.**

—— [Another edition, in the Modi character.] pp. 97, *lith.* मुंबई १८६० [*Bombay*, 1860.] 8°. **14139. c. 12.**

—— [Another edition.] pp. 106. मुंबई १८३७ [*Bombay*, 1867.] 8°. **14139. c. 30.**

VISHṆU ṢĀSTRĪ CHIPḶŪṆKAR. *See* VISHṆU KṚISHṆA CHIPḶŪṆKAR.

VISHṆU SUNDARA CHHATRE. *See* DE MORGAN (A.) De Morgan's Elements of Algebra: translated into the Marathi language by George Ritso Jervis ... assisted by Vishnoo Soonder Chutray. 1848. 8°. **14139. b. 5.**

VISHṆU VĀSUDEVA SĀṬHYE GONDHAḶEKAR. त्रैराशिक समूह [Trairāṣika samūha. Exercises in arithmetic with solutions, in two parts, viz.: Pt. I. consisting of 250 original exercises on the rule of three; and Pt. II. containing 130 exercises from Kero Lakshmaṇa Chhatre's "Treatise on Arithmetic." Fourth edition.] pp. 168. पुणें १८७७ [*Poona*, 1877.] 8°. **14139. b. 11.**

VISHṆU YEṢAVANTA DURVE. मारिसकृत हिंदुस्थानच्या इतिहासांतील लढाया तह व प्रसिद्ध पुरुषांविषयीं संक्षिप्त माहिती *etc.* [Hindusthānachyā itihāsāntīl laḍhāyā. A short account of remarkable battles, treaties, and personages in Indian history. Compiled from "Morris' History of India."] pp. 21. अलीबाग १८७७ [*Alibagh*, 1877.] 8°. **14139. e. 16(1.)**

VIṢVANĀTHA, *Kavi.* नौकाक्रीडन [Naukākrīḍana. A poem on the sports of Krishṇa and the milkmaids in the boat. Third edition.] pp. 10, *lith.* मुंबई १७७७ [*Bombay*, 1855.] 12°. **14140. a. 1(7.)**

VIṢVANĀTHA MAHĀDEVA GOKHALE. History of Hindoostan. Composed for children, in easy verse, by Wishvanath Mahadeo Gocklay (हिंदुस्थानाचा इतिहास) [Hindusthānāchā itihāsa.] pp. ii. 126, *lith.* *Poona*, 1863. 8°. **14139. e. 7.**

VIṢVANĀTHA NĀRĀYAṆA MAṆḌALIK, *C.S.I.* *See* ELPHINSTONE (*Hon.* M.) The history of India ..... Translated ... by Vishvanáth Náráyan Mandlik. 1861-62. 8°. **14139. e. 10.**

—— *See* HARI KEṢAVAJĪ. Elements of political economy ... Compiled ... by Hari Késhowaji ... and Vishwanáth Náráyan Mandlik. 1854. 8°. **14139. c. 7.**

—— हिन्दुधर्म शास्त्र [Hindudharma ṣāstra. A work on the principles of Hindu law in two parts. Part II. contains an annotated translation of the Yājñavalkyasmṛiti and Nīlakaṇṭha Mīmāṃsakabhaṭṭa's Vyavahāramayūkha.] मुंबई १८८२-८३ [*Bombay*, 1882-83.] 8°.

Part I. is of the second edition.

14137. g. 11.

VIṢVANĀTHA PAÑCHĀNANA BHAṬṬĀCHĀRYA TARKĀLAṄKĀRA. Nyāya bhārati, or the translation of Nyāya siddhānta muktâvali of [Viṣvanātha, a Sanskrit commentary on the Bhāshāparichchheda, a work on] Nyāya philosophy by Bhîmâchārya Jhaḷakikara, *etc.* (न्यायभारती.) 2 pt. *Bombay*, 1882–84. 8°.

The text of the Bhāshāparichchheda is given throughout, and that of the Siddhānta-muktāvalī in pt. 2 which contains the Anumāna and succeeding khaṇḍas. **14048. d. 49.**

VIṢVANĀTHA RĀMACHANDRA KĀḶE. तंतुवाद्य. सतार शिकण्याचें पहिलें पुस्तक [Tantuvādya. Instruction on the Indian guitar. Second edition.] pp. 124. मुंबई १८८१ [*Bombay*, 1881.] 12°. **14139. a. 47.**

VIṬHṬHALA, *Poet.* विठ्ठलकृत बिल्हण-चरित्र (रसमंजरी) [Bilhaṇa charitra, or The life of Bilhaṇa Miṣra, a poet of Kashmir, also Rasamañjarī. Two poems by V.] *See* PERIODICAL PUBLICATIONS.—*Poona.* काव्येतिहास-संग्रह [Kāvyetihāsa saṅgraha.] Vol. II. Nos. 5–12, and VII. Nos. 1–3. [1878, *etc.*] 8°. **14072. d. 37.**

VIṬHṬHALA BĀPŪJĪ KARMARKAR. The Himalayas. हिमालयवर्णनम् । A Sanskrit prize poem. By Vithal Bapujee Karmarkar. Translated in Marathi verse by Govind Wasudev Canitkar. pp. iv. 15. मुंबई १८७५ [*Bombay*, 1875.] 8°. **14076. c. 46.**

VIṬHṬHALA BHAGAVANTA LEMBHE. श्रियाळ नाटक [Ṣriyāḷa nāṭaka. A drama, in five acts, on king Ṣriyāla sacrificing his son to Ṣiva.] pp. 66, ii. मुंबई १८८१ [*Bombay*, 1881.] 12°. **14140. a. 8(3.)**

VIṬHṬHAḶA DĀSA. अथ तुळसीमाहात्म्य प्रारंभ [Tuḷasīmāhātmya. A poem, founded on a section of the Skandapurāṇa, extolling the virtues of the tulasī plant, or sacred basil. Second edition.] ff. 76. १७८४ [*Bombay?* 1862.] *obl.* 8°. **14137. d. 10(4.)**

VIṬHṬHALA HARI LIMAYE. Sadu Salgar, a famine narrative. (सदु सलगर अथवा दुष्काल वर्णन.) pp. 54. *Poona*, 1880. 16°. **14139. f. 22.**

VIṬHṬHALA KṚISHṆĀJĪ KĀYAKIṆĪKAR. *See* PURĀṆAS. — Skandapurāṇa. — *Gokarṇamāhātmya.* श्री गोकर्णमाहात्म्य प्रारंभः ॥ [Gokarṇamāhātmya. Translated by V. K. K.] [1875.] *obl.* 8°. **14137. e. 9.**

VIṬHṬHALA KṚISHṆĀJĪ KĀYAKIṆĪKAR. गणित याही विद्यार्थी करितां प्रसिद्ध केला. लीलावती चमत्कारिक हिशेब. [Līlāvatī. A collection of practical and entertaining mathematical exercises.] pp. 130. मुंबई १८७७ [*Bombay*, 1877.] 12°. **14139. a. 27(3.)**

VIṬHṬHALARĀVA ṢIVADEVA VINCHURKAR. विठ्ठलराव शिवदेव विंचुरकर यांची कारकीर्द. [An account of the life of V. Ṣ. V.] *See* PERIODICAL PUBLICATIONS.—*Poona*. काव्येतिहास-संग्रह [Kāvyetihāsa saṅgraha.] Vol. III. and IV. [1878, *etc.*] 8°. **14072. d. 37.**

VIṬHṬHALA ṢĀSTRĪ TARLEKAR. *See* KṚISHṆA RAGHUNĀTHAJĪ. Agamprakash. आगमप्रकाश [With extracts from the Tantras. Sanskrit text, with translations by V. Ṣ. T.] 1884. 8°. **14137. d. 3.**

VIṬHṬHALA VĀMANA GANDYE. हिंदुस्थानाचा भूगोल [Hindusthānāchā bhūgola. A short geography of India. Second edition.] pp. 31. धुळें १८७७ [*Dhulia*, 1877.] 12°. **14139. d. 31(3.)**

VOPADEVA. बोपदेवशतक. यांचें मराठी भाषांतर. [Ṣataṣlokī. A Sanskrit medical treatise in 100 stanzas by Vopaveda, with a Marathi paraphrase by Kṛishṇa Ṣāstrī Bhāṭavaḍekar.] pp. vi. 80, *lith.* मुंबई १८६० [*Bombay*, 1860.] 4°. **14043. d. 6.**

VYUTPATTI-RATNĀKARA. Vyutpatti Ratnakara. व्युत्पत्तिरत्नाकर [A glossary of Sanskrit words, explained in Marathi, Canarese and English.] *See* PERIODICAL PUBLICATIONS.—*Dharwar*. काव्यनाटकादर्श [Kāvyanāṭakādarṣa.] [1882, *etc.*] 8°. **14076. d. 35.**

WAMAN DHONDDEW KARWAY. *See* VĀMANA DHOṆḌADEVA KARVE.

WELLESLEY (ARTHUR) *Duke of Wellington. Life. See* VINAYĀKA KOṆḌADEVA OK. The life of the Duke of Wellington.

WHO. भाव कोणावर ठेवावा याचा विचार [Bhāva koṇāvar ṭhevāvā.] In whom shall we trust? [A Christian tract.] pp. 24. मुंबई [*Bombay*,] 1843. 12°. **14137. a. 2(7.)**

WILDER (R. G.) *See* BIBLE.—New Testament.—*Luke.* Commentary on the Gospel according to Luke. By the Rev. R. G. W. 1875. 8°. **3061. dd. 1.**

WILSON (JOHN) *D.D., Missionary of the Free Church of Scotland. See* MORA BHAṬṬA DĀṆḌEKAR. An exposure of the Hindu religion, in reply to Mora Bhatta Dandekar, by ... J. W. 1832. 8°. **4506. cc. 3.**

—— हिंदु धर्म प्रसिद्धीकरण [Hindudharma prasiddhikaraṇa.] ... Exposure of the Hindoo religion by the Rev. J. W. pp. 111. मुंबई १८३२ [*Bombay*, 1832.] 8°. **14137. b. 5(11.)**

—— दुसरें हिंदूधर्मप्रसिद्धीकरण ... A second exposure of the Hindu religion; in reply to Náráyana Ráo of Satárá: including strictures on the Vedánta. pp. 166. *Bombay*, 1835. 8°. **14137. b. 5(12.)**

—— A second exposure of the Hindu religion, *etc.* pp. 179. *English. Bombay, Surat* [printed], 1834. 8°. **4506. cc. 8.**

—— Idiomatical sentences illustrative of the phraseology and structure of the English and Maráthí languages. [Translated from J. D. Pearson's Bakyabolee in English and Bengali.] Second edition. pp. 330. *Bombay*, 1839. 12°. **12906. bbb. 8.**

WISHVANATH MAHADEO GOCKLAY. *See* VIṢVANĀTHA MAHĀDEVA GOKHALE.

WORSHIP. देवाचें भजन करण्याची रीत [Devāchen bhajana karaṇyāchī rīta.] The true worship of God. pp. 17. मुंबई १८४१ [*Bombay*, 1841.] 12°. **14137. a. 2(8.)**

YĀJÑAVALKYA. *See* VIṢVANĀTHA NĀRĀYAṆA MAṆḌALIK, *C.S.I.* हिन्दुधर्म शास्त्र [Hindudharma ṣāstra, containing a translation of the Yājñavalkyasmṛiti.] [1883.] 8°. **14137. g. 11.**

—— याज्ञवल्क्यस्मृति मिताक्षरव्यवहाराध्याय *etc.* [The Vyavahārādhyāya of Yājñavalkya's Smṛiti with Vijñeṣvara's Mitākshara, and a Marathi translation of both by Bhikājī Ṣāstrī Moghe, the whole followed by a Sanskrit-Marathi glossary. Edited by Janārdana Mahādeva Gurjar.] ff. 5, 22, 464, 13. मुंबई १८७९ [*Bombay*, 1879.] 8°. **14038. d. 25.**

YAṢAVANTA RĀVA. [*Miracles.*] *See* SAKHĀRĀMA SONĀR. यशवंतराव महाराज यांचा पवाडा [Yaṣavanta Rāva yāñchā pavāḍā.]

YAṢAVANTA VĀSUDEVA ĀṬHALE. हिंदु लोकांतील विवाहकाल [Hindu lokāntīl vivāhakāla. A lecture on the proper marriageable age for Hindus.] pp. 12. *See* BOMBAY, *City of.—Hindu Union Club.* हेमंत व्याख्यानमाला. [Hemanta vyākhyānamālā.] Vol. II. No. 4. [1886, *etc.*] 8°. **14139. c. 26**

INDEX OF ORIENTAL TITLES.

[The references in this Index are to the names of the authors or other headings under which the works are catalogued. In the case of anonymous works, which are catalogued under their titles, the phrase "in loco" is used in referring to them. Oriental titles only are entered in this Index, or those in which English words occur only as forming an essential part of an Oriental title.]

Abalāmitra.
See PERIODICAL PUBLICATIONS.—*Alibagh.*
Abhaṅga.
See CHĀṄGADEVA.
——— *See* JÑĀNADEVA.
——— *See* MUKTĀ BĀĪ.
——— *See* NIVṚITTINĀTHA.
——— *See* RĀMADĀSA SVĀMĪ, *Son of Sūryopanta.*
——— *See* SOPĀNADEVA.
——— *See* TUKĀRĀMA.
Abhaṅga bāḷakrīḍechc.
See NĀMADEVA.
Abhaṅgāchā gathā.
See NILOBĀ RĀYA.
Abhimanyu vivāha.
See ABHIMANYU.
Adbhuta chamatkāra saṅgraha.
See ADBHUTA CHAMATKĀRA.
Adbhuta Rāmāyaṇa.
See VĀLMĪKI.
Ādiṣāstra va Īṣvarajñāna.
See KEṢAVACHANDRA SENA.
Āgamanigama grantha.
See MAINĀNĀTHA.
Āgamaprakāṣa.
See KṚISHṆA RAGHUNĀTHAJĪ.
Ahīmahī ākhyāna.
See ANANTA, *Kavi.*
Aitihāsika-goshṭī [*in loco*].
——— nāṭakamālā [*in loco*].
Ajāmiḷākhyāna.
See VĀMANA PAṆḌITA.

Alandīchī yātrā.
See ALANDĪ.
Alaṅkāraviveka.
See KṚISHṆA ṢĀSTRĪ RĀJVĀḌE.
Amaruṣataka.
See AMARU.
Āmchī kuṭumba-vyavasthā.
See BHAVĀNARĀVA PĀVAGĪ.
Amṛitasāgara.
See PRATĀPA SIṂHA, *Raja of Jaipur.*
Ānandalaharī.
See EKANĀTHA.
Aneka janmanirṇaya.
See TRANSMIGRATION.
—— kavikṛita kavitā.
See MARATHI ANTHOLOGY.
—— vidyāmūlatattva saṅgraha.
See KṚISHṆA ṢĀSTRĪ CHIPLŪṆKAR.
Aṅgadaṣishṭāī.
See BALLĀLA DĀDO.
Āṅgre gharāṇyāchā itihāsa.
See RĀVAJĪ HARI AṬHVALE.
Aṅkagaṇita [*in loco*].
——— *See* KERO LAKSHMAṆA CHHATRE.
Aṅkalipi [*in loco*].
Annapūrṇāshṭaka.
See ṢAṄKARA ACHĀRYA.
Anubhavalaharī [*in loco*].
Anubhavāmṛita padabodhinī.
See JÑĀNADEVA.
Anusmṛiti.
See MAHĀBHĀRATA.—*Selections.*
Aplyā nikṛishṭāvasthechīṇ kāraṇeṇ.
See ANANTA MĀDHAVARĀVA MORE.
—— rāhaṇyāchyā rīti āṇi ārogyaṣāstra.
See KṚISHṆARĀVA BĀ[ḶĀJĪ ?] BULEL.

Ārabī goshṭī.
 See Persian Tales.
Āratīsaṅgraha.
 See Vāsudeva Moreṣvara Potadār.
Āratyā [*in loco*].
Āratyāpañchaka.
 See Gaṅgādhara Dīkshita.
Arjadāsta.
 See Ekanātha.
Arjuna garvaparihāra.
 See Arjuna.
Arjunāchī bakhar.
 See Nāro Āpājī Goḍbole.
Arjunagītā.
 See Mahābhārata.—*Selections*.
Ārogyarakshakavidyā.
 See Chintāmana Ananta Limaye.
Ārogyarakshaṇa.
 See Public Health.
Arthaṣāstra paribhāshā.
 See Mill (J. S.)
Ārya mātṛivilāsa.
 See Gaṅgādhara Viṭhṭhala Mogre.
Āryamitra.
 See Periodical Publications.—*Poona*.
Āryāṣataka.
 See Mudgala Āchārya.
Ārya vaidyaka va pāṣchimātya vaidyaka.
 See Bhālachandra Kṛishṇa Bhāṭavaḍekar.
Aṣru, tyāṇchī utpatti āṇe yojanā.
 See Kānhobā Raṇchhoḍdās Kīrtikar.
Aṣvaparīkshā.
 See Nakuḷa.
Aṣvinī ākhyāna.
 See Aṣvinī.
Ātmānubhava.
 See Keṣava Sakhārāma Ṣāstrī.
Aushadhavidyā.
 See Nārāyaṇa Dājī.
Avichāra, paṣchāttāpa va prāyaṣchitta.
 See Hindus.
Āyushya vartana kramāvishayīṇ ṣrutismṛitīṇchyā [ājñā.
 See Vishṇu Paraṣurāma Ṣāstrī Paṇḍita.
Bābājīchī bakhar.
 See Bābājī Raghunātha Marāṭhe.
Babhruvāhana ākhyāna.
 See Ṣrīdhara.
Baḍoḍe Sarkārchī taināti phauj.
 See Baroda, *Native State of*.
Bāgāīta.
 See Ṣaṅkara Ṣāstrī Gokhale.
Bahār i dānish.
 See ʻInāyat Allāh.
Bahurūpī santakheḷ.
 See Govinda Morobā Kārlekar.
Baitāl-pachīsī [*in loco*].
Bakhar Marāṭhyāṇchī.
 See Duff (J. G.)
Bakhtyār-nāmā.
 See Bakhtyār.
Bālabodhamuktāvalī.
 See Æsop.
Bālacharita.
 See Ānandatanaya.
Bāḷājī Viṣvanātha nāṭaka.
 See Rāvajī Hari Āṭhvale.
Bālakrīḍā.
 See Dāmodara Panta.
Bāḷakrīḍeche abhaṅga.
 See Nāmadeva.
——————
 See Tukārāma.
Bāḷamitra.
 See Berquin (A.)
Bālasaṅgopana.
 See Kṛishṇa Ṣāstrī Goḍbole.
Bāla Ṣivājī nāṭaka.
 See Sītārāma Narahara Ḍhavḷe.
Bālavaidya.
 See Janārdana Hari Āṭhalye.
Bālavivāhāchyā sambandhāneṇ hitāhita vichāra.
 See Vāmana Ābājī Moḍak.
Bālavivāha duḥkha-darṣana prahasana.
 See Ananta Nārāyaṇa Paṇḍita.
Bālavyākaraṇa.
 See Bāḷa Ṣāstrī.
Bāli vānarāchī bakhar.
 See Nāro Āpājī Goḍbole.
Bāpū Gokhale yāṇcheṇ charitra.
 See Ṣaṅkara Tukārāma Ṣāligrām.
Bārākhaḍyā.
 See Marāṭhi Spelling Book.
Barhāḍ ṣālāpatraka.
 See Periodical Publications.—*Poona*.
Bene Israēl lokāṇchā itihāsa.
 See Taḷkar (H. J.)
Betāḷapañchaviṣī.
 See Baitāl-pachīsī.
Bhadrāyu satvadarṣana nāṭaka.
 See Vāsudeva Chintāmaṇa Bāpaṭ.
Bhagavadgītā.
 See Mahābhārata.—*Bhagavadgītā*.
——————
 See Mahābhārata.—*Selections*.
——————
 See Uddhava Chidghana.
Bhagavadgītecheṇ sāra.
 See Nesbit (R.)
Bhāgavata.
 See Purāṇas.—*Bhāgavatapurāṇa*.
Bhāgavata āryā.
 See Moropanta.
Bhajanāṇchī paddhati.
 See Forms.
Bhaktalīlāmṛita.
 See Mahīpati.
Bhaktāmara-stotra.
 See Mānatuṅgāchārya.
Bhaktisāra.
 See Māḷu Narahari.
Bhaktivijaya.
 See Mahīpati.
Bhāmāvilāsa nāṭaka.
 See Dattātraya Vāsudeva Joglekar.

Bharatabhāva.
See Vāmana Paṇḍita.
Bhāratavarshīya prāchīna aitihāsika keṣa.
See Raghunātha Bhāskara Godbole.
——— vanaushadhisaṅgraha.
See Pāṇḍuraṅga Gopāla Mantrī.
Bhāshāmañjarī [in loco].
Bhāshāntara pāṭhamālā.
See Dvārakānātha Rāghobā Tarkhaḍkar.
Bhāū Sāhebāṇchī bakhar.
See Bhāū Sāheb.
Bhāva koṇāvar ṭhevāvā.
See Who.
Bhāvachandrikā.
See Mahābhārata.—Bhagavadgītā.
Bhāvadīpikā.
See Lakshmaṇa Govindabhāū Ashṭaputre.
Bhavānī-ashṭaka [in loco].
Bhāvārthasindhu.
See Vishṇu Bhikājī, called Brahmachārī.
Bhikshuka [in loco].
Bhīmasenāchī bakhar.
See Nāro Āpājī Godbole.
Bhishmastavarāja.
See Mahābhārata.—Selections.
Bhajana sadbodha mālikā.
See Nānā Koḷekar, also called Sanmatidāsa.
Bhrama-nirāsa.
See Rāmachandra Bhikājī Guñjīkar.
Bhrāntikṛita chamatkāra.
See Shakspere (W.)
Bhūgola āṇi khagola vishayaka saṃvāda.
See Dialogues.
Bhūgolācheṇ varṇana.
See Candy (T.)
Bhūgola khagola.
See Sullivan (R.) LL.D.
Bhūgola ṣāstra. Gaṇitabhāga.
See Bāḷa Gaṅgādhara Ṣāstrī Jāmbhekar.
Bhūgolavidyā.
See Rāmachandra Vishṇu.
Bhūmitī.
See Pasley (Sir C. W.)
Bhūpāḷyā [in loco].
Bhūtala vishayaka vidyechīṇ mūlatattveṇ.
See Blanford (H. F.)
Bhūvarṇana.
See Geikie (A.)
Bījagaṇitāchīṇ mūlatattveṇ.
See Haddon (J.) M.A.
Bījagaṇita mūlapīṭhikā.
See De Morgan (A.)
Bijāpur-varṇana.
See Sītārāma Rāmachandra Gaikvāḍ.
Bilhaṇa charitra.
See Viṭhṭhala, Kavi.
Bodhakathā [in loco].
Bodhalyācheṇ abhaṅga.
See Bodhala.
Bodhapar padeṇ.
See Kṛishṇajī Ballāḷa Ṭhākura.
Brahmadvesha
See Rāvajī Hari Āṭhvale.
Brahmajñānapar abhaṅga.
See Tukārāma.
Brāhmaṇajātīchyā vidhavā vishayīṇ prakaraṇa.
See Brahmans.
Brāhmaṇakanyā vivāhavichāra.
See Svadeṣa Hitechchhu.
Brāhmaṇavarṇācheṇ mūḷa.
See Haug (M.)
Brahmasmṛiti.
See Shāhū III., Raja of Satara.
Brahmastuti. [stuti.
See Purāṇas. — Bhāgavatapurāṇa.—Brahma-
Brahmendra Svāmī yāṇcheṇ charitra.
See Brahmendra Svāmī.
British Parliament ... kelele kāyade.
See Rāmachandra Govinda Taḷvarkar.
Buddhabāvanī [in loco.]
Chakravibhu.
See Vishṇudāsa.
Chamatkārika goshṭī.
See Farrar ( ) Mrs.
———
See Nāro Āpājī Godbole.
Champubhārata.
See Ananta Bhaṭṭa, the Poet.
Champūrāmāyaṇa.
See Bhojarāya Paṇḍita.
Chandrahāsa rājyāchī bakhar.
See Nāro Āpājī Godbole.
Chandrāvaḷī ākhyāna.
See Moreṣvara, Son of Dhuṇḍi.
Chāṅgadeva charitra.
See Nilobā Rāya.
Chāṅgle mulge.
See Good Boys.
Charpaṭapañjarī.
See Ṣaṅkara Āchārya.
Chautheṇ pustaka.
See Marathi Fourth Book.
Cheṇḍuphaḷī.
See Anantasuta.
Chhatrapati Sambhājī Mahārāja.
See Nāgeṣarāva Vināyaka Bāpaṭ.
Chikitsāsāra.
See Gopāladāsa.
Chitrasena gandharva nāṭaka.
See Dattātraya Vāsudeva Jogḷekar.
Chovīsanāvāṇche abhaṅga,
See Chovīsanāva.
Chyavana bhārgavāchī bakhar.
See Nāro Āpājī Godbole.
Daivasenī.
See Mādhavarāva, also called Bājābā Rāmachandra Pradhāna.
Ḍākṭar va vaidya.
See Prahasanasaṅgraha.
Dāmājīchī rasad.
See Amīr Chand.
Dambhahāraka.
See Periodical Publications.—Bombay.
Dānavrata.
See Narahari.

Dāsabodha.
See Rāmadāsa Svāmī, *Son of Sūryopanta.*
Daṣamaskandhāchyā āryā.
See Moropanta.
Daṣāvatārāche ṣloka.
See Daṣāvatāra.
Deṣavyavahāra vyavasthā.
See Hari Keṣavajī.
Devāchen bhajana karaṇyāchī rīta.
See Worship.
Devāchyā dāhā ājñā.
See Ten Commandments.
Dhākaṭe Shāhū Mahārāja yāñchen charitra.
See Malhār Rāmarāva Chiṭṇīs.
Dhāṇve [*in loco*].
Dharmasindhusāra.
See Kāṣīnātha Upādhyāya.
Dharmottejaka gīten.
See Revival Hymns.
Dhruvākhyāna.
See Uddhava Chidghana.
Dhuḷākshara [*in loco*].
Dīparatnākara.
See Rāmānanda.
Divāḷīchī lūṭ.
See Lakshmaṇa Gaṅgājī Toḍāvār.
Dīwānī kāma chālaviṇyāchā kāyadā.
See India.—*Legislative Council.*
Dnyanodaya [*i.e.* Jñānodaya].
See Periodical Publications.—*Ahmadnagar.*
Draupadī vastraharaṇa.
See Kiṅkara, *Kavi.*

———— *See* Tukārāma.
Durdaivī Murād va daivavān Salāudīn.
See Vināyaka Nārāyaṇa Bhāgavata.
Durgāstotra [*in loco*].
Dusreṇ pustaka.
See Berar Second Book.

———— *See* Marathi Second Book.
Ekādaṣīmāhātmāche abhaṅga.
See Tukārāma.
Ekādaṣīmāhātmya.
See Purāṇas.
Ekāksharī-ṣloka [*in loco*].
Ekanāthacharitra.
See Ekanātha.
Ekanātha Mahārāja yāñchen charitra.
See Dhoṇḍo Bālakṛishṇa Sahasrabuddhe.
Ekanāthī Bhāgavata.
See Ekanātha.
Gajagaurī-ākhyāna.
See Gajagaurī.
Gajagaurīvrata.
See Basvaliṅga.
Gajendramoksha.
See Mahābhārata.—*Selections.*

———— *See* Vāmana Paṇḍita.
Galiohar [*i.e.* Gulliver] yāchā vṛittānta.
See Swift (J.) *Dean of St. Patrick's.*
Gamatīchen pahilen pustaka.
See Nāro Āpājī Godbole.
Ganeṣapratāpa.
See Purāṇas.—*Gaṇeṣapurāṇa.*
Gaṇeṣapurāṇa āryā.
See Gaṇapatarāva Harihara Paṭavardhana.
Gaṅgālaharī.
See Jagannātha Paṇḍitarāja.
Gaṅgāmṛitaprasāda.
See Jagannātha Paṇḍitarāja.
Gaṅgāvarṇanā.
See Pāṇḍuraṅga Veṅkaṭeṣa Chintāmaṇi Peṭkar.
Garbhakāṇḍa [*in loco*].
Gāruḍa.
See Ekanātha.
Garuḍākhyāna.
See Garuḍa.
Gāruḍyāchā tamāshā.
See Gāruḍa.
Gatabhartṛikā rodana.
See Nārāyaṇa Keṣava Vaidya.
Gāyanaprakāra [*in loco*].
Gilpin charitra.
See Cowper (W.) *the Poet.*
Gītābhāvachandrikā.
See Bāḷājī Sundarajī.
Gokarṇamāhātmya.
See Purāṇas.— Skandapurāṇa.—*Gokarṇamāhātmya.*
Gopīgīta.
See Ananta, *Kavi.*

———— *See* Purāṇas.—Bhāgavatapurāṇa.—*Gopīgītā.*
Govindāshṭaka [*in loco*].
Grahasādhanāchīn koshṭaken.
See Kero Lakshmaṇa Chhatre.
Gṛihyasūtra.
See Āṣvalāyana.
Gulistān.
See Sa'dī.
Guṇotkarsha nāṭaka.
See Vāsudeva Vāmana Ṣāstrī Khare.
Gurucharitra.
See Sarasvati Gaṅgādhara.
Hambīrarāva āṇi Putaḷābāī.
See Vishṇu Janārdana Paṭavardhana.
Hanumāndvādaṣa nāma.
See Rāmadāsa Svāmī, *Son of Sūryopanta.*
Hanumantajanma.
See Purāṇas.—Brahmāṇḍapurāṇa.—*Vyaṅkaṭagirimāhātmya.*
Hari āṇi Trimbak.
See Govinda Ṣaṅkara Ṣāstrī Bāpaṭ.
Haripāṭha.
See Jñānadeva.
Haripāṭhāche abhaṅga.
See Jñānadeva.
Hariṣchandrākhyāna.
See Hariṣchandra.

———— *See* Mukteṣvara.
Hariṣchandra nāṭaka.
See Sokar Bāpūjī Trilokekar.
Hariṣchandra satvadarṣana nāṭaka.
See Raghunātha Ṣaṅkara Ṣāstrī Abhyaṅkar.

Hariṣchandropākhyāna.
See MOROPANTA.
Harivijaya.
See ṢRĪDHARA.
Hastāmalaka.
See EKANĀTHA.
———
See ṢAṄKARA ACHĀRYA.
Hemāḍapantakṛīta nīti.
See HEMĀḌAPANTA.
Hemanta vyākhyānamālā.
See BOMBAY, *City of.—Hindu Union Club.*
Hiḍimbavadha.
See BĀJĀBĀ BĀLĀJĪ NENE.
Himālayavarṇana.
See VIṬHṬHALA BĀPŪJĪ KARMARKAR.
Hindudharma prasiddhīkaraṇa.
See WILSON (J.) *D.D., F.R.S.*
Hindudharma ṣāstra.
See VIṢVANĀTHA NĀRĀYAṆA MAṆḌALIK, *C.S.I.*
Hindudharmatattva.
See GAṄGĀDHARA ṢĀSTRĪ PHAḌKE.
Hindu lokāṇchyā lagnakāryāṇt Sarkār nako.
See NĀRĀYAṆA BHĀSKARA RĀNAḌE and NĀRĀYAṆA VĀMANA ṬIḶAKA CHIKHALGĀNVKAR.
Hindu lokāntīl vivāhakāla.
See YAṢAVANTA VĀSUDEVA ĀṬHALE.
Hindusthānāchā arvachīna koṣa.
See RAGHUNĀTHA BHĀSKARA GOḌBOLE.
——— bhūgola.
See BĀPŪ PURUSHOTTAMA JOṢĪ ṬOṄKEKAR.
———
See VIṬHṬHALA VĀMANA GANDYE.
——— itihāsa.
See ELPHINSTONE (*Hon.* M.)
———
See MORRIS (H.) *of the Madras Civil Service.*
———
See MURRAY (H.)
———
See VIṢVANĀTHA MAHĀDEVA GOKHALE.
——— saṃkshipta itihāsa.
See VINĀYAKA KOṆḌADEVA OK.
Hindusthānācheṇ varṇana.
See CANDY (T.)
Hindusthānāchī ṣakāvaḷī.
See MACCUDDEN (T.)
Hindusthānāchyā itihāsāntīl ... saṃkshipta māhitī.
See PĀṆḌURAṄGA MOREṢVARA POTADĀR.
——— itihāsāntīl laḍhāyā.
See VISHṆU YEṢAVANTA DURVE.
Hindusthāna deṣāchyā sthitivishayīṇ vichāra.
See KĀṢĪNĀTHA TRIMBAK KHARE.
Hindusthānāntīl Ingliṣāṇchyā rājyāchā itihāsa.
See BĀḶA GAṄGĀDHARA ṢĀSTRĪ JĀMBHEKAR.
——— ṣilpaṣāstra.
See NAPIER (F.) *Baron Napier.*
——— tisrī rāshṭrīya-sabhā.
See KĀṢĪNĀTHA TRIMBAK KHARE.
Hiṅgalāja devīcheṇ stotra.
See BĀḶA YAJÑEṢVARA GURJAR.
Hiṣebāṇcheṇ pahileṇ pustaka.
Hiṣeb ratnamālā.
See NĀRO RAGHUNĀTHA MOHOḶKAR.
Hitopadeṣa [*in loco*].
Holkarāṇchī kaifiyat.
HOLKAR, *Family of.*
Hṛidayadarpaṇa.
See HEART BOOK.
Ibrī pahileṇ pustaka.
See RĀJPURKAR (J. E.)
Ijevar prathama upāya.
See ESMARCH (F.)
Inglāṇḍāchā vṛittānta.
See DAVYS (G.) *Bishop of Peterborough.*
Inglaṇḍ deṣāchī bakhar.
See ENGLAND.
Ingliṣ bhāshechā vyākaraṇāchī mūḷapīṭhikā.
See STEVENSON (J.) *D.D.*
—— tisreṇ pustaka.
See HOWARD (E. I.)
—— vyākaraṇa.
See ENGLISH GRAMMAR.
—— vyākaraṇāchī mūlapīṭhikā.
See DĀDOBĀ PĀṆḌURAṄGA TARKHAḌKAR.
Ingrejī vyākaraṇāchā saṃkshepa.
See MURRAY (L.)
Isāp nītikathā.
See ÆSOP.
Isrāelās hitopadeṣa.
See JEWS.
Isrāelī dharmācheṇ khareṇ svarūpa.
See RĀJPURKAR (J. E.)
Īṣvarācheṇ pavitratva.
See FARRAR (C. P.)
Īṣvaranityopāsanā.
See BRĀHMA SAMĀJ.—*Ahmadabad Prāthanā* [*Samāj.*
Īṣvara smaraṇapūrvaka ... lokavartana.
See RĀJĀRĀMA ṢĀSTRĪ BOḌAS.
Īṣvarokta ṣāstradhārā.
See MUIR (J.) *D.C.L.*
Itihāsarūpa darṣikā.
See BAḶAVANTA HARĪ JOṢĪ BORGĀṆVAKAR.
Itihāsāvarīl nibandha.
See VISHṆU KṚISHṆA CHIPḶŪṆKAR.
Jāgatijota.
See RĀMACHANDRA AMṚITA DUGAL.
Jamākharchāchī māhitī.
See GOPĀLA YAJÑEṢVARA BHIḌE.
Jamākharchāchī paddhati.
See VĀSUDEVA BĀḶAKṚISHṆA LOṬLĪKAR.
Jānakīpariṇaya nāṭaka.
See RĀMABHADRA DĪKSHITA.
Jarāsandhavadha nāṭaka.
See SAKHĀRĀMA BĀḶAKṚISHṆA SARNĀIK.
Jarīmarī vishayīṇ.
See CHOLERA.
Jaṣās taseṇ purvaṇī.
See RĀJĀRĀMA RĀMAKṚISHṆA BHĀGAVATA.
Jātibheda [*in loco*].
Jātibheda vivekasāra.
See HINDU.
Jayadrathavadha.
See VĀMANA PAṆḌITA.

Jayapāḷa.
See Vināyaka Janārdana Kīrtane.
Jñānādarṣa.
See Periodical Publications.—*Bombay.*
Jñānadevāchā gāthā.
See Jñānadeva.
Jñānadeva charitra.
See Raghunāthabovā Bhiṅgārkar.
Jñāneṣvara Mahārājāṇcheṇ charitra.
See Baḷavanta Khaṇḍojī Pārakh.
Jñāneṣvarī.
See Jñānadeva.
Jñānodaya.
See Periodical Publications.—*Ahmadnagar.*
Jyā bayakāṇs leṇkreṇ āhet tyāṇs subodha.
See Address.
Jyotiḥṣāstra.
See Kṛishṇa Ṣāstrī Goḍbole.

———

See Lockyer (J. N.)
Jyotisharatna. }
Jyotishasāra. }
See Ṣukadeva.
Kabīrādi . . . keleliṇ padeṇ.
See Kabīr.
Kahāṇyā.
See Vishṇu Dinkar Vaidya Kalyāṅkar.
Kaikeyīche ṣloka.
See Vāsudeva.
Kāḷakarmaṇūk.
See Āshṭamkar (A. S.)
Kālidāsa chāturya nāṭaka.
See Vāmana Gopāla Keḷkar.
Kaliviḍambana.
See Nīlakaṇṭha Dīkshita.
Kāliyamardana nāṭaka.
See Sakhārāma Bāḷakṛipshṇa Sarnāīk.
Kaliyuga [*in loco*].
Kālpanika vijñānāvishayeṇ.
See Stevenson (J.) *D.D.*
Kāmakandalā nāṭaka.
See Ekanātha Gaṇeṣa Bhāṇḍāre.
Kandukākhyāna.
See Ānandatanaya.
Kaṇsa rājyāchī bakhar.
See Nāro Āpājī Goḍbole.
Kāphar deṣāchī mulgī.
See African Girl.
Kaptān Kuk sāheb tyāche vṛittānta.
See Bingley (W.) *Rev.*
Kārāgīr lokāṇche kāmāvishayeṇ.
See Kāṣīnātha Mahādeva Thatte.
Karmavipāka [*in loco*].
Karṇa rājyāchī bakhar.
See Nāro Āpājī Goḍbole.
Karuṇāmṛita bhīmāshṭaka.
See Rāmadāsa Svāmī, *Son of Sūryopanta.*
Karuṇāmṛitastotra.
See Devīdāsa.
Karuṇāpar abhaṅga.
See Tukārāma.
Kāṣīkhaṇḍa.
See Purāṇas.—Skandapurāṇa.—*Kāṣīkhaṇḍa.*
Kāṣīpratāpa.
See Purāṇas.
Kaumudīmahotsāha.
See Rāmachandra Bhikājī Guñjīkar.
Kavicharitra.
See Janārdana Rāmachandrajī.
Kavitādarṣa.
See Gaṇeṣa Baḷavanta Limaye.
Kavitādīpikā. }
Kavitārthadīpikā. }
See Kāṣīnātha Bahirava Limaye.
Kavitārthamālā.
See Vināyaka Govinda Limaye.
Kavitāsāra saṅgraha.
See Paraṣurāma Panta Goḍbole.
Kāvyadoshavirechana.
See Benjamin (S.)
Kāvyanāṭakādarṣa.
See Periodical Publications.—*Dharwar.*
Kāvyenduṣekhara.
See Sakhārāma Bālakṛishṇa Sarnāīk.
Kāvyetihāsa saṅgraha.
See Periodical Publications.—*Poona.*
Kāyājīvasamvāda.
See Rāmakṛishṇa Hari Bhāgavata.
Kekāsāra. }
Kekāvalī. }
See Moropanta.
Kerokṛita aṅkagaṇita . . . . praṣnasamudāya.
See Nāro Raghunātha Mohoḷkar.
Kharaḍyāchyā svārīchī bakhar.
See Mādhava Rāva II., *Peshwa.*
Kharyā dharmāchiṇ chinheṇ.
See Marks.
Khristi dharmāchyā pramāṇeṇ.
See Christianity.
Khristi dharma Īṣvaradatta āhe, *etc.*
See Nīlakaṇṭha Gore (N.)
Khusrū rājāchā itihāsa.
See Rollin (C.)
Kīchakāchī bakhar.
See Nāro Āpājī Goḍbole.
Kimiyā.
See Trimbak Sakhārāma Ṣirvalkar.
Kirāta.
See Kurūlkar (A. D.)
Kīrtana-taraṅgiṇī.
See Rāvajī Ṣrīdhara Gondhaḷekar.
Kishkindhyākāṇḍa.
See Rāmadāsa Svāmī, *Son of Sūryopanta.*
Konkaṇastha Brāhmaṇāṇchī gotramālikā.
See Sadāṣiva Bajyābā Ṣāstrī.
Koshṭakeṇ.
See Nāro Āpājī Goḍbole.
Kṛishikarmāntargata rasāyanaṣāstra.
See Bāḷakṛishṇa Ātmārāma Gupte.
Kṛishṇacharitra.
See Vāmana Paṇḍita.
Kṛishṇāchī bakhar.
See Nāro Āpājī Goḍbole.
Kṛishṇajanma.
See Devanātha.

Krishṇajanma. }
Krishṇajayantī. }
See Śrīdhara.
Krishṇakumārī.
See Bhāū Dīkshita Sātārkar.
Krishṇalīlā ākhyāna.
See Dāmodara Panta.
Kshaitra saṅkuchchheda.
See Drew (W. H.)
Kshamāstotra.
See Rāmakrishṇa Hari Bhāgavata.
Kshatriyavaṃṣodgamamālā.
See Kshatriyavaṃṣa.
Kulina striyāṇ sāṭhīṇ gāṇīṇ.
See Gāṇīṇ.
Kuṭumbāchā mitra.
See Family Friend.
Kuvarajī Mahārāja yāṇcheṇ charitra.
See Kuvarajī.
Laghubodha.
See Raghunātha Achārya.
—— lekhanapaddhati.
See Gajānanabhāū Vaijya.
—— praṣnottarāvalī.
See United States of America.—*Methodist* [*Episcopal Church.*
—— pūrṇāṅka.
See Nārāyaṇa Yajñeṣvara Bhiḍe.
—— vākyavṛitti.
See Śaṅkara Āchārya.
—— vyākaraṇa.
See Gaṅgādhara Rāmachandra Ṭilaka.
Lagnayantra [*in loco*].
Lahān mulāṇkaritāṇ gaṇita.
See Bruce (H. J.)
Lahukuṣāchī bakhar.
See Lava Kuṣa.
Lahūkuṣākhyāna.
See Śrīdhara.
Lakshmī ashṭaka.
See Lakshmī.
Lalitasaṅgraha.
See Rāmajī Dhāyājī.
Lārḍ Bekan [*i.e.* Lord Bacon] yāchen charitra.
See Govinda Nārāyaṇa Kāṇe.
Lavakuṣākhyāna.
See Śrīdhara.
Lāvaṇyā.
See Rāma Joṣī.
————
See Śaṅkara Tukārāma Ṣāligrām.
Lekhanadīpikā [*in loco*].
Lekhanakalpataru.
See Hemādrī.
Lekhanapaddhatī [*in loco*].
Lenkrāchī pahilī pothī.
See First Book.
Līlāvatī [*in loco*].
————
See Viṭhṭhala Krishṇājī Kāyakiṇīkar.
Lipidhāra.
See Baker (F. P.)
Lohamārga.
See Vishṇu Chimṇājī Karve.
Lulit sungurh [*i.e.* Lalitasaṅgraha].
See Rāmājī Dhāyājī.
Mādhavanidāna. }
Mādhavārthaprakāṣikā. }
See Mādhava, *Son of Indukara.*
Madhva-mata.
See Bhīmāchārya Jhalkīkar.
Mahābhārata [*in loco*].
————
See Janārdana Bālājī Moḍak.
————
See Moropanta.
Mahanmaṇimālā.
See Vināyaka Koṇḍadeva Ok.
Mahārāshṭra bhāshechā koṣa.
See Bāla Ṣāstrī Ghagve.
—— bhāshecheṇ vyākaraṇa.
See Dādobā Pāṇḍuraṅga Tarkhaḍkar.
————
See Gaṅgādhara Ṣāstrī Phaḍke.
—— deṣācheṇ varṇana.
See Esdaile (D. A.)
Mahimnaḥ stotra.
See Pushpadanta.
Mālavikāgnimitra.
See Kālidasa.
Malhārī charitra.
See Balavanta Khaṇḍerāva Peshve.
Malhār Rāva Mahārāja nāṭaka.
See Nārāyaṇa Bāpujī Kāniṭkar.
Mallārimāhātmya.
See Purāṇas.—Brahmāṇḍapurāṇa.—*Mallāri-* [*māhātmya.*
Mallavidyā prakāṣaka.
See Sītārāma Ballāla Mahājan.
Manāche ṣloka.
See Rāmadāsa Svāmī, *Son of Sūryopanta.*
Manaṣchandrabodha [*in loco*].
Mañjughoshā.
See Nāro Sadāṣiva Risbuḍ.
Manoramā nāṭaka.
See Mahādeva Bālakrishṇa Chitḷe.
Manorañjaka.
See Nāro Bhāskara Khera.
———— Damayantī.
See Gaṇeṣa Vināyaka Kāniṭkar.
Mantrarāmāyaṇa.
See Moropanta.
Mānusha indriyavijñānaṣāstra. }
———— ṣarīraṣāstra. }
See Bhikājī Amṛita.
Manusmṛiti.
See Manu.
Marāṭhī bhāshechā navīna koṣa.
See Raghunātha Bhāskara Godbole.
—— bhāshecheṇ navīna vyākaraṇa.
See Krishṇa Ṣāstrī Godbole.
———— vyākaraṇa.
See Dādobā Pāṇḍuraṅga Tarkhaḍkar.
—— dusre pustakāntīl ṣabdārtha.
See Sadāṣiva Viṭhṭhala Pālkar.
—— kavitānvayārtha saṅgraha.
See Rāvajī Hari Āṭhvale.

Marāṭhī kramika tīn pustakāntīl kavitāṉche anvaya [va artha.
See Vishṇu Bhagavān Limaye.
—— laghu vyākaraṇa.
See Dādobā Pāṇḍuraṅga Tarkhaḍkar.
—— pahileṉ Moḍī pustaka.
See Bālājī Bhikājī Piṅge.
—— prachārāntīl mhaṇī.
See Gaṅgādhara Govinda Sāpkar.
—— sāhāvyā iyattechā gaṇita vishaya.
See Hari Nārāyaṇa Limaye.
—— saṃsārachopaḍī.
See Saṃsārachopaḍī.
Marāṭhyāṉchī bakhar.
See Duff (J. G.)
Mārkaṇḍeya ākhyāna.
See Ānandatanaya.
Mārkaṇḍeyapurāṇa.
See Purāṇas.—*Mārkaṇḍeyapurāṇa.*
Mārutījanma [*in loco*].
——————— [*girimāhātmya.*
See Purāṇas.—Brahmāṇḍapurāṇa.—*Vyaṅkaṭa-*
Mārutīstotra.
See Rāmadāsa Svāmī, *Son of Sūryopanta.*
Masūrikā va gostanaroga saṃskāra.
See Trimbaka Sakhārāma Śirvalkar.
Mataparīkshā.
See Muir (J.) *D.C.L.*
Matsyapurāṇa āṇi Ibrī Śāstra.
See Purāṇas.—*Matsyapurāṇa.*
Maujechyā chār ghaṭaka.
See Mahādeva Chimṇājī Āpṭe.
Mayūrakavi stuti.
See Rāmachandra Baḍve.
Mitāksharā.
See Vijñāneśvara.
Mitrachandra.
See Pāṇḍuraṅga Govinda Parakhī.
Moḍī bālabodha tisre bukāntīl śabdārtha.
See Nārāyaṇa Hari.
—— dusreṉ pustaka.
See Bālājī Bhikājī Piṅge.
———————
See Sītārāma Viśvanātha Paṭavardhana.
—— tisreṉ pustaka.
See Sītārāma Viśvanātha Paṭavardhana.
—— vachanapaddhati.
See Vishṇu Moreśvara Thatte.
—— vachanasāra.
See Vāsudeva Moreśvara Potadār.
Moḍīcheṉ pahileṉ pustaka.
See Sītārāma Viśvanātha Paṭavardhana.
Mora L. L. B.
See Nārāyaṇarāva Bhāgavata.
Moropantakṛita prakaraṇeṉ.
See Moropanta.
Moṭhā vichāra.
See Enquiry.
Mṛichchhakaṭika nāṭaka.
See Śūdraka.
Mṛityuñjaya charitra.
See Uddhava Chidghana.
Mudrārākshasa.
See Viśākhadatta.
Muktamālā.
See Lakshmaṇa Moreśvara Śāstrī Haḷbe.
Mulāṉkaritāṉ Marāṭhī gāṇeṉ.
See Morris (R.)
Mulāṉsāṭhīṉ bodhāchyā goshṭī.
See Stories.
Mūḷastambha [*in loco*].
———————
See Purāṇas.—*Śivapurāṇa.*
Mulīṉchā kheḷ.
See Nārāyaṇa Vishṇu Jośī.
Mumbaīcheṉ varṇana.
See Govinda Nārāyaṇa.
Mūrkhāṉchīṉ lakshaṇeṉ.
See Mukteśvara.
Mūrkhaśataka [*in loco*].
Mūrtoṉchā uchchheda.
See Idols.
Mustering kārkunās madat.
See Kṛishṇajī Gaṇeśa Dongre.
Nābhikapurāṇa.
See Bhāratī Viśvanātha.
Nāgānanda nāṭaka.
See Harshadeva.
Nāganātha charitra.
See Uddhava Chidghana.
Nāgpūrkar Bhoṉsalyāṉchī bakhar.
See Kāśīrāva Rājeśvara Gupta.
——————— vaṃśāvala.
See Nagpur.
——————— Bhoṉsalyāṉchyā sambandhāche kāgadpa- [tra.
See Nagpur.
Nakulāchī bakhar.
See Nāro Āpājī Godbole.
Nalākhyāna āryā.
See Moropanta.
Nalākhyānāchī bakhar.
See Mahābhārata.—*Nalopākhyāna.*
Nāradanīti [*in loco*].
Nārāyaṇabali.
See Dāmodara Vishṇu Sapre.
Nārāyaṇabodha.
See Rāmajī Gaṇojī Chaugule.
Nārāyaṇa Rāva Peshwe yāṉcheṉ charitra.
See Pāṇḍuraṅga.
Nārāyaṇa Rāvyāchī bakhar.
See Nārāyaṇa Rāva.
Nāsiketākhyāna.
See Tukārāma.
Nāṭaka thorle Mādhava Rāva Peshwe yāṉjvar.
See Vināyaka Janārdana Kīrtane.
Nātha-līlāmṛita.
See Ādinātha.
Naukākrīḍana.
See Viśvanātha.
Navagrahastotra.
See Mahīpati.
Navanātha grantha.
See Mālu Narahari.
Navanīta.
See Paraśurāma Panta Godbole.
Navīna laghu hitopadeśa.
See Maxims.

Nibandhamālā.
See Periodical Publications.—*Poona*.
Niḥṣāstravāda parīkshā.
See Bābā Padmanjī.
Nītidarpaṇa.
See Vishṇu Ṣāstrī.
Nītijñānāchī paribhāshā.
See Esdaile (D. A.).
Nītikathā [*in loco*].
Nītimandira.
See Govindaṣaṅkara Sāstrī Bāpaṭ.
Nītipar kavitā [*in loco*].
Nityapāṭhāche abhaṅga.
See Tukārāma.
Nyāyabhāratī. }
Nyāya siddhānta muktāvalī. } [Tarkālaṅkāra.
See Viṣvanātha Pañchānana Bhaṭṭāchārya
Oḷīvar oḷ.
See Mortimer (F. L.) *Mrs.*
Padabhāvānukāriṇī.
See Lakshmaṇa Govindabhāū Ashṭaputre.
Pāḍavahī [*in loco*].
Paḍeṉ [*in loco*].
———
See Kabīr.
Padyātmaka laghu hitopadeṣa.
See Vināyaka Yaṣavanta Berḍe.
Pahileṉ pustaka.
See Berar First Book.
———
See Bhāskara Dāmodara.
Pākaṣāstra.
See Rāvajī Hari Āṭhvale.
Pāḷaṇe [*in loco*].
Pāl āṇi Vharjiniyā [*i.e.*, Paul and Virginia].
See Saint Pierre (J. H. B. de).
Pālīchī kārikā.
See Pāl.
Pānapatchī laḍhāī.
See Panipat.
Pañchāṅga.
See Ephemerides.
Pañcharatna.
See Mahābhārata.—*Selections*.
Pañchatantra [*in loco*].
Pañchatantrasāra.
See Govindaṣaṅkara Ṣāstrī Bāpaṭ.
Pāñchaveṉ pustaka.
See Marathi Fifth Book.
Pañchīkaraṇa.
See Rāmadāsa Svāmī, *of Haidarabad*.
Pañchopākhyāna.
See Pañchatantra.
Pāṇḍavāṉchī bakhar.
See Rāma Ṣāstrī.
Pāṇḍavapratāpa.
See Ṣrīdhara.
Paṇḍharīmāhātmya.
See Ṣrīdhara.
Paṇḍitā Ramābāī ... pravāsa.
See Ramābāī, *Paṇḍitā*.
Pāṇḍuraṅgamāhātmya.
See Ṣrīdhara.
Pāṇḍuraṅgastotra.
See Mahīpati.
Pāṇipatchī bakhar.
See Raghunātha Yādava.
Pāradhī ākhyāna.
See Pāradhī.
Paramadharmatattva.
See Sītārāma Rāvajī Junnarkar.
Paramānandalaharī.
See Ṭikārāma.
Parameṣvarāchyā ārādhanecheṉ pustaka.
See Gopīnātha Sadāṣivajī Hāṭe.
Parimāṇamālā [*in loco*].
Pārvatī-pariṇaya.
See Bāṇa.
Paṣchāttāpāchī goshṭa.
See Repentance.
Pāṭhāvali.
See Paraṣurāma Panta Goḍbole.
Patrikeche abhaṅga.
See Tukārāma.
Patteṉ yādī waghairah.
See Patteṉ.
Pavanavijaya.
See Mukundarāja.
Pāvasāvishayīṉ vichāra.
See Enquiry.
Pavitra Bhāgīpaṇāchyā vidhisāṭhīṉ rāga.
See Liturgies.—England, *Church of*.—*Book of*
Peshwyāṉchī bakhar. [*Common Prayer*.
See Kṛishṇajī Vināyaka Sohanī.
Phiryādī karaṇyāchyā mudatī *etc.*
See India.—*Legislative Council*.
Prabhūchyā prārthanevar ṭīkā.
See Lord's Prayer.
Prabodhachandrodaya nāṭaka.
See Kṛishṇamiṣra.
Prāchīna āryavidyā va rīti.
See Gopāla Hari Deṣmukh.
Prahasanasaṅgraha [*in loco*].
Prakaraṇeṉ.
See Vāmana Paṇḍita.
Prākṛita kavitecheṉ pahileṉ pustaka.
See Mahādeva Govinda Ṣāstrī.
Pramilārjuna nāṭaka.
See Mahādeva Vināyaka Kelkar.
Prārthanā Samājāchā dharma svabuddhikalpita.
See Nīlakaṇṭha Gore (N.)
Prasannarāghava nāṭaka.
See Jayadeva.
Praṣnabhairava.
See Bhairava Jyotirvid.
Praṣna soḍaviṇyācheṉ sādhana.
See *Bell* (A.) *of Edinburgh*.
Praṣnottara ratnamālikā [*in loco*].
Praṣnottara saṅgraha.
See Kalyāṇa Sītārāma Chitre.
Prayāgamāhātmya. [*hātmya*.
See Purāṇas.—Matsyapurāṇa.—*Prayāgamā-*
Puṇeṉ jilhācheṉ varṇana.
See Sītārāma Viṣvanātha Paṭavardhana.
——— Prārthanā Samājāche niyama.
See Brāhma Samāj.—*Poona Prārthanā Samāj*.

Puṇeṉ shahr.
See SĪTĀRĀMA RĀMACHANDRA GĀIKVĀḌ.
Purrum dhurma tutwa [*i.e.* Paramadharmatattva].
See SĪTĀRĀMA RĀVAJĪ JUNNARKAR.
Purushasūkta.
See VEDAS.—Ṛigveda.—*Purushasūkta.*
Pushpavāṇavilāsa.
See KĀLIDĀSA, *pseud.*
Putanāvadha.
See ĀNANDATANAYA.
Rādhāvilāsa.
See MAṄGĪṢA.
Rājā Pratāpādityācheṉ charitra.
See VAIJANĀTHA ṢARMĀ.
Rājavyavahāra koṣa.
See RAGHUNĀTHA NĀRĀYAṆA.
Rāmamantra ṣloka.
See RĀMADĀSA SVAMĪ, *Son of Sūryopanta.*
Rāma rājyāchī bakhar.
See NĀRO APĀJĪ GOḌBOLE.
Rāmāryā.
See MUDGALA ACHĀRYA.
Rāmāṣvamedha.
See PURĀṆAS.–Padmapurāṇa.–*Rāmāṣvamedha.*
Rāmavijaya.
See ṢRĪDHARA.
Rambhā Ṣuka saṃvāda.
See MUKTEṢVARA.
———
See RAMBHĀ ṢUKA.
Rasakallola.
See GAṄGĀDHARA, *Kavi.*
Rāsakrīḍā.
See HĀĪM (D.)
———
See VISHṆUDĀSA.
Rasamañjarī.
See VIṬHṬHALA.
Rasāyanaṣāstra.
See HARI KEṢAVAJĪ.
———
See RĀMAJĪ GAṆOJĪ CHAUGULE.
Ratnakoṣa.
See BĀLAKṚISHṆA MALHĀR BĪḌKAR.
Ratnaprabhā.
See LAKSHMAṆA MOREṢVARA ṢĀSTRĪ HALBE.
Rāvaṇa rājyāchī bakhar.
See NĀRO ĀPĀJĪ GOḌBOLE.
Ribbī Pethāhyā yāche pravāsa.
See PETHAHIĀH ben JACOB, *of Ratisbon.*
Rogī va vaidya.
See BĀLAKṚISHṆA DINKAR VAIDYA KALYĀṆKAR.
Rukmiṇīsvayaṃvara.
See EKANĀTHA.
———
See RUKMIṆĪ.
———
See SAKHĀRĀMATANAYA.
Ṣabarī lalita nāṭaka.
See DATTĀRĀMA MOREṢVARA MANVĀCHĀRYA
Ṣabdaratnākara.
See MĀDHAVA CHANDROBĀ.
Ṣabdasaṅgraha.
See GOVINDA RĀMAKṚISHṆA PHAṆSALKAR.
———
See VĀSUDEVA MOREṢVARA POTADĀR and NĀRĀYAṆA MOREṢVARA KARANDĪKAR.
Ṣabdasiddhinibandha.
See JANĀRDANA HARI ĀṬHALYE.
———
See VINĀYAKA ṢĀSTRĪ DIVEKAR and GOVIṄDA VIṬHṬHALA MAHĀJAN.
Sabhāparva.
See MUKTEṢVARA.
Sadācharaṇāchyā goshṭī.
See STORIES.
Saddarshana-Chintanikâ [*i.e.* Shaddarṣanachintanikā.]
See PERIODICAL PUBLICATIONS.—*Poona.*
Saddharmadīpa.
See PERIODICAL PUBLICATIONS.—*Alibagh.*
Sadu Salgar.
See VIṬHṬHALA HARI LIMAYE.
Sahadevamatācheṉ jyotisharatna.
See NĀRO ĀPĀJĪ GOḌBOLE.
Sahāveṉ pustaka.
See MARATHI SIXTH BOOK.
Sakhūcheṉ charitra.
See SAKHU.
Sākreṭīs tyācheṉ charitra.
See ROLLIN (C.)
Ṣakuntalākhyāna.
See MOROPANTA.
Ṣakuntalā nāṭaka.
See KĀLIDĀSA.
Ṣālihotraṭīkā.
See NAKŪḶA.
Samaṣlokī.
See VĀMANA PAṆḌITA.
———
See VĀSUDEVĀTMAJA.
Sāṃbasadāṣiva.
See HOMER.
Sambhājī Rāje yāṉcheṉ charitra.
See MALHĀR RĀMARĀVA CHIṬṆĪS.
Sambhāshaṇāchīṉ sopīṉ vākyeṉ.
See BOMBAY, *Presidency of.* — *Government* [*Schools.*
Sambhāshaṇeṉ.
See POONA.
Saṃkshipta bhūgolavarṇana.
See PARAṢURĀMA PANTA GOḌBOLE.
——— bhūgolavidyā.
See GAṆEṢA LAKSHMAṆA ḌHORE.
Saṃsārachopaḍī [*in loco*].
Saṃskṛita āṇi Mahārāshṭra dhātukoṣa.
See VISHṆU PARAṢURĀMA ṢĀSTRĪ PAṆḌITA.
——— bhāshecheṉ lahān pustaka.
See KṚISHṆA ṢĀSTRĪ CHIPḶŪṆKAR.
——— kavi Bāṇa Bhaṭṭa.
See BĀṆA.
——— prākṛitakoṣa.
See ANANTA ṢĀSTRĪ TAḶKAR.
——— vidyecheṉ punarujjīvana.
See NĀRĀYAṆA VISHṆU BĀPAṬ.
——— vyākaraṇa.
See ṢRĪKṚISHṆA RAGHUNĀTHA ṢĀSTRĪ TAḶEKAR.

Sāmudrika [*in loco*].
Samūla-purāṇārthaprakāṣa.
See PURĀṆAS.
Saṅgativipāka nāṭaka.
See DATTO VINĀYAKA GOKHALE.
Saṅgīta Balisatva-darṣana.
See VĀMANA GAṆEṢA JOṢĪ KELṢIKAR.
—— Indrasabhā nāṭaka.
See VĀSUDEVA NĀRĀYAṆA DONGRE.
—— Kāmakandalā nāṭaka
See VĀMANA ĀTMĀRĀMA BHĀṆḌĀRĪ.
—— mīmāṃsaka.
See PERIODICAL PUBLICATIONS.—*Poona*.
—— sanjīvanī.
See VĀSTĀD MURĀRBĀ GONVEKAR.
Ṣanimāhātmya.
See MAHĪPATI.
Saṅkalita Rāmāyana.
See VĀMANA PAṆḌITA.
Saṅkaṭanāṣana ṣloka.
See GAṆAPATI.
Sanmārgadīpikā.
See GOVINDA NĀRĀYĀṆA KSHĪRASĀGARA.
Santalīlāmṛita.
See MAHĪPATI.
Saptaṣatī.
See PURĀṆAS.—Mārkaṇḍeyapurāṇa.—*Devīmāhātmya.*
Saraḷaregha trikoṇamiti.
See PARAṢURĀMA PANTA GOḌBOLE.
Sarasvatīmaṇḍala.
See RĀMACHANDRA BHIKĀJĪ GUÑJĪKAR.
Sarkārche kar.
See GAṆEṢA RĀMACHANDRA KILOSKAR.
Sarvadeṣāntīl nivaḍak mhaṇī.
See SADĀṢIVA VIṢVANĀTHA.
Sārvajanika ārogya.
See BHĀLACHANDRA KṚISHṆA BHĀṬAVAḌEKAR.
Sarvasaṅgraha [*in loco*].
————
See PERIODICAL PUBLICATIONS.—*Poona*.
Sāshṭī urf Ṭhāṇyāchī bakhar.
See ṬHĀṆĀ.
Ṣāstravachanamālā.
See BIBLE.—*Appendix*.
Ṣāstravaidyaka.
See GOPĀLA ṢIVARĀMA VAIDYAKA.
Ṣāstra va rūḍhi yāṇchyā balābalāvishayīṇ vichāra.
See KĀṢINĀTH TRIMBAKA TELANG, *C.I.E.*
Ṣatamukha Rāvaṇa vadha.
See MUKTEṢVARA.
Sātārā jilhyācheṇ varṇana.
See BALAVANTA VĀSUDEVA JOGḶEKAR.
Satārvādya.
See VĀMANA DHOṆḌADEVA KARVE.
Ṣataṣlokī.
See VOPADEVA.
Ṣatyanārāyaṇapūjā.
See PURĀṆAS.—Skandapurāṇa.—*Satyanārāyaṇavratakathā.*
Satyanirūpaṇa.
See GOVINDA NĀRĀYAṆA.
Sauri Vikrama nāṭaka.
See DATTĀTRAYA VĀSUDEVA JOGḶEKAR.
Savāī [*in loco*].
Savāī Mādhava Rāva Peshwe yāṇcheṇ nāṭaka.
See KĀṢĪNĀTHA MAHĀDEVA THATTE.
Sāvitrī ākhyāna.
See ṢRĪDHARA.
Sāvitrīchī bakhar.
See NĀRO ĀPĀJĪ GOḌBOLE.
Ṣoṭakīvishayīṇ.
See KĀṢĪNĀTHA MAHĀDEVA THATTE.
Shabda sangraha [i.e. Ṣabdasaṅgraha].
See GOVINDA RĀMAKṚISHṆA PHAṆSALKAR.
Shaḍdarṣanachintanikā.
See PERIODICAL PUBLICATIONS.—*Poona*.
Siddhāntakaumudī.
See BHAṬṬOJĪDĪKSHITA.
Siddhāntaṣiromaṇi prakāṣa.
See RĀMACHANDRA SŪBĀJĪ BĀPŪ.
Ṣikandar bādshāhcheṇ charitra.
See VINĀYAKA KOṆḌADEVA OK.
Ṣikshaka.
See DVĀRAKĀNĀTHA NĀRĀYAṆA RAṆADIVE.
—— va vidyārthī tyāṇchā mitra.
See MAHĀDEVA VIṬHṬHAḶA RĀHĀḶKAR.
Sīmantinī nāṭaka.
See DĀMODARA EKANĀTHA PĀṬSAKAR.
Siṃhāsana battīsī.
See VIKRAMĀDITYA, *King of Ujjayinī*.
Ṣiṣupālavadha nāṭaka.
See VĀMANA EKANĀTHA ṢĀSTRĪ KEMKAR.
Sītāsvayaṃvara.
See ANANTA, *Kavi*.
————
See CHINTĀMAṆI.
————
See VĀMANA PAṆḌITA.
———— nāṭaka.
See LAKSHMAṆA ṢAṄKARA ABHYAṄKAR.
Ṣivachhatrapatīcheṇ charitra.
See KṚISHṆAJĪ ANANTA, *Sabhāsad*.
Ṣivagītā.
See PURĀṆAS.—Padmapurāṇa.—*Ṣivagītā*.
Ṣivājī mahārāja yāṇs . . . . upadeṣa.
See EKANĀTHA AṆṆĀJĪ JOṢĪ.
Ṣivalīlāmṛita.
See ṢRĪDHARA.
Ṣivaparākrama varṇana.
See RAGHUNĀTHA YĀDAVA CHITRAGUPTA.
Ṣivarātrī māhātmyāche abhaṅga.
See NĀMADEVA.
Ṣīvastuti.
See VĀMANA PAṆḌITA.
Ṣivatattvaprakāṣa.
See PURĀṆAS.—*Ṣivapurāṇa*.
Ṣloka Rāmamantrāche.
See RĀMADĀSA SVĀMĪ, *Son of Sūryopantu*.
Soḷā somvār [*in loco*].
Somavatīpūjā.
See PURĀṆAS.—Bhavishyottarapurāṇa.—*Somavatīpūjā.*
Sphuṭa abhaṅga.
See TUKĀRĀMA.
—— āryā va ṣloka.
See SPHUṬA ĀRYĀ.
Sphuṭajyotisha [*in loco*].

Ṣrāvaṇa ākhyāna.
See Devanātha.
Ṣrīdattabodha.
See Srīdatta.
Ṣrīharasiddhīdevī.
See Nāro Bhāskara Khera.
Ṣrīmanta chhatrapati dhākaṭe Rāma Rāje yāṉcheṉ charitra.
——— Sambhājī yāṉcheṉ charitra.
See Malhār Rāmarāva Chiṭṇīs.
——— Panta pradhāna yāṉchī ṣakāvalī.
See Peshwas.
Ṣṛiṅgārasundara.
See Dattātraya Vāsudeva Joglekar.
Ṣṛiṅgārika sphuṭa ṣloka [*in loco*].
Ṣrīpālacharitra.
See Aṇṇāpā Āpā Vāḍakar.
Sṛishṭijñāna.
See Gaṇeṣa Kṛishṇa Āpṭe.
——— paribhāshā.
See Sakhārāma Bāpūṣeṭ Daṇḍekar.
Sṛishṭiṣāstra.
See Bālājī Prabhākara Moḍak.
Ṣriyāla nāṭaka.
See Viṭhṭhala Bhagavanta Lembhe.
Sthālīpāka.
See Janābāī.
Strīcharitra.
See Rāmajī Gaṇojī Chaugule.
Strīpurusha tulanā.
See Tārābāī Ṣinde.
Strīrogavijñāna.
See Aṇṇā Moreṣvara Kuṇṭe.
Strīvidyā vaichitryadarṣana prahasana.
See Strīvidyā.
Striyāṉchī kharī yogyatā.
See Vāsudeva Gopāla Bhāṇḍārkar.
Subantaprakāṣa.
See Kṛishṇa Ṣāstrī Bhāṭavaḍekar.
Subhadrāharaṇa.
See Moropanta.
Subodhamālinī.
See Kṛishṇarāva Bhāskarajī Rele.
Subodha padeṉ [*in loco*].
Subodhinī.
See Chāṇakya.
Sudāma-charitra.
See Kiṅkara, *Kavi.*
———
See Sudāma.
Sudarṣana charitra nāṭaka.
See Anantadīkshita Joṣī Chipḷūṇkar.
Sudarṣana Ṣaṣīkalā [*in loco*].
Ṣūdrakamalākara.
See Kamalākara Bhaṭṭa, *Son of Ramakṛishṇa* [*Bhaṭṭa.*
Ṣukabāhāttarī.
See Ṣukasaptati.
Ṣukacharitra.
See Amṛitarāya.
Ṣuka Rambhā saṃvāda.
See Kiṅkara, *Kavi.*
———
See Uddhava Chidghana.
Ṣukla Yajurvedīya Brāhmaṇa.
See Nārāyaṇa Viṭhṭhala Vaidya.
Ṣukranīti.
See Ṣukra.
Sulochanā āṇi Mādhava.
See Rāmachandra Bhikājī Gokhale.
Sulochanāsatī nāṭaka.
See Bāḷakṛishṇa Lele.
Sundarakāṇḍa.
See Rāmadāsa Svāmī, *Son of Sūryopanta.*
Sūpaṣāstra.
See Rāmachandra Sakhārāma Gupte.
Surasa abhaṅga.
See Tukārāma.
—— āratyā.
See Āratyā.
—— lāvaṇyā.
See Rāvajī Ṣrīdhara Gondhaḷekar.
—— padeṉ.
See Kabīr.
Sūryastuti.
See Vāmana Paṇḍita.
Svachchhatā kī pahilī pustaka.
See Cuningham (J. M.)
Svadeṣakalyāṇachandrikā.
See Keṣava Sadāṣiva Risbūḍ.
Svādhyāya [*in loco*].
Svapnādhyāya [*in loco*].
Swedenborg hyāṉchyā matāvishayīṉ, *etc.*
See Dādobā Pāṇḍuraṅga Tarkhaḍkar.
Syamantakopākhyāna.
See Ṣyāmā, *Kavi.*
Talmud [*in loco*].
Tantuvādya.
See Viṣvanātha Rāmachandra Kāle.
Tārakādarṣa.
See Bābājī Viṭhṭhala Kuḷakarṇī Mālvaṇkar.
Taruṇī ṣikshāṇa nāṭikā.
See Nārāyaṇa Bāpujī Kāniṭkar.
Tāṭakāvadha.
See Ānandatanaya.
Tāṭīche abhaṅga.
See Jñānadeva.
———
See Muktābāī.
Tattvavichāra.
See Gaṇeṣa Ṣāstrī Abhyaṅkar.
Thālīpāka.
See Janābāī.
Thorle Rājā Rāma yāṉcheṉ charitra prakaraṇa.
—— Shāhū Mahārājā yāṉcheṉ charitra.
See Malhār Rāmarāva Chiṭṇīs.
Tīn Rājakanyāṉchī goshṭa.
See Tīn Rājakanyā.
Tīrthāvaḷīche abhaṅga.
See Nāmadeva.
Tisreṉ pustaka.
See Bāḷakṛishṇa Lakshmaṇa Bāpaṭ.
———
See Marathi Third Book.
Toṇḍāche hiseb.
See Gaṅgādhara Govinda Sāpkar.

Trairāṣika samūha.
See Vishṇu Vāsudeva Sāṭhye Gondhaḷekar.
Triṣaṅku Rājyāchī bakhar.
See Nāro Apājī Godbole.
Triveṇī Pramātha.
See Gopāla Govinda Dābak.
Tryambaka varṇana.
See Bāḷakṛishṇa Bābājī Karkare and Gopāla Bāḷakṛishṇa Vaidya.
Tryambakī.
See Tryambaka.
Tukārāma Bābāchī gāthā.
——— Bābāchyā abhaṅgāṇchī gāthā.
See Tukārāma.
——— charitra.
See Mahīpati.
——— svargārohaṇāche abhaṅga.
See Tukārāma.
Tuḷasī ākhyāna.
See Vishṇudāsa.
Tuḷasīmāhātmya.
See Viṭhṭhaḷa Dāsa.
Turk va Raṣiyan lokāṇche laḍhāīchā itihāsa.
See Gaṇeṣa Moreṣvara Sovanī.
Udbhidjanyapadārtha.
See Govinda Nārāyaṇa.
Uddhāramahimā [*in loco*].
Ujaḷṇī.
See Aṅkalipī.
Ujaḷṇīcheṇ pahileṇ pustaka.
See Ujaḷṇī.
Umāvilāsa.
See Sadāṣiva, *Kavi*.
Unnati mhaṇaje kāy.
See Nārāyaṇa Vishṇu Bāpaṭ.
Upāsanāṇchyā ... veḷīṇ gāvayāchīṇ padyeṇ.
See Gaṅgādhara Bāḷakṛishṇa Gadre.
Upayogi jñānāchā pustaka samūha.
See Brougham (H.) *Baron Brougham and Vaux*.
Upayukta aksharalipī āṇi aṅkalipī
See Nāro Raghunātha Moholkar.
———
See Vināyaka Govinda Limaye.
——— aṅkalipī.
See Nāro Raghunātha Moholkar.
——— chamatkārā saṅgraha.
See Bhāū Govinda Sāpkar.
——— jñānasāra.
See Kāṣīnātha Mahādeva Thatte.
——— kathāsaṅgraha.
See Nārāyaṇa Rāmachandra Sohanī.
Utsavaprakāṣa.
See Kṛishṇa Ṣāstrī Rājvāḍe.
Uttaragītā.
See Mahābhārata.—*Uttaragītā*.
Uttara Koṇkaṇāntīl Ṣukla Yajurvedīya Brāhmaṇa.
See Nārāyaṇa Viṭhṭhala Vaidya.
Uttararāmacharitra.
See Bhavabhūti.
Vāchanamālā.
See Nārāyaṇa Bhāī Dāṇḍekar.
Vāchanapāṭhamāḷā.
See MacCulloch (J.M.) *D.D.*
Vachanasāra.
See Vāsudeva Moreṣvara Potadar.
Vāchanavidyā.
See Marathi Primer.
Vaidyakasaṅgraha.
See Bāpū Ṣāstrī Moghe.
Vaidyāmṛita.
See Moreṣvara, *Son of Māṇika Bhaṭṭa*.
Vaidyaprakāṣa.
See Raṅgo Sakhārāma Lāḷe Kīkvīkar.
Vaidyasārasaṅgraha.
See Raghunātha Ṣāstrī Dāṇtye and Kṛishṇa Ṣāstrī Bhāṭavaḍekar.
Vaidyatattva.
See Sakhārāma Arjuna.
Vaikuṇṭhāche abhaṅga.
See Tukārāma.
Vakāsura bakhar.
See Vakāsura.
Vākyavṛitti.
See Ṣaṅkara Achārya.
Vāmanacharitra.
See Moropanta.
—— nāṭaka.
See Vāmana Gaṇeṣa Joṣī Kelṣīkar.
Vastraharaṇāche abhaṅga.
See Tukārāma.
Vaṭasāvitrīkathā.
See Purāṇas.—Skandapurāṇa.— *Vaṭasāvitrī-kathā*
Vatsalāharaṇa nāṭaka.
See Dāmodara Harī Chitḷe.
Vedāṅgajyotisha.
See Lagadha.
Vedāṇvishayīṇ.
See Haug (M).
Vedārthayatna.
See Vedas.—*Rigveda*.
Veṇīsaṃhāra nāṭaka.
See Nārāyaṇa Bhaṭṭa, called Mṛigarājalakshmaṇa.
Veṇu.
See Gaṇeṣa Mahādeva Limaye.
Veshadhārī Pañjābī [*in loco*].
Vidhavāṣrumārjana.
See Dādobā Pāṇḍuraṅga. Tarkhaḍkar.
Vidhavāvivāha.
See Īṣvarachandra Vidyāsāgara.
—— saṃhārasāra.
See Sītārāma Panta.
Vidyā-vṛiddhīchyā kāmīṇ āmchī anāsthā.
See Rāmachandra Bhikājī Guñjīkar.
Viduranīti.
See Mahābhārata.—*Viduranīti*.
Vidyunmārga.
See Vishṇu Chimṇājī Karve.
Vigrahakoṣa.
See Gopāla Ṣāstrī Ghāṇṭe.
Vikramacharitra.
See Haridāsa.
Vikramorvaṣī nāṭaka.
See Kālidāsa.
Vinchūrkar gharāṇyāchā itihāsa.
See Hari Raghunātha Gāḍgīḷ.

Vishṇu Bhāskara Karmarkar yāṉcheṉ charitra.
See Tukārāma Nāthujī.
Vishṇunamastotra.
See Jñānadeva.
Viṣvāsu kuttā.
See Dog.
Vivāha-kālāvishayīṉ ṣārīra-ṣāstrācheṉ mata.
See Moreṣvara Gopāla Deṣmukh.
Vivāhavijñāna.
See Sakhārāma Arjuna.
Vivekasindhu.
See Mukundarāja.
Vividha jñānavistāra.
See Periodical Publications.—*Bombay.*
Viydya-prakash [*i.e.* Vaidyaprakāṣa].
See Raṅgo Sakhārāma Lāḷe Kikvīkar.
Vṛihannalāchī bakhar.
See Nāro Āpājī Goḍbole.
Vṛikshavarṇana.
See Govinda Nārāyaṇa.
Vṛittadarpaṇa.
See Paraṣurāma Panta Goḍbole.
Vyākaraṇa sambandhī sope dhaḍe.
See Lessons.
Vyaṅkateṣastotra.
See Devīdāsa.
Vyavahāradarpaṇa.
See Ṣaṅkara Ṣāstrī Gokhale.
Vyavahāramayūkha.
See Nīlakaṇṭha Mīmāṃsakabhaṭṭa.
Vyavahāropayogī nāṭaka.
See Govinda Nārāyaṇa.
Vyutpattipradīpa.
See Govinda Ṣaṅkara Ṣāstrī Bāpaṭ.
Vyutpatti-ratnākara [*in loco*].
Wáchan Páth Málá [*i.e.* Vāchanapāṭhamālā].
See MacCulloch (J. M.) *D.D.*
Yājñavalkyasmṛiti.
See Yājñavalkya.
Yaṣavanta Rāva yāṉchā pavāḍā.
See Sakhārāma Sonār.
Yātrākalpalatā.
See Gaurīṣaṅkara Ṣāstrī.
Yuddhakāṇḍa.
See Rāmadāsa Svāmī, *Son of Sūryopanta.*
Yukliḍche saralarekhā gaṇitāchīṉ mūlatattveṉ.
See Euclid.
Yuropāntīl vanadevatāṉchyā goshṭī.
See Bellairs (H.)

SUBJECT-INDEX.

AGRICULTURE.

Bāgāīta. Ṣaṅkara Ṣāstrī Gokhale.
Jāgatījota. Rāmachandra Amṛita Dugal.
Kṛishikarmāntargata rasāyanaṣāstra. Bāḷakṛishṇa Ātmārāma Gupte.
Ṣetakīvishayīṇ. Kāṣīnātha Mahādeva Thatte.
Upayukta jñānasāra. Kāṣīnātha Mahādeva Thatte.
Vṛikshavarṇana. Govinda Nārāyaṇa.
Vyavahāradarpaṇa. Ṣaṅkara Ṣāstrī Gokhale.

ARTS.

Divālīchī lūṭ. Lakshmaṇa Gaṅgājī Toḍāvār.
Gāruḍyāchā tamāshā. Gāruḍa.
Hindusthānāntīl ṣilpaṣāstra. Napier (F.) *Baron Napier.*
Kārāgīr lokāṇche kāmāvishayīṇ. Kāṣīnātha Mahādeva Thatte.
Laghu lekhanapaddhati. Gajānanabhāū Vaijya.
Lohamārga. Vishṇu Chimṇājī Karve.
Pākaṣāstra. Rāvajī Hari Āṭhvale.
Sūpaṣāstra. Rāmachandra Sakhārāma Gupte.
Upayukta jñānasāra. Kāṣīnātha Mahādeva Thatte.
Vidyunmārga. Vishṇu Chimṇājī Karve.
Vyavahāradarpaṇa. Ṣaṅkara Ṣāstrī Gokhale.

ASTROLOGY and DIVINATION.

Pālīchī kārikā. Pāl.
Praṣnabhairava. Bhairava Jyotirvid.
Sahadevamatāchen jyotisharatna. Nāro Apājī Goḍbole.
Sāmudrika. Sāmudrika.
Sphuṭajyotisha. Sphuṭajyotisha.
Svapnādhyāya. Svapnādhyāya.
Vedāṅgajyotisha. Lagadha.

ASTRONOMY.

Jyotiḥṣāstra. Kṛishṇa Ṣāstrī Goḍbole.
———— Lockyer (J. N.)
Jyotisharatna. } Ṣukadeva.
Jyotishasāra. }
Lagnayantra. Lagnayantra.
Siddhāntaṣiromaṇiprakāṣa. Rāmachandra Sūbājī Bāpū.
Tārakādarṣa. Bābājī Viṭhṭhala Kuḷakarṇī Mālvaṇkar.
Vedāṅgajyotisha. Lagadha.

BIOGRAPHY.

Bābājīchī bakhar. Bābājī Raghunātha Marāṭhe.
Bāpū Gokhale yāṇchen charitra. Ṣaṅkara Tukārāma Ṣāligrām.
Bhāū Sāhebāṇchī bakhar. Bhāū Sāheb.
Brahmendra Svāmī yāṇchen charitra. Brahmendra Svāmī.
Chhatrapati Sambhājī Mahārāja. Nāgeṣarāva Vināyaka Bāpaṭ.
Dhākaṭe Shāhū Mahārāja yāṇchen charitra. Malhār Rāmarāva Chiṭṇīs.
Ekanāthacharitra. Ekanātha.
Ekanātha Mahārāja yāṇchen charitra. Dhoṇḍo Bāḷakṛishṇa Sahasrabuddhe.
Jñānadeva charitra. Raghunāthabovā Bhiṅgārkar.
Jñāneṣvara Mahārājāṇchen charitra. Baḷavanta Khaṇḍojī Pārakh.
Kavicharitra. Janārdana Rāmachandrajī.
Kharaḍyāchyā svārīchī bakhar. Mādhava Rāva II., *Peshwa.*
Kuvarajī Mahārāja yāṇchen charitra. Kuvarajī.
Lārḍ Bekan yāṇchen charitra. Govinda Nārāyaṇa Kāṇe.
Mahanmaṇimālā. Vināyaka Koṇḍadeva Ok.
Nārāyaṇa Rāva Peshwe yāṇchen charitra. Pāṇḍuraṅga.
Nārāyaṇa Rāvyāchī bakhar. Nārāyaṇa Rāva.
Rājā Pratāpādityāchen charitra. Vaijanātha Ṣarmā.
Sākretīs tyāchen charitra. Rollin (C.)
Sambhājī Rāje yāṇchen charitra. Malhār Rāmarāva Chiṭṇīs.
Ṣikandar bādshāhchen charitra. Vināyaka Koṇḍadeva Ok.
Ṣivachhatrapatichen charitra. Kṛishṇajī Ananta, *Sabhāsad.*
Ṣrīmanta chhatrapati dhākaṭe Rāma Rāje yāṇchen charitra. } Malhār Rāmarāva Chiṭṇīs.
———— Sambhājī yāṇchen charitra. }
Thorle Rājā Rāma yāṇchen charitra prakaraṇa. } Malhār Rāmarāva Chiṭṇīs.
—— Shāhū Mahārājā yāṇchen charitra. }

N

Vikramacharitra. Haridāsa.
Vishṇu Bhāskara Karmarkar yāṇcheṇ charitra. Tukārāma Nāthujī.

CASTE.

Bhramanirāsa. Rāmachandra Bhikājī Guñjīkar.
Brahmadvesha. Rāvajī Hari Āṭhvale.
Brāhmaṇavarṇācheṇ mūḷa. Haug (M.)
Jasās taseṇ purvaṇī. Rājārāma Rāmakṛishṇa Bhāgavata.
Jātibheda. Jātibheda.
Jātibheda vivekasāra. Hindu.
Konkaṇastha Brāhmaṇāṇchī gotramālikā. Sadāsiva Bajyābā Ṣāstrī.
Kshatriyavaṃṣodgamamālā. Kshatriyavaṃṣa.
Madhvamata. Bhīmāchārya Jhalkīkar.
Nābhikapurāṇa. Bhāratī Visvanātha.
Prāchīna Āryavidyā va rīti. Gopāla Hari Deshmukh.
Sarasvatīmaṇḍala. Rāmachandra Bhikājī Guñjīkar.
Ṣūdrakamalākara. Kamalākara Bhaṭṭa.
Ṣukla Yajurvedīya Brāhmaṇa. Nārāyaṇa Viṭhṭhala Vaidya.

CHRONOLOGY.

Hindusthānāchī ṣakāvalī. MacCudden (T.)
Itihāsarūpa darṣikā. Balavanta Hari Joṣī Borgāṇvakar.

DICTIONARIES, VOCABULARIES, and GLOSSARIES.

Bhāratavarshīya prāchīna aitihāsika koṣa. Raghunātha Bhāskara Goḍbole.
Hindusthānāchā arvachīna koṣa. Raghunātha Bhāskara Goḍbole.
Mahārāshṭra bhāshechā koṣa. Bāḷa Ṣāstrī Ghagve.
Marāṭhī bhāshechā navīna koṣa. Raghunātha Bhāskara Goḍbole.
——— dusre pustakāntīl ṣabdārtha. Sadāṣiva Viṭhṭhala Pālkar.
Mustering kārkunās madat. Kṛishṇajī Gaṇeṣa Dongre.
Rājavyavahāra koṣa Raghunātha Nārāyaṇa.
Ratnakoṣa. Bāḷakṛishṇa Malhār Biḍkar.
Ṣabdaratnākara. Mādhava Chandrobā.
Ṣabdasaṅgraha. Govinda Rāmakṛishṇa Phaṇsalkar.
——————— Vāsudeva Moreṣvara Potadār.
Saṃskṛita āṇi Mahārāshṭra dhātukoṣa. Vishṇu Paraṣurāma Ṣāstrī Paṇḍita.
Vigrahakoṣa. Gopāla Ṣāstrī Ghāṇṭe.
Vyutpattiratnākara. Vyutpattiratnākara.

DIVINATION. See ASTROLOGY.

DRAMA.

Aitihāsika nāṭakamālā. Aitihāsika Nāṭakamālā.
Bāḷājī Visvanātha nāṭaka. Rāvajī Hari Āṭhvale.
Bāla Ṣivājī nāṭaka. Sītārāma Narahara Dhavḷe.
Bālavivāha duḥkha-darṣana prahasana. Ananta Nārāyaṇa Paṇḍita.
Bhadrāyu satvadarṣana nāṭaka. Vāsudeva Chintāmaṇa Bāpaṭ.
Bhāmāvilāsa nāṭaka. Dattātraya Vāsudeva Jogḷekar.
Bhrāntikṛita chamatkāra. Shakspere (W.)
Chitrasena gandharva nāṭaka. Dattātraya Vāsudeva Jogḷekar.
Dākṭar va vaidya. Prahasanasaṅgraha.
Guṇotkarsha nāṭaka. Vāsudeva Vāmana Ṣāstrī Khare.
Hariṣchandra nāṭaka. Sokar Bāpūjī Trilokekar.
Hariṣchandra satvadarṣana nāṭaka. Raghunātha Ṣaṅkara Ṣāstrī Abhyaṅkar.
Jānakīpariṇaya nāṭaka. Rāmabhadra Dīkshita.
Jarāsandhavadha nāṭaka. Sakhārāma Bāḷakṛishṇa Sarnāīk.
Jayapāḷa. Vināyaka Janārdana Kīrtane.
Kālidāsa chāturya nāṭaka. Vāmana Gopāla Keḷkar.
Kāliyamardana nāṭaka. Sakhārāma Bāḷakṛishṇa Sarnāīk.
Kāmakandalā nāṭaka. Ekanātha Gaṇeṣa Bhāṇḍāre.
Lalitasaṅgraha. Rāmajī Dhāyājī.
Mālavikāgnimitra. Kālidāsa.
Malhār Rāva Mahārāja nāṭaka. Nārāyaṇa Bāpujī Kāniṭkar.
Manoramā nāṭaka. Mahādeva Bāḷakṛishṇa Chitḷe.
Maujechyā chār ghaṭaka. Mahādeva Chimṇājī Āpṭe.
Mora L. L. B. Nārāyaṇarāva Bhāgavata.
Mṛichchhakaṭika nāṭaka. Ṣūdraka.
Mudrārākshasa. Viṣākhadatta.
Nāgānanda nāṭaka. Harshadeva.
Nāṭaka thorle Mādhava Rāva Peshwe yāṇjvar. Vināyaka Janārdana Kīrtane.
Pārvatī-pariṇaya. Bāṇa.
Prabodhachandrodaya nāṭaka. Kṛishṇamiṣra.
Prahasanasaṅgraha. Prahasanasaṅgraha.
Pramilārjuna nāṭaka. Mahādeva Vināyaka Keḷkar.
Prasannarāghava nāṭaka. Jayadeva.
Rāsakrīḍā. Haīm (D.)
Ṣabarī lalita nāṭaka. Dattārāma Moreṣvara Manvāchārya.
Ṣakuntalā nāṭaka. Kālidāsa.
Saṅgativipāka nāṭaka. Datto Vināyaka Gokhale.
Saṅgīta Balisatva-darṣana. Vāmana Gaṇeṣa Joṣī Keḷsīkar.
—— Indrasabhā nāṭaka. Vāsudeva Nārāyaṇa Dongre.
—— Kāmakandalā nāṭaka. Vāmana Ātmārāma Bhāṇḍārī.
Sauri Vikrama nāṭaka. Dattātraya Vāsudeva Jogḷekar.
Savāī Mādhava Rāva Peshwe yāṇcheṇ nāṭaka. Kāṣīnātha Mahādeva Thatte.

Sīmantinī nāṭaka. Dāmodara Ekanātha Pāṭsakar.
Śiśupālavadha nāṭaka. Vāmana Ekanātha Śāstrī Kemkar.
Sītāsvayaṃvara nāṭaka. Lakshmaṇa Śaṅkara Abhyaṅkar.
Śriyāla nāṭaka. Viṭhṭhala Bhagavanta Lembhe.
Strīvidyā vaichitryadarśana prahasana. Strīvidyā.
Sudarśana charitra nāṭaka. Anantadīkshita Jośī Chipḷūṇkar.
Śūdrakamalākara. Kamalākara Bhaṭṭa.
Sulochanāsatī nāṭaka. Bāḷakrishṇa Lele.
Taruṇī śikshaṇa nāṭikā. Nārāyaṇa Bāpujī Kāniṭkar.
Uttararāmacharitra. Bhavabhūti.
Vāmanacharitra nāṭaka. Vāmana Gaṇeśa Jośī Kelśīkar.
Vatsalāharaṇa nāṭaka. Dāmodara Harī Chitle.
Veṇīsaṃhāra nāṭaka. Nārāyaṇa Bhaṭṭa, called Mṛigarājalakshmaṇa.
Vikramorvaśī nāṭaka. Kālidāsa.
Vyavahāropayogī nāṭaka. Govinda Nārāyaṇa.

ETHICS.

Hemāḍapantakṛita nīti. Hemāḍapanta.
Marāṭhī prachārāntīl mhaṇi. Gaṅgādhara Govinda Sāpkar.
Nāradanīti. Nāradanīti.
Nārāyaṇabodha. Rāmajī Gaṇojī Chaugule.
Navīna laghu hitopadeśa. Maxims.
Nītidarpaṇa. Vishṇu Śāstrī.
Nītijñānāchī paribhāshā. Esdaile (D. A.)
Nītikathā. Nītikathā.
Nītimandira. Govindaśaṅkara Śāstrī Bāpaṭ.
Nītipar kavitā. Nītipar Kavitā.
Padyātmaka laghu hitopadeśa. Vināyaka Yaśavanta Berḍe.
Sanmārgadīpikā. Govinda Nārāyaṇa Kshīrasāgara.
Sarvadeśāntīl nivaḍak mhaṇi. Sadāśiva Viśvanātha.
Satyanirūpaṇa. Govinda Nārāyaṇa.
Strīcharitra. Rāmajī Gaṇojī Chaugule.
Subodhinī. Chāṇakya.
Śukranīti. Śukra.
Viduranīti. Mahābhārata.—*Viduranīti.*

GAMES.

Gamatīcheṇ pahileṇ pustaka. Nāro Āpājī Godbole.
Mallavidyā prakāśaka. Sītārāma Ballāla Mahājan.
Mulīṇchā khel. Nārāyaṇa Vishṇu Jośī.
Upayukta chamatkāra saṅgraha. Bhāū Govinda Sāpkar.

GEOGRAPHY

Bhūgola āṇi khagola vishayaka saṃvāda. Dialogues.
Bhūgolācheṇ varṇana. Candy (T.)
Bhūgola khagola. Sullivan (R.) *LL.D.*
Bhūgola śāstra. Bāḷa Gaṅgādhara Śāstrī Jāmbhekar.
Bhūgolavidyā. Rāmachandra Vishṇu.
Bhūtala vishayaka vidyechīṇ mulatattveṇ. Blanford (H. F.)
Bhūvarṇana. Geikie (A.)
Hindusthānāchā bhūgola. Bāpū Purushottama Jośī Ṭoṅkekar.
——— Viṭhṭhala Vāmana Gandye.
Saṃkshipta bhūgolavarṇana. Paraśurāma Panta Godbole.
——— bhūgolavidyā. Gaṇeśa Lakshmaṇa Dhore.
Srishṭijñāna paribhāshā. Sakhārāma Bāpūśeṭ Dāṇḍekar.

GRAMMARS.

Alaṅkāraviveka. Krishṇa Śāstrī Rājvāḍe.
Bālavyākaraṇa. Bāḷa Śāstrī.
Ingliś bhāshechā vyākaraṇāchī mūḷapīṭhikā. Stevenson (J.) *D.D.*
——— vyākaraṇa. English Grammar.
——— vyākaraṇāchī mūlapīṭhikā. Dādobā Pāṇḍuraṅga Tarkhaḍkar.
Ingrejī vyākaraṇāchā saṃkshepa. Murray (L.)
Kaumudīmahotsāha. Rāmachandra Bhikājī Guñjīkar.
Laghu vyākaraṇa. Gaṅgādhara Rāmachandra Tilaka.
Mahārāshṭra bhāshecheṇ vyākaraṇa. Dādobā Pāṇḍuraṅga Tarkhaḍkar.
——— Gaṅgādhara Śāstrī Phaḍke.
Marāṭhī bhāshecheṇ navīna vyākaraṇa. Krishṇa Śāstrī Godbole.
——— laghu vyākaraṇa. Dādobā Pāṇḍuraṅga Tarkhaḍkar.
Pāṭhāvali. Paraśurāma Panta Godbole.
Śabdasiddhinibandha. Janārdana Hari Āṭhalye.
——— Vināyaka Śāstrī Divekar.
Saṃskṛita bhāshecheṇ lahān pustaka. Krishṇa Śāstrī Chipḷūṇkar.
——— vyākaraṇa. Śrīkrishṇa Raghunātha Śāstrī Taḷekar.
Siddhāntakaumudī. Bhaṭṭojīdīkshita.
Subantaprakāśa. Krishṇa Śāstrī Bhāṭavaḍekar.
Vṛittadarpaṇa. Paraśurāma Panta Godbole.
Vyākaraṇa sambandhī sope dhaḍe. Lessons.
Vyutpattipradīpa. Govinda Śaṅkara Śāstrī Bāpaṭ.

HINDU PHILOSOPHY.

Āgamanigama grantha. Mainānātha.
Anubhavalaharī. Anubhavalaharī.
Anubhavāmṛita padabodhinī. Jñānadeva.
Ātmānubhava. Keśava Sakhārāma Śāstrī.
Bahurūpī santakheḷ. Govinda Morobā Kārlekar.
Bhagavadgītā. Mahābhārata.—*Bhagavadgītā.*
Bhagavadgītecheṇ sāra. Nesbit (R.)
Bhāvachandrikā. Mahābhārata.—*Bhagavadgītā.*

Bhāvārthasindhu. Vishṇu Bhikājī Gokhale.
Dāsabodha. Rāmadāsa Svāmī.
Dīparatnākara. Rāmānanda.
Gītābhāvachandrikā. Bāḷājī Sundarajī.
Hastāmalaka. Ekanātha.
———— Ṣaṅkara Āchārya.
Jñāneṣvarī. Jñānadeva.
Kālpanika vijñānāvishayin. Stevenson (J.) *D.D.*
Laghubodha. Raghunātha Āchārya.
Laghuvākyavṛitti. Ṣaṅkara Āchārya.
Manaṣchandrabodha. Manaṣchandrabodha.
Mūḷastambha. Mūḷastambha.
———— Purāṇas.—*Ṣivapurāṇa.*
Nyāyabhāratī. Viṣvanātha Pañchānana Bhaṭṭāchārya.
Pañchīkaraṇa. Rāmadāsa Svāmī, *of Haidarabad.*
Paramadharmatattva. Sītārāma Rāvajī Junnarkar.
Praṣnottara ratnamālikā. Praṣnottara ratnamālikā.
Ṣrīdattabodha. Ṣrīdatta.
Vākyavṛitti. Ṣaṅkara Āchārya.
Vivekasindhu. Mukundarāja.

HISTORY.

Aṅgre gharāṇyāchā itihāsa. Rāvajī Hari Āthvale.
Bakhar Marāṭhyāṇchī. Duff (J. G.)
Bene Isrāel-lokāṇchā itihāsa. Talkar (H. J.)
Bhāū Sāhebāṇchī bakhar. Bhāū Sāheb.
Hindusthānāchā itihāsa. Elphinstone (*Hon.* M.)
———— Morris (H.)
———— Murray (H.)
———— Viṣvanātha Mahādeva Gokhale.
———— saṃkshipta itihāsa. Vināyaka Koṇḍadeva Ok.
Hindusthānāchen varṇana. Candy (T.)
Hindusthānāchyā itihā-āntīl . . . saṃkshipta māhitī. Pāṇḍuraṅga Moreṣvara Potadār.
———— itihāsāntīl laḍhāyā. Vishṇu Yesavanta Durve.
Hindusthānāntīl Ingliṣāṇchyā rājyāchā itihāsa. Bāḷa Gaṅgādhara Ṣāstrī Jāmbhekar.
Holkarāṇchī kaifiyat. Holkar, *Family of.*
Inglāṇḍāchā vṛittānta. Davys (G.)
Ingland deṣāchī bakhar. England.
Itihāsāvarīl nibandha. Vishṇu Krishṇa Chipḷuṇkar.
Khusrū rājāchā itihāsa. Rollin (C.)
Mahārāshṭra deṣāchen varṇana. Esdaile (D. A.)
Marāṭhyāṇchī bakhar. Duff (J. G.)
Nāgpūrkar Bhonsalyāṇchī bakhar. Kāṣīrāva Rājeṣvara Gupta.
———— vaṃṣāvala. Nagpur.
Pānapatchī laḍhāī. Panipat.
Pānipatchī bakhar. Raghunātha Yādava.
Peshwyāṇchī bakhar. Krishṇajī Vināyaka Sohanī.
Sāshṭī urf Ṭhāṇyāchī bakhar. Ṭhāṇā.
Ṣrīmanta Panta pradhāna yāṇchī ṣakāvalī. Peshwas.
Vinchūrkar gharāṇyāchā itihāsa. Hari Raghunātha Gāḍgīḷ.

LAW.—English.

British Parliament . . . kelele kāyade. Rāmachandra Govinda Talvarkar.
Dīwāṇī kām chālaviṇyāchā kāyadā. India.—*Legislative Council.*
Phiryādī karaṇyāchyā mudatī, *etc.* India.—*Legislative Council.*
Praṣnottara saṅgraha. Kalyāṇa Sītārāma Chitre.
Vāchanamālā. Nārāyaṇa Bhāī Dāṇḍekar.

LAW.—Hindu.

Manusmṛiti. Manu.
Mitākshara. Vijñāneṣvara.
Vyavahāramayūkha. Nīlakaṇṭha Mīmāṃsaka-bhaṭṭa.
Yājñavalkyasmṛiti. Yājñavalkya.

LETTERS.

Lekhanakalpataru. Hemādrī.
Lekhanapaddhati. Lekhanapaddhati.
Lipidhārā. Baker (F. P.)
Nāgpūrkar Bhoṇsalyāṇchyā . . . kāgadpatra. Nagpur.
Patteṇ yādī waghairah. Patteṇ.

LITERARY CRITICISM.

Kāvyadoshavirechana. Benjamin (S.)
Saṃskṛita kavi Bāṇa Bhaṭṭa. Bāṇa.
———— vidyecheṇ punarujjīvana. Nārāyaṇa Vishṇu Bāpaṭ.
Svādhyāya. Svādhyāya.

MATHEMATICS.

Aṅkagaṇita. Aṅkagaṇita.
———— Kero Lakshmaṇa Chhatre.
Aṅkalipi. Aṅkalipi.
Bhūmiti. Pasley (*Sir* C. W.)
Bījagaṇitāchiṇ mūlatattveṇ. Haddon (J.) *M.A.*
Bījagaṇita mūlapiṭhikā. De Morgan (A.)
Grahasādhanāchiṇ koshṭakeṇ. Kero Lakshmaṇa Chhatre.
Hiṣebāṇcheṇ pahileṇ pustaka. } Nāro Raghunātha Moholkar
Hiṣeb ratnamālā. }
Jamākharchāchī māhitī. Gopāla Yajñeṣvara Bhiḍe.
Jamākharchāchī paddhati. Vāsudeva Bāḷakrishṇa Loṭlīkar.
Kerokṛita aṅkagaṇita . . . . praṣnasamudāya. Nāro Raghunātha Moholkar.
Koshṭakeṇ. Nāro Āpājī Godbole.
Kshaitra saṅkuchchheda. Drew (W. H.)
Laghu pūrṇāṅka. Nārāyaṇa Yajñeṣvara Bhiḍe.
Lahāṇ mulāṇkaritāṇ gaṇita. Bruce (H. J.)
Līlāvatī. Viṭhṭhala Krishṇājī Kāyakiṇīkar.
Marāṭhī sāhāvyā iyattechā gaṇita. Hari Nārāyaṇa Limaye.
Pāḍavahī. Pāḍavahī.
Parimāṇamālā. Parimāṇamālā.

Praşna soḍaviṇyāchen sādhana. BELL (A.)
Saraḷaregha trikoṇamiti. PARAŞURĀMA PANTA GODBOLE.
Toṇḍāche hişeb. GAṄGĀDHARA GOVINDA SĀPKAR.
Trairāşika samūha. VISHṆU VĀSUDEVA SĀṬHYE.
Ujaḷṇī. AṄKALIPI.
Ujaḷṇīchen pahileṇ pustaka. UJAḶṆĪ.
Upayukta aksharalipi. VINĀYAKA GOVINDA LIMAYE.
——— aṅkalipi. NĀRO RAGHUNĀTHA MOHOḶKAR.
Yukliḍche saralarekhā gaṇita. EUCLID.

MEDICINE.

Amṛitasāgara. PRATĀPA SIṂHA, *Raja of Jaipur.*
Ārogyarakshakavidyā. CHINTĀMANA ANANTA LIMAYE.
Ārogyarakshaṇa. PUBLIC HEALTH.
Ārya vaidyaka, *etc.* BHĀLACHANDRA KṚISHṆA BHĀṬAVAḌEKAR.
Aşru, tyāṇchī utpatti āṇi yojanā. KĀNHOBĀ RAṆCHHOḌDĀS KĪRTIKAR.
Aşvaparīkshā. NAKUḶA.
Aushadhavidyā. NĀRĀYAṆA DĀJĪ.
Bālavaidya. JANĀRDANA HARI ĀṬHALYE.
Bhāratavarshīya vanaushadhisaṅgraha. PĀṆḌURAṄGA GOPĀLA MANTRĪ.
Chikitsāsāra. GOPĀLADĀSA.
Garbhakāṇḍa. GARBHAKĀṆḌA.
Ijevar prathama upāya. ESMARCH (F.)
Mādhavanidāna. MĀDHAVA, *Son of Indukara.*
Mānusha indriyavijñānaşāstra. } BHIKĀJĪ AMṚITA.
——— şarīraşāstra. }
Masūrikā va gostanaroga. TRIMBAKA SAKHĀRĀMA ŞIRVALKAR.
Şālihotraṭīkā. NAKUḶA.
Sārvajanika ārogya. BHĀLACHANDRA KṚISHṆA BHĀṬAVAḌEKAR.
Şāstravaidyaka. GOPĀLA ŞIVARĀMA VAIDYAKA.
Strīrogavijñāna. AṆṆĀ MOREŞVARA KUṆṬE.
Svachchhatā kī pahilī pustaka. CUNINGHAM (J. M.)
Tryambakī. TRYAMBAKA.
Udbhidjanya padārtha. GOVINDA NĀRĀYAṆA.
Vaidyakasaṅgraha. BĀPŪ ŞĀSTRĪ MOGHE.
Vaidyāmṛita. MOREŞVARA, *Son of Māṇika Bhaṭṭa.*
Vaidyaprakāşa. RAṄGO SAKHĀRĀMA LĀḶE KIKVĪKAR.
Vaidyasārasaṅgraha. RAGHUNĀTHA ŞĀSTRĪ DĀNTYE and KṚISHṆA ŞĀSTRĪ BHĀṬAVAḌEKAR.
Vaidyatattva. SAKHĀRĀMA ARJUNA.

MUSIC.

Saṅgīta sañjīvanī. VASTĀD MURĀRBĀ GONVEKAR.
Satārvādya. VĀMANA DHOṆḌADEVA KARVE.
Tantuvādya. VIŞVANĀTHA RĀMACHANDRA KĀḶE.

MYTHOLOGICAL TALES.

See TALES. — MYTHOLOGICAL.

PERIODICAL LITERATURE.

(See under the heading "PERIODICAL PUBLICATIONS" in the body of the Catalogue.)

POETRY.

Abhaṅga. CHĀṄGADEVA.
——— JÑĀNADEVA.
——— MUKTĀ BĀĪ.
——— NIVṚITTINĀTHA.
——— RĀMADĀSA SVĀMĪ, *Son of Sūryopanta.*
——— SOPĀNADEVA.
——— TUKĀRĀMA.
Abhaṅga bāḷakrīḍeche. NĀMADEVA.
Abhaṅgāchā gāthā. NIḶOBĀ RĀYA.
Adbhuta Rāmāyaṇa. VĀLMĪKI.
Amaruşataka. AMARU.
Ānandalaharī. EKANĀTHA.
Aneka kavikṛita kavitā. MARATHI ANTHOLOGY.
Anusmṛiti. MAHĀBHĀRATA.—*Selections.*
Āratīsaṅgraha. VĀSUDEVA MOREŞVARA POTADĀR.
Āratyā. ĀRATYĀ.
Āratyāpañchaka. GAṄGĀDHARA DĪKSHITA.
Arjadāsta. EKANĀTHA.
Arjunagītā. MAHĀBHĀRATA.—*Selections.*
Ārya mātṛivilāsa. GAṄGĀDHARA VIṬHṬHALA MOGRE.
Āryāşataka. MUDGALA ĀCHĀRYA.
Bahurūpī santakheḷ. GOVINDA MOROBĀ KĀRLEKAR.
Bālacharita. ĀNANDATANAYA.
Bhagavadgītā. MAHĀBHĀRATA.—*Bhagavadgītā.*
——— MAHĀBHĀRATA.—*Selections.*
——— UDDHAVA CHIDGHANA.
Bhāgavata. EKANĀTHA.
Bhāgavata āryā. MOROPANTA.
Bhaktalīlāmṛita. MAHĪPATI.
Bhaktāmara-stotra. MĀNATUṄGĀCHĀRYA.
Bhaktisāra. MĀLU NARAHARI.
Bhaktivijaya. MAHĪPATI.
Bharatabhāva. VĀMANA PAṆḌITA.
Bhāvachandrikā. MAHĀBHĀRATA.—*Bhagavadgītā.*
Bhavānī-ashṭaka. BHAVĀNĪ ASHṬAKA.
Bhīshmastavarāja. MAHĀBHĀRATA.—*Selections.*
Bhūpāḷyā. BHŪPĀḶYĀ.
Bilhaṇa charitra. VIṬHṬHALA, *Kavi.*
Bodhalyācheṇ abhaṅga. BODHALA.
Bodhapar paḍeṇ. KṚISHṆAJĪ BALLĀLA ṬHĀKURA.
Brahmajñānapar abhaṅga. TUKĀRĀMA.
Buddhabāvanī. BUDDHABĀVANĪ.
Champūbhārata. ANANTA BHAṬṬA, *the Poet.*
Champūrāmāyaṇa. BHOJARĀYA PAṆḌITA.
Chāṅgadeva charitra. NIḶOBĀ RĀYA.
Charpaṭapañjarī. ŞAṄKARA ĀCHĀRYA.
Chovīsanāvāṇche abhaṅga. CHOVĪSANĀVA.
Daivasenī. MĀDHAVARĀVA, also called BĀJĀBĀ RĀMACHANDRA PRADHĀNA.
Dānavrata. NARAHARI.
Dāsabodha. RĀMADĀSA SVĀMĪ, *Son of Sūryopanta.*
Daşamaskandhāchyā āryā. MOROPANTA.
Daşāvatārāche şloka. DAŞĀVATĀRA.
Dhāṇve. DHĀṆVE.
Dīparatnākara. RĀMĀNANDA.
Durgāstotra. DURGĀSTOTRA.
Ekādaşīmāhātmāche abhaṅga. TUKĀRĀMA.
Ekādaşīmāhātmya. PURĀṆAS.
Ekāksharī-şloka. EKĀKSHARĪ ŞLOKA.
Ekanāthī Bhāgavata. EKANĀTHA.

Gajagaurīvrata. Basvaliṅga.
Gajendramoksha. Mahābhārata.—*Selections.*
——— Vāmana Paṇḍita.
Gaṇeṣapurāṇa āryā. Gaṇapatarāva Harihara Paṭavardhana.
Gaṅgālaharī. } Jagannātha Paṇḍitarāja.
Gaṅgāmṛitaprasāda. }
Gaṅgāvarṇanā. Pāṇḍuraṅga Veṅkaṭeṣa Chintāmaṇi Peṭkar.
Gāruḍa. Ekanātha.
Gāyanaprakāra. Gāyanaprakāra.
Gopīgīta. Ananta, *Kavi.*
Govindāshṭaka. Govindāshṭaka.
Gurucharitra. Sarasvati Gaṅgādhara.
Hanumāndvādaṣa nāma. Rāmadāsa Svāmī, *Son of Sūryopanta.*
Hanumantajanma. Purāṇas.—Brahmāṇḍapurāṇa.—*Vyaṅkaṭagirimāhātmya.*
Haripāṭhāche abhaṅga. Jñānadeva.
Harivijaya. Ṣrīdhara.
Himālayavarṇana. Viṭhṭhala Bāpūjī Karmarkar.
Hiṅgalāja devīcheṇ stotra. Bāḷa Yajñeṣvara Gurjar.
Jñānadevāchā gāthā. Jñānadeva.
Kabīrādi . . . keleliṇ padeṇ. Kabīr.
Karuṇāmṛita bhīmāshṭaka. Rāmadāsa Svāmī, *Son of Sūryopanta.*
Karuṇāmṛita stotra. Devīdāsa.
Karuṇāpar abhaṅga. Tukārāma.
Kavitādarṣa. Gaṇeṣa Baḷavanta Limaye.
Kavitādīpikā. } Kāṣīnātha Bahirava Limaye.
Kavitārthadīpikā. }
Kavitārthamālā. Vināyaka Govinda Limaye.
Kavitāsāra saṅgraha. Parasurāma Panta Goḍbole.
Kāvyenduṣekhara. Sakhārāma Bālakṛishṇa Sarnāīk.
Kāyājīvasaṃvāda. Rāmakṛishṇa Hari Bhāgavata.
Kekāsāra. } Moropanta.
Kekāvalī. }
Kīrtana-taraṅgiṇī. Rāvajī Ṣrīdhara Gondhalekar.
Kishkindhyākāṇḍa. Rāmadāsa Svāmī, *Son of Suryopanta.*
Krishṇacharitra. Vāmana Paṇḍita.
Kshamāstotra. Rāmakṛishṇa Hari Bhāgavata.
Kulina striyāṇ sāṭhīṇ gāṇiṇ. Gāṇīṇ.
Lakshmī ashṭaka. Lakshmī.
Lāvaṇyā. Rāma Joṣī.
——— Saṅkara Tukārāma Ṣāligrām.
Mahābhārata. Mahābhārata.
——— Janārdana Bālājī Moḍak.
——— Moropanta.
Mahimnaḥ stotra. Pushpadanta.
Manāche ṣloka. Rāmadāsa Svāmī, *Son of Sūryopanta.*
Manorañjaka. Nāro Bhāskara Khera.
Mantrarāmāyaṇa. Moropanta.
Mārkaṇḍeya ākhyāna. Ānandatanaya.
Marutījanma. Mārutijanma.
——— Purāṇas.—Brahmāṇḍapurāṇa.—*Vyaṅkaṭagirimāhātmya.*
Mārutīstotra. Rāmadāsa Svāmī.
Mayūrakavi stuti. Rāmachandra Baḍve.
Moropantakṛita prakaraṇeṇ. Moropanta.
Mṛityuñjaya charitra. Uddhava Chidghana.
Mūrkhāṇchiṇ lakshaṇeṇ. Mukteṣvara.
Mūrkhaṣataka. Mūrkhaṣataka.
Nāganātha charitra. Uddhava Chidghana.
Nalākhyāna āryā. Moropanta.
Nalākhyānāchī bakhar. Mahābhārata.—*Nalopākhyāna.*
Nārāyaṇabali. Dāmodara Vishṇu Sapre.
Nāsiketākhyāna. Tukārāma.
Nātha-līlāmṛita. Ādinātha.
Navagrahastotra. Mahīpati.
Navanātha grantha. Mālu Narahari.
Navanīta. Parasurāma Panta Goḍbole.
Nityapāṭhāche abhaṅga. Tukārāma.
Padeṇ. Padeṇ.
——— Kabīr.
Pāḷane. Pāḷane.
Pañcharatna. Mahābhārata.—*Selections.*
Pāṇḍavapratāpa. }
Paṇḍharīmāhātmya. } Ṣrīdhara.
Pāṇḍuraṅgamāhātmya. }
Pāṇḍuraṅgastotra. Mahīpati.
Pāradhī ākhyāna. Pāradhī.
Patrikeche abhaṅga. Tukārāma.
Prakaraṇeṇ. Vāmana Paṇḍita.
Pushpavāṇavilāsa. Kālidāsa, *pseud.*
Rādhāvilāsa. Maṅgīṣa.
Rāmamantra ṣloka. Rāmadāsa Svāmī, *Son of Sūryopanta.*
Rāmāryā. Mudgala Āchārya.
Rāmavijaya. Ṣrīdhara.
Rambhā Ṣuka saṃvāda. Mukteṣvara.
——— Rambhā Ṣuka.
Rasakallola. Gaṅgādhara, *Kavi.*
Rāsakrīḍā. Vishṇudāsa.
Rasamañjarī. Viṭhṭhala.
Sabhāparva. Mukteṣvara.
Samaṣlokī. Vāmana Paṇḍita.
——— Vāsudevātmaja.
Sāṃbasadāṣiva. Homer.
Ṣanimāhātmya. Mahīpati.
Saṅkalita Rāmāyaṇa. Vāmana Paṇḍita.
Saṅkaṭanāṣana ṣloka. Gaṇapati.
Sanmārgadīpikā. Govinda Nārāyaṇa Kshīrasāgara.
Sarvasaṅgraha. Sarvasaṅgraha.
Ṣataṣlokī. Vopadeva.
Savāī. Savāī.
Ṣivājī mahārāja yāṇs . . . . upadeṣa. Ekanātha Aṇṇājī Joṣī.
Ṣivalīlāmṛita. Ṣrīdhara.
Ṣivaparākrama varṇana. Raghunātha Yādava Chitragupta.
Ṣivarātrī māhātmyāche abhaṅga. Nāmadeva.
Ṣivastuti. Vāmana Paṇḍita.
Ṣloka Rāmamantrāche. Rāmadāsa Svāmī, *Son of Sūryopanta.*
Solā somvār. Solā Somvār.
Sphuṭa abhaṅga. Tukārāma.
——— āryā va ṣloka. Sphuṭa Āryā.

Ṣrīharasiddhīdevī. Nāro Bhāskara Khera.
Sthālīpāka. Janābāī.
Subodha paden. Subodha Paden.
Ṣukacharītra. Amṛitarāya.
Ṣuka Rambhā saṃvāda. Kiṅkara, *Kavi*.
——— Uddhava Chidghana.
Sundarakāṇḍa. Rāmadāsa Svāmī, *Son of Sūryopanta*.
Surasa abhaṅga. Tukārāma.
——— āratyā. Āratyā.
——— lāvaṇyā. Rāvajī Ṣrīdhara Gondhaḷekar.
——— paden. Kabīr.
Sūryastuti. Vāmana Paṇḍita.
Svadeṣakalyāṇachandrikā. Keṣava Sadāṣiva Risbūḍ.
Tāṭīche abhaṅga. Jñānadeva.
——— Muktābāī.
Tīrthāvaḷīche abhaṅga. Nāmadeva.
Tukārāma Bābāchī gāthā. Tukārāma.
——— svargārohaṇāche abhaṅga. Tukārāma.
Tulasī ākhyāna. Vishṇudāsa.
Tuḷasīmāhātmya. Viṭhṭhaḷa Dāsa.
Umāvilāsa. Sadāṣiva, *Kavi*.
Upayukta kathāsaṅgraha. Nārāyaṇa Rāmachandra Sohanī.
Utsavaprakāṣa. Kṛishṇa Ṣāstrī Rājvāḍe.
Vāmanacharitra. Moropanta.
Vishṇunamanastotra. Jñānadeva.
Vyaṅkaṭeṣastotra. Devīdāsa.
Yaṣavanta Rāva yāṇchā pavāḍā. Sakhārāma Sonār.
Yuddhakāṇḍa. Rāmadāsa Svāmī, *Son of Sūryopanta*.

POLITICAL TREATISES.

Baḍode Sarkārchī tainātī phauj. Baroda, *Native State of*.
Sarkārche kar. Gaṇeṣa Rāmachandra Kiloskar.

PURĀṆAS. See RELIGION.—Hindu.

READERS.

Bārākhaḍyā. Marathi Spelling Book.
Bhāshāntara pāṭhamālā. Dvārakānātha Rāghobā Tarkhaḍkar.
Bodhakathā. Bodhakathā.
Chauthen pustaka. Marathi Fourth Book.
Dhuḷākshara. Dhuḷākshara.
Dusren pustaka. Berar Second Book.
——— Marathi Second Book.
Ibrī pahilen pustaka. Rājpurkar (J. E.)
Ingliṣ tisren pustaka. Howard (E. J.)
Lekhanadīpikā. Lekhanadīpikā.
Lenkrāchī pahilī pothī. First Book.
Marāṭhī pahilen Moḍī pustaka. Bālājī Bhikājī Piṅge.
Moḍī bālabodha tisre bukāntīl ṣabdārtha. Nārāyana Hari.
——— dusren pustaka. Bālājī Bhikājī Piṅge.
——— Sītārāma Viṣvanātha Paṭavardhana.
Moḍī tisren pustaka. Sītārāma Viṣvanātha Paṭavardhana.
——— vachanapaddhati. Vishṇu Moreṣvara Thatte.
——— vachanasāra. Vāsudeva Moreṣvara Potadār.
Moḍīchen pahilen pustaka. Sītārāma Viṣvanātha Paṭavardhana.
Pahilen pustaka. Berar First Book.
——— Bhāskara Dāmodara.
Pānchaven pustaka. Marathi Fifth Book.
Prākṛita kavitechen pahilen pustaka. Mahādeva Govinda Ṣāstrī.
Sahāven pustaka. Marathi Sixth Book.
Sambhāshaṇāchīn sopīn vākyen. Bombay, *Presidency of.—Government Schools*.
Samsārachopaḍī. Saṃsārachopaḍī.
Ṣikshaka va vidyārthī. Mahādeva Viṭhṭhala Rāhāḷkar.
Tisren pustaka. Bāḷakṛishṇa Lakshmaṇa Bāpaṭ.
——— Marathi Third Book.
Vāchanapāṭhamāḷā. MacCulloch (J. M.) *D.D.*
Vachanasāra. Vāsudeva Moreṣvara Potadār.
Vāchanavidyā. Marathi Primer.

RELIGION.—Brahmist.

Ādiṣāstra va Īṣvarajñāna. Keṣavachandra Sena.
Brahmasmṛiti. Shāhū III., *Raja of Satara*.
Īṣvaranityopāsana. Brāhma Samāj.—*Ahmadabad Prārthanā Samāj*.
Parameṣvarāchyā ārādhanechen pustaka. Gopīnātha Sadāṣivajī Hāṭe.
Prārthanā Samājāchā dharma. Nīlakaṇṭha Gore (N.)
Puṇen Prārthanā Samājāche niyama. Brāhma Samāj.—*Poona Prārthanā Samāj*.
Upāsanāṇchyā . . . veḷīn gāvayāchīn padyen. Gaṅgādhara Bāḷakṛishṇa Gadre.

RELIGION.—Christian.

Alandīchī yātrā. Alandī.
Aneka janmanirṇaya. Transmigration.
Avichāra, paṣchāttāpa va prāyaṣchitta. Hindus.
Bhajanāṇchī paddhati. Forms.
Bhāva koṇāvar thevāvā. Who.
Chāṇgle mulge. Good Boys.
Devāchen bhajana karaṇyāchī rīta. Worship.
Devāchyā dāhā ājñā. Ten Commandments.
Dharmottejaka gīten. Revival Hymns.
Hṛidayadarpaṇa. Heart Book.
Isrāelās hitopadeṣa. Jews.
Īṣvarāchen pavitratva. Farrar (C. P.)
Īṣvarokta ṣāstradhārā. Muir (J.) *D.C.L.*
Jarīmarī vishayīn. Cholera.
Jyā bāykāṇs lenkren āhet tyāṇs subodha. Address.
Kharyā dharmāchīn chihnen. Marks.
Khristi dharmāchyā pramāṇen. Christianity.
Khristi dharma Īṣvaradatta āhe, *etc*. Nīlakaṇṭha Gore (N.)
Kuṭumbāchā mitra. Family Friend.

Laghu prasnottarāvalī. UNITED STATES OF AMERICA.—*Methodist Episcopal Church.*
Mataparīkshā. MUIR (J.) *D.C.L.*
Matsyapurāṇa āṇi Ibrī Ṣāstra. PURĀṆAS.—*Matsyapurāṇa.*
Mothā vichāra. ENQUIRY.
Mulāṇkaritāṇ Marāṭhī gāṇeṇ. MORRIS (R.)
Mūrtoṇchā uchchheda. IDOLS.
Niḥṣāstravāda parīkshā. BĀBĀ PADMANJĪ.
Olīvar ol. MORTIMER (F. L.) *Mrs.*
Paschāttāpāchī goshṭa. REPENTANCE.
Pāvasāvishayīṇ vichāra. ENQUIRY.
Pavitra Bhāgīpaṇāchyā vidhisāṭhīṇ rāga. LITURGIES.—England, *Church of.*—*Book of Common Prayer.*
Prabhūchyā prārthanevar ṭīkā. LORD'S PRAYER
Sambhāshaṇeṇ. POONA.
Ṣāstravachanamālā. BIBLE.—*Appendix.*
Swedenborg hyāṇchyā matāvishayīṇ, *etc.* DĀDOBĀ PĀṆḌURAṄGA TARKHAḌKAR.
Uddhāramahimā. UDDHĀRAMAHIMĀ.

RELIGION.—HINDU.

(*Including* PURĀṆAS.)

Āgamaprakāṣa. KṚISHṆA RAGHUNĀTHAJĪ.
Āyushya vartana kramāvishayīṇ. VISHṆU PARAṢURĀMA ṢĀSTRĪ PAṆḌITA.
Bhāgavata. PURĀṆAS.—*Bhāgavatapurāṇa.*
——— āryā. MOROPANTA.
Bhaktalīlāmṛita. MAHĪPATI.
Bhaktisāra. MĀLU NARAHARI.
Bhaktivijaya. MAHĪPATI.
Bhāvadīpikā. LAKSHMAṆA GOVINDABHĀŪ ASHṬAPUTRE.
Brāhmaṇa varṇācheṇ mūla. HAUG (M.)
Brahmastuti. PURĀṆAS.—Bhāgavatapurāṇa.—*Brahmastuti.*
Dharmasindhusāra. KĀṢĪNĀTHA UPĀDHYĀYA.
Ekanāthī Bhāgavata. EKANĀTHA.
Gaṇeṣapratāpa. PURĀṆAS.—*Gaṇeṣapurāṇa.*
Gaṇeṣapurāṇa āryā. GAṆAPATARĀVA HARIHARA PAṬAVARDHANA.
Gokarṇamāhātmya. PURĀṆAS.—Skandapurāṇa. *Gokarṇamāhātmya.*
Gopīgītā. PURĀṆAS. — Bhāgavatapurāṇa. — *Gopīgītā.*
Gṛihyasūtra. ĀṢVALĀYANA.
Gurucharitra. SARASVATI GAṄGĀDHARA.
Hindudharma prasiddhīkaraṇa. WILSON (J.)
——— ṣāstra. VIṢVANĀTHA NĀRĀYAṆA MAṆḌALIK, *C.S.I.*
——— tattva. GAṄGĀDHARA ṢĀSTRĪ PHAḌKE.
Karmavipāka. KARMAVIPĀKA.
Kāṣīkhaṇḍa. PURĀṆAS.—Skandapurāṇa.—*Kāṣīkhaṇḍa.*
Kāṣīpratāpa. PURĀṆAS.
Mallārimāhātmya. PURĀṆAS. — Brahmāṇḍapurāṇa.—*Mallārimāhātmya.*
Mārkaṇḍeyapurāṇa. PURĀṆAS. — *Mārkaṇḍeyapurāṇa.*
Mūlastambha. PURĀṆAS.—*Ṣivapurāṇa.*
Nāthalīlāmṛita. ĀDINĀTHA.
Padabhāvānukāriṇī. LAKSHMAṆA GOVINDABHĀŪ ASHṬAPUTRE.
Paramānandalaharī. ṬĪKĀRĀMA.
Pavanavijaya. MUKUNDARĀJA.
Prayāgamāhātmya. PURĀṆAS.—Matsyapurāṇa.—*Prayāgamāhātmya.*
Purushasūkta. VEDAS.—Ṛigveda.—*Purushasūkta.*
Rāmāṣvamedha. PURĀṆAS.—Padmapurāṇa.—*Rāmāṣvamedha.*
Samūla-purāṇārthaprakāṣa. PURĀṆAS.
Santalīlāmṛita. MAHĪPATI.
Saptaṣatī. PURĀṆAS. — Mārkaṇḍeyapurāṇa.—*Devīmāhātmya.*
Ṣāstra va rūḍhi yāṇchyā balābalāvishayīṇ vichāra. KĀṢĪNĀTHA TRIMBAK TELANG, *C.I.E.*
Satyanārāyaṇapūjā. PURĀṆAS.—Skandapurāṇa. —*Satyanārāyaṇavratakathā.*
Ṣivagītā. PURĀṆAS.—Padmapurāṇa.—*Ṣivagītā.*
Ṣivatattvaprakāṣa. PURĀṆAS.—*Ṣivapurāṇa.*
Somavatīpūjā. PURĀṆAS.—Bhavishyottarapurāṇa. —*Somavatīpūjā.*
Tattvavichāra. GAṆEṢA ṢĀSTRĪ ABHYAṄKAR.
Uttaragītā. MAHĀBHĀRATA.—*Uttaragītā.*
Vaṭaṣāvitrīkathā. PURĀṆAS.—Skandapurāṇa.—*Vaṭaṣāvitrīkathā.*
Vedārthayatna. VEDAS.—*Ṛigveda.*
Yātrākalpalatā. GAURĪṢAṄKARA ṢĀSTRĪ.

RELIGION.—JAIN.

Bhajana sadbodhamālikā. NĀNĀ KOḶEKAR.
Bhaktāmarastotra. MĀNATUṄGĀCHĀRYA.
Ṣrīpālacharitra. AṆṆĀPĀ ĀPĀ VĀḌAKAR.
Treatise on Jain ... usages. PADMARĀJA [*Addenda*].

RELIGION.—JEWISH.

Isrāelī dharmācheṇ khareṇ svarūpa. RĀJPURKAR (J. E.)
Talmud. TALMUD.

SCIENCES.

Anekavidyā mūlatattva saṅgraha. KṚISHṆA ṢĀSTRĪ CHIPḶŪṆKAR.
Kārāgīr lokāṇche kāmāvishayīṇ. KĀṢĪNĀTHA MAHĀDEVA THATTE.
Kimiyā. TRIMBAK SAKHĀRĀMA ṢIRVALKAR.
Rasāyanaṣāstra. HARI KEṢAVAJĪ.
——— RĀMAJĪ GAṆOJĪ CHAUGULE.
Sṛishṭijñāna. GAṆEṢA KṚISHṆA ĀPṬE.
Upayogī jñānāchā pustaka samūha. BROUGHAM (H.)

SOCIOLOGY.

Āmchī kuṭumba vyavasthā. BHAVANARĀVA PĀVAGĪ.
Āplyā nikṛishṭāvasthechīṇ kāraṇeṇ. ANANTA MĀDHAVARĀVA MORE.
—— rāhaṇyāchyā rīti āṇi ārogyaṣāstra. KṚISHNARĀVA BĀ[ḶĀJĪ?] BULEL.
Arthaṣāstra paribhāshā. MILL (J. S.)
Bālasaṅgopana. KṚISHṆA ṢĀSTRĪ GOḌBOLE.

Bālavivāhāchyā . . . vichāra. Vāmana Ābājī Moḍak.
Bhikshuka. Bhikshuka.
Brāhmaṇajātīchyā vidhavāvishayīṇ. Brahmans.
Brāhmaṇakanyā vivāhavichāra. Svadeṣa Hitechchhu.
Deṣavyavahāra vyavasthā. Hari Keṣavajī.
Gatabhartṛikā rodana. Nārāyaṇa Keṣava Vaidya.
Hemanta vyākhyānamālā. Bombay, *City of.—Hindu Union Club.*
Hiṇdu lokāṇchyā lagnakāryāṇt Sarkār nako. Nārāyaṇa Bhāskara Rāṇaḍe.
Hindu lokāntīl vivāhakāla. Yaṣavanta Vāsudeva Āṭhalye.
Hindusthāna deṣāchya sthitivishayīṇ. } Kāṣīnātha Trimbak Khare.
Hindusthānāntīl tisrī rāshṭrīya-sabhā. }
Iṣvara smaraṇapūrvaka . . . lokavartana. Rājārāma Sāstrī Boḍas.
Kaliviḍambana. Nīlakaṇṭha Dīkshita.
Kaliyuga. Kaliyuga.
Strīpurusha tulanā. Tārābāī Ṣinde.
Strīyāṇchī kharī yogyatā. Vāsudeva Gopāla Bhāṇḍārkar.
Subodhamālinī. Kṛishṇarāva Bhāskarajī Reḷe.
Unnati mhaṇaje kāy. Nārāyaṇa Vishṇu Bāpaṭ.
Vidhavāṣrumārjana. Dādobā Pāṇḍuraṅga Tarkhaḍkar.
Vidhavāvivāha. Īṣvarachandra Vidyāsāgara.
———— saṃhārasāra. Sītārāma Panta.
Vidyā-vṛiddhīchyā kāmīṇ āmchī anāsthā. Rāmachandra Bhikājī Guñjīkar.
Vivāha-kālāvishayīṇ ṣārīra-ṣāstrācheṇ mata. Moreṣvara Gopāla Deṣmukh.
Vivāhavijñāna. Sakhārāma Arjuna.

TALES.—Original.

Adbhuta chamatkāra saṅgraha. Adbhuta Chamatkāra.
Aitihāsika goshṭi. Aitihāsika Goshṭī.
Chamatkārika goshṭī. Nāro Āpājī Goḍbole.
Chhatrapati Sambhājī Mahārāja. Nāgeṣarāva Vināyaka Bāpaṭ.
Hambīrarāva āṇi Putaḷābāī. Vishṇu Janārdana Paṭavardhana.
Hari āṇi Trimbak. Govinda Ṣaṅkara Ṣāstrī Bāpaṭ.
Kahāṇyā. Vishṇu Dinkar Vaidya Kalyāṅkar.
Kāḷakarmaṇūk. Ashṭamkar (A. S.)
Kirāta. Kurūḷkar (A. D.)
Kṛishṇakumārī. Bhāū Dīkshita Sātārkar.
Līlāvatī. Līlāvatī.
Mañjughoshā. Nāro Sadāṣiva Risbuḍ
Mitrachandra. Pāṇḍuraṅga Govinda Parakhī
Muktamālā. } Lakshmaṇa Moreṣvara Ṣāstrī Halbe.
Ratnaprabhā. }
Rogī va vaidya. Bāḷakṛishṇa Dinkar Vaidya Kalyāṅkar.
Sadu Salgar. Viṭhṭhala Hari Limaye.
Sakhūcheṇ charitra. Sakhu.
Ṣikshaka. Dvārakānātha Nārāyaṇa Raṇadive.
Ṣṛiṅgārasundara. Dattātraya Vāsudeva Jogḷekar.
Ṣrīpālacharitra. Aṇṇāpā Āpā Vāḍakar.
Sulochanā āṇi Mādhava. Rāmachandra Bhikājī Gokhale.
Triveṇī Pramātha. Gopāla Govinda Dābak.
Veṇu. Gaṇeṣa Mahādeva Limaye.
Veshadhārī Pañjābī. Veshadhārī Pañjābī.

TALES.—Mythological.

Abhimanyu vivāha. Abhimanyu.
Ahīmahī ākhyāna. Ananta. *Kavi.*
Ajāmiḷākhyāna. Vāmana Paṇḍita.
Aṅgadaṣishṭāī. Ballāḷa Dādo.
Arjuna garvaparihāra. Arjuna.
Arjunāchī bakhar. Nāro Āpājī Goḍbole.
Aṣvinī ākhyāna. Aṣvinī.
Babhruvāhana ākhyāna. Ṣrīdhara.
Bāḷakrīḍā. Dāmodara Panta.
Bāḷakrīḍeche abhaṅga. Nāmadeva.
———— Tukārāma.
Bāli vānarāchī bakhar. } Nāro Āpājī Goḍbole.
Bhīmasenāchī bakhar. }
Chakravibhu. Vishṇudāsa.
Chandrahāsa rājyāchī bakhar. Nāro Āpājī Goḍbole.
Chandrāvaḷī ākhyāna. Moreṣvara, *Son of Dhuṇḍi.*
Cheṇḍuphaḷī. Anantasuta.
Chyavana bhārgavāchī bakhar. Nāro Āpājī Goḍbole.
Dhruvākhyāna. Uddhava Chidghana.
Draupadī vastraharaṇa. Kiṅkara, *Kavi.*
———— Tukārāma.
Gajagaurī-ākhyāna. Gajagaurī.
Garuḍākhyāna. Garuḍa.
Hariṣchandrākhyāna. Hariṣchandra.
———— Mukteṣvara.
Hariṣchandropākhyāna. Moropanta.
Hiḍimbavadha. Bājābā Bālājī Nene.
Jayadrathavadha. Vāmana Paṇḍita.
Kaikeyīche ṣloka. Vāsudeva.
Kandukākhyāna. Ānandatanaya.
Kaṇsa rājyāchī bakhar. } Nāro Āpājī Goḍbole.
Karṇa rājyāchī bakhar. }
Kīchakāchī bakhar. }
Kṛishṇāchī bakhar. }
Kṛishṇajanma. Devanātha.
Kṛishṇajanma. } Ṣrīdhara.
Kṛishṇajayantī }
Kṛishṇalīlā ākhyāna. Dāmodara Panta.
Lahukuṣāchī bakhar. Lava Kuṣa.
Lahūkuṣākhyāna. Ṣrīdhara.
Malhārī charitra. Balavanta Khaṇḍerāva Peshve.
Nakulāchī bakhar. Nāro Āpājī Goḍbole.
Naukākrīḍana. Viṣvanātha.
Putanāvadha. Ānandatanaya.
Rāma rājyāchī bakhar. } Nāro Āpājī Goḍbole.
Rāvaṇa rājyāchī bakhar. }

Rukmiṇīsvayaṃvara. Ekanātha.
——— Rukmiṇī.
——— Sakhārāmatanaya.
Śatamukha Rāvaṇavadha. Mukteśvara.
Sāvitrī ākhyāna. Śrīdhara.
Sāvitrīchī bakhar. Nāro Āpājī Goḍbole.
Sītāsvayaṃvara. Ananta, *Kavi.*
——— Chintāmaṇi.
——— Vāmana Paṇḍita.
Śrāvaṇa ākhyāna. Devanātha.
Subhadrāharaṇa. Moropanta.
Sudāma-charitra. Kiṅkara, *Kavi.*
——— Sudāma.
Syamantakopākhyāna. Śyāmā, *Kavi.*
Tāṭakāvadha. Ānandatanaya.
Triśaṅku rājyāchī bakhar. Nāro Āpājī Goḍbole.
Vakāsura bakhar. Vakāsura.
Vastraharaṇāche abhaṅga. Tukārāma.
Vṛihannalāchī bakhar. Nāro Āpājī Goḍbole.

TALES.—Translations from Oriental Works.

Ārabī goshṭī. Persian Tales.
Bahār i dānish. ʻInāyat Allāh.
Baitāl pachīsī. Baitāl Pachīsī.
Bakhtyār-nāma. Bakhtyār.
Bhāshāmañjarī. Bhāshāmañjarī.
Damājīchī rasad. Amīr Chand.
Gulistān. Sāʻdī.
Hitopadeśa. Hitopadeśa.
Manorañjaka Damayantī. Gaṇeśa Vināyaka Kāniṭkar.
Pañchatantra. Pañchatantra.
——— sāra. Govinda Śaṅkara Śāstrī Bāpaṭ.
Siṃhāsana battīsī. Vikramāditya, *King of Ujjayinī.*
Śukabāhāttarī. Śukasaptati.

TALES.—Translations from European Works.

Bālabodhamuktāvalī. Æsop.
Bālamitra. Berquin (A.)
Chamatkārika goshṭī. Farrar ( ) *Mrs.*
Durdaivī Murād, *etc.* Vināyaka Nārāyaṇa Bhāgavata.
Galivhar yāchā vṛittānta. Swift (J.)
Gilpin charitra. Cowper (W.) *the Poet.*
Isāp nītikathā. Æsop.
Kāphar deśāchī mulgī. African Girl.
Mulāṇsāṭhīṇ bodhāchyā goshṭī. Stories.
Pāl āṇi Vhārjiniyā. Saint Pierre (J. H. B. de).
Sadācharaṇāchyā goshṭī. Stories.
Tīn rājakanyāṇchī goshṭa. Tīn Rājakanyā.
Viśvāsu kuttā. Dog.
Yuropāntīl vanadevatāṇchyā goshṭī. Bellairs (H.)

TOPOGRAPHY.

Bijāpur varṇana. Sītārāma Rāmachandra Gaikvāḍ.
Mumbaīcheṇ varṇana. Govinda Nārāyaṇa.
Puṇeṇ jilhācheṇ varṇana. Sītārāma Viśvanātha Paṭavardhana.
Puṇeṇ shahr. Sītārāma Rāmachandra Gaikvāḍ.
Sāshṭī urf Ṭhāṇyāchī bakhar. Ṭhāṇā.
Sātārā jilhyācheṇ varṇana. Balavanta Vāsudeva Joglekar.
Tryambaka varṇana. Bālakṛishṇa Bābājī Karkare.

TRAVELS.

Kaptān Kuk sāheb tyāche vṛittānta. Bingley (W.)
Paṇḍitā Ramābāī . . . pravāsa. Ramābāī.
Ribbī Pethāhyā yāche pravāsa. Pethahiah ben Jacob.

VOCABULARIES. See DICTIONARIES.

Gilbert & Rivington, Lim., St. John's House, Clerkenwell Road, London, E.C.

ADDENDA.

AGARKAR (G. G.) *See* Gopāla Gaṇeśa Āgarkar.

ALBU (Israel). חק לישראל. A statute unto Israel. Containing an abridged account of the religious duties of the Israelite, especially elucidating those [which] refer to divine service ... Translated [from the English] into Marathi by Benjamin Samson Ashtumker. ... इस्राएलांचा विधि [Isrāelānchā vidhi.] pp. 122. मुंबई १८८७ [*Bombay*, 1887.] 8°. **14137. b. 16.(1.)**

ANANTA, *Kavi.* अनंतकविकृत द्रौपदीस्वयंवर [Draupadī-svayaṃvara. A poem on the Mahābhārata story of the marriage of Draupadī.] [1888.] *See* Periodical Publications.—*Poona.* काव्येतिहास-संग्रह [Kāvyetihāsa saṅgraha.] Vol. xi. No. 6-8. [1878, *etc.*] 8°. **14072. d. 37.**

AṆṆĀJĪ BALLĀḶA BĀPAṬ INDURKAR. रसरत्नमाला. [Rasaratnamālā. A collection of chemical recipes, compiled from various Sanskrit sources, with translations in Marathi.] Pt. I. pp. iv. 146, ii. पुणें १८८८ [*Poona*, 1888.] 8°. **14043. d. 42.**

AṆṆĀ MOREŚVARA KUṆṬE. *See* Jñānadeva. श्री ज्ञानदेवकृत अमृतानुभव *etc.* [Amṛitānubhava. Edited by A. M. K. with an explanatory and critical introduction, and a glossary of difficult terms.] [1889.] 4°. **14137. e. 11.**

ANTĀJĪ RĀMACHANDRA HARḌĪKAR. *See* Bāḷājī Janārdana Bhānu, also called Nānā Phaḍṇavīs. लेखरत्नमाला [Lekharatnamālā. Compiled and edited by A. R. H.] [1887.] 8°. **14139. e. 27.(1.)**

ĀSHṬAMKAR (Benjamin Samson). *See* Albu (I.) חק לישראל. A statute unto Israel ... Translated ... by Benjamin Samson Ashtumker. [1887.] 8°. **14137. b. 16.(1.)**

ĀSHṬAMKAR (Benjamin Samson). הנסתרות והנגלות Curiosities of Judaism. Facts, opinions, anecdotes and remarks relating to [the] Hebrew nation. Compiled ... by Benjamin Samson Ashtumker. ... इस्राएली धर्मांतील नवलाचें वृत्त. [Isrāelī dharmāntīl navalācheṇ vṛitta.] pp. 90. मुंबई १८८७ [*Bombay*, 1887.] 8°. **14137. b. 16.(2.)**

BAITĀL PACHĪSĪ. वेताळपंचविशी [Baitāl pachīsī. Translated by Sadāśiva Kāśīnātha Chhatre. Another edition.] pp. 173. मुंबई १८८९ [*Bombay*, 1889.] 16°. **14139. f. 32.**

BĀḶĀBOVĀ JÑĀNEŚVARĪ. *See* Bhaktitattvāmṛita. अथ श्रीभक्तितत्वामृतग्रंथ प्रारंभः [Bhaktitattvāmṛita. Edited with a Marathi paraphrase by B. J.] [1889.] *obl. fol.* **14028. e. 31.**

BĀḶĀJĪ JANĀRDANA BHĀNU, also called NĀNĀ PHAḌṆAVĪS. लेखरत्नमाला अथवा नाना फडणविसांचे निवडक पत्रांचा संग्रह [Lekharatnamālā. Letters of B. J. Bh., the Prime Minister of Mādhava Rāva II., chiefly with reference to the British rule, and the wars with the Marathas. Compiled and edited with a preface by Antājī Rāmachandra Harḍīkar.] pp. ii. viii. 53. १८८७ [*Poona*, 1887.] 8°. **14139. e. 27.(1.)**

BĀḶĀJĪ PRABHĀKARA MOḌAK. A short history of the Kolhapur principality. कोल्हापूर प्रांताचा संक्षिप्त इतिहास. [Kolhāpūra prāntāchā saṃkshipta itihāsa.] pp. 40. मुंबई १८८८ [*Bombay*, 1888.] 8°. **14139. e.**

BĀḶAKṚISHṆA ĀTMĀRĀMA GUPTE. दारू पिणें [Dārū piṇeṇ. A lecture condemning the use of spirituous liquors.] pp. 10. [1890.] *See* Bombay, *City of.—Hindu Union Club.* हेमंत व्याख्यानमाला [Hemanta vyākhyānamālā.] Vol. v. No. 2. [1886, *etc.*] 8°. **14139. c. 26.**

BĀḶAKṚISHṆA ĀTMĀRĀMA GUPTE. The Industrial arts of India. Compiled in Marathi (from Mr. Mukharji's "Art-manufactures of India" and other sources) by Rao Saheb Balkrishna Atmaram Gupte. (देशी हुन्नर) [Deṣī hunar.] pp. 207, 22. *Poona*, 1889. 8°. **14139. e. 32.**

BĀḶAKṚISHṆA BĀPŪ ĀCHĀRYA and MORO VINĀYAKA ṢIṄGṆE. A descriptive account of Bombay. Being an outline of events both past and present, with maps. By Bálkrishna Bápu Ácharya and Moro Vináyak Shingne. (मुंबईचा वृत्तांत) [Mumbaīchā vṛittānta.] pp. iv. xiv. 377, 33. *Bombay*, 1889. 8°. **14139. e. 31.**

BALAVANTARĀVA MALHĀRĪ DUDVAḌKAR. संतमेळा [Santameḷā. A collection of religious songs by famous Marathi poets. Compiled by B. M. D. Second edition.] pp. 144. मुंबई १८९० [*Bombay*, 1890.] 16°. **14140. a. 38.**

BĀḶA YAJÑEṢVARA GURJAR. धर्मौदार्य [Dharmaudārya. A lecture on religious toleration.] pp. 11. [1889.] *See* BOMBAY, *City of.—Hindu Union Club.* हेमंत व्याख्यानमाला [Hemanta vyākhyānamālā.] Vol. iv. No. 4. [1886, *etc.*] 8°. **14139. c. 26.**

BALLĀLA, *Marathi translator. See* PURĀṆAS.—Gaṇeṣapurāṇa. — *Gaṇeṣagītā.* अथ प्राकृतटीकासहित गणेशगीता प्रारंभः [Gaṇeṣagītā. Sanskrit text, accompanied by a Marathi commentary by B.] [1887.] *obl.* 8°. **14016. d. 49.**

BHAḌALĪ. अथ बृहज्ज्योतिषार्णवे षष्ठे मिश्रस्कंधे भाडलीमत ज्योतिषवर्णनं नाम पंचविंशोऽध्यायः प्रारभ्यते [Bhāḍalī-mata jyotishavarṇana. A work on astrology and divination, containing the sayings of Bhaḍalī, the daughter of Uddhaḍa Joṣī, who was also called Sahadeva, and forming the 25th chapter of the 6th section of the Bṛihajjyotishārṇava. Mostly in the original Hindi, but also partly in Gujarati, and partly in Marathi.] ff. 37. बाँबे सिटी १८८८ [*Bombay*, 1887.] *obl.* 4°. **14158. h. 10.**

BHAKTITATTVĀMṚITA. अथ श्रीभक्तितत्त्वामृतग्रंथ प्रारंभः [Bhaktitattvāmṛita. A Sanskrit work in verse, in 42 chapters, professing to be extracted from a larger work entitled Matsyendra-saṃhitā, and giving the life of Matsyendranātha and other holy men. Edited with a Marathi paraphrase by Bāḷābovā Jñāneṣvarī.] मुंबई १८१० [*Bombay*, 1889.] *obl. fol.* **14028. e. 31.**

BHĀŪ SĀHEB. श्रीमंत भाऊ साहेब यांची कैफियत [Ṣrīmanta Bhāū Sāheb yāṅchī kaiphiyat. An account of the Maratha Empire during the time of Sadāṣiva Rāva. Edited with critical notes by Kāṣīnātha Nārāyaṇa Sāne.] [1887.] *See* PERIODICAL PUBLICATIONS.—*Poona.* काव्येतिहास-संग्रह [Kavyetihāsa saṅgraha.] Vol. x. Nos. 1-3. [1878, *etc.*] 8°. **14072. d. 37.**

BHAVABHŪTI. *See* VĀMANA ṢĀSTRĪ ISLĀMPŪRKAR. Pranayi Mádhava. Translated [or rather, adapted] from Sanskrit [Mālatī Mādhava of Bhavabhūti.] 1889. 12°. **14139. f. 36.**

BHĪMĀCHĀRYA JHAḶKĪKAR and RĀJĀRĀMA GAṆEṢA BOḌAS. वेदार्थोद्धारः। दयानन्दकृत वेदव्याख्यान खण्डनात्मकः [Vedārthoddhāra. A critical refutation of Dayānānda Sarasvati's views regarding the Vedas, as the sole authority in matters of doctrine. Sanskrit text, with translations into Marathi and Gujarati.] pp. 4, 4, 4. मुंबापुरी १८७५ [*Bombay*, 1875.] 8°. **14028. d. 18.**

BHĪMARĀVA SĪTĀRĀMA ṢĀLIGRĀM. चनबसाप्पा मल्लाप्पा वारद यांच्या मुंबई दुकानांतील अडत मजुरी वगैरेचे दर *etc.* [The rates of remuneration as agency charges in the shop of Chanbasāppā Mallāpā Vārad, and general information on the trade of Bombay.] pp. viii. xiii. 92. मुंबई १८८८ [*Bombay*, 1888.] 12°. **14139. c. 30.**

BHŪSHAṆA, *Kavi.* शिवराजभूषण काव्य ... Shivarajabhushana. A work in the Brija language on the figures of speech by the poet Bhushana ... Edited by Janardan Balaji Modak. [1888.] *See* PERIODICAL PUBLICATIONS.—*Poona.* काव्येतिहास-संग्रह [Kāvyetihāsa saṅgraha.] Vol. xi. No. 8-11. [1878, *etc.*] 8°. **14072. d. 37.**

BIBLE. पवित्र शास्त्र . . . The Holy Bible. [With improvements sanctioned by the Marathi translation sub-committee, carried out under the editorial supervision of A. Hazen.] pp. 1402. *Bombay*, 1872. 8°. **3070. h. 24.**

—— पवित्र शास्त्र . . . The Holy Bible . . . Old Testament. *Bombay*, 1882. 8°. **3070. h. 29.**

Imperfect; wanting the New Testament.

—— पवित्र शास्त्र . . . The Holy Bible in the Maratta language. pp. 1373, 442. *Bombay*, 1886, 83. 12°. **3068. de. 19.**

The Old Testament is printed in double columns, with **33** *lines; the New in long lines with* **31.**

BIBLE.—NEW TESTAMENT.—*Gospels.* The Gospel of Matthew, (Mark, Luke, John.) 4 pt. मुबई १८७३ [*Bombay*, 1873.] 8°. **3070. de. 36.**

Printed in the Modi character.

—— *Luke.* The Gospel of Luke. लुकानें केलेलें शुभवर्तमान. pp. 234, *Mar.* and *Engl.* १८७७ *Bombay* [1877.] 12°. **3070. aaa. 20.**

—— The Gospel of Luke in Marathi and English. [A reprint.] pp. 234. मुबई १८८३ [*Bombay*, 1883.] 12°. **3070. de. 29.**

—— *John, Gospel of.* The Gospel according to St. John in English and Maráthí ... Second edition. pp. 189. *Bombay*, 1882. 8°. **3070. de. 27.**

BRĀHMA DHARMA. श्री ब्राह्मधर्म [Brāhma dharma. A collection of Brahmist maxims, compiled from the Upanishads and other Sanskrit works, translated into Marathi verse by Pratāpasiṃha Mahārāja.] ff. 52, 7. पुणें ब्राह्मसंवत ५८ [*Poona*, 1887.] *obl.* 12°. **14137. a. 15.**

The compiler of the Sanskrit original is here erroneously said to be Devendranātha Ṭhākura.

CANDY (THOMAS). Idiomatic sentences, English and Maráthí. (भाषणसांप्रदायिक वाक्यें.) [Bhāshaṇa sāmpradāyika vākyeṇ.] Second edition. pp. 275. *Bombay*, 1888. 12°. **14140. g. 45.**

CHINTĀMAṆA MOREŚVARA ĀPṬE. पुतळा बाई [Putaḷā Bāī. An historical tale of the early days of the rule of Śivājī.] pp. ii. 178. पुणें १८८९ [*Poona*, 1889.] 12°. **14139. f. 37.**

CHITRAGUPTA. शिवाजी महाराजांची बखर [Śivājī Mahārājāṇchī bakhar. An account of the life of Śivājī. Edited with notes by Kāśīnātha Nārāyaṇa Sāne.] [1888.] *See* PERIODICAL PUBLICATIONS.—*Poona.* काव्येतिहास-संग्रह [Kāvyetihāsa saṅgraha.] Vol. xi. No. 2-9. [1878, *etc.*] 8°. **14072. d. 37.**

CICERO (MARCUS TULLIUS). सिसरोकृत नीतिविषयक चार निबंध. [Nītivishayaka chār nibandha. Four treatises on morals, being a Marathi translation of Cicero's 'De officiis,' 'De senectute,' and 'De amicitia,' and of one of Lord Burleigh's 'Letters to his son.'] मुंबई १८८९ [*Bombay*, 1889.] 12°. **14139. c.**

COTTIN (SOPHIE). Elizabeth, or The Exiles of Siberia. A tale in French [by S. Cottin] ... Translated from English into Maráthí by Govind Shankar Shástri Bápat. pp. xiv. 132. *Bombay*, 1889. 12°. **14139. f. 34.**

DĀBHĀḌE, *Senāpati.* सेनापति दाभाडे व गायकवाड यांची हकीगत [Senāpati Dābhāḍe ... yāṇchī hakīgat. An account of the Chieftain Dābhāḍe and the Gaikwar of Baroda. Edited with notes by Kāśīnātha Nārāyaṇa Sāne.] [1886-87.] *See* PERIODICAL PUBLICATIONS.—*Poona.* काव्येतिहास-संग्रह [Kāvyetihāsa saṅgraha.] Vol. ix. No. 10—vol. x. no. 1. [1878, *etc.*] 8°. **14072. d. 37.**

DĀMODARA GAṆEŚA JOŚĪ. *See* RĀVAJĪ ŚRĪDHARA GONDHAḶEKAR. कीर्तनतरंगिणी [Kīrtana-taraṅgiṇī. Pt. i. Another edition.] [1889.] 8°. **14140. c. 40.**

DATTĀTRAYA VĀSUDEVA JOGḶEKAR. Independent widows and their youthful daughters. [A social drama in two acts.] स्वतंत्र विधवा आणि त्यांच्या तरुण मुली. [Svatantra vidhavā āṇi tyāṇchyā taruṇa mulī.] pp. 34. मुंबई १८८८ [*Bombay*, 1888.] 12°. **14140. f. 27.(2.)**

DAYĀNANDA SARASVATĪ. *See* BHĪMĀCHĀRYA JHAḶKĪKAR and RĀJĀRĀMA GAṆEŚA BOḌAS. वेदार्थोद्धारः। [Vedārthoddhāra. A critical refutation of D. S.'s views regarding the Vedas, as the sole authority in matters of doctrine.] [1875.] 8°. **14028. d. 18.**

DINKAR (M. B.) *See* MAHĀDEVA BHĀGAVATA DINKAR.

EKANĀTHA. *See* KRISHṆĀJĪ NĀRĀYAṆA KĀKAḌE. भजनी संतखेळ [Bhajanī santakhela. A collection of obscure stanzas by Ekanātha and other Marathi poets.] [1888, *etc.*] 12°. **14140. a. 37.**

GAṆAPATARĀVA VIŚRĀMA DEŚĀĪ. Deserved punishment, or Death of one Sileman Sidhi in Baroda. A drama in 3 acts ... by Ganapatráo Vishrám Desái. (योग्य शासनादर्श नाटक अथवा सिलेमान सिद्धीचा मृत्यु) [Yogya śāsanādarśa nāṭaka, also called Silemān Siddhīchā mṛityu.] pp. 100. *Bombay*, 1887. 12°. **14140. e. 12.**

GAṆEŚA JANĀRDANA ĀGĀŚE. सुंदरेची संक्रांत [Sundarechī saṅkrānta. A short tale.] pp. 17. मुंबई १८८८ [*Bombay*, 1888.] 12°. **14139. f. 33.(1.)**

GANEṢA SĪTĀRĀMA GOḶVALKAR. *See* SANKEṢVARA. श्री जगद्गुरु मठ संकेश्वर यांणीं . . . शास्त्र निर्णय ठरविला [A decision regarding the expiatory penance required of G. S. G. for having gone to England.] [1888.] 12°. **14137. d.**

GAṄGĀDHARA, *Kavi.* *See* JAGANNĀTHA PAṆḌITARĀJA. भामिनीविलास [Bhāminīvilāsa. Translated into verse by G.] [1886-87.] 8°. **14072. d. 37.**

GOPĀLA BĀVA. [*Life.*] *See* RĀJĀRĀMA MANOHARA DIVĀṆJĪ BUDHAKAR. जयराम स्वामी चरित्र [Jayarāma Svāmī charitra.]

GOPĀLA GAṆEṢA ĀGARKAR. वाक्यमीमांसा आणि वाक्यांचें पृथक्करण. [Vākya mīmāṃsā.] An inquiry into the nature of sentences with an analysis of them. By G. G. Agarkar. pp. x. xi. 120. पुणें १८८८ [*Poona,* 1888.] 12°. **14140. g.**

GOPĀLA RĀJĀRĀMA RAṄGANĀTHA. आपा साहेब नाटक [Āpā Sāheb nāṭaka. A drama on the murder of Bāla Sāhib, Raja of Nagpur, by Āpā Sāhib, his cousin and successor.] *See* PERIODICAL PUBLICATIONS.—*Pen.* नाट्यकथामाला Natya-kathamala. Vol. ii. No. 1-5. [1887, *etc.*] 8°. **14140. f. 30.**

GOVARDHANADĀSA LAKSHMĪDĀSA. श्री रामदास स्वामीचे चरित्राची बखर [Śrī Rāmadāsa Svāmīche charitra. A legendary account of the life of Rāmadāsa Svāmī, the popular saint and poet, and the religious preceptor of Śivājī. Second edition.] pp. viii. 536, viii. मुंबई १८१० [*Bombay,* 1889.] 12°. **14139. d. 33.**

GOVINDA KṚISHṆA ṬILAK. महाराज प्रतापसिंह विजयनगरचा राजपुत्र [Mahārāja Pratāpa Siṃha. A drama in 5 acts.] pp. 150. पुणें १८९० [*Poona,* 1890.] 12°. **14140. e. 18.**

GOVINDA ṢAṄKARA ṢĀSTRĪ BĀPAṬ. *See* COTTIN (S.) Elizabeth, or The Exiles of Siberia . . . Translated . . . by Govind Shankar Shástri Bápat. 1889. 12°. **14139. f. 34.**

HARI KṚISHṆA DĀMLE. Selections from Maráthi writers for translation into English. Standard VI. Third edition, revised and enlarged, with a glossary of difficult words and phrases. भाषांतराकरितां उतारे [Bhāshāntarākaritāṉ utāre.] pp. iv. vi. 180. १८८७ *Poona* [1887.] 12°. **14140. g. 44.**

HAZEN (ALLEN). *See* BIBLE. पवित्र शास्त्र . . . [With improvements carried out under the supervision of A. H.] 1872. 8°. **3070. h. 24.**

HĪRĀLĀLA GOPĀLA. शास्त्रार्थ [Śāstrārtha. Opinions of learned Pandits on the question as to whether a member of the Vaiṣya caste is empowered to perform religious ceremonies, as prescribed in the Vedas. Partly in Hindi, and partly in Marathi.] pp. 44. मुंबई १८८७ [*Bombay,* 1887.] 8°. **14154. e. 24.**

HUTTON (CHARLES) *LL.D.* A Maratha treatise on arithmetic. [Translated from the English of Dr. Hutton] by Captain Georgo Jervis [assisted by Jagannātha Ṣāstrī Kramavanta]. (गणितवृत्ति) [Gaṇitavṛitti.] Second edition, Pt. I. pp. 125. १८२६ *Bombay* [1826.] 12°. **14139. a. 48.**

HYMN BOOK. इस्राएल मुलांकरितां हिब्रू व मराठी गीतें. (Hymn book [in Hebrew and Marathi for Jewish children]. गीतांचें पुस्तक) [Gītāṉcheṉ pustaka.] pp. 16, 20. *Bombay,* 1887. 8°. **1979. e. 67.**

JAGANNĀTHA PAṆḌITARĀJA. भामिनीविलास [Bhāminīvilāsa. A Sanskrit poem translated into Marathi verse by Gaṅgādhara.] [1886-87.] *See* PERIODICAL PUBLICATIONS.—*Poona.* काव्येतिहाससंग्रह [Kāvyetihāsa saṅgraha.] Vol. ix. No. 11-Vol. x. No. 3. [1878, *etc.*] 8°. **14072. d. 37.**

JAGANNĀTHA ṢĀSTRĪ KRAMAVANTA. *See* HUTTON (C.) *LL.D.* A Maratha treatise on arithmetic. [Translated from the English] by Captain George Jervis [assisted by J. Ṣ. K.] [1826.] 12°. **14139. a. 48.**

JANĀRDANA BĀḶĀJĪ MODAK. *See* BHŪSHAṆA, *Kavi.* शिवराजभूषण काव्य . . . Shivaraja-bhushana . . . Edited by J. B. M. [1888.] 8°. **14072. d. 37.**

—— *See* JAYARĀMA SVĀMĪ. जयरामस्वामी . . . यांच्या चरित्राची बखर [Jayarāma Svāmī . . . yāṉchyā charitrāchī bakhar.] . . . Edited by J. B. M. [1888.] 8°. **14072. d. 37.**

—— *See* MARATHA EMPIRE. मराठी साम्राज्याची छोटी बखर [Marāṭhī sāmrājyāchī chhoṭī bakhar.] . . . Edited by J. B. M. [1888.] 8°. **14072. d. 37.**

JANĀRDANA DĀMODARA KOLHAṬKAR. आमची धर्मादाय पद्धति [Āmchī dharmādāya paddhati. A lecture on the best method of dispensing charities in large towns in India.] pp. 14. [1890.] *See* BOMBAY, *City of.—Hindu Union Club.* हेमंत व्याख्यानमाला [Hemanta vyākhyānamālā.] Vol. v. No. 3. [1886, *etc.*] 8°. **14139. c. 26.**

JAYARĀMA SVĀMĪ. [*Life.*] *See* RĀJĀRĀMA MANOHARA DIVĀṆJĪ BUDHAKAR. जयराम स्वामी चरित्र [Jayarāma Svāmī charitra.]

—— जयरामस्वामी वडगांवकर त्यांचे गुरु परमगुरु व शिष्य प्रशिष्य यांच्या चरित्रांची बखर [Jayarāma Svāmī . . . yāṇchyā charitrāchī bakhar.] . . . A description of the miracles worked by Jayarama Svami of Vadagaon, his two predecessors and four successors. Edited by Janardan Balaji Modak. [1888.] *See* PERIODICAL PUBLICATIONS.—*Poona.* काव्येतिहास-संग्रह [Kāvyetihāsa saṅgraha.] Vol. xi. Nos. 1-3. [1878, *etc.*] 8°. **14072. d. 37.**

JAYAVANTA (D. B.) कपटजाल नाटक अथवा एका गृहस्थाचा भोळसरपणा [Kapaṭajāla nāṭaka. A drama in five acts.] *See* PERIODICAL PUBLICATIONS.—*Pen.* नाट्यकथामाला Natya-kathamala. Vol. iii. Nos. 4-6. [1887, *etc.*] 8°. **14140. f. 30.**

JERVIS (GEORGE RITSO). *See* HUTTON (C.) *LL.D.* A Maratha treatise on arithmetic. [Translated from the English] by Captain George Jervis [assisted by Jagannātha Śāstrī Kramavanta]. [1826.] 12°. **14139. a. 48.**

JÑĀNADEVA. *See* KRISHṆĀJĪ NĀRĀYAṆA KĀKAḌE. भजनी संतखेळ [Bhajanī santakhela. A collection of obscure stanzas by Jñānadeva and other Marathi poets.] [1888, *etc.*] 12°. **14140. a. 37.**

—— श्री ज्ञानदेवकृत अमृतानुभव व त्यावरील श्रीशिवकल्याणकृत अमृतानुभवविवरण नित्यानंदैक्यदीपिका [Amṛitānubhava. Another edition of Jñānadeva's Anubhavāmṛita, with a commentary by Śivakalyāṇa, entitled Nityānandaikya-dīpikā. Edited by Aṇṇā Moreśvara Kuṇṭe, with an explanatory and critical introduction, and a glossary of difficult terms.] मुंबई १८१० [*Bombay,* 1889.] 4°. **14137. e. 11.**

JYOTISHA-CHAKRA. ज्योतिषचक्र [Jyotisha-chakra, or The wheel of fortune. Followed by an extract in Sanskrit from the Sāmudrika, called Hastarekhāvichāraṇa, on palmistry.] मुंबई [*Bombay,* 1860?] *s. sh. fol.* **14003. e. 2.(3.)**

KĀLIDĀSA. [MEGHADŪTA.] Meghaduta kavya by Mahakavi Shri Kalidasa. Edited with Kavyarthadipika, a Marathi commentary and critical notes, by Vaman Shastri Islampurkar. (मेघदूत काव्य) Second revised edition. pp. xvii. 274. *Bombay,* 1889. 8°. **14072. cc. 40.**

—— [VIKRAMORVAŚĪ.] संगीत विक्रमोर्वशी नाटक [Vikramorvaśī nāṭaka. A Sanskrit play of Kālidāsa, freely translated by Keśava Moreśvara Kāṇe.] *See* PERIODICAL PUBLICATIONS.—*Pen.* नाट्यकथामाला Natya-kathāmala. Vol. ii. Nos. 5-10. [1887, *etc.*] 8°. **14140. f. 30.**

KĀNHOBĀ RAṆCHHODDĀS KĪRTIKAR. जलधिज वर्णन [Jaladhija varṇana. A lecture on marine vegetable and animal life.] [1890.] *See* BOMBAY, *City of.—Hindu Union Club.* हेमंत व्याख्यानमाला [Hemanta vyākhyānamālā.] Vol. v. No. 6. [1886, *etc.*] 8°. **14139. c. 26.**

Incomplete; wanting all after p. 8.

KĀṢĪNĀTHA NĀRĀYAṆA SĀNE. *See* BHĀŪ SĀHEB. श्रीमंत भाऊ साहेब यांची कैफियत [Śrīmanta Bhāū Sāheb yāṇchī kaiphiyat. Edited with notes by K. N. S.] [1887.] 8°. **14072. d. 37.**

—— *See* CHITRAGUPTA. शिवाजी महाराजांची बखर [Śivājī Mahārājāṇchī bakhar. Edited with notes by K. N. S.] [1888.] 8°. **14072. d. 37.**

—— *See* DĀBHĀḌE, *Senāpati.* सेनापति दाभाडे . . . यांची हकीगत [Senāpati Dābhāḍe yāṇchī hakīgat. Edited with notes by K. N. S.] [1886-87.] 8°. **14072. d. 37.**

—— *See* MALHĀR RĀMARĀVA CHIṬṆĪS. राजनीति [Rājanīti. Edited with notes by K. N. S.] [1887-88.] 8°. **14072. d. 37.**

KĀṢĪNĀTHA SAMBHĀJĪ. श्री हरिविजय कथारस आणि श्री कृष्णाविषयीं ख्रिस्ती इत्यादि मतवादी लोकांच्या कुतर्कांचें खंडन [Harivijaya kathārasa. An account of the life and exploits of Krishṇa, founded on the Harivijaya of the poet Śrīdhara, written specially in refutation of the unfavourable views held by Christian authors as to the moral character of the Hindu god.] pp. iii. 197, vi. मुंबई १८८७ [*Bombay,* 1887.] 12°. **14137. d. 19.**

KĀṢĪNĀTHA TRIMBAK TELANG, *C.I.E.* *See* LESSING (G. E.) शाहणा नेथन [Śāhaṇā Nathan, or Nathan the Wise. A dramatic poem, translated, with an introductory preface and notes, by K. T. T.] [1887.] 8°. **14140. f. 29.**

KĀŞĪNĀTHA TRIMBAK TELANG, *C.I.E.* **सामाजिक विषयासंबंधी तोडजोड.** [Sāmājika vishayā-sambandhī toḍjoḍ. A lecture on social progress.] pp. 22. [1889.] *See* BOMBAY, *City of.—Hindu Union Club.* **हेमंत व्याख्यानमाला** [Hemanta vyākhyānamālā.] Vol. iv. No. 6. [1886, *etc.*] 8°. **14139. c. 26.**

KĀŞĪNĀTHA VĀMANA KĀṆE. **स्थावर जंगमात्मक सृष्टीविषयीं माहिती** [Sthāvara jaṅgamātmaka sṛishṭī-vishayīṉ māhitī. A lecture on the universe.] pp. 21. [1889.] *See* BOMBAY, *City of.—Hindu Union Club.* **हेमंत व्याख्यानमाला** [Hemanta vyākhyā-namālā.] Vol. iv. No. 5. [1886, *etc.*] 8°. **14139. c. 26.**

KEŞAVA MOREŞVARA KĀṆE. *See* KĀLIDĀSA. **संगीत विक्रमोर्वशी नाटक** [Vikramorvaşī nāṭaka. A free translation by K. M. K.] [1887, *etc.*] 8°. **14140. f. 30.**

KEŞAVA VĀMANA PEṬHE. **आमचे कलाकौशल्यांत सुधारणा करण्यास कोणकोणते उपाय योजिले पाहिजेत?** [Āmche kalākauşalyāṉt sudhārṇā karaṇyās upāya. A lecture suggesting means for the improvement of native arts and industries.] pp. 25. [1889.] *See* BOMBAY, *City of.—Hindu Union Club.* **हेमंत व्याख्यानमाला** [Hemanta vyākhyānamālā.] Vol. iv. No. 3. [1886, *etc.*] 8°. **14139. c. 26.**

KṚISHṆĀJĪ NĀRĀYAṆA KĀKAḌE. **भजनी संतखेळ आणि एकनाथी भारूड संग्रह** [Bhajanī santakhela. A collection of obscure and difficult stanzas by Tukārāma, Ekanātha, Jñānadeva, Nāmadeva and other Marathi poets, usually recited or sung by Vaishṇava pilgrims or devotees. Compiled by K. N. K.] **मुंबई १८८८** [*Bombay*, 1888, *etc.*] 12°. *In progress.* **14140. a. 37.**

KṚISHṆĀJĪ VĀSUDEVA KHARE. **मौन यौवना** [Mauna yauvanā, or The speechless maiden. A Marathi tale written conjointly by K. V. Kh., Vāsudeva Raṅganātha Şirvaḷkar and Vināyaka Trimbak Moḍak.] pp. 299. *Poona*, 1889. 8°. *See* POONA.—*Poona Night Club.* Entertainment Series. No. i. 1889, *etc.* 8°. **14139. g. 23.**

KṚISHṆĀPPĀ. [*Life.*] *See* RĀJĀRĀMA MANOHARA DIVĀṆJĪ BUDHAKAR. **जयराम स्वामी चरित्र** [Jayarāma Svāmī charitra.]

LESSING (GOTTHOLD EPHRAIM). **शाहणा नेथन** [Şāhaṇā Nathan, or Nathan the Wise. A dramatic poem, translated by Kāşīnātha Trimbak Telang, with an introductory preface and notes, from the English versions of R. D. Boylan and Dr. A. Wood, and by a comparison with the German original of G. E. L.] pp. xiv. xix. 160, ii. **मुंबई १८८७** [*Bombay*, 1887.] 8°. **14140. f. 29.**

LITURGIES.—JEWS.—*Daily Prayers.*—The Daily Prayers [according to the Spanish rite] translated from Hebrew into Marathi by Joseph Ezekiel Rajpurkar. [With the Hebrew text.] (**नित्याची प्रार्थना**) [Nityāchī prāthanā.] pp. vii. 374, 374, 17. vii. *Bombay*, 1889. 8°. **1972. cc. 11.**

—— *Fast-day Prayers.* The Jewish Propitiatory Prayer: or a prayer for the forgiveness of sins. Translated from Hebrew into Marathi by J. E. Rajpurker. **סליחות पापाच्या क्षमेसाठीं प्रार्थना** [Pāpāchyā kshamesāṭhīṉ prārthanā.] pp. 60. *Bombay*, 1859. 8°. **14137. b. 17.**

MĀDHAVARĀVA NĀRĀYAṆA MĀṄKAR. *See* RAṄGANĀTHA SVĀMĪ. **अथ रंगनाथी योगवासिष्ठसारटीका प्रारंभः** [Yogavāsishṭhasāra-ṭikā. Edited, with a life of the author and a glossary by M. N. M.] [1890.] *obl.* 8°. **14137. e. 13.**

MĀDHAVA ŞAṄKARA SOVANĪ. *See* SŪNṚITAVĀDĪ, *Son of Vişveşvara Mahāprasādi.* **श्री कौतुकचिंतामणि** [Kautuka-chintāmaṇi. Edited, with a Marathi translation and preface, by M. Ş. S.] [1886.] 8°. **14053. a. 10.**

MAHĀDEVA BĀVA. [*Life.*] *See* RĀJĀRĀMA MANOHARA DIVĀṆJĪ BUDHAKAR. **जयराम स्वामी चरित्र** [Jayarāma Svāmī charitra.]

MAHĀDEVA BHĀGAVATA DINKAR. **पदरत्नमहोदधि.** [Padaratna-mahodadhi. A collection of poems by ancient and modern Marathi poets, chiefly in praise of Hindu deities.] pp. ii. xviii. 350. **मुंबई १८८९** [*Bombay*, 1889.] 8°. **14140. b. 16.**

MAHĀDEVA VINĀYAKA KEḶKAR. **रत्नमाला आणि प्रतापचंद्र** [Ratnamālā āṇi Pratāpachandra. A romance.] pp. ii. 184. **मालवण १८८८** [*Malwan*, 1888.] 8°. **14139. g. 20.**

MAHĀDEVA VYAṄKATEṢA RAHĀḶKAR. नारायणराव आणि गोदावरी [Nārāyaṇa Rāva āṇi Godāvarī. A tale. Second edition.] pp. iv. 257. पुणें १८९० [*Poona*, 1890.] 8°. **14139. g. 22.**

MAHĪPATI. *See* MŪRKAR MAṆḌALĪ. श्रीभक्तलीलामृत कथारस [Bhaktalīlāmṛita kathārasa. A prose adaptation of Mahīpati's Bhaktalīlāmṛita.] [1890.] 8°. **14140. b. 17.**

—— —— श्रीसंतलीलामृत कथारस. [Santalīlāmṛita kathārasa. An adaptation in prose of Mahīpati's Santalīlāmṛita.] [1888.] 12°. **14140. b. 14.**

—— अथ श्री भक्तविजय ग्रंथ प्रारंभः [Bhaktivijaya. Third edition.] मुंबई १८८७ [*Bombay*, 1887.] *obl.* 4°. **14140. d. 20.**

MALHĀR RĀMARĀVA CHITṆĪS. राजनीति [Rājanīti. A treatise on the duties of kings. Edited, with critical notes by Kāṣīnātha Nārāyaṇa Sāne.] [1887-88.] *See* PERIODICAL PUBLICATIONS.—*Poona.* काव्येतिहास-संग्रह [Kāvyetihāsa saṅgraha.] Vol. x. No. 5-vol. xi. No. 1. [1878, *etc.*] 8°. **14072. d. 37.**

MANAṢCHANDRABODHA. अथ मनश्चंद्रबोधस्य प्रारंभः [Another edition.] मुंबई १८८६ [*Bombay*, 1886.] *fol.* 8°. **14140. d. 21.**

MĀṆIK PRABHU. [*Life.*] *See* RĀMACHANDRA BOVĀ SOLĀPURKAR. प्रसिद्ध . . . श्रीमाणिक प्रभु यांचें चारित्र [Māṇik Prabhu yāṉcheṉ charitra.] [1889.] 12. **14139. d. 34.**

MANOHARA NĀṬAKA. Manohara nâṭaka. A play in six acts. (मनोहर नाटक) pp. x. 163. *Bombay*, 1890. 12°. **14140. e. 17.**
No. xi. of "Potdar's Moral and Interesting Book Series."

MARATHA EMPIRE. मराठी साम्राज्याची छोटी बखर [Marāṭhī sāmrājyāchī chhoṭī bakhar.] A chronicle of the Maratha Empire from A.D. 1550-1818. Edited with notes by Janardan Balaji Modak. [1888.] *See* PERIODICAL PUBLICATIONS.—*Poona.* काव्येतिहास-संग्रह [Kāvyetihāsa saṅgraha.] Vol. xi. Nos. 4-11. [1878, *etc.*] 8°. **14072. d. 37.**

MORO VINĀYAKA ṢIṄGṆE. *See* BĀLAKṚISHṆA BĀPŪ ĀCHĀRYA and MORO VINĀYAKA ṢIṄGṆE. A descriptive account of Bombay. 1889. 8°. **14139. e. 31.**

MUHAMMAD, *Shaikh.* अथ योगसंग्राम प्रारंभ ॥ [Yoga-saṅgrāma. A treatise in verse and in 18 chapters, on Yoga philosophy by a Muhammadan convert to Hinduism. With an introductory preface containing a life of the author by Ṣivarāma Sītārāma Vāgḷe.] मुंबई १८८९ [*Bombay*, 1889.] *obl.* 8°. **14137. e. 12.**

MUKHARJI (T. N.) *See* TRAILOKYANĀTHA MUKHOPĀDHYĀYA.

MUNĪṢVARA SVĀMĪ. [*Life.*] *See* RĀJĀRĀMA MANOHARA DIVĀṆJĪ BUDHAKAR. जयराम स्वामी चरित्र [Jayarāma Svāmī charitra.]

MŪRKAR MAṆḌALĪ. श्रीभक्तलीलामृत कथारस आणि हिंदुलोकांचें मूर्तिपूजन [Bhaktalīlāmṛita kathārasa. A prose adaptation of Mahīpati's Bhaktalīlāmṛita, or Account of the lives and miracles of Vaishṇava saints. Followed by an essay, entitled Hindulokāṉcheṉ mūrtipūjana, or an Apology for Hindu idol-worship.] pp. ii. 317, 14. मुंबई १८९० [*Bombay*, 1890.] 8°. **14140. b. 17.**

—— श्रीहरिविजय कथारस आणि श्रीकृष्णाविषयीं खिस्ती इत्यादि मतवादी लोकांच्या कुतर्कांचें खंडण [Harivijaya kathārasa. A prose adaptation of Ṣrīdhara's Harivijaya, followed by a vindication of the life and character of Krishṇa from the hostile criticisms of Christian and other writers. Second edition.] pp. iii. iii. 227, 14, ii. मुंबई १८८९ [*Bombay*, 1889.] 12°. **14140. b. 15.**

—— श्रीसंतलीलामृत कथारस आणि आमचे अलिकडील सुधारलेले विद्वान. [Santalīlāmṛita kathārasa. An adaptation in prose of Mahīpati's Santalīlāmṛita, or Lives of Vaishṇava saints. Followed by an essay on the true principles of moral and social progress in Hindu communities.] pp. ii. 202, 25, ix. मुंबई १८८८ [*Bombay*, 1888.] 12°. **14140. b. 14.**

—— श्रीशिवलीलामृत कथारस आणि आमच्या शैववैष्णवांतील वखेडा. [Ṣivalīlāmṛita kathārasa. A prose adaptation of Ṣrīdhara's Ṣivalīlāmṛita. Followed by an essay in support of Ṣiva-worship.] मुंबई १८८९ [*Bombay*, 1889.] 12°. **14140. a. 40.**

NĀMADEVA. *See* KRISHṆĀJĪ NĀRĀYAṆA KĀKAḌE. भजनी संतखेल [Bhajanī santakhela. A collection of obscure passages by Nāmadeva and other Marathi poets.] [1888, *etc.*] 12°. **14140. a. 37.**

NĀNĀ PHADṆAVĪS. *See* BĀḶĀJĪ JANĀRDANA BHĀNU.

NARAHARI. नरहरिकृत गंगारत्नमाला [Gaṅgāratnamālā. A poem.] [1888.] *See* PERIODICAL PUBLICATIONS.—*Poona.* काव्येतिहास-संग्रह [Kāvyetihāsa saṅgraha.] Vol. xi. Nos. 1-6. [1878, *etc.*] 8°. **14072. d. 37.**

NĀRĀYAṆA BĀPUJĪ KĀNIṬKAR. श्रीशिवाजी नाटक [Ṣivājī nāṭaka. An historical drama, embodying the principal incidents in the life of Ṣivājī.] pp. iv. 137. पुणें १८८९ [*Poona,* 1889.] 12°. **14140. e. 15.**

—— तरुणीशिक्षण नाटिका [Taruṇī ṣikshaṇa nāṭikā. Second edition.] pp. xvi. ii. 151. पुणे १८९० [*Poona,* 1890.] 12°. **14140. e. 19.**

NĀRĀYAṆA GAṆEṢA MAṆḌALIK. *See* PERIODICAL PUBLICATIONS.—*Pen.* नाट्यकथामाला Natya-kathamala. A monthly magazine, *etc.* [Edited by N. G. M.] [1887, *etc.*] 8°. **14140. f. 30.**

—— तरुण पुरुष [Taruṇa purusha. A Marathi novel.] *See* PERIODICAL PUBLICATIONS. — *Pen.* नाट्यकथामाला Natya-kathamala. Vol. i.-vol. iii. No. 1. [1887, *etc.*] 8°. **14140. f. 30.**

NĀRĀYAṆA HARI BHĀGAVATA. भार्याप्रमाद अथवा पति विटंबन नाटक [Bhāryāpramāda, also called Pati viṭambana nāṭaka. A drama in six acts in disapproval of modern social reform, and high-class education, especially in the case of native women.] *See* PERIODICAL PUBLICATIONS.—*Pen.* नाट्यकथामाला Natya-kathamala. Vol. i. Nos. 9-12. [1887, *etc.*] 8°. **14140. f. 30.**

—— [Another edition.] pp. पेण: १८८८ [*Pen,* 1888.] 8°. **14140. f. 28.(2.)**

—— हुंडा प्रहसन [Huṇḍā prahasana. A farce in 11 scenes.] *See* PERIODICAL PUBLICATIONS.—*Pen.* नाट्यकथामाला Natya-kathamala. Vol. i. No. 2-7. [1887, *etc.*] 8°. **14140. f. 30.**

—— मसलत फसली अथवा राजविजय नाटक [Rājavijaya nāṭaka. An historical drama.] *See* PERIODICAL PUBLICATIONS.—*Pen.* नाट्यकथामाला Natya-kathamala. Vol. i. No. 8-vol. iii. No. 1. [1887, *etc.*] 8°. **14140. f. 30.**

NĀRĀYAṆA VĀMANA ṬIḶAKA CHIKHALGĀNVKAR. तीन विधवा [Tīn vidhavā. A tale on the evils of existing marriage customs amongst Brahmans.] pp. 43. पुणें १८८७ [*Poona,* 1887.] 12°. **14139. f.**

NĀRĀYAṆA VISHṆU BĀPAṬ. *See* RĀMAKṚISHṆA GOPĀLA BHĀṆḌĀRKAR. Early history of the Dekkan down to the Mahomedan conquest . . . Translated . . . by Nârâyaṇa Vishṇu Bâpat. 1887. 8°. **14139. e. 29.**

NĀRO ĀPĀJĪ GOḌBOLE. गोत्रमालिका कोंकणस्थ ब्राह्मणांची [Gotramālikā. The gotras, or family names of Konkani Brahmans, and lists of upanāma, or surnames of persons belonging to each gotra. Fifth edition.] pp. 32, *lith.* पुणें १८८८ [*Poona,* 1888.] 16°. **14137. c. 18.**

PADMARĀJA, *B., Jain Pandit.* A Treatise on Jain Law and Usages. [Consisting of a selection of verses from Sanskrit authorities, accompanied by translations into English, Canarese, and Marathi.] pp. 38. *Bombay,* 1886. 8°. **14038. b. 8.**

PERIODICAL PUBLICATIONS.—PEN. नाट्यकथामाला Natya-kathamala. A monthly magazine, comprising a series of Marathi dramas, novels, *etc. etc.* [Edited by Nārāyaṇa Gaṇeṣa Maṇḍalik.] पेण: १८०९ [*Pen,* 1887, *etc.*] 8°. **14140. f. 30.**
In progress.

POONA. — *Poona Night Club.* Entertainment Series of the Night Club. *Bombay,* 1889, *etc.* 8°.
In progress. **14139. g. 23.**

PRATĀPASIMHA MAHĀRĀJA. *See* BRĀHMA DHARMA. श्री ब्राह्मधर्म [Brāhma dharma. Translated into Marathi verse by P. M.] [1887.] *obl.* 12°. **14137. a. 15.**

PURĀṆAS.—GAṆEṢAPURĀṆA.—*Gaṇeṣagītā.* अथ प्राकृतटीकासहित गणेशगीता प्रारंभः [Gaṇeṣagītā. A work in 11 *adhyāyas,* stated to be a portion of the Pauranic compilation called Gaṇeṣapurāṇa. Sanskrit text, accompanied by a commentary in Marathi by Ballāla, and followed by 17 shorter works, in Sanskrit, Marathi, or both languages, and chiefly in praise of Gaṇeṣa.] पुणें [*Poona,* 1887.] *obl.* 8°. **14016. d. 49.**
Pagination irregular.

PURUSHOTTAMA BHĀSKARA ḌOṄGRE. भीमसिंग आणि पद्मिनी नाटक [Bhīma Siṃha āṇi Padminī nāṭaka. An historical drama of Bhīma Siṃha, Raja of Mewar, and his queen Padminī.] pp. 116. मुंबई १८८९ [*Bombay,* 1889.] 8°. **14140. f. 31.**

PURUSHOTTAMA BHĀSKARA ḌOṄGRE. जरठोद्वाह [Jaraṭhodvāha. A drama condemning the practice of marrying young girls to rich old men.] pp. 188. मुंबई १८९० [*Bombay*, 1890.] 8°. **14140. f. 32.**

RĀGHO NĀRĀYAṆA DEVḶE. वाटसराची गोष्ट [Vāṭsarāchī goshṭa. Tales of a traveller. Second edition.] pp. 44, *lith.* पुणें १८४७ [*Poona*, 1847.] 8°. **14139. g.**

RAGHUNĀTHA RĀMAKṚISHṆA BHĀGAVATA. *See* VIṬHOBĀ AṆṆĀ. विठोबा अण्णाकृत पदसमूह [Padasamūha. Edited, with notes, by R. R. Bh.] [1890.] 8°. **14140. b.**

RĀJĀRĀMA GAṆEŚA BOḌAS. *See* BHĪMĀCHĀRYA JHAḶKĪKAR and RĀJĀRĀMA GAṆEŚA BOḌAS. वेदार्थोद्धारः । [Vedārthoddhāra.] [1875.] 8°. **14028. d. 18.**

RĀJĀRĀMA MANOHARA DIVĀṆJĪ BUDHAKAR. जयराम स्वामी चरित्र [Jayarāma Svāmī charitra. A biography of a successive line of six famous devotees, *i.e.* of Kṛishṇāppā and of his disciples Jayarāma Svāmī, Gopāla Bāva, Viṭhṭhala Svāmī, Munīśvara Svāmī and Mahādeva Bāva, all residents of Wadgaon, near Satara.] pp. ii. 226. पुणें १८११ [*Poona*, 1889.] 8°. **14139. e. 30.**

RĀJĀRĀMA PRĀSĀDĪ. राजाराम प्रासादीकृत पदें [Paden. Miscellaneous poems.] [1887.] *See* PERIODICAL PUBLICATIONS.—*Poona.* काव्येतिहास-संग्रह [Kāvyetihāsa saṅgraha.] Vol. x. Nos. 10-12. [1878, *etc.*] 8°. **14072. d. 37.**

RĀJĀRĀMA RĀMAKṚISHṆA BHĀGAVATA. ब्राह्मण व ब्राह्मणीधर्म किंवा वेद व वैदिकधर्म [Brāhmaṇa va Brāhmaṇī dharma. A lecture on Brahmans and the religion of the Vedas.] pp. 32, ii. [1889.] *See* BOMBAY, *City of.—Hindu Union Club.* हेमंत व्याख्यानमाला [Hemanta vyākhyānamālā.] Vol. iv. No. 2. [1886, *etc.*] 8°. **14139. c. 26.**

—— मोगल व मोगली धर्म [Mogal va Mogalī dharma. A lecture on the Mongols and their religion.] pp. 13. [1890.] *See* BOMBAY, *City of.—Hindu Union Club.* हेमंत व्याख्यानमाला [Hemanta vyākhyānamālā.] Vol. v. No. 1. [1886, *etc.*] 8°. **14139. c. 26.**

RĀJPURKAR (JOSEPH EZEKIEL). *See* LITURGIES.—Jews.—*Daily Prayers.* The Daily Prayers, translated from Hebrew into Marathi by J. E. R. 1889. 8°. **1972. cc. 11.**

—— *See* LITURGIES.—Jews.—*Fast-day Prayers.* The Jewish Propitiatory Prayer . . . Translated . . . by J. E. R. 1859. 8°. **14137. b. 17.**

RĀMACHANDRA BALLĀLA GOḌBOLE. संक्रांतीचा हलवा [Saṅkrāntichā halvā. An account of the life of Vastupāla, the minister of Lavaṇaprasāda, one of the ancient kings of Gujarat. Founded on a Sanskrit poem by Someṣvara Deva, entitled Kīrtikaumudī.] pp. ii. 28, ii. पुणें १८८८ [*Poona*, 1888.] 8°. **14139. e. 27.(2.)**

RĀMACHANDRA BHIKĀJĪ GUÑJĪKAR. *See* ŚRĪ-KṚISHṆA RĀMAKṚISHṆA ŚĀSTRĪ ĀṬHALYE. सन्धिप्रकाश [Sandhi-prakāṣa. Compiled chiefly from the Kaumudī-mahotsāha of R. Bh. G.] [1890.] 12°. **14139. a.**

RĀMACHANDRA BHIKĀJĪ JOṢĪ. A higher Marathi grammar, by Ramchandra Bhikaji Joshi. (प्रौढबोध मराठी व्याकरण). [Prauḍhabodha Marāṭhī vyākaraṇa.] pp. xii. 312, ii. *Poona*, 1889. 12°. **14140. g. 46.**

RĀMACHANDRA BOVĀ SOLĀPURKAR. प्रसिद्ध सत्पुरुष दत्तावतारिक श्रीमाणिक प्रभु यांचें चरित्र [Māṇik Prabhu yāñcheṇ charitra. The life of Māṇik Prabhu, a Rājayogī Vedānta devotee of the Deccan, who was popularly believed to be an incarnation of the god Dattātreya.] pp. ix. 209. पुणें १८११ [*Poona*, 1889.] 12°. **14139. d. 34.**

RĀMADĀSA SVĀMĪ, *Son of Sūryopanta.* [*Life.*] *See* GOVARDHANADĀSA LAKSHMĪDĀSA. श्री रामदास स्वामीचे चरित्रांची बखर [Śrī Rāmadāsa Svāmīche charitra.] [1889.] 12°. **14139. d. 33.**

RĀMAKṚISHṆA GOPĀLA BHĀṆḌĀRKAR. Early history of the Dekkan down to the Mahomedan conquest. By Dr. Râmakrishṇa Gopâl Bhâṇdârkar, translated into Marâṭhi by Nârâyaṇa Vishṇu Bâpat. (दक्खनचा प्राचीन इतिहास) [Dakkhanchā prāchīna itihāsa.] pp. iv. ii. ii. 302. *Bombay*, 1887. 8°. **14139. e. 29.**

RĀMAYYĀ VENKAYYĀ ĀYYĀVĀRU. ख्रिस्ती बंधुजनांस विनंती [Khristī bandhujanāṇs vinantī. An anti-Christian tract, addressed to Christians in the form of a letter. Second edition.] pp. 36. मुंबई १८८७ [*Bombay*, 1887.] 16°. **14137. c.**

RAṄGANĀTHA SVĀMĪ. अथ रंगनाथी योगवासिष्ठसार-टीका प्रारंभः [Yogavāsishṭhasāra-ṭīkā. A metrical paraphrase of the Yogavāsishṭha, a Sanskrit philosophical poem. Edited, with a life of the author, and a glossary, by Mādhavarāva Nārāyaṇa Māṅkar.] मुंबई [*Bombay*, 1890.] *obl.* 8°. **14137. e. 13.**

RĀVAJĪ ŚRĪDHARA GONDHAḶEKAR. कीर्तनतरंगिणी [Kīrtana-taraṅgiṇī. Another edition.] Pt. i. and ii. पुणें १८८९ [*Poona*, 1889.] 8°. **14140. c. 40.**

Pt. i. is of the 5th and Pt. ii. of the 3rd edition.

SADĀŚIVA KĀŚĪNĀTHA CHHATRE. *See* BAITĀL PACHĪSĪ. वेताळपंचविशी [Translated by S. K. Chh.] [1889.] 16°. **14139. f. 32.**

SADĀŚIVA VĀMANA KĀṆE प्रयागांतील राष्ट्रीय सभेची हकीकत [Prayāgāntīl rāshṭrīya sabhechī hakīkat. An account of the proceedings of the Indian National Congress held at Allahabad.] pp. 17. [1889.] *See* BOMBAY, *City of*.—*Hindu Union Club*. हेमंत व्याख्यानमाला [Hemanta vyākhyānamālā.] Vol. iv. No. 7. [1886, *etc.*] 8°. **14139. c. 26.**

SAṂSKṚITA PUSTAKAMĀLĀ. अथ संस्कृतपुस्तकमाला [Saṃskṛita pustakamālā. A course of easy lessons in Sanskrit.] Pt. i. मुंबई १८८९ [*Bombay*, 1889.] 12°. **14139. a.**

SĀMUDRIKA. *See* JYOTISHA-CHAKRA. ज्योतिषचक्र [Jyotisha-chakra. Followed by an extract from the Sāmudrika, called Hastarekhāvichāraṇa.] [1860 ?] *s. sh. fol.* **14003. e. 2.(3.)**

ŚAṄKARA DĀJĪ ŚĀSTRĪ PADE. सुंदरा बाई अथवा साध्वी - - स्त्रीचरित्र [Sundarā Bāī, or The virtuous wife. A Marathi tale.] *See* PERIODICAL PUBLICATIONS.—*Pen.* नाट्यकथामाला Natya-kathamala. Vol. iii. No. 2-3. [1887, *etc.*] 8°. **14100. f. 30.**

ŚAṄKARA MORO RĀNAḌE. अतिपीडचरित नाटक [Atipīḍacharita nāṭaka. An adaptation of Shakespere's drama "King Lear." Second edition.] pp. xxvii. 171. पुणें १८८९ [*Poona*, 1889.] 12°. **14140. e. 14.**

ŚAṄKARA TUKĀRĀMA ŚĀLIGRĀM. बापू गोखले यांचें चरित्र [Bāpū Gokhale yāṉcheṉ charitra. Third edition.] pp. 147, xvi. मुंबई १८८९ [*Bombay*, 1889.] 12°. **4139. d. 35.**

SAṄKEŚVARA. श्री जगद्गुरु मठ संकेश्वर यांणीं . . . शास्त्र निर्णय ठरविला [A decision arrived at by the high-priest of the temple at Saṅkeśvara regarding the expiatory penance required of Gaṇeśa Sītārāma Goḷvalkar, a Subhadar of the Holkar State, for having gone to England.] pp. 14, viii. पुणें १८८८ [*Poona*, 1888.] 12°. **14137. d.**

SHAKESPERE (WILLIAM). *See* ŚAṄKARA MORO RĀNAḌE. अतिपीडचरित नाटक [Atipīḍacharita nāṭaka. An adaptation of Shakespere's "King Lear."] [1889.] 12°. **14140. e. 14.**

SĪTĀRĀMA NARAHARA ḌHAVḶE. शिवदिग्विजय अथवा तरुण शिवाजी नाटक [Śiva-digvijaya nāṭaka. A drama on the youth and conquests of Śivājī.] pp. v. iii. 278. मुंबई १८८९ [*Bombay*, 1889.] 12°. **14140. e. 16.**

ŚIVĀJĪ, *Raja of Satara.* [*Life.*] *See* CHITRAGUPTA. शिवाजी महाराजांची बखर [Śivājī Mahārājāṉchī bakhar.]

ŚIVAKALYĀṆA. *See* JÑĀNADEVA. श्री ज्ञानदेवकृत अमृतानुभव *etc.* [Amṛitānubhava. With a commentary by Ś., entitled Nityānandaikya-dīpikā.] [1889.] 4°. **14137. e. 11.**

ŚIVARĀMA SĪTĀRĀMA VĀGḶE. *See* MUHAMMAD, *Shaikh.* अथ योगसंग्राम प्रारंभः ॥ [Yogasaṅgrāma. With an introductory preface containing a life of the author by Ś. S. V.] **14137. e. 12.**

SOMEŚVARA DEVA. *See* RĀMACHANDRA BALLĀLA GODBOLE. संक्रांतीचा हलवा [Saṅkrāntīchā halvā. An account of the life of Vastupāla, founded on a Sanskrit poem by S. D. entitled Kīrtikaumudī.] [1888.] 8°. **14139. e. 27.(2.)**

SPENCER (HERBERT). *See* VĀSUDEVA GAṆEŚA SAHASRABUDDHE. Sikshana mimansa, or The analysis of the theory of education from H. S.'s famous essay on education, *etc.* [1889.] 8°. **14140. h. 28.**

ŚRĪDHARA. *See* KĀŚĪNĀTHA SAMBHĀJĪ. श्री हरिविजय कथारस [Harivijaya kathārasa. Founded on the Harivijaya of the poet Śrīdhara.] [1887.] 12°. **14137. d. 19.**

—— *See* MŪRKAR MAṆḌALĪ. श्रीहरिविजय कथारस [Harivijaya kathārasa. A prose adaptation of Śrīdhara's Harivijaya.] [1889.] 12°. **14140. b. 15.**

—— —— श्रीशिवलीलामृत कथारस [Śivalīlāmṛita kathārasa. A prose adaptation of Śrīdhara's Śivalīlāmṛita.] [1889.] 12°. **14040. a. 40.**

ṢRĪKṚISHṆA RĀMAKṚISHṆA ṢĀSTRĪ ĀṬHALYE. सन्धिप्रकाश [Sandhi-prakāṣa. The Sanskrit rules of Sandhi explained in Marathi. Compiled chiefly from the Kaumudī-mahotsāha, or Rules of Sanskrit grammar, of Rāmachandra Bhikājī Guñjīkar.] pp. ii. 48, vii. मुंबई १८९० [*Bombay*, 1890.] 12°. **14139. a.**

SUBANDHU. *See* VĀMANA DĀJĪ OK. वासवदत्ता कथासार [Vāsavadattā kathāsāra. An abridged version of the Sanskrit romance of Subandhu.] [1889.] 32°. **14139. f.**

ṢŪDRAKA. *See* VĀMANA ṢĀSTRĪ ISLĀMPŪRKAR. Chárudatta and Vasantasená. Translated [or rather, adapted] from the Sanskrit work [Mṛichchhakaṭika of Ṣūdraka]. 1889. 12°. **14139. f. 35.**

SŪNṚITAVĀDĪ, *Son of Viṣveṣvara Mahāprasādi.* श्री कौतुकचिंतामणि [Kautuka-chintāmaṇi. A collection of magical recipes in Sanskrit verse, compiled by S. from several sources. Edited, with a Marathi translation and preface, by Mādhava Ṣaṅkara Sovanī.] pp. iv. 10, 248, x. पुणें १८८८ [*Poona*, 1886.] 8°. **14053. a. 10.**

TOṬAKĀCHĀRYA. श्री तोटकाचार्यकृत श्रीमच्छंकराचार्य स्तोत्र [Ṣaṅkarāchārya stotra. A Sanskrit hymn in praise of Ṣaṅkara Āchārya, whose pupil the author is said to have been. Edited, with a Marathi translation, by Vāsudeva Hari Āṭhalye.] pp. 7. रत्नागिरी १८८८ [*Ratnagiri*, 1887.] 16°. **14076. a.**

TRAILOKYANĀTHA MUKHOPĀDHYĀYA. *See* BĀLAKṚISHṆA ĀTMĀRĀMA GUPTE. The Industrial arts of India. Compiled ... (from Mr. Mukharji's "Art-manufactures of India") *etc.* 1889. 8°. **14139. e. 32.**

TRIGONOMETRY. Plane and spherical trigonometry, compiled from original English works into Marathee. (सरळरेघ आणि गोलीय त्रिकोणमिति) [Saralaregha āṇi golīya trikoṇamiti.] pp. 168, *lith.* *Rutnagiri*, 1854. 8°. **14139. a. 2.(2.)**

TUKĀRĀMA. *See* KRISHṆĀJĪ NĀRĀYAṆA KĀKAḌE. भजनी संतखेळ [Bhajanī santakhela. A collection of obscure stanzas by Tukārāma and other Marathi poets.] [1888, *etc.*] 12°. **14140. a. 37.**

—— श्री तुकारामबावा आणि त्यांचे शिष्य यांच्या अभंगांची गाथा [The complete poems of Tukārāma, and of his disciple Niḷobā, with introductory poems, eulogistic and biographical, by various authors. Edited by Tukārāma Tātyā.] मुंबई १८८९ [*Bombay*, 1889.] 8°. **14140. c. 41.**

Wanting Vol. 3, containing the poems of Niḷobā.

TUKĀRĀMA TĀTYĀ. *See* TUKĀRĀMA. श्री तुकारामबावा आणि त्यांचे शिष्य यांच्या अभंगांची गाथा [The complete poems of Tukārāma. Edited by T. T.] [1889.] 8°. **14140. c. 41.**

VĀMANA ĀBĀJĪ MOḌAK. हिंदुलोकांत ऐक्याची वृद्धि होण्यास हरकती व त्या दूर होण्याचे उपाय [Hindulokāṇt aikyāchī vṛiddhi hoṇyās harakatī. A lecture suggesting means for furthering the improvement and social unity of Hindu society.] pp. 13. [1889.] *See* BOMBAY, *City of.—Hindu Union Club.* हेमंत व्याख्यानमाला [Hemanta vyākhyānamālā.] Vol. iv. No. 1. [1886, *etc.*] 8°. **14139. c. 26.**

—— युरोपाच्या इतिहासापासून आपल्या लोकांनीं काय शिकावें [Yuropāchyā itihāsāpāsūn āpalyā lokāṇnīṇ kāy ṣikāveṇ, or "What should we learn from the history of Europe?" A lecture urging social and political advancement.] pp. 15. [1890.] *See* BOMBAY, *City of.—Hindu Union Club.* हेमंत व्याख्यानमाला [Hemanta vyākhyānamālā.] Vol. v. No. 4. [1886, *etc.*] 8°. **14139. c. 26.**

VĀMANA DĀJĪ OK. वासवदत्ता कथासार [Vāsavadattā kathāsāra. An abridged version of Vāsavadattā, a Sanskrit romance by Subandhu.] pp. 24, iv. मुंबई १८८९ [*Bombay*, 1889.] 32°. **14139. f.**

VĀMANA EKANĀTHA ṢĀSTRĪ KEMKAR. *See* RĀVAJĪ ṢRĪDHARA GONDHAḶEKAR. कीर्तनतरंगिणी [Kīrtana-taraṅgiṇī. Pt. ii. Another edition.] [1889.] 8°. **14140. c. 40.**

VĀMANA ṢĀSTRĪ ISLĀMPURKAR. *See* KĀLIDĀSA. [Meghaduta.] Meghaduta kavya . . . Edited with Kavyarthadipika, a Marathi commentary and critical notes, by Vaman Shastri Islampurkar. 1889. 8°. **14072. cc. 40.**

—— Chárudatta and Vasantasená. [A tale] translated [or rather, adapted] from the Sanskrit work [Mṛichchhakaṭika of Ṣūdraka] by Pandit Vaman Shastri Islampurkar. (चारुदत्त आणि वसंतसेना). pp. viii. 279. *Bombay*, 1889. 12°. **14139. f. 35.**

No. iv. of "Potdar's Moral and Interesting Book Series."

—— Pranayi Mádhava. Translated [or rather, adapted] from Sanskrit [Mālatī Mādhava of Bhavabhūti] by Pandit Vaman Shástri Islámpurkar. (प्रणयिमाधव.) pp. vi. 272. Bombay, 1889. 12°. **14139. f. 36.**

No. v. of "Potdar's Moral and Interesting Book Series."

VASTUPĀLA. [*Life.*] *See* RĀMACHANDRA BALLĀLA GODBOLE. संक्रांतीचा हलवा [Saṅkrāntīchā halvā.]

VĀSUDEVA GAṆEŚA SAHASRABUDDHE. Sikshana mimansa, or The analysis of the theory of education from Herbert Spencer's famous essay on education by Vasudev Ganesh Sahasrabudhe. (शिक्षणमीमांसा). pp. xxviii. 261. १८८९ *Bombay*, [1889.] 8°. **14140. h. 28.**

VĀSUDEVA GOPĀLA BHĀṆḌĀRKAR. सोनें व रुपें यांचा हिंदुस्थानांत खप [Sonen va rupen yānchā Hindusthānānt khap. A lecture on the consumption of gold and silver in India, advising their conversion into safe investments, instead of into ornaments and jewellery.] pp. 11. [1890.] *See* BOMBAY, *City of.* — *Hindu Union Club.* हेमंत व्याख्यानमाला [Hemanta vyākhyānamālā.] Vol. v. No. 8. [1886, *etc.*] 8°. **14139. c. 26.**

VĀSUDEVA HARI ĀṬHALYE. *See* TOṬAKĀCHĀRYA. श्री तोटकाचार्यकृत श्रीमच्छंकराचार्य स्तोत्र [Śaṅkarāchārya stotra. Edited, with a Marathi translation, by V. H. Ā.] [1887.] 16°. **14076. a.**

VĀSUDEVA JOGḶEKAR PHAḌNAVĪS. द्वैतखंडनपूर्वक अद्वैत प्रतिपादक वेदांतसार [Vedāntasāra. The substance of Vedānta philosophy, being a refutation of the *dvaita*, or dual, and a support of the *advaita*, or non-dual system. With numerous quotations from Sanskrit writers.] pp. xiv. 230. पुणें १८८७ [*Poona*, 1887.] 8°. **14137. d. 18.**

VĀSUDEVA MOREŚVARA POTADĀR. स्त्रीपुरुषांनीं नांवें घेण्याची पद्धत आणि मनोरंजक उखाणे व म्हणी [Strīpurushāṇnīṇ nāṇveṇ gheṇyāchī paddhata. A book of riddles, proverbs, and of modes in which husbands and wives express one another's names.] 4 pt. मुंबई १८८८ [*Bombay*, 1888.] 32°. **14139. a. 49.**

VĀSUDEVA RAṄGANĀTHA ŚIRVAḶKAR. मौन यौवना [Mauna yauvanā, or The speechless maiden. A Marathi tale written conjointly by V. R. Ś., Krishṇājī Vāsudeva Khare and Vināyaka Trimbak Moḍak.] pp. 299. *Poona*, 1889. 8°. *See* POONA.— *Poona Night Club.* Entertainment Series. No. i. 1889, *etc.* 8°. **14139. g. 23.**

VINĀYAKA GOVINDA LIMAYE. Discription [*sic*] of a pilgrimage to Shree Setubandha Rameshwar. सेतुबंधरामेश्वर यात्रावर्णन [Setubandha Rāmeśvara yātrāvarṇana.] मुंबई १८८७ [*Bombay*, 1887.] 12°. **14139. d. 23.(2.)**

—— History of the Native States. Chapter I. The history of large native states, wars, treaties, the former and present regal jurisprudence and treaties with the English government, *etc.* (एतद्देशीय संस्थानांचा इतिहास) [Etadveśīya saṃsthānānchā itihāsa.] pp. vii. 131. *Bombay*, 1887. 12°. **14139. e. 28.**

VINĀYAKA HARI PRABHU ŚINAKAR. भारतभैषज्यप्रभावदिग्दर्शन नाटक [Bhāratabhaishajyaprabhāvadigdarṣana nāṭaka. A drama showing the superiority of the Indian over the European systems of medicine.] pp. viii. 92. [*Bombay*, 1887.] 16°. **14140. e. 13.**

VINĀYAKA TRIMBAK MOḌAK. मौन यौवना [Mauna yauvanā, or The speechless maiden. A Marathi tale, written conjointly by V. T. M., Krishṇājī Vāsudeva Khare and Vāsudeva Raṅganātha Śirvaḷkar.] pp. 299. 1889. *See* POONA. — *Poona Night Club.* Entertainment Series. No. i. 1889, *etc.* 8°. **14139. g. 23.**

VĪREŚVARA SADĀŚIVA CHHATRE. कामनाकल्पवृक्ष [Kāmanā-kalpavṛiksha. Sanskrit slokas with their meanings, short stories, dramas, Pauranic legends, a vocabulary of useful terms in Marathi and English, and other miscellaneous compositions.] पुणें १८८८ [*Poona*, 1888.] 8°. **14139. g. 21.**

Each composition has a separate pagination.

VISHṆU DINKAR VAIDYA KALYĀṆKAR. कहाण्या [Kahāṇyā. Pt. i. Second edition.] मुंबई १८८८ [*Bombay*, 1888.] 12°. **14139. f. 33.(2.)**

VISHṆU KRISHṆA BHĀṬAVAḌEKAR. कॉर्नलॉ लीग [An account of the successful efforts made by the Anti-corn-law League to get the duty on corn removed.] pp. 12. [1890.] *See* BOMBAY, *City of.*—*Hindu Union Club.* हेमंत व्याख्यानमाला [Hemanta vyākhyānamālā.] Vol. v. No. 7. [1886, *etc.*] 8°. **14139. c. 26.**

VIṬHOBĀ AṆṆĀ. विठोबा अण्णाकृत पदसमूह [Padasamūha. A collection of poems, chiefly on mythological subjects, by V. A. and a few by other poets. Edited, with notes, by Raghunātha Rāmakṛishṇa Bhāgavata. Second edition.] pp. viii. 68. मुंबई १८९० [*Bombay*, 1890.] 8°. **14140. b.**

VIṬHṬHALA SVĀMĪ. [*Life.*] *See* RĀJĀRĀMA MANOHARA DIVĀṆJĪ BUDHAKAR. जयराम स्वामी चरित्र [Jayarāma Svāmī charitra.]

YESU, *Kavi.* उमाजी नायकाचा पवाडा [Umājī Nā'ikāchā pavāḍā. A poem extolling the prowess of Umājī Nā'ik, a notorious dacoit of the Dekhan.] pp. 8. मुंबई १८८८ [*Bombay*, 1888.] 16°. **14140. a. 39.(2.)**

YOGAVĀSISHṬHA. *See* RAṄGANĀTHA SVĀMĪ. अथ रंगनाथी योगवासिष्ठसारटीका प्रारंभः [Yogavāsishṭhasāraṭīkā. A metrical paraphrase of the Yogavāsishṭha.] [1890.] 8°. **14137. e. 13.**

INDEX OF ORIENTAL TITLES (ADDENDA).

Āmche kalākauṣalyāṇt sudhārṇā karaṇyās upāya.
See Keṣava Vāmana Peṭhe.
Āmchī dharmādāya paddhati.
See Janārdana Dāmodara Kolhaṭkar.
Amṛitānubhava.
See Jñānadeva.
Āpā Sāheb nāṭaka.
See Gopāla Rājārāma Raṅganātha.
Atipīḍacharita nāṭaka.
See Ṣaṅkara Moro Rānaḍe.
Bhāḍalī mata jyotishavarṇana.
See Bhaḍalī.
Bhajanī santakhela.
See Krishṇājī Nārāyaṇa Kākaḍe.
Bhaktalīlāmṛita kathārasa.
See Mūrkar Maṇḍalī.
Bhaktitattvāmṛita [*in loco*].
Bhāminīvilāsa.
See Jagannātha Paṇḍitarāja.
Bhāratabhaishajyaprabhāvadigdarṣana nāṭaka.
See Vināyaka Hari Prabhu Ṣinakar.
Bhāryā-pramāda.
See Nārāyaṇa Hari Bhāgavata.
Bhāshaṇa sāmpradāyika vākyeṇ.
See Candy (T.)
Bhāshāntarakaritāṇ utāre.
See Hari Krishṇa Dāmle.
Bhīma Simha āṇi Padminī nāṭaka.
See Purushottama Bhāskara Ḍoṅgre.
Brāhmadharma [*in loco*].
Brāhmaṇa va Brāhmaṇīdharma.
See Rājārāma Rāmakṛishṇa Bhāgavata.
Chārudatta āṇi Vasantasenā.
See Vāmana Ṣāstrī Islāmpūrkar.
Dakkhanchā prāchīna itihāsa.
See Rāmakṛishṇa Gopāla Bhāṇḍārkar.
Dārū pineṇ }
Deṣī hunar. }
See Bāḷakṛishṇa Ātmārāma Gupte.
Dharmaudārya.
See Bāḷa Yajñeṣvara Gurjar.
Draupadī-svayamvara.
See Ananta, *Kavi.*
Etadveṣīya saṃsthānāṇchā itihāsa.
See Vināyaka Govinda Limaye.
Gaṇeṣagītā.
See Purāṇas.—Gaṇeṣapurāṇa.—*Gaṇeṣagītā.*
Gaṅgāratnamālā.
See Narahari.
Gaṇitavṛitti.
See Hutton (C.) *LL.D.*
Gītāṇcheṇ pustaka.
See Hymn Book.
Gotramālikā.
See Nāro Āpājī Goḍbole.
Harivijaya kathārasa.
See Kāṣīnātha Sambhājī.
Harivijaya kathārasa.
See Mūrkar Maṇḍalī.
Hastarekhāvichāraṇa.
See Jyotishachakra.
Hindulokāṇcheṇ mūrtipūjana.
See Mūrkar Maṇḍalī.
Hindulokāṇt aikyāchī vṛiddhi hoṇyās harakatī.
See Vāmana Ābājī Moḍak.
Huṇḍā prahasana.
See Nārāyaṇa Hari Bhāgavata.
Isrāelāṇchā vidhi.
See Albu (I.).
Isrāelī dharmāntīl navalācheṇ vṛitta.
See Āshṭamkar (B. S.)
Jaladhija varṇana.
See Kānhobā Raṇchhoḍdās Kīrtikar.
Jaraṭhodvāha.
See Purushottama Bhāskara Ḍoṅgre.
Jayarāma Svāmī charitra.
See Rājārāma Manohara Divāṇjī Budhakar.
Jayarāma Svāmī yāṇchyā charitrāchī bakhar.
See Jayarāma Svāmī.
Jyotishavarṇāna.
See Bhaḍalī.
Kāmanā-kalpavṛiksha.
See Vīreṣvara Sadāṣiva Chhatre.
Kapaṭajāla nāṭaka.
See Jayavanta (D. B.)
Kautuka-chintāmaṇi. [*sādi.*
See Sūnṛitavādī, *Son of Viṣreṣvara Mahāpra-*
Kāvyārthadīpikā.
See Vāmana Ṣāstrī Islāmpurkar.
Khristī bandhujanāṇs vinantī.
See Rāmayyā Venkayyā Āyyāvāru.
Kolhāpūr prāntāchā saṃkshipta itihāsa.
See Bāḷājī Prabhākara Moḍak.
Lekharatnamālā. [Phaḍṇavīs.
See Bāḷājī Janārdana Bhānu, also called Nānā
Mahārāja Pratāpa Simha.
See Govinda Krishṇa Ṭiḷak.
Māṇik Prabhu yāṇcheṇ charitra.
See Rāmachandra Bovā Solāpurkar.
Manohara nāṭaka [*in loco*].

Marāṭhī sāmrājyāchī chhoṭī bakhar.
See Maratha Empire.
Mauna yauvanā.
See Krishṇājī Vāsudeva Khare.
Meghadūta kāvya.
See Kālidāsa.
Mogal va Mogalī dharma.
See Rājārāma Rāmakṛishṇa Bhāgavata.
Mumbaīchā vṛittānta. [Vināyaka Ṣingṇe.
See Bālakṛishṇa Bāpū Āchārya and Moro
Nārāyaṇa Rāva āṇi Godāvarī.
See Mahādeva Vyaṅkateṣa Rahāḷkar.
Nāṭya-kathāmālā.
See Periodical Publications.—*Pen.*
Nītivishayaka chār nibandha.
See Cicero (M. T.)
Nityāchī prārthanā.
See Liturgies.—Jews.—*Daily Prayers.*
Nityānandaikya-dīpikā.
See Ṣivakalyāṇa.
Padaratna-mahodadhi.
See Mahādeva Bhāgavata Dinkar.
Pada-samūha.
See Viṭhobā Aṇṇā.
Padeṇ.
See Rājārāma Prasādī.
Pāpāchyā kshamesāṭhīṇ prārthanā.
See Liturgies.—Jews.—*Fast-day Prayers.*
Pati-viṭambana nāṭaka.
See Nārāyaṇa Hari Bhāgavata.
Praṇayī Mādhava.
See Vāmana Ṣāstrī Islampūrkar.
Prauḍhabodha Marāṭhī vyākaraṇa.
See Rāmachandra Bhikājī Josī.
Prayāgāntīl rāshṭrīya sabhechī hakīkat.
See Sadāṣiva Vāmana Kāṇe.
Putaḷā Bāī.
See Chintāmaṇa Moreṣvara Āpṭe.
Rājanīti.
See Malhār Rāmarāva Chiṭṇīs.
Rājavijaya nāṭaka.
See Nārāyaṇa Hari Bhāgavata.
Rasaratnamālā.
See Aṇṇājī Ballāḷa Bāpaṭ Indurkar.
Ratnamālā āṇi Pratāpachandra.
See Mahādeva Vināyaka Keḷkar.
Ṣāhaṇā Nathan.
See Lessing (G. E.)
Sāmājika vishayā-sambandhī toḍjoḍ.
See Kāṣīnātha Trimbak Telang, *C.I.E.*
Saṃskṛita pustakamālā [*in loco*].
Sandhi-prakāṣa.
See Ṣrīkṛishṇa Rāmakṛishṇa Ṣāstrī Āṭhalye.
Ṣaṅkarāchārya stotra.
See Toṭakāchārya.
Saṅkrāntīchā halvā.
See Rāmachandra Ballāḷa Goḍbole.
Santalīlāmṛita kathārasa.
See Mūrkar Maṇḍalī.
Santamelā.
See Balavantarāva Malhārī Duḍvaḍkar.
Saralaregha āṇi golīya trikoṇamiti.
See Trigonometry.
Ṣāstrārtha.
See Hīrālāla Gopāla Ṣarmā.
Senāpati Dābhāḍe . . . yāṇchī hakīgat.
See Dābhāḍe, *Senāpati.*
Setubandha Rāmeṣvara yātrāvarṇana.
See Vināyaka Govinda Limaye.
Ṣikshaṇa-mīmāṃsā.
See Vāsudeva Gaṇeṣa Sahasrabuddhe.
Silemān Siddhīchā mṛityu.
See Gaṇapatarāva Viṣrāma Deṣāī.
Ṣiva-digvijaya nāṭaka.
See Sītārāma Narahara Ḍhāvḷe.
Ṣivājī Mahārājāṇchī bakhar.
See Chitragupta.
Ṣivājī nāṭaka.
See Nārāyaṇa Bāpujī Kāṇiṭkar.
Ṣivalīlāmṛita kathārasa.
See Mūrkar Maṇḍalī.
Ṣivarāja-bhūshaṇa.
See Bhūshaṇa, *Kavi.*
Soneṇ va rupeṇ yāṇchā khap.
See Vāsudeva Gopāla Bhāṇḍārkar.
Ṣrīmanta Bhāū Sāheb yāṇchī kaiphiyat.
See Bhāū Sāheb.
Ṣrī Rāmadāsa Svāmīche charitra.
See Govardhanadāsa Lakshmīdāsa.
Sthāvara jaṅgamātmaka sṛishṭi.
See Kāṣīnātha Vāmana Kāṇe.
Strīpurushāṇnīṇ nāṇveṇ gheṇyāchī paddhata.
See Vāsudeva Moreṣvara Potadār.
Sundarā Bāī.
See Ṣaṅkara Dājī Ṣāstrī Paḍe.
Sundarechī saṅkrānta.
See Gaṇeṣa Janārdana Āgāṣe.
Svatantra vidhavā, *etc.*
See Dattātraya Vāsudeva Jogḷekar.
Taruṇa purusha.
See Nārāyaṇa Gaṇeṣa Maṇḍalik.
Tīn vidhavā.
See Nārāyaṇa Vāmana Ṭiḷak.
Umājī Nā'ikāchā pavāḍā.
See Yesu, *Kavi.*
Vākya mīmāṃsā.
See Gopāla Gaṇeṣa Āgarkar.
Vāsavadattā kathāsāra.
See Vāmana Dājī Ok.
Vāṭsarāchī goshṭa.
See Rāgho Nārāyaṇa Devḷe.
Vikramorvaṣī nāṭaka.
See Kālidāsa.
Yogasaṅgrāma.
See Muhammad, *Shaikh.*
Yogya ṣāsanādarṣa nāṭaka.
See Gaṇapatarāva Viṣrāma Deṣāī.
Vedārthoddhāra. [Gaṇeṣa Boḍas.
See Bhīmāchārya Jhaḷkīkar and Rājārāma
Vedāntasāra.
See Vāsudeva Jogḷekar Phaḍnavīs.
Yogavāsishṭhasāra-ṭīkā.
See Raṅganātha Svāmī.
Yuropāchyā itihāsāpāsūn kāy ṣikāveṇ.
See Vāmana Abājī Moḍak.

SUBJECT-INDEX (ADDENDA).

ARTS.

Āmche kalākauṣalyāṇt sudhārṇā karaṇyās upāya. Keṣava Vāmana Peṭhe.
Hastarekhāvichāraṇa. Jyotishachakra.
Kautuka-chintāmaṇi. Sūnṛitavādī.
Rasaratnamālā. Aṇṇājī Ballāḷa Bāpaṭ Indurkar.

ASTROLOGY and DIVINATION.

Bhāḍalī mata jyotishavarṇana. Bhaḍalī.

BIOGRAPHY.

Jayarāma Svāmī charitra. Rājārāma Manohara Divāṇjī Budhakar.
——————yāṇchyā charitrāchī bakhar. Jayārāma Svāmī.
Māṇik Prabhu yāṇcheṇ charitra. Rāmachandra Bovā Solāpurkar.
Saṅkrāntīchā halvā. Rāmachandra Ballāla Goḍbole.
Senāpati Dābhāḍe . . . yāṇchī hakīgat. Dābhāḍe, *Senāpati.*
Ṣivājī Mahārājāṇchī bakhar. Chitragupta.
Ṣrīmanta Bhāu Sāheb yānchī kaiphiyat. Bhāu Sāheb.
Ṣrī Rāmadāsa Svāmīche charitra. Govardhanadāsa Lakshmīdāsa.

CASTE.

Gotramālikā. Nāro Āpājī Goḍbole.
Ṣāstrārtha Hīrālāla Gopāla Ṣarmā.

DRAMA.

Āpā Sāheb nāṭaka. Gopāla Rājārāma Raṅganātha.
Atipīḍacharita nāṭaka. Ṣaṅkara Moro Rānaḍe.
Bhāratabhaishajyaprabhāvadigdarṣana nāṭaka. Vināyaka Hari Prabhu Ṣinakar.
Bhāryā-pramāda. Nārāyaṇa Hari Bhāgavata.
Bhīma Siṃha āṇi Padminī nāṭaka. Purushottama Bhāskara Ḍoṅgre.
Huṇḍā prahasana. Nārāyaṇa Hari Bhāgavata.
Jaraṭhodvāha. Purushottama Bhāskara Ḍoṅgre.
Kapaṭajāla nāṭaka. Jayavanta (D. B.)
Mahārāja Pratāpa Siṃha. Govinda Krishṇa Tilak.
Manohara nāṭaka. Manohara nāṭaka.
Pati-viṭambana nāṭaka. Nārāyaṇa Hari Bhāgavata.
Rājavijaya nāṭaka. Nārāyaṇa Hari Bhāgavata.
Ṣāhaṇā Nathan. Lessing (G. E.).
Silemān Siddhīchā mṛityu. Gaṇapatarāva Viṣrāma Deṣāi.
Ṣiva-digvijaya nāṭaka. Sītārāma Narahara Ḍhāvle.
Ṣivājī nāṭaka. Nārāyaṇa Bāpujī Kāniṭkar.
Svatantra vidhavā. Dattātraya Vāsudeva Joglekar.
Vikramorvaṣī nāṭaka. Kālidāsa.
Yogya ṣāsanādarṣa nāṭaka. Gaṇapatarāva Viṣrāma Deṣāi.

ETHICS.

Nītivishayaka chār nibandha. Cicero (M. T.)
Rājanīti. Malhār Rāmarāva Chiṭṇīs.

GRAMMARS.

Prauḍhabodha Marāṭhī vyākaraṇa. Rāmachandra Bhikājī Joṣī.
Sandhi-prakāṣa. Ṣrīkṛishṇa Rāmakṛishṇa Ṣāstṛī Āṭhalye.
Vākya mīmāṃsā. Gopāla Gaṇeṣa Āgarkar.

HINDU PHILOSOPHY.

Amṛitānubhava. Jñānadeva.
Yogasaṅgrāma. Muhammad, *Shaikh.*

HISTORY.

Dakkhanchā prāchīna itihāsa. Rāmakṛishṇa Gopāla Bhāṇḍārkar.
Etadveṣīya saṃsthānāṇchā itihāsa. Vināyaka Govinda Limaye.
Kolhāpur prāntāchā itihāsa. Bāḷājī Prabhākara Moḍāk.
Marāṭhī sāmrājyāchī chhoṭī bakhar. Maratha Empire.
Mogal va Mogalī dharma. Rājārāma Rāmakṛishṇa Bhāgavata.
Mumbaīchā vṛittānta. Bāḷakṛishṇa Bāpu Āchārya.

LETTERS.

Lekharatnamālā. Bāḷājī Janārdana Bhānu.

MATHEMATICS.

Gaṇitavṛitti. Hutton (C.) *LL.D.*
Saralaregha āṇi goḷiya trikoṇamiti. Trigonometry.

s

POETRY.

Bhajanī santakhela. Kṛishṇājī Nārāyaṇa Kākaḍe.
Bhaktitattvāmṛita. Bhaktitattvāmṛita.
Bhāminīvilāsa. Jagannātha Paṇḍitarāja.
Draupadī-svayaṃvara. Ananta, *Kavi.*
Gaṇeṣagītā. Purāṇas.—Gaṇeṣapurāṇa.—*Gaṇeṣagītā.*
Gaṅgāratnamālā. Narahari.
Meghadūta kāvya. Kālidāsa.
Padaratna-mahodadhi. Mahādeva Bhāgavata Dinkar.
Pada-samūha. Viṭhobā Aṇṇā.
Paḍeṇ. Rājārāma Prasādī.
Ṣaṅkarāchārya stotra. Toṭakāchārya.
Santamelā. Balavantarāva Malhārī Dudvaḍkar.
Ṣivarāja-bhūshaṇa. Bhūshṇa, *Kavi.*
Umājī Nā'īkāchā pavāḍā. Yesu, *Kavi.*

READERS.

Bhāshaṇa sāmpradāyika vākyeṇ. Candy (T.)
Bhāshāntarakaritāṇ utāre. Hari Kṛishṇa Dāmle.
Kāmānā-kalpavṛiksha. Vīreṣvara Sadāṣiva Chhatre.
Saṃskṛita pustakamālā. Saṃskṛita Pustakamālā.

RELIGION.—Brahmist.

Brāhmadharma. Brāhmadharma.

RELIGION.—Hindu.

Brāhmaṇa vā Brāhmaṇīdharma. Rājārāma Rāmakṛishṇa Bhāgavata.
Harivijaya kathārasa. Kāṣīnātha Sambhājī.
Hindulokāṇcheṇ mūrtipūjana. Mūrkar Maṇḍalī.
Vedāntasāra. Vāsudeva Jogḷekar Phaḍnavīs.
Vedārthoddhāra. Bhīmāchārya Jhaḷkīkar.

RELIGION.—Jewish.

Gītāṇcheṇ pustaka. Hymn Book.
Isrāelāṇchā vidhi. Albu (I.)
Isrāelī dharmāntīl navalācheṇ vṛitta. Āshṭamkar (B. S.)
Nityāchī prārthanā.—Liturgies.—Jews.—*Daily Prayers.*
Pāpāchyā kshamesāṭhīṇ prārthanā. Liturgies.—Jews.—*Fast-day Prayers.*

SCIENCES.

Jaladhija varṇana. Kānhobā Raṇchhoḍdās Kīrtikar.
Sthāvara jaṅgamātmaka sṛishṭi. Kāṣīnātha Vāmana Kāṇe.

SOCIOLOGY.

Āmchī dharmādāya paddhati. Janārdana Dāmodara Kolhaṭkar.
Dāru piṇeṇ / Deṣī hunar } Bāḷakṛishṇa Ātmārāma Gupte.
Dharmaudārya. Bāḷa Yajñeṣvara Gurjar.
Hindulokāṇt aikyāchī vṛiddhi hoṇyās harakatī. Vāmana Ābājī Moḍak.
Prayāgāntīl rāshṭrīya sabhechī hakīkat. Sadāṣiva Vāmana Kāṇe.
Sāmājika vishayā-sambandhī toḍjoḍ. Kāṣīnātha Trimbak Telang.
Ṣikshaṇa-mīmāṃsā. Vāsudeva Gaṇeṣa Sahasrabuddhe.
Soneṇ va rupeṇ yānchā khap. Vāsudeva Gopāla Bhāṇḍārkar.
Yuropāchyā itihāsāpāsūn kāy ṣikāveṇ. Vāmana Ābājī Moḍak.

TALES.—Original.

Mauna yauvanā. Kṛishṇājī Vāsudeva Khare.
Nārāyaṇa Rāva āṇi Godāvarī. Mahādeva Vyaṅkateṣa Rahāḷkar.
Putaḷā Bāī. Chintāmaṇa Moreṣvara Āpṭe.
Ratnamālā āṇi Pratāpachandra. Mahādeva Vināyaka Kelkar.
Sundarā Bāī. Ṣaṅkara Dājī Ṣāstrī Pade.
Sundarechī saṅkrānta. Gaṇeṣa Janārdana Āgāṣe.
Taruṇa purusha. Nārāyaṇa Gaṇeṣa Maṇḍalik.
Tīn vidhavā. Nārāyaṇa Vāmana Ṭiḷak.
Vāṭsarāchī goshṭa. Rāgho Nārāyaṇa Devḷe.

TALES.—Translations from Oriental Works.

Chārudatta āṇi Vasantasenā. Vāmana Ṣāstrī Islāmpūrkar.
Praṇayī Mādhava. Vāmana Ṣāstrī Islāmpūrkar.
Vāsavadattā kathāsāra. Vāmana Dājī Ok.

TRAVELS.

Setubandha Rāmeṣvara yātrāvarṇana. Vināyaka Govinda Limaye.

GILBERT & RIVINGTON, LIMITED, ST. JOHN'S HOUSE, CLERKENWELL, LONDON.

CATALOGUE OF GUJARATI BOOKS.

CATALOGUE

OF

GUJARATI BOOKS.

'ABBĀS, *Saiyid.* માતમે હસનેન. [Mātam i Ḥasanain. Elegiac verses on the death of Ḥasan and Ḥusain.] pp. 24. અહમદાબાદ ૧૮૮૦ [*Ahmadabad,* 1880.] 12°. **14148. d. 5(14.)**

'ABD al-ḲĀDIR ibn LUḲMĀN. *See* 'ALĪ ZAIN al-'ĀBIDĪN, *Fourth Imām,* called AL-SAJJĀD. رسالة الكاملة [Risālah i Kāmilah. Arabic text, with a translation by 'A. al-Ḳ.] [1887.] 12°. **14519. b. 13(3.)**

—— *See* ḲUR'ĀN. قران نوا ترجمة گجراتي زبان ما [The Koran, with an interlineary translation and marginal notes by 'A. al-Ḳ.] [1879.] 8°. **14507. c. 13.**

'ABD al-KARĪM, called MUDARRIS. બુદ્ધિ દર્પણ. (The Buddhi Darpan, or the mirror of wisdom. Translated from an Urdu essay by Munshi Abdul Karim, who writes under the nom de plume of Mudarris.) pp. 16. *Bombay,* 1877. 8°. **14146. e. 20(1.)**

'ABD al-LAṬĪF. *See* TALAKCHAND TĀRĀCHAND. રમુજે હિકમત. [Rumūz i ḥikmat. Translated with the assistance of 'A. al-L.] [1884.] 12°. **14148. a. 13.**

ABDUL KARĪM. *See* 'ABD AL-KARĪM, called MUDARRIS.

ABHIMANYU. અભીમન્યુનો ચકરાવો. [Abhimanyuno chakrāvo. A poem on the exploits of Abhimanyu.] pp. 119. *lith.* મુંબઈ ૧૯૧૮ [*Bombay,* 1862.] 8°. **14148. b. 9.**

ABŪ ṬĀHIR, *Tarsūsī.* દારાબ નામું *etc.* [Dārāb-nāmuṇ. An account of the life of Dārāb, son of Bahman, one of the ancient kings of Persia, translated from the Persian of Abū Ṭāhir. Second edition.] pp. viii. 121. મુંબાઈ [*Bombay,* 1883.] 8°. **14146. g. 18.**

—— ફરામરજ નામું [Farāmurz-nāmuṇ. An account of the wars and exploits of Farāmurz, son of Rustam, being a translation by Jahāngīr Bejanjī Karānī, from the Persian original of Abū Ṭāhir. Second edition.] Vol. I. and II., pp. x. 278. મુંબાઈ [*Bombay,* 1883.] 8°. **14146. g. 19.**

ACADEMIES.

BOMBAY.

Bombay Branch of the Royal Asiatic Society.

The Vandidád Sádé of the Pársís in the Zand language, but Gujarátí character, with a Gujarátí translation, paraphrase and comment; according to the traditional interpretation of the Zoroastrians. By . . . Frámjí Aspandiárjí, and other Dasturs. 2 vol. *Bombay,* 1842. 8°. **761. f. 1, 2.**

The Vispard of the Pársís in the Zand language, but Gujarátí character, with a Gujarátí translation, paraphrase, and comment; according to the traditional interpretation of the Zoroastrians. By . . . Frámjí Aspandiárjí and other Dasturs. pp. 137. *Bombay,* 1843. 8°. **761. f. 5.**

The Yaçna of the Pársís in the Zand language, but Gujarátí character, with a Gujarátí translation, paraphrase, and comment; according to the traditional interpretation of the Zoroastrians. By . . . Frámjí Aspandiárjí, and other Dasturs. 2 pt. *Bombay*, 1843. 8°. **761. f. 3.**

Zartoshtī Dīnnī Kholkarnārī Maṇḍalī.

જરતોશતી દીનની ખોલકરનારી મંડલીનો પાંચ વરસનો મુખતેસર હેવાલ. [A report of the proceedings of the Zartoshtī Dīnnī Kholkarnārī Maṇḍalī, or Society for the advancement of the Zoroastrian religion, for five years from A.D. 1864. With a preface by Kāwusjī Edaljī Kāṅgā, Secretary to the Society.] pp. 24. મુંબઈ ૧૮૬૯ [*Bombay*, 1869.] 8°. **14144. i. 4(2.)**

LONDON.

Society for the Diffusion of Useful Knowledge.

Library of useful knowledge. उपयोगी ज्ञाननो पुस्तकसमूह. आरंभकथन [Upayogī jñānanī pustakasamūha.] (Preliminary treatise, translated into the Goojratee language) [by G. R. Jervis, with the assistance of Jagannātha Ṣāstrī.] pp. 158. मुंबई १८३० [*Bombay*, 1830.] 8°. **14146. e. 14.**

ĀCHĀRĀṄGA. श्री आचारांग जी [Āchārāṅga. The first *aṅga* of the Jain canon, Prakrit text, Sanskrit commentaries, and a *bālāvabodha*, or exposition in Gujarati, by Pārṣvachandra Sūrī.] 2 pt. कलकत्ता १९३६ [*Calcutta*, 1880.] 4°. **14100. f. 7.**

ĀDARBĀD MĀRĀSPAND. Pand nâmah i Âdarbâd Mârâspand . . . Comprising the original Pehlevi text . . . a complete translation in Gujerathee and a glossary in Gujerathee and English . . . by Herbad Sheriarjee Dadabhoy. pp. 23, 124. *Bombay*, 1869. 8°. **761. e. 13.**

—— અનદરજે આતરેપાતનો તરજુમો [Andaraz i Âtarpât. Another edition of the Pandnāmah of Ā. M., with a different Gujarati translation.] *See* PESHOTAN BAHRĀMJĪ SANJĀNĀ. Ganjesháyagán, *etc.* 1885. 8°. **761. g. 2.**

ĀDARJĪ KĀWUSJĪ MASTER. દસ્કત શિક્ષક ગુજરાતી તથા બાળબોધ (Daskat shikshak, or a Guide to a beautiful Gujarati and Balbodh hand-writing, in six numbers, *etc.*) No. 1 and 2. *Bombay*, 1885. 8°. **14150. a. 21.**

AḌHIDVĪPA. अढी द्वीपनो नकसो [Aḍhidvīpano nakso. A mythological map of the part of India considered specially sacred by the Jains.] [*Bombay*, 1882?]. **Map. 52430. (13.)**

ĀDĪTRĀMA JOITĀRĀMA. મેઘજીની મોંકાણ. Meghajīnī mohkāṇ. A poem on the sufferings caused by want of rain.] pp. 16. अमदावाद १८७७ [*Ahmadabad*, 1877.] 16°. **14148. d. 13(14.)**

ADNĀ. *See* ARDSHER BAHRĀMJĪ PAṬEL.

AERPAT MEHERJIBHAI PALANJI MADAN. *See* MIHRJĪBHĀĪ PĀLANJĪ MĀDAN.

ĀGHĀ ḤASAN, *Saiyid*, called AMĀNAT. ઈંદરસભા [Indrasabhā. A fairy tale in verse, translated by Kuṇvarjī Haṭhīsaṅga, with the assistance of Muḥammad 'Ārif.] pp. 114. અમદાવાદ ૧૮૭૫ [*Ahmadabad*, 1875.] 12°. **14148. d. 12.**

AHMADABAD. — *Jainadharma-pravartaka Sabhā.* श्री जैन प्रार्थना माळा ॥ [Jaina prārthanāmālā. Jain hymns, published by the Jainadharma-pravartaka Sabhā.] Pt. I. अमदावाद १९४१ [*Ahmadabad*, 1884.] 12°. **14144. f. 7.**

—— श्री मल्लि जिन माहात्म्य [Malli Jina māhātmya. A brief account in verse of the life of Mallinātha, a Jain saint.] pp. 40. અમદાવાદ ૧૮૮૭ [*Ahmadabad*, 1887.] 16°. **14144. f. 1.(3.)**

—— प्रार्थनावळी. [Prārthanāvalī. Another collection of Jain hymns, with an introductory prayer.] pp. 16. अमदावाद १८८५ [*Ahmadabad*, 1885.] 12°. **14144. f. 12(4.)**

AKHĀ. અખાની વાણી. [Akhānī vāṇī. Vedantic poems by Akhā, a saint of the seventeenth century.] pp. 216. મુંબઈ: ૧૮૮૪ [*Bombay*, 1884.] 8°. **14148. e. 15.**

—— ब्रह्मज्ञानी अखा भक्तना छपा . . . तथा बुल्लाशाहनी सी हरफी. [Brahmajñānī Akhā Bhaktanā chhapā, Vedantic verses by Akhā, followed by Sīharfī, a Panjabi poem by Bullā Shāh.] pp. vii. 102. मुंबई १८८४ [*Bombay*, 1884.] 8°. **14144. d. 6.**

AKSHARAGAṆITA. અક્ષરગણિત [Aksharagaṇita. Algebra for the use of schools. Second edition.] pp. 177. મુંબઈ ૧૮૬૬ [*Bombay*, 1866.] 12°. **14146. c. 18.**

ALBERT, *Prince Consort of Victoria, Queen of Great Britain and Ireland.* *See* MĪNŪCHIHRJĪ KĀWUSJĪ SHĀPURJĪ LANGRĀNĀ, called MANSUKH. Prince Albert. Selections from . . . a Gujarati poem. 1870. 8°. **14148. f. 8.**

'ALĪ ibn ABĪ ṬĀLIB, *Caliph.* A Mehzur given by Huzrut Ally to a Parsee . . . and to the whole Parsee nation. Translated . . . by Sorabjee Jamsetjee Jejeebhoy. *See* MUḤAMMAD, *the Prophet.* Tuqviuti-din-i-Mazdiasna. 1851. 8°.
14144. i. 3.

'ALĪ ZAIN al-'ĀBIDĪN, *Fourth Imām,* called al-SAJJĀD. رسالة الكاملة ترجمة الادعيه في صحيفة الكاملة [Risālah i Kāmilah, or the Prayer-book of 'A. Z. al-'A., called Ṣaḥīfat i-Kāmilah. Arabic text, with a translation in the Arabic character by 'Abd al-Ḳādir ibn Luḳmān.] pp. 204, *lith.* ١٢٩٤ [*Bombay,* 1877.] 12°.
14519. b. 13(3.)

AMĀNAT. *See* ĀGHĀ ḤASAN, *Saiyid,* called AMĀNAT.

AMBĀLĀLA DĀMODARA JOṢĪ. *See* BHARTṚIHARI. भर्तृहरिकृत नीतिशतक *etc.* [Nītiṣataka. With a translation by A. D. J.] [1878.] 8°.
14072. cc. 14.

AMBĀLĀLA SĀKARLĀLA. અર્થશાસ્ત્ર . . . [Arthaṣāstra. A treatise] based on Mill's Principles of political economy . . . by Ambalal Sakerlal. pp. vii. 319, iii. अमदावाद १८७५ [*Ahmadabad,* 1875.] 8°.
14146. e. 16.

AMBIKĀ. श्री अंबिका काव्य. [Ṣrī Ambikākāvya. A collection of verses in praise of the goddess Ambikā, or Pārvatī.] pp. xii. 228. અમદાવાદ ૧૮૮૧ [*Ahmadabad,* 1881.] 12°. **14148. e. 9.**

AMĪCHAND MOTĪCHAND. अंबाजीना छंद नी चोपडी. [Ambājīnā chhanduī chopaḍī. Verses in praise of the goddess Durgā.] pp. 32. સુરત ૧૯૩૩ [*Surat,* 1877.] 16°. **14148. d. 4(5.)**

AMṚITALĀLA NĀRĀYAṆADĀSA LAHERI. નરસીંહ મેહેતાનું માહમેરૂં તથા હુંડી. [Narasiṃha Mehetānuṇ māhmeruṇ tathā huṇḍī. A dramatised version of the legendary story of the bill of exchange of the saint Narsī Mehetā.] pp. 31. મુંબઈ ૧૮૮૩ [*Bombay,* 1883.] 12°. **14148. c. 19(1.)**

ĀNANDAJĪ KHETASĪ. श्री जैनप्रबोध पुस्तक. भाग पहेलो. [Jainaprabodha. A collection of Jain hymns, prayers and religious maxims.] pp. xxiv. 600. मुंबापुरी १९३९ [*Bombay,* 1883.] 12°.
14144. f. 17.

ĀNANDAJĪ VAHĀLJĪ RĀJGAR. *See* DATTĀTRAYA. नारसिंहावतार नाटक. [Nārasiṃhāvatāra nāṭaka. A drama, translated from the Marathi of Dattātraya by Ā. V. R.] [1881.] 16°. **14148. c. 3.**

ĀNANDARĀVA CHAMPĀJĪ. *See* ROBERTSON (W.) *D.D., the Historian.* The life of Columbus. Translated into Gujaráti . . . . by . . . Ánandráo Chápáji. 1867. 12°. **14146. f. 19.**

—— A Dictionary, English, Marathi, Gujarati and Sanskrit . . . by Ánandráv Chápáji. Pt. 1, 2. *Bombay,* 1885. 4°. **760. k. 9.**

No more published.

ĀNANDĪBAĪ JOṢĪ. Anandibai Joshi, M.D. [A brief account of her perseverance in learning English, and of her journey to America, and obtaining the degree of M.D. in the Female Medical College of Philadelphia.] આનંદીબાઈ જોશી pp. 16. ગોધરા ૧૮૮૭ [*Godhra,* 1887.] 32°.
14146. f. 24.

ANANTAPRASĀDA TRIKAMLĀLA. राणक देवी. [Rāṇak Devī. A tale of female valour and constancy.] pp. 212. अमदावाद १८८३ [*Ahmadabad,* 1883.] 8°. **14148. a. 28.**

—— ત્રિદંપતિ વર્ણન. [Tridampati varṇana, or the Three married couples. A tale showing the unhappy results of ill-assorted marriages.] pp. iv. 164. राधनपुर १८८० [*Radhanpur,* 1880.] 12°.
14148. c. 12.

AṄKAGAṆITA. અંકગણિત. [Aṅkagaṇita. An elementary arithmetic.] pp. viii. 177. મુંબઈ ૧૮૫૯ [*Bombay,* 1859.] 12°. **14146. c. 21.**

ĀṄKNĪ CHOPAḌĪ. આંકની ચોપડી [Āṅknī chopaḍī. The Gujarati alphabet and alphabetical tables.] pp. 44. સુરત ૧૮૬૦ [*Surat,* 1860.] 16°.
14146. c. 22.

ANUYOGADVĀRA. श्री अनुयोगद्वार जो सूत्र [Anuyogadvāra. A Jain canonical text, with a Sanskrit commentary and a Gujarati commentary by Mohana.] pp. 660. कलकत्ता १९३६ [*Calcutta,* 1879.] *obl.* 4°. **14100. f. 11.**

ARABIAN NIGHTS. The Gujarati translation of the Arabian Nights' Entertainments, illustrated. In two volumes; by three Parsee students. pp. viii. 446. *Bombay,* 1865. 8°. **14148. b. 11.**

ARABIAN NIGHTS [*continued*]. અરેબિયન નાઈટસ [The Arabian Nights translated by Dāmodara Īṣvaradāsa.] Vol. I.—IV. મુંબઈ [*Bombay*, 1880, *etc.*] 8°. **14148. b. 24.**

—— ધી અરેબીઅન નાઈટસ ઈઆને હજાર અને એક રાત [Hazār ane ek rāt. The Arabian Nights translated into Gujarati. Illustrated.] Nos. 14-16. મુંબઈ [*Bombay*, 1882.] 4°. **14148. b. 28.**

The illustrations are reproductions of those in Galland's French translation published at Paris in 1865.

ARDASEER FRAMJEE MOOS. *See* ARDSHER FRĀMJĪ MUS.

ARDASIR SORABJEE DUSTOOR. *See* ARDSHER SOHRĀBJĪ DASTŪR.

ARDĀ VIRĀF. અર્દા વિરાફ નામું [Ardā Virāf-nāmuṇ. The Zoroastrian description of heaven and hell. Followed by translations of the Gosht i Fryāno, the Hādokht Nask, and the Ekvīs nasko.] pp. xi. 83. મુંબાઈ [*Bombay*, 1885.] 8°. **14144. i. 15.**

ARDSHER BAHRĀMJĪ PAṬEL, called ADNĀ. અસલાજી *etc.* [Aslājī. A tale of Parsi social life. Second edition.] pp. viii. 80. મુંબઈ ૧૮૮૫ [*Bombay*, 1885.] 8°. **14148. b. 35(1.)**

—— કંજુસના કરમની કાહણી [Kanjusnā karmanī kāhanī. A drama in three acts on Parsi social life.] pp. v. 71, xi. ૧૮૮૪ [*Bombay*, 1884.] 8°. **14148. c. 20(3.)**

ARDSHER ḌOSĀBHĀĪ MUNSHĪ. *See* JALĀL al-DĪN MĪRZĀ, *Ḳājār*. A history of the ancient Parsis . . . Translated into Goozerattee . . . by Ardaseer Dossabhaee Moonshee. 1871. 8°. **14146. g. 5.**

ARDSHER FRĀMJĪ MUS. હિંદુસ્થાનમાં મુસાફરી [Hindusthānamāṇ musāfirī.] (Journal of travels in India, by Ardaseer Framjee Moos . . . with [an English preface, table of contents, and an English translation of some of the passages of the work, a] map, and numerous illustrations in chromolithographs, *etc.*) Vol. I. pp. xxxiii. xii. 40, 292. *Bombay*, 1871. 8°. **14146. h. 12.**

ARDSHER RUSTAMJĪ FĪROZJĪ. *See* ZAND-AVASTĀ. ખુરદે અવસતા બા માએની [Khurdah Avastā. With a Gujarati translation by A. R. F.] [1861.] 8°. **761. g. 6.**

ARDSHER SOHRĀBJĪ DASTŪR. The schoolboy's guide. Being a collection of a few English idioms, phrases, *etc.*, alphabetically arranged by Ardasir Sorabjee Dustoor. pp. 100. *Bombay*, 1878. 12°. **14150. a. 33.**

ARJUNAGĪTĀ. અરજુનગીતા [Arjunagītā. Advice given to Arjuna by Kṛishṇa, in verse.] pp. 21, *lith.* [*Bombay*, 1860 ?] 16°. **14148. d. 5(1.)**

ĀRYA-HITECHCHHU SABHĀ. *See* BROACH.—*Ārya-hitechchhu Sabhā.*

ASFANDIYĀRJĪ BARJORJĪ PANTHAKĪ. Commentaries on the Zoroastrian religious ceremonies, as compared with the present medical science. Compiled by Mobed Aspundiarji Burjorji Punthakee . . . ખુલાસે દીને જરથોસ્તી [Khulāsah i dīn i Zartoshtī.] Part I. pp. 50. મુંબઈ ૧૮૮૨ [*Bombay*, 1882.] 8°. **14144. i. 9.**

ĀTMABODHA. आत्मबोध अने जीवनी उत्पत्ति [Ātmabodha ane jīvanī utpatti. A Jain philosophical treatise on the origin of the soul, on life and the end of existence. Followed by Jain hymns.] pp. 98. १८८६ [*Bombay*, 1886.] 32°. **14144. f. 18.**

ĀTMĀRĀMA KEṢAVAJĪ DVIVEDĪ. પૃથિરાજ ચહુઆણ. (દિલ્લીનો છેલ્લો રજપુત રાજા.) [Pṛithirāja chahuāṇ. Tales of Pṛithvīrāja, the last king of Delhi, compiled chiefly from the Hindi of Chand. Second edition.] pp. xi. 136. મુંબઈ ૧૮૮૪ [*Bombay*, 1884.] 8°. **14148. b. 14.**

ĀTMARAÑJANA. श्री आत्मरंजन [Ātmarañjana. Hymns to Jain saints, and religious maxims.] pp. 40. અમદાવાદ ૧૮૮૬ [*Ahmadabad*, 1886.] 12°. **14144. f. 1.(2.)**

ATONEMENT. The True Atonement. ખરૂં પરાએશચીત [Kharu prāyaṣchitta] pp. 52. *Bombay*, 1853. 16°. **14144. a. 3.(3.)**

No. 24 *of the "Bombay Tract and Book Society's Series."*

ÁTREPÁT MÁRÁSPANDÁN. *See* ĀDARBĀD MĀRĀS-PAND.

AYAVANTĪ SUKUMĀRA. અયવંતી સુકુમારનો તેર ઢાલીઓ. [Ayavantī Sukumārano tera ḍhālio. Songs about A. S., a Jain prince who became an ascetic, and concerning two holy Jain women.] pp. 48, *lith.* મુબાપુરી ૧૯૪૦ [*Bombay,* 1884.] 12°. **14144. f. 12.(2.)**

ĀYURVEDASĀRA-SAṄGRAHA. आयुर्वेदसारसंग्रह [Āyurvedasāra-saṅgraha. A collection of medical works, consisting of Sanskrit texts with Gujarati translations, and also Gujarati treatises on modern systems of medicine.] *Bombay,* [1885, *etc.*] 8°.

In progress. **14043. c. 33.**

B. N. B. *See* Nosnīrwānjī Shahriyārjī Ginwālā. The Parsee girl of the period. [An English essay with a Gujarati translation by B. N. B.] 1884. 8°. **14146. e. 15.(2.)**

BAHMAN ASFANDIYĀR, *King of Persia.* બહમન નામું [Bahman-nāmuṇ. A short history of Persia during the reign of B. A. Second edition.] pp. viii. 247. મુંબઈ ૧૮૮૨ [*Bombay,* 1882.] 8°. **14146. g. 7.**

BAHMANJĪ BAHRĀMJĪ PAṬEL. ઈરાનની મુખ્‌તેસર તવારીખ [Irānnī mukhtasar tawārīkh. A concise history of Persia, in the form of letters, up to the fall of the Sassanian dynasty. Third edition.] pp. 84. મુંબઈ ૧૮૮૦ [*Bombay,* 1880.] 12°. **14146. g. 16.**

—— પારસી પ્રકાશ ... Parsee Prakash, being a record of important events in the growth of the Parsee community in Western India, chronologically arranged from the date of their immigration into India to the year 1860 A.D. Vol. I. Originally issued from 1878 to 1888 in 11 parts. Compiled by Bomanjee Byramjee Patell. *Bombay,* 1888.

In progress. **14146. h. 3.**

BAHMANJĪ ḌOSĀBHĀĪ. *See* Ḍosābhāī Sohrābjī. A new self-instructing work entitled Idiomatic Sentences ... With notes explanatory and illustrative, to which are added copious vocabularies ... by B. D. 1873. 4°. **752. k. 11.**

BAHMANJĪ JAMSHEDJĪ MISTRĪ. *See* Zand-Avastā. ખુરદેહ અવસતા [Short morning and evening prayers from the Khurdah Avastā. With explanatory notes in Gujarati by B. J. M.] [1881.] 16°. **761. a. 18.**

BAHMANJĪ ṬEHMULJĪ PRABHU. ગુજરાતી શીખામણની નીતિ [Ṣikhāmaṇanī nīti. Moral maxims, taken from the author's Bodhavachana; with a glossary. Second edition.] pp. 59, *lith.* મુંબઈ ૧૯૧૧ [*Bombay,* 1855.] 8°. **14146. e. 19.**

In Devanagari and Gujarati characters.

—— [Third edition.] pp. 55, *lith.* મુંબઈ ૧૯૧૩ [*Bombay,* 1857.] 8°. **14146. e. 18.**

—— [Another edition.] pp. 23. [*Bombay,* 1859?] 12°. **14150. a. 23.**

Without title-page, and containing only a portion of the work. In Gujarati characters only.

BAHRĀMJĪ FARĪDUNJĪ MARZBĀN. *See* Naẕīr Aḥmad, *Khān Bahādur.* મેરાતુલ અરૂસ, *etc.* [Mirāt al-ʻarūs. A Hindustani tale translated by B. F. M.] [1878.] 8°. **14148. b. 22.**

BAHRĀMJĪ MIHRBĀNJĪ MALABĀRĪ. નીતિવિનોદ ... Niti-vinod, or Pleasures of Morality. [Poems] by Behramji Mervanji Malabari. pp. xxviii. 216, xxxvi. *Bombay,* 1875. 12°. **14146. e. 11.**

—— વિલ્સનવિરહ [Wilson-viraha. A poem on the late Dr. Wilson of Bombay.] pp. ii. 57. xi. મુમ્બઈ ૧૮૭૮ [*Bombay,* 1878.] 8°. **14146. g. 4.**

BAHRĀM RUSTAM KHUSRAU. સરનામેએ રાજ યજદાની. [Sar-nāmah i rāz i yazdānī, or The great secrets of God. A description of the ceremonies connected with the investiture of a young Zoroastrian with the sacred garment and waist-string. Translated from the Persian of B. R. Kh. by Pālanjī Jīvanjī Hātaryā.] pp. viii. 72. મુંબઈ ૧૮૮૬ [*Bombay,* 1886.] 12°. **14144. h. 5.**

BAITĀL PACHĪSĪ. *See* Ṣāmala Bhaṭa. મડાપચીશીની વારતા. [Maḍāpachīsīnī vārtā. A paraphrase in verse of the Baital Pachīsī.] [1862.] 8°. **14148. b. 7.**

BĀḶACHANDRĀCHĀRYA. करुणा वज्रायुध नाटक [Karuṇāvajrāyudha nāṭaka. A Sanskrit drama, founded on a Jain legend, translated by Nārāyaṇa-bhārthī Yaṣavantabhārthī.] pp. 67. અમદાવાદ ૧૮૮૬ [*Ahmadabad,* 1886.] 8°. **14148. c. 25.**

BĀḶA GAṄGĀDHARA ṢĀSTRĪ JĀMBHEKAR. History of British India. Translated from the abridged [Marathi] work of ... Bál Gangádhar Shástri Jámbhekar by Ranchodás Girdharbhái. (હિંદુસ્થાનમાંહેલ ઈંગ્લિશના રાજ્યનો ઇતિ-

હુાસ) [Hindusthānamāṇhel Ingliṣnā rājyano itihāsa.] Second edition, pp. 220. *Bombay*, 1855. 8°.
14146. g. 10.

BĀḶĀJĪ BHAGAVĀNJĪ DAVE. डाकोरयात्रामहात्म्य [Ḍākor-yātrā māhātmya. A poem in praise of Dakor, a celebrated place of pilgrimage. Followed by a few miscellaneous poems.] pp. 36. अमदावाद १९३६ [*Ahmadabad*, 1879.] 16°.
14148. d. 5(13.)

BĀḶĀJĪ VIṬHṬHALA GĀṆVASKAR. वेदोक्त संस्कार प्रकाश [Vedokta-saṃskāra-prakāṣa. A treatise on the principal Hindu purificatory ceremonial rites, according to the teaching of the Vedas. With quotations from the Sanskrit.] pp. iv. 178. મુંબઈ ૧૯૩૮ [*Bombay*, 1881.] 12°. **14144. b. 8.**

BĀḶAKHEḶA. બાળખેળ .... બાળકો તથા ખાનગી કુટુંબો માટે [Bāḷakheḷa. An English-Gujarati primer. Second edition.] pp. iv. 60. મુંબઈ ૧૮૬૫ [*Bombay*, 1865.] 16°.
14150. a. 24(1.)

BALARĀMA, *Sādhu.* अथ श्री विवेकसार प्रारंभः [Vivekasāra. A work in fifteen sections on the doctrines of the Vaishṇava sect of Nārāyaṇa Svāmī; consisting of Sanskrit slokas with a paraphrase in Gujarati prose.] ff. 72. नडियाद १९४४ [*Nadiad*, 1884.] *obl.* 4°. **14033. d. 18.**

BĀLUBHĀĪ MANMOHANADĀSA DALĀL. દુઃખી દીવાળી [Duḥkhī Dīvāḷī. A tale showing the evil results of marrying young girls to old men, and of prohibiting widow-marriage.] સુરત [*Surat*, 1886.] 12°. **14148. a. 35(2.)**

BĀṆA. શ્રીમદ્-બાણભટ્ટ-વિરચિત કાદમ્બરીનું સટીક ગુજરાતી ભાષાન્તર. [Kādambarī. Translated from the Sanskrit of Bāṇa, with notes and a glossary, by Chhaganlāla Harilāla.] pp. xxviii. vi. 458. મુંબઈ ૧૮૮૪ [*Bombay*, 1884.] 8°.
14148. b. 34.

BANDAGĪ. બંદગી. [Bandagī. Prayers and hymns for Parsi children.] 2nd edition, pp. xviii. 214. ૧૨૪૮ [*Bombay*, 1879.] 64°. **14144. h. 1.**

BĀPUJĪ MĀṆEKJĪ PASTĀKIĀ. Pupils' Progress. No. 2. . . . By B. M. Pastakia. [Containing a vocabulary of words in an English reader, explained in Gujarati.] pp. 82. *Bombay*, 1878. 12°.
14150. a. 30.

BARJORJĪ PĀLANJĪ DEṢĀI and PĀLANJĪ BARJORJĪ DEṢĀI. History of the Sassanides: being a chronicle of the Parsee monarchs of the Sassanian dynasty of ancient Persia, collated from the works of Rawlinson, Ferdusi, and other authors, European and Oriental .... by Barjorji Pálanji Desái and Pálanji Barjorji Desái. (તવારીખે સાસાનીઆન). [Tavārīkh i Sāsāniyān.] pp. xvi. 480. *Bombay*, 1880. 8°. **14146. h. 5.**

BARODA, *Native State of.* ગાયકવાડી ન્યાયપ્રકાશ. [Gāyakavāḍī nyāyaprakāṣa. A collection of circular orders and resolutions, issued by the Government of Baroda from the year A.D. 1879. Compiled by Paramānandadāsa Bholābhāī Pārekh.] Pt. I. pp. iv. 76, ii. xxvii. અમદાવાદ ૧૮૮૧ [*Ahmadabad*, 1881.] 8°. **14146. a. 7.**

BARTH (CHRISTIAN GOTTLOB). છોકરાંને સારૂ પવિત્રલેખની વાર્તા ઉપરથી કરેલાં સુવૃત્તાંતો [Pavitralekhanī vārtā.] Barth's Bible Stories. New Testament. pp. v. 207. સુરત ૧૮૬૦ [*Surat*, 1860.] 12°. **14144. a. 7.**

BARTHOLD. બર્થોલ્ડ અથવા ચાતુર્યતા ચમત્કારિક તથા સમયોચિત ઉત્તર. [Barthold, or the adventures of a peasant. Translated by Raṇchhoḍbhāī Udayarāma from an English version of the original Italian.] pp. 131. અમદાવાદ ૧૯૨૧ [*Ahmadabad*, 1865.] 12°. **14148. a. 7.**

BEHJAD RUSTAM. *See* ṠAD-DAR. સદ્દરે બેહેરે તવીલ [Ṡad-dare behere tavīl. Translated from the Persian by B. R.] [1881.] 8°.
14144. i. 24.

BEHRAMJI MERVANJI MALABARI. *See* BAHRĀMJĪ MIHRVĀNJĪ MALABĀRĪ.

BERQUIN (ARNAUD). Berquin's Children's Friend. Translated into Gujráti [from the Marathi translation by Sadāṣiva Kāṣīnātha Chhatre, entitled "Bālamitra."] (गुजराती बाळमित्र.) Vol. I. Fourth edition. pp. ix. 225. *Bombay*, 1860. 12°.
14144. a. 20.

In the Devanagari character.

BHAḌALĪ. अथ बृहज्ज्योतिषार्णवे षष्ठे मिश्रस्कंधे भाडलीमत ज्योतिषवर्णनं नाम पंचविंशोऽध्यायः प्रारभ्यते [Bhāḍalī-mata. A work on astrology and divination, containing the sayings of Bhaḍalī, the daughter of Uddhaḍa Joṣī, who was also called Sahadeva, and forming the 25th chapter of the 6th section of the Brihajjyotishārṇava. Mostly in the original Hindi, but partly in Gujarati and in Marathi.] ff. 37. बाँबे १८०८ [*Bombay*, 1887.] *obl.* 4°. **14158. h. 10.**

BHAGAVĀNLĀLA BĀPĀLĀLA. The Arya Praja or a play showing the miserable condition of the rising generation of this well-known Aryavartta, by Bhugwanlal Bapalal. (आर्य प्रजा.) pp. 212. *Baroda*, 1882. 12°. **14148. c. 21.**

BHAGAVATĪ-SŪTRA. अथ भगवती सूत्र [Bhagavatī sūtra. The fifth *aṅga* of the Jain canon. Prakrit text, with Sanskrit commentaries, and a Gujarati commentary by Megharāja.] pp. 1936. बनारस १८८२ [*Benares*, 1882.] *obl.* 4°. **14100. f. 9.**

BHAGAVATPRASĀDA, *Priest of the Svāmīnārāyaṇa Sect.* [*Life*]. *See* KOṬHĀRĪ GOVARDHANA. श्री भगवतप्रसादाख्यान *etc.*

BHĀĪDĀSA DAYĀRĀMA. દેશી હિસાબ ગણવાની સેહેલી રીતો [Deśī hisāb gaṇvānī sehelī rīto. Simple methods of solving arithmetical problems.] pp. 44. સુરત ૧૮૭૫ [*Surat*, 1875.] 16°. **14150. a. 2.(2.)**

—— ગુજરાતી ભાષામાં વાકય રચનાના નિયમો. [Gujarātī bhāshāmāṉ vākya rachanānā niyamo. The rules of syntax of the Gujarati language.] pp. 39. સુરત ૧૯૩૪ [*Surat*, 1878.] 16°. **14150. a. 26.(6.)**

BHĀLAṆA, also called **PURUSHOTTAMAJĪ.** *See* PURĀṆAS. — Mārkaṇḍeyapurāṇa. — *Devīmāhātmya.* सप्तशती [Saptaśatī. Translated into verse by Bh.] [1887.] 8°. **14148. e. 12.**

BHĀNUDATTA. *See* VĀLJĪ LAKSHMĪRĀMA DAVE. रसमंजरी [Rasamañjarī. Adapted from the Sanskrit of Bh.] [1877]. 16°. **14146. c. 2.**

BHARTṚIHARI. भर्तृहरिकृत नीतिशतकम् *etc.* [Nītiśataka. Sanskrit text, with a Gujarati translation by Ambālāla Dāmodara Joṣī.] pp. 32. मुंबई १८७८ [*Bombay*, 1878.] 8°. **14072. cc. 14.**

—— भर्तृहरिकृत वैराग्यशतक. [Vairāgyaśataka. Sanskrit text, with a Gujarati translation by Mahānanda Bhāīśaṅkara.] pp. ii. 47. अमदाबाद १९३४ [*Ahmadabad*, 1878.] 8°. **14072. d. 39.**

BHAVABHŪTI. महाकवि श्रीभवभूतिप्रणीत मालतीमाधव प्रकरण. [Mālatīmādhava. A Sanskrit drama, translated with copious notes by Maṇilāla Nabhubhāī Dvivedī.] pp. xiv. 153. ii. મુંબઈ ૧૮૮૦ [*Bombay*, 1880.] 8°. **14148. b. 17.**

BHĀVA MIŚRA. भावप्रकाशस्य पूर्वखण्डे प्रथमो भाग: [Bhāvaprakāśa. A work on medicine, Sanskrit text with Gujarati translation.] *See* ĀYURVEDASĀRASAṄGRAHA आयुर्वेदसारसंग्रह Pt. I. *etc.* [1885, *etc.*] 8°. **14043. c. 33.**

BHAVĀNĪŚAṄKARA NARASIṂHARĀMA. ભવાની કાવ્ય સુધા. पुस्तक १ लुं. ग्रंथ २ लो. [Bhavānī kāvya sudhā. Miscellaneous poems.] Vol. I. pt. I. pp. ii. 63. અમદાવાદ ૧૮૭૭ [*Ahmadabad*, 1877.] 16°. **14148. d. 23.**

BHAVAVAIRĀGYAŚATAKA. भववैराग्यशतक [Bhavavairāgyaśataka. A philosophical poem in 104 Prakrit verses, with a Gujarati commentary.] *See* BHĪMASIṂHA MĀṆAKA. प्रकरणरत्नाकर [Prakaraṇaratnākara.] Vol. III. pp. 813-832. [1878, *etc.*] 4°. **14100. e. 3.**

BHĪKHĪ. ગામડેની ભીખીને મુંબઈ શેહેરે ભખી! [Gāmḍenī Bhīkhīne Mumbai shehare bhakhī. A tale on the miseries of Bhīkhī, a country girl who was married to a worthless Parsi of Bombay.] pp. 316. મુંબઈ ૧૮૮૩ [*Bombay*, 1883.] 12°. **14148. a. 25.(1.)**

BHĪMAJĪ RĀVAJĪ MAHĀJAN. राजमित्र नाटक [Rājamitra nāṭaka. A drama, describing the immoral practices of native chieftains.] pp. viii. 86. मुंबई १८८७ [*Bombay*, 1887.] 12°. **14148. c. 26.(3.)**

BHĪMASIṂHA MĀṆAKA. *See* SŪTRAKṚITĀṄGA. श्रीसूयगडंग-सूत्र *etc.* [Edited with prefaces and indices in Gujarati by Bh. M.] [1881.] 4°. **14100. e. 2.**

—— શ્રી જૈનકાવ્યપ્રકાશ. [Jainakāvyaprakāśa. A collection of Jain prayers, hymns and poems by various authors. Compiled by Bh. M.] Pt. I. pp. xxiv. 480, *lith.* મુંબાપુરી ૧૯૩૯ [*Bombay*, 1883.] 8°. **14144. g. 6.**

—— प्रकरण-रत्नाकर [Prakaraṇaratnākara. A collection of Jain works in Sanskrit, Prakrit, or old Gujarati, generally accompanied by a translation in modern Gujarati. Edited by Bh. M.] 4 vol. मुम्बापुरी १८७८ [*Bombay*, 1878, *etc.*] 4°. **14100. e 3.**

Imperfect, wanting Vols. 1 and 2.

BHOGĪLĀLA MAHĀNANDA BHAṬṬA. *See* KRISHNAMIŚRA. प्रबोधचंद्रोदयनाटक. [Prabodhachandrodaya nāṭaka. Translated by Bh. M. Bh.] [1881.] 8°. **14148. c. 15.**

—— श्रवणपितृभक्ति नाटक [Śravaṇapitṛibhakti nāṭaka. A drama in five acts based on a popular legend.] pp. 99. મુંબઈ ૧૮૭૯ [*Bombay*, 1879.] 8°. **14148. c. 14.**

BHOGĪLĀLA PRĀṆAVALLABHADĀSA. Gujarâti deshi hisâb, or Mental arithmetic. Part II. by Râo Sâhib Bhogilâl Prânavallabhadâs. (દેશી હિસાબ) pp. ii. 66. *Bombay*, 1877. 12°. **14146. c. 19.**

BHOWSAR TRIBHOWUNDASS GIRDHURDASS KHUMBATI. *See* TRIBHUVANADĀSA GIRDHARADĀSA KHAMBĀTĪ.

BHŪGOḶA-JÑĀNA. ભૂગોળ જ્ઞાન [Bhūgoḷa-jñāna. An elementary geography.] Pt. II. pp. 80. મુંબઈ ૧૮૭૬ [*Bombay*, 1876.] 12°. **14146. f. 10.**

Imperfect, wanting pt. I.

BHUGWANLAL BAPALAL. *See* BHAGAVĀNLĀLA BĀPĀLĀLA.

BHŪPATRĀYA HARAGOVINDA DĀTĀR. Kanya vikraya dosh darshak. कन्याविक्रय दोषदर्षक. [An essay on the evil consequences of marrying young girls to rich old men. Compiled by Bh. H. D. with the assistance of Narottama Nityānanda Sabhāmantrī.] pp. 56. અમદાવાદ ૧૮૮૧ [*Ahmadabad*, 1881.] 12°. **14146. e. 8.(3.)**

BIBLE. The Holy Bible, containing the Old and New Testaments, translated from the originals into the Goozuratee language, by the Serampore missionaries. Vol. 5, containing the New Testament. pp. 675. *Serampore*, 1820. 8°.

3068. bb. 11.

No more of this edition appears to have been published.

—— [Another copy.] **3068. bb. 9.**

—— The Holy Bible, containing the Old and New Testaments, in the Goojurattee language, translated by the Surat missionaries. .... ધરમ પુશતક *etc.* 4 vol. *Surat*, 1828, 29, 27. 4°.

1110. h. 1-4.

—— પુરાતન સ્થાપનાનું પુસ્તક ... The Holy Scriptures in Gujarati. [The translation by J. Skinner and W. Fyvie, improved by the Bombay Auxiliary Book Society.] pp. ii. 1256. *Surat*, 1861. 8°. **3068. bb. 19.**

Only the Old Testament.

Appendix.

—— Daily prayers and promises from the Holy Scriptures. પરતીદીનની પરારથનાઓ [Pratidinanī prārthanāo.] pp. 60, ii. સુરત ૧૮૬૧ [*Surat*, 1861.] 12°. **14144. a. 2(12.)**

OLD TESTAMENT.

—— *Pentateuch.* પુરાતન સ્થાપનાનું પુસ્તક ... The five Books of Moses, *etc.* [Revised from the translation of J. Skinner and W. Fyvie.] pp. 279. *Surat*, 1858. 8°. **3070. d. 9.**

—— *Genesis.—Appendix.* *See* TRIBHUVANADĀSA RĀMADĀSA. આદમાખ્યાન *etc.* [Ādamākhyāna. The Bible history of Adam and Eve in verse.] [1875.] 16°. **14144. a. 16.**

—— *Chronicles.* પુરાતન સ્થાપનાનું પુસ્તક ... The two Books of Chronicles. Translated into Gujarati [by R. Young]. pp. 540-629. *Surat*, 1859. 8°. **3070. bb. 16.**

—— *Psalms.* The Psalms of David, translated into Gujarati verse ... by J. Glasgow. દાઊદનાં ગીતો *etc.* pp. vi. 452. *Surat*, 1856. 12°.

3089. bb.

—— OLD TESTAMENT.—*Appendix.* Abridgment of the Old Testament Scriptures; designed for the Gujeratí speaking population: by James McKee. (જુના ધર્મપુસ્તકનો સંક્ષેપ) [Junā Dharmapustakno saṃkshepa.] pp. iv. 149. *Surat*, 1852. 8°.

3068. b. 17.

NEW TESTAMENT.

—— The New Testament ... in the Goojurattee language, translated by the Surat missionaries. પરભુ તથા તારનાર ઈશુ ખરીશટનો નવો બંદોબશત, *etc.* pp. 591. *Surat*, 1827. 4°.

1410. l. 1.

—— આપણ પ્રભુ તથા ત્રાતા ઈશુ ખ્રીસ્તની નવીન સ્થાપના ... The New Testament ... Translated ... into the Gujarati language [by J. Skinner and W. Fyvie, and revised by Hormuzjī Pestanjī, Dhanjībhāi Naurozjī and Dr. Wilson.] pp. 703. *Surat*, 1857. 12°. **3068. b. 30.**

New Testament (*continued*).

—— ઈંજીલ-ઈ-મુકદસ . . . The New Testament in Gujaráti, adapted to the usage of the Pársis and others. pp. 488. *Bombay*, 1864. 8°. **3070. cc. 25.**

—— આપણા પ્રભુ તથા તારનાર ઈશુ ખ્રીસ્તનો નવો કરાર *etc.* [A revised edition.] pp. 878. *W. Raymond, Mission Press; Surat*, 1867. 8°. **3070. g. 8.**

—— *Matthew.* पेहेलो भाग मती जो [The Gospel of Matthew, translated into the Kachhi dialect of Gujarat, by J. Gray.] pp. 156. [*Bombay?*] 1834. 8°. **3070. b. 24.**

—— —— The Gospel according to Matthew in English and Goojaratee. [Translated by J. Taylor, and revised by J. Skinner and W. Fyvie.] pp. 175. *Surat*, 1840. 8°. **3068. bb. 1.**

—— —— ઈશુ ખ્રીશટના શારા શમાચાર માથીઊના બનાવેલા. The Gospel of St. Matthew. [Revised by the Rev. Dr. Wilson.] pp. 90. [*Bombay*,] 1844. 12°. **3068. aaa. 25.**

—— —— ઈશુના રાજની આગનાઓ ને તેઓ શંબંધીના વીચારો. Sermon on the Mount, with commentary. pp. 82. મુંબઈ ૧૮૫૪ [*Bombay*, 1854.] 12°. **3070. aaa. 21.**

—— *Mark.* Mark. મારકનો લખેલી સુવાર્તા . . . Bombay Auxiliary Society. pp. 69. શુરત [*Surat*,] 1865. 8°. **3068. b. 1.**

—— *John, Gospel of.* શારા શમાચાર ઈહોતના બનાવેલા. The Gospel of John. [Translated by J. Skinner and W. Fyvie.] pp. 58. *American Mission Press*, [*Surat?*,] 1842. 8°. **3070. bb. 19.**

—— *Acts.* The Acts of the Apostles in English and Goojuratee. [Translated by J. Skinner and W. Fyvie.] pp. 192. *Surat*, 1841. 8°. **3068. bb. 4.**

—— [Another copy.] **3068. cc. 2.**

BLANFORD (Henry Francis). Physical Geography . . . Translated into Gujarati by R. S. Mahipatram Rupram Nilkanth. (भूतळविद्या) [Bhūtaḷavidyā.] pp. vi. 169. *Bombay*, 1881. 12°. **14146. f. 6.**

BODHAKATHĀ. બોધકથા. [Bodhakathā. A moral and instructive reading-book for children.] Pt. I. pp. 55, *lith.* મુંબઈ ૧૭૭૬ [*Bombay*, 1854.] 16°. **14150. a. 20.(2.)**

BOMANJEE BYRAMJEE PATELL. *See* Bahmanjī Bahrāmjī Patel.

BOMBAY, *City of.—Kapadia Amusing Club.* Rules and bye-laws of the Kapadia Amusing Club. કાપડીઆ રમુજી મંડળીના ધારાઓ. pp. 8. મુંબઈ ૧૯૪૧ [*Bombay*, 1885.] 12°. **14146. e. 9.(2.)**

—— *Saurāshṭra Jñānaprasāraka Maṇḍaḷī.* *See* Purāṇas. — *Skandapurāṇa.* स्कंदपुराणार्थप्रकाश. . . . [Skandapurāṇa. Translated by the Saurāshṭra Jñānaprasāraka Maṇḍaḷī.] [1885, *etc.*] 8°. **14144. d. 7.**

—— *Government of.—Department of Public Instruction.* મુંબઈ ઈલાકાના કેળવણી ખાતાની બુક દીપોના ધારા. [Rules for the regulation of School Depots of the Government of Bombay.] pp. 42. મુંબાઈ ૧૮૮૧ [*Bombay*, 1881.] 8°. **14146. a. 8.**

—— *Presidency of.—Anglo-Vernacular Schools.* School dialogues . . . for the use of Anglo-Vernacular schools in the Bombay Presidency. [Translated from the Marathi by Ranjit.] (વાતચીતના શેહલાં વાકયો) [Vātchītnā ṣchalāṉ vākyo.] pp. 31. *Eng.* and *Guj.* *Bombay*, 1865. 16°. **14150. a. 26.(3.)**

—— *Court of Ṡadr Dīwānī 'Adālat.* Borradaile's Gujarát Caste Rules. [Collected by him by order and under the authority of the Bombay Ṡadr Dīwānī 'Adālat.] Published from the original answers of the Castes . . . by [or rather, at the instance and cost of] Sir Munguldass Nathoobhoy, Knight C.S.I. under the superintendence of [or rather, edited by] Ráo Bahádur Nána Morojí. [Vol. II. edited by Gokaḷdāsa Viṭhṭhaladāsa Saraiyā.] 2 vol. *Bombay*, 1884-87. 8°. **14146. a. 14.**

BONNYCASTLE (John). *See* Jervis (G. R.) A course of Mathematics in the Goojratee language . . . . Translated from the works of Dr. Charles Hutton and Mr. Bonnycastle. 1828. 4°. **14146. d. 5 and 6.**

BORRADAILE (Harry). *See* Bombay, *Presidency of.—Court of Ṡadr Dīwānī 'Adālat.* Borradaile's Gujarát Caste Rules, *etc.* 1884-87. 8°. **14146. a. 14.**

BRĀHMA DHARMA. ब्राह्मधर्म्मः [Brāhma dharma. A collection of Brahmist maxims, in Sanskrit, compiled from the Upanishads and other Sanskrit works, accompanied by a Gujarati translation by Nārāyaṇa Hemachandra.] pp. 170. મુંબઈ ૧૯૪૩ [*Bombay*, 1887.] 32°. **14028. a. 22.**

The compilation of the Sanskrit quotations is erroneously ascribed in this edition to Devendranātha Ṭhākura.

BRAHMAN. એક ડોશી તથા બરાહ્મણની વાતચીત [Ek ḍoṣī tathā Brāhmaṇanī vātchīt. A conversation between an old woman and a Brahman on Christianity.] pp. 27. સુરત ૧૮૬૦ [*Surat*, 1860.] 12°. **14144. a. 2.(8.)**

BRĀHMA SAMĀJ. ब्राह्मधर्म्ममतसार [Brāhmadharma matasāra. A collection of Brahmist hymns, translated from the Bengali into Sanskrit verse, and Gujarati prose, by Nārāyaṇa Hemachandra. Followed by a short catechism in Gujarati.] pp. 30. મુંબઈ [*Bombay*, 1882.] 32°. **14028. a. 17.**

—— *Ahmadabad Prārthanā Samāj.* बालसंध्योपासना. [Bālasandhyopāsanā. Brahmist prayers and hymns for the use of children.] pp. 16. अमदावाद १९३६ [*Ahmadabad*, 1880.] 12°. **14144. a. 17.(3.)**

—— —— ईश्वर प्रार्थना माळा . गद्य पद्य गायन सहित [Īṣvaraprārthanāmālā. Brahmist prayers and hymns, published by the Ahmadabad Brāhma Samāj. Second edition.] pp. x. 225, xxi. अमदावाद १९३१ [*Ahmadabad*, 1875.] 8°. **14144. a. 23.**

—— —— [Third edition.] pp. xv. 220. अमदावाद १९३५ [*Ahmadabad*, 1879.] 8°. **14144. a. 24.**

—— —— Part ii. pp. 68. अमदावाद १९३० [*Ahmadabad*, 1880.] 8°. **14144. a. 25.**

—— —— ईश्वरोपासना [Īṣvaropāsanā. Brahmist prayers and hymns in use by the Ahmadabad Prārthanā Samāj.] pp. 87. अमदावाद १९३६ [*Ahmadabad*, 1880.] 12°. **14144. a. 22.**

BROACH.—*Ārya-hitechchhu Sabhā.* સજોડા સુખદર્શક નાટક [Sajoḍā sukha-darṣaka nāṭaka. A drama, shewing that it is better for a girl to marry a poor, but well-educated and well-conducted man, than one of a rich family and vicious habits.] pp. 35. ભરૂચ ૧૮૮૬ [*Broach*, 1886.] 12°. **14148. c. 26.(2.)**

BULĀKĪ CHAKUBHĀI. યુવરાજ યાત્રા [Yuvarājayātrā. A description in verse of the festivities at Bombay in honour of the visit of the Prince of Wales.] pp. 16. અમદાવાદ ૧૯૩૨ [*Ahmadabad*, 1875.] 16°. **14148. d. 13.(5.)**

BUNDEHESH. બુનદેહેશ કેતાબ [Bundehesh, or The book of Creation. A work on cosmogony and cosmography, translated from the Pehlevi. Edited, with an introductory preface, by Peshotan Rustam.] 3 pt. મુંબઈ ૧૮૭૭ [*Bombay*, 1877.] 8°. **14144. i. 14.**

BUTT, afterwards SHERWOOD (Mary Martha). હેનરી તથા તેહેના ચાકર શંભુની વાત [Henrī tathā tehenā chākar.] Henry and his bearer. [Translated from the English of M. M. B.] pp. 97. સુરત ૧૮૫૧ [*Surat*, 1851.] 16°. **14144. a. 4.**

BUZURGMIHR. ગંજે શાઇગાન કેતાબનો તરજુમો [Ganj i shāegān, or the Precepts of Buzurgmihr. Pehlevi text and Gujarati translation.] *See* Peshotan Bahrāmjī Sanjāṇa. Ganjesháyagán, *etc.* 1885. 8°. **761. g. 2.**

CANDY (Thomas). A manual of geography ... Vol. I., translated into Gujarati by Chotalal Sevakram. (ભૂગોલનું વર્ણન) [Bhūgolanuṉ varṇana.] pp. xi. 253. *Bombay*, 1868. 8°. **14146. g. 15.**

CATECHISM. શવાલ જવાબની પેહેલી પોથી [Sawāl jawābnī pehelī pothī.] Elementary catechism. [A treatise on the principles of Christianity.] pp. 32. સુરત ૧૮૬૧ [*Surat*, 1861.] 16°. **14144. a. 3.(6.)**

CHALYĀKHYĀNA. ચલ્યાખ્યાન પ્રારંભ. [Chalyākhyāna. A popular legend in verse.] pp. 9, *lith.* મુંબાઈ ૧૯૩૧ [*Bombay*, 1874.] 12°. **14148. a. 2.(6.)**

CHAMANLĀLA NARASIṂHADĀSA. *See* Uttamarāma Umedchand and Chamanlāla Narasiṃhadāsa. દીલગીરીનો દેખાવ [Dilgirino dekhāva.] [1875.] 16°. **14148. d. 13.(3.)**

—— *See* Uttamarāma Umedchand and Chamanlāla Narasiṃhadāsa. ગુલચમન ગાયન [Gulchaman gāyan.] [1875.] 12°. **14148. d. 1.(6.)**

CHAMPION (Edme). અદમી ચાંપીઅન Edme Champion. [A Christian tract.] pp. 24. સુરત ૧૮૫૯ [*Surat*, 1859.] 12°. **14144. a. 1.(9.)**

CHAND *See* Ātmārama Kesavajī Dvivedī. પૃથિરાજ ચહુઆણ *etc.* [Prithirāja chahuāṇ. Tales of Prithvī Rāja, compiled chiefly from the Hindi of Ch.] [1884.] 8°. **14148. b. 14.**

CHAND RĀJĀ. ચંદરાજા અને ગુણાવલી રાણીના કાગલ, *etc.* [Chand rājā ane Guṇāvalī rāṇīnā kāgal, or The letters of king Chand and queen Guṇāvalī; a Jain legend. Followed by hymns by Vīravijaya in praise of the saint Pārsvanātha.] pp. 56, *lith.* મુંબાપુરી [*Bombay*, 1884.] 16°. **14144 f. 12.(1.)**

CHANDRA MAHATTARĀCHĀRYA. सप्ततिकानामा षष्ठ कर्मग्रंथ [Saptatikā. The sixth of the Jain Karmagranthas, attributed to Ch. M., with a Gujarati commentary.] *See* Bhīmasiṃha Māṇaka प्रकरण-रत्नाकर Vol. iv. pp. 773-927. [1878, *etc.*] 4°. **14100. e. 3.**

CHANDRA SŪRI. संग्रहणीसूत्र [Saṅgrahaṇī-sūtra. Prakrit text with a Gujarati commentary.] *See* Bhīmasiṃha Māṇaka प्रकरण-रत्नाकर Vol. iv. pp. 33—184. [1876, *etc.*] 4°. **14100. e. 3.**

CHANDRIKĀ. ચંદ્રિકા અંક ૧ લો. [Chandrikā. Miscellaneous poems.] Pt. i. pp. 22. મુંબઈ ૧૮૬૫ [*Bombay*, 1865.] 12°. **14148. d. 9.(1.)**

CHARITRASAṄGRAHA. ચરિત્ર સંગ્રહ. શ્રી પાંડવ ચરીત્ર સહીત [Charitrasaṅgraha. A collection of Jain legends, philosophical and other works.] pp. 200, 200. અમદાવાદ ૧૮૮૪ [*Ahmadabad*, 1884.] 8°. **14144. g. 9.**

CHATURBHUJA DĀSA. મધુમાલતીની વારતા. [Madhu Mālatīnī vārtā. A tale in verse.] pp. 115, *lith.* મુંબઈ ૧૭૭૭ [*Bombay*, 1855.] 8°. **14148. b. 4.(3.)**

CHATURBHUJA PRĀṆAJĪVANA. *See* Merāmaṇajī. प्रवीनसागर ॥ [Pravīṇasāgara. Edited by Ch. P.] [1882.] 4°. **14154. i. 1.**

CHATURBHUJA VĀLJĪ JERĀJĀṆĪ KHAMBHĀLIĀVĀLĀ. ભાટીઆ કુલોત્પતી ગ્રંથ [Bhāṭiā kulotpatti grantha. A treatise on the genealogy of the Bhāṭiā caste, proving them to be of Rajput descent.] pp. iv. 63. મુંબઈ ૧૮૮૬ [*Bombay*, 1886.] 8°. **14146. e. 20.(3.)**

CHAURĀSĪ VĀRTĀ. चोराशी वैष्णवनी वारता . . . તરજુમો કરનાર શાસ્ત્રી પ્રાણવલ્લભ [*sic*] ભગવાનજી [Chaurāsī Vaishṇavanī vārtā. Stories of 84 Vaishṇava saints, translated by Prāṇavallabha Bhagavānjī from the Braj-bhāshā original.] pp. 126. अमदावाद १९३७ [*Ahmadabad*, 1881.] 12°. **14144. b. 2.**

CHHA BHĀĪ. છભાઈનું રાસ [Chha bhāinuṇ rās. A Jain story in verse. Second edition.] pp. 56, *lith.* મુંબઈ ૧૯૩૪ [*Bombay*, 1877.] 12°. **14148. a. 2.(7.)**

CHHAGANLĀLA HARILĀLA. *See* Bāṇa શ્રીમદ્બાણભટ્ટ-વિરચિત કાદમ્બરીનું સટીક ગુજરાતી ભાષાન્તર. [Kādambarī. Translated by Chh. H.] [1884.] 8°. **14148. b. 34.**

CHHOṬĀLĀLA MOHANALĀLA. *See* Maṇilāla Harilāla and Chhoṭālāla Mohanalāla. મોંઘવારીની મોહોકણ. [Monghavārīnī mohkāṇ.] [1877.] 16°. **14148. d. 13.(15.)**

CHHOṬĀLĀLA PREMĀNANDA TRAVĀḌĪ. *See* Krishṇa Raṇchhoḍa Travāḍī and Chhoṭālāla Premānanda Travāḍī. राजेश्री भुधरभाइ धनेश्वरनो रासडो तथा परजोयो. [Bhudharabhāi Dhanesvarano rāsḍo.] [1875.] 12°. **14148. d. 5.(7.)**

CHHOṬĀLĀLA SEVAKARĀMA. *See* Candy (T.) A manual of geography by T. Candy . . . Vol. I. translated into Gujarati by Chotalal Sevakram. 1868. 8°. **14146. g. 15.**

—— *See* Morris (H.) *of the Madras Civil Service.* A history of India, in Gujarati, ... by Chhotálál Sevakarám. 1875. 8°. **14146. g. 13.**

—— *See* Shakspere (W.) Selected tales from Shakespeare, translated into Gujarati by . . . Chotálál Savekrám, *etc.* 1867. 12°. **14148. a. 10.**

—— *See* Vrinda. વૃંદસતસઈ [Vrinda sat-saī. Translated from the Braj-bhāshā by Chh. S.] [1886.] 12°. **14148. e. 17.**

CHIMANALĀLA NARSIDĀSA. महाराजा मलहाररावनो रासडो [Mahārājā Malhār Rāvano rāsḍo. Verses on the trial and deposition of Malhār Rāva, Gaikwar of Baroda.] pp. 16. अमदावाद १९३१ [*Ahmadabad*, 1875.] 12°. **14148. d. 13.(8.)**

CHISTEY (N. P.) *See* Niẓām al-Dīn, *Chishtī*, called Hāmī.

CHOTALAL SEVAKRAM. *See* Chhoṭālāla Sevakarāma.

CHRISTIAN MINISTERS. ખરીશટી પાદરીઓ શામાટે આ દેશમાં આએવા. [Khristī pādrīo ṣāmāṭe ā deṣamāṇ āevā.] Why have Christian Ministers come to this country? [A Christian tract.] pp. 12. *Surat*, 1839. 12°.
14144. a. 1.(2.)

CHRISTIANS. ખરીશટના વીશવાશીઓની ઊતરાવલી. [Khristnā viṣvāsīonī uttarāvalī.] An apology for Christians. pp. 38. ૧૮૫૩ [*Surat*, 1856.] 12°. **14144. a. 1.(5.)**

CHUNĪLĀLA BĀPUJĪ MODĪ. *See* DEFOE (D.) Robinson Crusoe. [Translated by Ch. B. M.] [1881.] 12°. **14148. a. 29.**

CLIVE (ROBERT) *Baron Clive.* લોર્ડ કલાઈવ, હિંદુસ્તાનમાં અંગ્રેજી રાજ્યનો પાયો સ્થાપનાર .... A sketch of Lord Clive, the founder of the British empire in India. pp. xiii, 110. મુંબઈ ૧૮૬૬ [*Bombay*, 1866.] 12°. **14146. f. 15.**

CONCERTINA. કૅાનસરટીનામાં વગાડવાના ગાયણો [Kānsartīnāmāṇ vagāḍvānā gāyaṇo. An arrangement of music suited for a concertina of 20 keys.] pp. 16. મુંબઈ ૧૮૮૦ [*Bombay*, 1880.] 16°. **14146. c. 6.**

COPY-SLIPS. સ્ટાન્ડર્ડ કાપી સ્લીપ્સ [Standard copy-slips. Fourth edition.] 4 pt. સુરત ૧૮૭૭ [*Surat*, 1877.] 8°. **14150. a. 22.**
In Devanagari and Gujarati characters.

COTTIN (SOPHIE). इलीजावेथ अथवा सैबीरीयानुं देशपार करेलुं कुटुंब. [Elizabeth, or The exiles of Siberia. Translated from an English version of the French of S. C.] pp. ii. 113. અમદાવાદ ૧૯૩૧ [*Ahmadabad*, 1875.] 8°. **14148. b. 13.**

COWASJEE NOWROSJEE VESUWALA. *See* KĀVASJĪ NAVAROJĪ VESUWĀLĀ.

CRICKET. ક્રિકેટ: તેની પુરતી સમજ તથા સર્વે જાતના કાયદા સાથે. [The rules of cricket, translated from the English.] pp. 45. મુંબઈ [*Bombay*, 1887.] 12°. **14146. c. 24.**

CURTIS (T. B.) *Gujarati Translator.* *See* HOWARD (E. I.) Howard's Rudimentary English grammar translated into Gujarati .... and revised by T. B. C. [1865.] 12°. **14150. a. 29.**

ḌĀHYĀBHĀĪ AMBĀRĀMA. हिंदुस्ताननी भूगोळ [Hindustānanī bhūgoḷa. Geography of India.] pp. 48. સુરત ૧૯૩૩ [*Surat*, 1876.] 12°.
14150. a. 26.(4.)

ḌĀHYĀBHĀĪ GHELĀBHĀĪ PANḌITA. *See* PARĀṢARA. श्री पाराशरधर्मशास्त्र *etc.* [Pārāṣaradharmaṣāstra. With a Gujarati translation by Ḍ. Gh. P.] [1869.] 8°. **14038. c. 27.**

DALAL (B. M.) *See* BĀLUBHĀĪ MANMOHANADĀSA DALĀL.

DALPATRĀMA AMBĀRĀMA. गुरुनी सत्ताविषे निबंध [Gurunī sattā vishe nibandha. A treatise on the authority of Gurus.] pp. 34. મુંબઈ ૧૮૫૯ [*Bombay*, 1859.] 8°. **14146. e. 15.(1.)**

—— विषयीं गुरुविषे निबंध [Vishayīṇ guru vishe nibandha. A treatise on the corrupt practices of worldly-minded Gurus.] pp. 28. મુંબઈ ૧૮૫૯ [*Bombay*, 1859.] 8°. **14144. i. 4.(1.)**

DALPATRĀMA ḌĀHYĀBHĀĪ, *Kavi, C.I.E.* *See* MERĀMAṆAJĪ. प्रवीनसागर॥ [Pravīnasāgara. A Hindi poem, with a commentary in Gujarati by D. Ḍ.] [1882] 4°. **14154. i. 1.**

—— Gujarati Kavyasankshepa, or Selections from Gujarati poets, by Kavi Dalpatrám Dáhyábhái. (गूजराती काव्य संक्षेप) pp. ii. 194, xiii. मुंबई १८७५ [*Bombay*, 1875.] 8°. **14148. f. 7.**

—— Gujarati Pingal, or Prosody by Kavi Dalpatrám Dáyábhái (गुजराती पिंगळ) Third edition. pp. 70. *Bombay*, 1875. 12°. **14146. c. 3.**

—— Selections from the Gujaráti poets by Dalpatrám Dayábhái. (काव्यदोहन. એટલે ગુજરાતી ભાષાની કવિતાનો સારસંગ્રહ.) [Kāvyadohana] 3 pt. *Ahmedabad*, 1862. 8°. **14148. f. 14.**

—— 2nd Series. pp. xii, 448, xi. *Ahmedabad*, 1865. 8°. **14148. e. 4.**

—— Third edition [of the First Series.] pp. 352, xxiv. *Bombay*, 1866. 8°. **14148. f. 9.**

—— The Gujarâti Kâvyadôhana. Expurgated and revised by R. S. Mahipatrâm R. Nilkanth, C.I.E. pp. viii. 520. *Bombay*, 1886. 8°.
14148. e. 13.

—— સંપઅને લક્ષ્મિવચે સંવાદ [Sampayanen lakshmīvache saṃvāda. A poem.] pp. ii. 38, *lith.* સુરત ૧૮૫૨ [*Surat*, 1852.] 8°. **14148. e. 3.(1.)**

—— ज्ञाति निबंध. [Jñāti-nibandha. An essay on Hindu castes. Fourth edition.] pp. 150. અમદાવાદ ૧૮૮૭ [*Ahmadabad*, 1887.] 16°.
14146. e. 24.

DALPATRĀMA PRĀṆAJĪVANA KHAKHKHAR. કચ્છની ભૂગોળવિદ્યા [Kachchhnī bhūgoḷavidyā. An account of the Province of Cutch, its history, religion, and ancient buildings.] pp. vi. 110. મુંબઈ ૧૯૩૧ [*Bombay*, 1875.] 12°. **14146. f. 5.**

—— [Second edition.] pp. xi. 108. મુંબઈ ૧૮૮૦ [*Bombay*, 1880.] 12°. **14146. f. 22.**

DĀMAJĪ MAKANDĀSA. *See* HARAJĪVANADĀSA GOVINDARĀMA and DĀMAJĪ MAKANDĀSA. गोहिल राज्यनो इतिहास *etc.* [Gohil rājyano itihāsa.] [1880.] 12°. **14146. f. 11.**

DĀMODARA ĪŚVARADĀSA. *See* ARABIAN NIGHTS. અરેબિયન નાઈટસ. [The Arabian Nights tales, translated by D. Ī.] [1880, *etc.*] 8°. **14148. b. 24.**

DĀMODARA RATANSĪ SOMĀṆĪ. નવો ઓખા હરણ [Okhāharaṇa. A poem on the story of Ushā and Aniruddha.] pp. 16. મુંબઈ ૧૮૭૯ [*Bombay*, 1879.] 16°. **14148. d. 1.(8.)**

—— रुक्ष्मणी हरणनो गायनरुपी आपेरा. [Rukshmiṇī haraṇa. A dramatized version of the story of the abduction of Rukshmiṇī by Krishṇa.] pp. 18. મુંબઈ ૧૮૮૦ [*Bombay*, 1880.] 12°. **14148. c. 13.(1.)**

—— सदेवंत सावलींगानी गायनरुपी नाटक [Sadevanta Sāvaliṅgānī gāyanarūpī nāṭaka. A dramatized version of the popular story of Sadevanta and Sāvaliṅga.] pp. 23. મુંબઈ ૧૮૮૨ [*Bombay*, 1882.] 16°. **14148. c. 13.(3.)**

DATTĀTRAYA. नारसिंहावतार नाटक. [Nārasiṃhāvatāra nāṭaka. A drama on the Narasiṃha, or man-lion incarnation of Vishṇu. Translated from the Marathi of D. by Ānandajī Vahāljī Rājgar.] pp. 43. अमदावाद १८८१ [*Ahmadabad*, 1881.] 16°. **14148. c. 3.**

DAY (THOMAS) *Author of "Sandford and Merton."* A glossary of difficult words and phrases occurring in History of Sandford and Merton. Part I. pp. 50. *Bombay*, 1879. 8°. **14150. b. 4.(3.)**

DAYĀLAJĪ RAṆCHHOḌA. હાજરજવાબી પ્રધાનની વાર્તા [Hāzir-javābī pradhānanī vārtā. Anecdotes of a minister's ready wit and shrewdness.] pp. ii. 72. अमदावाद १९३२ [*Ahmadabad*, 1875.] 12°. **14148. a. 26.**

DAYĀLA RĀVAJĪ. મોતીના હિશાબની ગણતરીની ચોપડી [Motīnā hisābnī chopaḍī. Useful money tables.] pp. 172. મુંબઈ ૧૮૭૫ [*Bombay*, 1875.] 12°. **14146. c. 23.**

DAYĀNANDA SARASVATI. *See* BHĪMĀCHĀRYA JHALKĪKAR and RĀJĀRĀMA GAṆEŚA BODAS वेदार्थोद्धार: *etc.* [Vedārthoddhāra. A critical refutation of D. S.'s views regarding the Vedas as the sole authority in matters of doctrine.] [1875.] 8°. **14028. d. 18.**

DAYĀRĀMA, *Kavi.* દયારામકૃત કાવ્યસંગ્રહ [Dayārāmakṛita kāvyasaṅgraha. The complete works of Dayārāma. Edited by Narmadāśaṅkara Lālaśaṅkara. Second edition.] pp. xxiii. 658. મુંબઈ ૧૮૬૫ [*Bombay*, 1865.] 8°. **14148. e. 5.**

—— દયારામકૃત કવિતા [Dayārāmakṛita kavitā. The poetical works of Dayārāma. A revised edition by Raṇchhoḍalāla Galurāma.] Pt. i. *lith.* અમદાવાદ ૧૯૨૨ [*Ahmadabad*, 1865.] 8°. **14148. f. 6.**

—— દયારામકૃત કવિતા તથા ચરચુરણ કિર્તન [Another edition of D.'s works, with verses by other poets, chiefly in praise of Krishṇa.] pp. 276, *lith.* અમદાવાદ ૧૮૮૦ [*Ahmadabad*, 1880.] 8°. **14148. f. 13.**

—— દયારામકૃત કવિતા [Another edition of D.'s poetical works, with copious notes.] *See* PRĀCHĪNA KĀVYA प्राचीन काव्य No. 3 of 1886. [1885, *etc.*] 8°. **14148. e. 12.**

DEFOE (DANIEL). Robinson Crusoe. [Translated from the English by Chunīlāla Bāpujī Modī.] राबिन्सन् क्रूसोनुं चरित्र Pt. i. pp. ii. 202. મુંબઈ ૧૮૮૧ [*Bombay*, 1881.] 12°. **14148. a. 29.**

DESTROYER. The destroyer of superstition. No. 1. Pantheism. ભરમની તોડનારી વાણી [Bhramnī toḍnārī vāṇī.] Second edition. pp. 59. *Bombay*, 1853. 16°. **14144. a. 3.(2.)**

No. 21 of the Bombay Tract and Book Society's Series.

DEVACHANDRA. अथ श्री पंडित देवचंद्रजीकृत आगमसार लिख्यते [Āgamasāra. A Jain philosophical treatise, in the Devanagari character.] *See* BHĪMASIṂHA MĀṆAKA. प्रकरण-रत्नाकर [Prakaraṇa-ratnākara.] Vol. i. pp. 139-179. [1876, *etc.*] 4°. **14100. e. 3.**

DEVACHANDRA अथ श्री देवचंद्रजिकृत श्री आगमसार [Āgamasāra. Another editon.] *See* JAINAṢĀSTRA. જૈન સાસ્ત્ર કથા સંગ્રહ [Jainaṣāstra kathā saṅgraha.] pp. 370-417. [1883.] 8°. **14144. g. 8.**

—— [Another edition.] *See* NĀTHĀ LALUBHĀI. જૈન કાવ્ય સાર સંગ્રહ [Jainakāvya sārasaṅgraha.] pp. 370—385. [1882.] 8°. **14144. g. 23.**

—— पंडित श्री देवचंद्रगणि विरचित बालावबोध सहित चतुर्विंशतिजिन स्तवन, तथा विंशति विहरमानजिन स्तवन. [Chaturviṃṣati Jina stavana. A collection of hymns in old Hindi addressed to the 24 Jain Tīrthankaras, with a commentary in Gujarati. Followed by Viṃṣati Viharamān Jina stavana, or 20 hymns to the saint Viharamān.] pp. ii. 168. मुंबापुरी १९४० [*Bombay*, 1884.] 8°. **14144. g. 4.**

—— अथ श्री देवचंद्रजीकृत नयचक्रसारनुं बालावबोध लिख्यते [Nayachakrasāra. A Jain metaphysical treatise on the doctrine of existence and non-existence, in Sanskrit verse, accompanied by a Gujarati commentary.] *See* BHĪMASIṂHA MĀṆAKA. प्रकरण-रत्नाकर [Prakaraṇa-ratnākara.] Vol. i. pp. 181-254. [1876, *etc.*] 4°. **14100. e. 3.**

DEVAPRABHU SŪRI. અથ શ્રીપાંડવ ચરીત્ર. [Pāṇḍavacharitra. Stories of Jain saints, in imitation of the Mahābhārata account of the Pāṇḍavas, being a Gujarati prose translation of a Sanskrit poem by D. S.] *See* CHARITRA-SAṄGRAHA. ચરિત્ર સંગ્રહ *etc.* [1884.] 8°. **14144. g. 7.**

—— અથ શ્રીપાંડવ ચરીત્ર. [Another edition.] *See* JAINAṢĀSTRA. જૈન સાસ્ત્ર કથા સંગ્રહ, *etc.* [1884.] 8°. **14144. g. 9.**

DEVAJĪ UKĀBHĀI MAKVĀṆĀ. કવિ નાગજીનું જન્મ ચરિત્ર. [Kavi Nāgjīnūṇ janmacharitra. A biographical sketch of the life of the poet Nāgjī, and a collection of his poems with accompanying commentaries.] pp. iv. 110. અમદાવાદ ૧૮૮૫ [*Ahmadabad*, 1885.] 12°. **14148. d. 9.(3.)**

DEVENDRA SŪRI. अथ बालावबोध सहित बंधस्वामित्वाख्य तृतीय कर्मग्रंथः प्रारभ्यते [Bandhasvāmitva. The third of the Jain Karmagranthas, with a Gujarati commentary.] *See* BHĪMASIṂHA MĀṆAKA. प्रकरण-रत्नाकर [Prakaraṇa-ratnākara.] Vol. iv. pp. 455-497. [1876, *etc.*] 4°. **14100. e. 3.**

DEVENDRA SŪRI. कर्मविपाकनामे कर्मग्रंथ १ [Karmavipāka. The first of the Jain ethical works called Karmagranthas, with a Gujarati commentary by Matichandra.] *See* BHĪMASIṂHA MĀṆAKA प्रकरण-रत्नाकर Vol. iv. pp. 305-411. [1876, *etc.*] 4°. **14100. e. 3.**

—— अथ शतकनामा पंचम कर्मग्रंथः ॥ [Ṣataka. The fifth of the Jain Karmagranthas, with a commentary in old Gujarati by Yaṣaḥsoma.] *See* BHĪMASIṂHA MĀṆAKA प्रकरण-रत्नाकर Vol. iv. pp. 605-772. [1878, *etc.*] 4°. **14100. e. 3.**

DHANJĪBHĀI NAVAROJĪ. *See* BIBLE.—*New Testament.* આપણા પ્રભુ . . . નવીન સ્થાપના . . . The New Testament . . . [Revised by Dh. N.] 1857. 12°. **3068. b. 30.**

DHARMA. ધરમનાં તરાજવાં [Dharmanāṇ tarājavāṇ, or The balance of religion. A Christian tract.] pp. 108. શુરત ૧૮૫૪ [*Surat*, 1854.] 16°. **14144. a. 3.(4.)**

—— ધર્મ એ શું છે? [Dharma e ṣuṇ chhe, or What is religion? An anonymous tract condemning idolatry, and urging a life of strict morality.] pp. 24. મુંબઈ ૧૮૮૮ [*Bombay*, 1888.] 12°. **14144. a.**

DHARMĀNANDA SVĀMĪ. भागवत धर्म. [Bhāgavatadharma. A poem on the religious duties of the followers of the Bhāgavata sect of the Vaishṇavas.] pp. 164. अमदावाद १९३६ [*Ahmadabad*, 1879.] 12°. **14144. b. 5.**

DHARMASAMṢODHAKA, *pseud.* स्वाभाविक धर्म. Natural religion. [Svābhāvika dharma. A Brahmist treatise.] pp. 88. अमदावाद १९३७ [*Ahmadabad*, 1881.] 12°. **14144. a. 17.(2.)**

DHARMAVIVECHANA. धर्मविवेचन [Dharmavivechana. A religious treatise founded on a Marathi work.] pp. 84. अमदावाद १९३२ [*Ahmadabad*, 1876.] 8°. **14144. a. 21.**

DHĪRĀ BHAKTA. ધીરા ભકતની કવિતા [Dhīrā Bhaktanī kavitā. An annotated edition of the poetical works of Dh. Bh.] *See* PRĀCHĪNA KĀVYA प्राचीन काव्य No. 2 of 1887. [1885, *etc.*] 8°. **14148. e. 12.**

DHĪRAJRĀMA DALPATRĀMA. Anatomy descriptive and súrgical in Gujráti . . . Part I. Osteo-

logy. નિર્દેશક એવં શસ્ત્ર શારીર વિદ્યા [Śārīravidyā.] pp. v. viii. 254. *Bombay*, 1875. 8°.
14146. b. 10.

—— સંસ્કૃત ભાષાનું વ્યાકરણ. ભાગ ૧ લો. [Saṃskṛita bhāshānuṇ vyākaraṇa. Part I. of a Sanskrit grammar, partly in Sanskrit, partly in Gujarati.] pp. 4, 47, 4, 55. મુંબઈ ૧૯૧૮ [*Bombay*, 1861.] 8°. **14092. b. 27.**

DIL-KHUSH, *pseud.* ફેસાદે ફેબરવારી *etc.* [Fasād i February. An account of the Muhammadan riots which occurred at Bombay in February, 1874.] pp. x. 372. મુંબઈ ૧૨૪૪ [*Bombay*, 1875.] 12°. **14148. d. 18.**

DINKARD. The Dinkard. The original Péhlwi text; the same transliterated in Zend characters; translations of the text in the Gujrati and English languages [the former by the editor, the latter by Ratanshāh Erachshāh Kohiyār from the Gujarati]; a commentary and a glossary of select terms. By Peshotun Dustoor Behramjee Sunjana. 5 vol. *Bombay*, 1874, *etc.* 8°. **761. g. 10.**
In progress.

DĪNSHĀH HORMASJĪ. *See* ZAND-AVASTĀ. પાક ખોરદેહ અવસતા [Khurdah-Avastā. With an interlineary translation and notes by D. H.] [1874.] 32°. **761. a. 16.**

DĪPACHAND DEVACHAND and JAVERĪ CHHAGANLĀLA. सिद्धाचलनुं वर्णन. [Siddhāchala-nuṇ varṇana. A description of the Jain temples at Palitana in Kathiawar, together with a collection of Jain hymns and prayers.] pp. iv. 168. अमदावाद १८८७ [*Ahmadabad*, 1887.] 16°. **14144. f. 19.**

DĪPTIVIJAYA. श्री मंगलकलश कुमारनो रास [Maṅgalakalaṣa kumārno rās. A Jain legend in verse.] pp. 92. श्रीमुंबापुरी १९४२ [*Bombay*, 1886.] 12°. **14144. f. 10.**

DOL. ડોલ ઘાલુ સુધરેલને ચાબકા અથવા હીંદુ સુધરેલોની ઠગાઈ [Ḍol ghālu sudharelno chābakā, or A whip to correct vicious practices. A poem on Hindu social reform.] pp. 16. મુંબઈ ૧૮૬૫ [*Bombay*, 1865.] 16°. **14148. d. 8.(3.)**

DOSĀBHAĪ FRĀMJĪ KARĀKĀ. Travels in Great Britain by Dosabhoy Framjee (ગરેટ બરીટન બાતેની મુસાફરી) [Greṭ Briṭan bātenī musāpharī.] pp. xx. 314. *Bombay*, 1861. 4°. **14146. h. 10.**

DOSĀBHAĪ HORMASJĪ BĀMJĪ. સંસાર કોષ *etc.* (Sansár kosh, or a Gujrati-English vocabulary of articles of commerce and general utility. Compiled by Dosabhui Hormasji Bumji.) pp. 95. *Bombay*, 1875. 12°. **14150. a. 32.**

DOSĀBHAĪ SOHRĀBJĪ. Idiomatical Sentences in the English, Hindostanee, Goozratee and Persian languages, in six parts ... by Dossabhaee Sorabjee. *Bombay*, 1843. 4°. **753. k. 5.**

—— A new self-instructing work entitled Idiomatic Sentences, in the English, Gujarati, Hindustani, and Persian languages, ... in seven parts. [Enlarged from the first edition of D.S.'s Idiomatic Sentences.] With notes explanatory and illustrative, to which are added copious vocabularies ... by Bahmanji Dosabhai, Munshi. With a memoir of the late Mr. D. S. pp. xviii. 427, 290. *Bombay*, 1873. 4°. **752. k. 11.**

DOSSABHAEE SORABJEE. *See* DOSĀBHAĪ SOHRĀBJĪ.

DUKĀḶ. दुकाळनो गरबो [Dukāḷno garbo. A poem on the scarcity of grain during the famine of 1876.] pp. 16. સુરત ૧૯૩૩ [*Surat*, 1877.] 16°. **14148. d. 13.(11.)**

DUNJEEBHOY NOUROJEE. *See* DHANJĪBHĀĪ NAVAROJĪ.

EDALJĪ DĀDĀBHAĪ MISTRI. ગુલ અને બુલબુલ [Gul ane Bulbul. A drama in two acts.] pp. 23. મુંબઈ ૧૮૮૦ [*Bombay*, 1880.] 12°. **14148. c. 10.(1.)**

EDALJĪ DĀRĀBJĪ JĀMĀSP ĀSĀVĀLĀ. *See* PESHOTAN BAHRĀMJĪ SAÑJĀNĀ. તફસીરે ગાહે ગાસાની [Tafsīr i gāh i gāsānī. A refutation of the Farmān i dīn of E. D. J. Ā.] [1867.] 8°. **14144. i. 26.**

EDALJĪ DOSĀBHAĪ. The history of Guzerat, compiled by Eduljee Dossabhoy. (ગુજરાતના ઈતિહાસ) pp. 149, *lith. Ahmedabad*, 1850. 8°. **14146. h. 7.**

EDALJĪ FRĀMJĪ DHOṆḌĪ. સીતમે હસરત અને નેકીએ નેકબખ્ત યાને કરણી તેવી પારઊતરણી. [Sitam i hasrat. A drama in four acts on the triumph of good over evil.] pp. 111. મુંબઈ ૧૮૮૧ [*Bombay*, 1881.] 8°. **14148. c. 16.**

EDALJĪ JAMSHEDJĪ KHORĪ. જાલેમ જોર [Jālem jor, *i.e.* Ẕālim zor. A drama in five acts.] pp. 108. મુંબઈ ૧૮૭૬ [*Bombay*, 1876.] 8°. **14148. c. 10.(2.)**

—— Popular natural history in the Guzeratee language in four volumes. Compiled . . . by Edaljee Jamsetjee Khory. Volume i. (પ્રાણીવિદ્યા) [Prāṇividyā.] pp. x. 240. *Bombay*, 1880. 4°. **14146. d. 8.**

EDALJĪ KERSĀSPJĪ ĀNṬIYĀ. જરતોશ્તી ધર્મ શિક્ષક [Zartoshtī dharma ṣikshaka. A catechism of the Zoroastrian religion. Second edition.] pp. 80. મુંબઈ ૧૮૮૦ [*Bombay*, 1880.] 12°. **14144. h. 4.**

EDMUND. એદમંદ વીશેની વારતા [Edmund visheni vārtā.] History of Edmund. [A Christian tract.] pp. 32. સુરત ૧૮૬૧ [*Surat*, 1861.] 12°. **14144. a. 2.(10.)**

EDULJEE DOSSABHOY. *See* EDALJĪ ḌOSĀBHĀĪ.

EKVĪS NASKO. એકવીસ નસ્કો [Ekvīs nasko, or the contents of 21 Zoroastrian sacred books which have been lost.] *See* ARDĀ VIRĀF. અર્દા વિરાફ નામું [Ardā Virāf-nāmuṉ.] [1885.] 8°. **14144. i. 15.**

ELPHINSTONE (*Hon.* MOUNTSTUART). The history of India, the Hindu and Mahomedan periods, by the Hon. M. E., translated into Gujaráti, (from his Marathi version of 1862,) by Vishvanáth Náráyan Mandlik. Introduction. (હિન્દસ્થાનનો ઇતિહાસ) [Hindusthānano itihāsa.] pp. xii. 370. *Bombay*, 1862. 8°. **14146. g. 9.**

This part is a translation of Vol. III. of the Marathi version, i.e. of the first three books of the original.

ENCOURAGEMENT. देशी कारीगरीने उत्तेजन [Deṣī kārīgarīne uttejana.] Encouragement to native industry. 2 pt. અમદાવાદ ૧૮૭૬-૭૭ [*Ahmadabad*, 1876-77.] 12°. **14146. c. 15.**

Pt. I. is of the 2nd edition.

EPHEMERIDES. સંવત ૧૯૪૪ ના ચૈતરથી સંવત ૧૯૪૫ ના ફાગણ સુધીનું પંચાંગ. [A Jain almanac for the Ṣaka year 1810, or 1888-89 A.D.] [*Ahmadabad*, 1888.] *s. sh. fol.* **14003. e. 2.(8.)**

ERACHJĪ SOHRĀBJĪ MEHRJĪRĀṆĀ. રેહબરે દીને જરથુશતી [Rahbar i dīn i Zartoshtī. Outlines of the Zoroastrian religion, in the form of a catechism.] pp. viii. 232. મુંબઈ ૧૨૩૮ [*Bombay*, 1869.] 8°. **14144. i. 12.**

EUCLID. ભૂમિતિનાં મૂળતત્વોના પેહેલા છ સ્કંધો [Bhūmitināṉ mūḷatattva. Lardner's "First six books of the elements of Euclid," translated by J. Graham, with the assistance of Nandaṣaṅkaya Tulajāṣaṅkara.] 2 pt. મુંબઈ ૧૮૬૬-૫૯ [*Bombay*, 1866-59.] 8°. **14146. c. 20.**

Pt. i. is of the 2nd edition.

EXISTENCE. દેવસિદ્ધાંત [Devasiddhānta.] The existence and attributes of God. [A Christian tract.] pp. 51. સુરત ૧૮૫૨ [*Surat*, 1852.] 12°. **14144. a. 2.(1.)**

F. B. The folk-lore of Gujarat: being legends and stories of the prince and peasantry of Gujarat and Kathiavad, from oral tradition only. (ગુજરાત તથા કાઠીઆવાડ દેશની વારતા) Pt. ii. and iii. *Bombay*, 1874. 12°. **14148. a. 32.**

Imperfect; wanting pt. I.

FAKĪRBHĀĪ KĀṢĪDĀSA. *See* HARIṢAṄKARA MEHTĀ. છેલની વારતા [Chhelnī vārtā. Edited by F. K.] [1875.] 8°. **14148. e. 6.**

—— —— [1886.] 8°. **14148. b. 37.**

—— गुजराती चोथी चोपडीना अर्थ [Gujarātī chothī chopaḍīnā artha. A glossary to T. C. Hope's "Gujarati Fourth Book," with a brief account of Gujarat.] pp. 80. સુરત ૧૮૮૦ [*Surat*, 1880.] 12°. **14150. a. 2.(4.)**

FERDUSI. *See* FIRDAUSĪ.

FIRDAUSĪ. *See* BARJORJĪ PĀLANJĪ and PĀLANJĪ BARJORJĪ. History of the Sassanides: . . . collated from the works of . . . Ferdusi, and other authors, *etc.* 1880. 8°. **14146. h. 5.**

FLOWER GATHERERS. ફુલ વીણનારી છોકરીઓની વાત. The Flower gatherers. [Phula vīṇanārī chhokrionī vāt. A Christian tract.] pp. 33. સુરત ૧૮૬૨ [*Surat*, 1862.] 16°. **14144. a. 14.**

FORBES (ALEXANDER KINLOCH). *See* GOPĀLAJĪ TRIBHUVANADĀSA. ગુજરાત દેશનો ઇતિહાસ. [Gujarāt deṣano itihāsa. Compiled from A.K.F.'s "Râs Mâlâ."] [1875.] 12°. **14146. f. 13.(1.)**

—— *See* KRISHṆAJĪ. The Ratna Mālā. Translated by . . . A. K. F. [1868.] 8°. **760. d. 31.**

FORBES (ALEXANDER KINLOCH). Rás Málá; translated into Gujaráti ... by Ranachhodabhái Udayarám. With a memoir of the author by Mansukharám Suryarám ... With illustrations from drawings by the author. Vol. I. (रासमाळा) pp. xii. xliii. 551. *Bombay,* 1869. 8°. **14146. h. 6.**

—— Râs Mâlâ; रासमाला or Hindoo annals of the Province of Goozerat, in Western India. ... With illustrations, principally architectural, from drawings by the author. 2 vol. *London,* 1856. 8°. **9056. g.**

FRĀMJĪ ASFANDIYĀRJĪ. *See* ZAND-AVASTĀ. The Vandidád Sádé ... with a Gujaráti translation, paraphrase and comment ... By ... Frámjí Aspandiárjí. 1842. 8°. **761. f. 1, 2.**

—— —— The Vispard ... with a Gujaráti translation, paraphrase, and comment ... By ... Frámjí Aspandiárjí. 1843. 8°. **761. f. 5.**

—— —— The Yaçna ... with a Gujaráti translation, paraphrase, and comment ... By ... Frámjí Aspandiárjí. 1843. 8°. **761. f. 3.**

FRĀMJĪ DĪNSHĀJĪ PĪṬĪṬ. મુંબઈથી યૂરોપ તરફના પ્રવાસની નોંધ પત્રીકા [Mumbaithī Yurop tarafnā pravāsnī nondh patrikā. A diary of a journey made from Bombay to Europe in 1881.] 2nd edition. pp. xv. 352. મુંબઈ ૧૮૮૪ [*Bombay,* 1884.] 8°. **14146. h. 11.**

—— યૂરોપ, અમેરીકા, જાપાન અને ચીન તરફની મુસાફરીની નોંધ [Yūrop ... tarafnī musāfirīnī nondh. An account of travels in Europe, America, Japan and China.] pp. xxvii. 623. મુંબાઈ ૧૮૮૯ [*Bombay,* 1889.] 8°. **14146. g. 23.**

FRĀMJĪ KĀVASJĪ MEHETĀ. *See* ZAND-AVASTĀ. પાક ખોરદેહ અવસતા [Khurdah Avastā. Edited with a translation in Gujarati by F. K. M.] [1881.] 32°. **761. a. 20.**

FRĀMJĪ MINUCHEHRJĪ JĀMĀSP ĀSĀJĪNĀ. જરથોશતી ધર્મ બોધ [Zartoshtī dharma bodha. Lessons on the Zoroastrian religion for Parsi children.] Pt. I. pp. vi. 66. મુંબઈ ૧૮૮૦ [*Bombay,* 1880.] 12°. **14144. h. 3.**

—— [Second edition.] pp. vi. 66. ૧૮૮૨ [*Bombay,* 1882.] 12°. **14144. h. 6.**

FYVIE (WILLIAM). *See* BIBLE. પુરાતન સ્થાપનાનું પુસ્તક ... The Holy Scriptures in Gujarati. [The translation by Messrs. Skinner and Fyvie.] 1861. 8°. **3068. bb. 19.**

—— —— Old Testament.—*Pentateuch.* પુરાતન સ્થાપનાનું પુસ્તક ... The five books of Moses. [Revised from the translation of Messrs. Skinner and Fyvie.] 1858. 8°. **3670. d. 9.**

—— —— NEW TESTAMENT. આયણ પ્રભુ ... ઈશુ ખ્રીસ્તની नवीन स्थापना ... The New Testament ... translated into the Gujarati language [by Messrs Skinner and Fyvie.] 1857. 12°. **3068. b. 30.**

—— —— *Matthew.* The Gospel according to Matthew ... [Revised by Messrs. Skinner and Fyvie.] 1840. 8°. **3068. bb. 1.**

—— —— *John, Gospel of.* શારા શમાચાર ઈહોનના બનાવેલા. The Gospel of John. [Translated by Messrs. Skinner and Fyvie.] 1842. 8°. **3070. bb. 19.**

—— —— *Acts.* The Acts of the Apostles ... [Translated by Messrs. Skinner and Fyvie.] 1841. 8°. **3068. bb. 4.**

—— A manual for public worship ... મંડલીના ભજનની રીત. [Maṇḍalīnā bhajananī rīta.] pp. 133. *Surat,* 1839. 8°. **14144. a. 19.(1.)**

—— A vocabulary, English and Goojurattee, to which is added a selection of fables, etc. ... ફરહંગ તથા શીખાંમણની પોથી pp. 200. *Surat,* 1828. 8°. **622. f. 8.**

GAJRĀMĀRU. ગજરા મારૂજીની રશીલી વાર્તા. [Gajrāmārujīnī rasīlī vārtā. A popular romance.] pp. 122. iii. अमदावाद १८७७ [*Ahmadabad.* 1877.] 12°. **14148. a. 21.**

—— [Another edition.] pp. 81. अमदावाद १८८० [*Ahmadabad,* 1880.] 12°. **14148, a. 2.(9.)**

GAṆAPATARĀMA RĀJĀRĀMA BHAṬṬA. प्रताप नाटक. *etc.* [Pratāpa nāṭaka. An historical drama on the wars between Pratāpa Siṃha, Raja of Udaipur, and the emperor Akbar of Delhi.] pp. xxiv. 186. અમદાવાદ ૧૮૮૩ [*Ahmadabad,* 1883.] 8°. **14148. c. 22.**

GAṆAPATARĀMA RĀJĀRĀMA MEHETĀ. भरुच जिल्लानो केळवणी खातानो इतिहास [Bharūch jillāno keḷavaṇī khātāno itihāsa. An account in verse of the spread of education in the district of Broach.] pp. 100. અમદાવાદ ૧૯૩૪ [*Ahmadabad*, 1877.] 12°. **14146. f. 12.**

GAṆAPATARĀMA VIṢVANĀTHA. *See* PURĀṆAS.—Padmapurāṇa.—*Rāmāṣvamedha.* ગણુપતરામકૃત રામાશ્વમેધ [Rāmāṣvamedha. Translated into verse by G. V.] [1881.] 8°. **14144. d. 4.**

GAṄGĀDHARA ṢĀSTRĪ PHAḌKE. The Principles of Gujarati grammar, comprising the substance of a Gujarati grammar; written by Gangadhar Shastri Phadake and other Pandits . . . Translated, arranged and briefly illustrated by H. N. Ramsay. pp. iv. ii. 88. *Bombay*, 1842. 8°. **12906. c. 17.**

GAṄGĀṢAṄKARA JAYAṢAṄKARA. *See* KĀLIDĀSA. [*Supposititious works.*] અથ રતિ સ્વયંવર . . . Rati swayamvara . . . Formerly composed [or rather translated] by Kavi Gangashankar Jeyshankar. 1884. 12°. **14148. d. 25.**

—— *See* PURĀṆAS.—Padmapurāṇa.—*Sābhramatīmāhātmya.* साभ्रमती महात्म्य. [Sābhramatīmāhātmya. Translated by G. J.] [1876.] 8°. **14144. d. 3.**

GARBĀVALĪ. બાળ લગન નિષેખક ગરબાવળી [Bāḷalagna nishedhaka garbāvalī. Garbī songs on the evil consequences of child-marriages.] pp. 25. अमदावाद १९३३ [*Ahmadabad*, 1877.] 16°. **14148. d. 6.(8.)**

—— ગરબાવલી [Garbāvalī. A collection of miscellaneous Garbī songs, or ballads usually sung by women.] pp. 37, *lith.* મુંબઈ ૧૮૨૧ [*Bombay*, 1864.] 16°. **14148. d. 6.(1.)**

—— મનોરંજક ગરબાવળી. [Manorañjaka garbāvalī. Another collection of songs.] pp. 88. अमदावाद १८७५ [*Ahmadabad*, 1875.] 16°. **14148. d. 6.(2.)**

—— સ્ત્રી મનોરંજક ગરબાવળી [Strī manorañjaka garbāvaḷī. A collection of songs usually sung by women.] pp. 70. અમદાવાદ ૧૮૮૦ [*Ahmadabad*, 1880.] 12°. **14148. d. 6.(7.)**

—— [Another edition of the preceding.] pp. 66. અમદાવાદ ૧૮૮૧ [*Ahmadabad*, 1881.] 12°. **14148. d. 6.(8.)**

GAṬṬŪLĀLA GHANAṢYĀMAJĪ. *See* PERIODICAL PUBLICATIONS. — *Bombay.* આર્યસમુદય Aryasamudaya. [A monthly literary periodical, edited by G. Gh.] [1888, *etc.*] 8°. **14150. c. 13.**

GAṬṬU LĀLAJĪ. *See* GOVARDHANA LĀLAJĪ, also called GAṬṬU LĀLAJĪ.

GAURĪṢAṄKARA PRABHĀṢAṄKARA. गरबावळी (વડોદરા કેળવણી ખાતાને માટે). [Garbāvaḷī. A collection of Garbi songs by various authors. Compiled by G. P.] pp. 31. અમદાવાદ ૧૮૭૭ [*Ahmadabad*, 1877.] 16°. **14148. d. 6.(5.)**

GĀYANAPRAKĀRA. અથ શ્રી ગાયનપ્રકાર પ્રારંભઃ [Gāyanaprakāra. A collection of love songs, and miscellaneous poems.] pp. 13, *lith.* [*Surat*, 1860 ?] 16°. **14148. d. 4.(1.)**

—— ગાયન પ્રકાર. [Another and a larger collection of songs.] pp. 47. સુરત ૧૮૭૭ [*Surat*, 1877.] 12°. **14148. d. 1.(7.)**

GEIKIE (ARCHIBALD). Science primers in Gujarati. Physical Geography by Professor A. G. Translated into Gujarati by Rao Saheb Mahipatram R. Nilkanth. (भूगोळ विद्या.) [Bhūgolavidyā] pp. ii. 114. *Bombay*, 1880. 16°. **14146. c. 13.**

GHELĀBHĀĪ LĪLĀDHARA. જૈન વિવેક વાણી યાને જૈન ધર્મ સાર સંગ્રહ. [Jaina viveka vāṇī, or Jainadharma sārasaṅgraha. A collection of Jain prayers in Prakrit, with Gujarati explanations, and of Jain prayers and songs in Gujarati by various authors. Compiled by Gh. L.] Pt. I. મુંબઈ ૧૮૮૮ [*Bombay*, 1888, *etc.*] 8°.
In progress. **14144. g. 26.**

GHULĀM MUHAMMAD, *Rānderī.* ખીરસતી અને મોહંમદી ધરમનો ચુકાદો. [Khristī ane Mohammadī dharmano chukādo. Muhammadan arguments against Christianity.] pp. 34. સુરત ૧૩૦૫ હીજરી. [*Surat*, 1888.] 8°. **14144. b.**

GINWALLA (N. S.) *See* NASARVĀNJĪ SHEHRIYĀRJĪ GINWĀLĀ.

GIRDHARA. गिरधरकृत रामायण. [Rāmāyaṇa. An abridged translation in verse.] pp. 320. અમદાવાદ ૧૮૮૧ [*Ahmadabad*, 1881.] 8°. **14148. f. 11.**

GIRDHARALĀLA HARAKISANDĀSA. શ્રીમદ ગોસ્વામી શ્રીજીવનલાલજી મહારાજનું જન્મ ચરિત્ર. [Ṣrī Jīvanalālajī Mahārājanuṉ janmacharitra. A poem on the life of Jīvanalāla, a Vaishṇava Raja of the Vallabha sect.] pp. 30. મુંબઈ ૧૮૮૦ [*Bombay*, 1880.] 12°. **14148. d. 2.(7.)**

GIRDHARALĀLA HARIVALLABHADĀSA and **KEṢAVALĀLA RAṆCHHOḌḌĀSA JOṢĪ.** स्वदेश हितदर्शक. [Svadeṣa hitadarṣaka. A treatise in prose and verse on progress in trade and education, and on the reform of moral and social evils.] pp. 76. अमदावाद १९३३ [*Ahmadabad*, 1877.] 16°. **14146. e. 8.(1.)**

GIRIJĀṢAṄKARA MULJĪ. बाळलग्नथी बनती बिना [Bāḷalagnathī bantī binā. A poem on the evil consequences of early marriage institutions.] pp. 186. अमदावाद १९३३ [*Ahmadabad*, 1877.] 16°. **14148. d. 19.**

GĪTAGRANTHA. ગીતગ્રંથ. [Gītagrantha. Christian hymns, both original and translations from the English.] pp. 84. શુરત૧૮૫૮ [*Surat*, 1858.] 12°. **14144. a. 2.(5.)**

GLASGOW (JAMES). *See* BIBLE.—Old Testament.—*Psalms*. The Psalms of David, translated into Gujarati verse . . . by J. G. 1856. 12°. **3089. bb.**

GOKAḶDĀSA VIṬHALADĀSA SARAIYĀ. *See* BOMBAY, *Presidency of.—Court of Ṣadr Dīwānī 'Adālat.* Borradaile's Gujarát Caste Rules, *etc.* [Vol. II. edited by G. V. S.] 1884-87. 8°. **14146. a. 14.**

GOKULAJĪ SAMPATHIRĀMA JHĀLĀ. *Life.* *See* MANASUKHARĀMA SŪRYARĀMA TRIPĀṬHĪ. सुज्ञ गोकुलजी संपत्तिराम झाला:

GOOD TIDINGS. શરવ લોકને શાડ્ર વધામણી. Good tidings. [Sarva lokane sādu vadhāmaṇī. A Christian tract.] pp. 24. શુરત ૧૮૫૯ [*Surat*, 1859.] 12°. **14144. a. 2.(7.)**

GOPĀLAJĪ TRIBHUVANADĀSA. ગુજરાત દેશનો ઈતિહાસ [Gujarāt deṣano itihāsa. A short history of the Province of Gujarat, taken from A. K. Forbes' "Râs mâlâ."] pp. 62. મુંબઈ ૧૯૩૧ [*Bombay*, 1875.] 12°. **14146. f. 13.(1.)**

GOSHT i FRYĀNO. ગોશ્તે ફ્રયાનો [Gosht i Fryāno. A Zoroastrian story showing the conquest of good over evil.] *See* ARDĀ VIRĀF. અર્દા વિરાફ નામું [Ardā Virāf-nāmuṇ.] [1885.] 8°. **14144. i. 15.**

GOVARDHANADĀSA LAKSHMĪDĀSA. મલ્હાર-વિરહ શતક [Malhār-viraha ṣataka. One hundred stanzas on the trial and deposition of Malhār Rāva, Gaikwar of Baroda.] pp. 24, *lith.* પુના ૧૯૩૨ [*Poona*, 1875.] 12°. **14148. d. 13.(4.)**

GOVARDHANA LĀLAJĪ, also called **GAṬṬU LĀLAJĪ.** Cutch Mahodaya or Address to . . . Shree Khengarji Bahadur on his enstallation [*sic*] from the people of Cutch . . . A.C. 1884. कच्छमहोदय. [A Sanskrit poem, accompanied by a Gujarati prose translation by Mūlaṣaṅkara Rāmajī. Followed by five other Sanskrit poems on the same subject, entitled Mānapatra, by various authors, with prose translations by Keṣavalāla Harirāma.] pp. 48, 36, 68, ii. मुंबा १८८४ [*Bombay*, 1884.] 8°. **14070. d. 30.**

GOVINDALĀLA BĀLĀJĪ. *See* INDIA.—*High Courts of Judicature.* ઈંડયન લા રીપોર્ટસ. [Indian Law Reports. Translated by G. B.] [1877.] 8°. **14146. a. 3.**

—— *See* INDIA.—*Legislative Council.* દિવાની નવો કાયદો, *etc.* [Diwānī navo kāyado. A summary of the Civil Procedure Code. Translated from the English by G. B.] [1877.] 16°. **14146. a. 1.**

—— —— હિંદુસ્તાનનો પુરાવનો કાયદો. [Hindustānano purāvano kāyado. The Indian Evidence Act. Translated into Gujarati, with a commentary and index by G. B.] [1881.] 8°. **14146. a. 11.**

—— હિંદુશાસ્ત્રની ડાયજેસ્ટ. [Hindu ṣāstranī ḍāyjest. A digest of Hindu Law, containing abstracts of rulings of the High Courts of Calcutta, Bombay, Madras, and the North-West Provinces, from A.D. 1862 to 1877.] pp. xviii. 180. અમદાવાદ ૧૮૭૭ [*Ahmadabad*, 1877.] 16°. **14144. b. 3.**

GRAHAM (JAMES). *See* EUCLID. ભૂમિતિનાં મૂળતત્વોના પેહેલા છ સ્કંધો. [Lardner's Euclid. Translated by J. G.] [1866-59.] 8°. **14146. c. 20.**

GRANT (SIR ALEXANDER) *Bart.* Catalogue of native publications in the Bombay Presidency up to 31st December, 1864. Prepared under orders of Government by Sir A. Grant, Bart. Second edition, with numerous additions and corrections. pp. 35, 239. *Bombay*, 1867. 8°. **752. e. 14.**

GRAY (JAMES). *See* BIBLE.—New Testament.—*Matthew.* पेहेलो भाग मतो जो [The Gospel of Matthew. Translated into Kachhi by J. G.] 1834. 8°. **3070. b. 24.**

GREEN (HENRY) *Superintendent of Government Schools in Gujarat.* A collection of English phrases with their idiomatic Gujarati equivalents. Third edition. pp. 233. *Bombay,* 1858. 8°. **12907. c. 15.**

—— Sixth edition. pp. 233. *Bombay,* 1869. 8°. **12906. c. 25.**

—— Seventh edition. pp. 233. *Bombay,* 1881. 8°. **14150. b, 9.**

GUIDE. A guide to the Moral Class book. [Containing the meanings and derivations of words in English and Gujarati.] pp. 138. *Surat,* 1875. 12°. **14150. a. 31.**

GUJARATI HYMN BOOK. Goojuratee Hymn Book ... ગીતની પોથી [Gītanī pothī.] Second edition. pp. 155. *Surat,* 1839. 12°. **14144. a. 1.(1.)**

GUJARĀTĪ NAVO KHARḌO. ગુજરાતી નવો ખરડો [Gujarātī navo kharḍo. A copy-book in Gujarati and Devanagari characters.] pp. 48. મુંબઈ [*Bombay,* 1875 ?] 12°. **14150. a. 40.**

GUJARATI TREATISE. A Goojrat,hee treatise on the management of schools. (निशाळनी पद्धति) [Niṣāḷnī paddhati.] pp. 40. *Bombay,* 1824. 8°. **14150. b. 4.(1.)**

GULĀBCHAND DAYĀLJĪ and LAKSHMĪDĀSA KAHĀNJĪ ṬHAKKAR. શ્રી આદીશ્વરનો શ્લોકો [Ādīṣvarano ṣloko. An account in verse of the Jain saint Ādinātha.] pp. 16. મુંબઈ ૧૯૪૨ [*Bombay,* 1886.] 12°. **14144. f. 1.(1.)**

GULĀBCHAND LAKSHMĪCHAND. *See* MAHĀBHĀRATA.—*Aṣvamedhaparva.* અશ્વમેધ [Aṣvamedhaparva. A verse translation by G. L.] [1857.] 8°. **14148. f. 2.**

GUṆASUNDARA. *See* NEMICHANDRA. अथ श्रीषष्टिशतक बालावबोध व्याख्या सहित प्रारंभः [Shashṭi ṣataka. With a translation into Gujarati couplets, and a verbal explanation and commentary by G.] [1876, *etc.*] 4°. **14100. e. 3.**

HĀDOKHT NASK. હાદોખ્ત નસ્ક [Hādokht nask, or The efficacy of the Zoroastrian Ashem-vohu prayer.] *See* ARDĀ VIRĀF અર્દા વિરાફ નામું [Ardā Virāf-nāmuṇ.] [1885.] 8°. **14144. i. 15.**

HĀMĪ. *See* NIẒĀM al-DĪN, *Chishtī,* called HĀMĪ.

HAMILTON (W. H.) *See* MANCHERJĪ KĀVASJĪ SHĀPURJĪ LANGRĀNĀ, called MANSUKH. Prince Albert. Selections from the prize translation [into English] of a Gujarati poem ... The translation by W. H. H. 1870. 8°. **14148. f. 8.**

HAMSARATNA MUNI. अथ श्री उपमितिभवप्रपंच वार्त्तिकरूपं लिख्यते [Upamiti bhavaprapañcha. Legendary stories inculcating Jain virtues; being a Gujarati translation from H. M.'s prose abridgment of Siddharshi Gaṇi's original Sanskrit work in verse, which is said to consist of 16,002 *slokas.*] *See* BHĪMASIMHA MĀṆAKA. प्रकरण-रत्नाकर [Prakaraṇa-ratnākara.] Vol. i. pp. 439-582. [1876, *etc.*] 4°. **14100. e. 3**

HARAGOVINDA AMATHĀRĀMA JOSĪ. શ્રી વીશ્વકર્માયનમોસ્તુ. સીલ્પકર્મ. શુથારોના નીત્યનેમનેસારૂ. [Ṣilpakarma. A compilation of invocatory Sanskrit verses to be addressed by artificers to the god Viṣvakarmā, with rubrical directions in Gujarati.] pp. 8. સુરત ૧૮૮૭ [*Surat,* 1887.] 16°. **14028. b.**

The Sanskrit verses are in Gujarati characters.

HARAGOVINDA DVĀRAKĀDĀSA KĀNṬĀWĀLĀ. *See* PRĀCHĪNA KĀVYA. प्राचीन काव्य [Prāchīna kāvya. Edited, with copious notes, by H. D. K.] [1885, *etc.*] 8°. **14148. e. 12.**

—— अंधेरी नगरीनो गर्धवसेन [Andherī nagarīno gardhavasena. A tale descriptive of the disorder prevailing in mismanaged Native States.] pp. 280. અમદાવાદ ૧૮૮૧ [*Ahmadabad,* 1881.] 8°. **14148. b. 21.**

—— गुजरात वर्नेक्युलर सोसाईटीना हेतु, तेनो उपयोग etc. [Gujarāt Varnākyular Sosāiṭinā hetu, *etc.* A tract on the objects, use and advantages of the Gujarati Vernacular Society.] pp. 12. अमदावाद १८८३ [*Ahmadabad,* 1883.] 12° **14146. e. 9.(1.)**

—— राणी रूपसुंदरी [Rāṇī Rūpasundarī. An historical novel.] pp. 82. अमदावाद [*Ahmadabad,* 1885.] 12°. **14148. a. 9.(2.)**

HARAGOVINDA KEṢAVALĀLA SHĀH. *See* PARAMĀNANDADĀSA BHOḶĀBHĀĪ PĀREKH. गायकवाडी राज्यनो इतिहास [Gāyakavāḍī rājyano itihāsa. Compiled with the assistance of H. K. Sh.] [1877.] 12°. **14146. f. 21.**

HARAJĪVANADĀSA GOVINDARĀMA and DĀMAJĪ MAKANDĀSA. गोहिल राज्यनो इतिहास. भाग २ लो. संस्थान भावनगर [Gohil rājyano itihāsa. An account of the administration of the Gohelwar division of the Kathiawar Agency. Pt. I. The Bhaunagar State.] pp. vii. 126. અમદાવાદ ૧૮૮૦ [*Ahmadabad*, 1880.] 12°. **14146. f. 11.**

HARAJĪVANA UTTAMARĀMA MEHETĀ. *See* NĀRĀYAṆA BĀPUJĪ KĀNIṬKAR. Malharrao Maharaj. A historical drama . . . Translated into Gujrathi by Harjivan Uttamram Meheta. [1876.] 12°. **14148. c. 6.**

HARAKISANDĀSA HARAJĪVANADĀSA. અથ શ્રી જૈનધર્મ દીલખુશ સ્તવનાવલી [Jainadharma dil-khush stavanāvalī. Hymns in praise of Jain saints. Compiled by H. H.] pp. 37, *lith.* મુંબઈ ૧૯૩૩ [*Bombay*, 1876.] 12°. **14144. f. 4.(5.)**

HARARĀYA BĀPUBHĀĪ DEṢĀI. અનાવિલ ગ્રહસ્થોમાં થયલા નવા નિયમો [Anāvil grihasthomāṉ thayelā navā niyamo. Rules for the reduction of marriage expenses, for the performance of funeral rites and other matters in connection with the Anāvil caste, which were passed at a meeting of the Anāvil Hitechchhu Maṇḍalī. Signed by H. B. D. as President of that Society.] pp. 14. સુરત ૧૮૮૮ [*Surat*, 1888.] 8°. **14146. e.**

HARIKṚISHṆA BAḶADEVA BHAṬṬA. काव्यनिमज्जन [Kāvyanimajjana. Extracts from the writings of popular poets of Gujarat, with a vocabulary, and explanations of difficult words and phrases.] pp. x. 276, 12. સુરત ૧૮૮૭ [*Surat*, 1887.] 8°. **14148. e. 18.**

HARILĀLA HARSADRĀYA DHRUVA. *See* MUGDHĀVABODHA AUKTIKA. The Mugdhâvabodha auktika, or A grammar . . . of the Gujerati language . . . Edited by H. H. Dh. 1889. 8°. **14150. b. 20.**

HARILĀLA MOHANALĀLA. ભૂગોળનો ઉપયોગ કરવાની રીતિનો ગ્રંથ [Bhūgoḷano upayoga karvānī rītino grantha. A catechism on geography.] pp. 34. મુંબઈ ૧૯૨૩ [*Bombay*, 1863.] 12°. **14146. f. 9.**

HARIṢAṄKARA MEHETĀ. છેલની વારતા [Chhelnī vārtā. Tales in verse, edited by Fakīrbhāī Kāṣīdāsa. Second edition.] pp. 264. अमदावाद १८७५ [*Ahmadabad*, 1875.] 8°. **14148. e. 6.**

—— [Another edition.] pp. 256. मुंबई १८८६ [*Bombay*, 1886.] 8°. **14148. b. 37.**

HARIṢCHANDRA, *Rājā.* હરીચંદ્ર આખ્યાન [Harichandrākhyāna. A poem on the story of king Hariṣchandra.] pp. 142, *lith.* મુંબઈ ૧૭૭૭ [*Bombay*, 1855.] 16°. **14148. d. 1.(2.)**

HARLEZ (CHARLES DE) *See* ZAND-AVASTĀ. Yaçna and the Gathas . . . from "Avesta, livre sacre du Zoroastrisme . . . par C. de H," *etc.* 1885. 12°. **14144. i. 11.**

HARSADRĀYA SUNDARALĀLA. ધીરા મારૂજીની વારતા [Dhīrā Mārujīnī vārtā. A tale in prose and verse on the adventures of Dhīrā Māru, a prince of Malwa. Translated from the Marwari by H. S.] pp. 128, *lith.* અમદાવાદ ૧૯૩૨ [*Ahmadabad*, 1875.] 12°. **14148. a. 12.**

ḢĀTIM ṬĀ'Ī. હાતમ નામું [Ḣātam-nāmuṉ, or The adventures of Ḣātim Ṭā'ī. A romance, translated from the Persian. Third edition.] pp. 163. મુંબાઈ [*Bombay*, 1887.] 12°. **14148. b. 38.**

HARŪN al-RASHĪD, *Caliph.* હરૂન નાટક [Harūn nāṭaka. A drama in five acts on the life of the Caliph H. al-R.] pp. 92. મુંબઈ [*Bombay*, 1880.] 8°. **14148. c. 10.(3.)**

ḢASAN, *Mīr.* Badraimunir Bainazir. [An Urdu poem by Mīr Ḣasan] translated into Guzeratee verse by N. P. Chistey (Hami). (બદરેમુનીર બેનજીર) pp. 192. *Ahmedabad*, 1879. 12°. **14148. a. 16.**

ḢASAN RAḢMAT ALLĀH. મસજીદ ફસ હલાઈ મેમણ મોહલાની હીસાબ. સંવત ૧૯૦૯ થી ૧૯૩૪ સુધી. [An account of the income and expenses of the mosque in the Halāi Meman quarter of Bombay, from the Samvat year 1909 to 1934.] pp. 343. viii. મુંબઈ ૧૮૮૦ [*Bombay*, 1880]. 8°. **14150. e. 1.**

HAṬṬHI SIMHA. હઠીસિંહકૃત અંજનશિલાકાના ઢાળીયાં [Añjanaṣilākānā ḍhāliyāṉ. Verses on the installation of a Jain idol by H. S., a merchant of Ahmadabad. Followed by several Bāramāsā poems.] pp. 56, *lith.* મુંબાપુરી ૧૯૪૦ [*Bombay*, 1884.] 16°. **14144. f. 12.(3.)**

HEMACHANDRA ĀCHĀRYA. અથ શ્રી રામ ચરીત્ર પારંભતે [Rāmacharitra, or The story of Rāma and Lakshmaṇa.] *See* JAINAṢĀSTRA. જૈન સાસ્ત્ર કથા સંગ્રહ. [Jainaṣāstra kathāsaṅgraha.] [1883.] 8°. **14144. g. 8.**

HEMACHANDRA ĀCHĀRYA. [Rāmacharitra. Another edition.] *See* NĀTHĀBHĀI LALUBHĀI. જૈન કાવ્ય સાર સંગ્રહ. [Jainakāvya sārasangraha.] pp. 1-169. [1882.] 8°. **14144. g. 23.**

HIKĀYAT i LATĪF. *See* MĀṆEKJĪ DĀDĀBHĀĪ ARJĀNĪ. A glossary of words occurring in Hikayat-e-latif, *etc.* 1888. 8°. **757. f. 29.(2.)**

—— *See* NAVAROJĪ ĀDARJĪ TĀTĀ. A glossary of words occurring in Hékáyet-e-latif, *etc.* 1884. 12°. **757. cc. 5.(2.)**

HINDUISM. Questions on Hinduism. હીંદુઓને શારૂ અરાડ અરાડ માણકાની માલા [Hinduone sādu arāḍ arāḍ māṇkānī mālā. In 5 chapters, each containing 18 questions. A Christian tract.] pp. 70. શુરત ૧૮૫૯ [*Surat,* 1859.] 12°. **14144. a. 2.(6.)**

HINDUS. The touchstone of truth and falsehood; conversations between two Hindus on Hinduism and Christianity. શત તથા અશતની પરીક્ષા [Ṣat tathā aṣatnī parīkshā.] pp. 121. *Engl.* and *Guj. Bombay,* 1852. 12°. **14144. a. 9.**

One of the Bombay Tract and Book Society's Series.

HĪRĀCHAND KĀNJĪ. *See* AKHĀ. Works of Brahmadnyani Akhabhakta ... Published [with an introductory preface in Gujarati] by H. K. [1864.] 8°. **14148. e. 19.**

—— *See* JASVAT SIṂHA, *Maharaja.* Bhashabhushan ... with Luptopama vilasa ... and Upama sangraha, with commentaries in Gujarati ... by Kavi H. K. 1866. 12°. **14158. c. 8.**

—— *See* MANORADĀSA, called SACHCHIDĀNANDA BRAHMATĪRTHA. सनत्सुजातीय आख्यान *etc.* [Sanatsujātīya ākhyāna. Edited by H. K.] [1864.] 8°. **14148. b. 3.(2.)**

—— ગાયન શતક (Gayan Shatak by Kavi Hirachand Kanji.) [Miscellaneous poems.] 3 pt. *Bombay,* 1863-65. 16°. **14148. d. 3.**

Pts. i. and ii. are of the 2nd edition.

—— Gujrati Koshavali, or A garland of 13 Gujrati lexicons. Compiled by Kavi Hirachand Kanji. કોશાવળી ગુજરાતી કોશ ૧૩ ની pp. viii. xxi. 322. *Bombay,* 1865. 12°. **14150. a. 39.**

—— Koomarika bodha. Instructions to girls by Kavi Hirachand Kanji. કુમારિકા બોધ *etc.* 2nd edition. pp. iv. 42. *Bombay,* 1864. 16°. **14148. d. 8.(2.)**

HĪRĀCHAND KĀNJĪ. કુમાર બોધ [Kumāra bodha. Moral and instructive poems for boys.] pp. viii. v. 30. મુંબઈ ૧૮૬૩ [*Bombay,* 1863.] 16°. **14148. d. 8.(1.)**

—— Nāmārtha-bodha, or Explanation of names applied to men according to their natures, by Kavi Hirāchand Kānji. નામાર્થ બોધ *etc.* pp. 95. *Bombay,* 1864. 16°. **14148. d. 10.**

—— Vairágbodha. [Verses on the renunciation of worldly pleasures.] વૈરાગ બોધ. pp. 16. મુબઈ ૧૯૨૧ [*Bombay,* 1865.] 16°. **14148. d. 8.(4.)**

HĪRAJĪ HAṂSARĀJA. विवेकसार [Vivekasāra. A treatise on the Jain religion, with an account of the lives of Jain saints, and a collection of Jain hymns.] pp. 232. बनारस १८७९ [*Benares,* 1879.] 8°. **14144. g. 20.**

HOMER. Pope's Homer's Iliad. Book I. Containing meanings ... and explanation of numerous words, phrases and sentences both in English and Gujrati. Together with a useful portion of mathematical geography [in English]. pp. 74. *Surat,* 1875. 16°. **14150. a. 2.(1.)**

—— Notes [in English with occasional equivalents in Gujarati] on the Fourth Book of Pope's Homer's Iliad. pp. 75. *Bombay,* 1881. 12°. **14150. a. 1.(5.)**

HOPE (THEODORE CRACRAFT). ભૂગોળવિદ્યા [Bhūgoḷavidyā. An elementary geography.] 2 pt. મુંબઈ, અમદાવાદ, ૧૮૬૮-૬૩ [*Bombay, Ahmadabad,* 1868-63.] 12°. **14146. f. 7.**

Pt. i. is of the 8th, and Pt. ii. of the 3rd edition.

—— ગુજરાતી ભાષાનું વ્યાકરણ [Gujarātī bhāshānuṇ vyākaraṇa. A Gujarati grammar for the use of vernacular schools. Second edition.] pp. iv. 47. મુંબઈ ૧૮૬૦ [*Bombay,* 1860.] 12°. **14150. a. 37.**

—— [Fourth edition.] pp. 44. મુંબઈ ૧૮૬૪ [*Bombay,* 1864.] 12°. **14150. a. 36.**

—— [Fifth edition.] pp. 44. મુંબઈ ૧૮૬૭ [*Bombay,* 1867.] 12°. **14150. a. 35.**

—— [Sixth edition.] pp. 44. મુંબઈ ૧૮૭૦ [*Bombay,* 1870.] 12°. **14150. a. 38.**

HOPE (Theodore Cracraft). પેહેલી ચોપડી [Pehelī chopaḍī. Gujarati First Book.] pp. 52. મુંબઈ ૧૮૬૦ [*Bombay*, 1860.] 16°. **14150. a. 3.**

—— [Third edition.] pp. 52. મુંબઈ ૧૮૬૩ [*Bombay*, 1863.] 16°. **14150. a. 4.**

—— Gujaráti First Book. (ગુજરાતી પેહેલી ચોપડી) Twelfth edition. pp. 52. *Bombay*, 1877. 16°. **14150. a. 24.(2.)**

—— હોપ શાહેબની બનાવેલી ગુજરાતી પેહેલી ચોપડીના અગરેજી તથા ગુજરાતી અર્થ. [Gujarātī peheli chopaḍīnā . . . artha. A vocabulary of difficult words occurring in T. C. H.'s Gujarati First Book.] pp. 15. મુંબઈ ૧૮૮૧ [*Bombay*, 1881.] 16°. **14150. a. 26.(10.)**

—— બીજી ચોપડી [Bījī chopaḍī. Gujarātī Second Book.] pp. vi. 68. મુંબઈ ૧૮૬૦ [*Bombay*, 1860.] 12°. **14150. a. 5.**

—— Fourth edition. pp. vi. 58. મુંબઈ ૧૮૬૫ [*Bombay*, 1865.] 12°. **14150. a. 6.**

—— Gujarati Second Book. (ગજરાતી બીજી ચોપડી) Ninth edition. pp. ix. 62. *Bombay*, 1874. 12°. **14150. a. 7.**

—— ત્રીજી ચોપડી [Trījī chopaḍī. Gujarati Third Book.] pp. viii. 114. મુંબઈ ૧૮૬૧ [*Bombay*, 1861.] 12°. **14150. a. 8.**

—— —— [Another edition.] pp. viii. 100. મુંબઈ ૧૮૬૩ [*Bombay*. 1863.] 12°. **14150. a. 9.**

—— Gujaráti Third Book. Seventh edition. pp. xi. 114. *Bombay*, 1874. 12°. **14150. a. 10.**

—— ચોથી ચોપડી [Chothī chopaḍī. Gujarati Fourth Book.] pp. viii. 151. મુંબઈ ૧૮૬૦ [*Bombay*, 1860.] 12°. **14150. a. 11.**

—— [A reprint.] મુંબઈ ૧૮૬૦ [*Bombay*, 1862.] 12°. **14150. a. 12.**

—— Gujarati Fourth Book. (ગુજરાતી ચોથી ચોપડી.) Eighth edition. pp. viii. 154. *Bombay*, 1874. 12°. **14150. a. 13.**

—— Eleventh edition. pp. viii. 154. *Bombay*, 1879. 12°. **14150. a. 14.**

—— *See* Fakīrbhāī Kāsīdāsa. **गुजराती चोथी चोपडीना अर्थ** [Gujarātī chothī chopaḍīnā artha. A glossary to T. C. H.'s "Gujarati Fourth Book."] [1880.] 12°. **14150. a. 2.(4.)**

HOPE (Theodore Cracraft). પાંચમી ચોપડી [Pāñchmī chopaḍī. Gujarātī Fifth Book.] pp. vi. 180. મુંબઈ ૧૮૬૦ [*Bombay*, 1860.] 12°. **14150. a. 15.**

—— Gujaráti Fifth Book. (ગુજરાતી પાંચમી ચોપડી) Twelfth edition. pp. vii. 186. *Bombay*, 1880. 12°. **14150. a. 16.**

—— છઠી ચોપડી [Chhaṭhī chopaḍī. Gujarati Sixth Book.] pp. vii. 244. મુંબઈ ૧૮૬૧ [*Bombay*, 1861.] 12°. **14150. a. 17.**

—— સાતમી ચોપડી [Sātamī chopaḍī. Gujarati Seventh Book.] pp. iv. 284. મુંબઈ ૧૮૬૧ [*Bombay*, 1861.] 12°. **14150. b. 5.**

—— Gujarati Seventh Book, *etc.* ગુજરાતી સાતમી ચોપડી) Sixth edition. pp. iv. 245. *Bombay*, 1875. 8°. **14150. b. 12.**

HORMASJĪ KHURSHEDJĪ. વ્યાકરણ [Vyākaraṇa. An elementary Gujarati grammar.] pp. 34. મુંબઈ ૧૮૮૦ [*Bombay*, 1880.] 12°. **14150. a. 26.(7.)**

HORMASJĪ PĀLANJĪ MEHRJĪ. કુદરતી એલમે ઈલાહી [Kudratī ilm i Ilāhī. Lessons in natural history.] pp. 130. મુંબઈ ૧૮૭૫ [*Bombay*, 1875.] 12°. **14144. i. 17.**

HORMASJĪ PESTANJĪ. *See* Bible.—*New Testament.* આયણ પ્રભુ . . . નવીન સ્થાપના . . . The New Testament . . . Revised by Hormusjee Pestonjee, *etc.* 1857. 12°. **3068. b. 30.**

HOWARD (Edward Irving). English Series. Second Book. Part I. (Part II.) Translated into Gujarati (with pronunciations and explanatory notes). અંગ્રેજી બિજી ચોપડી [Angrejī bījī chopaḍī.] pp. 100, 128. *Bombay*, 1865. 12°, 8°. **14150. b. 11.**

Pt. i. is of 12° and pt. ii. of 8° size.

—— A guide to beginners, or the pronunciation and the meanings of English terms, with the meanings of the sentences, occurring in the work entitled the English Primer, by E. I. H. . . . In Gujarati tongue by a student (વિદયાર્થીઓનો મદદગાર). [Vidyārthiono madadgār.] pp. 56. *Bombay*, 1865. 16°. **14150. a. 18.**

—— Howard's English Primer translated into Gujaratee with pronunciation of words. pp. 48. મુંબઈ ૧૮૮૧ [*Bombay*, 1881.] 16°. **14150. a. 26.(8.)**

HOWARD (Edward Irving). Howard's English Primer, literally and idiomatically translated into Gujarati for the use of schools and private students. pp. 68. *Engl.* and *Guj.* *Bombay,* 1881. 16°. **14150. a. 26.(9.)**

A different translation from the preceding, and containing the whole of the English text.

—— [Another edition.] pp. 66. *Ahmedabad,* 1881. 16°. **14150. a. 20.(1.)**

—— Howard's Rudimentary English grammar, translated into Gujarati by Luxminarayan Shionarayan, and revised by T. B. Curtis .... ઈંગ્લિશ વ્યાકરણની મુળપીઠિકા [Ingliṣ vyākaraṇanī mūlapīthikā.] pp. ii. 107. અમદાવાદ ૧૮૬૫ [*Ahmadabad,* 1865.] 12°. **14150. a. 29.**

HUKM MUNIJĪ. अध्यात्म प्रकरण संग्रह [Adhyātma prakaraṇa-saṅgraha. A treatise on the principles of Jain philosophy.] pp. viii. 726. अमदावाद १८८० [*Ahmadabad,* 1880.] 8°. **14144. g. 10.**

—— ज्ञानप्रकाश प्रकरण संग्रह [Jñānaprakāṣa prakaraṇa-saṅgraha. A treatise on Jain religion and philosophy, together with a collection of Jain hymns.] pp. 621. अमदावाद १८८७ [*Ahmadabad,* 1887.] 8°. **14144. g. 25.**

HUMAN DEPRAVITY. શધલાં માણશ ભરશટ તે શંબંધીની વાત [Sadhlāṇ māṇaṣ bharṣaṭ.] Human depravity. [A Christian tract.] pp. 8. ૧૮૫૭ [*Surat,* 1857.] 12°. **14144. a. 1.(8.)**

HUTTON (Charles) *LL.D.* *See* Jervis (G. R.) A course of Mathematics in the Goojratee language. ... Translated from the works of Dr. C. H., *etc.* 1828. 4°. **14146. d. 5.**

ICHASUNKER AMTHARAM VYAS. *See* Ichchhāṣaṅkara Amathārāma Vyāsa.

ICHCHHĀRĀMA SŪRYARĀMA DEṢĀI. ગંગા એક ગુર્જર વાર્તા. (Gangā. A Gurjar tale.) pp. 323. *Bombay,* 1888. 8°. **14148. b. 39.**

—— Hind and Brittania.—A political picture. By Ichharam Suryaram Desai. (હિન્દ અને બ્રિટાનિયા) pp. 32, 239. *Bombay,* 1885. 8°. **14146. f. 2.**

—— Selections from the Gujarati poets. ... Compiled by Itcharam Suryaram Desai (બૃહત્ કાવ્યદોહન) [Bṛihat kāvyadohana.] People's edition. *Bombay,* 1886, *etc.* 8°. **14148. e. 14.**

In progress. To be completed in ten parts. Pt. i. is of the 2nd edition.

ICHCHHĀṢAṄKARA AMATHĀRĀMA VYĀSA. बत्रीसाना बीगाडनी बुमो. [Batrisānā bigāḍnī bumo. An account in verse of disastrous floods at Ahmadabad.] pp. 24. અમદાવાદ ૧૮૭૫ [*Ahmadabad,* 1875.] 16°. **14148. d. 13.(2.)**

—— Jugglery exposed ... by Ichasunker Amtharam Vyas. જાદુકપટપ્રકાશ. [Jādukapaṭaprakāṣa.] 2 vol. *Ahmedabad,* 1873-72. 8°. **14146. c. 16.**

Vol. I. is of the 3rd edition.

ILLUSTRATIONS. The illustrations of music, or a series of popular English and Guzratee songs with hints to English music by a Parsee student. (ગાયણ પ્રકાશ) [Gāyaṇaprakāṣa.] Pt. i. pp. 39. *Engl.* and *Guj.* *Bombay,* 1864. 4°. **14146. d. 7.**

'INĀYAT ALLĀH. *See* Ṣāmala Bhaṭa. જાહાંદાર શાહા બાદશાની વારતા [Jahāndār Shāh bādshāhnī vārtā. A metrical adaptation of the Bahār i dānish, or Persian tales of 'I. A.] [1850.] 8°. **14148. b. 2.**

—— —— [1884.] 8°. **14148. b. 29.**

INDIA. હિંદુસ્તાનનો સંક્ષિપ્ત ઈતિહાસ [Hindustānano saṃkshipta itihāsa. A concise history of India from the Muhammadan period, to the year A.D. 1861. With chronological tables.] pp. vii. 181. મુંબઈ ૧૮૭૫ [*Bombay,* 1875.] 12°. **14146. f. 13.(3.)**

—— [Second edition, greatly abridged.] pp. 86, xvi. મુંબઈ ૧૮૭૭ [*Bombay,* 1877.] 12°. **14146. f. 14.**

—— Outlines of the history of India. हिंदुस्ताननना इतिहासनो संक्षेप.) [Hindustānanā itihāsano saṃkshepa.] pp. 104. મુંબઈ ૧૮૭૭ [*Bombay,* 1877.] 12°. **14146. f. 18.**

—— The Opium trade as carried on between India and China, with a history of the insurrection in China. (હીનદુશથાન અને ચીન વચેના અફીમનો વેપાર) [Aphīmno vepār.] pp. x. 250. *Bombay,* 1854. 8°. **14146. g. 11.**

—— *High Courts of Judicature.* ઈંડયન લા રીપોર્ટસ. [Indian Law Reports, being decisions of the High Courts of India, passed in 1875-77. Translated by Govindalala Bālājī.] અમદાવાદ ૧૮૭૭ [*Ahmadabad,* 1877.] 8°. **14146. a. 3.**

INDIA.—*Legislative Council.* See SOHRĀBJĪ SHĀPURJĪ BANGĀLĀ. The Parsee Marriage and Divorce Act 1865: (Act No. XV. of 1865) the Parsee Chattels Real Act: (Act No. IX. of 1837) the Parsee Succession Act: (Act No. XXI. of 1865) and the Indian Succession Act 1865 (Act No. X. of 1865) with ... Guzeratteo translation. 1868. 8°. **760. h. 14.**

—— —— हिंदुस्तानना फोजदारी कायदो. પેનલકોડ ટીકાસાથે. [Hindustānano faujdārī kāyado. The Indian Penal Code] Act No. XLV. of 1860, and No. XXVII. 1870. [With notes.] pp. 240. અમદાવાદ ૧૯૩૪ [*Ahmadudad*, 1878.] 8°. **14146. a. 6.**

—— —— Notes on the Indian Penal Code, Act 45 of A.D. 1860. સને ૧૮૬૦ ના હીંદુસ્તાનના ફોજદારી કાયદાના આકટ ૪૫ ઊપરની ટીકા. [Compiled by Trikamrāya Udayaṣaṅkara.] pp. 48, 380. અમદાવાદ ૧૮૮૧ [*Ahmadabad*, 1881.] 8°. **14146. a. 9.**

—— —— The Indian Evidence Act. Act No. I. of 1872. હિંદુસ્તાનનો પુરાવાનો આકટ. [Hindustānano purāvāno Act. Edited with notes by Vījavalava Jeṭhābhāī.] pp. vi. 112. अमदावाद १९३० [*Ahmadabad*, 1880]. 8°. **14146. a. 2.**

—— —— [Another edition. With a commentary and index by Vrajarāya Sākarlāla and Govindalāla Bālājī.] pp. 28, 274. અમદાવાદ ૧૮૮૧ [*Ahmadabad*, 1881.] 8°. **14146. a. 11.**

—— —— ફોજદારી કામ ચલાવવાનો રીત બાબતનો કાયદો. [Faujdārī kāmchalāvavāno rīt. The Code of Criminal Procedure, or Act X. of 1872, with notes, and Act XI. of 1872.] pp. ii. 252, lvi. अमदावाद १९३३ [*Ahmadabad*, 1877.] 8°. **14146. a. 4.**

—— —— દિવાની નવો કાયદો. (સન ૧૮૭૭ નો આકટ ૧૦ મો) *etc.* [Dīwānī navo kāyado. A summary of the Civil Procedure Code, or Act X. of 1877, translated from the English by Govindalāla Bālājī.] pp. iv. 223. અમદાવાદ ૧૮૭૭ [*Ahmadabad*, 1877.] 16°. **14146. a. 1.**

—— —— માજીસ્ત્રેટનો પરીક્ષાનો કાયદો [Mājistreṭno parīkshāno kāyado. The Indian Penal Code, the Code of Criminal Procedure, and other laws, compiled for the use of Indian Magistrates.] अमदावाद १९३४ [*Ahmadabad*, 1877.] 8°. **14146. a. 5.**

ĪRĀNSHĀH ibn **MALAKSHĀH.** See ṢAD-DAR. સદ્દરે બેહેરે તવીલ [Ṣad-daro behere tavīl. Translated by Īrānshāh from a Persian metrical version of the Pehlevi original.] [1881.] 8°. **14124. i. 24.**

ĪṢVARA BĀROṬ. हरिरस. [Harirasa. A devotional poem addressed to the god Hari. With introductory verses by Pūrṇānanda Mahānanda Bhaṭṭa.] ff. iv. 16. १९३३ [*Bombay*, 1877.] *obl.* 12°. **14148. d. 15.**

ITCHARAM SURYARAM DESAI. See ICHCHHĀRĀMA SŪRYARĀMA DESĀI.

JAGAJJĪVANA DALPATRĀMA. वैदकनो सारसंग्रह [Vaidakno sārasaṅgraha. A treatise on the native system of medicine, taken from a Hindustani work. Second edition.] pp. 114. अमदावाद १९३० [*Ahmadabad*, 1880.] 12°. **14146. b. 8.**

—— [Third edition.] pp. vi. 89. अमदावाद १९३१ [*Ahmadabad*, 1881.] 8°. **14146. b. 7.**

JAGAJJĪVANADĀSA CHUNĪLĀLA. ફડીઆઓનો જુલમ [Phaḍiyāono julam. Verses on the unjust dealings of grain merchants during a time of scarcity.] pp. 8. અમદાવાદ ૧૯૩૩ [*Ahmadabad*, 1877.] 16°. **14148. d. 13(16.)**

JAGANNĀRĀYAṆA. ઈસુપરિક્ષા [Īsu-parīkshā. An anti-Christian tract in confutation of the doctrine of the Divinity of Christ. Translated into Gujarati from the Hindi of J. by the Ārya-dharma-pustaka-prasāraka Maṇḍalī of Surat.] pp. 32. અમદાવાદ ૧૮૮૮ [*Ahmadabad*, 1888.] 32°. **14144. b.**

JAGANNĀTHA ṢĀSTRĪ. See ACADEMIES, *etc.*—London.—*Society for the Diffusion of Useful Knowledge.* Library of useful knowledge. (Prelimnary treatise, translated into the Goojratee language) [by G. R. Jervis, with the assistance of J. Ṣ.] [1830.] 8°. **14146. e. 14.**

JAHĀNGĪR. જેહાંગીર નામું [Jahāngīr-nāmuṇ. An account of the exploits of Jahāngīr, the son of Rustam. Translated by Ṭemuljī Navarojī Sanjāṇā from the Persian.] pp. viii. 209. મુંબઈ ૧૮૭૫ [*Bombay*, 1875.] 8°. **14146. g. 6.**
Imperfect; wanting pp. 41—48.

JAHĀNGĪR BAHRĀMJĪ MARZBĀN. See TAYLOR (M.) તારા બાઈ [Tārā: a Mahratta tale. Translated by J. B. M.] [1886.] 8°. **14148. a. 33.**

JAHĀNGĪR BAHRĀMJĪ MARZBĀN. મુંબાઇથી કાશ્મીર [Mumbāithī Kāshmīr. An account of a journey to Kashmir and back. With illustrations.] pp. xxiii. 171, 3, 86. મુંબઈ ૧૮૮૭ [*Bombay*, 1887.] 8°. **14146. f. 26.**

JAHĀNGĪR BEJANJĪ KARĀṆĪ. *See* Abū Ṭāhir, *Tarsūsī.* ફરામરઝ નામું [Farāmurz-nāmuṉ. A translation by J. B. K. from the Persian original of Abū Ṭāhir.] [1883.] 8°. **14146. g. 19.**

—— *See* Periodical Publications.—*Bombay.* જ્ઞાનવર્ધક [Jñānavardhaka. A monthly magazine, edited by J. B. K.] [1884.] 8°. **14150. c. 3.**

JAHĀNGĪRSHĀH ARDSHER ṬALI'YĀRKHĀN. Mundra and Koolin, or India in the eighteenth century. By Jihangirshah Ardeshir Tale-yarkhan. (મુંદ્રા અને કુલીન.) pp. x. 218. *Ahmedabad*, 1884. 8°. **14148. b. 16.**

JAINADHARMA. श्री जैन धर्म ग्यान प्रदीपक पुस्तक [Jainadharma gyān-pradīpaka. The Paḍikamana, and other Jain prayers and hymns, and religious maxims, partly in Marwari, and partly in Gujarati.] pp. ii. iii. 264. पुना १९४४ [*Poona*, 1887.] 8°. **14154. h. 12.**

—— [Fourth edition.] pp. vi. 304. पुना १९४७ [*Poona*, 1890.] 8°. **14154. h. 16.**

JAINADHARMA-PRASĀRAKA SABHĀ. *See* Bhaunagar.—*Jainadharma-prasāraka Sabhā.*

JAINADHARMA-PRAVARTAKA SABHĀ. *See* Ahmadabad.—*Jainadharma-pravartaka Sabhā.*

JAINADHARMA-SIDDHĀNTA. श्री जैन धर्म सिद्धांत सार पुस्तक [Jainadharma-siddhānta sāra. A treatise on Jain religious observances, with a collection of prayers and hymns, partly in Hindi and partly in Gujarati.] pp. ii. iv. 190. पुना १९४६ [*Poona*, 1889.] 8°. **14144. g. 33.**

JAINAṢĀSTRA. જૈન સાસ્ત્ર કથા સંગ્રહ [Jainaṣāstra kathāsaṅgraha. A collection of Jain legends, philosophical works, prayers and hymns in praise of Jain saints, by various authors.] અમદાવાદ ૧૮૮૩ [*Ahmadabad*, 1883.] 8°. **14144. g. 8.**

—— [A reprint of the above, with the addition of the Pāṇḍavacharitra of Devaprabhu Sūri.] અમદાવાદ ૧૮૮૪ [*Ahmadabad*, 1884.] 8°. **14144. g. 9.**

JAINAVṚITTA. जैन वृत्त शिक्षापत्रि [Jainavṛitta ṣikshāpatri. Instructions on the performance of twelve Jain religious observances.] pp. 50. અમદાવાદ [*Ahmadabad*, 1887.] 16°. **14144. f. 1.(4.)**

JAINS, *Digambara Sect of.* बंबैमें शुद्ध दिगम्बराम्नाय मन्दिर निर्म्माणार्थ पत्रिका [A letter addressed to the followers of the Digambara sect of Jains appealing for funds for the erection of a temple at Bombay.] pp. 16. १९२० [*Bombay*, 1888.] 16°. **14144. f.**

JALĀL al-DĪN MĪRZĀ, *Ḳājār.* A history of the ancient Parsis from the original Persian work [the Nāmah i Khusrawān] compiled by Prince Jalal Kajar of Persia. Translated into Goozerattee . . . by Ardaseer Dossabhace Moonshee. (પુરાતન પારસીઓની તવારીખ) [Purātan Pārsīonī tavārīkh.] With portraits of the kings. pp. 37, 147. *Bombay*, 1871. 8°. **14146. g. 5.**

JALAL KAJAR. *See* Jalāl al-Dīn Mīrzā, *Ḳājār.*

JĀL ANE RODĀBE. ઈરાની નાટક મંડલીના જાલ અને રોદાબેના પ્રારસી ખેલનો ગુજરાતી સાર [Jāl ane Rodābe. An adaptation of a Persian drama.] pp. 12. મુંબઈ ૧૮૮૦ [*Bombay*, 1880.] 12°. **14148. c. 9(1.)**

JĀMĀSPJĪ MINUCHEHRJĪ JĀMĀSP-ASĀNĀ. *See* Ratanjī Rustamjī Kāṅgā. રૂવાંનની ચાર દાહડાની ક્રીઆ વીશે [Rūvānnī chār dāhāḍānī kriyā vishe. With an explanation of three lectures given by J. M. J.] [1875.] 12°. **14144. h. 7(2.)**

—— *See* Ṣad-dar. સદ્દરબેહેરે રે તવીલ [Ṣad-dare behere tavīl. Edited by J. M. J.] [1881.] 8°. **14144. i. 24.**

JAMBUDVĪPA. जंबुद्वीपनो नकसो [Jambudvīpano nakso. Map of India according to Jain mythology.] [*Bombay*, 1882 ?] **Map. 52430.(12.)**

JAMSHED, *King of Persia.* [*Life.*] *See* Jīvanajī Jamshedjī Modī. જમશેદ, હોમ અને આતશ. [Jamshed, homa ane ātash.] **14144. i. 23.**

JAMSHEDJĪ FRĀMJĪ BACHĀBHĀĪ RABĀḌĪ. દીનબેહ માઝદીયશની [Dīnbeh Mazdayasnī. A brief account of the ancient kings of Persia, and of the arrival of the Parsis in India; together with a sketch of their religious and moral duties.] pp. 139, xx. સુરત ૧૮૮૭ [*Surat*, 1887.] 8°. **14146. g. 21.**

JAMSHEDJĪ FRĀMJĪ BACHĀBHĀĪ RABĀḌĪ. રોઆનની ક્રિયા [Rūvānnī kriyā. A treatise on the due performance of Parsi funeral obsequies.] pp. 56. સુરત ૧૮૮૮ [*Surat,* 1888.] 8°. **14144. i. 29.**

JAMSHEDJĪ PĀLANJĪ KĀPADIĀ. *See* MALCOLM (*Sir* J.) *General.* તવારીખે કદીમ ઈરાન .... History of Ancient Persia from Sir John Malcolm, with latest modern researches. By Jamshedjee Pallonjee. 1868. 4°. **14146. h. 1.**

—— The history of the commonwealth of the Magian monarchies which arose out of the fragments of Alexander's conquest of Persia . . . in II. Vols. and V. Parts by Jamshedjee Pallonjee. (તવારીખે મલુકે તવાયફે જરથોસ્તીઆન) [Tavārīkh i mulūk i tavā'if i Zartoshtiyān.] Vol. i. pt. 1. *Bombay,* 1881. 8°. **14146. h. 4.**

Wanting all other parts.

JANĀRDANA BHĀSKARA KRAMAVANTA. *See* ŚUKADEVA. જ્યોતિષસાર । [Jyotishasāra. With J. Bh. K.'s Marathi commentary translated into Gujarati.] [1864?] 4°. **14053. d. 11.**

JANI (B. R.) *See* BHAGUBHĀĪ RĀMAŚAṄKARA JĀNĪ.

JAŚOVIJAYAJĪ. *See* YAŚOVIJAYAJĪ.

JASVAT SIṂHA, *Maharaja.* Bhashabhushan by . . . Maharajah Jaswatsinhji . . . with Luptopama vilasa . . . and Upama sangraha [Hindi treatises on rhetoric]. With [a preface and] commentaries in Gujarati . . . by Kavi Hirachand Kanji. pp. xv. 123. *Bombay,* 1866. 12°. **14158. c. 8.**

JAVERĪ CHHAGANLĀLA. *See* DĪPACHAND DEVACHAND and JAVERĪ CHHAGANLĀLA. सिद्धाचलनुं वर्णन [Siddhāchala-nuṇ varṇana.] **14144. f. 19.**

JAVERĪLĀLA UMIĀŚAṄKARA YĀJÑIKA. *See* MANU. मानवधर्मशास्त्र अथवा मनुस्मृति (Mănava-dharma-śăstra .... translated into Gujaráti by Jáverilál Umiáshankar Yájṇik.) 1871. 8°. **14146. a. 10.**

—— *See* KĀLIDĀSA. Sakuntalá .... a Sanskrit drama ... translated into Gujarátí prose and verse .... by Javerilál Umiáshankar Yajñik. 1867. 8°. **14148. c. 1.**

JAYAKṚISHṆA, *Pupil of Rāmadāsa.* *See* RĀMADĀSA SVĀMĪ, *of Haidarabad.* श्रीपंचीकरण [Pañchīkaraṇa. With a commentary by J.] [1881.] 12°. **14048. b. 10.**

—— —— [1885.] 12°. **14048. b. 14.**

JAYAKṚISHṆA JĪVANARĀMAJĪ. *See* KṚISHṆA-MIŚRA. प्रबोधचंद्रोदय नाटक [Prabodhachandrodaya nāṭaka. Translated with the assistance of J. J.] [1881.] 8°. **14148. c. 15.**

JAYATASI. शेठ कयवन्ना शाहनो रास. [Śeṭh Kayavannā Shāhno rās. A Jain legend.] pp. 80. मुंबई १९४१ [*Bombay,* 1884.] 12°. **14144. f. 14.**

JEEJEEBHOY (*Sir* JAMSETJEE) *Baronet.* [*Life.*] *See* MANCHERJĪ KĀVASJĪ LANGRĀNĀ, called MANSUKH. ગંજનામું, *etc.* [Ganj-nāmuṇ.] Chap. viii.

—— [*Life*] *See* MANCHERJĪ KĀVASJĪ LANGRĀNĀ, called MANSUKH. સર જમશેદજી બારોનેટ [Sir Jamṣedjī Baronet.]

—— [*Life*] *See* NASĪM. ગોહેરે જીંદગી [Gauhar i zindagī.]

—— મરહુમ નેકનામદાર... સર જમસેદજી જીજીભાઈ *etc.* [A short sketch of the life of Sir J. J.] pp. 35. મુંબઈ ૧૮૭૭ [*Bombay,* 1877.] 16°. **14146. f. 16(1.)**

JERVIS (GEORGE RITSO). *See* ACADEMIES, *etc.*—London.—*Society for the Diffusion of Useful Knowledge.* Library of useful knowledge. (Preliminary treatise, translated into the Goojratee language) [by G. R. J.] [1830.] 8°. **14146. e. 14.**

—— *See* PASLEY (*Sir* C. W.) Goojeratee version of a course of practical geometry . . . Translated by . . G. R. J. 1826. 4°. **14146. d. 1.**

—— A Course of mathematics in the Goojratee language. Vol. I. consisting of arithmetic and book-keeping. (Vol. II. consisting of elements of algebra, logarithms, elements of geometry, application of algebra to geometry, plane trigonometry, mensuration : with tables of logarithms.) Translated from the works of Dr. Charles Hutton and Mr. Bonnycastle, by ... G.R.J. (शिक्षामाला) [Śikshāmālā.] *lith. Bombay,* 1828. 4°. **14146. d. 5.**

—— भूमिति व्याख्या [Bhūmiti vyākhyā. Elements of geometry, being Pt. 3. of Vol. ii. of G. R. J.'s "Course of mathematics in the Goojratee language."] pp. 219. [*Bombay,* 1828.] 4°. **14146. d. 4.**

—— बीज गणित [Bījagaṇita. The elements of Algebra, being Pt. 1 of Vol. ii. of G. R. J.'s "Course of mathematics in the Goojratee language."] pp. 226. [*Bombay,* 1828.] 4°. **14146. d. 2.**

JERVIS (George Ritso). सिधी लिटी त्रिकोणमिति व्याख्या [Sidhīliṭī trikoṇamiti. Plane trigonometry and logarithms; being Pts. 2–4 of Vol. ii. of G. R. J.'s "Course of mathematics in the Goojratee language."] pp. 57, 26. [*Bombay*, 1828.] 4°. **14146. d. 3.**

JESHANGBHĀĪ TRIKAMDĀSA PAṬEL. વિજિયા વૈધવ્ય દુઃખ દર્શક નાટક. [Vijiyā vaidhavya duḥkhadarṣaka nāṭaka. A play in 11 acts on the hardships of Hindu widowhood.] pp. 120, xii. અમદાવાદ ૧૮૮૪ [*Ahmadabad*, 1884.] 12°. **14148. c. 24.**

JESHANGDĀSA TRIKAMDĀSĀ PAṬEL. માણક શાહ ચરીત્ર [Mānak Shāh charitra. A tale in verse.] pp. 67. અમદાવાદ ૧૮૮૩ [*Ahmadabad*, 1883.] 16°. **14148. d. 29.**

JESUS CHRIST. ઈશા મશીહ તથા મહમદની બાબતની વાત [Īṣā Masīh tathā Muhammadnī bābatnī vāt.] Concerning Jesus the Messiah, and Mahummed. pp. 42. શુરત ૧૮૪૩ [*Surat*, 1843.] 8°. **14144. a. 19(2.)**

—— ઈશુ ખરીશટના મરણ તથા તેહેના શજીવન [Īṣu Khristnā maraṇa. A Christian tract on the death and resurrection of Jesus Christ.] pp. 28. [*Surat*, 1860 ?] 12°. **14144. a. 1(10.)**

—— ઈશુ ખરીશટ વીશે પેગંબરોનાં વચનોથી ખરીશટી ધરમની શાબીતીનું પુશતક. [Īṣu Khrisṭ vishe pustaka. The fulfilment of the prophecies concerning Jesus Christ, as evidences of the Christian religion.] pp. 67. શુરત ૧૮૪૯ [*Surat*, 1849.] 12°. **14144. a. 1(3.)**

JEṬHĀLĀLA HARAJĪVANA. મોટું काव्यदोहन. [Moṭuṇ kāvyadohana. Selections from the writings of popular poets of Gujarat.] pp. iv. 404. અમદાવાદ ૧૮૮૬ [*Ahmadabad*, 1886.] 8°. **14148. f. 15.**

JEṬHA MALLAJĪ. *See* Ātmārāmajī Ānandavijayajī. सम्यकत्व शल्योद्धार [Samyaktva ṣalyoddhāra. A controversial tract, in refutation of the Samakitasāra of J. M.] [1888.] 8°. **14144. g. 30.**

JIHANGIRSHAH ARDESHIR TALE-YARKHAN. *See* Jahāngīrshāh Ardsher Tāli'yārkhān.

JINADĀSA. લાવણી સંગ્રહ. [Lāvaṇī saṅgraha. A collection of Jain verses by J. and other poets.] Pt. I. pp. viii. 152. મુંબઈ ૧૮૩૮ [*Bombay*, 1882.] 12°. **14148. d. 20.**

JINAVALLABHA. अथ बालावबोधसहित षडशीतिकाख्य चतुर्थ कर्मग्रंथः प्रारभ्यते [Shadaṣīti. The fourth of the Jain Karmagranthas, Prakrit text, with a Gujarati commentary by Yaṣaḥsoma.] *See* Bhīmasiṃha Māṇaka. प्रकरण-रत्नाकर [Prakaraṇa-ratnākara.] Vol. iv. pp. 498–604. [1876, *etc.*] 4°. **14100. e. 3.**

JINODAYA SŪRI. हंसराज वत्सराजनो रास. [Haṃsarāja Vatsarājano rās. The story of the two princes Haṃsarāja and Vatsarāja. A Jain tale in verse.] pp. 133. मुंबापुरी १९३१ [*Bombay*, 1881.] 12°. **14144. f. 5.**

JITĀMALA SVĀMĪ. अथ भ्रमविद्धंशण ग्रंथ प्रारंभः [Bhramavidhvaṃṣana. A Jain religious treatise consisting of Prakrit verses with a gloss and commentary in Gujurati, compiled by J. S.] ff. 174, *lith.* मुंबई १९४० [*Bombay*, 1883.] *obl. fol.* **14100. f. 5.**

JĪVĀBHIGAMA. स्थानांगनाम्नस्तृतीयांगस्योपांग जीवाभिगम नाम सूत्रम् १४ ॥ [Jīvābhigama. The 3rd *upāṅga*, and 14th work in the Siddhānta or Jain canon. Sanskrit text and commentary, with a Gujarati paraphrase.] ff. 1114. अमदावाद १९८३ [*Ahmadabad*, 1883.] *obl.* 4°. **14100. f. 6.**

JĪVANABHEDAVĀṆĪ. જીવનભેદવાણી [Jīvanabhedavāṇī. A Christian tract in refutation of Hinduism.] Pt. I. pp. 40. ૧૮૫૮ *Surat*, [1858.] 32°. **14144. a. 12.**

JĪVANAJĪ JAMSHEDJĪ MODĪ. જમશેદ, હોમ અને આતશ. [Jamshed, homa ane ātash. A life of the emperor Jamshed, with dissertations on sacrificial rites, and on fire-worship amongst the Parsis.] pp. xvi. 210. મુંબઈ ૧૮૮૪ [*Bombay*, 1884.] 8°. **14144. i. 23.**

JĪVANALĀLAJĪ, *Mahārāja.* [*Life.*] *See* Girdharalāla Harakisandāsa. શ્રીમદગોસ્વામી શ્રીજીવનલાલજી મહારાજનું જન્મ ચરિત્ર. [Ṣrī Jīvanalālajī Mahārājanuṇ janmacharitra.]

JÑĀNASĀRA. *See* [Addenda] Ānandaghana. अथ श्री आनंदघनकृत ऋषभप्रमुख चोवीस जिन स्तुति *etc.* [Chovīsa Jina stuti. With a Gujarati commentary by Jñānasāra.] [1876, *etc.*] 4°. **14100. e. 3.**

JÑĀNAVIMALA SŪRI. *See* Yaṣovijaya. अथ श्रीमद्यशोविजयजी उपाध्यायकृत आठ दृष्टीनी सज्झा *etc.* [Yogadrishṭi. Accompanied by a Gujarati translation by Jñ. S.] [1876. *etc.*] 4°. **14100. e. 3.**

JÑĀNAVIMALA SŪRI. શ્રી જ્ઞાનવિમલ સૂરિ વિરચિત શ્રી શ્રીચંદ કેવલીનો રાસ. [Srīchand Kevalīno rās. A Jain legend in verse, with occasional notes.] pp. ii. 358. મુમ્બા ૧૯૪૨ [*Bombay*, 1886.] 8°. **14144. g. 14.**

JOHNSON (SAMUEL) *LL.D.* Johnson's Rasselas: હબશી દેશના રાજકુમાર રાસલસનું ચરિત્ર. . . Translated by Shapurjí Edaljí. Part I. pp. iv. 76. *Bombay*, 1866. 12°. **14148. a. 9.(1.)**

JOSEPH, *the Patriarch.* ઇઊશફનું ચરીતર [Yūsufnuṇ charitra.] History of Joseph. [A Christian tract.]. pp. 40. શુરત ૧૮૫૪ [*Surat*, 1854] 12°. **14144. a. 2.(2.)**

JUNAGARH. જુનાગઢનો ભોમીયો [Junāgaḍhno bhomiyo. Travels in Junagarh.] pp. 119. સુરત ૧૯૩૩ [*Surat*, 1877.] 12°. **14146. f. 3.**

KABĪR. [*Life.*] *See* VĀLJĪ BECHAR. Sources of the Kabīr religion. [1881.] 8°. **14144. b. 4.**

KAHĀNDĀSA MAÑCHHĀRĀMA. Natural philosophy for beginners. Being familiar illustrations of the laws of motion and mechanics, translated into Gujarati [from the English] by Kahándás Manchárám. Second edition, revised by Nushirvánji Chándábhai. (યંત્રશાસ્ત્રનાં મૂળ) [Yantraṣāstranāṇ mūḷa.] pp. viii. 205. *Bombay*, 1856. 12°. **14146. c. 9.**

KAIKHUSRAU HORMASJĪ ĀLPAIWĀLĀ. Prize essay on the advantages and necessity of railways in the Bombay presidency . . . મુંબઈ ઈલાકામા લોહોડાની સડક *etc.* pp. iv. 89. મુંબઈ ૧૮૫૩ [*Bombay*, 1853.] 8°. **14146. c. 14.**

KAIKHUSRAU NAVAROJĪ KĀBRĀJĪ. દુખિયારી બચું [Dukhiyārī Bachuṇ. A Parsi tale.] Pt. iv. મુંબા ૧૮૮૬ [*Bombay*, 1886.] 8°. **14148. b. 27.**

Incomplete; wanting pts. i.-iii. and concluding parts.

—— નિંદાખાનું. [Nindā khānuṇ. A Parsi play, in three acts, adapted from Sheridan's "School for scandal."] pp. 107. મુંબઈ ૧૮૮૩ [*Bombay*, 1883.] 8°. **14148. c. 20.(1.)**

KĀLIDĀSA, *the Sanskrit poet.* Ṣakuntalá recognised by the ring. A Sanskrit drama, in seven acts, by Kálidás, translated into Gujaráti prose and verse, chiefly from the Sanskrit text by Prof. Mon. Williams, by Javerilál Umiáshankar Yajñik. (અભિજ્ઞાન શકુન્તલ નાટક) pp. xxvi. 204. *Bombay*, 1867. 8°. **14148. c. 1.**

KĀLIDĀSA, *the Sanskrit poet.* विक्रमोर्वशी त्रोटक [Vikramorvaṣī troṭaka. A Sanskrit play translated, with an introductory preface, and notes, by Raṇchhoḍbhāī Udayarāma.] pp. ix. 152. मुंबई १९२४ [*Bombay*, 1868.] 12°. **14148. c. 11.**

—— [*Supposititious works.*] અથ રતિ સ્વયંવર . . . Rati swayamvara, or The Choice Merriage [*sic*] of Rati. Formerly composed [or rather translated into verse] by Kavi Gangashankar Jeyshankar [from a Sanskrit work ascribed to K.] Second edition. pp. xvi. 144. *Ahmedabad*, 1884. 12°. **14148. d. 25.**

KĀLIDĀSA, *of Wassawad.* શ્રી પ્રહ્લાદ આખ્યાન ॥ [Prahlādākhyāna. The mythological story of Prahlāda in verse.] pp. 140, *lith.* મુંબઈ ૧૯૧૧ [*Bombay*, 1854.] 8°. **14148. b. 3(1.)**

Imperfect; wanting pp. 49-52.

—— [Another edition.] pp. 99, *lith.* મુંબઈ ૧૯૨૧ [*Bombay*, 1864.] 8°. **14148. b. 4.(8)**

KĀLIDĀSA DEVAṢAṄKARA. रूपदेवजीना गरबा. [Rūpadevajīnā garbā. Garbī songs concerning Rūpadeva, the Raja of Alirajpur, a small State in the province of Malwa.] pp. 23. અમદાવાદ ૧૯૩૪ [*Ahmadabad*, 1877.] 12°. **14148. d. 6.(4.)**

KĀLIDĀSA DEVAṢAṄKARA PAṆḌYĀ. The Gujarát Rájasthán, or The native states of Gujarát. By Kálidáss Devshankar Pandyá. (ગુજરાત રાજસ્થાન) pp. xvi. 560. *Ahmedabad*, 1884. 8°. **14146. h. 8.**

KĀLIDĀSA GOVINDAJĪ. *See* ṢAṄKARA ĀCHĀRYA. श्री विवेकचूडामणि: [Vivekachūḍāmaṇi. With a prose translation by K. G.] [1886.] 12°. **14043. b. 22.**

KĀLIKĀCHĀRYA. पंनवणासूत्र [Pannavaṇā, called in Sanskrit Prajñāpanā-sūtra, a canonical work of the Jains, Prakrit text with Sanskrit commentary and translation and a Gujarati commentary by Paramānanda.] ff. 6, 849, 37. बनारस १९४१ [*Benares*, 1884.] *obl.* 4°. **14100. f. 10.**

The commentary or ṭabbā was composed A.D. 1819.

KALYĀṆACHANDAJĪ JAYACHANDAJĪ. લોકાગચ્છીય શ્રાવકસ્ય સાર્થપંચ પ્રતિક્રમણસૂત્ર, *etc.* [Lokāgachchhīya ṣrāvakasya sārtha pañcha pratikramaṇasūtra. A collection of Jain prayers and hymns of the Lokagachchha branch of the

Svetāmbara sect. Partly in Prakrit with explanations in Gujarati. Second edition.] pp. vi. 236, *lith.* મોહમયી ૧૯૩૯ [*Bombay*, 1883.] 8°.
14144. g. 18.

KĀMĀ (K. R.) *See* KHURSHEDJĪ RUSTAMJĪ KĀMĀ.

KĀMĀVATĪ. કામાવતીની વારતાની ચોપડી [Kāmāvatīnī vārtā, or The story of Karaṇa and Kāmāvatī. A love tale in verse.] *lith.* મુંબઈ ૧૯૧૪ [*Bombay*, 1857.] 12°. **14148. a. 14.(3.)**

Imperfect; wanting all after p. 104.

—— કરણ કામાવતીની વારત્તા [Another edition.] pp. 188, *lith.* અમદાવાદ ૧૯૩૧ [*Ahmadabad*, 1875.] 12°. **14148. a. 15.**

KANAKASUNDARA. श्री वीतरागायनमः अथ श्री हरिचंदराजानो रास प्रारंभः [Harichand Rājāno rās, or the story of King Hariṣchandra. A Jain legend in verse.] pp. 112. [*Bombay*, 1884.] 16°.
14144. f. 3.

KANHAIYĀLĀLA MOTILĀLA MUNSHĪ. Evil friendship's mirror, by Kanialal Motilal Munshi. (કુમિત્ર દર્પણ) [Kumitra darpaṇa. A drama in five acts.] pp. 147. *Ahmedabad*, 1886. 12°.
14148. c. 26.(1.)

KAPADIA AMUSING CLUB. *See* BOMBAY, *City of.*—*Kapadia Amusing Club.*

KARAM 'ALĪ RAHĪM, *Nānjiāni.* A collection of select Persian proverbs and familiar sayings with their English and Gujaráti equivalents. pp. 14, 12, 14. *Bombay*, 1882. 8°. **757. cc. 9.**

—— દુનિયા દર્પણ [Duniyā-darpan, or The mirror of the world. A social drama in six acts.] pp. 79. મુંબઈ ૧૮૮૫ [*Bombay*, 1885.] 12°.
14148. c. 19.(2.)

KARMAGRANTHAS. [For the six Jain works included under this collective title, with Gujarati commentaries.] *See* BHĪMASIṂHA MĀṆAKA. प्रकरणरत्नाकर [Prakaraṇa-ratnākara.] Vol. iv. [1876, *etc.*] 4°. **14100. e. 3.**

KARMASTAVA. कर्मस्तवनामा द्वितीय कर्मग्रंथ [Karmastava. The second of the Jain Karmagranthas, Prakrit text with a paraphrase and commentary in Gujarati.] *See* BHĪMASIṂHA MĀṆAKA. प्रकरणरत्नाकर Vol. iv. pp. 412-454. [1876, *etc.*] 4°.
14100. e. 3.

KARSANDĀS MŪLJĪ. *Memoir. See* MAHĪPATRĀMA RŪPARĀMA NĪLAKAṆṬHA, *C. I. E.* उत्तम कपोळ करसनदास चरित्र . . . A memoir of the reformer K. M.

—— નીતિવચન [Nītivachana] . . . Moral essays. Second edition. pp. viii. 232. મુંબઈ ૧૮૬૫ [*Bombay*, 1865.] 16°. **14146. e. 4.**

—— Travels in England by Karsandás Múlji. Second edition, revised and enlarged with numerous illustrations. (ઈંગ્લંડમાં પ્રવાસ) [Inglaṇḍmāṇ pravāsa.] pp. xxiv. 424, iv. *Bombay*, 1867. 8°. **14146. h. 13.**

—— ઈંગલંડમાં પ્રવાસ [Chapter I. only of K. M.'s "Travels in England."] pp. 48. મુંબઈ ૧૮૬૪ [*Bombay*, 1864.] 8°. **14146. h. 14.**

—— વેદ ધર્મ તથા વેદ પછીનાં ધર્મ પુસ્તકો [Vedadharma. A treatise on the religion of the Vedas.] pp.31. મુંબઈ ૧૮૬૬ [*Bombay*, 1866.] 12°.
14144. b. 1.

KATHIAWAR. કાઠીઆવાડ સર્વસંગ્રહ [Kāṭhiāvāḍ sarvasaṅgraha. An account of the Province of Kathiawar, being a translation by Narmadāṣaṅkara Lālaṣaṅkara of Vol. VIII. of the Gazetteer of the Bombay Presidency.] pp. ii. 611. મુંબઈ ૧૮૮૬ [*Bombay*, 1886.] 8°. **14146. h. 15.**

KĀVASJĪ EDALJĪ KĀNGĀ. *See* ACADEMIES, *etc.*—Bombay.—*Zartoshtī Dīnnī Kholkarnārī Maṇḍalī.* જરતોશતી દીનની ખોલ કરનારી મંડલીનો પાંચ વરસનો મુખતેસર હેવાલ [A concise report of the proceedings of the Zartoshtī Dīnnī Kholkarnārī Maṇḍalī. With a preface by K. E. K.] [1869.] 8°. **14144. i. 4.(2.)**

—— *See* ZAND-AVASTĀ. Khordeh Avesta . . . transliterated and translated into Gujerati, with copious explanatory notes, by K. E. K. 1880. 8°.
14144. i. 20.

—— —— વંદીદાદની . . . ગુજરાતી તરજુમો . . . Vendidad, translated, . . . with grammatical and explanatory notes, by K. E. K. [1864-66.] 8°.
761. d.

—— —— 1874. 8°. **14144. i. 25.**

—— —— 1884. 8°. **14144. i. 22.**

—— —— Yaçna and Vispered translated into Gujerati . . . with critical and explanatory notes, by K. E. K. 1886. 8°. **14144. i. 19.**

KĀVASJĪ DĪNSHĀH KIASH. *See* SA'DĪ. The Gulistan of Shaik Sadi .. Translated .. with copious explanatory notes, by Kawasji Dinshaw Kiash. 1879. 8°. **14148. b. 12.**

KĀVASJĪ NAVAROJĪ VESUWĀLĀ. Studies from British poets with a short account of their biographies and their writings in Gujarati, by Cowasjee Nowrosjee Vesuwala. (વિલાયતના કવીશ્વરો) [Vilāyatnā kavīṣvaro.] pp. v. 282. *Bombay*, 1880. 8°. **14148. e. 8.**

KĀVASJĪ PESTANJĪ. દીલચમન ગાયણ સંગ્રહ [Dilchaman gāyaṇasaṅgraha. A collection of miscellaneous songs by modern composers.] Pt. I. pp. xx. 228. મુંબઈ ૧૮૭૯ [*Bombay*, 1879.] 8°. **14148. e. 7.**

KAVESARĪ KALĀMO. કવેસરી કલાંમો [Kavesarī kalāmo. Moral instruction in verse.] pp. ii. 34. મુંબાઈ ૧૮૭૫ [*Bombay*, 1875.] 12°. **14148. d. 2.(5.)**

KAVI HIRACHAND KANJI. *See* HĪRĀCHAND KĀNJĪ, *Kavi.*

KAVITĀSAṄGRAHA. કવિતા સંગ્રહ [Kavitāsaṅgraha. Miscellaneous poems. Fourth edition.] pp. viii. 177. મુંબઈ ૧૮૬૬ [*Bombay*, 1866.] 12°. **14148. d. 16.**

KEṢARA VIMALA. अथ सूक्तमुक्तावली प्रारंभः [Sūktamuktāvalī. A Jain treatise in verse on the means of attaining final beatitude.] *See* BHĪMASIṂHA MĀṆAKA. प्रकरण-रत्नाकर [Prakaraṇa-ratnākara.] Vol. ii. pp. 110-124. [1876, *etc.*] 4°. **14100. e. 3.**

KEṢAVALĀLA HARIRĀMA. *See* GOVARDHANA LĀLAJĪ, also called GAṬṬU LĀLAJĪ. Cutch mahodaya . . . [Followed by Mānapatra, or a collection of five Sanskrit poems, with prose translations by K. H.] [1884.] 8°. **14070. d. 30.**

—— *See* PURĀṆAS.—*Bhāgavatapurāṇa.* श्रीमद् भागवत भाषांतर. Bhágavata bháshántara. [Translated by K. H.] [1885.] 4°. **14144. e. 1.**

—— —— *Devībhāgavatapurāṇa.* श्रीमद् भगवती भागवत भाषांतर Bhagavati Bhágavata bháshántara. [Translated by K. H.] [1885, *etc.*] 8°. **14144. e. 3.**

KEṢAVALĀLA MAGANLĀLA. અમદાવાદમાં બત્રીસાની રેલનો રોળ [Ahmadābādmāṇ batrīsānī relno roḷ. An account in verse of disastrous floods at Ahmadabad.] pp. 32. અમદાવાદ ૧૮૭૫ [*Ahmadabad*, 1875.] 12°. **14148. d. 13.(1.)**

—— ધર્મપ્રકાસ *etc.* [Dharmaprakāṣa. A Sanskrit work on the religious duties of Vaishṇavas, with interpretation and commentary in Gujarati.] pp. viii. 103. અમદાવાદ ૧૮૭૫ [*Ahmadabad*, 1875.] 12°. **14033. a. 4.**

KEṢAVALĀLA RAṄCHHOḌDĀSA JOṢĪ. *See* GIRDHARALĀLA HARIVALLABHADĀSA and KEṢAVALĀLA RAṄCHHOḌDĀSA JOṢĪ. स्वदेश हितदर्शक [Svadeṣa hitadarṣaka.] [1877.] 16°. **14146. e. 8.(1.)**

KEṢAVALĀLA ṢIVARĀMA. जैनबाळज्ञानसुबोध. [Jaina bālajñāna subodha. An explanation of Jain prayers and religious ceremonies, for the instruction of children.] pp. 48. અમદાવાદ ૧૮૮૮ [*Ahmadabad*, 1888.] 12°. **14144. f.**

KEṢAVARĀMA VIṢVANĀTHA JOṢĪ. कमळा दुःखदर्शक नाटक. [Kamaḷā duḥkhadarṣaka nāṭaka. A drama in 3 acts on the evil consequences of child-marriages, and the miseries of widowhood.] pp. 68. સુરત ૧૮૮૩ [*Surat*, 1883.] 8°. **14148. c. 20.(2.)**

KEVAḶADĀSA AMĪCHAND. સાબરનો સાખો અને બલીસાનો બેહાલ [Sābarno sākho. Verses describing the floods, cholera and other calamities which befel the people of Gujarat during the Saṃvat year 1932.] pp. 16. અમદાવાદ ૧૮૭૫ [*Ahmadabad*, 1875.] 16°. **14148. d. 13.(7.)**

KHEḌĀVĀḶ BRAHMANS. खेडावाळ ज्ञाति समस्ते करेला ठरावो [Kheḍāvāḷ jñāti samaste karelā ṭharāvo. Resolutions passed at a meeting of Kheḍāvāḷ Brahmans at Vadal condemning child-marriages and polygamy.] pp. vi. 40. અમદાવાદ ૧૮૮૬ [*Ahmadabad*, 1886.] 8°. **14146. e. 20.(2.)**

KHĪMAJĪ PREMAJĪ MEHETĀ. राणपुरनी मख्तेसर हकीकत [Rāṇpurnī mukhtaṣar hakīkat. A brief account of Ranpur and its Rajput chieftains.] pp. 46. અમદાવાદ ૧૮૭૫ [*Ahmadabad*, 1875.] 12°. **14146. f. 13.(2.)**

KHURSHEDJĪ MINUCHEHRJĪ KAṬELI. દુવા નાંમસેતાએશને [Du'ā nām setāyishne. A treatise on Zoroastrian worship, containing translations of prayers from various Pehlevi sources.] pp. vii. 177. મુંબઈ ૧૮૭૨ [*Bombay*, 1872.] 8°. **14144. i. 16.**

KHURSHEDJĪ NASARVĀNJĪ PESTANJĪ. નકલીઆતનામું [Nakliyāt-nāmuṇ. Moral tales for Parsi children, taken from the English.] pp. 437. મુંબઈ ૧૮૬૯ [*Bombay,* 1869.] 12°. **14148. a. 8.**

KHURSHEDJĪ RUSTAMJĪ KĀMĀ. ભાશાણો. જરતોસતી ધરમને લગતી બાબદો ઊપર [Bhāṣāno. Lectures delivered at Bombay on the principles of the Zoroastrian religion.] pp. vi. 266. મુંબઈ ૧૮૬૯ [*Bombay,* 1869.] 8°. **14144. i. 5.**

—— પેગમબર અશો જરતોશતના જનમારાનો એહેવાલ, અવસતા ઊપરથી [An account of the life of Zoroaster, based on the Zand Avastā. With quotations from the original Pehlevi, accompanied by Gujarati translations and notes.] pp. xxi. 434. મુંબઈ ૧૮૭૦ [*Bombay,* 1870.] 8°. **14144. i. 7.**

—— ઇઅજદેજરદી તારીખ [Yazdagirdī tārīkh. A treatise on the difference of one month's time, which happens between the Indian and Persian methods of calculating the Parsi year.] pp. 74. મુંબઈ ૧૮૭૦ [*Bombay,* 1870.] 8°. **14144. i. 4.(3.)**

—— જરતોશતી અભીઆસ Zartoshtī abhyas. [Researches in Zend literature, and the Zand Avastā.] Nos. 1-11. મુંબઈ ૧૮૬૬-૬૯ [*Bombay,* 1866-69.] 8°. **14144. i. 6.**

KHUSHĀLRĀYA SĀRĀBHĀĪ. છોટા ઊદેપુરના દીવાન રા. બા. ખુશાલરાય સારાભાઈના પેનસન લેવાને પ્રસંગે ભરાયેલો દરબાર, *etc.* [A brief account of the official career of Kh. S. Diwan of the Chhota Udaipur State, and of a public meeting held on the occasion of his retirement on pension.] pp. 34. અમદાવાદ ૧૮૮૮ [*Ahmadabad,* 1888.] 16°. **14146. f. 15.(2.)**

KHUSRAU, *Amīr.* બાગો બાહાર યાને ચાર દરવેશનો કીસ્સો. [Bāgh o Bahār. The Persian romance of Amīr Khusrau, translated into Gujarati by Rustam Irānī.] pp. ii. 234. મુંબઈ [*Bombay,* 1884.] 8°. **14148. b. 36.**

KHUSRAU NOSHĪRWĀN, *King of Persia.* અન્દરજે ખુસરોએ કોબાતાંત [Andaraz i Khusro Kovātāt, or the Precepts of King Khusrau. Pehlevi text and Gujarati translation.] *See* PESHOTAN BAHRĀMJĪ SANJĀNĀ. Ganjesháyagán, *etc.* 1885. 8°. **761. g. 2.**

KHUSROE KAVĀTĀN, *King of Persia. See* KHUSRAU NOSHĪRWĀN.

KĪKĀBHĀĪ PRABHUDĀSA. હોળી સંગ્રહ. [Holī-saṅgraha. A collection of songs sung during the Holī festival.] pp. 72. સુરત ૧૮૮૧ [*Surat,* 1881.] 16°. **14144. b. 6.(3.)**

KOSHṬAKA. કોષ્ટકની ચોપડી [Koshṭakanī chopaḍī. Tables of English and Indian weights and measures.] pp. 16, *lith.* મુંબઈ ૧૯૨૦ [*Bombay,* 1863.] 16°. **14150. a. 26.(2.)**

KOṬHĀRĪ GOVARDHANA. श्रीभगवतप्रसादाख्यान [Bhagavat Prasādākhyāna. A sketch in verse of the life of Bhagavat Prasāda, high priest of the Ṣvāmīnārāyaṇa sect in Gujarat.] pp. 54. સુરત ૧૯૩૭ [*Surat,* 1881.] 16°. **14146. f. 16.(2.)**

KṚIPĀŚAṄKARA DOLATRĀMA TRAVĀḌĪ. स्त्रीनीतिधर्म दर्शक [Strīnītidharma darṣaka. A treatise in favour of female education, and social improvement.] pp. 175. અમદાવાદ ૧૯૩૩ [*Ahmadabad,* 1877.] 12°. **14146. e. 5.**

KṚISHṆADĀSA. ગુલ બકાવલી [Gul i bakāwalī. A love-tale in Gujarati verse, taken from the Persian of 'Izzat Allāh.] pp. 198, *lith.* મુંબઈ ૧૭૮૫ [*Bombay,* 1863.] 8°. **14148. b. 10.**

—— ગુલબકાવલીની વાર્તા. [Another edition.] pp. 126. अमदावाद १९३६ [*Ahmadabad,* 1880.] 12°. **14148. a. 27.**

—— [Another edition.] pp. 154. અમદાવાદ ૧૯૩૭ [*Ahmadabad,* 1881.] 12°. **14148. a. 20.**

—— રામાયણ. [Rāmāyaṇa. A poem on the story of Rāma.] *See* SOMACHAND KĀLIDĀSA. ज्ञान उपदेश [Jñāna-upadeṣa.] pp. 61-70. [1885.] 12°. **14148. e. 10.**

KṚISHṆAJĪ. The Ratna Mālā [by K.]. Translated [into English from a portion of the Gujarati original] by . . . A. K. Forbes. pp. 84. [*Bombay,* 1868.] 8°. **760. d. 31.**

Reprinted from the Journal of the Bombay Branch of the Royal Asiatic Society.

—— [Another copy.] *Bombay,* 1872? 8°. **14148. e. 2.**

KṚISHṆAMIŚRA. प्रबोधचन्द्रोदय नाटक [Prabodhachandrodaya nāṭaka. A Sanskrit drama, translated by Bhogīlāla Mahānanda Bhaṭṭa, with the assistance of Jayakṛishṇa Jīvanarāmajī.] pp.ii.97. મુંબઈ ૧૯૩૭ [*Bombay,* 1881.] 8°. **14148. c. 15.**

KRISHNA RANCHHODA TRAVĀḌĪ and CHHOṬALĀLA PREMĀNANDA TRAVĀḌĪ. राजेश्री भुधरभाइ धनेश्वरनो रासडो तथा परजीयो. [Bhudharabhāī Dhaneṣvarano rāsḍo. An elegy on the death of Bhudharabhāī Dhaneṣvara.] pp. 12. અમદાવાદ ૧૮૭૫ [*Ahmadabad*, 1875.] 12°. **14148. d. 5.(7.)**

KRISHNA ŚĀSTRĪ BHĀṬAVADEKAR. *See* RAGHUNĀTHA ŚĀSTRĪ DĀNTYE and KRISHNA ŚĀSTRĪ BHĀṬAVADEKAR. વૈદ્યસારસંગ્રહ [Vaidyasārasaṅgraha.] [1862.] 8°. **14146. b. 1.**

KRISHNA ŚĀSTRĪ CHIPLŪNKAR. An elementary grammar of the Sanskrit language, ... compiled and prepared [in Marathi] by Krishna Shastri Chiploonkur, ... Translated into Gujarati by Rao Saheb Myaram Shambhonath. (संस्कृत भाषेचें लहान व्याकरणाचें पुस्तक) [Saṃskṛita vyākaraṇa.] pp. 62. *Bombay*, 1867. 12°. **14150. b. 13.**

KSHEMAHARSHA. चंदन मालयागिरीनो रास . . . तथा शालिभद्र शाहनो रास. [Chandan Mālyāgirīno rās, and Śālibhadra Shāhno rās. Two Jain legends in verse, the former by Kshemaharsha, the latter by Matisārajī.] pp. 112. मुंबई १९४० [*Bombay*, 1884.] 12°. **14144. f. 2.**

KUMUDACHANDRA. कुमुदचंद्राचार्य विरचित महाप्रभाविक श्री कल्याण मंदिर स्तोत्र [Kalyāṇa mandira stotra. A Jain hymn in Sanskrit, accompanied by a verbal explanation in Gujarati, a verse translation in Hindi, and a Sanskrit commentary.] pp. 104. मुंबापुरी १९४४ [*Bombay*, 1888.] 8°. **14033. a. 23.**

KUNVARJĪ HAṬHĪSAṄGA. *See* ĀGHĀ ḤASAN, *Saiyid*, called AMĀNAT. ઇંદરસભા [Indrasabhā. Translated by K. H.] [1875.] 12°. **14148. d. 12.**

KUNVAR VIJAYAJĪ. अध्यात्मसार प्रश्नोत्तर ग्रंथ [Adhyātmasāra praṣnottara. A Jain philosophical treatise in the form of a dialogue between a Guru and his disciple.] pp. xii. 148. मुंबापुरी १९४० [*Bombay*, 1884.] 8°. **14144. g. 5.**

ḲUR'ĀN. قران نوا ترجمه گجراتي زبان ما [The Koran. Arabic text, with an interlineary translation, and marginal notes in Gujarati, and in the Arabic character, by ʻAbd al-Ḳādir ibn Lukmānjī.] pp. 797, iii. *lith.* بمبئي ١٢٩٦ [*Bombay*, 1879.] 8°. **14507. c. 13.**

The title-page and colophon are dated 1295.

KURJĪ PRĀGJĪ. *See* MAHĀBHĀRATA. भारतार्थ प्रकाश. The Bhartarth Prakash. [Vols. i.-vi. translated by K. P.] [1877, *etc.*] 8°. **14148. e. 1.**

LABDHIVIJAYA, *Muni*. मुनि लब्धि विजयजी कृत हरिबल मच्छीनो रास [Haribal Machchhīno rās. A Jain legend in verse, on the conversion of a fisherman, his great regard for animal life, and reward of his piety.] pp. 292. १८८९ [*Bombay*, 1889.] 16°. **14144. f. 20.**

LĀBHAVIJAYA, *Pandit*. श्रीजैनकाव्यसंग्रह [Jainakāvya saṅgraha. A collection of hymns in praise of Jain saints.] pp. 78. मोहमयी १९३१ [*Bombay*, 1881.] 12°. **14144. f. 4.(7.)**

LAILĀ MAJNŪN. લયેલા મજનું [Lailā Majnūn. A drama in four acts, adapted from the popular Persian romance. Second edition.] pp. 36. મુંબઈ ૧૮૮૧ [*Bombay*, 1881.] 12°. **14148. c. 13.(2.)**

LAKSHMĪDĀSA KAHĀNJĪ ṬHAKKAR. *See* GULĀBCHAND DAYĀLJĪ and LAKSHMĪDĀSA KAHĀNJĪ ṬHAKKAR. શ્રી આદીશ્વરનો શ્લોકો [Ādīṣvarano ṣloko.] [1886.] 12°. **14144. f. 1.(1.)**

LAKSHMĪNĀRĀYAṆA ŚIVANĀRĀYAṆA. *See* HOWARD (E. I.). Howard's Rudimentary English grammar, translated into Gujarati by Luxminarayan Shivnarayan. [1865.] 12°. **14150. a. 29.**

LĀLA, *Kavi*. *See* AKHĀ. Works of Brahmadnyani Akhabhakta. [Preceded by a poem by L. in eulogy of Karaṇṣī Raṇmal.] [1864.] 8°. **14148. e. 19.**

LĀLĀ BĀROṬ. સાતઅવતારની સદેવંતસાવલિંગાની વારતા [Sāt avatāranī Sadevanta Sāvaliṅgānī vārtā. The legend of the seven births of Sadevanta Sāvaliṅga, in prose and verse.] pp. 344, *lith.* મુંબઈ ૧૯૩૩ [*Bombay*, 1877.] 8°. **14148. b. 32.**

LĀLADĀSAJĪ. લાલદાસજી કૃત પદસંગ્રહ [Padasaṅgraha. A collection of songs addressed to the god Kṛishṇa.] pp. xii. 168, *lith.* અમદાવાદ ૧૮૮૬ [*Ahmadabad*, 1886.] 8°. **14148. f. 12.**

LĀLAṢAṄKARA UMIĀṢAṄKARA TRAVĀḌĪ. Elementary arithmetic, treated synthetically in Gujarati by Lálshankar Umiashankar Travádi. (અંકગણિતનાં મૂળતત્વ.) [Aṅkagaṇitanāṇ mūlatattva.] pp. ii. 209. *Bombay*, 1877. 12°. **14146. c. 17.**

LĀLCHAND LALUBHĀĪ. धना साळीभद्रनी जैनी नाटक [Dhanā Sāḷibhadra. A Jain religious drama on the attainment of salvation by asceticism and meditation.] pp. 32. અમદાવાદ ૧૮૮૭ [*Ahmadabad*, 1887.] 16°. **14148. c. 27.**

LALLU VALYAM. श्री विजयराजेंद्र सूरिजीनुं जन्म चरित्र. [Vijaya Rājendra Sūrijīnuṇ janmacharitra. The life of Vijaya Rājendra, a Jain priest, in verse.] pp. 16. अमदावाद १८८८ [*Ahmadabad*, 1888.] 16°. **14144. f.**

LÁLSHANKAR UMIASHANKAR TRAVÁDI. *See* LĀLAŚAṄKARA UMIĀŚAṄKARA TRAVĀḌĪ.

LALUBHĀĪ JAMNĀDĀSA. બાગનો ગરબો [Bāgno garbo. Garbi songs.] pp. 15. સુરત ૧૯૩૪ [*Surat*, 1877.] 12°. **14148. d. 6.(3.)**

LALUBHĀĪ PRĀṆAVALLABHADĀSA. રા. સા. લલુભાઈ પ્રાણવલ્લભદાસે . . . વાંચેલા નિબંધ [An essay read by L. P. on the 17th August, 1887, at a meeting of the Gujarat Vernacular Society, on the progress of Gujarati literature and education.] pp. 18. અમદાવાદ ૧૮૮૭ [*Ahmadabad*, 1887.] 8°. **14146. e. 20.(6.)**

LALU PĪTĀMBARA. ધોળ તથા પદવિગેરેનો સંગ્રહ [Dhoḷ tathā padavigereno saṅgraha. A collection of Vaishṇava songs, compiled by L. P.] pp. 278. અમદાવાદ ૧૮૮૧ [*Ahmadabad*, 1881.] 12°. **14144. f. 6.**

LAMB (CHARLES) *the Essayist.* *See* M., B. F. Lamb's Tales' complete glossary, *etc.* 1875. 16°. **14150. a. 2.(2.)**

—— *See* SHAKSPERE (W.) Selected tales from Shakespeare, [by C. L.] translated into Gujarati. 1867. 12°. **14148. a. 10.**

LARDNER (DIONYSIUS). *See* EUCLID. ભૂમિતિનાં મૂળતત્વોના પેહેલા છ સ્કંધો. [Lardner's "First six books of the elements of Euclid," translated into Gujarati.] [1866-59.] 8°. **14146. c. 20.**

LAVA KUSA. લવ કુશ આખ્યાન પ્રારંભ. [Lava Kuṣākhyāna. The story of Lava and Kuṣa, sons of Rāma.] pp. 62, *lith.* મુંબઈ ૧૯૧૫ [*Bombay*, 1858.] 16°. **14148. a. 2.(4.)**

LIFE. એક મુએલો છોકરો જીવતો [Ek muelo chhokro jīvato.] . . . Life from the dead. [A Christian tract.] pp. 49. શુરત ૧૮૫૪ [*Surat*, 1854.] 12°. **14144. a. 2.(3.)**

LIPIDHĀRĀ. લિપીધારા તથા અંકની ચોપડી. [Lipidhārā. A spelling-book, and arithmetical tables for schools.] pp. 46. મુંબઈ ૧૮૫૪ [*Bombay*, 1854.] 8°. **14150. b. 4.(2.)**

LOKANĀLA. अथ लोकनाल द्वत्रिंशिका बालावबोध सहित प्रारंभः [Lokanāla-dvatriṃṣikā. Thirty-two Prakrit verses on Jain cosmogony, with verbal and explanatory commentaries in Gujarati.] *See* BHĪMASIṂHA MĀṆAKA. प्रकरण-रत्नाकर [Prakaraṇa-ratnākara.] Vol. ii. pp. 720-736. [1876, *etc.*] 4°. **14100. e. 3.**

LUXMINARAYAN SHIVNARAYAN. *See* LAKSHMĪNĀRĀYAṆA ṢIVANĀRĀYAṆA.

M., B. F. Lamb's Tales' complete glossary. Containing meanings, other words, roots, of numerous words and all the idiomatic sentences and phrases explained both in English and Gujerati, by B. F. M. pp. 68. *Surat*, 1875. 16°. **14150. a. 2.(3.)**

M. D. A. *See* MĀṆEKJĪ DĀDĀBHĀĪ ARJĀNĪ.

MAC KEE (JAMES). *See* BIBLE.—Old Testament. —*Appendix.* Abridgment of the Old Testament Scriptures . . . by James McKee. 1852. 8°. **3068. b. 17.**

MĀDIGĀN i CHATRANG. માદીગાને ચતરંગ [Mādigan i chatrang. An account of the introduction of the game of chess into Persia. Pehlevi text and Gujarati translation.] *See* PESHOTAN BAHRĀMJĪ SANJĀNĀ. Ganjesháyagán, *etc.* 1885. 8°. **761. g. 2.**

MAGANLĀLA VAKHATCHAND. ગુજરાત દેશનો ઇતિહાસ [Gujarāt deṣano itihāsa. A history of Gujarat. Second edition.] pp. 60. મુંબઈ ૧૮૬૪ [*Bombay*, 1864.] 8°. **14146. g. 17.**

—— [Fourth edition.] pp. 126. મુંબઈ ૧૮૬૮ [*Bombay*, 1868.] 12°. **14146. f. 23.**

—— હોળી નિબંધ [Hoḷī-nibandha. A treatise exposing some of the pernicious practices peculiar to the Holī festival.] pp. ii. 64, *lith.* અમદાવાદ ૧૮૫૧ [*Ahmadabad*, 1851.] 16°. **14144. b. 6.(1.)**

MAGANRĀMA NARAHARARĀMA. મનોરંજક વારતા તથા ટૂચકા સંગ્રહ. [Manorañjaka vārtā. A collection of entertaining tales and anecdotes.] pp. 146. સુરત ૧૮૮૧ [*Surat*, 1881.] 12°. **14148. a. 23.**

MAHĀBHĀRATA. भारतार्थ प्रकाश. The Bhartarth Prakash. [A prose translation of the Mahābhārata, appearing in monthly parts. Vol. i.-vi. translated by Kurjī Prāgjī. Vol. vii. and succeeding volumes, translated by Maṇiṣaṅkara Mahānanda.] मुंबई १८७७ [*Bombay*, 1877, *etc.*] 8°.
In progress. **14148. e. 1.**

—— Aṣvamedhaparva. અશ્વમેધ [Aṣvamedhaparva. A verse translation by Gulābchand Lakshmīchand.] pp. 316, *lith.* મુંબઈ ૧૯૧૪ [*Bombay*, 1857.] 8°. **14148. f. 2.**

—— Bhagavadgītā. अथ श्रीमद्भगवद्गीता प्रारंभः [Bhagavadgītā. Sanskrit text, with a commentary in Gujarati.] ff. 131, *lith.* મુંબઈ [*Bombay*, 1860?]. *obl.* 8°. **14065. b. 4.**

—— Nalopākhyāna. *See* Premānanda Bhaṭa. નલ રાજાનું આખ્યાન. [Nala rājānuṇ ākhyāna. An episode of the Mahābhārata in verse.] [1858.] 8°. **14148. b. 4.(4.)**

—— Udyogaparva. *See* Manoradāsa, called Sachchidānanda Brahmatīrtha. सनत्सुजातीय आख्यान *etc.* [Sanatsujātīya ākhyāna. A paraphrase in verse of a philosophical treatise, taken from the Udyogaparva of the Mahābhārata.] [1864.] 8°. **14148. b. 3.(2.)**

—— Vanaparva. *See* Manoradāsa, called Sachchidānanda Brahmatīrtha. सनत्सुजातीय आख्यान *etc.* [Sanatsujātīya ākhyāna and Bandīnuṇ ākhyāna. A paraphrase in verse of two philosophical treatises; the latter taken from the Vanaparva of the Mahābhārata.] [1864.] 8°. **14148. b. 3.(2.)**

—— Viduranīti. વિદુરનીતિ [Viduranīti, or The morals of Vidura. An extract from the Udyogaparva, translated from the Sanskrit.] pp. 160, *lith.* મુંબઈ ૧૭૭૮ [*Bombay*, 1857.] 12°. **14148. d. 14.**

—— [Another edition.] *See* Periodical Publications.—*Nadiad.* आत्मज्ञान वर्धक [Ātmajñānavardhaka.] [1884.] 8°. **14150. c. 9.**

MAHĀDEVA GOPĀLA ṢĀSTRĪ. *See* Raghunātha Ṣāstrī Dāntye and Krishṇa Ṣāstrī Bhāṭavadekar. વૈદ્યસારસંગ્રહ [Vaidyasārasaṅgraha. Translated by M. G. Ṣ.] [1862.] 8°. **14146. b. 1.**

MAHĀNANDA BHĀĪṢAṄKARA. *See* Bhartṛihari. भर्तृहरिकृत वैराग्यशतक [Vairāgya-ṣataka. With a Gujarati version by M. Bh.] [1878.] 8°. **14072. d. 37.**

MĀHĀSUKHARĀMA NARBHERĀMA. आर्योद्वयनी उत्कंठा [Āryodvayanī utkaṇṭhā. Verses on the decline of commerce and civilization in India, and exhortations to industry.] pp. 54. अमदावाद १८३४ [*Ahmadabad*, 1877.] 16°. **14148. d. 8.(5.)**

—— मेघराजाने विनंती पत्र. [Megharājāne vinantīpatra, or A petition to the king of the clouds for rain. A poem.] pp. 8. અમદાવાદ ૧૮૭૭ [*Ahmadabad*, 1877.] 12°. **14148. d. 13.(13.)**

—— माहासुखराम कृत रसीक पदमाळा [Rasika padamālā. Miscellaneous poems.] pp. iii. 102. અમદાવાદ ૧૮૭૭ [*Ahmadabad*, 1877.] 16°. **14148. d. 5.(10.)**

MAHĪPATRĀMA RŪPARĀMA NĪLAKAṆṬHA, *C. I. E.* *See* Blanford (H. F.) Physical Geography .... Translated ... by R. S. Mahipatram Rupram Nilkanth. 1881. 12°. **14146. f. 6.**

—— *See* Dalpatrāma Ḍāhyābhāī, *Kavi, C. I. E.* The Gujarâti Kâvyadôhana. Expurgated and revised by R. S. Mahipatrâm R. Nilkanth, C. I. E. 1886. 8°. **14148. e 13.**

—— *See* Geikie (A.) Science primers in Gujarati. Physical Geography ... translated ... by Rao Saheb Mahipatram R. Nilkanth. 1880. 16°. **14146. c. 13.**

—— *See* Narmadāṣaṅkara Lālaṣaṅkara. The Narmagadya ... Expurgated and edited by Ráosáhib Mahipatrám Rúprám Nilkanth. 1880. 8°. **14150. e. 4.**

—— *See* Roscoe (H. E.) Science primers in Gujarati. Chemistry ... translated ... by Rao Saheb Mahipatram R. Nilkanth. 1880. 16°. **14146. c. 12.**

—— *See* Wells (T. L.) Anglo-Gujarâti Translation Series. Part V. ... Edited by R. S. Mahipatram R. Nilkanth. 1881. 12°. **14150. a. 34.**

—— उत्तम कपोळ करसनदास मुळजी चरित्र [Karsandās Muljī charitra.] ... A memoir of the reformer Karsandas Mulji. [With an introductory biographical sketch in English.] pp. xxx. 167. અમદાવાદ ૧૮૭૭ [*Ahmadabad*, 1877.] 8°. **14146. g. 12.**

—— [Second edition.] pp. 142. અમદાવાદ ૧૮૮૭ [*Ahmadabad*, 1887.] 12°. **14146. f. 25.**
Without the English portion of the first edition.

MAHĪPATRĀMA RŪPARĀMA NĪLAKAṆṬHA. Life of Akabar. Compiled by Rao Saheb Mahipatram Rupram. અકબર ચરિત્ર. [Akbarcharitra.] pp. 118. અમદાવાદ ૧૮૮૪ [*Ahmadabad*, 1884.] 8°. **14146. h. 9.**

—— A manual of Gujarati etymology, compiled by Rao Saheb Mahipatram R. Nilkanth. (व्युत्पत्तिप्रकाश) [Vyutpattiprakāṣa.] pp. vi. 75. *Bombay*, 1881. 8°. **14150. b. 15.**

—— A manual of the history of India, compiled by Ráo Sáhib Mahipatrám Rúprám Nílkanth. (ભરતખંડનો ઈતિહાસ.) [Bharatakhaṇḍano itihāsa.] Second edition. pp. xxxix. 200. *Bombay*, 1880. 12°. **14146. f. 20.**

—— Third edition. pp. ii. 36, 194. *Bombay*, 1881. 12°. **14146. f. 4.**

—— A new grammar of the Gujarati language, by Rao Sahib Mahipatram Ruparam Nilkantha. गूजराती भाषानुं नवुं व्याकरण. [Gujarātī bhāshānuṇ navuṇ vyākaraṇa.] pp. 67. मुंबई १८८० [*Bombay*, 1880.] 12°. **14150. a. 28.**

—— सधराजेसंघ. अथवा सिद्धराज जयसिंहदेवनी वार्त्ता. [Sadharājesaṅgha, or The story of Siddharāja Jayasiṃha, the Rajput Chief. An historical tale.] pp. ii. 146. અમદાવાદ ૧૮૮૦ [*Ahmadabad*, 1880.] 8°. **14144. g. 22.**

—— A short history of Guzerat, by Ráo Sáheb Mahipatrám Rúprám Nilkanth . . . ગૂજરાતનો બાળબોધક ઈતિહાસ [Gujarātno bāḷabodhaka itihāsa.] pp. 33. *Bombay*, 1877. 12°. **14146. f. 13.(4.)**

—— वनराज चावडो. गूर्जरी राज्य अने गूर्जरी प्रजा. [Vanarāja Chāvaḍo. An account of the Rajput kings of Gujarat of the Chāvada dynasty, particularly of king Vanarāja, his father Jayaṣekhara, and his son Yogarāja. Second edition.] pp. 225. અમદાવાદ ૧૮૮૦ [*Ahmadabad*, 1880.] 8°. **14148. b. 31.**

MALABARI (BEHRAMJI MERVANJI). *See* BAHRĀMJĪ MEHRVĀNJĪ MALABĀRĪ.

MALCOLM (*Sir* JOHN) તવારીખે કદીમ ઈરાન [Tavārīkh i kadīm Irān.] . . . . History of Ancient Persia from Sir J. M. with latest modern researches by Jamshedjee Pallonjee. pp. xiv. 201, 186. *Bombay*, 1868. 4°. **14146. h. 1.**

MALLINĀTHA, *Jain saint.* [*Life.*] *See* AHMADABAD.—*Jainadharma-pravartaka Sabhā.* श्री मल्लि जिन माहात्म्य [Malli Jina māhātmya.]

MAN. એક માણસે પોતાના સહુ પાડ પડોસીઓને મારીનાંખ્યા તેની કથા. The man who killed his neighbours. [A Christian tract.] pp. 24. શુરત ૧૮૫૮ [*Surat*, 1858.] 12°. **14144. a. 2.(4.)**

MANĀJĀT. મોનાજાત ગુજરાતી બેતોમાં [Manājāt. Zoroastrian hymns.] pp. iv. 39. મુંબઈ ૧૮૭૪ [*Bombay*, 1874.] 12°. **14144. h. 7.(1.)**

MANAMOHANADĀSA RAṆCHHODDĀSA. *See* PURĀṆAS.—*Bhāgavatapurāṇa.* શ્રીમદ ભાગવતની કથાનો સાર [Ṣrīmadbhāgavatanī kathāno sāra. An abstract of the contents of each chapter of the Bhāgavatapurāṇa, translated by M. R. from the Marathi.] [1881.] 8°. **14144. d. 2.**

MANASSUKHARĀMA SŪRYARĀMA TRIPĀṬHĪ. *See* FORBES (A. K.) Rás Málá . . . . translated into Gujaráti . . . With a memoir of the author by Mansukharám Suryarám. 1869. 8°. **14146. h. 6.**

—— सुज्ञ गोकुलजी संपत्तिराम झाला [Sujña Gokulajī Sampattirāma Jhālā.] . . . The life and letters of Gokulaji Sampattirâma Zâlâ: and his views of the Vedânta [with a brief sketch of his life in English] by Manassukharâma Sûryarâma Tripâṭhî. pp. xlv. 311. મુંબઈ ૧૯૩૭ [*Bombay*, 1881.] 8°. **14146. g. 3.**

MĀNATUNGĀCHĀRYA. भक्तामर स्तोत्र. [Bhaktāmara-stotra. A Jain hymn, Sanskrit text, with a Hindi verse translation by Hemarāja, devotional hymns, also in Hindi, by Devavijaya, and accompanied by a verbal interpretation in Gujarati.] pp. 116. मुंबाई १९४१ [*Bombay*, 1884.] 16°. **14100. a. 8.**

MANCHERJĪ HOSHANGJĪ JĀGOS. પારસીઓનું લીસ્ટ *etc.* [Pārsīonuṇ list, or An alphabetically arranged list of the names of Parsis residing in various towns in India.] pp. 140. મુંબઈ ૧૮૮૩ [*Bombay*, 1883.] 8°. **14150. e. 7.**

MANCHERJĪ JAMSHEDJĪ. એસકી બાનુ તથા એસકી ધણીનો ગરબો [Eskī bānu tathā eskī dhaṇīno garbo, or The foppish Parsi gentleman and his foppish wife. A poem.] pp. 16. સુરત ૧૮૮૦ [*Surat*, 1880.] 16°. **14148. d. 1.(9.)**

MANCHERJĪ KĀVASJĪ LANGRĀNĀ, called MANSUKH. આતશનાં કેબલાની ખુબી [Ātashnāṉ kebalānī khubī. A course of lectures on fire-worship by the Zoroastrians.] pp. iv. 100. મુંબઈ ૧૮૮૭ [*Bombay*, 1887.] 8°. **14144. i. 27.**

—— ગંજનામું ઇઆને સખુનોનો ખજ્નેનો દસ ભાગમાં [Ganj-nāmuṉ. A collection of the author's compositions in prose and verse, in ten chapters.] મુંબઈ ૧૮૬૩ [*Bombay*, 1863.] 4°. **14146. h. 2.**

—— મનસુખી મનાજાત અને અરજ ગુજરાતી [Mansūkhī manājāt.] (Prayers, hymns, and entreaties to Heaven, or Discourses upon sacred and various other subjects, composed in Gujrati verse and prose by Munsookh, alias Mr. Muncherjee Cowasjee Shapoorjee. No. V.) *Bombay*, 1872. 12°. **14144. i. 8.(1.)**
Incomplete; wanting pt. i.-iv.

—— પારસી ધારા પરની નુકતેચીની [Pārsī dhārā parnī nuktechinī. Criticisms on the Parsi laws, pointing out defects and the necessity for their alteration.] pp. 132. મુંબઈ ૧૮૮૮ [*Bombay*, 1888.] 12°. **14146. e. 25.**

—— Prince Albert. Selections from the prize translation [into English] of a Gujarati poem [chap. x. of the author's Ganj-nāmah] . . . by a Parsee poet named Muncherjee Cawasjee S. L., alias "Munsookh." . . . The translation by W. H. Hamilton. pp. iv. 201. *Bombay*, 1870. 8°. **14148. f. 8.**

—— સર જંમશેદજી બારોનેટ [Sir Jamshedjī Baronet. The life of Sir Jamsetjee Jeejeebhoy, in verse.] pp. xiv. 300. મુંબઈ ૧૮૬૧ [*Bombay*, 1861.] 12°. **14146. f. 1.**

MAÑCHHĀRĀMA GHELĀBHĀĪ. વડોદરાના મલહારરાવ ગાયકવાડનો ગરબો. [Baḍodarānā Malhār Rāva garbo. Verses on the trial of Malhār Rāva, Gaikwar of Baroda, for conspiring to poison Colonel Phayre, the British Resident.] pp. 55. સુરત ૧૯૩૧ [*Surat*, 1861.] 16°. **14148. d. 1.(4.)**

—— ચતુર સિંગ [Chatura Siṃha. A moral tale for boys.] pp. 160. સુરત ૧૯૩૩ [*Surat*, 1877.] 16°. **14148. a. 6.**

—— પરણેલા પીડાએ મરે ને કુંવારો કોહોડે મરે. [Parṇelo pīḍāe mare, ne kuṉvāro kohoḍe mare. A short tale contrasting married with unmarried life.] pp. 27. સુરત ૧૯૩૩ [*Surat*, 1877.] 16°. **14148. a. 11.(2.)**

MAÑCHHĀRĀMA GHELĀBHĀĪ. સાવકી માથકી છોકરાંઓ ઊપર પડતાં દુઃખ. [Sāvakī māthakī chhokrāṉo upar paḍtāṉ duḥkha. A drama in three acts on the miseries inflicted by stepmothers on their stepchildren.] pp. 119. સુરત ૧૮૮૦ [*Surat*, 1880.] 12°. **14148. c. 9.(2.)**

MAṆḌANA, *Son of Kshetra, of Chittor.* मिस्त्रितुं वास्तुशास्त्र तेमाथी अथ वास्तुसार नाम ग्रंथ *etc.* [Vāstusāra. A work on architecture in Sanskrit, with a Gujarati translation.] pp. 59, *lith.* अमदावाद १९३५ [*Ahmadabad*, 1878.] 8°. **14053. cc. 50.**

MĀṆEKJĪ BARJORJĪ MINUCHEHR HOMJĪNĀ. બરજોનામું [Barjo-nāmuṉ. A historical account of the wars between the ancient kings of Persia and Turkey.] Pts. ix. and xiv.-xvi. મુંબઈ ૧૮૭૫-૭૭ [*Bombay*, 1875-77.] 8°. **14146. g. 14.**
Incomplete; wanting all other parts.

—— ભાઈઓ બઈરી કરો તો જોઈને કુવો પુરજો! [Bhāio bairī karo to joine kuvo purjo. A tale of Parsi domestic life.] pp. ii. 157. મુંબઈ ૧૮૮૧ [*Bombay*, 1881.] 12°. **14148. a. 24.(3.)**

—— ભકિત નીતિ તથા વૈરાગ્ય બોધક કવિતા [Bhakti . . . bodhaka kavitā. Selections from the works of popular poets of Gujarat on devotion, morality and the abandonment of worldly pleasures. Compiled by M. B. M.] મુંબઈ ૧૮૮૭ [*Bombay*, 1887, *etc.*] 8°. **14148. e. 20.**
In progress.

—— ગામડેની ગલાલવહુ અને મુંબઈ શેહેરની ડીયર એમી! [Gāmḍenī Galālvahu. An amusing sketch of Parsi social life.] pp. 229. મુંબઈ ૧૮૮૧ [*Bombay*, 1881.] 12°. **14148. a. 24.(2.)**

—— હિંદુ દેવતાઓની ચિત્રમાળા [Hindu devatāonī chitramāḷā. Pictures and descriptions of Hindu gods.] pp. 40. મુંબઈ ૧૮૮૭ [*Bombay*, 1887.] 4°. **14144. e. 9.**

—— કાણી કુબાઈનાં કરતુક! [Kāṇī Kubāīnāṉ kartuk. A Parsi tale.] pp. 384. મુંબઈ ૧૮૮૫ [*Bombay*, 1885.] 12°. **14148. a. 25.(2.)**

—— સલુકની દીકરીનું જરા કોઠું તો જુવો! [Saluknī dikrinuṉ jarā kothuṉ to juvo! A tale illustrative of Parsi social life.] pp. 158. મુંબઈ ૧૮૮૦ [*Bombay*, 1880.] 12°. **14148. a. 24.(1.)**

—— [Second edition.] pp. 158. મુંબઈ ૧૮૮૬ [*Bombay*, 1886.] 12°. **14148. a. 35.(1.)**

MĀṆEKJĪ DĀDĀBHĀĪ ARJĀNĪ. A glossary of words occurring in Hikayat-e-latif [or Persian anecdotes, explained in English and Gujarati.] With the correct pronunciation of each word in Guzerati. pp. 46. *Bombay,* 1888. 8°.
757. f. 29.(2.)

MĀṆEKJĪ DĀRĀBJĪ ADRIANWĀLĀ. હોરમજદ યષ્ટ ઊપરથી હોરમજદની સીફત વીશેની શરેહ [Hormuzdnī sifat. An essay on the attributes of the Supreme God, as taught in the Yashts and other portions of the Zoroastrian scriptures.] pp. 16. મુંબઈ ૧૨૫૧ [*Bombay,* 1881.] 8°.
14144. i. 21.

MAṄGALADĀSA NATHŪBHĀI, *K. C. S. I. See* BOMBAY, *Presidency of.—Court of Śadr Dīwānī 'Adālat.* Borrodaile's Gujarát Caste Rules. Published . . . by [or rather, at the instance and cost of] Sir Munguldass Nathoobhoy, Knight C. S. I. 1884-87. 8°. **14146. a. 14.**

MAṄGAḶĀ GAURĪ. અથ શ્રી મંગળ વિચાર. [Maṅgaḷavichāra. Thoughts on Vedānta philosophy.] pp. 104. સુરત ૧૯૩૬ [*Surat,* 1879.] 16°.
14144. b. 7.

MAṆIBHĀĪ JASBHĀĪ. *See* SHAKSPERE (W.) Selected tales from Shakespeare, translated into Gujarati by . . . Manibhái Jusbhái. 1867. 12°.
14148. a. 10.

—— A digest of local customs in the Province of Cutch relating to trade and giras. કચ્છ દેશ સીરસ્તા સંગ્રહ. [Compiled by M. J., Diwan of Cutch.] pp. xii. 182. *Bombay,* 1885. 8°.
14146. g. 8.

MAṆILĀLA HARILĀLA and CHHOṬĀLĀLA MOHANALĀLA. મોંઘવારીની મોહોકણ. [Monghavārīnī mohkāṇ. A poem on the dearness of grain in consequence of drought.] pp. 11. अमदावाद १९३३ [*Ahmadabad,* 1877.] 16°. **14148. d. 13.(15.)**

MAṆILĀLA NABHUBHĀĪ DVIVEDĪ. *See* BHAVABHŪTI. महाकवि श्रीभवभूतिप्रणीत मालतीमाधव प्रकरण. [Mālatīmādhava. Translated with copious notes by M. N. D.] [1880.] 8°. **14148. b. 17.**

—— Siddhânta-sâra. An outline of the history of thought in India, terminating with an attempt to point out the basis of a universal religion. [With a preface and introductory synopsis of the work in English.] (સિધ્ધાન્તસાર) pp. xxxi. iv. iii. 387. *Bombay,* 1889. 16°. **14144. c. 4.**

MAṆIŚAṄKARA GOVINDAJĪ. વ્યાધિરોધ વિદ્યા [Vyādhirodha vidyā. A treatise on the preservation of health, and the treatment of Indian diseases. Fourth edition.] *See* MOREŚVARA, *Son of Māṇaka Bhaṭṭa.* વૈદ્યામૃત [Vaidyāmrita.] pp. 57-85. [1889.] 12°. **14043. c. 37.**

MAṆIŚAṄKARA LALUBHĀĪ. મણિશંકર કૃત કાવ્ય *etc.* [Maṇisaṅkarakṛita kāvya. Miscellaneous poems.] Pt. I. pp. 34. અમદાવાદ ૧૯૩૨ [*Ahmadabad,* 1875.] 12°. **14148. d. 5.(8.)**

MAṆIŚAṄKARA MAHĀNANDA. *See* MAHĀBHĀRATA. भारतार्थ प्रकाश. The Bhartarth Prakash. [Vol. vii. and succeeding volumes, translated by M. M.] [1877, *etc.*] 8°. **14148. e. 1.**

MANOHARA VĀṆĪ. મનોહર વાણી [Manohara vāṇī. A Christian poem.] pp. 36. સુરત ૧૮૫૮ [*Surat,* 1858.] 16°. **14144. a. 5.**

MANORADĀSA, called SACHCHIDĀNANDA BRAHMATĪRTHA. सनत्सुजातीय आख्यान तथा बंदीनुं आख्यान [Sanatsujātīya ākhyāna, and Bandīnuṇ ākhyāna. A paraphrase in verse, with an intermixture of Hindi, of two Sanskrit philosophical treatises by M., the former being taken from the Udyogaparva, and the latter from the Vanaparva of the Mahābhārata. Edited by Hīrāchand Kānjī.] pp. 86. मुंबई १९२० [*Bombay,* 1864.] 8°.
14148. b. 3.(2.)

MANSUKH. *See* MANCHERJĪ KĀVASJĪ LANGRĀNĀ, called MANSUKH.

MANU. मानवधर्मशास्त्र अथवा मनुस्मृति. (Mănavadharma-śāstra or Manusmṛiti, being the Institutes of Manu . . . . translated into Gujaráti by Jáverilál Umiáshankar Yájṇik.) pp. lvii. viii. 267. *Bombay,* 1871. 8°. **14146. a. 10.**

MARZBAN (J. B.) *See* JAHĀNGĪR BAHRĀMJĪ MARZBĀN.

MATICHANDRA. *See* DEVENDRA SŪRI. अथ श्री कर्मविपाक *etc.* [Karmavipāka. With a commentary by M.] [1876, *etc.*] 4°. **14100. e. 3.**

MATISĀRAJĪ. श्रीशालिभद्र शाहनो रास प्रारंभः [Śālibhadra Shāhno rās. A Jain legend in verse.] *See* KSHEMAHARSHA. चंदन मालयागिरीनो रास [Chandan Mālyāgirīno rās.] pp. 51-111. [1884.] 12°.
14144. f. 2.

MAULĀ-BAKHSH GHISHE-KHĀN. संगीतानुभव. [Saṅgītānubhava. A treatise on Indian music.] मुंबई १९४४ [*Bombay,* 1888, *etc.*] 8°. **14150. b. 19.**
In progress.

MAYĀRĀMA ṢAMBHUNĀTHA. *See* KRISHṆA ṢĀSTRĪ CHIPLŪṆKAR. An elementary grammar of the Sanskrit language .... Translated into Gujarati by Rao Saheb Myaram Shambhonath. 1867. 12°. **14150. b. 13.**

MAYO ṢIVADĀSA. સોમપ્રદોષની કથા અથવા સીમંતિની આખ્યાન [Somapradoshanī kathā, also called Sīmantinī ākhyāna. A mythological story of the princess Sīmantinī, and her protection by the god Ṣiva for observing the Somapradosha festival. Taken from the Brahmottarakhaṇḍa of the Skandapurāṇa.] pp. 23. સુરત ૧૮૭૭ [*Surat,* 1877.] 16°. **14144. b. 6.(2.)**

MEGHARĀJA. *See* BHAGAVATĪ-SŪTRA. अथ भगवती सूत्र [Bhagavatī. With a Gujarati commentary by M.] [1882.] *obl.* 4°. **14100. f. 9.**

—— *See* RĀJAPRAṢNĪYA. श्री रायपसेणी ० [Rāyapaseṇī, or Rājapraṣnīya. With a Gujarati commentary by M.] [1880.] 4°. **14100. e. 5.**

—— *See* SAMAVĀYĀṄGA. समवायांग [Samavāyāṅga. With a Gujarati *ṭabba* or explanation by M.] [1880.] *obl.* 4°. **14100. f. 8.**

—— *See* STHĀNĀṄGA. स्थानाङ्ग सूत्र ... मेघराजगणि कृत भाषा टीका सहित [Sthānāṅga. With a Gujarati commentary by M.] [1880.] *obl.* 4°. **14100. f. 3.**

MEHETĀJĪ DEVAJĪ UKĀBHĀĪ MAKVĀṆĀ. *See* DEVAJĪ UKĀBHĀĪ MAKVĀṆĀ.

MEHEṬĀJĪ KHĪMAJĪ PREMAJĪ. *See* KHĪMAJĪ PREMAJĪ MEHETĀ.

MEHRJĪBHĀĪ PĀLANJĪ MĀDAN. *See* ZAND AVASTĀ. Yaçna and the Gathas ... Translated ... by Aerpat Meherjibhai Palanji Madan. 1885. 12°. **14144. i. 11.**

MEHRVANJEE HORMUSJEE MEHTA. *See* MEHRVĀNJĪ HORMASJĪ MEHETĀ.

MEHRVĀNJĪ HORMASJĪ MEHETĀ. Conversations on Chemistry, Translated into Goojurathee, and published with the English original; by Meherwanjee Hormusjee Mehta. (રસાયનશાસ્ત્ર સંબંધી વાતચીત) [Rasāyanaṣāstra sambandhī vātchīt.] pp. ii. 265. *Bombay,* 1851. 12°. **14146. c. 11.**

MEHRVĀNJĪ HORMASJĪ MEHETĀ and NAVAROJĪ RUSTAMJĪ LĀḌ. The English and Goojratee scholar's assistant; comprising a vocabulary, English and Goojratee, together with the rudimental principles of English grammar, accompanied by a literal Goojratee translation ... by Mehrvanjee Hormusjee Mehta and Nowrojee Rustomjee. pp. vi. 56. *Bombay,* 1840. 8°. **14150. b. 3.**

The vocabulary is without pagination.

MERĀMAṆAJĪ. प्रवीनसागर ॥ सटीक ॥ [Pravīṇasāgara. A romance in Hindi verse, introducing matters relating to geography, chiromancy, music, medicine, Yoga philosophy, and various other subjects. Edited by Chaturbhuja Prāṇajīvana, with a running commentary in Gujarati, begun by Ranmal Adābhāi, and completed by Dalpatrāma Ḍāhyābhāi.] pp. iv. 1179, xxxvi. अमदावाद १८८२ [*Ahmadabad, Rajkot,* printed, 1882.] 4°. **14154. i. 1.**

MERCY. દયા કરવી તે વાત વીશે [Dayā karvī.] Mercy. [A Christian tract.] pp. 42. ૧૮૫૮ *Surat,* [1858.] 12°. **14144. a. 1.(7.)**

MILL (JOHN STUART). *See* AMBALĀLA SĀKARLĀLA. અર્થશાસ્ત્ર ... [Arthaṣāstra. A treatise] based on Mill's Principles of political economy, *etc.* 1875. 8°. **14146. e. 16.**

MOBED RATANJĪ RUSTAMJĪ KĀṄGĀ. *See* RATANJĪ RUSTAMJĪ KĀṄGĀ.

MOHANA. *See* ANUYOGADVĀRA. श्री अनुयोगद्वार ० [Anuyogadvāra. With a Gujarati commentary by M.] [1879.] *obl.* 4°. **14100. f. 11.**

MOHANALĀLA KUVERA TRAVĀḌĪ. श्रीमंत सरकार समशेर बहादुर गायकवाड माहाराजना राज्यनो इतिहास. [Gāyakavāḍa Mahārājanā itihāsa. A history of the Gaikwar Chiefs of Baroda.] Pt. I. pp. 72. અમદાવાદ ૧૮૩૧ [*Ahmadabad,* 1875.] 8°. **14146. g. 1.**

MOHANARĀMA DALPATRĀMA. गोपाळ गुण वर्णन [Gopāla guṇavarṇana. A eulogistic poem, in praise of Gopāla Rāva, late Judge of the Small Cause Court at Ahmadabad.] pp. 23. અમદાવાદ ૧૮૭૭ [*Ahmadabad,* 1877.] 16°. **14148. d. 13.(12.)**

MOHANA VIJAYAJĪ. ચંદ રાજાનો રાસ [Chand Rājāno rās. The story of king Chand. A Jain legend in verse.] pp. 132. અમદાવાદ ૧૮૮૨ [*Ahmadabad,* 1882.] 8°. **14144. g. 19.**

MOREṢVARA, *Son of Māṇaka Bhaṭṭa.* વૈદ્યામૃત. [Vaidyāmṛita. A treatise on medicine in Sanskrit verse, accompanied by a Gujarati prose translation by Kālidāsa Govindajī. Followed by Vyādhirodha vidyā, a short article on the preservation of health, and the treatment of Indian diseases, by Maṇiṣaṅkara Govindajī. Second edition.] pp. vi. 85. મુંબઈ ૧૮૮૯ [*Bombay*, 1889.] 12°. **14043. c. 37.**

MOROBĀ KĀNHOBĀ. ઘાશીરામ કોટવાલ ... Ghasiram Kotwāl. [A tale, shewing the cruelties practised by the police at Poona, during the time of the Peshwas. Translated] from the Maráthi [of M. K.] into Gujráti by Shakerrám Dalpatrám. pp. iv. xvi. 205. *Bombay*, 1865. 12°. **14148. a. 22.**

MORRIS (Henry) *of the Madras Civil Service.* A history of India, in Gujarati, being a translation of Morris' History of India, by Chhotálál Sevakarám. (હિંદુસ્તાનનો ઇતિહાસ.) [Hindustanano itihāsa.] Fourth edition. pp. xvii. 217. *Bombay*, 1875. 8°. **14146. g. 13.**

MORTIMER (Favell Lee) *Mrs.* Peep of Day. અરૂણોદય. [Aruṇodaya, translated from the English of Mrs. F. L. M.] pp. 180. સુરત ૧૮૭૪ [*Surat*, 1874.] 16°. **14144. a. 15.**

MOTĪLĀLA MANASSUKHARĀMA SHĀH. ગુજરાતી શબ્દાર્થ કોષ [Gujarātī ṣabdārtha kosha. A vocabulary of Gujarati words, chiefly technical and colloquial, which are not to be found in existing Gujarati dictionaries.] pp. 94. अमदावाद १८८६ [*Ahmadabad*, 1886.] 12°. **14150. b. 18.**

—— [Second edition.] pp. 102. અમદાવાદ ૧૮૮૮ [*Ahmadabad*, 1888.] 12°. **14150. b. 21.**

MOTĪRĀMA MAÑCHHARĀMA. ચંડીકાનો ગરબો [Chaṇḍīkāno garbo. A poem in praise of the goddess Durgā, based on the Chaṇḍīpātha, or Devīmāhātmya, a section of the Mārkaṇḍeyapurāṇa.] pp. 38, *lith.* અમદાવાદ ૧૯૩૧ [*Ahmadabad*, 1875.] 12°. **14148. d. 4.(4.)**

MOTĪṢĀ. મોતીશાનાં ઢાળીઆં [Motīṣānāṇ ḍhāḷiāṇ. Verses in praise of Jain saints and pilgrimages.] pp. 32. અમદાવાદ ૧૮૮૫ [*Ahmadabad*, 1885.] 12°. **14144. f. 12.(5.)**

MUGDHĀVABODHA AUKTIKA. The Mugdhâvabodha auktika, or A grammar for beginners of the Gujerati language [by a pupil of Devasundara] ... मुग्धावबोधमौक्तिकम् ॥ Edited by H. H. Dhruva. *Bombay*, 1889. 8°. **14150. b. 20.**

The first number of a series of works on old Gujarati literature, entitled "Prâchîna Gujerâti Sâhitya Ratnamâlâ."

MUHAMMAD, *the Prophet.* *See* Jesus Christ, ઈશા મશીહ *etc.* Concerning Jesus the Messiah, and Mahummed. [1843.] 8°. **14144. a. 19.(2.)**

—— Tuqviutí-din-i-Mazdiasna, or a Mehzur or Certificate, given by Huzrut Mahomet, the Prophet of the Moosulmans, on behalf of Mehdi-Furrookh bin-Shukhsan ..., and another Mehzur given by Huzrut Ally to a Parsee named Behramshád-bin-Kheradroos and to the whole Parsee nation. Translated into Goozrathee from the Persian version of the original Arabic ... by Sorabjee Jamsetjee Jejeebhoy. (તકવીઅતે દીને માજદીઅસનાં) pp. 78, 46. *Bombay*, 1851. 8°. **14144. i. 3.**

MUHAMMAD 'ĀRIF. *See* Āghā Hasan, *Saiyid*, called Amānat. ઈંદરસભા [Indrasabhā. Translated with the assistance of M. 'Ā.] [1875.] 12°. **14148. d. 12.**

MUKTĀNANDA. રૂકમીણી વીવાની ચોપડી [Rukmiṇī vivāṇī chopaḍī. A poem on the marriage of Krishṇa and Rukmiṇī.] pp. 16, *lith.* અમદાવાદ ૧૮૭૪ [*Ahmadabad*, 1874.] 16°. **14148. d. 5.(6.)**

MŪLAṢAṄKARA RĀMAJĪ. *See* Govardhana Lālajī, also called Gaṭṭu Lālajī. Cutch mahodaya ... [A Sanskrit poem, with a prose translation by M. R.] [1884.] 8°. **14070. d. 30.**

MUNCHERJEE CAWASJEE S. L. *See* Mancherjī Kāvasjī Langrānā, called Mansukh.

MUNISUNDARA SŪRI. अथ श्री मुनिसुंदरसूरिकृत अध्यात्मकल्पद्रुमो बालावबोध सहितः प्रारभ्यते [Adhyātma-kalpadruma. A work in Sanskrit verse in 16 chapters, on Jain doctrine and discipline, with a Gujarati paraphrase by Ratnachandra.] *See* Bhīmasiṃha Māṇaka. प्रकरण-रत्नाकर [Prakaraṇa-ratnākara.] Vol. ii. pp. 9-96. [1876, *etc.*] 4°. **14100. e. 3.**

—— अथ श्री मुनी सुंदरीसुरकृत श्री अध्यात्मकल्पद्रुमनो अर्थ प्रारंभ्यते [Adhyātma-kalpadruma. Paraphrased in Gujarati by Ratnachandra.] *See* JAINAŚĀSTRA. જૈન સાસ્ત્ર કથા સંગ્રહ. pp. 102-172. [1883.] 8°. **14144. g. 8.**

—— [Another edition.] *See* CHARITRASAṄGRAHA ચરિત્ર સગ્રહ. pp. 102-172. [1884.] 8°. **14144. g. 7.**

MUNSOOKH. *See* MANCHERJĪ KĀVASJĪ LANGRĀNĀ, called MANSUKH.

MYARAM SHAMBHONATH. *See* MAYĀRĀMA ŚAMBHUNĀTHA.

NĀGAJĪ KALYĀṆAJĪ. [*Life.*] *See* DEVAJĪ UKĀBHĀĪ MAKVĀṆĀ. કવિ નાગજીનું જન્મ ચરિત્ર. [Kavi Nāgjīnuṇ janmacharitra. A biographical sketch of the life of the poet Nāgajī.]

NAGĪNDĀSA MAÑCHHĀRĀMA GHELĀBHĀĪ. બાળવિધવા રૂપસુંદરી [Bāḷavidhavā Rūpasundarī. A drama in three acts on the miseries of child-widowhood.] pp. 120. સુરત ૧૮૮૫ [*Surat,* 1885.] 12°. **14148. d. 27.**

—— રંગિલી ને છબિલી અથવા સરસ્વતીનો શણગાર. [Raṅgilī ne Chhabilī. A drama in three acts on the adventures of two educated girls.] pp. 92. સુરત ૧૮૮૮ [*Surat,* 1888.] 8°. **14148. c. 29.**

NĀNĀBHĀĪ RUSTAMJĪ RĀṆĪNĀ. *See* SHAKSPERE (WILLIAM.) શેકસપીર નાટક. [Shakspere's plays, translated by N. R. R.] [1865.] 8°. **14148. b. 19.**

—— હોમલો હાઊ ... Homlo Háu or Cheating play never thrives. A comedy in three acts. pp. 106, xi. મુંબઈ: ૧૮૮૮ [*Bombay,* 1888.] 8°. **14148. c. 14.(2.)**

—— કાળાં મેંઢાં અથવા સંસાર સુખના શત્રુ. [Kāḷāṇ meṇḍhāṇ. Black sheep, or social pests. A play in three acts.] pp. xix. 180. મુંબઈ ૧૮૮૫ [*Bombay,* 1885.] 12°. **14148. c. 18.(2.)**

NĀNĀ MOROJĪ. *See* BOMBAY, *Presidency of.— Court of Ṣadr Dīwānī 'Adālat.* Borradaile's Gujarát Caste Rules. Published ... under the superintendence of [or rather, edited by] Ráo Bahádur Náná Morojí. 1884-87. 8°. **14146. a. 14.**

NANDALĀLA. *See* SOMAPRABHĀCHĀRYA. सप श्री शृंगारवैराग्यतरंगिणी प्रारंभः [Śriṅgāravairāgya-taraṅgiṇī. With a Gujarati translation and gloss by N.] [1876, *etc.*] 4°. **14100. e. 3.**

—— —— [1883.] 8°. **14144. g. 8.**

—— —— [1884.] 8°. **14144. g. 7.**

NANDA RĀJĀ. नंदराजा अने सती सुलोचनाना नाटकमां गवातां गायनो. [Nanda Rājā ane satī Sulochanā. A drama in verse on the popular story of King Nanda and his wife Sulochanā.] pp. 18. અમદાવાદ ૧૮૮૨ [*Ahmadabad,* 1882.] 12°. **14148. c. 18.(1.)**

NANDAŚAṄKARA TULJĀŚAṄKARA. *See* EUCLID. ભૂમિતિનાં મૂળતત્વોના પેહેલા છ સ્કંધો. [Lardner's Euclid, translated with the assistance of N. T.] [1866-59.] 8°. **14146. c. 20.**

—— *See* RĀMAKṚISHṆA GOPĀLA BHĀṆḌĀRKAR. સંસ્કૃત માર્ગોપદેશિકા [Mārgopadeśikā. Translated into Gujarati by N. T.] [1868.] 8°. **14085. b. 10.**

—— —— 1875. 8°. **14085. b. 17.**

—— કરણ ઘેલો ગુજરાતનો છેલો રજપુત રાજા. [Karaṇ Ghelo, or the Rajput prince of Gujarat. An historical novel.] pp. 356. મુંબઈ ૧૮૬૬ [*Bombay,* 1866.] 8°. **14148. b. 8.**

NARASIMHA MEHETĀ. *See* NṚISIMHA MEHETĀ.

NĀRĀYAṆA BĀPUJĪ KĀNIṬKAR. Malharrao Maharaj. A historical drama in seven acts in Marathi by Narayen Bapuji Kanitkar. Translated into Gujrathi by Harjivan Uttamram Meheta. (મલ્હારરાવ મહારાજ નાટક). pp. vi. 170. મુંબઈ ૧૮૭૬ [*Bombay,* 1876.] 12°. **14148. c. 6.**

NĀRĀYAṆABHĀRTHĪ YAŚAVANTABHĀRTHĪ. *See* BĀLACHANDRĀCHĀRYA. करुणा वज्रायुध नाटक [Karuṇāvajrāyudha nāṭaka. Translated by N. Y. from the Sanskrit.] [1886.] 8°. **14148. c. 25.**

—— *See* PURĀṆAS.— Mārkaṇḍeyapurāṇa.— *Devīmāhātmya.* सप्तशती [Saptaśatī. Translated in verse by Bhālaṇa. With an introductory sketch of the life and writings of the poet, by N. Y.] [1887.] 8°. **14148. e. 12.**

NĀRĀYAṆA BHAṬṬA, called MṚIGARĀJALAKSHMAN. Veni Sanhár Nátak. A drama in six acts, translated from Sanscrit and Marathi, by Sukheshwar Bápuji Shastri. (વેણીસંહાર નાટક) pp. 123. *Bombay*, 1867. 12°. **14148. c. 4.**

NĀRĀYAṆA HEMACHANDRA. *See* BRĀHMA SAMĀJ. ब्राह्मधर्म्ममतसार [Brāhmadharma matasāra. Translated into Gujarati prose by N. H.] [1882.] 32°. **14028. a. 17.**

—— —— [1887.] 32°. **14028. a. 22.**

—— *See* UPANISHADS. श्वेताश्वतरोपनिषद्ना सार [Selections from the Śvetāśvatara Upanishad, with a prose translation by N. H.] [1881.] 8°. **14010. c. 30.(1.)**

—— आर्यधर्मनीति [Āryadharmanīti. A collection of moral verses in Sanskrit, with a Gujarati prose translation.] pp. 118. મુંબઈ ૧૮૮૦ [*Bombay*, 1880.] 12°. **14085. c. 32.**

—— जातिभेद अने भोजनविचार [Jātibheda ane bhojanavichāra. Caste and consideration of diet, being verses from various early Sanskrit authors, with a translation, notes and preface in Gujarati. Compiled by N. H. with a view of modifying current caste prejudices as to diet.] pp. 39. *Sansk.* and *Guj.* મુંબઈ ૧૮૮૧ [*Bombay*, 1881.] 12°. **14028. c. 42.**

—— પુનર્વિવાહ શાસ્ત્રસંમત છે. [Punarvivāha śāstrasammata chhe. A treatise in favour of widow-marriage, with numerous Sanskrit quotations in support of the question.] pp. 40. મુંબઈ ૧૮૮૬ [*Bombay*, 1886.] 12°. **14146. e. 21.(2.)**

—— वैराग्य. [Vairāgya. A tract on a Brahmist view of asceticism.] pp. 20. અમદાવાદ [*Ahmadabad*, 1883.] 32°. **14144. a. 18.**

—— जरतोस्त धर्मनीति. અર્થાત્ સદ્ધર્મ વચન સંગ્રહ. [Zartosht dharmanīti, or the principles of the Zoroastrian religion, being a commentary on passages in the Zand Avastā, and other sacred books of the Parsis.] Pt. vi. મુંબઈ ૧૯૩૭ [*Bombay*, 1881.] 8°. **14144. i. 10.**

NĀRĀYAṆA HĪRĀCHAND KĀNŪNĪ. ज्ञाननो बगीचो. એટલે ધર્મતત્વભાસ્કર યાને જૈનધર્મ સંબંધી કાયદાની આવૃતી બીજી [Dharmatattva-bhāskara. A digest of the principles of the Jain religion. Second edition.] pp. iv. 80. અમદાવાદ ૧૮૮૯ [*Ahmadabad*, 1889.] 12°. **14144. g. 32.**

NARBHERĀMA KĀŚĪRĀMA DAVE. બાળવિધવા રૂપવંતી દુઃખ દર્શક [Bāḷavidhavā rūpavantī duḥkhadarṣaka. A novel on the unfortunate condition of Hindu widows.] Pt. i. pp. 234. મુંબઈ ૧૮૭૭ [*Bombay*, 1877.] 12°. **14148. c. 7.**

NARBHERĀMA MAÑCHHĀRĀMA. नभु कविता [Nabhu kavitā. Miscellaneous verses.] pp. 48. શુરત ૧૮૭૭ [*Surat*, 1877.] 16°. **14148. d. 5.(11).**

NARMADĀŚAṄKARA LĀLAŚAṄKARA. *See* DAYĀRĀMA. દયારામકૃત કાવ્યસંગ્રહ [Dayārāmakṛita kāvyasaṅgraha. Edited by N. L.] [1865.] 8°. **14148. e. 5.**

—— *See* KATHIAWAR. કાઠીઆવાડ સર્વસંગ્રહ [Kāṭhiāvāḍ sarvasaṅgraha. Translated by N. L.] [1886.] 8°. **14146. h. 15.**

—— *See* PREMĀNANDA BHAṬA. Premánand's Nalákhyán. Students' edition, prepared by Kavi Narmadáshankar Lálashankar. 1880. 12°. **14148. a. 30.**

—— અલંકારપ્રવેશ [Alaṅkārapraveṣa. A treatise on rhetoric. Second edition.] pp. viii. 48. મુંબઈ ૧૮૬૩ [*Bombay*, 1863.] 12°. **14146. c. 5.(2.)**

—— नर्मगद्य [Narmagadya. The prose works of N. L.] pp. iv. 486. મુંબઈ ૧૮૬૫ [*Bombay*, 1865.] 8°. **14150. e. 3.**

—— The Narmagadya, or The prose works of Kavi Narmadashankar Lálashankar. Part ii. *Bombay*, 1875. 8°. **14150. e. 5.**
Imperfect; wanting pt. 1.

—— The Narmagadya, . . . , expurgated and edited by Ráosáhib Mahipatrám Rúprám Nílkanth. (નર્મગદ્ય) 2nd edition, pp. ix. 647. *Bombay*, 1880. 8°. **14150. e. 4.**

—— નર્મકવિતા [Narmakavitā. The poetical works of N. L.] 3 vol. મુંબઈ ૧૮૬૨ [*Bombay*, 1862.] 12°. **14148. d. 22.**

—— [Second edition. With copious notes.] pp. xii. 440, iv. મુંબઈ ૧૮૬૬ [*Bombay*, 1886.] 4°. **14148. f. 18.**

—— [Third edition.] Pt. i. pp. vii. 135. મુંબઈ ૧૮૭૭ [*Bombay*, 1877.] 12°. **14148. d. 7.(1.)**
Wanting all other parts.

—— नर्मकोश [Narmakoṣa. A Gujarati dictionary, explained in Gujarati.] Pt. i. [A-Jeṭh.] મુંબઈ ૧૮૨૦ [*Bombay*, 1864.] 4°. **14150. b. 1.**

NARMADĀSAṄKARA LĀLASAṄKARA. નર્મકોશ ગુજરાતી શબ્દાર્થસંગ્રહ [Another edition.] pp. xxiv. 619. સુરત ૧૮૭૩ [*Surat*, 1873.] 4°. **14150. b. 2.**

—— નર્મવ્યાકરણ ગુજરાતી ભાષાનું વ્યાકરણ [Narmavyākaraṇa. A grammar of the Gujarati language.] Pt. i. pp. 42. મુંબઈ ૧૮૬૫ [*Bombay*, 1865.] 12°. **14150. a. 1.(4.)**

—— પિંગળપ્રવેશ. [Piṅgaḷapraveṣa. A treatise on prosody.] pp. 77. મુંબઈ ૧૮૬૦ [*Bombay*, 1860.] 12°. **14146. c. 5.(1.)**

NAROTTAMA AMARAJĪ. *See* PURĀṆAS.—*Śivapurāṇa.* श्री शिवपुराण भाषांतर Shri Shivpuran bhasanter. [Translated into prose by N. A.] [1884, *etc.*] 4°. **14144. e. 2.**

NAROTTAMA NITYĀNANDA SABHĀMANTRĪ. *See* BHŪPATARĀYA HARAGOVINDA DĀTĀR. Kanya vikraya dosh darshak, *etc.* [An essay compiled with the assistance of N. N. S.] [1881.] 12°. **14146. e. 8.(3.)**

NARSI MEHETĀ. *See* NṚISIṂHA MEHETĀ.

NASARVĀNJĪ CHĀNDĀBHĀĪ. *See* KAHĀNDĀSA MAÑCHHĀRAMA. Natural philosophy for beginners . . . Second edition, revised by Nushirvánji Chándábhai. 1856. 12°. **14146. c. 9.**

NASARVĀNJĪ FRĀMJĪ. મજ્દયસ્ન અથવા જરથોશ્તી ધર્મઃ તેનુ પડી ભાગવું. [Mazdayasna. A short account of the decline of the Zoroastrian religion.] pp. 9. મુંબઈ ૧૮૮૧ [*Bombay*, 1881.] 8°. **14144. i. 4.(4.)**

NASARVĀNJĪ HIRJĪBHĀĪ PAṬEL. દ્રવ્ય તથા રૂપાના મૂલની ન્યૂનતા વિષેનાં ભાષણઃ [Dravya tathā rupānā mūlanī nyūnatā vishenāṉ bhāshaṇa.] (Lectures on wealth and the silver question : . . . With copious notes in English by N. H. Patel.) pp. 215. *Bombay*, 1880. 8°. **14146. e. 12.**

NASARVĀNJĪ NAVAROJĪ PĀGHḌEWĀLĀ. ડુંગરવાડાનો ખેઆલ [Ḍungar vāḍāno kheyāl. A poem regarding the Towers of Silence, or Parsi burying-place.] pp. 8. મુંબઈ ૧૮૭૫ [*Bombay*, 1875.] 8°. **14148. e. 3.(2.)**

NASARVĀNJĪ RUSTAMJĪ VĀCHHĀ. નોશીરવાને સમનગાન અને શીરીને શીસતાન. [Noshīrwān i Samangān ane Shīrīn i Sīstān. A drama in four acts.] pp. xi. 110. મુંબઈ ૧૮૮૧ [*Bombay*, 1881.] 8°. **14148. c. 17.**

NASARVĀNJĪ SHĀPURJĪ TAVAḌIĀ. મિથ્ર અથવા મેહેર યજદઃ [Mithra, also called Meher Yazda. A prize essay on Mithra, the deity representing the dawn, as described in the Zand Avastā, and a comparison between it and similar deities in the mythologies of other religions.] pp. viii. 53. મુંબઈ ૧૮૮૮ [*Bombay*, 1888.] 8°. **14144. i. 28.(2.)**

NASARVĀNJĪ SHEHRIYĀRJĪ GINWĀLĀ. The Parsee girl of the period. [An English essay] by Mr. N. S. Ginwalla, of Broach. (હાલના જમાનાની પારસી છોકરીઓ.) [Hālnāṉ jamānānī Pārsī chhokrīo. With a Gujarati translation by B. N. B.] pp. 16, 15. *Bombay*, 1884. 8°. **14146. e. 15.(2.)**

—— Seven papers. On early death among native public men, or physical inferiority of natives. City and country life of Parsees. The vernacular press in the Bombay presidency. Infant marriage and enforced widowhood. The Indian ryot. An appeal to my countrymen for our beloved Queen, and A cheeta hunt in the Gaekwar's territory. By Nusserwanjee Sheriarjee Ginwalla, *etc.* [The first two in English and Gujarati, the rest in English only.] pp. 135. *Broach*, 1887. 8°. **14146. e. 20.(5.)**

NASĪM. ગોહેરે જીંદગી [Gauhar i zindagī. A short account in verse of the life of Sir Jamsetjee Jeejeebhoy.] pp. 52. મુંબઈ ૧૮૭૭ [*Bombay*, 1877.] 12°. **14148. e. 3.(3.)**

NĀTHĀBHĀĪ LALUBHĀĪ. જૈન કાવ્ય સાર સંગ્રહ. [Jaina kāvya sārasaṅgraha. Selections from the writing of Jain poets, compiled by N. L. Also Rāmacharitra, or the story of Rāma and Sītā, in prose, by Hemachandra Āchārya.] pp. 643. અમદાવાદ ૧૮૮૨ [*Ahmadabad*, 1882.] 8°. **14144. g. 23.**

—— મોહોટી પુજાસંગ્રહ *etc.* [Mohoṭī pūjāsaṅgraha. A collection of Jain hymns and prayers.] pp. 112, 52, 64, 48. અમદાવાદ ૧૮૮૧ [*Ahmadabad*, 1881.] 8°. **14144. g. 11.**

NĀTHĀṢAṄKARA PŪJĀṢAṄKARA ṢĀSTRĪ. *See* PRĀCHĪNA KĀVYA. प्राचीन काव्य [Prāchīna kāvya. Edited, with copious notes, by N. P. Ṣ.] [1885, *etc.*] 8°. **14148. e. 12.**

NATHURĀMA PITĀMBARAJĪ RĀVAḶ. परमपद बोधिनी. [Paramapada-bodhinī. A treatise on two forms of meditation, viz. the Rājayoga and the Haṭhayoga.] pp. 198. मांगरोळ १९४२ [*Mangrol, Ahmadabad* printed, 1886.] 12°. **14144. c. 1.**

NATHUṢAṄKARA UDAYAṢAṄKARA ḌHOLKIYĀ. કેહેવત માળા. [Kehevat māḷā. A collection of Gujarati proverbs and sayings.] pp. 32. અમદાવાદ ૧૮૮૮ [*Ahmadabad*, 1888.] 16°. **14146. e.**

NAUTAMARĀMA UTTAMARĀMA TRIVEDĪ. राजऋषि ग्रंथ. धर्म जिज्ञासु जनो सारु [Rājarishi grantha. A Vedānta religious work in the form of a dialogue between a king and a sage. In Devanagari characters.] pp. viii. 380. अमदावाद १९४० [*Ahmadabad*, 1884.] 4°. **14144. d. 9.**

NAVALARĀMA LAKSHMĪRĀMA. Bal-garbávalí, or A song-book for girls by Navalrám Lakshmírám. बाळ-गरबावळी pp. vi. 54. મુંબઈ ૧૮૭૭ [*Bombay*, 1877.] 12°. **14148. d. 7.(2.)**

NAVARĀTRĪ-PŪJANA. अथ नवरात्रीपूजन [Navarātrī-pūjana. The ritual for observing nine nights in honour of the goddess Kālī; consisting chiefly of extracts from Sanskrit sacred books, accompanied by a Gujarati version.] pp. 52. अमदावाद १९३६ [*Ahmadabad*, 1880.] *obl.* 12°. **14028. a. 18.**

NAVAROJĪ ĀDARJĪ TĀTĀ. A glossary of words occurring in Hékáyet-é-latif [or Persian anecdotes] by Nowrojee Adarjee Tata. pp. 52. *Bombay*, 1884. 12°. **757. cc. 5.(2.)**

—— A glossary of words occurring in Karimá [the Pand-nāmah, or Book of advice] of Shaik-Sáadi by Nowroji Adarji Tátá. Second edition, pp. 32. *Bombay*, [1881.] 12°. **757. cc. 5.(1.)**

NAVAROJĪ RUSTAMJĪ LĀḌ. *See* MEHRVĀNJĪ HORMASJĪ MEHETĀ and NAVAROJĪ RUSTAMJĪ LĀḌ. The English and Goojratee scholar's assistant, *etc.* 1840. 8°. **14150. b. 3.**

NAVATATTVA-PRAKARAṆA. नवतत्व प्रकरण मूल तथा गुर्जरभाषा बालावबोध. [Navatattva prakaraṇa. A philosophico-religious work of the Ṣvetāmbara Jains in Sanskrit, with a Gujarati paraphrase.] pp. 180. मुंबापुरी १९४० [*Bombay*, 1884.] 16°. **14100. a. 7.**

NAVĪNACHANDRA RĀYA. सद्धर्म दीपिका [Saddharma dīpikā. Principles of the Prārthanā Samāj of Ahmadabad, taken from the Sanskrit or Bengali of N. R.] pp. 15. અમદાવાદ ૧૮૮૭ [*Ahmadabad*, 1887.] 32°. **14144. a. 18.(2.)**

NAẒĪR AḤMAD, *Khān Bahādur.* મેરાતુલ એરૂસ, ઇઆને કન્યા દર્પણ. [Mirāt al-'arūs, or The bride's mirror. A Hindustani tale for women by N. A., translated by Bahrāmjī Farīdunjī Marzbān. Second edition.] pp. viii. 130. મુંબઈ ૧૮૭૮ [*Bombay*, 1878.] 8°. **14148. b. 22.**

—— તોબેહ નસુહ, યાને નસુહ નામનાં એક ગ્રુહસ્થે કીધેલા તોબાહ! [Taubat al-Nasūḥ. A Hindustani tale by N. A. translated into Gujarati.] pp. xiv. 201. મુંબઈ ૧૮૮૪ [*Bombay*, 1884.] 8°. **14148. b. 15.**

NEMICHANDRA. श्रीजिनेंद्राय नमः। अथ श्रीप्रवचनसारोद्धार ... प्रारभ्यते। [Pravachanasāroddhāra. Sanskrit text, with a Gujarati paraphrase by Padmamandira Gaṇi.] *See* BHĪMASIṂHA MĀṆAKA. प्रकरणरत्नाकर Vol. iii. pp. 1-568. [1876, *etc.*] 4°. **14100. e. 3.**

—— अथ श्रीषष्टिशतक बालावबोध व्याख्या सहित प्रारंभः [Shashṭi ṣataka. Jain religious precepts in Sanskrit couplets, with a translation into Gujarati couplets, and a verbal explanation and commentary, also in Gujarati, by Guṇasundara.] *See* BHĪMASIṂHA MĀṆAKA. प्रकरण रत्नाकर [Prakaraṇa-ratnākara.] Vol. ii. pp. 626-698. [1876, *etc.*] 4°. **14100. e. 3.**

NEW BIRTH. બીજા જનમની વાત [Bījā janmanī vāt.] New Birth. [A Christian tract.] pp. 12. ૧૮૫૩ [*Surat*, 1853.] 12°. **14144. a. 1.(4.)**

NISHKULĀNANDA. अथ श्री भक्तचिंतामणि ग्रंथ प्रारंभ. [Bhaktachintāmaṇi. A poem on the life and teachings of Sahajānanda Svāmī, the founder of the Svāmīnārāyaṇa sect.] ff. 428. नडियाद १९४० [*Nadiyad*, 1884.] *obl.* 4°. **14144. e. 8.**

—— पंचवरतमान तथा सांख्ययोगी बाइओनुं वरतमान [Pañcha vartamāna, and Sāṅkhyayogī bāionuṃ vartamāna. Two poems, the former showing the importance of the possession of five special vir-

tues; the latter admonishing women, who practise devotion according to the Sāṅkhya philosophy, to control their passions.] ff. 22, *lith.* अमदावाद १८८० [*Ahmadabad*, 1880.] *obl.* 16°.
14146. e. 7.

—— वचनविधि तथा चोमठपदो. [Vachanavidhi. Religions and moral advice in verse to followers of the Svāmīnārāyaṇa sect.] pp. 160. અમદાવાદ ૧૮૮૬ [*Ahmadabad*, 1886.] 16°
14144. c. 2.

NITYĀNANDA MUNI. *See* SAHAJĀNANDA SVĀMĪ. श्रीसहजानंद स्वामिनी लखेली शिक्षापत्री । [Sikshāpatrī. With N. M.'s commentary in Gujarati.] [1862.] 12°. **14076. a. 5.**

NIẒĀM al-DĪN, *Chishtī,* called HĀMĪ. *See* HASAN, *Mīr.* Badraimunir Bainazir, translated into Guzeratee verse by N. P. Chistey (Hami). 1879. 12°.
14148. a. 16.

—— *See* RAJAB ʿALĪ BEG, *Mīrzā*, called SURŪR. Fasanai agaib. [A romance, translated] into Guzerati verse by Hami. [1879.] 12°.
14148. a. 2.(8.)

—— વડોદરાના વિલાપ અટલે મલ્હારરાવ મહારાજનો રાસડો. [Baḍoda-rānā vilāpa. A poem, deploring the deposition of Malhār Rāva, Gaikwar of Baroda.] pp. 8. अमदावाद १८७५ [*Ahmadabad*, 1875.] 12°. **14148. d. 13.(9.)**

—— રાજનગરમાં રેલનો રોળ [Rājnagarmāṇ relno roḷ. A poem describing the distress caused by recent floods.] pp. 16. અમદાવાદ ૧૮૭૫ [*Ahmadabad*, 1875.] 16°. **14148. d. 13.(6.)**

NOWROJEE RUSTOMJEE. *See* NAVAROJĪ RUSTAMJĪ LĀḌ.

NṚISIṂHA MEHETĀ. નૃસિંહ મેહેતાનાં પદ. [A collection of poems by N. M., with notes and an introductory sketch of the poet's life.] *See* PRĀCHĪNA KĀVYA प्राचीन काव्य Vol. i. No. 3. [1885, *etc.*] 8°. **14148. e. 12.**

—— સુરતસંગ્રામ [Suratasaṅgrāma. Verses on the amours of Rādhā and Krishṇa. With copious notes.] *See* PRĀCHĪNA KĀVYA प्राचीन काव्य Vol. ii. No. 4. [1885, *etc.*] 8°. **14148. e. 12.**

NUSHIRVÁNJI CHÁNDÁBHAI. *See* NASARVĀNJĪ CHĀNDĀBHĀĪ.

NUSSERWANJEE SHERIARJEE GINWALLA. *See* NASARVĀNJĪ SHEHRIYĀRJĪ GINWĀLĀ.

OṂ, *pseud.* सुरेश चरित्र. [Sureśa-charitra. A tale in the form of a drama embodying Hindu philosophical beliefs.] Pt. i. pp. 271. अमदावाद १८८४ [*Ahmadabad*, 1884.] 12°. **14148. b. 23.**

PADA. पद राग धोरानो [Pada. Verses condemning idolatry and superstition.] pp. 7. अमदावाद [*Ahmadabad*, 1877.] 16°. **14144. a. 17.(1.)**

PADMAMANDIRA GAṆI. *See* NEMICHANDRA. श्रीजिनेंद्राय नमः । अथ प्रवचनसारोद्धार ... प्रारंभ्यते । [Pravachanasāroddhāra. With a Gujarati paraphrase by P. G.] [1876, *etc.*] 4°. **14100. e. 3.**

PADMAVIJAYA. *See* PŪJĀSAṄGRAHA. પુજાસંગ્રહ *etc.* [Pūjāsaṅgraha. Containing selections from the writings of P. and others.] [1884.] 8°.
14144. g. 15.

—— *See* YAŚOVIJAYA. *Begin.* अथ श्रीमद्यशोविजयजी ... कृत साडात्रणसोगाथानुं स्तवन, *etc.* [Sīmandhara-stavana, or °vijñapti. With a Gujarati commentary by P.] [1876, *etc.*] 4°. **14100. e. 3.**

—— —— अथ श्री श्रीमद्यशोविजयजी उपाध्यायकृत वीरस्तुतिरूप [Vīrastuti. Accompanied by an extensive commentary by P.] [1876, *etc.*] 4°.
14100. e. 3.

—— श्री जयानंद केवलीनो रास. [Jayānanda Kevalīno rās. A Jain legend in verse.] pp. ii. 382. १९४२ [*Bombay*, 1886.] 4°. **14144. g. 3.**

—— समरादित्य केवलीनो-रास. [Samarāditya Kevalīno rās. The story of Samarāditya, and other Jain legends, in verse.] pp. 464. १८८२ [*Bombay*, 1882.] 4°. **14144. g. 2.**

PAI. એક પઈની શી ચીંતા છે? [Ek painī śī chintā chhe. A Christian tract.] pp. 17. સુરત ૧૮૬૧ [*Surat*, 1861.] 12°. **14144. a. 2.(11.)**

PĀLAṆĀ. પાલણા પોથી. [Pālaṇā. Cradle songs.] pp. 12. મુંબઈ ૧૮૬૫ [*Bombay*, 1865.] 12°. **14148. d. 2.(2.)**

PĀLANJĪ BARJORJĪ DEṢĀI. *See* BARJORJĪ PĀLANJĪ DEṢĀI and PĀLANJĪ BARJORJĪ DEṢĀI. History of the Achæmenides. 1889. 8°. **14146. h. 16.**

—— —— History of the Sassanides. 1880. 8°.
14146. h. 5.

PĀLANJĪ JĪVANJĪ HĀṬARYĀ. *See* BAHRĀM RUSTĀM KHUSRAU. સરનામેએ રાજે યજદાની. [Sar-nāmah i rāz i yazdānī. Translated from the Persian by P. J. H.] [1886.] 12°. **14144. h. 5.**

PĀNĀCHAND MOJĪLĀLA DEṢĀI. વડોદરાના વાસીનું વલણ [Baḍodarānā vāsīnuṇ valan. A poem, exhorting the inhabitants of Baroda to abstain from adultery, and pointing out its evil consequences.] pp. 16. अमदावाद १९३३ [*Ahmadabad,* 1877.] 16°. **14148. d. 13.(18.)**

PAÑCHATANTRA. Punchopakhyan. [A collection of moral tales, taken from the Sanskrit Pañchatantra.] પંચોપાખ્યાન pp. 234, 20, *lith. Bombay,* 1833. 8°. **14148. a. 1.**

—— Goozrathee Punchopakhyan. [Another edition, illustrated.] pp. 278. *Bombay,* 1848. 8°. **14148. b. 1.**

—— પંચોપાખ્યાન ગુજરાતી. [Another edition. With illustrations and a glossary.] pp. iv. 244. મુંબઇ ૧૮૫૮ [*Bombay,* 1858.] 8°. **14148. b. 6.**

PĀṆḌAVAS. અથ શ્રી પાંડવવાલા મુલમંડાણના [Pāṇḍavavālā mulamanḍāṇanā. A poem on the exploits of the five Pāṇḍava princes.] pp. 212, *lith.* મુંબઇ ૧૯૧૮ [*Bombay,* 1862.] 8°. **14148. f. 3.**

PAṆḌYĀ PURUSHOTTAMA MAYĀRĀMA. *See* PURUSHOTTAMA MAYĀRĀMA PAṆḌYĀ.

PANNYĀSA RATNAVIJAYAGAṆI. आर्यानार्य देशज्ञापक चरचापत्र [Āryānārya deṣajñāpaka charchāpatra. Arguments in proof of the fact that the country of Sarath (Saurāshṭra) or Kathiawar was included in the limits of the ancient Āryakshetra, or country of the Āryas.] pp. 90. अमदावाद १९४३ [*Ahmadabad,* 1887.] 12°. **14146. g. 22.**

PĀNTRIṢA BOL. अथ श्री पांत्रीश बोलनो थोकडो प्रारंभः [Pāṇtriṣa bolno thokḍo. Information on 35 points connected with Jain religious observances, followed by 192 short maxims.] pp. 32. [*Bombay,* 1888.] 16°. **14144. f.**

PARAMĀNANDA. *See* KĀLIKĀCHĀRYA पंनवणा ० [Pannavaṇā. With a Gujarati commentary by P.] [1884.] *obl.* 4°. **14100. f. 10.**

PARAMĀNANDADĀSA BHOLĀBHĀĪ PĀREKH. *See* BARODA, *Native State of.* ગાયકવાડી ન્યાયપ્રકાશ, *etc.* [Gāyakavāḍī nyāyaprakāṣa. A collection of circular orders, resolutions, *etc.,* issued by the Baroda Administration, from the year A.D. 1879. Compiled by P. Bh. P.] [1881.] 8°. **14146. a. 7.**

—— बजावणी संबंधी सूचना. [Bajāvaṇī sambandhī sūchanā. Directions for the execution of processes issued by the Civil Courts of Baroda.] pp. 20. अमदावाद १९११ [*Ahmadabad,* 1877.] 12°. **14146. c. 7.**

—— गायकवाडी राज्यनो इतिहास [Gāyakavāḍī rājyano itihāsa. An account of the Baroda State, compiled by P. Bh. P. with the assistance of Haragovinda Keṣavalāla Shāh.] pp. v. 8. અમદાવાદ ૧૯૩૪ [*Ahmadadad,* 1877.] 12°. **14146. f. 21.**

PARĀṢARA. श्री पराशरधर्मशास्त्र *etc.* [Parāṣara dharmaṣāstra. Sanskrit text, with a Gujarati translation by Ḍāhyābhāī Ghelābhāī Paṇḍita.] pp. i. xii. 71, 93. मुबई १९२५ [*Bombay,* 1869.] 8°. **14038. c. 27.**

PARSIS. પારશીઓ ખોદાપરશત છે કે નહીં એ વાતનો વીચાર [Pārṣio khodāparast chhe ke nahīṇ.] . . . The polytheism of the Parsis, as set forth in the books of the Zoroastrian faith. Second edition. pp. 46. *Bombay,* 1861. 12°. **14144. h. 10.**

No. 5 of the Bombay Tract and Book Society's "Parsi Gujarathi Series."

PARSOTAM MĀDHAVAJĪ MEHETĀ. કપોલ ઉતપતીની કથા [Kapol utpattinī kathā. An account in verse of the traditional origin of the Kapol Banya caste, and of the Kandolia Brahmans. Together with verses in praise of the goddess Sāmodarī, or Parvatī, and other short poems.] pp. 44. મુંબઇ ૧૮૭૮ [*Bombay,* 1878.] 12°. **14146. e. 8.(2.)**

PĀRṢVACHANDRA SŪRI. *See* ĀCHĀRĀÑGA. श्री आचारांग ० [Āchārāñga. Prakrit text, with a commentary in Gujarati by P. S.] [1880.] 4°. **14100. f. 7.**

—— *See* SŪTRAKṚITĀÑGA. श्रीसूयगडांग-सूत्र *etc.* [Sūtrakṛitāñga. With a Gujarati paraphrase by P. S.] [1881.] 4°. **14100. e. 2.**

PASLEY (*Sir* CHARLES WILLIAM). Goojeratee version of a course of practical geometry, compiled by Lieutenant Colonel Pasley . . . Translated by Captain George Jervis. (कर्त्तव्य भूमिति) [Kartavya bhūmiti.] pp. x. 171. *Bombay,* 1826. 4°. **14146. d. 1.**

PASTAKIA (B. M.) *See* Bāpujī Māṇekjī Pastākiā.

PATEL (N. H.) *See* Nasarvanjī Hirjībhāī Paṭel.

PATH. શત ધરમનો મારગ. The path of truth. [Sat dharmano mārga. A Christian tract.] pp. 12. શુરત ૧૮૬૦ [*Surat*, 1860.] 8°. **14144. a. 2.(9.)**

PEARSON (John D.) *Rev., of Chinsurah.* *See* Wilson (J.) *D.D., F.R.S., etc.* Idiomatic Exercises .... Rendered into Goojeratee [from Dr. J. Wilson's version of J. D. P.'s Bengali Vākyāvalī.] 1850. 12° **12906. bbb. 9.**

PEHELĪ POTHĪ. પેહેલી પોથી [Pehelī pothī. A Gujarati primer.] pp. 28. *Surat*, 1860. 12°. **14150. a. 1.(2.)**

PEILE (James Braithwaite). Catalogue of native publications in the Bombay Presidency from 1st January 1865 to 30th June 1867, and of some works omitted in the previous catalogue. Prepared under orders of Government by J. B. P. pp. 120. *Bombay*, 1869. 8°. **752. e. 15.**

PERIODICAL PUBLICATIONS.

Bhaunagar.

जैन धर्म प्रकाश Jaina dharma prakash. [A monthly periodical of Jain religion, philosophy and legendary lore.] Vol. i. *etc.* भावनगर १९४१ [*Bhaunagar, Ahmadabad* printed, 1885, *etc.*] 12°. **14144. g. 17.**

In progress.

Bombay.

आर्य धर्मप्रकाश Arya dharma-prakash. [A monthly journal.] Vol. v. Nos. 10-12; Vol. vi. Nos. 1-5; Vol. x. Nos. 3-8. મુંબઈ ૧૮૭૭ [*Bombay*, 1877, *etc.*] 8°. **14150. c. 6.**

आर्यज्ञानवर्धक. The Aryajnana vardhaka. [A literary magazine.] Vol. i. Nos. 9 to 11. મુંબઈ ૧૮૮૨ [*Bombay*, 1882.] 8°. **14150. c. 5.**

आर्य्यप्रकाश. [Āryaprakāṣa. A monthly journal of religion and philosophy, published by the Ārya Samāj.] Vol. i.-iii. 6. મુંબઈ ૧૮૮૫ [*Bombay*, 1885, *etc.*] 8°. **14150. c. 12.**

આર્યસમુદય Aryasamudaya. [A monthly literary periodical devoted chiefly to Aryan religion and philosophy. Edited by Gaṭṭūlāla Ghanaṣyāmajī.] મુંબઈ ૧૯૪૫ [*Bombay*, 1888, *etc.*] 8°. **14150. c. 13.**

In progress.

PERIODICAL PUBLICATIONS.

Bombay (*continued.*)

بهجة الاخبار [Bahjat al-akhbār. A fortnightly literary magazine for Gujarati-speaking Muhammadans, in the Persian character.] Nos. 10, 11, *lith.* بمبئي [*Bombay*, 1877.] 8°. **14150. c. 7.**

બુદ્ધિવર્ધક ગ્રંથ .... Buddhivardhak magazine. [A monthly literary periodical.] Vol. i. *Bombay*, 1874. 12°. **14150. c. 2.**

ફુરસદ [Fursad, or Leisure time. A monthly literary and entertaining magazine.] Nos. 55-61. મુંબઈ ૧૮૭૭ [*Bombay*, 1877.] 8°. **14150. d. 4.**

[illegible]. હખ મજદયસ્નનામ. યાને મજદયસ્નીઓનો દોસ્ત. Hakha Mazdayasnanam or The friend of the Mazdayasnians. [A Parsi weekly journal.] Vol. i. & ii. *Bombay*, 1881-84. 4°. **14150. d. 5.**

Incomplete; wanting Nos. 43 and 44 of vol. ii.

જ્ઞાનવર્ધક [Jñānavardhaka. A monthly magazine, edited by Jahāngīr Bejanjī Karāṇī.] Vol. v. Nos. 5-11 and Vol. xii. મુંબઈ ૧૮૮૪ [*Bombay*, 1877-84.] 8°. **14150. c. 3.**

મીલાવડો [Mīlāvaḍo.] or The Miscellany. Vol. iv. મુંબઈ ૧૮૭૭ [*Bombay*, 1877.] 8°. **14150. c. 4.**

પારશી પંચ આપએખતીઆર Parsee Punch and Apyakhtiar. [A weekly illustrated paper.] Vol. xv. and xxi-xxvii. *Bombay*, 1869-81. 4°. **14150. d. 1.**

Imperfect; wanting Nos. 4 and 5 of Vol. xv.; No. 52 of Vol. xxi.; Nos. 11 and 52 of Vol. xxii; Nos. 1-22, 34, 50-52 of Vol. xxiii.; Nos. 1-10, and 34 of Vol. xxiv.; No. 50 of Vol. xxv.; and Nos. 19, 22 and 23 of Vol. xxvi.

Pickings from the Parsee Punch પારસી પંચમાંથી ચુંટી કાહાડેલાં ચીતરો. Vol. i. Nos. 1-6. *Bombay*, 1884. 8°. **14150. d. 2.**

પ્રિયંવદા. [Priyaṃvadā. A monthly social journal.] Vol. ii. No. 3. મુંબઈ ૧૮૮૬ [*Bombay*, 1886.] 8°. **14150. c. 11.**

રાસત દીને જરથોશતીઆંન યાને જરથોશતી દીનની રાસતી. [Rāst dīn i Zartoshtiyān. A Parsi monthly periodical, containing the text of the Zand Avastā with a Gujarati commentary, and matters concerning the Zoroastrian creed. Edited by Ratanjī Rustamjī Kāṅgā.] Vol. i. Nos. 1-3. મુંબઈ ૧૮૮૩ [*Bombay*, 1883.] 8°. **14150. e. 2.**

PERIODICAL PUBLICATIONS.

BOMBAY (*continued.*)

સ્ત્રીબોધ. [Strībodha. A monthly magazine for educated native women.] Vol. xii. મુંબઈ ૧૮૬૮ [*Bombay*, 1868.] 4°. **14150. d. 3.**

स्वदेश वत्सल [Svadeṣa vatsaḷa] or the Patriot. [A monthly periodical on science and literature.] Vol. i. Nos. 10-12; Vol. ii. Nos. 1-5. મુંબઈ ૧૮૭૭ [*Bombay*, 1877-78.] 8°. **14150. c. 10.**

वेदान्तप्रकाश. Vedânt Prakâsh. [A monthly serial intended to give translations of select Sanskrit works.] Vol. i and ii. મુંબઈ ૧૮૮૩ [*Bombay*, 1883, *etc.*] 8°. **14144. d. 8.**
In progress.

વિધ્યામિત્ર. Vidya Mitra. Literary friend. [A monthly literary magazine.] Vol. iv. Nos. 6-10. ૧૮૭૭ [*Bombay*, 1877.] 8°. **14150. c. 8.**

NARIAD.

आत्मज्ञान वर्धक [Ātmajñāna-vardhaka. A monthly periodical on Sanskrit literature, containing also translations of Sanskrit works on Vedantism.] Vol. ii. નડીઆદ ૧૮૮૪ [*Nariad*, 1884, *etc.*] 8°.
In progress. **14150. c. 9.**

SURAT.

ज्ञानदीपक Gnyandipuck. Lamp of Knowledge. [A monthly Christian magazine of religion and general literature. Partly in English and partly in Gujarati.] Vol. i.-vi. *Surat*, 1855-60. 8°. **14150. c. 1.**

સત્યોદય. [Satyodaya.] Dawn of Truth. [A Christian monthly magazine.] Vol. i. No. 6; Vol. xvi. No. 7-12; Vol. xvii. No. 1-3; and Vol. xxi. No. 4-6. *Surat*, 1862-82. 12°. **14144. a. 8.**

PESHOTAN BAHRĀMJĪ SANJĀṆĀ. *See* DINKARD. The Dinkard. The original Péhlwi text; . . . translations of the text in the Gujarati and English languages [the former by the editor]; a commentary and a glossary of select terms. By Peshotun Dustoor Behramjee Sunjana. 1874, *etc.* 8°. **761. g. 10.**

—— Ganjeshâyagân, Andarze Átrepât Márâspandân, Mâdigâne Chatrang, and Andarze Khusroe Kavâtân. The original Péhlvi text; . . . and translated into the Gujarati and English languages; a commentary and a glossary of select words, by Peshutan Dastur Behraniji Sanjana. *Bombay*, 1885. 8°. **761. g. 2.**

—— A grammar of the Pahlvi language. With quotations and examples from original works, and a glossary of words bearing affinity with the Semetic language, by Peshotun Dustoor Behramjee Sunjana. pp. xviii. 47, 459. *Bombay*, 1871. 8°. **761. e. 22.**

—— [Another copy.] **14150. b. 10.**

—— તફસીરે ગાહે ગાસાની [Tafsīr i gāhi gāsānī. A treatise on the reciting of the Gathas, with special reference to the month Isfandarmad; being a refutation of the Farmān i dīn of Dastūr Edaljī Dārābjī Jāmāsp Āsāvālā.] pp. 120. મુંબઈ ૧૮૬૭ [*Bombay*, 1867.] 8°. **14144. i. 26.**

PESHOTAN RUSTAM. *See* BUNDEHESH. બુનદેહેશ કેતાબ [Bundehesh. Edited, with an introductory preface, by P. R.] [1877.] 8°. **14144. i. 14.**

PESTANJĪ FRĀMJĪ VELĀTE. ગુલજારે આલમ યાને તશવીરે ખુબી [Gulzār i ʻālam, also called Tasbīr i khūbi. A Parsi account of the creation, and early history of the world.] pp. 158. મુંબઈ ૧૮૮૪ [*Bombay*, 1884.] 8°. **14144. i. 18.**

PESTANJĪ NAVAROJĪ. Dukha nivárana, or a compendium of the practice of medicine, containing a general description of diseases, . . . of their most recent and approved treatments, and of several prescriptions of Indian drugs, expressly adapted for family use. By Pestanji Naoroji. (દુઃખ નિવારણ) pp. viii. 566. *Bombay*, 1880. 8°. **14146. b. 5.**

PHARO. ફરો નઈં તો મરો [Pharo naiṇ to maro, or Repent else you will die. A Christian tract.] pp. 23. શુરત [*Surat*, 1860.] 16°. **14144. a. 3.(5.)**

PĪTĀMBARADĀSA TRIBHUVANADĀSA MEHETĀ. Hindu astrology, by Pitamberdas Tribhovandas Mehta. (જ્યોતિષ વિષે) [Jyotisha vishe. Second edition.] pp. iii. v. 159. *Ahmedabad*, 1877. 8°. **14146. c. 8.**

PĪTĀMBARA PURUSHOTTAMA. *See* PURĀṆAS.—Bhāgavatapurāṇa.—*Vedastuti.* अथ . . . वेदस्तुति [Vedastuti. With a commentary in Sanskrit and Gujarati by P. P.] 1877. 4°. **14016. e. 35.**

POONA CONVERSATIONS. પુના મધ્યે ધર્મ સંબંધી વાતચીત. [Punāmadhye dharmasambandhī vātchīt.] Poona Conversations. [A Christian tract.] pp. 106. શુરત ૧૮૫૧ [*Surat*, 1851.] 16°. **14144. a. 3.(1.)**

POPE (ALEXANDER) *the Poet.* *See* HOMER. Pope's Homer's Iliad, Book I. Containing meanings . . . and explanation of numerous words, *etc.* 1875. 16°. **14150. a. 2.(1).**

—— —— Notes on the Fourth Book of Pope's Homer's Iliad. 1881. 12°. **14150. a. 1.(5.)**

PRABHĀKARA RĀMACHANDRA PANDITA. अपभ्रष्ट शब्दप्रकाश [Apabhrashṭa ṣabdaprakāṣa. A vocabulary of corrupt forms of Sanskrit, Persian, Arabic, and other words, in use in Gujarati.] pp. v. 168. मुंबई १८८० [*Bombay*, 1880.] 8°. **14150. b. 16.**

PRABHĀṢAṄKARA ṢĀMALAJĪ. તેત્રીશાનો તડાકો [Tetrīṣāno taḍāko. A poem on the scarcity of grain prevailing in the province of Gujarat.] pp. 12. અમદાવાદ ૧૯૩૩ [*Ahmadabad*, 1877.] 16°. **14148. d. 13.(17.)**

PRĀCHĪNA KĀVYA. प्राचीन काव्य [Prāchīna kāvya. A collection of old Gujarati poems, published in tri-monthly parts. Edited, with copious notes, critical and otherwise, by Haragovinda Dvārakādāsa Kāṇṭāwālā and Nāthāṣaṅkara Pūjāṣaṅkara Ṣāstrī.] Vol. I, *etc.* અમદાવાદ ૧૮૮૫ [*Ahmadabad*, 1885, *etc.*] 8°. **14148. e. 12.**

In progress.

PRAKARAṆA-SAṄGRAHA. श्री प्रकरणसंग्रह प्रारंभ. [Prakaraṇa-saṅgraha. A collection of tracts on Jain religion and philosophy. Second edition.] ff. 200. मुंबई १९४४ [*Bombay*, 1888.] *obl.* 8°. **14144. g. 29.**

PRĀṆAJĪVANADĀSA MĀṆEKLĀLA. ન્યાતીવરા અથવા જમણવરા [Nyātīvarā. A dialogue between a Parsi and a Baniya, in which the former condemns the practice of celebrating caste dinners, which prevails amongst the merchants of Gujarat.] pp. 56. સુરત ૧૮૮૮ [*Surat*, 1888.] 16°. **14146. e. 26.(2.)**

PRĀṆAJĪVANA HARIHARA ṢĀSTRĪ. *See* DAṆḌIN. Dashakumára charitra . . . Translated into Gujarati by Shastri Pránjivan Harihar. [1889.] 8°. **14148. b. 40.**

PRĀṆALĀLA MATHURĀDĀSA. *See* ROBERTSON (W.) *D.D., the Historian.* The life of Columbus. Translated into Gujaráti . . . by Pránlál Mathurádás and Ánandráo Chápáji. 1867. 12°. **14146. f. 19.**

PRĀṆALĀLA ṢAMBHULĀLA DEṢĀI. मनहरमाळा नाटक शरदकांतो स्वयंवर आख्यान [Manaharamālā. A story, in the form of a drama, in ten scenes.] pp. xii. 204. અમદાવાદ ૧૯૩૪ [*Ahmadabad*, 1877.] 12°. **14148. c. 8.**

PRĀṆAVALLABHA BHAGAVĀNJĪ. *See* CHAURĀṢĪ VĀRTĀ. चोराशी वैष्नवनी वारता, *etc.* [Chaurāṣī Vaishṇavanī vārtā. Translated by P. Bh. from the Braj-bhasha original.] [1881.] 12°. **14144. b. 2.**

PRATĀPARĀYA ṢIVALĀLA MĀNKAḌ. मनोरंजक प्रतापकाव्य. [Manorañjaka Pratāpakāvya. A collection of poems by P. S. M.] pp. xii. 204. અમદાવાદ ૧૮૮૩ [*Ahmadabad*, 1883.] 8°. **14148. e. 16.**

PRATĀPA SIṂHA, *Raja of Jaipur.* અમૃતસાગર તથા પ્રતાપસાગર વૈદ્યકગ્રંથ (Amritsagur and Pratapsagur. Medical works [compiled by Raja P. S. and] translated into Guzerati from the Jepoory and the Hindoostani languages by Bhowsar Tribhowundass Girdhurdass Khumbati.) pp. xv. xiii. 684. *Surat*, 1878. 8°. **14146. b. 3.**

PRATIKRAMAṆA SŪTRAS. श्री. विधिपक्ष गच्छीय श्रावकस्य दैवसिकादिक पंच प्रतिक्रमण विधि. [Vidhipaksha gachchhīya ṣrāvakasya daivasikādika pañcha pratikramaṇa vidhi. A compilation of confessional formularies, and general hymns, for the daily use of the Jains of the Vidhipaksha gachchha. Prakrit text, with occasional Gujarati explanations.] pp. xiv. 336. मुंबाय्यपुरी १८८१ [*Bombay*, 1881.] 16°. **14100. a. 2.**

Text, and Gujarati explanations in Devanagari characters.

—— દૈવસિકતથા રાઈપ્રતિક્રમણાદિ મૂલસૂત્ર. [Daivasika tathā rāī pratikramaṇādi mūlasūtra. A smaller collection of Jain confessional formularies, and hymns for daily use, with occasional Gujarati explanations on ritual.] pp. iv. 116, *lith.* મુંબઈ ૧૯૩૮ [*Bombay*, 1881.] 16°. **14100. a. 1.**

In Gujarati characters.

PRATIKRAMAṆA SŪTRAS. प्रतिक्रमणनां सूत्र. [Pratikramaṇanāṇ sūtra. Another edition, slightly differing from the preceding.] pp. 56. અમદાવાદ ૧૯૩૮ [*Ahmadabad*, 1882.] 16°. **14100. a. 5.**

The titles of sections are in Devanagari, the text and explanations in Gujarati characters.

—— [Another edition.] pp. 56. અમદાવાદ ૧૯૩૮ [*Ahmadabad*, 1882.] 16°. **14100. a. 4.**

—— શ્રી પંચ પ્રતિક્રમણાદિ સૂત્રાણિ. [Pañcha pratikramaṇādi sūtrāṇi. A revised edition, edited by Ānandajī Khetaṣī.] pp. viii. 238, *lith.* શ્રીમુંબાપુરી ૧૮૮૨ [*Bombay*, 1882.] 16°. **14100. a. 3.**

—— દેવસી અને રાઈ પ્રતિક્રમણા સુત્ર. [A smaller collection of prayers, with the addition of several in Gujarati.] pp. 48. અમદાવાદ ૧૮૮૨ [*Ahmadabad*, 1882.] 8°. **14100. c. 1.**

PRAYĀGAJĪ ṬHĀKARSĪ. श्री प्रमाणसहस्री [Pramāṇasahasrī. A collection of 1000 select passages from Sanskrit works on the creation of the universe, on religious and social observances, and on the nature of Brahma. With translations and commentaries in Gujarati.] pp. xv. 82, 229, 13. મુંબઈ ૧૮૮૭ [*Bombay*, 1887.] 8°. **14085. d. 28.**

PREMAJĪ KHETASIṂHA KAJARIYĀ. શૃંગારદર્શન [Śriṅgāradarṣana. A collection of 40 Sanskrit verses from various classical poets, with Gujarati translations.] મુંબઈ ૧૮૭૭ [*Bombay*, 1877.] 8°. **14072. b. 4.**

PREMĀNANDA. *See* PURĀṆAS.—Bhāgavatapurāṇa.—*Saptamaskandha.* सप्तमस्कंध [Saptamaskandha. Translated in verse by P.] [1886.] 8°. **14148. e. 12.**

—— અથ અભીમન્યુનું મોટુ આખીઆન [Abhimanyunuṇ moṭu ākhyāna. A mythological story in verse.] pp. 84, *lith.* મુંબઈ ૧૯૧૧ [*Bombay*, 1854.] 8°. **14148. b. 4.(1.)**

—— હારમાળા [Hāramālā. A poem by P., with notes and a glossary.] *See* PRĀCHĪNA KĀVYA प्राचीन काव्य Vol. i. No. 1. [1885, *etc.*] 8°. **14148. e. 12.**

—— लक्ष्मणा हरण अने दाणलीला. [Lakshmaṇāharaṇa, and Dānalīlā. Two mythological poems, with notes.] *See* PRĀCHĪNA KĀVYA प्राचीन काव्य. Vol. i. No. 4. [1885, *etc.*] 8°. **14148. e. 12.**

PREMĀNANDA. મૃદાલસા આખ્યાન. [Mṛidālaṣā ākhyāna. A mythological story in verse.] pp. 90, *lith.* અમદાવાદ ૧૮૮૩ [*Baroda, Ahmadabad*, printed, 1883.] 8°. **14148. b. 25.**

—— નલરાજાનું આખ્યાન, *etc.* [Nala rājānuṇ ākhyāna, or the story of king Nala. An episode of the Mahābhārata, in verse.] pp. 170, *lith.* મુંબાઈ ૧૭૮૦ [*Bombay*, 1858.] 8°. **14148. b. 4.(4.)**

—— નળઆખ્યાન [Nalākhyāna. Another edition.] pp. 106, *lith.* અમદાવાદ ૧૯૩૩ [*Ahmadabad*, 1876.] 8°. **14148. b. 26.**

—— Premánand's Nalákhyán. Students' edition, prepared by Kavi Narmadáshankar Lálashankar. (भट प्रेमानन्दकृत नळाख्यान.) Second edition. pp. 113. *Bombay*, 1880. 12°. **14148. a. 30.**

—— નરશી મેહેતાની હુંડી [Narṣī Mehetānī huṇḍī, or The bill of exchange of Narsī Mehetā. A satirical poem, together with other short poems, and a few couplets by Ṣāmaḷa Bhaṭa.] pp. 106, *lith.* મુંબઈ ૧૭૮૪ [*Bombay*, 1862.] 12°. **14148. d. 5.(3.)**

—— [Another edition.] pp. 80, *lith.* મુંબઈ ૧૭૮૬ [*Bombay*, 1864.] 12°. **14148. d. 11.**

—— નૃસિંહ મેહેતાની હુંડી [Another edition, annotated.] *See* PRĀCHĪNA KĀVYA प्राचीन काव्य Vol. iii. No. 1. [1885, *etc.*] 8°. **14148. e. 12.**

—— ઓખાહરણ. [Okhāharaṇa. A poem on the story of Ushā and Aniruddha.] pp. 104, *lith.* મુંબઈ ૧૯૨૦ [*Bombay*, 1863.] 8°. **14148. f. 4.**

—— રૂકમીણીહરણ [Rukmiṇīharaṇa. A poem on the marriage of Krishṇa and Rukmiṇī.] pp. 136, *lith.* મુંબઈ ૧૭૭૭ [*Bombay*, 1855.] 16°. **14148. d. 1.(3.)**

—— [Another edition.] pp. 135, *lith.* મુંબઈ ૧૯૧૪ [*Bombay*, 1857.] 16°. **14148. a. 14.(2.)**

—— સુદામચરીત્ર [Sudāmacharitra. The story of Sudāma in verse.] pp. 50, *lith.* મુંબઈ ૧૯૧૪ [*Bombay*, 1857.] 16°. **14148. a. 2.(3.)**

—— વિવેક વણજારો. [Viveka vaṇajhāro. A philosophical poem.] pp. 24. *lith.* અમદાવાદ ૧૮૭૫ [*Ahmadabad*, 1875.] 12°. **14148. d. 5.(9.)**

PRĪTAMA. પ્રીતમકૃત कविता [Kavitā. Miscellaneous poems. With notes.] *See* PRĀCHĪNA KĀVYA. प्राचीन काव्य Vol. vi. No. 2. [1885, *etc.*] 8°. **14148. e. 12.**

PŪJĀSAṄGRAHA. पुजा संग्रह. સર્વે જૈનધર્મના શોખીલા સજ્જનોને વાસ્તે. [Pūjāsaṅgraha. A selection of Jain prayers and hymns from the writings of Vīravijaya, Rūpavijaya, Padmavijaya and others. Edited by Sāṅkalchand Mahāsukharāma.] pp. 131. અમદાવાદ ૧૮૭૫ [*Ahmadabad*, 1875.] 8°. **14144. g. 1.**

—— પુજાસંગ્રહ, *etc.* [Another edition, with much additional matter.] pp. 196. अमदावाद १८८४ [*Ahmadabad*, 1884.] 8°. **14144. g. 15.**

PURĀṆAS. प्राकृत एकादशी महात्म्य [Ekādaṣīmāhātmya. Selections from different Purāṇas on the celebration of the eleventh day in each half month, translated from the Sanskrit by Raṇchhodlāla Galurāma.] pp. 207. अमदावाद १९३३ [*Ahmadabad*, 1877.] 8°. **14144. d. 5.**

BHĀGAVATAPURĀṆA.

—— श्रीमद् भागवत भाषांतर Bhágavata bháshántara. [Translated by Keṣavalāla Harirāma from the Sanskrit, with the help of Ṣrīdhara Svāmī's commentary.] pp. 780. મુંબઈ ૧૮૮૫ [*Bombay*, 1885.] 4°. **14144. e. 1.**

—— શ્રીમદ ભાગવતની કથાનો સાર [Ṣrīmadbhāgavatanī kathāno sāra. An abstract of the contents of each chapter of the Bhāgavatapurāṇa, translated by Manamohanadāsa Raṇchhoḍdāsa from the Marathi.] pp. 152. अमदावाद [*Ahmadabad*, 1881.] 8°. **14144. d. 2.**

—— *Gopīgītā.* ગોપીગીત આ ગોપીગીતમાં શ્લોક સંસ્કૃતને તેની ટીકા એટલ અરથ ગુજરાતીમાં. [Gopīgītā. The thirty-first canto of the tenth book of the Bhāgavatapurāṇa, Sanskrit text, with a commentary in Gujarati.] pp. 13, *lith.* મુંબઈ ૧૯૧૪. [*Bombay*, 1857.] 12°. **14016. a. 5.**

—— *Saptamaskandha.* सप्तमस्कंध [Saptamaskandha. The seventh skandha of the Bhāgavatapurāṇa, translated in verse by Premānanda. With copious notes.] *See* PRĀCHĪNA KĀVYA. प्राचीन काव्य Vol. ii. No. 1. [1885, *etc.*] 8°. **14148. e. 12.**

BHĀGAVATAPURĀṆA (*continued*).

—— *Vedastuti.* अथ अन्वयटीकासहिता वेदस्तुतिः प्रारभ्यते ॥ [Vedastuti. Sanskrit text, with a Gujarati commentary by Pītāmbara Purushottama.] ff. 17. मुंबई १९३३ [*Bombay*, 1877.] 4°. **14016. e. 35.**

DEVĪBHĀGAVATAPURĀṆA.

—— श्रीमद् भगवती भागवत भाषांतर. Bhagavati Bhágavata bháshántara. [The Devībhāgavatapurāṇa translated into prose by Keṣavalāla Harirāma.] મુંબઈ ૧૮૮૫ [*Bombay*, 1885, *etc.*] 8°. **14144. e. 3.**

In progress.

MĀRKAṆḌEYAPURĀṆA.

—— *Devīmāhātmya.* *See* MOTĪRĀMA MAÑCHHĀRĀMA. ચંડીકાનો ગરબો [Chaṇḍīkāno garbo. A poem based on the Devīmāhātmya.] [1875.] 12°. **14148. d. 4.(4.)**

—— *See* RĀMABHAKTA ṢIVADĀSA. ચંડીપાઠપ્રાકૃત. [Chaṇḍīpāṭha, or Devīmāhātmya, adapted by Rāmabhakta Ṣivadāsa.] [1875.] 8°. **14144. i. 14.**

—— सप्तशती [Saptaṣatī, or Devīmāhātmya. Translated into verse by Bhālaṇa, who is also called Purushottamaji. With critical notes, and an introductory sketch of the life and writings of the poet by Nārāyaṇabhārthī Yaṣavantabhārthī.] *See* PRĀCHĪNA KĀVYA. प्राचीन काव्य. Vol. iii. No. 3. [1885, *etc.*] 8°. **14148. e. 12.**

PADMAPURĀṆA.

—— *Rāmāṣvamedha.* ગણપતરામકૃત રામાશ્વમેધ [Rāmāṣvamedha. A verse translation by Gaṇapatarāma Viṣvanātha.] pp. 459, *lith.* અમદાવાદ ૧૮૮૧ [*Ahmadabad*, 1881.] 8°. **14144. d. 4.**

—— *Sābhramatīmāhātmya.* साभ्रमती महात्म्य. [Sābhramatīmāhātmya. A poem in praise of the river Sabarmati. An episode from the Padmapurāṇa, translated from the Sanskrit by Gaṅgāṣaṅkara Jayaṣaṅkara.] pp. 62. अमदावाद १९३२ [*Ahmadabad*, 1876.] 8°. **14144. d. 3.**

ṢIVAPURĀṆA.

—— श्री शिवपुराण भाषांतर. Shri Shivpuran bhasanter. [Translated into prose by Narottama Amarajī.] 4 vol. મુંબઈ ૧૮૮૪ [*Bombay*, 1884-87.] 4°. **14144. e. 2.**

SKANDAPURĀṆA.

—— स्कंदपुराणार्थप्रकाश. Skandapuránárthprakásh. [The Skandapurāṇa, translated by the Saurāshṭra Jñānaprasāraka Maṇḍaḷi.] મુંબઈ ૧૮૮૫ [*Bombay*, 1885, *etc.*] 8°. **14144. d. 7.**

In progress.

—— *Brahmottarakhaṇḍa.* See MAYO ṢIVADĀSA. સોમ પ્રદોષની કથા [Somapradoshanī kathā. A poem based on the Brahmottarakhaṇḍa of the Skandapurāṇa.] [1877.] 16°. **14144. b. 6.(2.)**

PŪRṆĀNANDA MAHĀNANDA BHAṬṬA. *See* ĪṢVARA BĀROṬ. हरिरस [Harirasa. With introductory verses by P. M. Bh.] [1877.] *obl.* 12°. **14148. d. 15.**

PURUSHOTTAMAJĪ. *See* BHĀLAṆA, also called PURUSHOTTAMAJĪ.

PURUSHOTTAMA KĀHĀNJĪ GĀṆDHE. गूजराती वेहेम. [Gujarātī vehem. Indian superstitions.] Pt. I. pp. 24. અમદાવાદ ૧૮૮૧ [*Ahmadabad*, 1881.] 12°. **14146. e. 2.**

PURUSHOTTAMA KAKAL. શ્રી અમદાવાદની વિશાશ્રીમાળી શ્રાવકની નાત તરફથી થયલ અષ્ટોત્રી સનાત્ર મહોત્સવ. [Ashṭotrī sanātra mahotsava. An account of a Jain religious ceremony, performed at Ahmadabad with the object of averting cholera.] pp. 16. અમદાવાદ ૧૮૮૮ [*Ahmadabad*, 1888.] 16°. **14144. f. 16.(2.)**

PURUSHOTTAMA MAYĀRĀMA PAṆḌYĀ. सुभाषित संग्रह [Subhāshita-saṅgraha. A collection of Sanskrit verses compiled by P. M. with a preface and translation in Gujarati prose.] pp. ii. 46, ii. મુંબઈ ૧૮૮૧ [*Bombay*, 1881.] 16°. **14085. b. 23.**

RĀDHĀ. રાધાજીના તેર મહીના [Rādhājīnā tera mahīnā. A poem in praise of Rādhā.] pp. 13, *lith.* મુંબઈ ૧૮૬૩ [*Bombay*, 1863.] 16°. **14148. d. 4.(3.)**

RADHANPUR, *Native State of.* રાધનપુર સ્વસ્થાનનો દીવાની નિબંધ [Rādhanpur svasthānano dīwānī nibandha. The Civil Procedure Code of the Native State of Radhanpur. Edited by Trikamlāla Kahānjī.] pp. 110, *lith.* અમદાવાદ ૧૮૩૦ [*Ahmadabad*, 1874.] 4°. **14146. a. 12.**

—— સ્વસ્થાન રાધનપુરનો ફોજદારી નિબંધ [Svasthāna Rādhanpurno phojdārī nibandha. The Criminal Procedure Code of the Native State of Radhanpur. Edited by Trikamlāla Kahānjī.] pp. 105, *lith.* અમદાવાદ ૧૮૩૧ [*Ahmadabad*, 1875.] 4°. **14146. a. 13.**

RĀGHUNĀTHA RĀVAJĪ. *See* UTTAMARĀMA UMEDCHAND and CHAMANLĀLA NARASIṀHADĀSA. દીલગીરીનો દેખાવ [Dilgirino dekhāva. An elegy on the death of R. R., late Secretary to the Ahmadabad municipality.] [1875.] 16°. **14148. d. 13.(3.)**

RAGHUNĀTHA ṢĀSTRĪ DĀNTYE and KRISHṆA ṢĀSTRĪ BHĀṬAVAḌEKAR. વૈદ્યસારસંગ્રહ [Vaidyasārasaṅgraha. A work on medicine, translated from the Marathi of R. Ṣ. D. and K. Ṣ. Bh. by Vishṇu Vāsudeva Goḍbole and Mahādeva Gopāla Ṣāstrī.] pp. xix. 298, *lith.* મુંબઈ ૧૮૬૨ [*Bombay*, 1862.] 8°. **14146. b. 1.**

RAJAB 'ALĪ BEG, *Mīrzā,* called SURŪR. Fasanai agaib. [A romance, translated from the Hindustani original of R. 'A. B.] into Guzerati verse by Hami . . . फ़साने अजाइब pp. 64. અમદાવાદ ૧૮૭૯ [*Ahmadabad*, 1879.] 12°. **14148. a. 2.(8.)**

RĀJĀ PARDEṢĪ. રાજા પરદેશીનો રાશ ઘણું વીશતાર શહીત [Rājā Pardeṣīno rās. An amplified version of a Jain legend.] pp. viii. 84, *lith.* મુંબાઈ [*Bombay*, 1884.] 16°. **14144. f. 15.**

RĀJAPRAṢNĪYA. श्री रायपसेणी जी सूत्र ० । [Rāyapaseṇī or Rājapraṣnīya. A canonical work of the Jains, Prakrit text with a Sanskrit commentary and a Gujarati commentary by Megharāja.] pp. 296. कलकत्ता १९३६ [*Calcutta*, 1880.] 4°. **14100. e. 5.**

RĀJĀRĀMA GAṆEṢA BOḌAS. *See* BHĪMĀCHĀRYA JHALKĪKAR and RĀJĀRĀMA GAṆEṢA BOḌAS. वेदार्थोद्धारः [Vedārthoddhāra.] [1875.] 8°. **14028. d. 18.**

RĀJENDRA SŪRI. भट्टारक श्री राजेंद्रसूरि विरचितः कल्पसूत्रस्य बालावबोधः प्रारभ्यते [Kalpasūtrasya bālāvabodha. An extensive commentary on the Kalpasūtra of Bhadrabāhu, specially designed for reading during the Paryūshaṇa, or period of fasting and religious meditation amongst the Jains.] ff. xx. 252. मुंबापुरी १८८८ [*Bombay*, 1888.] *obl.* 8°. **14144. g. 31.**

—— रसिक स्तवनावली [Rasika stavanāvalī. Hymns to several Jain saints.] pp. 80. अमदावाद १८८६ [*Ahmadabad*, 1886.] 12°. **14144. f. 9.**

RAJKOTE.—*Rajkumar College.* Recitations [from the works of English and Gujarati authors by students of the] Rajkumar College, 1877. pp. 20. [*Bombay,* 1877 ?] 4°. **14148. f. 17.**

RĀJYACHANDRA. राज्यचंद्रप्रणित मोक्षमाळा. [Mokshamāḷa. Lessons in the Jain religion, intended specially for the education of Jain children.] pp. viii. 183. अमदावाद १८८८ [*Ahmadabad,* 1888.] 8°. **14144. g. 27.**

RĀMABHAKTA ŚIVADĀSA. ચંડીપાઠપ્રાકૃત. [Chaṇḍīpāṭha or Devīmāhātmya. Adapted from the Sanskrit by R. Ś.] pp. 105, *lith.* અમદાવાદ ૧૮૭૫ [*Ahmadabad,* 1875.] 8°. **14144. i. 13.**

RĀMADĀSA SVĀMĪ, *of Haidarabad.* श्रीपंचीकरण [Pañchīkaraṇa. Verses on Vedānta philosophy, Sanskrit text, with a Gujarati commentary by Jayakṛishṇa. Second edition.] pp. xx. 281. १८८१ [*Bombay,* 1881.] 12°. **14048. b. 10.**

—— [Fourth edition.] pp. xix. 28. मुंबई १८८५ [*Bombay,* 1885.] 12°. **14048. b. 14.**

RAMAKADUṆ. રમકડું. નાદાનાં છોકરોને લશાચાની ચોપડી. [Ramakaḍuṇ. A primer for little children.] pp. 16, *lith.* અમદાવાદ ૧૯૫૧ [*Ahmadabad,* 1851.] 12°. **14150. a. 41.**

RĀMAKṚISHṆA GOPĀLA BHĀṆḌĀRKAR. સંસ્કૃત માર્ગોપદેશિકા. [Mārgopadeśikā, or First Book of Sanskrit, with translations into Gujarati by Nandaśaṅkara Tuljāśaṅkara.] pp. v. 112. મુંબઈ ૧૮૬૮ [*Bombay,* 1868.] 8°. **14085. b. 10.**

—— The Margopadesika, or First Book of Sanskrit . . . Translated into Gujarati by Nandashankar Tuljāshanker. Second edition. pp. vii. 118. *Bombay,* 1875. 8°. **14085. b. 17.**

RAMSAY (HORATIO N.) *See* GAṄGĀDHARA ŚĀSTRĪ PHADKE. The Principles of Gujarati grammar, . . . Translated, arranged and briefly illustrated by H. N. R. 1842. 8°. **12906. c. 17.**

RAṆCHHODBHĀĪ UDAYARĀMA. *See* FORBES (A. K.) Rás Málá; . . . . Translated into Gujaráti . . . by Ranachhodabhái Udayarám. 1869. 8°. **14146. h. 6.**

—— *See* KĀLIDĀSA. विक्रमोर्वशीत्रोटक [Vikramorvaśī nāṭaka. Translated, with an introductory preface and notes, by R. U.] [1868.] 12°. **14148. c. 11.**

RAṆCHHODBHĀĪ UDAYARĀMA. *See* SHAKSPERE (W.) Selected tales from Shakespeare, translated into Gujarati by Runchodebhái Ooderám. 1867. 12°. **14148. a. 10.**

—— आरोग्यतासूचक [Ārogyatāsūchaka. A treatise on the means of preserving health, adapted from the English.] pp. 58. મુંબઈ ૧૯૨૧ [*Bombay,* 1864.] 8°. **14146. b. 2.**

—— बाणासुर मदमर्दन ओखाहरण नाटक [Bāṇāsura madamardana. A drama on the mythological story of the abduction of Ushā, daughter of the demon-king Bāṇa, by Aniruddha, grandson of Kṛishṇa.] pp. 99. મુંબઈ ૧૮૮૭ [*Bombay,* 1887.] 12°. **14148. c. 28.**

—— जयकुमारीविजय नाटक [Jayakumārīvijaya nāṭaka. A drama in eight acts, directed chiefly against the evil practice of child-marriages.] pp. iv. 251. મુંબઈ ૧૯૨૦ [*Bombay,* 1864.] 12°. **14148. c. 5.**

—— ललिता दुःखदर्शक. [Lalitā duḥkhadarśaka. A drama in five acts.] pp. vi. 291. मुंबई १९२२ [*Bombay,* 1865.] 16°. **14148. c. 2.**

RAṆCHHODDĀSA GIRDHARBHĀĪ. *See* BĀLA GAṄGĀDHARA ŚĀSTRĪ JĀMBHEKAR. History of British India. Translated . . . by Ranchodás Girdharbhái. 1855. 8°. **14146. g. 14.**

RAṆCHHODJĪ UDHAVAJĪ. *See* YOGAVĀSISHṬHA-RĀMĀYAṆA. श्रीयोगवासिष्ठ महारामायण [Translated by R. U.] [1883, *etc.*] 8°. **14144. d. 8.**

RAṆCHHODLĀLA GALURĀMA. *See* DAYĀRĀMA, *Kavi.* દયારામકૃત કવિતા [Dayārāmakṛita kavitā. Revised by R. G.] [1865.] 8°. **14148. f. 6.**

—— *See* PURĀṆAS. प्राकृत एकादशी महात्म्य. [Ekādaśīmāhātmya. Translated from the Sanskrit by R. G.] [1877.] 8°. **14144. d. 5.**

RAṆCHHODLĀLĀ MOTĪRĀMA. सुंदर स्त्री विलास मनहर गरबावळी. [Sundara strīvilāsa. Garbi songs chiefly on the sports of Kṛishṇa. Second edition.] pp. ii. 120. अमदावाद १८८४ [*Ahmadabad,* 1884.] 16°. **14148. d. 26.**

RAṆCHHODLĀLA VIṬHṬHALADĀSA. શરીર સુખદર્શક [Śarīra sukhadarśaka.] (Mirror of health. Compiled from several medical works, by Runchorlal Vithuldass.) pp. 112. *Ahmadabad,* 1872. 12°. **14146. b. 9.**

RANCHODAS GIRDHARBHÁI. *See* RAṆCHHODDĀSA GIRDHARBHĀĪ.

RAṄGĪLADĀSA HARAKIṢANDĀSA. હીંદુઓમાં, તેરમા-સીમંત્તની જમણવારો શંબંધી આ ભાષણ. [An address to Hindus, showing the folly of giving expensive caste dinners on the death of a relative, and on other occasions.] pp. 18. સુરત ૧૮૭૮ [*Surat*, 1878.] 12°.
14146. e. 21.(1.)

RANJIT. *See* BOMBAY, *Presidency of.—Anglo-Vernacular Schools.* School dialogues . . . [Translated from the Marathi by R.] 1865. 16°.
14150. a. 26.(3.)

RANMAL ADĀBHĀI. *See* MERĀMAṆAJĪ. प्रवीनसागर॥ [Pravīṇasāgara. A Hindi poem, with a commentary in Gujarati by R. A.] [1882.] 4°.
14154. i. 1.

RATANJĪ RUSTAMJĪ KĀṄGĀ. *See* PERIODICAL PUBLICATIONS.—*Bombay.* રાસત દીને જરથોશતીઆંન *etc.* [Rāst dīn i Zartoshtiyān. A Parsi monthly periodical, edited by R. R. K.] [1883, *etc.*] 8°. **14150. e. 2.**

—— *See* ZAND-AVASTĀ. ઇનતેખાબે વંદીદાદ [Intikhāb i Vendidād. Edited with notes by R. R. K.] [1881.] 12°. **14144. h. 2.**

—— કબીશા વીશે તથા ગોશપદોના ખોરાક વીશે જરથોશતીઓને શુચના. [Kabīsā vishe. Suggestions to Zoroastrians on the subject of leap year, and against the use of a meat diet.] pp. 32. મુંબઈ ૧૨૪૪ [*Bombay*, 1875.] 12°.
14144. i. 8.(2.)

—— રૂવાંનની ચાર દાહાડાની કરીઆ વીશે [Rūvānnī chār dāhāḍānī kriyā vishe. A lecture on the funeral rites to be performed during the four days after the death of a Zoroastrian; with an explanation of three lectures on the subject given by Jāmāspjī Minuchehrjī Jamāsp-Asānā.] pp. 68. મુંબઈ ૧૮૭૫ [*Bombay*, 1875.] 12°.
14144. h. 7.(2.)

—— વાએજો. દરરોજની બંદગી વીશેની પુરજ તથા મુકતાદના દીવશો ઊપર કીરીઆ કરવા વીશે. [Vāejo. Zoroastrian sermons on the necessity of daily prayers, and the performance of the religious ceremony of the Muktād.] pp. 36. મુંબઈ ૧૨૪૫ [*Bombay*, 1875.] 12°.
14144. h. 7.(3.)

RATANJĪ RUSTAMJĪ KĀṄGĀ. જરથોશતી ટોલાનો અથવા કોમનો વડો કોણ તે વીશે ઊઠેલી ખટપટ, *etc.* [Zartoshtī ṭolāno vaḍo koṇ. A discussion, in the form of a dialogue between the author and a friend, on the agitation regarding the appointment of a suitable head for the Parsi community, and on other matters.] pp. 24. મુંબઈ ૧૮૭૭ [*Bombay*, 1877.] 8°. **14144. i. 8.(3.)**

RATANSHĀH ERACHSHĀH KOHIYĀR. *See* DINKARD. The Dinkard. The original Péhlwi text . . . translations in the Gujrati and English languages [the latter by R. E. K. from the Gujarati] *etc.* 1874, *etc.* 8°. **761. g. 10.**

RATANṢĪ SĀMAJĪ. સટ્ટા પરીણામ દર્શક [Saṭṭā pariṇāmadarṣaka. Verses on the evil results of speculation, and the advantages of honest trading.] pp. 55. મુંબઈ ૧૮૬૫ [*Bombay*, 1865.] 12°.
14148. d. 2.(3.)

RATNACHANDRA. *See* MUNISUNDARA SŪRI. अथ . . . अध्यात्मकल्पद्रुमो [Adhyātmakalpadruma. With a Gujarati explanation by R.] [1876, *etc.*] 4°.
14100. e. 3.

—— —— [1883.] 8°. **14144. g. 8.**

—— —— [1884.] 8°. **14144. g. 7.**

RATNAṢEKHARA. लघुक्षेत्रसमासप्रकरणः [Laghukshetrasamāsa. Sanskrit text, with a Gujarati commentary by Udayasāgara.] *See* BHĪMASIṂHA MĀNAKA. प्रकरण-रत्नाकर Vol. iv. pp. 185-299. [1876, *etc.*] 4°. **14100. e. 3.**

RAVACHAND JAYACHAND. *See* VĪRAVIJAYA. अथ पंडित श्रीवीरविजयजीकृत पूजाए आदि ॥ [Pūjāe ādī. Edited by R. J.] [1881.] 8°. **14144. g. 13.**

RĀVAJĪ RĀMAJĪ SĀVANT. સને ૧૮૮૦ ની સાલની કાઠીયાવાડ ગાઈડ તથા ડાયરી [Kāṭhiyāvāḍ gāid. Diary for the year 1880, and guide to Kathiawar.] pp. 128. અમદાવાદ ૧૯૩૬ [*Ahmadabad*, 1879.] 8°. **14150. e. 8.**

RAWLINSON (GEORGE). *See* BARJORJĪ PĀLANJĪ DEṢĀI and PĀLANJĪ BARJARJĪ DEṢĀI. History of the Sassanides . . . . Collated from the works of G. R. 1880. 8°. **14146. h. 5.**

REFUGE. The true refuge. ખરો આશ્રો [Kharo āsro. A Christian tract.] pp. 43. શુરત ૧૮૬૧ [*Surat*, 1861.] 16°. **14144. a. 3.(7.)**

REVĀSAṄKARA JAYASAṄKARA. સુધાસંચિત [Sudhāsañchita. A work on Hindu medicine in verse.] pp. iv. 710, *lith.* અમદાવાદ ૧૮૮૫ [*Ahmadabad*, 1885.] 8°. **14146. b. 6.**

RIPON, *Marquis of.* *See* ROBINSON (G. F. S.) *Marquis of Ripon.*

ṚITUVARṆANA. ઋતુવર્ણન. [Ṛituvarṇana. A poetical description of the seasons.] pp. 51. મુંબઈ ૧૮૬૧ [*Bombay*, 1861.] 12°. **14148. d. 2.(1.)**

ROBERTSON (WILLIAM) *D.D., the Historian.* The life of Columbus. Translated into Gujaráti from Robertson's History of America, Book ii., by Pránlál Mathurádás, and Ánandráo Chápáji. (કોલમ્બસનો વૃતાંત) [Kolambasno vṛittānta.] Fourth edition. pp. 144. *Bombay*, 1867. 12°. **14146. f. 19.**

—— [Sixth edition.] *Bombay*, 1877. 12°. **14146. f. 17.**

ROBINSON (GEORGE FREDERICK SAMUEL) *Marquis of Ripon.* India's farewell to Lord Ripon. [A Gujarati poem, with an English prose translation.] pp. 12, 11. [*Bombay*, 1884.] 12°. **14148. d. 9.(2.)**

ROSCOE (HENRY ENFIELD). Science primers in Gujarati. Chemistry by Professor H. E. R. Translated into Gujarati by Rao Saheb Mahipatram R. Nilkanth. (रसायन विद्या) [Rasāyana vidyā.] pp. iv. 111. *Bombay*, 1880. 16°. **14146. c. 12.**

RUMŪZ i DIL-KHUSH. રમુઝેદીલ ખુશ [Rumūz i dil-khush. A collection of humorous tales, fables, and anecdotes.] pp. 192. મુંબઈ ૧૮૬૨ [*Bombay*, 1862.] 8°. **14148. a. 3.**

RUNCHODEBHÁI OODERÁM. *See* RAṆCHHOḌBHĀĪ UDAYARĀMA.

RUNCHORLAL VITHULDASS. *See* RAṆCHHOḌLĀLA VIṬHṬHALADĀSA.

RŪPAJĪ JAYAKṚISHṆA. *See* VĀLMĪKI. શ્રી વાલ્મીકિ રામાયણ [Rāmāyaṇa. Translated by R. J.] [1882, *etc.*] 8°. **14148. e. 11.**

RŪPĀṆĪ BHĪMAJĪ KĀLIDĀSA. चंद्रसिंह-दीपमणी नाटक. [Chandrasiṃha Dīpamaṇī nāṭaka. A drama in five acts.] pp. 114. અમદાવાદ ૧૮૮૪ [*Ahmadabad*, 1884.] 12°. **14148. c. 23.**

RŪPAVIJAYA. *See* PŪJĀSAṄGRAHA. પુજાસંગ્રહ [Pūjāsaṅgraha. Containing selections from the writings of R. and others.] [1884.] 8°. **14144. g. 15.**

RŪPCHAND. *See* BANĀRASĪ DĀSA. अथ श्रीसमयसार [Samayasāra. With a Gujarati translation by R.] [1876, *etc.*] 4°. **14100. e 3**

RŪSHIRĀJA MAHĀRĀJA. बोधचिंतामणी [Bodhachintāmaṇī. A collection of 193 philosophical poems, of which 159 are by R. M. and the remaining 34 by his disciples Durlabharāma, Rāmānanda Brahmachārī and Jhumakharāma.] pp. vi. 118. अमदावाद १९३३ [*Ahmadabad*, 1877.] 8°. **14144. d. 1.**

In the Balabodha character.

RUSTAM ASFANDIYĀR. *See* ŚAD-DAR. સદદરે બેહેરે તવીલ [Śad-dare behere tavīl. Translated from the Persian by R. A.] [1881.] 8°. **14144. i. 24.**

RUSTAM ĪRĀNĪ. *See* KHUSRAU, *Amīr.* બાગો બાહાર *etc.* [Bāgh o Bahār. Translated by R. I.] [1882.] 8°. **14148. b. 36.**

—— દોખમે નોશીરવાન *etc.* [Dokhme Noshīrvān. A tale describing the visit of Caliph Hārūn al-Rashīd to the Towers of Silence. Translated from the Persian. Second edition.] pp. 31. મુંબઈ ૧૮૮૪ [*Bombay*, 1884.] 8°. **14148. b. 30.(2.)**

—— ગુન્ચ-એ-અવસ્તા *etc.* [Ghuncha i Avastā. A metrical adaptation of Zoroastrian prayers, taken from the Zand-Avastā.] pp. 21. મુંબઈ ૧૨૪૯ [*Bombay*, 1880.] 32°. **14144. h. 8.**

—— ગુલ શીરીના: ઈરાનની છેલ્લી શાહજાદી. [Gul Shīrīnā. An historical novel, describing the last struggles of the Zoroastrian rule in Persia, under the Emperor Shehriyār, and the exploits of his daughter Shīrīnā.] pp. vi. 230. મુંબાઈ [*Bombay*, 1889.] 8°. **14148. b. 41.**

RUSTAMJĪ NASARVĀNJĪ KHORE. The Bombay Materia Medica and their therapeutics. [Compiled from various native medical works, with the names of drugs in the Gujarati character] by Rustomjee Naserwanjee Khory. pp. 600, 39. *Bombay*, 1887. 8°. **7509. dd. 6.**

RUSTAM PESHOTAN, *Mobed.* સ્યાવશનામું. ગુજરાતી કવિતામાં [Siyāvash-nāmuṇ. An old

Gujarati poem on the history of Siyāvakhsh, son of Kaikāwus, king of Persia. Edited, with notes and a glossary, by Tehmuras Dīnshāh.] pp. xii. 284. મુંબઈ ૧૮૭૩ [*Bombay*, 1873.] 8°. **14146. g. 2.**

SACHCHIDĀNANDA BRAHMATĪRTHA. *See* MANORADĀSA, called SACHCHIDĀNANDA BRAHMATĪRTHA.

SADĀṢIVA KĀṢĪNĀTHA CHHATRE. *See* BERQUIN (A.) Berquin's Children's friend. Translated into Gujrátí [from the Marathi version of S. K. Chh.] 1860. 12°. **14144. a. 20.**

ṠAD-DAR. સદ્દરે બેહેરે તવીલ યાને સો બાબ અથવા સો દરવાજાની કેતાબ [Ṡad-dare behere tavīl, or The hundred gates. A popular exposition of the principles of the Zoroastrian religion, in 100 chapters; being a translation, by Mullā Rustam Asfandiyār and Mullā Behjad Rustam, of a Persian metrical version by Īrānshāh ibn Malakshāh of the Pehlevi original. With portions of the Persian transliterated. Second edition, revised and edited by Jāmāspjī Minuchehrjī Jāmāsp-Asānā.] pp. xix. 366. મુંબઈ ૧૮૮૧ [*Bombay*, 1881.] 8°. **14144. i. 24.**

SADEVANTA. શદેવંત શાવલીંગાની વારતા [Sadevanta Ṣāvaliṅgānī vārtā. A romance in verse.] pp. 67, *lith.* ૧૮૨૧ [*Bombay*, 1864.] 8°. **14148. b. 4.(7.)**

SAʻDĪ. *See* NAVAROJĪ ĀDARJĪ TĀTĀ. A glossary of words occurring in Karimá of Shaik-Sáádi, *etc.* [1881.] 12°. **757. cc. 5.(1.)**

—— The Gulistan of Shaik Sadi. Part iv. Translated into Gujarati with copious explanatory notes, *etc.*, by Kawasji Dinshaw Kiash. (શેખ સાદીનુ બનાવેલું ફારસી ગુલસ્તાન.) pp. xviii. 151-214. viii. *Bombay*, 1879. 8°. **14148. b. 12.**

ṢĀDIḲ ʻALĪ. مجموع النصائح [Majmūʻ al-naṣāʼiḥ. Moral precepts in verse, and in the Persian character.] pp. 208. ممبئي ١٢٩٤ [*Bombay*, 1878.] 8°. **14146. e. 17.**

SAHAJĀNANDA SVĀMĪ. [*Life.*] *See* NISHKULĀNANDA. अथ श्री भक्तचिंतामणि ग्रंथ प्रारंभ. [Bhaktachintāmaṇi.]

—— श्री सहजानंद स्वामिनी लखेली शिक्षापत्री । नित्यानंद मुनिनी लखेली टीकासाथे [Ṣikshāpatrī. Aphorisms on moral and religious duties, in Sanskrit, with a Gujarati commentary by Nityānanda Muni.] pp. 72. मुंबई १८६२ [*Bombay*, 1862.] 12°. **14028. b. 33.**

—— शिक्षापत्रीध्वान्तनिवारणेऽयक्रन्थः । अर्थात् स्वामिनारायणमत दोषदर्शनात्मक . . . श्यामजिना भाषान्तर कृतम् [An anonymous treatise in refutation of the doctrines of the Svāmīnārāyaṇa sect, as set forth in Sahajānanda's Ṣikshāpatrī. Sanskrit text, with a Gujarati translation by Ṣyāmajī Kṛishṇavarmā.] pp. 12, 16. મુંબઈ ૧૮૭૬ [*Bombay*, 1876.] 8°. **14028. c. 30.**

—— श्लोका लावणीओ अने गरबाओ [Ṣlokā lāvaṇio ane garbāo. Poems by various authors in praise of S. S.] pp. 76. अमदावाद १९३४ [*Ahmadabad*, 1877.] 12°. **14148. d. 24.**

—— श्रीहरिकृष्ण महाराजनो श्रीमुखसिद्धांत [Ṣrīmukha-siddhānta. Religious discourses delivered on various occasions to followers of the Svāmīnārāyaṇa sect.] 3 pt. *lith.* अमदावाद १९३४ [*Ahmadabad*, 1877.] 4°. **14144. e. 7.**

—— वचनामृत [Vachanāmrita. A philosophical treatise in verse, on the tenets of the Svāmīnārāyaṇa sect.] ff. 364. अमदावाद १९३३ [*Ahmadabad*, 1876.] *obl.* 4°. **14144. e. 4.**

—— [Another edition.] pp. 993. अमदावाद १९३३ [*Ahmadabad*, 1876.] *obl.* 8°. **14144. d. 10.**

—— [Another edition.] ff. 14, 82, 86, 75, 72. मुंबई १८७७ [*Bombay*, 1877.] *obl.* 4°. **14144. e. 5.**

SAJHĀYAMĀLĀ. सझायमाला [Sajhāyamāla. A collection of religious precepts in verse, compiled from the works of various Jain authors.] pp. xii. 556. अमदावाद १९३४ [*Ahmadabad*, 1877.] 8°. **14144. g. 12.**

—— મોહોટું સજાયમાળા સંગ્રહ. [A larger collection of religious maxims in verse.] pp. v. 256. અમદાવાદ ૧૮૮૭ [*Ahmadabad*, 1887.] 8°. **14144. g. 24.**

SAJHĀYO. સજ્યાઓ [Sajyāo, or more correctly Sajhāyo. Moral precepts in verse for followers of the Jain religion.] pp. ?4. अमदावाद १९३३ [*Ahmadabad*, 1877.] 16°. **14144. f. 4.(6.)**

ṢĀKERRĀMA DALPATRĀMA. *See* MOROBĀ KĀNHOBĀ. ઘાશીરામ કોટવાલ . . . Ghasiram Kotwal. [Translated] from the Maráthi into Gujráti by Shakerrám Dalpatrám. 1865. 12°.

14148. a. 22.

SALMON. (   ) *Lieut.* *See* BHĀVASINGHAJĪ MODAJĪ, *Jāḍejā.* *Begin.* To His Excellency the Right Honourable Baron Reay . . . The humble petition of Jadeja Bhowsingji Modji ... [charging Lieutenant Salmon with assault, and the use of abusive language.] 1886. 4°. **14146. a. 15.**

SALVATION. તારણ શું છે ને તેશી રીતે મલશે. Salvation. [Tāraṇa. A Christian tract.] pp. 34. ૧૮૫૭ [*Surat?* 1857.] 12°. **14144. a. 1.(6.)**

ṢAMAJĪ RAṆCHHOḌ. चंद्रास अने चद्रकळा. [Chandrās ane Chandrakaḷā. A tale arranged in the form of a drama.] pp. 128. મુંબઈ ૧૮૮૦ [*Bombay,* 1880.] 8°. **14148. b. 20.**

ṢĀMAJĪ RATANṢĪ. वडोदरामां विद्यादि विषे कविता. [Baḍodarāmāṉ vidyādi vishe kavitā. A poem on the state of education in Baroda.] અમદાવાદ ૧૮૭૮ [*Ahmadabad,* 1878.] 12°. **14148. d. 13.(19.)**

ṢĀMALA BHAṬA. અંગદવિષ્ટિ. [Aṅgadavishṭi. A poem by Ṣ. Bh. with notes and a glossary.] *See* PRĀCHĪNA KĀVYA प्राचीन काव्य. Vol. i. No. 2. [1885, *etc.*] 8°. **14148. e. 12.**

—— બરાસ કશતુરી [Barāsa Kasturī. A romance in verse.] pp. 194, *lith.* મુંબઈ ૧૭૮૫ [*Bombay,* 1863.] 8°. **14148. f. 5.**

—— જોહાંદાર શાહા બાદશાની વારતા [Jahāndar Shāh bādshāhnī vārtā. A metrical adaptation of the Bahār i dānish, or Persian tales of ʻInāyat Allāh.] pp. 500, *lith.* મુંબઈ ૧૮૫૦ [*Bombay,* 1850.] 8°. **14148. b. 2.**

—— [Another edition.] pp. 147. અમદાવાદ ૧૮૮૪ [*Ahmadabad,* 1884.] 8°. **14148. b. 29.**

—— કાસ્ટના ઘોડાની વારતા [Kāshṭhanā ghoḍānī vārtā, or The story of the wooden horse. A paraphrase in verse of the sixteenth tale of the Singhāsan Battīsī.] pp. 60, *lith.* મુંબઈ ૧૯૧૨ [*Bombay,* 1855.] 8°. **14148. b. 4.(2.)**

—— મદન મોહનાની વારતા [Madana Mohanānī vārtā. A romance in verse.] pp. 286, *lith.* મુંબઈ ૧૯૧૯ [*Bombay,* 1862.] 12°. **14148. a. 4.**

—— [Another edition.] pp. 285, *lith.* મુંબઈ ૧૯૨૦ [*Bombay,* 1863.] 12°. **14148. a. 5.**

—— સામળકૃત मदनमोहना [An annotated edition.] *See* PRĀCHĪNA KĀVYA. प्राचीन काव्य Vol. vi. No. 1. [1885, *etc.*] 8°. **14148. e. 12.**

ṢĀMALA BHAṬA. મડાપચીશીની વારતા. [Maḍāpachīsīnī vārtā. A paraphrase in verse of the collection of tales, entitled Baitāl Pachīsī.] pp. 283, *lith.* મુંબઈ ૧૯૧૯ [*Bombay,* 1862.] 8°. **14148. b. 7.**

—— માધવાનલની વારતાની ચોપડી [Mādhavānalanī vārtā. A paraphrase in verse of one of the stories of the Singhāsan Battīsī.] pp. 108, *lith.* મુંબઈ ૧૯૦૯ [*Bombay,* 1852.] 16°. **14148. a. 2.(1.)**

—— મેનાપોપટની વારતા. [Menāpopaṭnī vārtā. A metrical adaptation of one of the tales of the Singhāsan Battīsī.] pp. 78, *lith.* મુંબઈ ૧૮૬૪ [*Bombay,* 1864.] 12°. **14148. a. 2.(5.)**

—— અથ નંદબતરીશીની વારતા [Nanda battrīsīni vārtā. A tale in verse of king Nanda and his prime minister Vilochana.] pp. 62, *lith.* મુંબઈ ૧૯૧૯ [*Bombay,* 1862.] 8°. **14148. b. 5.(2.)**

—— [Another edition.] pp. 46, *lith.* મુંબઈ ૧૯૨૧ [*Bombay,* 1865.] 8°. **14148. b. 4.(9.)**

—— [Another edition.] pp. 64, *lith.* મુંબઈ ૧૮૮૫ [*Bombay,* 1885.] 8°. **14148. b. 35.(2.)**

—— [Another edition.] *See* PRĀCHĪNA KĀVYA. प्राचीन काव्य Vol. ii. No. 2. [1885, *etc.*] 8°. **14148. e. 12.**

—— આ પદમાવતીની વારતાની ચોપડી [Padmāvatīnī vārtā. The story of Padmāvatī in verse.] pp. 68, *lith.* મુંબઈ ૧૭૮૨ [*Bombay,* 1860.] 8°. **14148. b. 4.(5.)**

—— [Another edition.] pp. 72, *lith.* ૧૯૧૭ [*Bombay?* 1860.] 8°. **14148. b. 5.(1.)**

—— બતરીશ પુતલીમધેની પાનનાબીડાની વારતા [Pānanābiḍānī vārtā. A paraphrase in verse of one of the tales from the Singhāsan Battīsī.] pp. 158, *lith.* મુંબઈ ૧૭૭૭ [*Bombay,* 1855.] 16°. **14148. a. 2.(2.)**

—— પંચડંડની વારતાની ચોપડી [Pañcha daṇḍanī vārtā. A paraphrase in verse of the fifth tale of the Singhāsan Battīsī. Second edition.] pp. 118, *lith.* મુંબઈ ૧૯૧૬ [*Bombay,* 1859.] 16°. **14148. a. 17.**

—— બત્રીસ પુતળીની વારતામાંની ૧૭મી પંખીની વારતા [Paṅkhīnī vārtā. A paraphrase in verse of the seveneenth tale of the Singhāsnat Battīsī.] pp. 32. અમદાવાદ ૧૯૩૩ [*Ahmadabad,* 1877.] 8° **14148. b. 30.(1.)**

ṢĀMALA BHAṬA. सदेवंत ने शावळींगाना आठ भवनी रमोक वार्ता. [Sadevanta ne Ṣāvaliṅgānā .... vārtā. A popular tale in prose and verse, on the story of the eight births of Sadevanta and Ṣāvaliṅgā.] pp. 184. अमदावाद १९३४ [*Ahmadabad*, 1877.] 12°. **14148. a. 18.**

—— [Another edition.] pp. 184. अमदावाद १९३३ [*Ahmadabad*, 1877.] 12°. **14148. a. 19.**

—— Shamal Bhat's Chuppa, with meaning. શામળભટ્ટકૃત છપ્પા અર્થસહિત. pp. 17. મુંબઈ [*Bombay*, 1877.] 16°. **14148. d. 5.(12.)**

—— શુડા બહોતેરી [Sudābahoterī. A versified adaptation of the Ṣukasaptatī, or Seventy-two tales of a parrot. With illustrations.] pp. 470. અમદાવાદ ૧૮૮૦ [*Ahmadabad*, 1880.] 8°. **14148. b. 33.**

—— ઊદમકરમસંવાદ [Udyama karma saṃvāda. A tale in verse.] pp. 78, *lith.* મુંબઈ ૧૯૧૭ [*Bombay*, 1860.] 16°. **14148. d. 5.(2.)**

—— [Another edition.] pp. 88, *lith.* [*Bombay?* 1861 ?] 16°. **14148. d. 17.**

SAMAVĀYĀṄGA. समवायांग [Samavāyāṅga, The fourth *aṅga* of the Jain canon. Sanskrit text, with a Gujarati *ṭabba* or explanation by Megharāja.] [1880.] *obl.* 4°. **14100. f. 8.**

SĀMĀYAKA. सामायक तथा पडीकमणुं. પ્રાકૃત તથા દેશિ ભાષામાં. [Sāmāyaka and Paḍīkamaṇa. Jain devotional treatises in Prakrit and Gujarati.] pp. 80, *lith.* અમદાવાદ ૧૮૭૭ [*Ahmadabad*, 1877.] 8°. **14100. c. 8.**

—— सामायक सूत्र तथा चैत्यवंदन अर्थ सहित अने स्तवन चोय सज्झायो विगरे [Sāmāyaka. Sanskrit text, with a verbatim translation into Gujarati; followed by a form of salutation, and Jain hymns, and prayers in Gujarati.] pp. 4, 32. अमदावाद १९४१ [*Ahmadabad*, 1885.] 16°. **14100. a.**

SAMAYASUNDARA UPĀDHYĀYAJĪ. करकंडू आदिक चार प्रत्येक बुद्ध रास [Karakaṇḍū ādik chār pratyek Buddha rās. Four Jain legends.] pp. 104. मुंबानगरी १९४१ [*Bombay*, 1886.] 12°. **14144. f. 8.**

SAMSĀRACHOPAḌĪ. નાંનીશંશારચોપડી. [Saṃsārachopaḍī. Lessons in orthography, and useful numerical tables.] pp. 46, *lith.* ૧૯૧૮ [*Bombay*, 1862]. 16°. **14150. a. 26.(1.)**

SAMSĀRACHOPAḌĪ. શનશાર ચોપડી [Saṃsārachopaḍī. A manual of instruction in reading, writing, spelling, the elements of arithmetic, lessons in English and Hindustani alphabets, and various other useful matters.] pp. 500, *lith.* મુંબઈ ૧૭૮૫ [*Bombay*, 1864.] 8°. **14150. b. 6.**

This work contains all the matter of the preceding.

—— [Another edition.] pp. 504, *lith.* મુંબઈ ૧૭૮૫ [*Bombay*, 1864]. 8°. **14150. b. 7.**

—— [Another edition.] pp. 504, *lith.* મું૦ ૧૯૩૩ [*Bombay*, 1877]. 8°. **14150. b. 8.**

SAMYAKTVASVARŪPA-STAVA. अथ श्री सम्यक्त्वस्वरूपस्तव बालावबोध सहित प्रारंभः [Saṃyaktvasvarūpastava. A work in Prakrit verse in praise of *saṃyaktva* or Jain orthodoxy, with a commentary in Gujarati. By a pupil of Jñānasāgara.] *See* BHĪMASIṂHA MĀṆAKA प्रकरण-रत्नाकर [Prakaraṇa-ratnākara.] Vol. ii. pp. 577—625. [1876, *etc.*] 4°. **14100. e. 3.**

ṢANIṢCHARA. શનીશચર દેવતાની કથા. [Ṣaniṣchara devatānī kathā. A poem in praise of the god Saturn.] pp. 41, *lith.* મુંબઈ ૧૯૧૧ [*Bombay*, 1854.] 16°. **14148. d. 1.(1.)**

—— [Another edition.] pp. 29, *lith.* [*Bombay*, 1860 ?]. 16°. **14148. d. 4.(2.)**

—— [Another edition.] pp. 31, *lith.* મુંબઈ ૧૭૮૭ [*Bombay*, 1865]. 16°. **14148. d. 5.(5.)**

SĀṄKALCHAND MAHĀSUKHARĀMA. *See* PŪJĀSAṄGRAHA. पुजा संग्रह [Pūjāsaṅgraha. Edited by S. M.] [1875.] 8°. **14144. g. 1.**

—— દીલખુશ સ્તવનાવળી [Dil-khush stavanāvalī. Verses in praise of Jain saints.] pp. 56. અમદાવાદ [*Ahmadabad*, 1875 ?]. 16°. **14144. f. 4.(3.)**

SĀṄKALEṢVARA CHHAGANLĀLA DAVE. सुकनावली. [Sukanāvalī. A small work on divination, with numerous illustrations.] ff. 77, *lith.* अमदावाद १९३१ [*Ahmadabad*, 1881.] 16°. **14146. c. 1.**

ṢAṄKARA ĀCHĀRYA. प्रारंभ चर्पटपंजरी [Charpaṭapañjarī. A Sanskrit poem attributed to Ṣ. Ā., in 16 slokas, in praise of Vishṇu, with translations into Gujarati, Hindi and Marathi.] pp. 14, *lith.* मुंबई १९१५ [*Bombay*, 1859]. 8°. **14076. a. 3.**

—— श्री विवेकचूडामणि: [Vivekachūḍāmaṇi. A treatise on Vedānta philosophy. Sanskrit text, with a Gujarati prose translation by Kālidāsa Govindajī.] pp. 55, 90. मुंबई १८८६ [*Bombay*, 1886.] 12°. **14043. b. 22.**

ṢAṄKARA HARIBHĀĪ. કબીર સાહેબ ... તથા સમુદાય સંતની વાણી [Samudāya santanī vāṇī. A collection of Vaishṇava poems, some by Hindi and others by Gujarati poets. Compiled by Ṣ. H.] pp. vii. 198. મુંબઈ ૧૮૮૮ [*Bombay*, 1888.] 8°. **14158. e. 33.**

ṢAṄKARALĀLA MAHEṢVARA. શીઘ્રકવિ શંકરલાલ માહેશ્વરકૃત પાર્વતીપરિણયાંતર્ગત अनसूयाभ्युदय तथा भोगवतीभाग्योदयनुं ભાષાંતર [Anusūyābhyudaya and Bhogavatībhāgyodaya. Episodes from the author's Sanskrit romance Pārvatīpariṇaya.] pp. ii. 92. મુંબઈ ૧૯૪૦ [*Bombay*, 1883.] 16°. **14148. a. 31.**

ṢAṄKARA LIṄGAM. શંકર લીંગમ નામે એક હીંદુ ... તેની વારતા. [Ṣaṅkara Liṅgam tenī vārtā. The story of a Hindu convert to Christianity.] pp. 80. શુરત ૧૮૫૩ [*Surat*, 1853.] 12°. **14144. a. 6.**

ṢĀNTISŪRI. श्री जीवविचार प्रकरण [Jīvavichāraprakaraṇa. A Jain treatise on psychology in 51 Prakrit stanzas, accompanied by a *bālāvabodha* or verbal explanation in Gujarati.] pp. 64. मुंबापुरी १९४१ [*Bombay*, 1885.] 16°. **14100. a. 9.**

ṢATRUÑJAYA. शत्रुंजय तीर्थमाला, रास, उद्धारादिक संग्रहग्रंथ. [Ṣatruñjaya tīrthamālā. A collection of songs by Jain poets in praise of the sacred hill of Ṣatruñjaya.] pp. 92. मोहमयी १९४१ [*Bombay*, 1884.] 12°. **14144. f. 13.**

SAUBHĀGAMĀLAJĪ. विबध रतन प्रकाश पुस्तक [Bibadha ratan prakāṣa. Instruction in the principles of the Jain religion in Prakrit, with an admixture of Gujarati.] pp. vi. 192. पुना १९४५ [*Poona*, 1888.] 16°. **14154. h. 14.**

SAURĀSHṬRA JÑĀNAPRASĀRAKA MAṆḌAḶĪ. *See* BOMBAY, *City of.—Saurāshṭra Jñānaprasāraka Maṇḍaḷī.*

SAVITĀNĀRĀYAṆA GAṆAPATINĀRĀYAṆA. अलंकारचंद्रिका [Alaṅkārachandrikā. A treatise on rhetoric compiled from various Sanskrit sources.] pp. x. 117. મુંબઈ ૧૮૮૦ [*Bombay*, 1880]. 12°. **14146. c. 4.**

SENTENCES. Short sentences, English and Gujarati, with a glossary of useful words for the use of schools and private families. Fifth edition. pp. 67. *Bombay*, 1881. 16°. **14150. a. 19.**

ṢERṢAṬĀ. શેરશટાનું વરણન [Ṣerṣaṭānuṇ varṇana. Caution in verse against rash speculation in shares.] pp. 22. મુંબઈ ૧૮૬૫ [*Bombay*, 1865.] 12°. **14148. d. 2.(4.)**

SHAKERRÁM DALPATRÁM. *See* ṢĀKERRĀMA DALPATRĀMA.

SHAKSPERE (WILLIAM). શેકસપીર નાટક અંક ૧ [Shakspere's plays, translated by Nānābhāī Rustamjī Rāṇīnā. Pt. I. containing a translation of "Comedy of Errors," and "Othello."] pp. viii. 182. મુંબઈ ૧૮૬૫ [*Bombay*, 1865.] 8°. **14148. b. 19.**

—— Selected tales from Shakespeare [by Charles Lamb] translated into Gujarati by Runchodebhái Ooderám, Chotálál Savekrám, and Manibhái Jusbhái. (शेक्सपियर कथासमाज.) pp. xv. 244. *Ahmadabad*, 1867. 12°. **14148. a. 10.**

SHĀPURJĪ EDALJĪ. *See* JOHNSON (S.) *LL.D.* Johnson's Rasselas ... Translated by Shápurjí Edaljí. 1866. 12°. **14148. a. 9.(1.)**

SHEHRIYĀRJĪ DĀDĀBHĀĪ. *See* ĀDARBĀD MARĀSPAND. Pandnâmah i Âdarbâd Mâraspand ... Comprising the original Pehlevi text ... a complete translation in Gujerathee and a glossary ... by Herbad Sheriarjee Dadabhoy. 1869. 8°. **761. e. 13.**

SHERIARJEE DADABHOY. *See* SHEHRIYĀRJĪ DĀDĀBHĀĪ.

SHERIDAN (*Right Hon.* RICHARD BRINSLEY BUTLER). *See* KAIKHUSRAU NAVAROJĪ KĀBRĀJĪ. નિંદાખાનું. [Nindā khānuṇ. A Parsi play, adapted from Sheridan's "School for Scandal."] [1883.] 8°. **14148. c. 20.(1.)**

SHERWOOD (MARY MARTHA). *See* BUTT, afterwards SHERWOOD (M. M.)

SIDDHARSHI GAṆI. *See* HAṂSARATNA MUNI. अथ श्री उपमितिभवप्रपंच वार्त्तिकरूपं लिख्यते [Upamitibhavaprapañcha. A Gujarati translation from Haṃsaratna Muni's prose abridgment of S. G.'s original Sanskrit work in verse.] [1876, *etc.*] 4°. **14100. e. 3.**

SĪTĀRĀMA RĀVAJĪ JUNARKAR. *See* ṢUKADEVA. જ્યોતીષસાર *etc.* [Jyotishasāra. With Janārdana Bhāskara Kramavanta's Marathi commentary translated into Gujarati by S. R. J.] [1864?] 4°. **14053. d. 11.**

SITĀYISH-NĀMAH. સેતાયશ નામું; આસમાની . . . પ્રારસી . . . તથા ગુજરાતી જુબાનમાં. [Sitāyish-nāmuṇ. A collection of Zoroastrian prayers in Zend, Persian and Gujarati.] pp. 176. મુંબાઈ [*Bombay*, 1884.] 32°. **761. a. 21.**
The Zend and Persian prayers are in the Gujarati character.

ṢIVADĀSA. દ્રૌપદીસહ્યંવર [Draupadī svayamvara. A poem on the marriage of Draupadī to the five Pāṇḍava princes, taken from the Mahābhārata.] pp. 131, *lith.* મુંબઈ ૧૯૧૨ [*Bombay*, 1855.] 12°. **14148. a. 14.(1.)**

—— द्रौपदीस्वयंवर अने एकादशीमहिमा [Another edition. Followed by Ekādaṣīmahimā, a poem on the sanctity of the eleventh day of each half-moon. With copious notes.] *See* PRĀCHĪNA KĀVYA. प्राचीन काव्य. Vol. iii. No. 4. [1885, *etc.*] 8°. **14148. e. 12.**

ṢIVALĀLA DHANEṢVARA. श्रीमद्रामायण. तुळसीकृत उपरथी, गुजराती भाषामां [Rāmāyaṇa. A verse adaptation by Ṣ. Dh. of the Hindi poem of Tulasīdāsa.] pp. v. 414, iii. मुंबई १९३१ [*Bombay*, 1875]. 4°. **14148. f. 16.**

SIYĀJĪ RĀVA, *Gaikwar of Baroda. Life. See* [Addenda.] BHAGUBHĀĪ RĀMAṢAṄKARA JĀNĪ. Life of His Highness Sir Sayajirao Gaikwar.

SKINNER (JAMES). *See* BIBLE. પુરાતન સ્થાપનાનું પુસ્તક . . . The Holy Scriptures in Gujarati. [Translated by J. S. and W. Fyvie.] 1861. 8°. **3068. bb. 19.**

—— Old Testament.—*Pentateuch.* પુરાતન સ્થાપનાનું પુસ્તક . . . The five Books of Moses. [Revised from the translation of J. S. and W. Fyvie.] 1858. 8°. **3070. d. 9.**

—— *New Testament.* આચણ પ્રભુ . . . ઈશુ ખ્રીસ્તની नवीन स्थापना . . . The New Testament . . . Translated . . . [by J. S. and W. Fyvie.] 1857. 12°. **3068. b. 30.**

—— —— *Matthew.* The Gospel according to Matthew . . . [Translated by J. Taylor, and revised by J. S. and W. Fyvie.] 1840. 8°. **3068. bb. 1.**

SKINNER (JAMES). *See* BIBLE.—New Testament.—*John, Gospel of.* શારા શમાચાર ઈહોનના બનાવેલા. The Gospel of John. [Translated by J. S. and W. Fyvie.] **3070. bb. 19.**

—— —— *Acts.* The Acts of the Apostles in English and Goojuratee. [Translated by J. S. and W. Fyvie.] 1841. 8°. **3068. bb. 4.**

ṢLOKĀ-SAṄGRAHA. શલોકા સંગ્રહ. [Slokā-saṅgraha. A collection of verses in honour of Jain saints.] Pt. i. મુંબઈ ૧૮૮૧ [*Bombay*, 1881.] 12°. **14148. d. 21.**

ṢOBHANA. शोभनकृतजिनस्तुति [Jinastuti. A Sanskrit hymn in praise of the 24 Tirthankaras, with a Gujarati commentary.] *See* BHĪMASIṂHA MĀṆAKA प्रकरण-रत्नाकर [Prakaraṇa-ratnākara.] Vol. iii. pp. 760-812. [1876, *etc.*] 4°. **14100. e. 3.**

ṢOBHĀVAHUJĪ. શોભાવહુજીકૃત કકોતા. [Kakotā. Short poems.] pp. 21, *lith.* મુંબઈ ૧૭૮૫ [*Bombay*, 1863.] 16°. **14148. d. 5.(4.)**

SOHRĀBJĪ HORMASJĪ. કલીઆનીના નવા દખ્માનો ગરબો [Kaliānīnā navā dakhmāno garbo. An account in verse of the ceremony at the opening of the new Tower of Silence at Kalyān on the 20th Nov. 1885.] pp. 32. મુંબઈ ૧૮૮૬ [*Bombay*, 1886.] 12°. **14144. h. 9.(1.)**

—— પારસી સ્ત્રી રમુજી નવા ગરબા [Parsī strī ramujī navā garbā. A collection of garbi songs for Parsi women.] pp. 87. મુંબઈ ૧૮૮૧ [*Bombay*, 1881.] 12°. **14148. a. 2.(10.)**

SOHRĀBJĪ JAMSHEDJĪ JĪJĪBHĀI. *See* MUḤAMMAD, *the Prophet.* Tuqviuti-din-i-Mazdiasna, or a Mehzur . . . given by Huzrut Mahomed . . . and another Mehznr given by Huzrut Ally . . . Translated into Goozrathee . . . by Sorabjee Jamsetjee Jejeebhoy. 1851. 8°. **14144. i. 3.**

—— Jowhur-é-zindéhgāni; or Human life, its duties and responsibilities. A lecture delivered . . . on the 27th of March 1856, by Sorabjee Jamsetjee Jejeebhoy. (જોહરે જીનદેહગાંની) pp. 81. *Bombay*, 1856. 12°. **14146. e. 10.**

—— Rāhé Pārsā; or a Guide to the religions. Being a translation from various works in Zend, Pehlvi, Arabic, Persian, English, Latin and Sanscrit, in elucidation of the question, Are we justified in killing animals? with suggestions on the means to be adopted to check the cruelty to animals which prevails in this country. By Sorabjee Jamsetjee Jejeebhoy. (રાહે પારસા) pp. xxxi. 394. *Bombay*, 1853. 8°. **14144. i. 1.**

SOHRĀBJĪ JAMSHEDJĪ READER. સર્વોપયોગી નુસખા સંગ્રહ [Sarvopayogī nuskhā saṅgraha. A collection of over 500 chemical, medical, culinary and other useful recipes.] Pt. I. pp. 76. મુંબઈ ૧૮૭૮ [*Bombay*, 1878.] 8°. **14146. b. 4.**

SOHRĀBJĪ KŪVARJĪ TĀSKAR. Persian Monajat for the Zorastrians in praise of the Almighty for His needful grace and help to them. [Accompanied by a Gujarati translation, the Persian verses, as well as the translation, being in Gujarati characters.] By Sorabji Kuvarji Taskar. (પારસી મોનાજાત) [Fārsī munājāt.] pp. 16. *Surat*, [1887.] 16°. **14144. h. 9.(2.)**

SOHRĀBJĪ SHĀPURJĪ BAṄGĀLĪ. ચુંટી કાહડેલાં લખાણો. [Chuṇṭī kāhāḍelān lakhāṇo. Selections from newspapers and other periodicals relating to the ancient history, language, literature, and social customs of the Parsis.] 2 vol. મુંબઈ ૧૮૮૦ [*Bombay*, 1880.] 8°. **14150. e. 6.**

—— The Parsee Marriage and Divorce Act 1865: (Act No. xv. of 1865.) the Parsee Chattels Real Act: (Act No. ix. of 1837.) the Parsee Succession Act: (Act No. xxi. of 1865.) and the Indian Succession Act 1865. (Act No. x. of 1865.) with an appendix and Guzeratte translation. Edited by Sorabjee Shapoorjee Bengalee. pp. viii. 243, 248. *Bombay*, 1868. 8°. **760. h. 14.**

—— જરતોસતી લોકોનાં ધરમ પુસતકો. [Zartoshtī lokonāṇ dharma pustako. Lessons on the Zoroastrian Scriptures.] pp. x. 197. મુંબઈ ૧૨૨૦ [*Bombay*, 1858.] 8°. **14144. i. 2.**

SOHRĀBSHĀH ḌOSĀBHĀĪ. *See* WILSON (J.) *D.D., F.R.S., etc.* Idiomatic Exercises . . . Rendered into Goojeratee by Sorabshaw Dossabhoy. 1850. 12°. **12906. bbb. 9.**

SOMACHAND KĀLIDĀSA. ज्ञान उपदेश. [Jñāna-upadeṣa. A collection of Hindi and Gujarati songs by Sūradāsa, Kabīr, Dayārāma, and other poets. Also the Rāmāyaṇa of Krishṇadāsa. Compiled by S. K.] pp. 91. અમદાવાદ ૧૮૮૫ [*Ahmadabad*, 1885.] 12°. **14148. e. 10.**

SOMAPRABHĀCHĀRYA. अथ श्री शृंगारवैराग्यतरंगिणी प्रारंभ [Sṛiṅgārāvairāgya-taraṅgiṇī. Sanskrit verses on asceticism and the temptations of female beauty, with a Gujarati translation and gloss by Nandalāla.] *See* BHĪMASIṂHA MĀṆAKA. प्रकरण-रत्नाकर [Prakaraṇa-ratnākara.] Vol. ii. pp. 217-241. [1876, *etc.*] 4°. **14100. e. 3.**

—— [Another edition.] *See* JAINASĀSTRA. જૈન સાસ્ત્ર કથા સંગ્રહ. pp. 173-200. [1883.] 8°. **14144. g. 8.**

—— [Another edition.] *See* CHARITRASAṄGRAHA. ચરિત્ર સંગ્રહ pp. 173-200. [1884.] 8°. **14144. g. 7.**

SORABJEE JAMSETJEE JEJEEBHOY. *See* SOHRĀBJĪ JAMSHEDJĪ JĪJĪBHĀĪ.

SORABSHAW DOSSABHOY. *See* SOHRĀBSHĀH ḌOSĀBHĀĪ.

STHĀNĀṄGA. स्थानाङ्ग सूत्र . . . मेघराजगणि कृत भाषा टीका सहित। [Sthānāṅga. The third of the *aṅgas* or leading canonical books of the Svetāmbara Jains. Sanskrit text and commentary, and a Gujarati commentary by Megharāja.] pp. 596. *Prakrit, Sansk.* and *Guj.* बनारस १८८० [*Benares*, 1880.] *obl.* 4°. **14100. f. 3.**

STRĪ GANEĀNT MĀLĀ. અસતરી ગનેઆંત માલા [Strī ganeānt mālā. Advice to Parsi Parsi women on social, hygienic, and educational matters; being a collection of articles and addresses by several Parsi writers.] pp. 228. મુમબાઈ ૧૮૫૯ [*Bombay*, 1859.] 12°. **14146. e. 3.**

SUIHARA DĀSA. રામાએણના ચંદરાવલા [Rāmāyaṇanā chandrāvalā. The story of the Rāmāyaṇa in verse.] pp. 271, *lith.* મુંબઈ ૧૯૧૫ [*Bombay*, 1858.] 8°. **14148. f. 1.**

ṢUKADEVA. જ્યોતીષસાર। આ ગ્રંથ સંસ્કૃત ગ્રંથ ઊપરથી જનાર્દન ભાસ્કર ભટ ક્રમવંત એઓએ મરાઠી ભાષામાં કરિઓ તેનુ ગુજરાતી ભાષાંતર [Jyotishasāra. A treatise on astrology, Sanskrit text, with Janārdana Bhāskara Kramavanta's Marathi commentary translated into Gujarati by Sītārāma Rāvajī Junarkar.] pp. xi. 142, 85, *lith.* મુંબઈ [*Bombay*, 1864?] 4°. **14053. d. 11.**

ṢUKASAPTATI. *See* ṢĀMALA BHAṬA. શુડાબહોતેરી. [Ṣuḍābahoterī. A versified adaptation of the Ṣukasaptati.] [1880.] 8°.
14148. b. 33.

SUKHEṢVARA BĀPUJĪ ṢĀSTRĪ. *See* NĀRĀYAṆA BHAṬṬA, called MṚIGARĀJALAKSHMAN. Veni Sanhár Nátak. A drama ... translated from Sanscrit and Marathi by Sukheshwar Bápuji Shastri. 1867. 12°. **14148. c. 4.**

SUMATI NĀGILA. सुमति नागिल चरित्र [Sumati Nāgila charitra. A tale in verse on the influence of good and evil gurus. With quotations from Sanskrit and Jaina Prakrit authors.] pp. viii. 155. अमदावाद १९३३ [*Ahmadabad*, 1876.] 8°.
14144. g. 21.

SUNDARA KĀMDĀR. શુંદર કામદારની વારતા [Sundara Kāmdārnī vārtā. A tale in verse.] pp. 138, *lith.* મુંબઇ ૧૯૧૮ [*Bombay*, 1862.] 8°.
14148. b. 4.(6.)

—— [Another edition.] pp. 114, *lith.* ૧૯૨૧ [*Bombay*, 1864.] 8°. **14148. b. 5.(3.)**

SUNDARA SŪRI. *See* MUṆISUNDARA SŪRI.

SŪTRAKṚITĀṄGA. श्रीसूयगडांग-सूत्र *etc.* [Sūtrakṛitāṅga, or Sūyagaḍāṅga. The second of the Jain Aṅgas. Sanskrit text, with a Gujarati paraphrase by Pārṣvachandra Sūri, and two Sanskrit commentaries. The whole edited with prefaces and indices in Gujarati by Bhīmasiṃha Māṇaka.] pp. 28, 1020. मुंबापुरी १९०२ [*Bombay*, 1881.] 4°. **14100. e. 2.**

SVADEṢA SUBHECHCHHANĀR, *pseud.* બાળ ગાયણ [Bālagāyaṇa. Miscellaneous poems.] pp. 35. મુંબઈ ૧૯૬૫ [*Bombay*, 1865.] 12°.
14150. a. 1.(3.)

SVĀMĪ NĀRĀYAṆA. *See* SAHAJĀNANDA SVĀMĪ.

ṢYĀMAJĪ KRISHṆA VARMĀ. *See* SAHAJĀNANDA SVĀMĪ. शिक्षापत्रीध्वान्तनिवारणेऽयद्ग्रन्थः [An anonymous treatise, in refutation of the doctrines of the Svāmīnārāyaṇa sect. Sanskrit text, with a translation by Ṣ. K. V.] [1876.] 8°.
14028. c. 30.

TALAKCHAND TĀRĀCHAND. રમુજે હિકમત. [Rumūz i ḥikmat. A work on medicine, translated from the Hindustani by T. T. with the assistance of Ḳāẓī 'Abd Al-Laṭīf.] pp. 120. સુરત ૧૮૮૪ [*Surat*, 1884.] 12°. **14148. a. 13.**

TASKAR (SORABJI KUVARJI). *See* SOHRĀBJĪ KŪVARJĪ TĀSKAR.

TAYLOR (JOSEPH VAN SOMEREN). *See* BIBLE.—New Testament.—*Matthew.* The Gospel according to Matthew in English and Goojaratee [Translated by J. van S. T.] 1840. 8°.
3068. bb. 1.

—— Daily food. [Texts of Scripture, and moral reflections for each day of the month, with five sermons on the observance of the Sabbath-day.] एक माहिनाने वास्ते दैनिक प्रसाद *etc.* [Dainika prasāda.] pp. ii. 113. સુરત ૧૮૭૪ [*Surat*, 1874.] 12°. **14144. a. 11.**

—— गुजराती भाषानुं व्याकरण [Gujarātī bhāshānuṇ vyākaraṇa.] . . . A grammar of the Gujaráti language. Second edition. pp. v. 237. सुरत: १९६८ [*Surat*, 1868.] 8°. **14150. b. 14.**

—— Third edition. pp. ii. 149. सुरत १९७५ [*Surat*, 1875.] 12°. **14150. a. 27.**

—— मुक्तिमुक्तावली. (Mukti Muktāvalī : or The old old story. Translated [from the English] by J. van S. T.) ff. 16. *Surat*, 1874. *obl.* 16°.
15144. a. 13.

TAYLOR (MEADOWS). તારાબાઈ. [Tārā : a Mahratta tale. Translated by Jahāngīr Bahrāmjī Marzbān from the English of M. T.] pp. vii. 408. મુંબઈ ૧૮૮૬ [*Bombay*, 1886.] 8°. **14148. a. 33.**

TEHMURAS DĪNSHĀH. *See* RUSTAM PESHOTAN, *Mobed.* સ્યવશનામું [Syavash-nāmuṇ. Edited, with notes and a glossary, by T. D.] [1873.] 8°.
14146. g. 2.

ṬEMULJĪ NAVAROJĪ SANJĀNĀ *See* JAHĀNGĪR. જેહાંગીર નામું [Jahāngīr-nāmuṇ. Translated by Ṭ. N. S. from the Persian.] [1875.] 8°.
14146. g. 6.

TEN COMMANDMENTS. પરમેશવરના મોહોટા દશ હુકમ વગેરે. The Ten Commandments, *etc.* [A Christian tract.] pp. 12. *Surat*, 1860? 12°.
14144. a. 10.

ṬHAKAR DAYĀLA RĀVAJĪ. *See* DAYĀLA RĀVAJĪ.

THREE WORLDS. તરી લોકની વાત. The three worlds. [Trilokanī vāt. A Christian tract.] pp. 22. સુરત ૧૮૬૧ [*Surat*, 1861.] 12°.
14144. a. 2.(13.)

TRIBHUVANADĀSA GIRDHARADĀSA KHAMBĀTĪ. *See* PRATĀPA SIṂHA, *Raja of Jaipur.* અમૃતસાગર તથા પ્રતાપસાગર *etc.* (Amritsagur and Pratapsagur . . . Translated into Gujerati . . . . by Bhowsar Tribhowundass Girdhurdass Khumbati.) 1878. 8°. **14146. b. 3.**

TRIBHUVANADĀSA RĀMADĀSA. આદમાખ્યાન, અથવા મૂળ પુરૂષ. [Ādamākhyāna. The Bible history of Adam and Eve. A Christian tract in verse.] pp. 46. अमदावाद १९३१ [*Ahmadabad*, 1875.] 16°. **14144. a. 16.**

TRIKAMLĀLA KAHĀNJĪ. *See* RADHANPUR, *Native State of.* રાધનપુર સ્વસ્થાનનો દીવાની નિબંધ. [The Civil Procedure Code of the Native State of Radhanpur. Edited by T. K.] [1874.] 4°. **14146. a. 12.**

—— —— સ્વસ્થાન રાધનપુર ફોજદારી નિબંધ. [The Criminal Procedure Code of the Native State of Radhanpur. Edited by T. K.] [1875.] 4°. **14146. a. 13.**

TRIKAMRĀYĀ UDAYAṢAÑKARA. *See* INDIA.—*Legislative Council.* Notes on the Indian Penal Code, *etc.* [Compiled by T. U.] [1881.] 8°. **14146. a. 9.**

TULASĪ, *of Kuntarpur.* ધ્રુવ આખ્યાન [Dhruvākhyāna. The legend of Dhruva, the polar star.] pp. 166, *lith.* [*Bombay*, 1860 ?] 16°. **14148. a. 11.(1.)**

TULASĪDĀSA. *See* ṢIVALĀLA DHANEṢVARA. श्रीमद्रामायण. [Rāmāyaṇa. Adapted from the Hindi poem of Tulasīdāsa.] [1875.] 4°. **14148. f. 16.**

TULJĀRĀMA JHĪṆĀRĀMA. મેઘલીલા અથવા ચોત્રીશાની ચમક [Meghalīlā. A poem on the heavy rains which fell in Cutch in the Samvat year 1934.] pp. 23. મુંબઈ ૧૯૩૪ [*Bombay*, 1878.] 12°. **14148. d. 2.(6.)**

UDAYASĀGARA. *See* RATNAṢEKHARA. लघुक्षेत्रसमासप्रकरण [Laghukshetrasamāsa. Sanskrit text, with a Gujarati commentary by U.] [1878, *etc.*] 4°. **14100. e. 3.**

UMEṬĀ. उमेटानां ढाळीयां तथा स्तवनो [Umeṭānāṇ ḍhāḷiyāṇ tathā stavano. A description of the Jain ceremony of Ujamṇā performed at Umeṭā, and hymns in praise of several Jain saints.] pp. 38. અમદાવાદ ૧૯૩૩ [*Ahmadabad*, 1876.] 12°. **14144. f. 4.(4.)**

UMIĀRĀMA ṬHĀKORDĀSA DARU. કાયદે તાઊસ [Kāyade tāus. Instructions for playing on the tāus, a kind of Indian guitar.] Pt. i. pp. 34. સુરત ૧૮૮૯ [*Surat*, 1889.] 12°. **14146. c. 7.(2.)**

UPANISHADS. श्वेताश्वतरोपनिषद्‌ना सार [Selections from the Ṣvetāṣvatara Upanishad. Sanskrit text, with a translation into Gujarati prose by Nārāyaṇa Hemachandra.] pp. 12. મુંબઈ ૧૮૮૧ [*Bombay*, 1881.] 8°. **14010. c. 30.(1.)**

Forming pt. 5 of a series entitled "Saddharma-vachana-saṅgraha."

USHĀ. ઓખાહરણ નાટક [Okhāharaṇa nāṭaka. A drama on the abduction of Ushā by Aniruddha.] pp. 66. અમદાવાદ ૧૮૮૩ [*Ahmadabad*, 1883.] 12°. **14148. d. 28.**

UTTAMARĀMA DURLABHARĀMA. सुची निबंध [Suchī-nibandha. Elementary instructions in needlework and tailoring.] pp. 41. અમદાવાદ ૧૯૩૩ [*Ahmadabad*, 1877.] 12°. **14146. c. 10.**

—— टोळकनिबंध एटले टोळकिया ब्राह्मणोनी उत्पत्ति विशेनो ग्रंथ. [Ṭoḷak-nibandha. A treatise on the origin of the Ṭoḷkia Brahmans of Gujarat.] pp. 16. અમદાવાદ ૧૯૩૩ [*Ahmadabad*, 1877.] 12°. **14146. e. 20.(4.)**

UTTAMARĀMA UMEDCHAND and CHAMANLĀL NARASIṂHADĀSA. દીલગીરીનો દેખાવ [Dilgirino dekhāva. An elegy on the death of Raghunātha Rāvajī, late Secretary to the Ahmadabad municipality.] pp. 7. અમદાવાદ ૧૯૩૧ [*Ahmadabad*, 1875.] 16°. **14148. d. 13.(3.)**

—— ગુલચમન ગાયન [Gulchaman gāyana. Miscellaneous songs. Second edition.] pp. 60. અમદાવાદ ૧૮૭૫ [*Ahmadabad*, 1875.] 12°. **14148. d. 1.(6.)**

VĀGHJĪ ĀṢĀRĀMA OJHĀ. चांपराजहाडो ने सोनराणी. [Chāmparāja Hāḍo ne Sonarāṇī. An historical drama, in seven acts, of a Rajput king and his virtuous wife. Second edition.] pp. 151. અમદાવાદ ૧૮૮૭ [*Ahmadabad*, 1887.] 12°. **14148. c. 30.**

VAIDYARATNĀKARA. वैद्यरत्नाकर [Vaidyaratnākara. A Sanskrit work in verse on the treatment of diseases, with a Gujarati translation.] *See* ĀYURVEDASĀRA-SAÑGRAHA. आयुर्वेदसारसंग्रह Pt. I. *etc.* [1885, *etc.*] 8°. **14043. c. 33.**

VAJORGMITHRA. *See* Buzurgmihr.

VĀLJĪ BECHAR. Sources of the Kabir religion. [Containing an account of the life and teachings of Kabīr.] कबीर मतदर्शक ग्रंथ अथवा कबीर चरित्र [Kabīr matadarṣaka grantha.] pp. 336, viii. સુરત ૧૮૮૧ [*Surat*, 1881.] 8°. **14144. b. 4.**

VĀLJĪ LAKSHMĪRĀMA DAVE. रसमंजरी अथवा नायकनिरूपण [Rasamañjarī. An erotic poem, adapted from the Sanskrit original of Bhānudatta. With notes.] pp. vii. 76. અમદાવાદ [*Ahmadabad*, 1877.] 16°. **14146. c. 2.**

VALLABHARĀMA SŪRYARĀMA VYĀSA. નાત્યોમાં શેઠોના શાખા [Nātyomāṇ sethonā ṣākhā. A pamphlet in prose and verse on the tyrannous conduct of the village patels in Gujarat. Second edition.] pp. 34. અમદાવાદ [*Ahmadabad*, 1885.] 12°. **14146. e. 6.**

—— વલ્લભકૃત કાવ્ય [Vallabhakṛita kāvya. Vaishṇava poems, chiefly on mythological subjects.] 2 pt. *lith.* અમદાવાદ ૧૮૭૭-૮૮ [*Ahmadabad*, 1877-88.] 8°. **14148. f. 10.**

VĀLMĪKI. શ્રી વાલ્મીકિ રામાયણ [Rāmāyaṇa. Translated into Gujarati prose by Rūpajī Jayakrishṇa, from the Sanskrit.] મુંબઈ ૧૮૮૨ [*Bombay*, 1882, *etc.*] 8°. **14148. e. 11.**

In progress.

VARSĀDNĪ VADHĀMṆĪ. વરસાદની વધામણી [Varsādnī vadhāmṇī. A poem of thanksgiving for a timely fall of rain during a season of drought.] pp. 7. અમદાવાદ ૧૯૩૩ [*Ahmadabad*, 1876.] 16°. **14148. d. 13.(10.)**

VEDAMĀRGA HITECHCHHU, *pseud.* *See* Vedas.—Ṛigveda.—*Purushasūkta.* પુરૂષસૂકત: *etc.* [Purushasūkta. With a commentary by V. H.] [1863.] 8°. **14010. b. 1.**

VEDAS. *See* Bāḷājī Viṭhṭhala Gāṇvaskar. वेदोक्त संस्कार प्रकाश [Vedokta-saṃskāra-prakāṣa. A treatise on Hindu ceremonial rites, according to the Vedas.] [1881.] 12°. **14144. b. 8.**

—— Ṛigveda.—*Purushasūkta.* પુરૂષસૂકત: । સવ્યાખ્યાન: ભાષ્યાનુસાર: ગુજરાતી ભાષામાં પ્રકટ કરનાર વેદમાર્ગ હિતેચ્છુ : [Purushasūkta. Ṛigveda x. 90, Sanskrit text, with a commentary in Gujarati by Vedamārga Hitechchhu.] pp. i. 13. ૧૯૨૦ [*Bombay*, 1863.] 8°. **14010. b. 1.**

VIDYĀBHYĀSA. વિદ્યાભ્યાસની પોથી [Vidyābhyāsanī pothī. A reading-book for schools. Third edition.] pp. ii. 63. સુરત ૧૮૫૯ [*Surat*, 1859.] 12°. **14150. a. 1.(1.)**

VĪJAVALAVA JEṬHĀBHĀĪ. *See* India.—*Legislative Council.* The Indian Evidence Act, *etc.* [Edited with notes by V. J.] [1880.] 8°. **14146. a. 2.**

VIJAYA RĀJENDRA. [*Life.*] *See* Lallu Valyam. श्री विजयराजेंद्र सूरिजीनुं जन्म चरित्र [Vijaya Rājendra Sūrijīnuṇ janmacharitra.] [1888.] 16°.

VIKRAMĀDITYA, *King of Ujjayinī.* *See* Ṣāmala Bhaṭa. કાશ્ઠના ઘોડાની વારતા. [Kāshṭhanā ghoḍāni vārtā. A paraphrase in verse of the sixteenth tale of the Singhāsan Battīsī.] [1855.] 8°. **14148. e. 3.(2.)**

—— —— માધવાનલની વારતા [Mādhavānalanī vārtā. A paraphrase in verse of a portion of the Singhāsan Battīsī.] [1852.] 16°. **14148. a. 2.(1.)**

—— —— મેનાપોપટની વારતા. [Menāpopaṭnī vārtā. A verse adaptation of a portion of the Singhāsan Battīsī.] [1864.] 12°. **14148. a. 2.(5.)**

—— —— બતરીશ પુતલીમધેની પાનનાબીડાની વારતા [Pānanābiḍānī vārtā. A verse paraphrase of a tale from the Singhāsan Battīsī.] [1885.] 16°. **14148. a. 2.(2.)**

—— —— પંચડંડની વારતાની ચોપડી [Pañchaḍaṇḍanī vārtā. A paraphrase in verse of a portion of the Singhāsan Battīsī.] [1859.] 16°. **14148. a. 17.**

—— —— પંખીની વારતા [Paṅkhīnī vārtā. A verse paraphrase of the 17th tale of the Singhāsan Battīsī.] [1877.] 8°. **14148. b. 30.(1.)**

—— સીંહાસન બતરીશી [Singhāsan Battīsī, or The thirty-two tales of king Vikramāditya, translated into Gujarati.] pp. 117, *lith.* મુંબઈ ૧૯૦૯ [*Bombay*, 1852.] 8°. **14148. b. 18.**

VINAYAVIJAYA. श्री विनयविजयजी उपाध्यायकृत शांतसुधारस ग्रंथ अर्थ सहित प्रारंभः [Ṣāntasudhārasa. A Jain religious treatise in Sanskrit, with a commentary in Gujarati.] *See* Bhīmasiṃha Māṇaka. प्रकरणरत्नाकर [Prakaraṇa-ratnākara.] Vol. ii. pp. 124-174. [1876, *etc.*] 4°. **14100. e. 3.**

VINAYAVIJAYA. श्रीपालचरित्र अथवा श्रीपाल राजानो रास [Śrīpālacharitra, also called Śrīpāla rājā-no rās. A Jain legend in Hindi verse, on the story of Śrīpāla, king of Malwa, commenced by Vinayavijaya, and completed by Yaśovijaya. With an occasional commentary in Gujarati. Second edition.] ff. 92. [*Bombay*, 1876?] *obl.* 8°. **14154. h. 3.**

Printed in the form of the Devanagari character peculiar to Jain works.

—— अथ नवपदमावर्णनरूप श्री श्रीपाल राजानो रास प्रारंभ ॥ [Another edition, with an anonymous Gujarati commentary, differing from that in the preceding edition.] ff. 177. १९३४ [*Bombay*, 1877.] *obl.* 8°. **14154. h. 2.**

—— શ્રી શ્રીપાળ ચરીત્ર [Śrīpālacharitra. A Gujarati prose version of the Jain legend of king Śrīpāla.] *See* JAINAŚĀSTRA. જૈન સાસ્ત્ર કથા સંગ્રહ pp. 1-45. [1883.] 8°. **14144. g. 8.**

—— [Another edition.] *See* CHARITRASAṄGRAHA. ચરિત્ર સંગ્રહ pp. 1-45. [1884.] 8°. **14144. g. 7.**

VĪRACHANDA RĀGHAVAJĪ. રડવા કુટવાની હાનિકારક ચાલ વિષે નિબંધ [Raḍvā kuṭavānī hānijanak chāl. An essay condemning the practise of an excessive show of grief on the death of a near relative, common among the women of Gujarat.] pp. iv. 38. ૧૯૪૨ [*Ahmadabad*, 1887.] 16°. **14146. e. 21.(3.)**

VĪRAVIJAYA. *See* PŪJĀSAṄGRAHA. पुजा संग्रह *etc.* [Pūjāsaṅgraha. A selection of Jain prayers and hymns from the writings of V.] [1875.] 8°. **14144. g. 1.**

—— —— [1884.] 8°. **14144. g. 15.**

—— *See* YAŚOVIJAYA. अथ श्रीयशोविजयजी उपाध्यायकृत अध्यात्मसार ग्रंथ अर्थसहित प्रारंभ [Adhyātmasāra. With a Gujarati translation by V.] [1876, *etc.*] 4°. **14100. e. 3.**

—— —— [1883.] 8°. **14144. g. 8.**

—— ધમ્મિલ કુમારનો રાસ [Dhammil Kumārno rās. The story of Dhammil, the merchant's son, who gained a kingdom by virtue of his austerities. A Jain legend in verse.] pp. 344. ૧૯૪૨ [*Bombay*, 1886.] 12°. **14144. f. 11.**

—— પંડિત વીરવિજયજી કૃત શ્રી ગોડી પાર્શ્વનાથના ઢાલીયાં [Goḍi Pārśvanāthanā ḍhāliyāṇ. Hymns in praise of the god Pārśvanātha.] *See* CHAND RĀJĀ. ચંદરાજા અને ગુણાવલી રાણીના કાગલ, *etc.* pp. 15-55. [1884.] 16°. **14144. f. 12.(1.)**

—— अथ पंडित श्रीवीरविजयजीकृत पूजाए आदी ॥ [Pūjāe ādī. A collection of twenty-two Jain devotions in prose and verse, with occasional stanzas in Sanskrit and in Prakrit. Edited by Ravachand Jayachand.] pp. iv. 260. अमदावाद [*Ahmadabad*, 1881.] 8°. **14144. g. 13.**

Lithographed after the manner of Jain MSS.

—— थुळीभद्रनी शियळवेल. [Thuḷibhadranī śiyaḷvela. The story of Thulibhadra, a Jain saint and ascetic.] pp. 32. અમદાવાદ ૧૮૮૪ [*Ahmadabad*, 1884.] 12°. **14144. f. 16.**

VISHṆUŚARMAN. [For editions of the Pañchatantra ascribed to Vishṇuśarman.] *See* PAÑCHATANTRA.

VISHṆU VĀSUDEVA GOḌBOLE. *See* RAGHUNĀTHA ŚĀSTRĪ DĀNTYE and KṚISHṆA ŚĀSTRĪ BHĀṬAVAḌEKAR. વૈદ્યસારસંગ્રહ [Vaidyasārasaṅgraha. Translated by V. V. G.] [1862.] 8°. **14146. b. 1.**

VIŚRĀMA MULJĪ. ગોકુલ વૃંદાવનના ચંદ્રાવળા તથા બીજા ચંદ્રાવળા [Gokula Vṛindāvana chandrāvaḷā. Vaishṇava poems.] pp. 25. મુંબઈ ૧૯૧૯ [*Bombay*, 1862.] 16°. **14148. d. 1.(5.)**

VIŚVANĀTHA KHUSHĀLADĀSA. रोजपाठ [Rojapāṭha. Daily prayers and songs of followers of the Svāmīnārāyaṇa sect.] pp. 416. अमदावाद १९४४ [*Ahmadabad*, 1888.] 16°. **14144. c. 3.**

VIŚVANĀTHA NĀRĀYAṆA MAṆḌALIK, *C.S.I.* *See* ELPHINSTONE (*Hon.* M.) The history of India ... translated into Gujaráti, ... by Vishvanáth Náráyan Mandlik. 1862. 8°. **14146. g. 9.**

VIṬHṬHALADĀSA DHANJĪBHĀĪ. गूजरातना भीखारीओ. [Gujarātnā bhikhārio. A prize essay on the professional beggars of Gujarat. Second edition.] pp. 104, xvi. અમદાવાદ ૧૮૮૭ [*Ahmadabad*, 1887.] 12°. **14146. e. 23.**

—— મેવાડની જાહોજલાલી [Mevāḍnī jāh o jalālī. An historical account of Mewar and its greatness, from the time of the establishment of the kingdom till its decline in A.D. 1681.] pp. x. 260. અમદાવાદ [*Ahmadabad*, 1886.] 12°. **14146. g. 20.**

VITHTHALADĀSA DHANJĪBHĀĪ. पतिव्रता स्त्री [Pativratā strī, or The faithful wife. A tale. Second edition.] pp. 104. अमदावाद १९४२ [*Ahmadabad*, 1886.] 12°. **14148. a. 34.**

—— स्त्रीनीति धर्म. [Strīnītidharma, or The duties of women.] pp. ii. ii. 138. अमदावाद १९३३ [*Ahmadabad*, 1877.] 12°. **14146. e. 13.**

VRAJALĀLA KĀLIDĀSA ṢĀSTRĪ. गूजराती भाषानो इतिहास [Gujarātī bhāshāno itihāsa. A prize essay on the origin, the changes, and gradual development of the Gujarati language. Second edition.] pp. 100, xvi. અમદાવાદ ૧૮૮૭ [*Ahmadabad*, 1887.] 12°. **14146. e. 22.**

VRAJARĀYAJĪ. गोस्वामि श्रीमदुलालजि महाराजे . . . छपनभोग आरोगाव्यो. [Chhappanbhoganuṇ varṇana. An account of the Chhappan-bhoga festival, an important Vaishṇava ceremony performed at Dakor by Mahārāja Maṭulālajī, and priests of the Vallabha sect.] pp. 52. अमदावाद १९३६ [*Ahmadabad*, 1880.] 8°. **14144. g. 16.**

VRAJARĀYA SĀKARLĀLA. *See* INDIA.—*Legislative Council.* હિંદુસ્તાનનો પુરાવનો કાયદો. [Hindustānano purāvano kāyado. The Indian Evidence Act. With a commentary and index by V. S.] [1881.] 8°. **14146. a. 11.**

VṚINDA. વૃંદસતસઈ [Vṛinda sat-saī. Seven hundred and six stanzas, translated from the Brajbhasha of Vṛinda by Chhoṭālāla Sevakarāma.] pp. xii. 60. મુંબઈ ૧૮૮૬ [*Bombay*, 1886.] 12°. **14148. e. 17.**

VYĀSA VALLABHARĀMA SŪRAJRĀMA. *See* VALLABHARĀMA SŪRYARĀMA VYĀSA.

WELLS (T. L.). Anglo-Gujarâti Translation Series. Part v. . . . Edited by R. S. Mahipatram R. Nilkanth, . . . Sanctioned for use under standards vi. and vii. of High Schools. Second edition. pp. iv. ii. 119. *Bombay*, 1881. 12°. **14150. a. 34.**

—— English Exercises, Part i. . . . Third edition. Sanctioned for standard ii. of Anglo-Gujarati schools. અંગ્રેજી ભાષાંતર પાઠમાળા [Angrejī bhāshāntara pāṭhamālā.] pp. 112. *Bombay*, 1877. 8°. **14150. b. 17.**

WELL-WISHER. Hints to married women, by a well-wisher . . . સ્ત્રી ઉપયોગી સૂચના [Strī upayogī sūchanā.] 2 pt. *Bombay*, 1863. 16°. **14146. e. 1.**

WILLIAMS (*Sir* MONIER MONIER). *See* KĀLIDĀSA. Śakuntalá . . . translated into Gujaráti prose and verse, chiefly from the Sanskṛit text by Prof. Mon. Williams. 1877. 8°. **14148. c. 1.**

WILSON (JOHN) *D.D., F.R.S., Missionary of the Free Church of Scotland.* [*Life.*] *See* BAHRĀMJĪ MEHRVĀNJĪ MALABĀRĪ. વિલ્સનવિરહ [Wilsanviraha.]

—— *See* BIBLE.—*New Testament.* આયણ પ્રભુ . . . તવીન સ્થાપના . . . The New Testament . . . Revised by . . . Dr. Wilson. 1857. 12°. **3068. b. 30.**

—— —— *Matthew.* ઈશુ ખ્રીશતના શારા શમાચાર માથ્થીઊના બનાવલા. The Gospel of St. Matthew. [Revised by Dr. W.] 1844. 8°. **3068. aaa. 25.**

—— Idiomatic Exercises illustrative of the phraseology and structure of the English and Goojeratee languages. Rendered into Goojeratee [from Dr. Wilson's version of J. D. Pearson's Bengali Vākyāvalī] by Sorabshaw Dossabhoy. Second edition. pp. xxi. 370. *Bombay*, 1850. 12°. **12906. bbb. 9.**

—— [Another copy.] *Bombay*, 1850. 12°. **14150. a. 25.**

WODEHOUSE (CHARLES) *Acting Political Agent at Kathiawar.* *See* BHĀVASINGHAJĪ MOḌAJĪ, *Jāḍejā.* [Addenda.] *Begin.* To His Excellency the Right Honourable Baron Reay . . . The humble petition of Jadeja Bhowsingji Modji . . . [appealing against an order of C. W.] 1886. 4°. **14146. a. 15.**

YAŚAḤSOMA. *See* DEVENDRA SŪRI. अथ शतकनामा पंचम कर्मग्रंथः प्रारभ्यते [Śataka. With a Gujarati commentary by Y.] [1876, *etc.*] 4°. **14100. e. 3.**

—— *See* JINAVALLABHA. अथ बालावबोधसहित षडशीतिकाख्य चतुर्थ कर्मग्रंथः प्रारभ्य [Shaḍaśīti. With a Gujarati commentary by Y.] [1876, *etc.*] 4°. **14100. e. 3.**

YAŚOVIJAYA. *See* VINAYAVIJAYA. श्रीपालचरित्र [Śrīpālacharitra. A Jain legend in Hindi verse, commenced by Vinayavijaya, and completed by Yaṣovijaya. With an occasional commentary in Gujarati.] [1876?] *obl.* 8°. **14154. h. 3.**

—— अथ यशोविजयजी उपाध्यायकृत अध्यात्ममतपरीक्षा प्रारंभः [Adhyātmamata-parikshā. A work in Prakrit verse, with a Gujarati commentary by the author, on Jain philosophy, mainly controversial, and directed against the tenets of the Digambara sect from the Svetāmbara point of view.] *See* BHĪMASIṂHA MĀṆAKA. प्रकरण-रत्नाकर [Prakaraṇa-ratnākara. Vol. ii. pp. 273-344. [1876, *etc.*] 4°. **14100. e. 3.**

—— अथ श्रीयशोविजयजी उपाध्यायकृत अध्यात्मसार ग्रंथ अर्थसहित प्रारंभ. [Adhyātmasāra. A Jain philosophical treatise in Sanskrit verse, with a Gujarati translation by Vīravijaya.] *See* BHĪMASIṂHA MĀṆAKA. प्रकरण-रत्नाकर [Prakaraṇa-ratnākara.] Vol. i. pp. 583-730. [1876, *etc.*] 4°. **14100. e. 3.**

—— શ્રી અધ્યાત્મસાર નામા ગ્રંથનો બાળાબોધ પ્રારંભ [Adhyātmasāra. Translated into Gujarati by Vīravijaya.] *See* JAINAṢĀSTRA. જૈન સાસ્ત્ર કથા સંગ્રહ pp. 418-517. [1883.] 8°. **14144. g. 8.**

—— ચાવીશીનાં સ્તવન [Chovīṣinā stavana. Verses in praise of the twenty-four Jain Tirthankaras.] pp. 16, *lith* અમદાવાદ ૧૯૩૦ [*Ahmadabad*, 1874.] 16°. **14144. f. 4.(2.)**

—— अथ श्रीमद्यशोविजयजी उपाध्यायकृत द्रव्यगुण पर्यायनो रास *etc.* [Dravyaguṇa paryāyano rās. A Jain metaphysical treatise in Hindi verse, treating on moral fitness for final emancipation. Accompanied by a Gujarati commentary.] *See* BHĪMASIṂHA MĀṆAKA. प्रकरण-रत्नाकर [Prakaraṇa-ratnākara.] pp. 337-412. [1876, *etc.*] 4°. **14100. e. 3.**

—— અથ શ્રીમહાવીરસ્વામીના સત્યાવીસભવ વિગરેના ચારસ્તવનોનો સંગ્રહ *etc.* [Māhāvīrasvāmīnā .... stavanono saṅgraha. Verses in praise of Jain saints.] pp. 80, *lith.* મુંબઈ ૧૯૩૧ [*Bombay*, 1874.] 12°. **14144. f. 4.(1.)**

—— अथ श्री सीमंधर स्वामिनी विनतीरूप सवासो गाथानुं स्तवन अर्थसहित प्रारंभ [Savā-so gāthānuṇ stavana. Religious advice contained in 125 verses, with accompanying translations in modern Gujarati.] *See* BHĪMASIṂHA MĀṆAKA. प्रकरण-रत्नाकर [Prakaraṇa-ratnākara.] Vol. iii. pp. 730-759. [1876, *etc.*] 4°. **14100. e. 3.**

YASOVIJAYA. अथ श्रीमद्यशोविजयजी उपाध्याय कृत साडात्रणसोगाथानुं स्तवन अर्थ सहित प्रारंभ *End.* इति श्री सीमंधर जिनविज्ञप्तिः संपूर्णा [Sīmandhara-stavana, or ° vijñapti. A Hindi poem containing rules for the conduct of Sravakas, or secular Jains. With a Gujarati commentary by Padmavijaya.] *See* BHĪMASIṂHA MĀṆAKA. प्रकरण-रत्नाकर [Prakaraṇa-ratnākara.] Vol. i. pp. 1-138. [1876, *etc.*] 4°. **14100. e. 3.**

—— अथ श्री श्रीमद्यशोविजयजी उपाध्यायकृत वीरस्तुतिरूप [Vīrastuti, also called Mahāvīra-Jinastuti. The principles of the orthodox Jain religion in old Gujarati verse, forming a refutation of the religious views of the Ḍhuṇḍhakas. Accompanied by an extensive commentary by Padmavijaya.] *See* BHĪMASIṂHA MĀṆAKA. प्रकरण-रत्नाकर [Prakaraṇa-ratnākara.] Vol. iii. pp. 569-696. [1876, *etc.*] 4°. **14100. e. 3.**

—— अथ श्रीमद्यशोविजयजी उपाध्यायकृत आठ दृष्टीनी सझा *etc.* [Yogadṛishṭi. An exposition in Hindi verse of eight theories concerning *Yoga*, or abstract meditation. Accompanied by a Gujarati translation by Jñānavimala Sūri.] *See* BHĪMASIṂHA MĀṆAKA. प्रकरण-रत्नाकर [Prakaraṇa-ratnākara.] Vol. i. pp. 413-438. [1876, *etc.*] 4°. **14100. e. 3.**

YOGAVĀṢISHṬHA. The Yogavásishta. [A philosophical poem of the Mīmāṃsa school of philosophy. Translated from the Sanskrit.] યોગવાસિષ્ટ pp. vii. 198. *Bombay*, 1863. 12°. **14144. b. 9.**

—— श्रीयोगवासिष्ठमहारामायण [Translated into Gujarati prose by Raṇchhoḍjī Udhavajī.] *See* PERIODICAL PUBLICATIONS.—*Bombay.* वेदान्तप्रकाश. Vedânt Prakâsh. Vol. i and ii. [1883, *etc.*] 8°. **14144. d. 8.**

—— યોગવાસિષ્ટ [Another prose translation.] *See* PERIODICAL PUBLICATIONS.—*Nadiad.* आत्मज्ञान वर्धक [Âtmajñāna-vardhaka.] [1884, *etc.*] 8°. **14150. c. 9.**

YOUNG (ROBERT) *Bookseller and Orientalist, of Edinburgh.* *See* BIBLE.—Old Testament.—*Chronicles.* પુરાતન સ્થાપનાનું પુસ્તક ... The two Books of Chronicles. Translated into Gujarati [by R. Y.] 1859. 8°. **3070. bb. 16.**

—— Gujarati Exercises: or A new mode of learning to read, write, or speak the Gujarati language, on the Ollendorffian system. pp. iv. 500. *London*, 1860. 12°. **12906. b. 22.**

YŪSUF ṢĀLIḤ. મુખાલેફાતે બાઈબલ [Mukhālafāt i Baibal, or Contradictions of the Bible. An anti-Christian pamphlet by a Muhammadan.] pp. 10. સુરત. હીજરીસને ૧૩૦૫ [*Surat*, 1888.] 8°. **14144. a. 26.**

ZAND-AVASTĀ. *See* KHURSHEDJĪ RUSTAMJĪ KĀMĀ. જરતોશતી અભીઆસ. Zartoshti abhyas. [Researches in Zend literature, and the Zand-Avastā.] [1866-69.] 8°. **14144. i. 6.**

—— *See* MĀṆEKJĪ DĀRĀBJĪ ADRIANWĀLĀ. હોરમજદ યશ્ટ ઉપરથી હોરમજદની સીફત વીશેની શરેહ [Hormuzdnī sifat. An essay on the attributes of the Supreme God, as taught in the Yashts and other portions of the Zoroastrian Scriptures.] [1881.] 8°. **14144. i. 21.**

—— *See* NĀRĀYAṆA HEMACHANDRA. जरतोस्त धर्मनीति [Zartosht dharmanīti. A commentary on passages in the Zand-Avastā, and other sacred books of the Parsis.] [1881.] 8°. **14144. i. 10.**

—— *See* PERIODICAL PUBLICATIONS.—*Bombay*, રાસત દીને જરથોશતીઆંન *etc.* [Rāst dīn i Zartoshtiyān. A monthly periodical, containing the text of the Zand-Avastā with a Gujarati commentary.] [1883, *etc.*] 8°. **14150. e. 2.**

—— *See* RUSTAM ĪRĀNĪ. ગુન્ચ-એ-અવસ્તા *etc.* [Ghuncha i Avastā. A versified adaptation of some Zoroastrian prayers taken from the Zand-Avastā.] [1880.] 32°. **14144. h. 8.**

—— ખુરદે અવસતા બા માએની [Khurdah Avastā. Zend in Gujarati characters, with a Gujarati translation by Ardsher Rustamjī Fīrozjī.] pp. xi. 452. મુમબઈ ૧૨૩૦ [*Bombay*, 1861.] 8°. **761. g. 6.**

—— પાક ખોરદેહ અવસતા [Khurdah Avastā. Zend in Gujarati character, with an interlineary translation and notes in Gujarati by Dīnshāh Hormasjī. Second edition.] pp. xxviii. 620. મુંબઈ ૧૨૪૩ [*Bombay*, 1874.] 32°. **761. a. 16.**

—— Khordeh Avesta ... transliterated and translated into Gujerati with copious explanatory notes, by Kavasji Edalji Kanga. (ખોરદેહ અવસ્તા) pp. xvi. 280. *Bombay*, 1880. 8°. **14144. i. 20.**

—— પાક ખોરદેહ અવસતા [Khurdah Avastā. Edited, with a preface and an abridged translation in Gujarati, by Frāmjī Kāvasjī Mehetā.] pp. iv. 386. મુંબઈ ૧૮૮૧ [*Bombay*, 1881.] 32°. **761. a. 20.**

—— ખુરદેહ અવસતા [Short morning and evening prayers from the Khurdah Avastā, with explanatory notes in Gujarati by Bahmanjī Jamshedjī Mistrī. Second edition.] pp. 48. મુંબઈ ૧૮૮૧ [*Bombay*, 1881.] 16°. **761. a. 18.**

—— The Vandidád Sádé ... with a Gujarátí translation, paraphrase and comment, ... By ... Frámjí Aspandiárjí, and other Dasturs. 2 vol. *See* ACADEMIES, *etc.*—Bombay.—*Bombay Branch of the Royal Asiatic Society.* The Vandidád Sádé. 1842. 8°. **761. f. 1-2.**

—— વંદીદાદની ... ગુજરાતી તરજુમો ... Vendidad, translated into Gujerati with grammatical and explanatory notes. Part I. Fargards i. and ii. (Pt. II. Fargard xix. Pt. III. Yaçna ix. Hávaním.) By Kavasji Edalji Kanga. ૧૮૬૪-૬૬ [*Bombay*, [1864-66.] 8°. **761. d.**

—— Vendidad translated into Gujerati with explanatory notes, and a complete philological and grammatical glossary of all the words contained in the texts by Kavasji Edalji Kanga ... In two parts. *Bombay*, 1874. 8°. **14144. i. 25.**

Khurshedjī Rustamjī Kāmā's prize essay.

—— Second edition, pp. 272. *Bombay*, 1884. 8°. **14144. i. 22.**

—— ઈનતેખાબે વંદીદાદ [Intikhāb i Vandidād. An abridged translation of the Vendidād. Edited with notes by Ratanjī Rustamjī Kāngā.] pp. 156, xiii. મુંબઈ ૧૮૮૧ [*Bombay*, 1881.] 12°. **14144. h. 2.**

—— The Vispard ... with a Gujarátí translation, paraphrase and comment ... By ... Frámjí Aspandiárjí, and other Dasturs. *See* ACADEMIES, *etc.*—Bombay.—*Bombay Branch of the Royal Asiatic Society.* The Vispard, *etc.* 1843. 8°. **761. f. 5.**

—— The Yaçna ... with a Gujarátí translation, paraphrase and comment ... By ... Frámjí Aspandiárjí, and other Dasturs. *See* ACADEMIES, *etc.*—Bombay.—*Bombay Branch of the Royal Asiatic Society.* The Yaçna, *etc.* 1843. 8°. **761. f. 3.**

ZAND-AVASTĀ. Yaçna and the Gathas, with copious explanatory notes and an appendix containing some remarks on the Zend-Avesta ... from "Avesta, livre sacré du Zoroastrisme traduit du texte Zend par Mon. C. De Harlez." ... Translated into Gujarati by Aerpat Meherjibhai Palanji Madan. (યજશને અને ગાથાઓ) pp. xvi. 203. *Bombay,* 1885. 12°. **14144. i. 11.**

ZAND-AVASTĀ. Yaçna and Vispered translated into Gujerati from the original Zend texts, with critical and explanatory notes, by Kavasji Edalji Kanga. (યજશને તથા વીસ્પરદ નો ગુજરાતી તરજુમો) pp. 218, ii. *Bombay,* 1886. 8°. **14144. i. 19.**

ZOROASTER. [*Life.*] *See* KHURSHEDJĪ RUSTAMJĪ KĀMĀ. પેગમબર અશો જરતોશતના જનમારાનો એહેવાલ.

ADDENDA.

A., M. D. *See* MĀṆEKJĪ DĀDĀBHĀĪ ARJĀNĪ.

AKHĀ. Works of Brahmadnyani Akhabhakta [in 8 bks. preceded by a poem by Lāla Kavi in eulogy of Karaṇṣī Raṇmal, to whom the work is dedicated.] Published [with an introductory preface in Gujarati] by Kavi Hirachand Kanji. ब्रह्मज्ञानी अखाभक्तनी वाणी pp. xii. 215. मुंबई १८६४ [*Bombay*, 1864.] 8°. **14148. e. 19.**

AMṚITALĀLA ANOPARĀMA MEHETĀ, also called AFLĀTŪN. श्रीडंकपुर महारुद्र यज्ञनुं वर्णन अने मेवाडा ब्राह्मणनी ज्ञात विषे [Ḍaṅkpur Mahārudra yajñanuṉ varṇana. An account of the Mevāḍā caste of Brahmans, and of the celebration of the Mahārudra sacrifice at Dankpur.] pp. 62. અમદાવાદ ૧૮૮૮ [*Ahmadabad*, 1888.] 16°. **14146. e. 26.(1.)**

AMṚITALĀLA GOVARDHANADĀSA SHĀH and KĀṢĪRĀMA UTTAMARĀMA PAṆḌYĀ. The Hind Rajasthan ... [An account of the Native States of Central India, compiled from English and other sources] by Amratlal Goverdhandass Shah and Kashiram Uttamram Pandya. Vol. ii. *Ahmadabad*, 1889. 12°. **14146. f. 27.**

ĀNANDAGHANA. अथ श्री आनंदघनकृत ऋषभप्रमुख चोवीस जिन स्तुति *etc.* [Chovīsa Jinastuti. Hindi hymns in praise of the 24 Jain Tirthankaras. With a Gujarati commentary by Jñānasāra.] *See* BHĪMASIṂHA MĀṆAKA. प्रकरण-रत्नाकर [Prakaraṇa-ratnākara.] Vol. i. pp. 255-336. [1876, *etc.*] 4°. **14100. e. 3.**

ĀNANDAJĪ KHETAṢĪ. *See* PRATIKRAMAṆA SŪTRAS. શ્રી પંચ પ્રતિક્રમણાદિ સૂત્રાણિ. [Pañcha pratikramaṇādi sūtrāṇi. Edited by Ā. Kh.] [1882.] 16°. **14100. a. 3.**

ĀTMĀRĀMAJĪ ĀNANDAVIJAYAJĪ. सम्यक्त्व शल्योद्धार [Samyaktva ṣalyoddhāra. A controversial tract issued by the Tapa-Gachchha of the Svetāmbara sect of Jains; being a Gujarati translation, by the Jainadharmaprasāraka Sabhā at Bhaunagar, of the Hindi Samakita ṣalyoddhāra of Ā. Ā., which was written in refutation of the Samakitasāra of Jeṭha Mallajī of the Dhundiya sect, who condemns idol-worship, and the tenets of other sects of the Jains.] pp. xvi. 282. अमदावाद १९४३ [*Ahhmadabad*, 1888.] 8°. **14144. g. 30.**

BAHRĀMJĪ FARDUNJĪ MARZBĀN. *See* NAẒĪR AḤMAD, *Khān Bahādur.* [Addenda.] હોસનઆરા [Ḥusn-ārā. Translated from the Hindustani Banāt al-naʿsh by B. F. M.] [1890.] 8°. **14148. b. 43.**

BALADEVARĀMA KṚISHṆARĀMA BHAṬṬA. श्रीभोजसुबोध रत्नमाला. [Bhoja subodha ratnamālā. An account of the life, learning and administration of king Bhoja of Dhar, compiled from the Sanskrit Bhojaprabandha of Ballālā and other sources. With copious quotations from the Sanskrit, accompanied by translations of the same.] pp. viii. 189. મુંબઈ ૧૮૮૮ [*Bombay*, 1888.] 8°. **14146. g. 21.**

BALLĀLA. *See* BALADEVARĀMA KṚISHṆARĀMA BHAṬṬA. श्रीभोजसुबोध रत्नमाला [Bhoja subodha ratnamālā. Compiled chiefly from the Sanskrit Bhojaprabandha of Ballāla.] [1888.] 8°. **14146. g. 24.**

BANĀRASĪ DĀSA. अथ श्रीसमयसार नाटक बनारसीदास कृत *etc.* [Samayasāra. A work in Hindi verse on Jain religion, by a member of the Digambara sect. With a Gujarati translation by Rūpachandra.] *See* BHĪMASIṂHA MĀṆAKA. प्रकरण-रत्नाकर [Prakaraṇa-ratnākara.] Vol. ii. pp. 345-576. [1876, *etc.*] 4°. **14100. e. 3.**

BARJORJĪ ERACHJĪ BAJĀN. સપેન્તોમઈન્યુશ અને અંગ્રોમઈન્યુશ. [Sapentomainyusha ane

Angromainyusha. An essay on the creative and destructive attributes of God according to the Zoroastrian scriptures.] pp. 55. મુંબઈ ૧૮૮૯ [*Bombay*, 1889.] 8°. **14144. i 28.(1.)**

BARJORJĪ PĀLANJĪ DEṢĀI and PĀLANJĪ BARJORJĪ DEṢĀI. History of the Achæmenides: being a chronicle of the Parsee menarchs of the Achæmenian dynasty of ancient Persia, collated from the works of European and Oriental authors, with special reference to the latest researches in Achæmenian inscriptions and architecture. (તવારીખે હખામનીઆન) [Tavārīkh i Hakhāmaniyān.] pp. xii. 500. *Bombay*, 1889. 8°. **14146. h. 16.**

BHADRABĀHU. *See* RĀJENDRA SŪRI. भट्टारक श्री राजेंद्रसूरि विरचितः कल्पसूत्रस्य बालावबोधः प्रारभ्यते [Kalpasūtrasya bālāvabodha. An extensive commentary on the Kalpasūtra of Bhadrabāhu.] [1888.] *obl* 8°. **14144. g. 31.**

BHAGAVĀNLĀLA BĀPĀLĀLA SAIYAḌH. सति राणक देवी [Satī Rāṇak Devī. A tale of Rajput valour and female virtue.] pp. viii. 82. અમદાવાદ ૧૮૮૮ [*Ahmadabad*, 1888.] 12°. **14148. a. 36.**

BHAGUBHĀI RĀMAṢAÑKARA JĀNĪ. Life of His Highness Maharaja Sir Sayajirao Gaikwar, G.C.S.I. By Bhagubhai Ramshunker Jani. (શ્રીમંત ... નામદાર મહારાજા સર શિયાજીરાવ ગાયકવાડ ... નું જીવનચરિત્ર.) pp. xi. 58. *Bombay*, 1888. 8°. **14146. g. 25.**

BHĀṆA DĀSA. ભાણ દાસકૃત हस्तामलक [Hastāmalaka. A poem.] *See* PRĀCHĪNA KĀVYA. प्राचीन काव्य Vol. vi. No. 4. [1885, *etc.*] 8°. **14148. e. 12.**

BHAU, *Kavi.* કવિ ભાઊકૃત पांडव विष्टि [Pāṇḍavavishṭi. A poem on the Mahābhārata story of the Pāṇḍavas. With notes.] *See* PRĀCHĪNA KĀVYA. प्राचीन काव्य Vol. vi. No. 3. [1885, *etc.*] 8°. **14148. e. 12.**

BHAUNAGAR.—JAINADHARMA PRASĀRAKA SABHĀ. *See* ĀTMĀRĀMAJĪ ĀNANDAVIJAYAJĪ. सम्यक्त्व शल्योद्धार [Samyaktva ṣalyoddhāra. A translation, by the Jainadharmaprasāraka Sabhā at Bhaunagar, of the Hindi Samakita ṣalyoddhāra.] [1888.] 8°. **14144. g. 30.**

BHĀVASINGHAJĪ MOḌAJĪ, *Jāḍejā.* *Begin.* To His Excellency the Right Honourable Baron Reay, LL.D., C.I.E., Governor and President in Council, Bombay. The humble petition of Jadeja Bhowsingji Modji Girassia of Jivapur and Bhayad of Morbi [on behalf of himself and other members of the Girassia community, appealing against an order of Lieutenant-Colonel C. Wodehouse, Acting Political Agent at Kathiawar, rejecting a petition presented by them against Lieutenant Salmon, Assistant Political Agent, charging him with assault and the use of abusive language. With other papers relating to the case, partly in English and partly in Gujarati.] *Rajkot*, 1886. 4°. **14146. a. 15.**

BHĪMĀCHĀRYA JHALKĪKAR and RĀJĀRĀMA GAṆEṢA BODAS. वेदार्थोद्धारः। दयानन्दकृत वेदव्याख्यान खण्डनात्मकः [Vedārthoddhāra. A critical refutation of Dayānanda Sarasvati's views regarding the Vedas, as the sole authority in matters of doctrine. Sanskrit text, with translations into Gujarati and Marathi.] pp. 4, 4, 4. मुंबापुरी १८७५ [*Bombay*, 1875.] 8°. **14028. d. 18.**

BHOWSINGJI MODJI. *See* BHĀVASINGHAJĪ MOḌAJĪ.

BHŪRĀBHĀĪ BEHECHAR JOṢĪ. શ્રી અષ્ટાપદજી બીંબ પ્રતિષ્ઠા. [Ashṭāpadajī bimba pratishṭhā. An account, in verse, of the consecration of a Jain temple, and installation of the idol, at Kapadwanj.] pp. vii. 42. મુંબઈ ૧૮૮૮ [*Bombay*, 1888.] 8°. **14144. g. 28.**

CHUNĪLĀLA JAYACHAND. જૈન મતની પરીક્ષાનો પ્રત્યુત્તર [Jaina matanī parikshāno pratyuttara. A reply to an attack made on the Jain religion by Christian missionaries.] pp. 16. સુરત ૧૮૮૮ [*Surat*, 1888.] 16°. **14144. f.**

ḌĀHYĀBHĀĪ DALPATBHĀĪ DALĀL. Gujarati proverbs ... with their English equivalents arranged in alphabetical order by D. D. Dalal. pp. 21. *Surat*, 1889. 12°. **14146. e.**

DALAL (D. D.) *See* ḌĀHYĀBHĀĪ DALPATBHĀĪ DALĀL.

DĀMODARA KEṢAVAJĪ ṬHAKKAR. सस्ती सुखडी ने सिद्धपुरनी यात्रा [Sastī sukhaḍī ne Siddhapuranī yātrā. A denunciation, in verse, against the Maharajas or spiritual guides of the Vallabhi sect, charging them with immorality and unfitness for their high offices. Third edition.] pp. 32. અમદાવાદ ૧૮૮૮ [*Ahmadabad*, 1888.] 16°. **14144. c. 5.**

DANḌIN. Dashakumára charitra [or Adventures of Ten Princes. A series of Sanskrit tales] by Mahákavi Dandi. Translated into Gujarati by Shastri Piánjivan Harihar, *etc.* pp. iv. 176, v. *Bombay*, [1889.] 8°. **14148. b. 40.**

DEŠĪMITRAWĀLĀ. *See* NAGĪNDĀSA MAÑCHHĀRĀMA GHELĀBHĀĪ.

DHRUVA (H. H.) *See* HARILĀLA HARSADRĀYA DHRUVA.

DIGAMBARA JAINS. *See* JAINS, *Digambara Sect of.*

GAṄGĀDHARA ṢIVANĀRĀYAṆA ṢUKLA. કચ્છી કોષ્ટકો. [Kachchhī koshṭako. Tables of weights and measures, and arithmetical exercises for the use of schools in the province of Cutch.] pp. 32. મુંબઈ ૧૮૭૫ [*Bombay*, 1875.] 12°. **14150. a. 26.(5.)**

GAṬṬULĀLA GHANAṢYĀMAJĪ. *See* MAHĀBHĀRATA.—*Bhagavadgītā.* [Addenda.] समश्लोकी श्रीमद्भगवद्गीता [Edited, with a translation in verse, by G. Gh.] [1890.] 8°. **14060. c. 28.**

HEMACHANDRA ĀCHĀRYA. श्री जैन रामायण [Jaina Rāmāyaṇa. Another edition of Rāmacharitra, in Balbodha characters.] pp. 379. पुणा १८९० [*Poona*, 1890.] 8°. **14144. g. 34.**

ICHCHHĀRĀMA SŪRYARĀMA DEṢĀI. *See* KSHEMENDRA. [Addenda.] ચારૂચર્યા અથવા શુભ આચાર. [Chārucharyā. Translated by I. S. D. from the Sanskrit of Kshemendra.] [1889.] 12°. **14146. e.**

JAINADHARMA. श्री जैनधर्म ज्ञानप्रकाशक पुस्तक [Jainadharma jñānaprakāṣaka. A collection of Jain prayers and hymns, and of instructions to the monastic and lay classes of Jains.] pp. iv. 200. पुना १९४७ [*Poona*, 1890.] 8°. **14144. g. 35.**

KAIKHUSRAU NAVAROJĪ KĀBRĀJĪ. હીંદુસતાનનુ મેહેસુલ અને ઈનકમ ટાકસ. [Hindustānanuṇ mehesūl. Four papers on the revenues and taxation of India, and the Income tax, delivered at the Bombay branch of the East-India Association.] pp. 52. મુંબઈ ૧૮૭૧ [*Bombay*, 1871.] 8°. **14146. a.**

KĀLIDĀSA, *of Wassawad.* કાળિદાસકૃત सीता-स्वयंवर [Sītāsvayaṃvara. A poem on the marriage of Sītā. With notes.] *See* PRĀCHĪNA KĀVYA. प्राचीन काव्य. Vol. v. No. 1. [1885, *etc.*] 8°. **14148. e. 12.**

KĀLIDĀSA GOVINDAJĪ. *See* MOREṢVARA, *Son of Mānaka Bhaṭṭa.* વૈદ્યામૃત. [Vaidyāmṛita. Sanskrit text, with a Gujarati prose translation by K. G.] [1889.] 8°. **14043. c. 37.**

KĀṢĪRĀMA UTTAMARĀMA PAṆḌYĀ. *See* AMṚITALĀLA GOVARDHANADĀSA SHĀH and KĀṢĪRĀMA UTTAMARĀMA PAṆḌYĀ. The Hind Rajasthan. 1889. 12°. **14146. f. 27.**

KĀVASJĪ DĪNSHĀH KIASH. Ancient Persian Sculptures: or the monuments, buildings, bas-reliefs, rock inscriptions, *etc. etc.*, belonging to the kings of the Achæmenian and Sassanian dynasties of Persia. Containing about 100 plates, arranged with descriptive and historical matter, and itinerary notes, in English, Gujarati and Persian. By K. D. Kiash. pp. 234, (કદીમ નક્ષે ઈરાન) [Kadīm naksh i Irān.] *Bombay*, 1889. 8°. **14146. h. 17.**

KEṢAVALĀLA HARIVIṬHṬHALADĀSA. ગુર્જર અગ્રેસર મંડળની ચિત્રાવલી [Chitrāvalī.] The Gujarat portrait gallery, being a collection of the portraits and biographical sketches of leading men in Gujarát. Compiled by Keshavlál Harivithaldás. *Bombay*, 1889. 8°. **14146. g. 26.**

KIASH (K. D.) *See* KĀVASJĪ DĪNSHĀH KIASH.

KSHEMENDRA. ચારૂચર્યા અથવા શુભ આચાર. [Chārucharyā. A treatise on moral behaviour, translated by Ichchhārāma Sūryarāma Deṣāi from the Sanskrit original of Kshemendra.] મુંબઈ ૧૮૮૯ [*Bombay*, 1889.] 12°. **14146. e.**

LAKSHMAṆA DĀSA. તોરાની ઈશ્કી લાવણી સંગ્રહ [Torānī ʻishkī lāvaṇio. A collection of love-songs, partly in Gujarati and partly in Hindi.] pp. 36. અમદાવાદ ૧૮૮૯ [*Ahmadabad*, 1889.] 12°. **14148. d.**

MAHĀBHĀRATA.—BHAGAVADGĪTĀ. समश्लोकी श्रीमद्भगवद्गीता. [Bhagavadgītā. Sanskrit text, edited with a translation in Gujarati verse by Gaṭṭulāla Ghanaṣyāmajī.] pp. ii. 128. મુંબઈ ૧૮૯૦ [*Bombay*, 1890.] 8°. **14060. c. 28.**

Forms No. 6 of a series of separate publications from the Bombay periodical 'Aryasamudaya.'

MAHĪPATRĀMA RŪPARĀMA NĪLAKAṆṬHA. वनराज चावडो [Vanarāja Chāvaḍo. Third edition.] pp. 320. અમદાવાદ ૧૮૮૩ [*Ahmadabad*, 1883.] 8°. **14146. g. 27.**

NAGĪNDĀSA MAÑCHHĀRĀMA GHELĀBHĀĪ. Charitra mala. Biographies of the royal princes of Guzerat and Kathiavad. Vol. i. Containing the history of sixteen princes. By Nagindas Mancharam. (ચરિત્રમાળા) pp. 308. *Surat*, 1890. 4°. **14146. i. 1.**

NAZĪR AḤMAD, *Khān Bahādur.* હુસનઆરા [Ḥusn-ārā. A moral tale of Muhammadan social life, and the advantages of education. Translated by Bahrāmjī Fardunjī Marzbān from the Hindustani Banāt al-na'sh of N. A.] pp. 156. મુંબઈ ૧૮૯૦ [*Bombay*, 1890.] 8°. **14148. b. 43.**

RUSTAMJĪ HORMASJĪ MISTRĪ. દુશમન દારાબ [Dushman Dārāb. A tale of an unprincipled and criminal Parsi banker, written in imitation of Miss Braddon's novels.] pp. 208. મુંબઈ ૧૮૮૯ [*Bombay*, 1889.] 12°. **14148. b. 42.**

VĪRAJĪ. सुरेखाहरण [Surekhā-haraṇa. A poem on the elopement of Surekhā, i.e. Vatsalā, with Abhimanyu, son of Arjuna. With notes.] *See* PRĀCHĪNA KĀVYA. प्राचीन काव्य Vol. v. No. 2. [1885, *etc.*] 8°. **14148. e. 12.**

INDEX OF ORIENTAL TITLES.

[The references in this Index are to the names of the authors or other headings under which the works are catalogued. In the case of anonymous works, which are catalogued under their titles, the phrase "in loco" is used in referring to them. Oriental titles only are entered in this Index, or those in which English words occur only as forming an essential part of an Oriental title.]

Abhijñāna Ṣakuntalā nāṭaka.
  See Kālidāsa, *the Sanskrit poet.*
Abhimanyuno chakrāvo.
  See Abhimanyu.
Abhimanyunuṇ moṭu ākhyāna.
  See Premānanda.
Āchārānga [*in loco*].
Ādamākhyāna.
  See Tribhuvanadāsa Rāmadāsa.
Aḍhidvīpano nakso.
  See Aḍhidvīpa.
Adhyātmakalpadruma.
  See Munisundara Sūri.
Adhyātmamata-parīkshā.
  See Yaṣovijaya.
Adhyātma prakaraṇa saṅgraha.
  See Hukm Munijī.
Adhyātmasāra.
  See Yaṣovijaya.
Adhyātmasāra praṣnottara.
  See Kuṇvar Vijayajī.
Ādīṣvarano ṣloko.
  See Gulābchand Dayāljī and Lakshmīdāsa [Kahānjī Thakkar.
Āgamasāra.
  See Devachandajī.
Ahmadābādmāṇ batrīsānī relno roḷ.
  See Keṣavalāla Maganlāla.
Akbar-charitra.
  See Mahīpatrāma Rūparāma Nīlakaṇṭha, [*C.I.E.*
Akhānī vāṇī.
  See Akhā.
Akshara-gaṇita [*in loco*].
Alaṅkārachandrikā.
  See Savitānārāyaṇa Gaṇapatinārāyaṇa.
Alaṅkārapraveṣa.
  See Narmadāṣankara Lālaṣaṅkara.
Ambājīnā chhandnī chopaḍī.
  See Amīchand Motīchand.
Ambikākāvya.
  See Ambikā.
Amṛitasāgara.
  See Pratāpa Siṃha, *Raja of Jaipur.*
Anandibai Joshi.
  See Anandībāī Joṣī.
Anāvil gṛihasthomāṇ thayelā navā niyamo.
  See Hararāya Bāpubhāi Deṣāi.
Andaraz i Ātarpāt.
  See Ādarbād Mārāspand.
—— Khusro Kovātāt.
  See Khusrau Noshīrwān, *King of Persia.*
Andherī nagarīno gardhavasena.
  See Haragovinda Dvārakādāsa Kāṇṭāwālā.
Aṅgadavishṭi.
  See Sāmala Bhaṭa.
Angrejī ane Gujarātī pustaka.
  See Mehrvānjī Hormasjī Mehetā and Navarojī Rustamjī Lāḍ.
—— bhāshāntara pāṭhamālā.
  See Wells (T. L.)
—— bījī chopaḍī.
  See Howard (E. I.)
—— tathā Gujarātī vākyāvalī.
  See Wilson (J.) *D.D., F.R.S.*
Añjanaṣilākānā ḍhāliyāṇ.
  See Haṭṭhi Siṃha.
Aṅkagaṇita [*in loco*].
Aṅkagaṇitanāṇ mūlatattva.
  See Lālaṣaṅkara Umiāṣaṅkara Travāḍī.
Āṅknī chopaḍī [*in loco*].
Anusūyābhyudaya.
  See Ṣaṅkaralāla Maheṣvara.
Anuyogadvāra [*in loco*].
Apabhrashṭa ṣabdaprakāṣa.
  See Prabhākara Rāmachandra Paṇḍita.
Aphīmnā vepār.
  See India.

Ardā Virāf-nāmuṉ.
See Ardā Virāf.
Arjunagītā [*in loco*].
Ārogyatāsūchaka.
See Raṇchhoḍbhāī Udayarāma.
Arthaṣāstra.
See Ambālāla Sākarlāla.
Aruṇodaya.
See Mortimer (F. L.) *Mrs.*
Āryadharmanīti.
See Nārāyaṇa Hemachandra.
Āryadharmaprakāṣa. }
Āryajñānavardhaka. }
See Periodical Publications.—*Bombay.*
Āryānārya deṣajñāpaka charchāpatra.
See Pannyāsa Ratnavijaya Gaṇi.
Āryaprajā.
See Bhagavānlāla Bāpālāla.
Āryaprakāṣa. }
Āryasamudaya. }
See Periodical Publications.—*Bombay.*
Āryodvayanī utkaṇṭhā.
See Māhāsukharāma Narbherāma.
Aslājī.
See Ardsher Bahrāmjī Paṭel, called Adnā.
Ashṭāpadajī bimba pratishṭhā.
See Bhūrābhāī Behechar Joṣī. [Addenda.]
Ashṭotrī sanātra mahotsava.
See Purushottama Kakal.
Aṣvamedhaparva.
See Mahābhārata.—*Aṣvamedhaparva.*
Ātashnāṉ kebalānī khubī. [Mansukh.
See Mancherjī Kāvasjī Langrānā, called
Ātmabodha ane jīvanī utpatti.
See Ātmabodha.
Ātmajñāna-vardhaka.
See Periodical Publications.—*Nariad.*
Ātmarañjana [*in loco*].
Ayavanti Sukumārano tera ḍhālio.
See Ayavanti Sukumāra.
Āyurvedasāra-saṅgraha [*in loco*].
Baḍodarāmāṉ vidyādi vishe kavitā.
See Ṣāmajī Ratansī.
Baḍodarānā Malhār Rāva garbo.
See Mañchhārāma Ghelābhāī.
——— vāsinuṉ valaṉ.
See Pānāchand Mojīlāla Deṣāi.
——— vilāpa.
See Niẓām al-Dīn, *Chishtī,* called Hāmī.
Badrmunīr Benaẓīr.
See Ḥasan, *Mīr.*
Bāgh o Bahār.
See Khusrau, *Amīr.*
Bāgno garbo.
See Lalubhāī Jamnādāsa.
Bahjat al-akhbār.
See Periodical Publications.—*Bombay.*
Bahman-nāmuṉ.
See Bahman Asfandiyār, *King of Persia.*
Bajāvaṇī sambandhī sūchanā.
See Paramānandadāsa Bholābhāī Pārekh.
Bāḷagarbāvalī.
See Navalarāma Lakshmīrāma.
Bāḷagāyana.
See Svadeṣa subhechchhanār, *pseud.*
Bāḷakheḷa [*in loco*].
Bāḷalagna nishedhaka garbāvalī.
See Garbāvalī.
Bāḷalagnathī bantī binā.
See Girijāṣaṅkara Muljī.
Bāḷamitra.
See Berquin (A.)
Bāḷasandhyopāsanā. [*Samāj.*
See Brāhma Samāj.—*Ahmadabad Prārthanā*
Bāḷavidhavā Rūpasundarī.
See Naoīndāsa Mañchhārāma Ghelābhāī.
Bāḷavidhavā rupavantī duḥkhadarṣaka.
See Narbherāma Kāṣīrāma Dave.
Bāṇāsura madamardana.
See Raṇchhoḍbhāī Udayarāma.
Bandagī [*in loco*].
Bandhasvāmitva.
See Devendra Sūri.
Bandīnuṉ ākhyāna.
See Manoradāsa, called Sachchidānanda Brahmatīrtha.
Barāsa Kasturī.
See Ṣāmala Bhaṭa.
Barjo-nāmuṉ.
See Māṇekjī Barjorjī Minuchehr Homjīnā.
Batrisānā bigāḍnī bumo.
See Ichchhāṣaṅkara Amathārāma Vyāsa.
Bhāḍalī-mata.
See Bhaḍalī.
Bhagavadgītā.
See Mahābhārata.—*Bhagavadgītā.*
Bhāgavata.
See Purāṇas.—*Bhāgavatapurāṇa.*
Bhāgavatadharma.
See Dharmānanda Svāmī.
Bhagavata prasādākhyāna.
See Koṭhārī Govardhana.
Bhagavatī Bhāgavata.
See Purāṇas.—*Devībhāgavatapurāṇa.*
Bhagavatī-sūtra [*in loco*].
Bhāio bairī karo to joine kuvo purjo.
See Māṇekjī Barjorjī Minuchehr Homjīnā.
Bhaktachintāmaṇi.
See Nishkulānanda.
Bhaktāmara-stotra.
See Mānatuṅgāchārya.
Bhakti . . . bodhaka kavitā.
See Māṇekjī Barjorjī Minuchehr Homjīnā.
Bharatakhaṇḍano itihāsa. [*C.I.E.*
See Mahīpatrāma Rūparāma Nīlakaṇṭha,
Bhāratārthaprakāsa.
See Mahābhārata.
Bharūch jillāno keḷavaṇī khātāno itihāsa.
See Gaṇapatarāma Rājārāma Mehetā.
Bhāṣāno.
See Khurshedjī Rustamjī Kāmā.
Bhāshābhūshaṇa.
See Jasvat Siṃha, *Maharaja.*

Bhāṭiā kulotpatti grantha. [Liāvālā.
See Chaturbhuja Vālji Jerājāṇī Khambhā-
Bhavānī kāvya sudhā.
See Bhavānīṣaṅkara Narasiṃharāma.
Bhāvaprakāṣa.
See Bhāva Miṣra.
Bhavavairāgyaṣataka [*in loco*].
Bhogavatībhāgyodaya.
See Ṣaṅkaralāla Maheṣvara.
Bhoja subodha ratnamālā. [Addenda.]
See Baladevarāma Kṛishṇarāma Bhaṭṭa.
Bhramanī toḍnārī vāṇī.
See Destroyer.
Bhramavidhvāmsana.
See Jitāmala Svāmī.
Bhudharabhāī Dhaneṣvarano rāsḍo.
See Kṛishṇa Raṇchhoḍa Ṭravāḍī.
Bhūgoḷajñāna [*in loco*].
Bhūgoḷano upayoga karvānī rītino grantha.
See Harilāla Mohanalāla.
Bhūgoḷanuṇ varṇana.
See Candy (T.)
Bhūgoḷavidyā.
See Geikie (A.)
———
See Hope (T. C.)
Bhūmitināṇ mūlatattva.
See Euclid.
Bhūmiti vyākhyā.
See Jervis (G. R.)
Bhūtaḷavidyā.
See Blanford (H. F.)
Bibadha ratan prakāṣa.
See Saubhāgamālājī.
Bījagaṇita.
See Jervis (G. R.)
Bījā janmanī vāt.
See New Birth.
Bījī chopaḍī.
See Hope (T. C.)
Bodhachintāmaṇi.
See Rushirāja Mahārāja.
Bodhakathā [*in loco*].
Brāhma dharma [*in loco*].
——— matasāra.
See Brāhma Samāj.
Brahmajñānī Akhā Bhaktanā chhapā. }
——————— Bhaktanī vāṇī. }
See Akhā.
Bṛihat kāvyadohana.
See Ichchhārāma Sūryarāma Desāī.
Buddhidarpaṇa.
See ʻAbd al-Karīm, called Mudarris.
Buddhivardhaka.
See Periodical Publications.—*Bombay*.
Bundehesh [*in loco*].
Chalyākhyāna [*in loco*].
Chāmparāja Hāḍo ne Sonarāṇī.
See Vāghjī Āsārāma Ojhā.
Chandan Mālyāgirīno rās.
See Kshemaharsha.
Chaṇḍīkāno garbo.
See Motīrāma Mañchhārāma.
Chaṇḍīpāṭha.
See Rāmabhakta Ṣivadāsa.
Chand Rājā ane Guṇāvalī rāṇīnā kāgal.
See Chand Rājā.
Chand Rājāno rās.
See Mohana Vijayajī.
Chandrās ane Chandrakaḷā.
See Ṣāmajī Raṇchhoḍ.
Chandrasiṃha Dīpamaṇi nāṭaka.
See Rūpāṇī Bhīmajī Kālidāsa.
Chandrikā [*in loco*].
Charchāpatra.
See Pannyāsa Ratnavijaya Gaṇi.
Charitramālā. [Addenda.]
See Nagīndāsa Mañchhārāma Ghelābhāī.
Charitra-saṅgraha [*in loco*].
Charpaṭapañjarī.
See Ṣaṅkara Āchārya.
Chārucharyā.
See Kshemendra. [Addenda.]
Chatura Siṃha.
See Mañchhārāma Ghelābhāī.
Chaturviṃṣati Jina stavana.
See Devachandra.
Chaurāṣī Vaishṇavanī vārtā.
See Chaurāṣī Vārtā.
Chha bhāinuṇ rās.
See Chha bhāī.
Chhappā.
See Ṣāmala Bhaṭa.
Chhappan bhoganuṇ varṇana.
See Vrajarāyajī.
Chhaṭhī chopaḍī.
See Hope (T. C.)
Chhelnī vārtā.
See Hariṣaṅkara Mehetā.
Chitrāvalī. [denda.]
See Keṣavalāla Harivithṭhaladāsa. [Ad-
Chothī chopaḍī.
See Hope (T. C.).
Chovīsa Jina stuti.
See Ānandaghana. [Addenda].
Chovīsināṇ stavana.
See Yaṣovijaya.
Chuṇṭī kāḥāḍelāṇ lakhāṇo.
See Sohrābjī Shāpurjī Baṅgālī.
Cutch mahodaya [*i. e.* Kachchh-mahodaya].
See Govardhana Lālajī, also called Gaṭṭu Lālajī.
Dainika prasāda.
See Taylor (J. van S.).
Daivasika tatha rāī pratikramaṇādi mūlasūtra.
See Pratikramaṇa sūtras.
Ḍākor-yātrā māhātmya.
See Bāḷājī Bhagavānjī Dave.
Dānalīlā.
See Premānanda.
Ḍaṅkpur Mahārudra yajñanuṇ varṇana. [denda.]
See Amṛitalāla Anoparāma Mehetā. [Ad-
Dārāb-nāmuṇ.
See Abū Ṭāhir, *Tarsūsī*.

Daṣakumāra charitra.
See Daṇḍin. [Addenda.]
Daskat shikshak.
See Ādarjī Kāvasjī Master.
Dayā karvī.
See Mercy.
Dayārāmakṛita kāvyasaṅgraha.
See Dayārāma, *Kavi.*
Deṣī hisāb.
See Bhogīlāla Prāṇavallabhadāsa.
—— hisāb gaṇvānī sehelī rīto.
See Bhāidāsa Dayārāma.
—— kārīgarīne uttejana.
See Encouragement.
Devasiddhānta.
See Existence.
Devībhāgavatapurāṇa.
See Purāṇas.—*Devībhāgavatapurāṇa.*
Devīmāhātmya.
See Purāṇas.—Mārkaṇḍeyapurāṇa.—*Devīmāhātmya.*
Dhammil Kumārno rās.
See Vīravijaya.
Dhanā Sālibhadra.
See Lālchand Lalubhāī.
Dharma e ṣuṇ chhe.
See Dharma.
Dharmanāṇ tarājavāṇ.
See Dharma.
Dharmaprakāṣa.
See Keṣavalāla Maganlāla.
Dharmatattva-bhāskara.
See Nārāyaṇa Hīrāchand Kānūnī.
Dharmavivechana [*in loco*].
Dhīrā Bhaktanī kavitā.
See Dhīrā Bhakta.
Dhīrā Mārujīnī vārtā.
See Harsadrāya Sundaralāla.
Dhoḷ tathā padavigereno saṅgraha.
See Lalu Pītāmbara.
Dhruvākhyāna.
See Tulasī, *of Kuntarpur.*
Dilchaman gāyanasaṅgraha.
See Kāvasjī Pestanjī.
Dilgirino dekhāva.
See Uttamarāma Umedchand and Chamanlāl Narasiṃhadāsa.
Dilkhush stavanāvalī.
See Sāṅkalchand Mahāsukharāma.
Dīnbeh Mazdayasnī.
See Jamshedjī Frāmjī Bachābhāī Rabāḍī.
Dinkard [*in loco*].
Dīwānī navo kāyado.
See India.—*Legislative Council.*
Dokhme Noshirvān.
See Rustam Īrānī.
Ḍol ghālu sudhrelne chābakā.
See Ḍol.
Draupadī-svayaṃvara.
See Ṣivadāsa.
Dravyaguṇa paryāyano rās.
See Yaṣovijaya.
Dravya tathā rupānā mūlanī nyūnatā vishenāṇ bhāshaṇa.
See Nasarvānjī Hirjībhāī Paṭel.
Du'ā nām setāyishne.
See Khurshedjī Minucherjī Kaṭeli.
Duḥkhī Divālī.
See Bālubhāī Manmohanadāsa Dalāl.
Dukāḷno garbo.
See Dukāḷ.
Dukhanivāraṇa.
See Pestanjī Navarojī.
Dukhiyārī Bachuṇ.
See Kaikhusrau Navarojī Kābrājī.
Ḍungar vāḍāno kheyāl.
See Nasarvānjī Navarojī Pāghḍewālā.
Duniyā-darpan.
See Karam 'Alī Rahīm, *Nānjiānī.*
Dushman Dārāb.
See Rustamjī Hormasjī Mistrī. [Addenda.]
Edmund vishenī vārtā.
See Edmund.
Ekādaṣimāhātmya.
See Purāṇas.
Ek ḍoṣī tathā Brāhmaṇanī vātchīt.
See Brahman.
Ek māṇse . . . tenī kathā.
See Man.
Ek muelo chhokro jīvato.
See Life.
Ek painī ṣī chintā chhe.
See Pai.
Ekvīs nasko [*in loco*].
Eskī bānu tathā eskī dhaṇīno garbo.
See Mancherjī Jamshedjī.
Farāmurz-nāmuṇ.
See Abū Ṭāhir, *Tarsūsī.*
Fārsī munājāt.
See Sohrābjī Kūvarjī Tāskar.
Fasād i February.
See Dil-khush, *pseud.*
Fasānah i 'ajā'ib.
See Rajab 'Alī Beg, *Mīrzā,* called Surūr.
Faujdārī kām chalāvavāno rīt.
See India.—*Legislative Council.*
Fursad.
See Periodical Publications.—*Bombay.*
Gajrāmārujīnī rasīlī vārtā.
See Gajrāmāru.
Gāmḍenī Bhīkhīne Mumbai sheharc bhakhī.
See Bhīkhī.
——— Galālvahu.
See Māṇekjī Barjorjī Minucheer Homjīnā.
Gaṅgā.
See Ichchhārāma Sūryarāma Deṣāī.
Ganj-nāmuṇ.
See Mancherjī Kāvasjī Langrānā, called Mansukh.
Ganj i shāegān.
See Buzurgmihr.
Garbāvalī [*in loco*].
———
See Gauriṣaṅkara Prabhāṣaṅkara.
Gauhar i zindagī.
See Nasīm.
Gāyakavāḍa Mahārājanā itihāsa.
See Mohanalāla Kuvera Travāḍī.

Gāyakavāḍī nyāyaprakāṣa.
See Baroda, *Native State of.*
——— rājyano itihāsa.
See Paramānandadāsa Bhoḷābhāī Pārekh.
Gāyanaprakāra [*in loco*].
Gāyaṇaprakāṣa.
See Illustrations.
Gāyanaṣataka.
See Hīrāchand Kānjī.
Ghāṣīrāma koṭwāl.
See Morobā Kānhobā.
Ghuncha i Avastā.
See Rustam Rānī.
Gītagrantha [*in loco*].
Gītanī pothī.
See Gujarati Hymn Book.
Gnyandipuck.
See Jñānadīpaka.
Goḍi Pārṣvanāthanā ḍhāliyāṇ.
See Vīravijaya.
Gohil rājyano itihāsa. [Makandāsa.
See Harajīvanadāsa Govindarāma and Dāmajī
Gokula Vṛindāvana chandrāvaḷā.
See Visrāma Mulji.
Gopāla guṇavarṇana.
See Mohanalāla Dalpatrāma.
Gopīgītā.
See Purāṇas.—Bhāgavatapurāṇa.—*Gopīgītā.*
Gosht i Fryāno [*in loco*].
Greṭ Briṭan bātenī musāpharī.
See Ḍosabhāī Frāmjī Karākā.
Gujarāt deṣanī vārtā.
See F. B.
——— deṣano itihāsa.
See Gopālajī Tribhuvanadāsa.
———
See Maganlāla Vakhatchand.
——— Rājasthān.
See Kālidāsa Devaṣaṅkara Paṇḍyā.
——— Varnākyular Sosāitīnā hetu.
See Haragovinda Dvārakādāsa Kāṇṭāwālā.
Gujarātī bhāshāmāṇ vākya rachanānā niyamo.
See Bhāīdāsa Dayārāma.
——— bhāshāno itihāsa.
See Vrajalāla Kālidāsa Ṣāstrī.
———bhāshānuṇ laghu vyākaraṇa.
See Taylor (J. van S.)
——— navuṇ vyākaraṇa.
See Mahīpatrāma Rūparāma Nīlakaṇṭha.
——— vyākaraṇa.
See Hope (T. C.)
———
See Taylor (T. van S.)
——— bījī chopaḍī.
See Hope (T. C.)
——— chothī chopaḍīnā artha.
See Fakīrbhāī Kāṣīdāsa.
——— deṣī hisāb.
See Bhogīlāla Prāṇavallabhadāsa.
——— kāvyadohana. }
——— kāvyasaṃkshepa. }
See Dalpatrāma Ḍāhyābhāī, *Kavi, C.I.E.*
Gujarātī koshāvalī.
See Hīrāchand Kānjī.
——— navo khardo [*in loco*].
——— pāñchamī chopaḍī. }
——— pehelī chopaḍī. }
——— chopaḍīnāṇ artha. }
See Hope (T. C.)
——— piṅgala.
See Dalpatrāma Ḍāhyābhāī, *Kavi, C.I.E.*
——— ṣabdārtha kosha.
See Motīlāla Manassukharāma Shāh.
——— sātamī chopaḍī.
See Hope (T. C.)
——— vehem.
See Purushottama Kāhānjī Gāndhe.
Gujarātnā bhikhārio.
See Viṭhṭhaladāsa Dhanjībhāī.
Gujarātno bāḷabodhaka itihāsa.
See Mahīpatrāma Rūparāma Nīlakaṇṭha, *C.I.E.*
——— itihāsa.
See Edalji Ḍosābhāī.
Gul ane Bulbul.
See Edaljī Dādābhāī Mistri.
Gul i Bakāwalī.
See Kṛishṇadāsa.
Gulchaman gāyana. [Narasiṃhadāsa.
See Uttamarāma Umedchand and Chamanlāla
Gulistan.
See Sa'dī.
Gul Shīrīnā.
See Rustam Īrānī.
Gulzār i 'ālam.
See Pestanjī Frāmjī Velāte.
Gurunī sattā vishe nibandha.
See Dalpatrāma Ambārāma.
Habshī deṣnāṇ Rājkumār Rāsalasnuṇ charitra.
See Johnson (S.) *LL.D.*
Hādokht Nask [*in loco*].
Hakha Mazdayasnanam.
See Periodical Publications.—*Bombay.*
Hālnāṇ jamānānī Pārsī chhokrīo.
See Nasarvānjī Shehriyārjī Ginwālā.
Haṃsarāja Vatsarājano rās.
See Jinodaya Sūri.
Hāramālā.
See Premānanda.
Haribal Machchhino rās.
See Labdhivijaya, *Muni.*
Harichand Rājāno rās.
See Kanakasundara.
Harichandrākhyāna.
See Harischandra, *Rājā.*
Harirasa.
See Īsvara Bāroṭ.
Harūn nāṭaka.
See Harūn al-Rashīd, *Caliph.*
Hastāmalaka.
See Bhāṇa Dāsa. [Addenda.]
Hātam-nāmuṇ.
See Hātim Ṭā'ī.
Hāvanīm
See Zand-Avastā.

Hazār ane ek rāt.
See ARABIAN NIGHTS.
Hāzir-javābī pradhānanī vārtā.
See DAYĀLAJĪ RAṆCHHOḌA.
Henrī tathā tehenā chākar.
See BUTT, afterwards SHERWORD (M. M.)
Hind ane Brittania.
See ICHCHHĀRĀMA SŪRYARĀMA DEṢĀI.
Hind Rājasthāna. [Addenda.]
See AMṚITALĀLA GOVARDHANADĀSA SHĀH.
Hindu devatāonī chitramālā.
See MĀṆEKJĪ BARJORJĪ MINUCHEHR HOMJĪNĀ.
Hindu ṣāstranī ḍāyjest.
See GOVINDALĀLA BĀLĀJĪ.
Hinduone sādu araḍ araḍ māṇkānī mālā.
See HINDUISM.
Hindustānanā itihāsano saṃkshepa.
See INDIA.
Hindustānanī bhūgoḷa.
See ḌĀHYĀBHĀĪ AMBĀRĀMA.
Hindustānano faujdārī kāyado.
See INDIA.—*Legislative Council.*
———— itihāsa.
See MORRIS (H.) *of the Madras Civil Service.*
———— purāvano kāyado.
See INDIA.—*Legislative Council.*
———— saṃkshipta itihāsa.
See INDIA.
Hindustānanuṇ mehesūl. [Addenda.]
See KAIKHUSRAU NAVAROJĪ KĀBRĀJĪ.
Hindusthānamāṇhel Ingliṣnā rājyano itihāsa.
See BĀḶA GAṄGĀDHARA ṢĀSTRĪ JĀMBHEKAR.
Hindusthānamāṇ musāfirī.
See ARDSHER FRĀMJĪ MUS.
Hindusthānano itihāsa.
See ELPHINSTONE (*Hon.* M.)
Hoḷīnibandha.
See MAGANLĀLĀ VAKHATCHAND.
Hoḷīsaṅgraha.
See KĪKĀBHĀĪ PRABHUDĀSA.
Homlo Hāū.
See NĀNĀBHĀĪ RUSTAMJĪ RĀṆĪNĀ.
Hormuzdnī sifat.
See MĀṆEKJĪ DĀRĀBJĪ ADRIANWĀLĀ.
Ḥusn-ārā.
See NAẒĪR AḤMAD, *Khān Bahādur.* [Addenda.]
Indrasabhā.
See ĀGHĀ ḤASAN, *Saiyid*, called AMĀNAT.
Inglandmāṇ pravāsa.
See KARSANDĀS MŪLJĪ.
Inglish vyākaraṇanī mūḷapīṭhikā.
See HOWARD (E. I.)
Intikhāb i Vandidād.
See ZAND-AVASTĀ.
Irānnī mukhtasar tavārīkh.
See BAHMANJĪ BAHRĀMJĪ-PATEL.
Īṣā Masīh tathā Muhammadnī bābatnī vāt.
See JESUS CHRIST.
Īṣu Khristnā maraṇa. }
———— vishe pustaka. }
See JESUS CHRIST.
Īsu-parīkshā.
See JAGANNĀRĀYĀṆA.
Īṣvara prārthanāmālā. }
Īṣvaropāsana. } [Samāj.
See BRĀHMA SAMĀJ.—*Ahmadabad Prārthanā*
Jadukapaṭa-prakāṣa.
See ICHCHHĀṢAṄKARA AMATHĀRĀMA VYĀSA.
Jahāndār Shāh bādshāhnī vārtā.
See ṢĀMALA BHAṬA.
Jahāngīr-nāmuṇ.
See JAHĀNGĪR.
Jaina bālajñāna subodha.
See KEṢAVALĀLA ṢIVARĀMA.
Jainadharma dilkhush stavanāvalī.
See HARAKISANDĀSA HARAJĪVANADĀSA.
———— gyān-pradīpaka.
See JAINADHARMA.
———— jñānaprakāṣaka.
See JAINADHARMA. [Addenda.]
———— prakāṣa.
See PERIODICAL PUBLICATIONS.—*Bhaunagar.*
———— pravartaka Sabhā. [*Sabha.*
See AHMADABAD. —*Jainadharma-pravartaka*
———— sārasaṅgraha.
See GHELĀBHĀĪ LĪLĀDHARA.
———— siddhāntasāra.
See JAINADHARMA-SIDDHĀNTA.
Jaina kāvyaprakāṣa.
See BHĪMASIṂHA MĀṆAKA.
—— kāvyasaṅgraha.
See LĀBHAVIJAYA, *Pandit.*
—— kāvya sarasaṅgraha.
See NĀTHĀBHĀĪ LALUBHĀĪ.
—— matanī parīkshāno pratyuttara.
See CHUNĪLĀLA JAYACHAND. [Addenda.]
—— prabodha.
See ĀNANDAJĪ KHETAṢĪ.
—— prārthanāmālā. [*Sabhā.*
See AHMADABAD —*Jainadharma-pravartaka*
—— Rāmāyaṇa.
See HEMACHANDRA ĀCHĀRYA. [Addenda.]
—— ṣāstra kathāsaṅgraha.
See JAINAṢĀSTRA.
—— viveka vāṇī.
See GHELĀBHĀĪ LĪLĀDHARA.
—— vṛitta ṣikshāpatri.
See JAINAVṚITTA.
Jāl ane Rodābe [*in loco*].
Jālem jor.
See EDALJĪ JAMSHEDJĪ KHORI.
Jambudvīpano nakso.
See JAMBUDVĪPA.
Jamshed, homa ane ātash.
See JĪVANAJĪ JAMSHEDJĪ MODĪ.
Jātibheda ane bhojanavichāra.
See NĀRĀYAṆA HEMACHANDRA.
Jauhar i zindagānī.
See SOHRĀBJĪ JAMSHEDJĪ JĪJĪBHĀĪ.
Jayakumārīvijaya nāṭaka.
See RAṆCHHODBHĀĪ UDAYARĀMA.
Jayānanda Kevalīno rās.
See PADMAVIJAYA.
Jinastuti.
See SOBHANA.
Jīvābhigama [*in loco*].

Jīvanabhedavāṇī [*in loco*].
Jīvanacharitra.
See Bhagubhāī Rāmaṣaṅkara Jānī. [Addenda.]
Jīvavichāra-prakaraṇa.
See Ṣānti Sūri.
Jñānadipaka.
See Periodical Publications.—*Surat.*
Jñānaprakāṣa prakaraṇa-saṅgraha.
See Hukm Munijī.
Jñāna-upadeṣa.
See Somachand Kālidāsa.
Jñānavardhaka.
See Periodical Publications.—*Bombay.*
Jñāti-nibandha.
See Dalpatrāma Ḍāhyābhāī, *Kavi, C.I.E.*
Junā Dharmapustakno saṃkshepa.
See Bible.—Old Testament.—*Appendix.*
Junāgaḍhno bhomiyo.
See Junagarh.
Jyotishasāra.
See Ṣukadeva.
Jyotisha vishe.
See Pītāmbaradāsa Tribhuvanadāsa Mehetā.
Kabīr matadarṣaka grantha.
See Vāljī Bechar.
Kabīṣā vishe.
See Ratanjī Rustamjī Kāṅgā.
Kachchh deṣa sirishtah saṅgraha.
See Maṇibhāī Jasbhāī.
——— mahodaya.
See Govardhana Lālajī, also called Gaṭṭu Lālaji.
Kachchhī koshṭako.
See Gaṅgādhara Ṣivanārāyaṇa Ṣukla. [Addenda.]
Kachchhnī bhūgoḷavidyā.
See Dalpatrāma Prāṇajīvana Khakhkhar.
Kādambarī.
See Bāṇa.
Kadīm naksh i Irān.
See Kāvasjī Dīnshāh Kiash. [Addenda.]
Kakotā.
See Ṣobhāvahujī.
Kāḷāṇ meṇḍhāṇ.
See Nānābhāī Rustamji Rāṇinā.
Kaliāṇīnā navā dakhmāno garbo.
See Sohrābjī Hormasjī.
Kalpasūtrasya bālāvabodha.
See Rājendra Sūri.
Kalyāṇa mandira stotra.
See Kumudachandra.
Kamalā duḥkhadarṣaka nāṭaka.
See Keṣavarāma Viṣvanātha Joṣī.
Kāmāvatīnī vārtā.
See Kāmāvatī.
Kāṇī Kubāīnāṇ kartuk.
See Maṇekjī Barjorjī Minucheher Homjīnā.
Kanjusnā karmanī kāhanī.
See Ardsher Bahrāmjī Paṭel, called Adnā.
Kānsartīnāmāṇ vagāḍvānā gāyaṇo.
See Concertina.
Kanyāvikraya doshadarṣaka.
See Bhūpatrāya Haragovinda Dātār.
Kāpadiā ramujī maṇḍaḷinā dhārāo.
See Bombay, *City of.—Kapadia Amusing Club.*
Kapol utpattinī kathā.
See Parsotam Mādhavajī Mehetā.
Karakaṇḍū ādik chār pratyek Buddha rās.
See Samayasundara Upādhyāyajī.
Karaṇa Ghelo.
See Nandaṣaṅkara Tuljāṣaṅkara.
Karaṇa Kāmāvatīnī vārtā.
See Kāmāvatī.
Karmastava [*in loco*].
Karmavipāka.
See Devendra Sūri.
Karsandās Muljī charitra.
See Mahīpatrāma Rūparāma Nīlakaṇṭha.
Kartavya bhūmiti.
See Pasley (*Sir* C. W.)
Karuṇāvajrāyudha nāṭaka.
See Bālachandrāchārya.
Kāshṭhanā ghoḍānī vārtā.
See Ṣāmala Bhaṭa.
Kāṭhiāvāḍ gāiḍ.
See Rāvajī Rāmajī Sāvant.
——— sarvasaṅgraha.
See Kathiawar.
Kavesarī Kalāmo [*in loco*].
Kavi Nāgjīnūṇ janmacharitra.
See Devajī Ukābhāī Makvāṇā.
Kavitā.
See Dayārāma, *Kavi.*
———
See Dhīrā Bhakta.
———
See Prītama.
Kavitāsaṅgraha [*in loco*].
Kāvyadohana.
See Dalpatrāma Ḍāhyābhāī, *Kavi, C.I.E.*
———
See Ichchhārāma Suryarāma Deṣāī.
———
See Jeṭhālāla Harajīvana.
Kāvyanimajjana.
See Harikrishṇa Baḷadeva Bhaṭṭa.
Kāvyasaṃkshepa.
See Dalpatrāma Ḍāhyābhāī, *Kavi, C.I.E.*
Kāyade tāus.
See Umiyārāma Ṭhākordāsa Daru.
Kehevat māḷā.
See Nathuṣaṅkara Udayaṣaṅkara Ḍholkiyā.
Kharo āṣro.
See Refuge.
Kharu prāyaṣchitta.
See Atonement.
Kheḍāvāḷ jñāti samaste karelā ṭharāvo.
See Kheḍāvāḷ Brahmans.
Khordeh Avesta.
See Zand-Avastā.
Khristī ane Mohammadī dharmano chukādo.
See Ghulām Muhammad, *Rānderī.*
——— pādrīo sāmāṭe ā deṣamāṇ āevā.
See Christian Ministers.
Khristnā viṣvāsionī uttarāvali.
See Christians.
Khulāsah i dīn i Zartoshtī.
See Asfandiyārjī Barjorjī Panthakī.

Khurdah Avastā.
See Zand-Avastā.
Kolambasno vṛittānta.
See Robertson (W.) *D.D., the Historian.*
Koshṭakanī chopaḍī.
See Koshṭaka.
Kudrati ilm i Ilāhī.
See Hormasjī Pālanjī Mehrjī.
Kumārabodha. }
Kumārikābodha. }
See Hīrāchand Kānjī.
Kumitra darpaṇa.
See Kanhaiyālāla Motīlāla Munshī.
Lailā Majnūn [*in loco*].
Lakshmaṇā-haraṇa.
See Premānanda.
Lalitā duḥkhadarṣaka.
See Raṇchhoḍbhāī Udayarāma.
Lava Kuṣākhyāna.
See Lava Kuṣa.
Lāvaṇī saṅgraha.
See Jinadāsa.
Lipidhārā [*in loco*].
Lokāgachchhīya ṣrāvakasya pratikramaṇasūtra.
See Kalyāṇachandajī Jayachandajī.
Lokanāla dvatriṃṣikā.
See Lokanāla.
Luptopamā vilāsa.
See Jasvat Siṃha, *Maharaja.*
Madana Mohanānī vārtā. }
Madāpachīsīnī vārtā. }
Mādhavānalanī vārtā. }
See Sāmala Bhaṭa.
Madhu Mālatīnī vārtā.
See Chaturbhuja Dāsa.
Mādigān i chatrang [*in loco*].
Mahārājā Malhār Rāvano rāsḍo.
See Chimanalāla Narsīdāsa.
Mahāvīra Jinastuti.
See Yaṣovijaya.
Mājistreṭno parīkshāno kāyado.
See India.—*Legislative Council.*
Majmū'-al-naṣā'iḥ.
See Ṣādik 'Alī.
Mālatī mādhava.
See Bhavabhūti.
Malhār Rāva Mahārāja nāṭaka.
See Nārāyaṇa Bāpujī Kāniṭkar.
——— viraha ṣataka.
See Govardhanadāsa Lakshmīdāsa.
Malli Jina māhātmya.
See Ahmadabad. — *Jainadharma-pravartaka* [*Sabhā.*
Manaharamālā.
See Prāṇalāla Ṣambhulāla Deṣāī.
Manājāt [*in loco*].
Māṇak Shāh charitra.
See Jeshaṅgdāsa Trikamdāsa Paṭel.
Mānavadharmaṣāstra.
See Manu.
Maṇḍalīnā bhajananī rīt.
See Fyvie (W.)
Maṅgalakalaṣa kumārno rās.
See Dīptivijaya.
Maṅgaḷavichāra.
See Maṅgaḷā Gaurī.
Maṇiṣaṅkarakṛita kāvya.
See Maṇiṣaṅkara Lalubhāī.
Manohara vāṇī [*in loco*].
Manorañjaka garbāvalī.
See Garbāvalī.
——————— Pratāpakāvya.
See Pratāparāya Ṣivalāla Māṅkaḍ.
——————— vārtā.
See Maganrāma Naraharāma.
Mansūkhī manājāt.
See Mancherjī Kāvasjī Langrānā, called [Mansūkh.
Mārgopadeṣikā.
See Rāmakṛishṇa Gopāla Bhāṇḍārkar.
Mātam i Ḥasanain.
See 'Abbās, *Saiyid.*
Maṭulālaji . . . arogavyo.
See Vrajarāyajī.
Mazdayasna.
See Nasarvānjī Frāmjī.
Meghajīnī mohkāṇ.
See Ādītrāma Joitārāma.
Meghalīlā.
See Tuljārāma Jhīṇārāma.
Megharājāne vinantīpatra.
See Māhāsukharāma Narbherāma.
Meher Yazda.
See Nasarvānjī Shāpurjī Tavaḍiā.
Menāpopaṭnī vārtā.
See Sāmala Bhaṭa.
Mevāḍnī jāh o jalālī.
See Viṭhṭhaladāsa Dhanjībhāī.
Mīlāvaḍo.
See Periodical Publications.—*Bombay.*
Mirāt al-'arūs.
See Naẕīr Aḥmad, *Khān Bahādur.*
Mithra.
See Nasarvānjī Shāpurjī Tavaḍiā.
Mohoṭī pūjāsaṅgraha.
See Nāthābhāī Lalubhāī.
Mohoṭuṇ sajhāyamā'ā saṅgraha.
See Sajhāyamālā.
Mokshamālā.
See Rājyachandra.
Monghavārīnī mohkāṇ.
See Maṇilāla Harilāla and Chhoṭālāla [Mohanalāla.
Motīnā hisābnī chopaḍī.
See Dayāla Rāvajī.
Motiṣānāṇ ḍhāḷiāṇ.
See Motiṣā.
Moṭuṇ kāvyadohana.
See Jeṭhālāla Harajīvana.
Mṛidālaṣā ākhyāna.
See Premānanda.
Mugdhāvabodha auktika [*in loco*].
Mukhā'afāt i Baibal.
See Yūsuf Ṣāliḥ.
Muktimuktāvalī.
See Taylor (J. van S.)
Mumbāithī Kāshmīr.
See Jahāngīr Bahrāmjī Marzbān.

Mumbāithī Yūrop tarafnā pravāsnī nondh patrikā.
See Frāmjī Dīnshājī Pīṭīṭ.
Mundrā ane Kulin.
See Jahāngīrshāh Ardsher Ṫāli'yārkhān.
Nabhu kavitā.
See Narbherāma Mañchhārāma.
Nakliyāt-nāmuṉ.
See Khurshedjī Nasarvānjī Pestanjī.
Nala Rājānuṉ ākhyāna.
See Premānanda.
Nāmārthabodha.
See Hīrāchand Kānjī.
Nanda batrīṣīnī vārtā.
See Ṣāmala Bhaṭa.
Nanda Rājā ane satī Sulochanā.
See Nanda Rājā.
Narasiṃha Mehetānuṉ māhmeruṉ tathā huṇḍī.
See Amṛitalāla Nārāyaṇadāsa Laherī.
Nārasiṃhāvatāra nāṭaka.
See Dattātraya.
Narmagadya.
——— kavitā.
——— koṣa.
——— vyākaraṇa.
See Narmadāṣaṅkara Lālaṣaṅkara.
Narsī Mehetānī huṇḍī.
See Premānanda.
Nātyomāṉ ṣeṭhonā ṣākhā.
See Vallabharāma Sūryarāma.
Navarātrī-pūjana [*in loco*].
Navatattva-prakaraṇa [*in loco*].
Nayachakrasāra.
See Devachandra.
Nindā khānuṉ.
See Kaikhusrau Navarojī Kābrājī.
Niṣālnī paddhati.
See Gujarati Treatise.
Nītiṣataka.
See Bhartṛihari.
Nītivachana.
See Karsandās Mūljī.
Nītivinoda.
See Bahrāmjī Mehrvānjī Malabārī.
Noshīrwān i Samangān ane Shīrīn i Sīstān.
See Nasarvānjī Rustamjī Vāchhā.
Nyātīvara.
See Prāṇajīvanadāsa Māṇeklāla.
Okhāharaṇa.
See Dāmodara Ratansī Somānī.
——————
See Premānanda.
——————— nāṭaka.
See Ushā.
Pada [*in loco*].
Padasaṅgraha.
See Lāladāsajī.
Padmāvatīnī vārtā.
See Ṣāmala Bhaṭa.
Pālaṇā [*in loco*].
Pānanābiḍānī vārtā.
Pañcha daṇḍanī vārtā.
See Ṣāmala Bhaṭa.
Pañcha pratikramaṇādi sūtrāṇi.
See Pratikramaṇa sūtras.
Pañchatantra [*in loco*.]
Pañcha vartamāna.
See Nishkulānanda.
Pañchīkaraṇa.
See Rāmadāsa Svāmī, *of Haidarabad*.
Pāñchmī chopaḍī.
See Hope (T. C.)
Pañchopākhyāna.
See Pañchatantra.
Pāṇḍavacharitra.
See Devaprabhu Sūri.
Pāṇḍavavālā mulamaṇḍānanā.
See Pāṇḍavas.
Pāṇḍava-vishṭi.
See Bhau, *Kavi*. [Addenda.]
Pand-nāmah i Ādarbād Mārāspand.
See Ādarbād Mārāspand.
Paṅkhinī vārtā.
See Ṣāmala Bhaṭa.
Pannavaṇā.
See Kālikāchārya.
Pāṉtriṣa bolno thokḍo.
See Pāṉtriṣa bol.
Paramapada-bodhinī.
See Nathurāma Pītāmbarajī Rāvaḷ.
Parameṣvarnā mohoṭā daṣa hukm.
See Ten Commandments.
Pārāṣara dharmaṣāstra.
See Parāṣara.
Parṇelo pīḍāo mare, *etc.*
See Mañchhārāma Ghelābhāī.
Parsee Punch and Apyakhtiar.
See Periodical Publications.—*Bombay*.
Pārsī dhārā parnī nuktechinī. [Mansukh.
See Mancherjī Kāvasjī Langrānā, called
Pārsīo khodāparast chhe ke nahiṉ.
See Parsis.
Pārsīonūṉ list.
See Mancherjī Hoshangjī Jāgos.
Pārsīprakāṣa.
See Bahmanjī Bahrāmjī Paṭel.
Pārsī strī ramujī navā garbā.
See Sohrābjī Hormasjī.
Pativratā strī.
See Viṭṭhaladāsa Dhanjībhāī.
Pavitra lekhanī vārtā.
See Barth (C. G.)
Pehelī chopaḍī.
See Hope (T. C.)
Pehelī pothī [*in loco*].
Phaḍiyāono julam.
See Jagajjīvanadāsa Chunīlāla.
Pharo naiṉ to maro.
See Pharo.
Phula viṇanārī chhokrionī vāt.
See Flower Gatherers.
Piṅgalapraveṣa.
See Narmadāṣaṅkara Lālaṣaṅkara.
Prabodhachandrodaya nāṭaka.
See Kṛishṇa miṣra.

Prāchīna kāvya [*in loco*].
Prahlādākhyāna.
See Kālidāsa, *of Wassawad.*
Prajñāpanā.
See Kālikāchārya.
Prakaraṇa ratnākara.
See Bhīmasiṃha Māṇaka.
Prakaraṇa-saṅgraha [*in loco*].
Pramāṇa-sahasrī.
See Prayāgajī Ṭhākarsī.
Prāṇividyā.
See Edaljī Jamshedjī Khorī.
Prārthanāvalī. [*Sabhā.*
See Ahmadabad. — *Jainadharma - pravartaka*
Pratāpa nāṭaka.
See Gaṇapatarāma Rājārāma Bhaṭṭa.
Pratāpasāgara.
See Pratāpa Siṃha, *Raja of Jaipur.*
Pratidinanī prārthanāo.
See Bible.—*Appendix.*
Pratikramaṇanāṇ sūtra.
See Pratikramaṇa sūtras.
Pravachanasāroddhāra.
See Nemichandra.
Pravīṇasāgara.
See Merāmaṇajī.
Prithirāja chahuāṇ.
See Ātmārāma Keṣavajī Dvivedī.
Priyaṃvada.
See Periodical Publications.—*Bombay.*
Pūjāe ādī.
See Vīravijaya.
Pūjāsaṅgraha [*in loco*].
———
See Nāthābhāī Lalubhāī.
Punāmadhye dharmasambandhī vātchīt.
See Poona Conversations.
Punarvivāha ṣāstrasammata chhe.
See Nārāyaṇa Hemachandra.
Purātan Pārsīonī tavārīkh.
See Jalāl al-Dīn Mīrzā, *Ḳājār.*
Purushasūkta.
See Vedas.—Ṛigveda.—*Purushasūkta.*
Rābinsan Krusonī charitra.
See Defoe (D.)
Rādhājīnā tera mahīnā.
See Rādhā.
Rādhanpur svasthānano dīwānī nibandha.
See Radhanpur, *Native State of.*
Raḍvā kuṭavānī hāni-janak chāl.
See Vīrachanda Rāghavajī.
Rahbar i dīn i Zartoshtī.
See Erachjī Sohrābjī Mehrjīrāṇā.
Rāh i Pārsā.
See Sohrābjī Jamshedjī Jījībhāī.
Rājamitra nāṭaka.
See Bhīmajī Rāvajī Mahājan.
Rājā Pardesīno rās.
See Rājā Pardeṣī.
Rājapraṣnīya [*in loco*].
Rājarishi grantha.
See Nautamarāma Uttamarāma Trivedī.
Rajnagarmāṇ relno roḷ.
See Niẓām al-Dīn, *Chishtī*, called Hāmī.
Rāmacharitra.
See Hemachandra Āchārya.
Ramakaḍuṇ [*in loco*].
Rāmāṣvamedha. [*medha.*
See Purāṇas. — Padmapurāṇa. — *Rāmāṣva-*
Rāmāyaṇa.
See Girdhara.
———
See Kṛishṇadāsa.
———
See Ṣivalāla Dhaneṣvara.
———
See Vālmīki.
Rāmāyaṇanā chandrāvalā.
See Suihara Dāsa.
Rāṇak Devī.
See Anantaprasāda Trikamlāla.
Raṅgilī ne Chhabilī.
See Nagīndāsa Mañchhārāma Ghelābhāī.
Rāṇī Rūpasundarī.
See Haragovinda Dvārakādāsa Kāṇṭāwālā.
Rāṇpurnī mukhtaṣar ḥakīḳat.
See Khīmajī Premajī Mehetā.
Rāsalasnuṇ charitra.
See Johnson (S.) *LL.D.*
Rāsamālā.
See Forbes (A. K.)
Rasamañjarī
See Vālji Lakshmīrāma Dave.
Rasāyanaṣāstra sambandhī vātchīt.
See Mehrvānjī Hormasjī Mehetā.
Rasāyanavidyā.
See Roscoe (H. E)
Rasika padamālā
See Māhāsukharāma Narbherāma.
——— stavanāvalī.
See Rājendra Sūri.
Rāst dīn i Zartoshtiyān.
See Periodical Publications.—*Bombay.*
Rati-svayaṃvara.
See Kālidāsa. [*Supposititious works.*]
Ratnamālā.
See Kṛishṇajī.
Rāyapaseṇī.
See Rājapraṣnīya.
Risālah i kāmilah.
See ʻAlī Zain al-ʻĀbidīn, *Fourth Imām.*
Ṛituvarṇana [*in loco*].
Rojapāṭha.
See Viṣvanātha Khushāladāsa.
Rukmiṇīharaṇa.
See Premānanda.
Rukmiṇī vivānī chopaḍī.
See Muktānanda.
Rukshmaṇī haraṇa.
See Dāmodara Ratanṣī Somāṇī.
Rumūz i dil-khush [*in loco*].
——— ḥikmat.
See Talakchand Tārāchand.

Rūpadevajīnā garbā.
See Kālidāsa Devaṣaṅkara.
Rūvānnī chār dābāḍānī kriyā vishe.
See Ratanjī Rustamjī Kāṅgā.
——— kriyā.
See Jamshedjī Frāmjī Bachābhāī Rabāḍi.
Sābarno sākho.
See Kevaḷadāsa Amīchand.
Ṣabdārthakoṣa.
See Motīlāla Manassukharāma Shāh.
Sābhramatīmāhātmya. [*māhātmya.*
See Purāṇas. — Padmapurāna. — *Sābhramatī-*
Ṡad-dare behere tavīl.
See Ṡad-dar.
Saddharma dīpikā.
See Navīnachandra Rāya.
Sadevanta Ṣavaliṅgānī vārtā.
See Ṣadevanta.
————
See Ṣāmala Bhaṭa.
——— gāyanarūpī nāṭaka.
See Dāmodara Ratanṣī Somānī.
Sadharājesaṅgha. [*C.I.E.*
See Mahīpatrāma Rūparāma Nīlakaṇṭha,
Sadhlāṉ mānaṣ bharṣaṭ.
See Human Depravity.
Sajhāyamālā [*in loco*].
Sajhāyo [*in loco*].
Sajoḍā sukha-darṣaka nāṭaka.
See Broach.—*Ārya-hitechchhu Sabhā.*
Ṣakuntalā nāṭaka.
See Kālidāsa, *the Sanskrit poet.*
Ṣālibhadra Shāhno rās.
See Matisārajī.
Saluknī dikrinuṉ jarā kothuṉ to juvo.
See Māṇekjī Barjorjī Minuchehr Homjīnā.
Samarāditya Kevalīno rās.
See Padmavījaya.
Samavāyāṅga [*in loco*].
Sāmāyaka [*in loco*].
Samayasāra.
See Banārasī Dāsa. [Addenda.]
Sampayaneṉ lakshmivache saṃvāda.
See Dalpatrāma Ḍāhyābhāī, *Kavi, C.I.E.*
Saṃsārachopaḍī [*in loco*].
Saṃsārakoṣa.
See Ḍosābhāī Hormasjī Bāmjī.
Saṃskṛita bhāshānuṉ vyākaraṇa.
See Dhīrajrāma Dalpatrāma.
——— vyākaraṇa.
See Kṛishṇa Ṣāstrī Chipḷuṇkar.
Samudāya santanī vāṇī.
See Ṣaṅkara Haribhāī.
Samyaktva ṣalyoddhāra.
See Ātmārāmajī Ānandavijayajī. [Addenda.]
Saṃyaktvasvarūpa-stava [*in loco*].
Sanatsujātīya ākhyāna. [Brahmatīrtha.
See Manoradāsa, called Sachchidānanda
Saṅgītānubhava.
See Maulā-Bakhsh Ghishe-Khān.
Saṅgrahanī sūtra.
See Chandra Sūri.

Ṣaniṣchara devatānī kathā.
See Saniṣchara.
Ṣaṅkara Liṅgam tenī vārtā.
See Ṣaṅkara Liṅgam.
Sāṅkhyayogī bāionuṉ vartamāna.
See Nishkulānanda.
Sansár kosh.
See Saṃsārakoṣa.
Ṣāntasudhārasa.
See Vinayavijaya.
Sapentomainyusha.
See Barjorjī Erachjī Bajān. [Addenda.]
Saptamaskandha. [*kandha.*
See Purāṇas.—Bhāgavatapurāṇa.—*Saptamas-*
Saptaṣatī. [*hātmya.*
See Purāṇas.—Mārkaṇḍeyapurāṇa.—*Devīmā-*
Saptatikā.
See Chandra Mahattarāchārya.
Ṣarīra sukhadarṣaka.
See Raṇchhoḍlāla Viṭhṭhaladāsa.
Ṣārīravidyā.
See Dhīrajrāma Dalpatrāma.
Sar-nāmah i rāz i yazdānī.
See Bahrām Rustam Khusrau.
Sarva lokane sādu vadhāmaṇī.
See Good Tidings.
Sarvopayogī nuskhā saṅgraha.
See Sohrābjī Jamshedjī Reader.
Sasti sukhaḍī ne Siddhapuranī yātrā.
See Dāmodara Keṣavajī Ṭhakkar. [Addenda.]
Ṣataka.
See Devendra Sūri.
Sātamī chopaḍī.
See Hope (T. C.)
Sāt avatāranī Sadevanta Sāvaliṅgānī vārtā.
See Lālā Bāroṭ.
Ṣat dharmano mārga.
See Path.
Satī Rāṇak Devī. [denda.]
See Bhagavānlāla Bāpālāla Saiyaḍh. [Ad-
Ṣatruñjaya tīrthamālā.
See Ṣatruñjaya.
Sat-saī.
See Vṛinda.
Saṭṭā pariṇāmadarṣaka.
See Ratanṣī Sāmajī.
Ṣat tathā aṣatnī parīkshā.
See Hindus.
Satyodaya.
See Periodical Publications.—*Surat.*
Sāvakī māthakī chhokrāṉo upar padtāṉ duḥkha.
See Mañchhārāma Ghelābhāī.
Savā-so gāthānuṉ stavana.
See Yaṣovijaya.
Sawāl jawābnī pehelī pothī.
See Catechism.
Ṣekspīr kathāsamāja. }
——— nāṭaka. }
See Shakspere (W.)
Ṣerṣaṭānuṉ varṇana.
See Ṣersaṭā.

Seṭh Kayavanuā Shāhno rās.
See JAYATASĪ.
Shaḍaṣīti.
See JINAVALLABHA.
Shashṭi ṣataka.
See NEMICHANDRA.
Siddhāchalanuṇ varṇana. [GANLĀLA.
See DĪPACHAND DEVACHAND, and JAVERĪ CHHA-
Siddhānta-sāra.
See MAṆILĀLA NABHUBHĀĪ DVIVEDĪ.
Sidhilipī trikoṇamiti.
See JERVIS (G. R.)
Ṣīkhāmaṇaṇī nīti.
See BAHMANJĪ ṬEHMULJĪ PRABHU.
Ṣikshāmālā.
See JERVIS (G. R.)
Ṣikshāpatri.
See SAHAJĀNANDA SVĀMĪ.
Ṣilpakarma.
See HARAGOVINDA AMATHĀRĀMA JOṢĪ.
Sīmandhara-stavana. }
——— vijñapti. }
See YAṢOVIJAYA.
Sīmantinī ākhyāna.
See MAYO ṢIVADĀSA.
Singhāsan Battīsī.
See VIKRAMĀDITYA, *King of Ujjayinī*.
Sitam i ḥasrat.
See EDALJĪ FRĀMJĪ ḌHOṆḌĪ.
Sītāsvayamvara.
See KĀLIDĀṢA, *of Wassawad*. [Addenda.]
Sitāyish-nāmuṇ.
See SITĀYISH-NĀMAH.
Ṣivapurāṇa.
See PURĀṆAS.—*Ṣivapurāṇa*.
Siyāvash-nāmuṇ.
See RUSTAM PESHOTAN, *Mobed*.
Skandapurāṇārthaprakāṣa.
See PURĀṆĀS.—*Skandapurāṇa*.
Ṣlokā lāvaṇio ane garbāo.
See SAHAJĀNANDA SVĀMĪ.
Ṣlokā-saṅgraha [*in loco*].
Somapradoshanī kathā.
See MAYO ṢIVADĀSA.
Ṣravaṇapitṛibhakti nāṭaka.
See BHOGĪLĀLA MAHĀNANDA BHAṬṬA.
Ṣrīchand Kevalīno rās.
See JÑĀNAVIMALA SŪRI.
Ṣrī Jīvanalālajī Mahārājanuṇ janmacharitra.
See GIRDHARALĀLA HARAKISANDĀSA.
Ṣrīmadbhāgavatanī kathāno sāra.
See PURĀṆAS.—*Bhāgavatapurāṇa*.
Ṣrīmukhasiddhānta.
See SAHAJĀNANDA SVĀMĪ.
Ṣriṅgāradarṣana.
See PREMAJĪ KHETASIṂHA KAJARIYĀ.
Ṣriṅgāravairāgya-taraṅgiṇī.
See SOMAPRABHĀCHĀRYA.
Ṣrīpālacharitra. }
——— Rājāno rās. }
See VINAYAVIJAYA.
Sthānāṅga [*in loco*].
Strībodha.
See PERIODICAL PUBLICATIONS.—*Bombay*.
Strī ganeānt mālā [*in loco*].
Strī manorañjaka garbāvalī.
See GARBĀVALĪ.
Strīnītidharma.
See VIṬHṬHALADĀSA DHANJĪBHĀĪ.
——— darṣaka.
See KṚIPĀṢAṄKARA DOLATRĀMA TRAVĀḌĪ.
Strī upayogī sūchanā.
See WELL WISHER.
Subhāshita saṅgraha.
See PURUSHOTTAMA MAYĀRĀMA PAṆḌYĀ.
Suchīnibandha.
See UTTAMARĀMA DURLABHARĀMA.
Ṣuḍābahoterī.
See ṢĀMALA BHAṬA.
Sudāmacharitra.
See PREMĀNANDA.
Sudhāsañchita.
See REVĀṢAṄKARA JAYAṢAṄKARA.
Sujña Gokulajī Sampattirāma Jhālā.
See MANASSUKHARĀMA SŪRYARĀMA TRIPĀṬHI.
Sukanāvalī.
See SĀṄKALEṢVARA CHHAGANLĀLA DAVE.
Sūktamuktāvalī.
See KEṢARA VIMALA.
Sumati Nāgila charitra.
See SUMATI NĀGILA.
Sundara Kāmdārnī vārtā.
See SUNDARA KĀMDĀR.
——— strīvilāsa.
See RAṆCHHODLĀLA MOTĪRĀMA.
Suratasaṅgrāma.
See NṚISIṂHA MEHETĀ.
Surekhā-haraṇa.
See VĪRAJĪ. [Addenda.]
Sureṣa-charitra.
See OṂ, *pseud*.
Sūtrakṛitāṅga [*in loco*].
Svābhāvika dharma.
See DHARMASAṂṢODHAKA, *pseud*.
Svadeṣa hitadarṣaka.
See GIRDHARALĀLA HARIVALLABHADĀSA and KEṢAVALĀLA RAṆCHHODDĀSA JOṢĪ.
——— vatsala.
See PERIODICAL PUBLICATIONS.—*Bombay*.
Svasthāna Rādhanpurno phojdārī nibandha.
See RADHANPUR, *Native State of*.
Ṣvetāṣvataropanishadnā sāra.
See UPANISHADS.
Tafsīr i gāh i gāsānī.
See PESHOTAN BAHRĀMJĪ SAÑJĀNĀ.
Taḳwiyat i dīn i Mazdiasnāṇ.
See MUḤAMMAD, *the Prophet*.
Tārā.
See TAYLOR (M.)
Tāraṇa.
See SALVATION.
Tasbīr i khūbī.
See PESTANJĪ FRĀMJĪ VELĀTĪ.

Taubat al Naṣūḥ.
See NAẔĪR AḤMAD, *Khān Bahādur.*
Tavārīkh i Hakhāmaniyān.
See BARJORJĪ PĀLANJĪ DEṢĀI and PĀLANJĪ BARJORJĪ DEṢĀI. [Addenda.]
——— ḳadīm Irān.
See MALCOLM (*Sir* J.)
——— mulūk i tavā'if i Zartoshtiyān.
See JAMSHEDJĪ PĀLAṆJĪ KĀPAḌIĀ.
——— Sāsāniyān.
See BARJORJĪ PĀLANJĪ DEṢĀI and PĀLANJĪ BARJORJĪ DEṢĀI.
Tetrīṣāno taḍāko.
See PRABHĀṢAṄKARA ṢĀMALAJĪ.
Thuḷibhadranī ṣiyaḷvela.
See VĪRAVIJAYA.
Ṭoḷak nibandha.
See UTTAMARĀMA DURLABHARĀMA.
Torānī 'ishkī lāvaṇio.
See LAKSHMAṆA DĀSA. [Addenda.]
Tridampati varṇana.
See ANANTAPRASĀDA TRIKAMLĀLA.
Trijī chopaḍī.
See HOPE (T. C.)
Trilokanī vāt.
See THREE WORLDS.
Udyamakarma saṃvāda.
See ṢĀMALA BHAṬA.
Umeṭānāṇ ḍhāḷīyāṇ.
See UMEṬĀ.
Upamā saṅgraha.
See JASVAT SIṂHA, *Maharaja.*
Upamiti bhavaprapañcha.
See HAṂSARATNA MUNI.
Upayogī jñānanī pustakasamūha.
See ACADEMIES, *etc.*—London.—*Society for the Diffusion of Useful Knowledge.*
Uttama kapoḷ Karsandās Muljī charitra.
See MAHĪPĀTRĀMA RŪPARĀMA NĪLAKAṆṬHA, *C.I.E.*
Vachanāmṛita.
See SAHAJĀNANDA SVĀMĪ.
Vachanavidhi.
See NISHKULĀNANDA.
Vāejo.
See RATANJĪ RUSTAMJĪ KĀṄGĀ.
Vaidakno sārasaṅgraha.
See JAGAJJĪVANA DALPATRĀMA.
Vaidyāmṛita.
See MOREṢVARA, *Son of Māṇaka Bhaṭṭa.*
Vaidyaratnākara [*in loco*].
Vaidyasārasaṅgraha.
See RAGHUNĀTHA ṢĀSTRĪ DĀNTYE and KṚISHṆA ṢĀSTRĪ BHĀṬAVAḌEKAR.
Vairāgya.
See NĀRĀYAṆA HEMACHANDRA.
——— bodha.
See HĪRĀCHAND KĀNJĪ.
——— ṣataka.
See BHARTṚIHARI.
Vallabhakṛita kāvya.
See VALLABHARĀMA SURYARĀMA VYĀSA.
Vanarāja Chāvaḍo.
See MAHĪPATRĀMA RŪPARĀMA NĪLAKAṆṬHA, *C.I.E.*
Vandidād.
See ZAND-AVASTĀ.
Varsādnī vadhāmṇī [*in loco*].
Vāstusāra.
See MAṆḌANA, *Son of Kshetra, of Chittor.*
Vātchītuā ṣehalāṇ vākyo. [*Schools.*
See BOMBAY, *Presidency of.*—*Anglo-Vernacular*
Vedadharma.
See KARSANDĀS MULJĪ.
Vedāntaprakāṣa.
See PERIODICAL PUBLICATIONS.—*Bombay.*
Vedārthoddhāra.
See BHĪMĀCHĀRYA JHAḶKĪKAR and RĀJĀRĀMA GAṆEṢA BOḌAS. [Addenda].
Vedastuti.
See PURĀṆAS.—Bhāgavatapurāṇa.—*Vedastuti.*
Vedokta saṃskāra-prakāṣa.
See BĀḶĀJĪ VIṬHṬHALA GĀṈVASKAR.
Vendidad.
See ZAND-AVASTĀ.
Veṇīsaṃhāra nāṭaka. [LAKSHMAN.
See NĀRĀYAṆA BHAṬṬA, called MṚIGARĀJA-
Vidhipaksha gachchhīya ṣrāvakasya . . . pañcha pratikramaṇa vidhi.
See PRATIKRAMAṆA SŪTRAS.
Viduranīti.
See MAHĀBHĀRATA.—*Viduranīti.*
Vidyābhyāsanī pothī.
See VIDYĀBHYĀSA.
Vidyāmitra.
See PERIODICAL PUBLICATIONS.—*Bombay.*
Vidyārthīono madadgār.
See HOWARD (E. J.)
Vijaya Rājendra janmacharitra.
See LALLU VALYAM.
Vijiyā vaidhavya duḥkhadarṣaka nāṭaka.
See JEṢHAṄGBHĀĪ TRIKAMDĀSA PAṬEL.
Vikramorvaṣī troṭaka.
See KĀLIDĀSA, *the Sanskrit poet.*
Vilāyatuā kavīṣvaro.
See KĀVASJĪ NAVAROJĪ VESUWĀLĀ.
Viṃṣati Viharamāṇ Jina stavana.
See DEVACHANDRA.
Vīrastuti.
See YAṢOVIJAYA.
Vishayīṇ guru vishe nibandha.
See DALPATRĀMA AMBĀRĀMA.
Vispard. }
Vispered. }
See ZAND-AVASTĀ.
Vivekachūḍāmaṇi.
See ṢAṄKARA ĀCHĀRYA.
Vivekasāra.
See BALARĀMA, *Sādhu.*
———
See HĪRAJĪ HAṂSARĀJA.
Viveka vaṇajhāro.
See PREMĀNANDA.
Vyādhi-rodha vidyā.
See MAṆIṢAṄKARA GOVINDAJĪ.

Vyākaraṇa.
See HORMASJĪ KHURSHEDJĪ.
Vyutpattiprakāṣa.
See MAHĪPATRĀMA RŪPARĀMA NĪLAKAṆṬHA, *C.I.E.*
Wilsan-viraha.
See BAHRĀMJĪ MEHRVĀNJĪ MALABĀRĪ.
Yaçna.
See ZAND-AVASTĀ.
Yantraṣāstranān mūla.
See KAHĀNDĀSA MAÑCHHĀRĀMA.
Yazdagirdī tārīkh.
See KHURSHEDJĪ RUSTAMJĪ KĀMĀ.
Yogadṛishṭi.
See YAṢOVIJAYA.
Yogavāṣishṭha [*in loco*].
Yūrop . . . tarafnī musā firīnī nondh patrikā.
See FRĀMJĪ DĪNSHĀJĪ PIṬĪṬ.
Yūsufnuṇ charitra.
See JOSEPH, *the Patriarch.*
Yuvarājayātrā.
See BULĀKĪ CHAKUBHĀĪ.
Ẓālim zor.
See EDALJĪ JAMSHEDJĪ KHORĪ.
Zartosht dharmanīti.
See NĀRĀYAṆA HEMACHANDRA.
Zartoshtī abhyāsa.
See KHURSHEDJĪ RUSTAMJĪ KĀMĀ.
——— dharmabodha.
See FRĀMJĪ MINUCHEHRJĪ JĀMĀSP ĀSĀJĪNĀ.
——— dharmaṣikshaka.
See EDALJĪ KERSĀSPJĪ ĀṆṬIYĀ.
——— Dīnnī Kholkarnārī Maṇḍalīno hevāl.
See ACADEMIES, *etc.* — Bombay. — *Zartoshtī Dīnnī Kholkarnārī Maṇḍalī.*
——— lokonāṇ dharmapustako.
See SOHRĀBJĪ SHĀPURJĪ BANGĀLĪ.
——— ṭolāno vaḍo koṇ.
See RATANJĪ RUSTAMJĪ KĀṄGĀ.

SUBJECT-INDEX

ARTS.

Daskat shikshak. Ādarjī Kāvasjī Master.
Deṣī kārīgarīne uttejana. Encouragement.
Gujarātī navo khard̤o. Gujarātī navo khard̤o.
Jadukapaṭa-prakāṣa. Ichchhāṣaṅkara Amathārāma Vyāsa.
Mādigān i chatrang. Mādigān i chatrang.
Sarvopayogī nuskhā saṅgraha. Sohrābjī Jamshedjī Reader.
Suchīuibaudha. Uttamarāma Durlabharāma.
Vāstusāra. Maṇḍana, *Son of Kshetra.*

ASTROLOGY and DIVINATION.

Bhād̤alī-mata. Bhad̤alī.
Sukanāvalī. Sāṅkaleṣvara Chhaganlāla Dave.

ASTRONOMY.

Jyotishasāra. Ṣukadeva.
Jyotisha vishe. Pītāmbaradāsa Tribhuvanadāsa Mehetā.

BIOGRAPHY.

Akbar-charitra. Mahīpatrāma Rūparāma Nīlakaṇṭha.
Anandibai Joshi. Ānandībāī Joṣī.
Bhagavataprasādākhyāna. Koṭhārī Govardhana.
Bhaktachintāmaṇi. Nishkulānanda.
Charitramālā. Nagīndāsa Mañchhārāma Ghelābhāī.
Chitrāvalī. Keṣavalāla Harivithṭhaladāsa.
Dārāb-nāmuṇ. Abū Ṭāhir, *Tarsūsī.*
Gauhar i zindagī. Nasīm.
Jahāngīr-nāmuṇ. Jahāngīr.
Jamshed homa ane ātash. Jīvanajī Jamshedjī Modī.
Jīvanacharitra. Bhagubhāī Rāmaṣaṅkara Jānī.
Kabīr matadarṣaka grantha. Vāljī Bechar.
Karsandās Muljī charitra. Mahīpatrāma Rūparāma Nīlakaṇṭha.
Kavi Nāgjīnūṇ janmacharitra. Devajī Ukābhāī Makvāṇā.
Kolambasno vrittānta. Robertson (W.) *D.D.*
Malli Jina māhātmya. Ahmadabad.—*Jainadharma-pravartaka Sabhā.*
Ṣrī Jīvanalālajī Mahārājanun janmacharitra. Girdharalāla Harakisandāsa.
Sujña Gokulajī Sampattirāma Jhālā. Manassukharāma Sūryarāma Tripāṭhī.
Vijaya Rājendra janmacharitra. Lallu Valyam.

CASTE.

Anāvil gṛihasthomāṇ thayelā navā niyamo. Hararāya Bāpubhāī Desāī.
Bhāṭiā kulotpatti grantha. Chaturbhuja Vāljī Jerājānī.
Jātibheda ane bhojanavichāra. Nārāyaṇa Hemachandra.
Jñāti-nibandha. Dalpatrāma Ḍāhyābhāī, *Kavi.*
Kapol utpattinī kathā. Parsotam Mādhavajī Mehetā.
Nyātīvara. Prāṇajīvanadāsa Māṇeklāla.
Ṭolak-nibandha. Uttamarāma Durlabharāma.

CHRONOLOGY.

Yazdagirdī tārīkh. Khurshedjī Rustamjī Kāmā.

DICTIONARIES, VOCABULARIES, and GLOSSARIES.

Apabhrashṭaṣabdaprakāṣa. Prabhākara Rāmachandra Paṇḍita.
Gujarātī chothī chopaḍīnā artha. Fakīrbhāī Kāṣīdāsa.
———koshāvalī. Hīrāchand Kānjī.
———pehelī chopaḍīnā artha. Hope (T. C.)
———ṣabdārtha kosha. Motīlāla Manassukharāma Shāh.
Narmakoṣa. Narmadāṣaṅkara Lālaṣaṅkara.
Saṃsārakoṣa. Ḍosābhāī Hormasjī Bāmjī.

DIRECTORIES.

Kāṭhiāvāḍ gāiḍ. Rāvajī Rāmajī Sāvant.
Pārsīonuṇ list. Mancherjī Hoshangjī Jāgos.

DIVINATION. See ASTROLOGY.

DRAMA.

Āryaprajā. Bhagavānlāla Bāpālāla.
Bālavidhavā Rūpasundarī. Nagīndāsa Mañchhārāma Ghelabhāī.
Bāṇāsura madamardana. Ranchhoḍbhāī Udayarāma.
Chāmparāja Hāḍo ne Sonarāṇī. Vāghjī Āṣārāma Ojhā.
Chandrasiṃha Dīpamaṇi nāṭaka. Rūpāṇī Bhīmajī Kālidāsa.
Dhanā Sālibhadra. Lālchand Lalubhāī.
Duniyā-darpan. Karam ʿAlī Rahīm, *Nānjiānī.*

Gul ane Bulbul. Edaljī Dādābhāī Mistrī.
Harūn nāṭaka. Harūn al Rashīd, *Caliph*
Homlo Hāū. Nānābhāī Rustamjī Rāṇīnā.
Jāl ane Rodābe. Jāl ane Rodābe.
Jālem jor. Edaljī Jamshedjī Khorī.
Jayakumārīvijaya nāṭaka. Raṇchhoḍbhāī Udayarāma.
Kāḷāṇ meṇḍhāṇ. Nānābhāī Rustamjī Rāṇīnā.
Kamalā duḥkhadarṣaka nāṭaka. Keṣavarāma Viṣvanātha Joṣī.
Kanjusnā karmanī kāhanī. Ardsher Bahrāmjī Paṭel.
Karuṇāvajrāyudha nāṭaka. Bāḷachandrāchārya.
Kumitra darpaṇa. Kanhaiyālāla Motīlāla Munshī.
Lailā Majnūn. Lailā Majnūn.
Lalitā duḥkhadarṣaka. Raṇchhoḍbhāī Udayarāma.
Mālatīmādhava. Bhavabhūti.
Malhār Rāva Mahārāja nāṭaka. Nārāyaṇa Bāpujī Kāniṭkar.
Manaharamālā. Prāṇalāla Ṣambhulāla Deṣāī.
Nanda Rājā ane satī Sulochanā. Nanda Rājā.
Narasiṃha Mehetānuṇ māhmeruṇ tathā huṇḍī. Amṛitalāla Nārāyaṇadāsa Laherī.
Nārasiṃhāvatāra nāṭaka. Dattātraya.
Nindā khānuṇ. Kaikhusrau Navarojī Kābrājī.
Noshīrwān i Samangān. Nasarvānjī Rustamjī Vāchhā.
Okhāharaṇa nāṭaka. Ushā.
Prabodhachandrodaya nāṭaka. Krishṇamiṣra.
Pratāpa nāṭaka. Gaṇapatarāma Rājārāma Bhaṭṭa.
Rājamitra nāṭaka. Bhīmajī Rāvajī Mahājan.
Raṅgilī ne Chhabilī. Nagīndāsa Mañchhārāma Ghelābhāī.
Rukshmiṇī haraṇa. Dāmodara Ratanṣī Somāṇī.
Sadevanta Sāvaliṅgānī gāyanarūpī nāṭaka. Dāmodara Ratanṣī Somāṇī.
Sajoḍā sukha-darṣaka nāṭaka. Broach.—*Āryahitechchhu Sabhā.*
Ṣakuntalā nāṭaka. Kālidāsa, *the Sanskrit poet.*
Sāvakī māthakī chhokrāṇo upar paḍtāṇ duḥkha. Mañchhārāma Ghelābhāī.
Ṣekspīr kathāsamāja. } Shakspere (W.)
——— nāṭaka. }
Sitam i hasrat. Edaljī Frāmjī Ḍhoṇḍī.
Ṣravaṇapitṛibhakti nāṭaka. Bhogīlāla Mahānanda Bhaṭṭa.
Veṇīsaṃhāra nāṭaka. Nārāyaṇa Bhaṭṭa, called Mṛigarājalakshman.
Vijiyā vaidhavya duḥkhadarṣaka nāṭaka. Jeshangbhāī Trikamdāsa Paṭel. [poet.
Vikramorvaṣī troṭaka. Kālidāsa, *the Sanskrit*

ETHICS.

Andaraz i Ātarpāt. Ādarbād Mārāspand.
——— Khusro Kovātāt. Khusrau Noshīrwān, *King of Persia.*
Āryadharmanīti. Nārāyaṇa Hemachandra.
Ganj i shāegān. Buzurgmihr.
Kehevat mālā. Nathuṣaṅkara Udayaṣaṅkara Dholkiyā.
Nītiṣataka. Bhartṛihari.
Nītivachana. Karsandās Mūljī.
Nītivinoda. Bahrāmjī Mehrvānjī Malabārī.
Pand-nāmah i Ādarbād Mārāspand. Ādarbād Mārāspand.
Ṣikhāmaṇanī nīti. Bahmanjī Ṭehmuljī Prabhu.
Viduranīti. Mahābhārata.—*Viduranīti.*

GEOGRAPHY.

Adhidvīpano nakso. Adhidvīpa.
Bhūgoḷajñāna. Bhūgoḷajñāna.
Bhūgoḷano upayoga karvānī rītino grantha. Harilāla Mohanalala.
Bhūgoḷanuṇ varṇana. Candy (T.)
Bhūgoḷavidyā. Hope (T. C.).
Hindustānanī bhūgoḷa. Ḍāhyābhāī Ambārāma.
Jambudvīpano nakso. Jambudvīpa.

GLOSSARIES. See DICTIONARIES.

GRAMMARS.

Aṅgrejī ane Gujarātī pustaka. Mehrvānjī Hormasjī Mehetā and Navarojī Rustamjī Lāḍ.
Āṅknī chopaḍī. Āṅknī chopaḍī.
Gujarātī bhāshāmāṇ vākya rachanānā niyamo. Bhāīdāsa Dayārāma.
——— bhāshāno itihāsa. Vrajalāla Kālidāsa Ṣāstrī.
——— bhāshānuṇ laghu vyākaraṇa. Taylor (J. van S.)
——————— navuṇ vyākaraṇa. Mahīpatrāma Rūparāma Nīlakaṇṭha.
——————— vyākaraṇa. Hope (T. C.)
——————— Taylor (J. van S.)
Ingliṣ vyākaraṇanī mūḷapīṭhikā. Howard (E. I.)
Mugdhāvabodha auktika. Mugdhāvabodha auktika.
Narmavyākaraṇa. Narmadāṣaṅkara Lālaṣaṅkara.
Saṃskṛita bhāshānuṇ vyākaraṇa. Dhīrajrāma Dalpatrāma.
——— vyākaraṇa. Krishṇa Ṣāstrī Chipḷuṇkar.
Vyākaraṇa. Hormasjī Khurshedjī.
Vyutpattiprakāṣa. Mahīpatrāma Rūparāma Nīlakaṇṭha.

HINDU PHILOSOPHY.

Bandīnuṇ ākhyāna. Manoradāsa, called Sachchidānanda Brahmatīrtha.
Bhavavairāgyaṣataka. Bhavavairāgyaṣataka.
Maṅgaḷavichāra. Maṅgaḷā Gaurī.
Pañchīkaraṇa. Rāmadāsa Svāmī, *of Haidarabad.*
Paramapada-bodhinī. Nathurāma Pītāmbarajī Rāvaḷ.
Rājarishi grantha. Nautamarāma Uttamarāma Trivedī.
Sanatsujātīya ākhyāna. Manoradāsa, called Sachchidānanda Brahmatīrtha
Siddhānta-sāra. Maṇilāla Nabhubhāī Dvivedī.
Vivekachūḍāmaṇi. Ṣaṅkara Āchārya.
Yogadrishṭi. Yaṣovijaya.
Yogavāṣishṭha. Yogavāṣishṭha.

HISTORY.

Bahman-nāmuṇ. BAHMAN ASFANDIYĀR, *King of Persia.*
Barjo-nāmuṇ. MĀṆEKJĪ BARJORJĪ MINUCHEHR HOMJĪNĀ.
Bharatakhaṇḍano itihāsa. MAHĪPATRĀMA RŪPARĀMA NĪLAKAṆṬHA.
Chuṇṭī kāhāḍelāṇ lakhāṇo. SOHRĀBJĪ SHĀPURJĪ BAṄGĀLĪ.
Dārāb-nāmuṇ. ABŪ ṬĀHIR, *Tarsūsī.*
Dīnbeh Mazdayasnī. JAMSHEDJĪ FRĀMJĪ BACHĀBHĀĪ RABĀḌĪ.
Farāmurz-nāmuṇ. ABŪ ṬĀHIR, *Tarsūsī.*
Fasād i February. DIL-KHUSH, *pseud.*
Gāyakavāḍa Mahārājanā itihāsa. MOHANALĀLA KUVERA TRAVĀḌĪ.
Gohil rājyano itihāsa. HARAJĪVANADĀSA GOVINDARĀMA and DĀMAJĪ MAKANDĀSA.
Gujarāt deṣano itihāsa. GOPĀLAJĪ TRIBHUVANADĀSA.
—————— MAGANLĀLA VAKHATCHAND.
——— Rājasthān. KĀLIDĀSA DEVAṢAṄKARA PAṆḌYĀ.
Gujarātno bāḷabodhaka itihāsa. MAHĪPATRĀMA RŪPARĀMA NĪLAKAṆṬHA.
———— itihāsa. EDALJĪ DOSĀBHĀĪ.
Gulzār i ʿālam. PESTANJĪ FRĀMJĪ VELATE.
Hind Rājasthān. AMṚITALĀLA GOVARDHANADĀSA SHĀH.
Hindustānanā itihāsano saṃkshepa. INDIA.
Hindustānano itihāsa. MORRIS (H.)
———— saṃkshipta itihāsa. INDIA.
Hindusthānamāṇhel Ingliṣnā rājyano itihāsa. BĀLA GAṄGĀDHARA ṢĀSTRĪ JĀMBHEKAR.
Hindusthānano itihāsa. ELPHINSTONE (*Hon.* M.)
Irānnī mukhtaṣar tavārīkh. BAHMANJĪ BAHRĀMJĪ PAṬEL.
Jahāṅgīr-nāmuṇ. JAHĀNGĪR.
Kadīm nakṣh i Irān. KĀVASJĪ DĪNSHĀH KIASH.
Mevāḍnī jāh o jalālī. VIṬHṬHALADĀSA DHANJĪBHĀĪ.
Pārsīprakāṣa. BAHMANJĪ BAHRĀMJĪ PAṬEL.
Purātan Pārsīonī tavārīkh. JALĀL al-DĪN MĪRZĀ, *Kājār.*
Rāsamālā. FORBES (A. K.)
Ratnamālā. KṚISHṆAJĪ.
Takwiyat i dīn i Mazdiasnāṇ. MUHAMMAD, *the Prophet.*
Tasbīr i khūbī. PESTANJĪ FRĀMJĪ VELĀTE.
Tavārīkh i Hakhāmaniyān. BARJORJĪ PĀLANJĪ DEṢĀĪ and PĀLANJĪ BARJORJĪ DEṢĀĪ.
———— kadīm Irān. MALCOLM (*Sir* J.)
———— mulūk i tavāʾif i Zartoshtiyān. JAMSHEDJĪ PĀLANJĪ KĀPAḌIĀ.
———— Sāsāniyān. BARJORJĪ PĀLANJĪ DEṢĀĪ and PĀLANJĪ BARJORJĪ DEṢĀĪ.
Vanarāja Chāvaḍo. MAHĪPATRĀMĀ RŪPARĀMA NĪLAKAṆṬHA.

JAIN LITERATURE.

Āchārāṅga. ĀCHĀRĀṄGA.
Adhyātmakalpadruma. MUNISUNDARA SŪRI.
Adhyatmamata-parīkshā. YAṢOVIJAYA.
Adhyātmaprakaraṇa-saṅgraha. HUKM MUNIJĪ.
Adhyātmasāra. YAṢOVIJAYA.
———— praṣnottara. KUNVAR VIJAYAJĪ.
Āgamasāra. DEVACHANDAJĪ.
Anuyogadvāra. ANUYOGADVĀRA.
Ashṭāpadajī bimba pratishṭhā. BHŪRĀBHĀĪ BEHECHAR JOṢĪ.
Ashṭotrī sanātra mahotsava. PURUSHOTTAMA KAKAL.
Ātmabodha ane jīvanī utpatti. ĀTMABODHA.
Ātmarañjana. ĀTMARAÑJANA.
Bandhasvāmitva. DEVENDRA SŪRI.
Bhagavatī-sūtra. BHAGAVATĪ-SŪTRA.
Bhaktāmara-stotra. MĀNATUṄGĀCHĀRYA.
Bhramavidhvaṃsana. JITĀMALA SVĀMĪ.
Bibadha ratan prakāṣa. SAUBHĀGAMĀLAJĪ.
Charitra-saṅgraha. CHARITRA SAṄGRAHA.
Chaturviṃṣati Jina stavana. DEVACHANDRA.
Chovīsa Jina stuti. ĀNANDA GHANA.
Chovīsīnāṇ stavana. YAṢOVIJAYA.
Daivasika tatha rāī pratikramaṇādi mūlasūtra. PRATIKRAMAṆA SŪTRAS.
Dhammil Kumārno rās. VĪRAVIJAYA.
Dharmatattva-bhāskara. NĀRĀYAṆA HĪRĀCHAND KĀNŪNĪ.
Dilkhush stavanāvalī. SĀṄKAḶCHAND MAHĀSUKHARĀMA.
Dravyaguṇa paryāyano rās. YAṢOVIJAYA.
Goḍi Pārṣvanāthanā ḍhāliyāṇ. VĪRAVIJAYA.
Jaina bālajñāna subodha. KEṢAVALĀLA ṢIVARĀMA.
Jainadharma dilkhush stavanāvalī. HARAKISANDĀSA HARAJĪVANADĀSA.
———— gyān-pradīpaka. JAINADHARMA.
———— jñānaprakāṣaka. JAINADHARMA.
———— prakāṣa. PERIODICAL PUBLICATIONS. *Bhaunagar.*
———— pravartaka Sabhā. AHMADABAD.—*Jainadharma-pravartaka Sabhā.*
———— sārasaṅgraha. GHELĀBHAI LĪLĀDHARA.
———— siddhāntasāra. JAINADHARMA-SIDDHĀNTA.
Jaina kāvyaprakāṣa. BHĪMASIṂHA MĀṆAKA.
—— kāvyasaṅgraha. LĀBHAVIJAYA, *Pandit.*
—— kāvya sārasaṅgraha. NĀTHĀBHĀĪ LALUBHĀĪ.
—— matanī parīkshāno pratyuttara. CHUNĪLĀLA JAYACHAND.
—— prabodha. ĀNANDAJĪ KHETAṢĪ.
—— prārthanāmālā. AHMADABAD.—*Jainadharma-pravartaka Sabhā.*
—— Rāmāyaṇa. HEMACHANDRA ĀCHĀRYA.
—— ṣāstra kathāsaṅgraha. JAINAṢĀSTRA.
—— vṛitta ṣikshāpatrī. JAINAVṚITTA.
—— viveka vāṇī. GHELĀBHĀĪ LĪLĀDHARA.
Jinastuti. SOBHANA.
Jīvābhigama. JĪVĀBHIGAMA.
Jīvavichāra-prakaraṇa. ṢĀNTI SŪRI.
Jñānaprakāṣa prakaraṇa-saṅgraha. HUKM MUNIJĪ.
Kalpasūtrasya bālāvabodha. RĀJENDRA SŪRI.
Kalyāṇa mandira stotra. KUMUDACHANDRA.
Karakaṇḍū ādik chār pratyek Buddha rās. SAMAYASUNDARA UPĀDHYĀYAJĪ.
Karmastava. KARMASTAVA.
Karmavipāka. DEVENDRA SŪRI.
Lokāgachchhīya ṣrāvakasya pratikramaṇasūtra. KALYĀṆACHANDAJĪ JAYACHANDAJĪ.

Lokanāla-dvatrimṣikā. LOKANĀLA.
Mahāvīra Jinastuti. YAṢOVIJAYA.
Maṅgalakalaṣa kumārno rās. DĪPTIVIJAYA.
Mohoṭī pūjāsaṅgraha. NĀTHĀBHĀĪ LALUBHĀĪ.
Mohoṭuṇ sajhāyamālā saṅgraha. SAJHĀYAMĀLĀ.
Mokshamālā. RĀJYACHANDRA.
Navatattva-prakaraṇa.. NAVATATTVA-PRAKARAṆA.
Nayachakrasāra. DEVACHANDRA.
Pañcha pratikramaṇādi sūtrāṇi. PRATIKRAMAṆA SŪTRAS.
Pāṇḍavacharitra. DEVAPRABHU SŪRI.
Pannavaṇā. KĀLIKĀCHĀRYA.
Pāṇtriṣa bolno thokḍo. PĀṆTRIṢA BOL.
Prajñāpanā. KĀLIKĀCHĀRYA.
Prakaraṇa ratnākara. BHĪMASIṂHA MĀṆAKA.
Prakaraṇa-saṅgraha. PRAKARAṆA-SAṄGRAHA.
Prārthanāvalī. AHMADABAD.—*Jainadharma-pravartaka Sabhā.*
Pratikramaṇanāṇ sūtra. PRATIKRAMAṆA SŪTRAS.
Pravachanasāroddhāra. NEMICHANDRA.
Pūjāe ādī. VĪRAVIJAYA.
Pūjāsaṅgraha. PŪJĀSAṄGRAHA.
———— NĀTHĀBHĀĪ LALUBHĀĪ.
Rājā Pardeṣīno rās. RĀJĀ PARDEṢĪ.
Rājapraṣnīya. RĀJAPRAṢNĪYA.
Rasika stavanāvalī. RĀJENDRA SURI.
Rāyapaseṇī. RĀJAPRAṢNĪYA.
Sajhāyamālā. SAJHĀYAMĀLĀ.
Sajhāyo. SAJHĀYO.
Samavāyāṅga. SAMAVĀYĀṄGA.
Sāmāyaka. SĀMĀYAKA.
Samayasāra. BANĀRASĪ DĀSA.
Samyaktva ṣalyoddhāra. ATMĀRĀMAJĪ ĀNANDAVIJAYAJĪ.
Samyaktvasvarūpa-stava. SAMYAKTVASVARŪPA-STAVA.
Saṅgrahaṇī sūtra. CHANDRA SŪRI.
Ṣāntasudhārasa. VINAYAVIJAYA.
Saptatikā. CHANDRA MAHATTARĀCHĀRYA.
Ṣataka. DEVENDRA SŪRI.
Ṣatruñjaya tīrthamālā. ṢATRUÑJAYA.
Savā-so gāthānuṇ stavana. YAṢOVIJAYA.
Seṭh Kayavannā Shāhno rās. JAYATASĪ.
Shaḍaṣīti. JINAVALLABHA.
Shashṭi ṣataka. NEMICHANDRA.
Siddhāchalanuṇ varṇana. DĪPACHAND DEVACHAND, and JAVERĪ CHHAGANLĀLA.
Sīmandhara-stavana. } YAṢOVIJAYA.
————vijñapti. }
Ṣrīpālacharitra. } VINAYAVIJAYA.
———Rājāno rās. }
Sthānāṅga. STHĀNĀṄGA.
Sūktamuktāvalī. KEṢARA VIMALA.
Sūtrakṛitāṅga. SŪTRAKṚITĀṄGA.
Thuḷibhadranī siyaḷvela. VĪRAVIJAYA.
Umeṭānāṇ ḍhāḷiyāṇ. UMEṬĀ.
Upamiti bhavaprapañcha. HAMSARATNA MUNI.
Viṃṣati Viharamān Jina stavana. DEVACHANDRA
Vīrastuti. YAṢOVIJAYA.
Vivekasāra. HĪRAJĪ HAMSARĀJA.

LAW.—ENGLISH.

Dīwānī navo kāyado. } INDIA.—*Legislative Council.*
Faujdārī kām chalāvavāno rīt. }
Hindustānano faujdārī kāyado. }
———— purāvano kāyado. }
Hindustānanuṇ mehesūl. KAIKHUSRAU NAVAROJĪ KĀBRĀJĪ.
Mājistreṭno parīkshāno kāyado. INDIA.—*Legislative Council.*
Pārsī dhārā parnī nuktechinī. MANCHERJĪ KĀVASJĪ LANGRĀNĀ.

LAW.—HINDU.

Hindu ṣāstranī ḍāyjest. GOVINDALĀLA BĀḶĀJĪ.
Mānavadharmaṣāstra. MANU.
Pārāṣara dharmaṣāstra. PARĀṢARA.

LAW.—NATIVE STATES.

Bajāvaṇī sambandhī sūchanā. PARAMĀNANDADĀSA BHOLĀBHĀĪ PĀREKH.
Gāyakavāḍī nyāyaprakāṣa. BARODA, *Native State of.*
Kachchh deṣa sirishtah saṅgraha. MAṆIBHĀĪ JASBHĀĪ.
Rādhanpur svasthānano dīwānī nibandha. }
Svasthāna Rādhanpurno phojdārī nibandha. }
RADHANPUR, *Native State of.*

LITERARY COMPOSITION and RHETORIC.

Alaṅkārachandrikā. SAVITĀNĀRĀYAṆA GAṆAPATINĀRĀYAṆA.
Alaṅkārapraveṣa. NARMADĀṢANKARA LĀLAṢAṄKARA.
Bhāshābhūshaṇa. JASVAT SIṂHA, *Maharaja.*
Ganj-nāmuṇ. MANCHERJĪ KĀVASJĪ LANGRĀNĀ.
Gujarātī piṅgala. DALPATRĀMA ḌĀHYĀBHĀĪ, *Kavi.*
Luptopamā vilāsa. JASVAT SIṂHA, *Maharaja.*
Narmagadya. } NARMADĀṢAṄKARA LĀLAṢAṄKARA.
Piṅgalapraveṣa. }
Upamā saṅgraha. JASVAT SIṂHA, *Maharaja.*

MATHEMATICS.

Aksharagaṇita. AKSHARAGAṆITA.
Aṅkagaṇita. AṄKAGAṆITA.
Aṅkagaṇitanāṇ mūlatattva. LĀLAṢAṄKARA UMIĀṢAṄKARA TRAVĀḌĪ.
Bhūmitināṇ mūlatattva. EUCLID.
Bhūmiti vyākhyā. } JERVIS (G. R.)
Bījagaṇita. }
Deṣī hisāb. BHOGĪLĀLA PRĀṆAVALLABHADĀSA.
———— gaṇvānī sehelī rīto. BHĀIDĀSA DAYĀRĀMA.
Kachchhī koshṭako. GAṄGĀDHARA ṢIVANĀRĀYAṆA ṢUKLA.
Kartavya bhūmiti. PASLEY (*Sir* C. W.)
Koshṭakanī chopaḍī. KOSHṬAKA.
Lipidhārā. LIPIDHĀRĀ.
Motīnā hisābnī chopaḍī. DAYĀLA RĀVAJĪ.
Sidhlipī trikoṇamiti. } JERVIS (G.R.)
Ṣikshāmālā. }

MEDICINE.

Amṛitasāgara. PRATĀPA SIṂHA, *Raja of Jaipur.*
Ārogyatāsūchaka. RAṆCHHOḌBHĀĪ UDAYARĀMA.
Āyurvedasāra-saṅgraha. ĀYURVEDASĀRA-SAṄGRAHA.
Bhāvaprakāṣa. BHĀVA MISRA.
Dukhanivāraṇa. PESTANJĪ NAVAROJĪ.
Pratāpasāgara. PRATĀPA SIṂHA, *Raja of Jaipur.*
Rumūz i hikmat. TALAKCHAND TĀRĀCHAND.
Ṣarīra sukhadarṣaka. RAṆCHHOḌLĀLA VIṬHṬHALADĀSA.
Ṣārīravidyā. DHĪRAJRĀMA DALPATRĀMA.
Strī upayogī sūchanā. WELL WISHER.
Sudhāsañchita. REVĀṢAṄKARA JAYAṢAṄKARA.
Vaidakno sārasaṅgraha. JAGAJJĪVANA DALPATRĀMA.
Vaidyāmṛita. MOREṢVARA, *Son of Māṇaka Bhaṭṭa.*
Vaidyaratnākara. VAIDYARATNĀKARA.
Vaidyasārasaṅgraha. RAGHUNĀTHA ṢĀSTRĪ DĀNTYE and KṚISHṆA ṢĀSTRĪ BHĀṬAVAḌEKAR.
Vyādhi-rodha vidyā. MAṆIṢAṄKARA GOVINDAJĪ.

MUSIC.

Kānsartīnāmāṇ vagāḍvānā gāvaṇo. CONCERTINA.
Kāyade tāus. UMIYĀRĀMA ṬHĀKORDĀSA DARU.
Gāyaṇaprakāṣa. ILLUSTRATIONS.
Saṅgītānubhava. MAULĀ-BAKHSH GHISHE-KHĀN.

MYTHOLOGICAL TALES.

See TALES.—MYTHOLOGICAL.

PERIODICAL LITERATURE.

(See under the heading "PERIODICAL PUBLICATIONS" in the body of the Catalogue.)

POETRY.

Ādīṣvarano ṣloko. GULĀBCHAND DAYĀLJĪ and LAKSHMĪDĀSA KAHĀNJĪ ṬHAKKAR.
Ahmadābādmāṇ batrīsāni relno roḷ. KEṢAVALĀLA MAGANLĀLA.
Akhānī vāṇī. AKHĀ.
Ambājīnā chhandnī chopaḍī. AMĪCHAND MOTĪCHAND.
Ambikākāvya. AMBIKĀ.
Añjanaṣilākānā ḍhāliyāṇ. HAṬṬHI SIṂHA.
Arjunagītā. ARJUNAGĪTĀ.
Āryodvayanī ūtkaṇṭhā. MĀHĀSUKHARĀMA NARBHERĀMA.
Aṣvamedhaparva. MAHĀBHĀRATA.—*Aṣvamedhaparva.*
Ayavanti Sukumārano tera ḍhālio. AYAVANTI SUKUMĀRA.
Baḍodarāmāṇ vidyādi visho kavitā. ṢĀMAJĪ RATANṢĪ.
Baḍodarānā Malhār Rāva garbo. MAÑCHHĀRĀMA GHELĀBHĀĪ.
——— vāsinuṇ valaṇ. PĀNĀCHAND MOJILĀLA DEṢĀĪ.
——— vilāpa. NIZĀM al-DĪN, *Chishtī.*
Bāgno garbo. LALUBHĀĪ JAMNĀDĀSA.
Bālagarbāvalī. NAVALARĀMA LAKSHMĪRĀMA.
Bāḷagāyaṇa. SVADEṢA SUBHECHCHHANĀR, *pseud.*
Bāḷalagna nishedhaka garbāvalī. GARBĀVALĪ.
Batrisāuā bigāḍnī bumo. ICHCHHĀṢAṄKARA AMATHĀRĀMA VYĀSA.
Bhagavadgītā. MAHĀBHĀRATA.—*Bhagavadgītā.*
Bhakti . . . bodhaka kavitā. MĀṆEKJĪ BARJORJĪ MINUCHEHR HOMJĪNĀ.
Bhāratārthaprakāṣa. MAHĀBHĀRATA.
Bharūch jillāno keḷavaṇī khātāno itihāsa. GAṆAPATARĀMA RĀJĀRĀMA MEHETĀ.
Bhavānī kāvya sudhā. BHAVĀNĪṢAṄKARA NARASIṂHARĀMA.
Bhavavairāgyaṣataka. BHAVAVAIRĀGYAṢATAKA.
Bhudharabhāī Dhaneṣvarano rāsḍo. KṚISHṆA RAṆCHHOḌA TRAVĀḌĪ.
Bodhachintāmaṇi. ṚUSHIRĀJA MAHĀRĀJA.
Bṛihat kāvyadohana. ICHCHHĀRĀMA SŪRYARĀMA DEṢĀĪ.
Chaṇḍikāno garbo. MOTĪRĀMA MAÑCHHĀRĀMA.
Chandrikā. CHANDRIKĀ.
Charpaṭapañjarī. ṢAṄKARA ĀCHĀRYA.
Chappā. AKHĀ.
——— ṢĀMALA BHAṬA.
Ḍākor-yātrā māhātmya. BĀḶĀJĪ BHAGAVĀNJĪ DAVE.
Dhoḷ tathā padavigereno saṅgraha. LALU PĪTĀMBARA.
Dilchaman gāyanasaṅgraha. KĀVASJĪ PESTANJĪ.
Dilgirino dekhāva. UTTAMARĀMA UMEDCHAND and CHAMANLĀL NARASIṂHADĀSA.
Dukāḷno garbo. DUKĀḶ.
Ḍungar vāḍāno kheyāl. NASARVĀNJĪ NAVAROJĪ PĀGHḌEWĀLĀ.
Eskī bānu tathā eskī dhaṇīno garbo. MANCHERJI JAMSHEDJĪ.
Ganj-nāmuṇ. MANCHERJĪ KĀVASJĪ LANGRĀNĀ.
Garbāvalī. GARBĀVALĪ.
——— GAURĪṢAṄKARA PRABHĀṢAṄKARA.
Gāyanaprakāra. GĀYANAPRAKĀRA.
Gāyanaṣataka. HĪRĀCHAND KĀNJĪ.
Gokula Vṛindāvana chandrāvaḷā. VISRĀMA MULJĪ.
Gopāla guṇavarṇana. MOHANALĀLA DALPATRĀMA.
Gujarātī kāvyadohana. } DALPATRĀMA ḌĀHYĀBHĀĪ.
——— kāvyasaṃkshepa. }
Gulchaman gāyana. UTTAMARĀMA UMEDCHAND and CHAMANLĀL NARASIṂHADĀSA.
Hāramālā. PREMĀNANDA.
Harirasa. ĪṢVARA BĀROṬ.
Hastāmalaka. BHĀṆA DĀSA.
Hoḷisaṅgraha. KĪKĀBHĀĪ PRABHUDĀSA.
Indrasabhā. ĀGHĀ HASAN, *Saiyid.*
Jñāna-upadeṣa. SOMACHAND KĀLIDĀSA.
Kachchh-mahodaya. GOVARDHANA LĀLAJĪ.
Kakotā. ṢOBHĀVAHUJĪ.
Kavesarī Kalāmo. KAVESARĪ KALĀMO.
Kavitā. DAYĀRĀMA, *Kavi.*
——— DHĪRĀ BHAKTA.
——— PRĪTAMA.
Kavitāsaṅgraha. KAVITĀSAṄGRAHA.
Kāvyadohana. DALPATRĀMA ḌĀHYĀBHĀĪ.
——— ICHCHHĀRĀMA SŪRYARĀMA DEṢĀĪ.
——— JETHĀLĀLA HARAJĪVANA.
Kāvyanimajjana. HARIKṚISHṆA BALADEVA BHAṬṬA.
Kāvyasaṃkshepa. DALPATRĀMA ḌĀHYĀBHĀĪ.
Kāvyasaṅgraha. DAYĀRĀMA, *Kavi.*

Lāvaṇī-saṅgraha. JINADĀSA.
Mahārājā Malhār Rāvano rāsḍo. CHIMANALĀLA NARSĪDĀSA.
Malhārviraha ṣataka. GOVARDHANADĀSA LAKSHMĪDĀSA.
Maṇiṣaṅkarakṛita kāvya. MAṆIṢAṄKARA LALUBHĀĪ.
Manorañjaka garbāvalī. GARBĀVALĪ.
——— Pratāpakāvya. PRATĀPARĀYA ṢIVALĀLA MĀṄKAḌ.
Mātam i Ḥasanain. ʻABBĀS, *Saiyid.*
Meghajīnī mohkāṇ. ĀDĪTRĀMA JOITĀRĀMA.
Meghalīlā. TULJĀRĀMA JHĪṆĀRĀMA.
Megharājāne vinantīpatra. MĀHĀSUKHARĀMA NARBHERĀMA.
Monghavārīnī mohkāṇ. MAṆILĀLA HARILĀLA and CHHOṬĀLĀLA MOHANALĀLA.
Motīṣānāṇ ḍhaḷiāṇ. MOTĪṢĀ.
Moṭuṇ kāvyadohana. JEṬHĀLĀLA HARAJĪVANA.
Nabhu kavitā. NARBHERĀMA MAÑCHHĀRĀMA.
Nāmārthabodha. HĪRĀCHAND KĀNJĪ.
Narmakavitā. NARMADĀṢAṄKARA LĀLAṢAṄKARA.
Narsī Mehetānī huṇḍī. PREMĀNANDA.
Nītiṣataka. BHARTṚIHARI.
Pada. PADA.
Padasaṅgraha. LĀLADĀSAJĪ.
Pālaṇā. PĀLAṆĀ.
Pañcha vartamāna. NISHKULĀNANDA.
Pañchīkaraṇa. RĀMADĀSA SVĀMĪ, *of Haidarabad.*
Pāṇḍavavālā mulamaṇḍānanā. PĀṆḌAVAS.
Pārsī strī ramujī navā garbā. SOHRĀBJĪ HORMASJĪ.
Phaḍiyāono julam. JAGAJJĪVANADĀSA CHUNĪLĀLA.
Prāchīna kāvya. PRĀCHĪNA KĀVYA.
Rādhājīnā tera mahīnā. RĀDHĀ.
Rajnagarmāṇ reluo roḷ. NIẒĀM al-DĪN, *Chishtī.*
Rāmāyaṇa. GIRDHARA.
——— KṚISHṆADĀSA.
——— ṢIVALĀLA DHANEṢVARA.
——— VĀLMĪKI.
Rāmāyaṇanā chandrāvalā. SUHHARA DĀSA.
Rasamañjarī. VĀLJĪ LAKSHMĪRĀMA DAVE.
Rasika padamālā. MĀHĀSUKHARĀMA NARBHERĀMA.
Rati-svayaṃvara. KĀLIDĀSA, *the Sanskrit poet.*
Ṛituvarṇana. ṚITUVARṆANA.
Rūpadevajīnā garbā. KĀLIDĀSA DEVAṢAṄKARA.
Sābarno sākho. KEVALADĀSA AMĪCHAND.
Sampayanuṇ lakshmivache saṃvāda. DALPATRĀMA DĀHYĀBHĀĪ.
Samudāya santanī vāṇī. ṢAṄKARA HARIBHĀĪ.
Sāṅkhyayogī bāionuṇ vartamāna. NISHKULĀNANDA.
Sat-saī. VṚINDA.
Ṣilpakarma. HARAGOVINDA AMATHĀRĀMA JOṢĪ.
Siyāvash-nāmuṇ. RUSTAM PESHOTAN, *Mobed.*
Ṣlokā lāvaṇio ane garbāo. SAHAJĀNANDA SVĀMĪ.
Ṣlokā-saṅgraha. ṢLOKĀ-SAṄGRAHA.
Ṣṛiṅgāradarṣana. PREMAJĪ KHETASIṂHA KAJARIYĀ.
Ṣṛiṅgāravairāgya-taraṅgiṇī. SOMAPRABHĀCHĀRYA.
Strī manorañjaka garbāvalī. GARBĀVALĪ.
Subhāsita saṅgraha. PURUSHOTTAMA MAYĀRĀMA PAṆḌYĀ.
Sundara strīvilāsa. RAṆCHHOḌLĀLA MOTĪRĀMA.
Suratasaṅgrāma. NṚISIṂHA MEHETĀ.
Tetriṣāno taḍāko. PRABHĀṢAṄKARA ṢĀMALAJĪ.
Torānī ʻishkī lāvaṇio. LAKSHMAṆA DĀSA.
Vairāgya bodha. HĪRĀCHAND KĀNJĪ.
——— ṣataka. BHARTṚIHARI.
Vallabhakṛita kāvya. VALLABHARĀMA SŪRYARĀMA VYĀSA.
Varsādnī vadhāmṇī. VARSĀDNĪ VADHĀMṆĪ.
Vilāyatnā kaviṣvaro. KĀVASJĪ NAVAROJĪ VESUWĀLĀ.
Viveka vanajhāro. PREMĀNANDA.
Wilsan-viraha. BAHRĀMJĪ MEHRVĀNJĪ MALABĀRĪ.
Yuvarājayātrā. BULĀKĪ CHAKUBHĀĪ.

POLITICAL TREATISES.

Aphīmno vepār. INDIA.
Dravya tathā rupānā mūlanī nyūnatā vīshenāṇ bhāshaṇa. NASARVĀNJĪ HIRJĪBHĀĪ PAṬEL.
Hind ane Brittania. ICHCHHĀRĀMA SŪRYARĀMA DESĀĪ.

PURĀṆAS. See **RELIGION.—HINDU.**

READERS.

Angrejī bhāshāntara pāṭhamālā. WELLS. (T. L.)
——— bījī chopaḍī. HOWARD (E. I.)
——— tathā Gujarātī vākyāvalī. WILSON (J.) *D.D.*
Bāḷakhela. BĀḶAKHELA.
Bījī chopaḍī. HOPE (T. C.)
Bodhakathā. BODHAKATHA.
Chhaṭhī chopaḍī. / Chothī chopaḍī. } HOPE (T. C.)
Lipidhārā. LIPIDHĀRĀ.
Mārgopadeṣikā. RĀMAKṚISHṆA GOPĀLA BHĀṆḌĀRKAR.
Pāñchmī chopaḍī. / Pehelī chopaḍī. } HOPE (T. C.)
Pehelī pothī. PEHELĪ POTHĪ.
Ramakaḍun. RAMAKAḌUṆ.
Rumūz i dil-khush. RUMŪZ I DIL-KHUSH.
Saṃsārachopaḍī. SAṂSĀRACHOPAḌĪ.
Sātamī chopaḍī. / Trījī chopaḍī. } HOPE (T. C.)
Vātchītnā ṣehalāṇ vākyo. BOMBAY, *Presidency of.—Anglo-Vernacular Schools.*
Vidyābhyāsanī pothī. VIDYĀBHYĀSA.
Vidyārthīono madadgār. HOWARD (E.J.)

RELIGION.—BRAHMIST.

Bāḷasandhyopāsanā. BRĀHMA SAMĀJ.—*Ahmadabad Prārthanā Samāj.*
Brāhma dharma. BRĀHMA DHARMA.
——— matasāra. BRĀHMA SAMĀJ.
Īṣvaraprārthanāmālā. / Īṣvaropāsana. } BRĀHMA SAMĀJ.—*Ahmadabad Prārthanā Samāj.*
Saddharma dīpikā. NAVĪNACHANDRA RĀYA.
Svābhāvika dharma. DHARMASAṂṢODHAKA, *pseud.*
Vairāgya. NĀRĀYAṆA HEMACHANDRA.

RELIGION.—CHRISTIAN.

Adamākhyāna. TRIBHUVANADĀSA RĀMADĀSA.
Aruṇodaya. MORTIMER (F. L.) *Mrs.*
Bhramanī toḍnārī vāṇī. DESTROYER.

Bījā janmanī vāt. NEW BIRTH.
Dainika prasāda. TAYLOR (J. VAN S.)
Dayā karvī. MERCY.
Devasiddhānta. EXISTENCE.
Dharma e ṣuṇ chhe. } DHARMA.
Dharmanāṇ tarājavāṇ. }
Edmund visheṇī vārtā. EDMUND.
Ek muelo chhokro jīvato. LIFE.
Ek ḍosī tathā Brāhmaṇanī vātchīt. BRAHMAN.
Ek maṇse . . . teṇī kathā MAN.
Ek painī ṣī chintā chhe. PAI.
Gītagrantha. GĪTAGRANTHA.
Gītanī pothī. GUJARATI HYMN BOOK.
Hinduone sādu arāḍ arāḍ māṇkāṇī mālā. HINDUISM.
Īṣā Masīh tathā Muhammadnī bābatnī vāt. JESUS CHRIST.
Īṣu Khristnā maraṇa. } JESUS CHRIST.
——— vishe pustaka. }
Jīvanabhedavāṇī. JĪVANABHEDAVĀṆĪ.
Junā Dharmapustakno saṃkshepa. BIBLE.—Old Testament.—*Appendix.*
Kharo āṣro. REFUGE.
Kharu prāyaṣchitta. ATONEMENT.
Khristī pādrio sāmāṭe ā deṣamāṇ āevā. CHRISTIAN MINISTERS.
Khristnā viṣvāsionī uttarāvali. CHRISTIANS.
Maṇḍalīnā bhajananī rīt. FYVIE (W.)
Manohara vāṇī. MANOHARA VĀṆĪ.
Muktimuktāvalī. TAYLOR (J. VAN S.)
Parameṣvarnā mohoṭā daṣa hukm. TEN COMMANDMENTS.
Pavitra lekhanī vārtā. BARTH (C. G.)
Pharo naiṇ to maro. PHARO.
Phula viṇanārī chhokrionī vāt. FLOWER GATHERERS.
Pratidinanī prārthanāo. BIBLE.—*Appendix.*
Punāṁadhye dharmasambandhī vātchīt. POONA CONVERSATIONS.
Sadhlāṇ māṇāṣ bharṣaṭ. HUMAN DEPRAVITY.
Ṣaṅkara Liṅgam tenī vārtā. ṢAṄKARA LIṄGAM.
Sarva lokane sādu vadhāmaṇī. GOOD TIDINGS.
Ṣat dharmano mārgo. PATH.
Ṣat tathā aṣatnī parīkshā. HINDUS.
Sawāl jawābnī pehelī pothī. CATECHISM.
Tāraṇa. SALVATION.
Trilokanī vāt. THREE WORLDS.
Yūsufnuṇ charitra. JOSEPH, *the Patriarch.*

RELIGION.—HINDU.

Bhāgavata. PURĀṆAS.—*Bhāgavatapurāṇa.*
Bhāgavatadharma. DHARMĀNANDA SVĀMĪ.
Bhagavatī Bhāgavata. PURAṆAS.—*Devībhāgavatapurāṇa.*
Bhaktachintāmaṇi. NISHKULĀNANDA.
Chaṇḍīpātha. RĀMABHAKTA ṢIVADĀSA.
Chaurāṣī Vaishṇavanī vārtā. CHAURĀṢĪ VĀRTĀ.
Chhappan bhoganuṇ varṇana. VRAJARĀYAJĪ.
Ḍaṅkpur Mahārudra yajñanuṇ varṇana. AMṚITALĀLA ANOPARĀMA MEHETĀ.
Devībhāgavatapurāṇa. PURĀṆAS.—*Devībhāgavatapurāṇa.*
Devīmāhātmya. PURĀṆAS.—Mārkaṇḍeyapurāṇa.—*Devīmāhātmya.*
Dharmaprakāṣā. KEṢAVALĀLA MAGANLĀLA.
Dharmavivechana. DHARMAVIVECHANA.
Ekādaṣīmāhātmya. PURĀṆAS.
Gopīgītā. PURĀṆAS.—Bhāgavatapurāṇa.—*Gopīgītā.*
Hindu devatāonī chitramālā. MĀṆEKJĪ BARJORJĪ MINUCHEHR HOMJĪNĀ.
Īsu-parikshā. JAGANNĀRĀYAṆA.
Navarātri-pūjana. NAVARĀTRĪ-PŪJANA.
Pramāṇa-sahasrī. PRAYĀGAJĪ ṬHĀKARSĪ.
Purushasūkta. VEDAS.—Ṛigveda.—*Purushasūkta.*
Rāmāṣvamedha. PURĀṆAS.—Padmapurāṇa.—*Rāmāṣvamedha.*
Rojapāṭha. VIṢVANĀTHA KHUSHĀLADĀSA.
Sābhramatīmāhātmya. PURĀṆAS.—Padmapurāṇa. *Sābhramatīmāhātmya.*
Saptamaskandha. PURĀṆAS.—Bhāgavatapurāṇa.—*Saptamaskandha.*
Saptaṣatī. PURĀṆAS.—Mārkaṇḍeyapurāṇa.—*Devīmāhātmya.*
Sasti sukhaḍī ne Siddhapuranī yātrā. DĀMODARA KEṢAVAJĪ ṬHAKKAR.
Ṣikshāpatrī. SAHAJĀNANDA SVĀMĪ.
Ṣivapurāṇa. PURĀṆAS.—*Ṣivapurāṇa.*
Skandapurāṇārthaprakāṣa. PURĀṆAS.—*Skandapurāṇa.*
Ṣrīmadbhāgavatanī kathāno sāra. PURANAS.—*Bhāgavatapurāṇa.*
Ṣrīmukhasiddhānta. SAHAJĀNANDA SVĀMĪ.
Ṣvetāṣvataropanishadnā sāra. UPANISHADS.
Vachanāmṛita. SAHAJĀNANDA ṢVĀMĪ.
Vachanavidhi. NISHKULĀNANDA.
Vedadharma. KARSANDĀS MŪLJĪ.
Vedāntaprakāṣa. PERIODICAL PUBLICATIONS.—*Bombay.*
Vedārthoddhāra. BHĪMACHĀRYA JHAḶKĪKAR and RĀJĀRĀMA GAṆEṢA BOḌAS.
Vedastuti. PURĀṆAS.—Bhāgavatapurāṇa.—*Vedastuti.*
Vedokta saṃskāra-prakāṣa. BĀḶĀJĪ VIṬHṬHALA GĀṆVASKAR.
Vivekasāra. BALARĀMA, *Sādhu.*

RELIGION.—JAIN. See JAIN LITERATURE.

RELIGION.—MUHAMMADAN.

Khristī ane Mohammadī dharmano chukādo. GHULĀM MUḤAMMAD, *Rānderī.*
Mukhālafāt i Baibal. YŪSUF ṢĀLIḤ.
Risālah i kāmilah. 'ALĪ ZAIN al-'ĀBIDĪN, *Fourth Imām.*

RELIGION.—PARSI.

Ardā Virāf-nāmuṇ. ARDĀ VIRĀF.
Ātashnāṇ kebalānī khubī. MANCHERJĪ KĀVASJI LANGRĀNĀ.
Bandagī. BANDAGĪ.
Bhāṣāno. KHURSHEDJĪ RUSTAMJĪ KĀMĀ.
Bundehesh. BUNDEHESH.
Dinkard. DINKARD.
Dokhme Noshirvāu. RUSTAM ĪRĀNĪ.
Du'ā nām setāyishne. KHURSHEDJĪ MINUCHEHRĪ KAṬELI.

Ekvīs nasko. EKVĪS NASKO.
Fārsī munājāt. SOHRĀBJĪ KŪVARJĪ TĀSKAR.
Ghuncha i Avastā. RUSTAM ĪRĀNĪ.
Gosht i Fryāno. GOSHT i FRYĀNO.
Hādokht nask. HĀDOKHT NASK.
Hāvanīm. ZAND-AVASTĀ.
Hormuzdnī sifat. MĀṆEKJĪ DĀRĀBJĪ ADRIANWĀLĀ.
Intikhāb i Vandidād. ZAND-AVASTĀ.
Jamshed homa ane ātash. JĪVANAJĪ JAMSHEDJĪ MODĪ.
Kabīsā vishe. RATANJĪ RUSTAMJĪ KĀṄGA.
Kaliānīnā navā dakhmāno garbo. SOHRĀBJĪ HORMASJĪ.
Khulāsah i dīn i Zartoshtī. ASFANDIYĀRJĪ BARJORJĪ PANTHAKĪ.
Khurdah Avastā. ZAND-AVASTĀ.
Manājāt. MANĀJĀT.
Mansūkhī manājāt. MANCHERJĪ KĀVASJĪ LANGRĀNĀ.
Mazdayasna. NASARVĀNJĪ FRĀMJĪ.
Meher Yazda. NASARVĀNJĪ SHĀPURJĪ TAVAḌIĀ.
Mithra. NASARVĀNJĪ SHĀPURJĪ TAVAḌIĀ.
Pārsīo khodāparast chhe ke nahiṉ. PARSIS.
Rahbar i dīn i Zartoshtī. ERACHJĪ SOHRĀBJĪ MEHRJĪRĀṆĀ.
Rāh i Pārsā. SOHRĀBJĪ JAMSHEDJĪ JĪJĪBHĀĪ.
Rāst dīn i Zartoshtiyān. PERIODICAL PUBLICATIONS.—*Bombay*.
Rūvāunī chār dāhāḍāṇī kriyā vishe. RATANJĪ RUSTAMJĪ KĀṄGĀ.
——— kriyā. JAMSHEDJĪ FRĀMJĪ BACHĀBHĀĪ RABĀḌĪ.
Ṡad-dare behere tavīl. SAD-DAR.
Sapentomainyusha. BARJORJĪ ERACHJĪ BAJĀN.
Sar-nāmah i rāz i yazdānī. BAHRĀM RŪSTAM KHUSRAU.
Sitāyish-nāmuṉ. SITĀYISH-NĀMAH.
Tafsīr i gāh i gāsānī. PESHOTAN BAHRĀMJĪ SAÑJĀNĀ.
Vāejo. RATANJĪ RUSTAMJĪ KĀṄGĀ.
Vandidād. ZAND-AVASTĀ.
Vispard. } Vispered. } ZAND-AVASTĀ.
Yaçna. ZAND-AVASTĀ.
Zartosht dharmanīti. NĀRĀYAṆA HEMACHANDRA.
Zartoshtī abhyāsa. KHURSHEDJĪ RUSTAMJĪ KĀMĀ.
——— dharmabodha. FRĀMJĪ MINUCHEHRJĪ JĀMĀSP ĀSĀJĪNĀ.
——— dharmaṣikshaka. EDALJĪ KERSĀSPJĪ ĀṆṬIYĀ.
——— Dīnnī Kholkarnārī Maṇḍalīno hevāl. ACADEMIES, *etc.*—Bombay.—*Zartoshtī Dīnnī Kholkarnārī Maṇḍalī.*
——— lokonāṉ dharmapustako. SOHRĀBJĪ SHĀPURJĪ BANGĀLĪ.
——— ṭolāno vaḍo koṇ RATĀNJĪ RUSTAMJĪ KĀṄGĀ.

RHETORIC. See **LITERARY COMPOSITION.**

SCIENCES.

Bhūgolavidyā. GEIKIE (A.)
Bhūtaḷavidyā. BLANFORD (H. F.)
Kudrati ilm i Ilāhī. HORMASJĪ PĀLANJĪ MEHRJĪ.
Prāṇividyā. EDALJĪ JAMSHEDJĪ KHORĪ.
Rasāyanaṣāstra sambandhī vātchīt. MEHRVĀNJĪ HORMASJĪ MEHETĀ.
Rasāyanavidyā. ROSCOE (H. E.)
Upayogī jñānanī pustakasamūha. ACADEMIES, *etc.* London.—*Society for the Diffusion of Useful Knowledge.*
Yantraṣāstranāṉ mūla. KAHĀNDĀSA MAÑCHHĀRĀMA.

SOCIOLOGY.

Arthaṣāstra. AMBĀLĀLA SĀKARLĀLA.
Bāḷalagnathī bantī binā. GIRIJĀṢAṄKARA MULJĪ.
Buddhidarpaṇa. 'ABD AL-KARĪM' called MUDARRIS.
Chārucharyā. KSHEMENDRA.
Ḍol ghālu sudhrelne chābakā. DOL.
Gujarātī vehem. PURUSHOTTAMA KĀHĀNJĪ GĀṆDHE.
Gujarātnā bhikhārio. VIṬHṬHALADĀSA DHANJĪBHĀĪ.
Gurunī sattā vishe nibandha. DALPATRĀMA AMBĀRĀMA.
Hālnāṉ jamānānī Pārsī chhokrio. NASARVĀNJĪ SHEHRIYĀRJĪ GINWĀLĀ.
Holīnibandha. MAGANLĀLA VAKHATCHAND.
Jauhar i zindagānī. SOHRĀBJĪ JAMSHEDJĪ JĪJĪBHĀĪ.
Kanyāvikraya doshadarṣaka. BHŪPATRĀYA HARAGOVINDA DĀTĀR.
Kāpadiā ramujī maṇḍaḷīnā dhārāo. BOMBAY, *City of. Kapadia Amusing Club.*
Kheḍāvāḷ jñāti samaste karelā ṭharāvo. KHEḌĀVĀḶ BRAHMANS.
Kumārabodha. } Kumārikābodha. } HĪRĀCHAND KĀNJĪ.
Majmū'-al -naṡā'ih. SĀDIK 'ALĪ.
Nātyomāṉ ṣeṭhonā ṣākhā. VALLABHARĀMA SURYARĀMA.
Niṣālnī paddhati. GUJARATI TREATISE.
Punarvivāha ṣāstrasammata chhe. NĀRĀYAṆA HEMACHANDRA.
Raḍvā kuṭavānī hāni-janak chāl. VĪRACHANDA RĀGHAVAJĪ.
Sattā pariṇāmadarṣaka. RATANṢĪ SĀMAJĪ.
Ṣerṣaṭānuṉ varṇana. ṢERṢAṬĀ.
Strī ganeānt mālā. STRĪ GANEĀNT MĀLĀ.
Strīnītidharma. VIṬHṬHALADĀSA DHANJĪBHĀĪ.
——— darṣaka. KṚIPĀṢAṄKARA DOLATRĀMA TRAVĀḌĪ.
Svadeṣa hitadarṣaka. GIRDHARALĀLA HARIVALLABHADĀSA and KEṢAVALĀLA RAṆCHHOḌDĀSA JOṢĪ.
Vishayīṉ guru vishe nibandha. DALPATRĀMA AMBĀRĀMA.

TALES.—MYTHOLOGICAL.

Abhimanyuno chakrāvo. ABHIMANYU.
Abhimanyunuṉ moṭuṉ ākhyāna. PREMĀNANDA.
Aṅgadavishṭi. ṢĀMALA BHAṬA.
Dānalīlā. PREMĀNANDA.
Dhruvākhyāna. TULASĪ, *of Kuntarpur.*
Draupadī-svayaṃvara. ṢIVADĀSA.
Lakshmaṇā-haraṇa, PREMĀNANDA.
Lava Kuṣākhyāna. LAVA KUṢA.
Mṛidālaṣā ākhyāna. } Nala Rājānuṉ ākhyāna. } PREMĀNANDA.

Okhāharaṇa. Dāmodara Ratansī Somānī.
——— Premānanda.
Pāṇḍava-vishṭi. Bhau, *Kavi.*
Prahlādākhyāna. Kālidāsa, *of Wassawad.*
Rāma charitra. Hemachandra Āchārya.
Rukmiṇīharaṇa. Premānanda.
Rukmiṇī vivānī chopaḍī. Muktānanda.
Ṣaniṣchara devatānī kathā. Ṣaniṣchara.
Sīmantinī ākhyāna. Mayo Ṣivadāsa.
Sītāsvayaṃvara. Kālidāsa, *of Wassawad.*
Somapradoshanī kathā. Mayo Ṣivadāsa.
Surekhā-haraṇa. Vīrajī.

TALES.—Original.

Andherī nagarīno gardhavasena. Haragovinda Dvarākādāsa Kāṇṭāwālā.
Aslājī. Ardsher Bahrāmjī Paṭel.
Bāḷavidhavā rupavantī duḥkhadarṣaka. Narbherāma Kāṣīrāma Dave.
Barāsa Kasturī. Ṣāmala Bhaṭa.
Bhāio bairī karo to joine kuvo purjo. Māṇekjī Barjorjī Minucheher Homjīnā.
Chalyākhyāna. Chalyākhyāna.
Chandan Mālyāgirīno rās. Kshemaharsha.
Chand Rājā ane Guṇāvalī rāṇīnā kāgal. Chand Rājā.
Chand Rājāno rās. Mohana Vijayajī.
Chandrās ane Chandrakaḷā. Ṣāmajī Raṇchhoḍ.
Chatura Siṃha. Mañchhārāma Ghelābhāī.
Chha bhāinuṇ rās. Chha Bhāī.
Chhelnī vārtā. Hariṣaṅkara Mehetā.
Duḥkhī Divāḷī. Bālubhāī Manmohanadāsa Dalāl.
Dukhiyārī Bachuṇ. Kaikhusrau Navarojī Kābrājī.
Dushman Dārāb. Rustamjī Hormasjī Mistrī.
Gajrāmārujīnī raṣīlī vārtā. Gajrāmāru.
Gāmḍenī Bhīkhīne Mumbai shehare bhakhī. Bhīkhī.
——— Galālvahu. Māṇekjī Barjorjī Minucheher Homjīnā.
Gaṅgā. Ichchhārāma Sūryarāma Desāī.
Gujarāt deṣanī vārtā. F. B.
Gul Shīrīnā. Rustam Īrānī.
Haṃsarāja Vatsarājano rās. Jinodaya Sūri.
Haribal Machchhīno rās. Labdhivijaya, *Muni.*
Harichand Rājāno rās. Kanakasundara.
Harichandrākhyāna. Hariṣchandra, *Rājā.*
Hāzir-javābī pradhānanī vārtā. Dayālajī Raṇchhoḍa.
Jayānanda Kevalīno rās. Padmavijaya.
Kāmāvatīnī vārtā, Kāmāvatī.
Kāṇī Kubāīnāṇ kartuk. Maṇekjī Barjorjī Minucheher Homjīnā.
Karaṇa Ghelo. Nandaṣaṅkara Tuljāṣaṅkara.
Karaṇa Kāmāvatīnī vārtā. Kāmāvatī.
Madana Mohanānī vārtā. Ṣāmala Bhaṭa.
Madhu Mālatīnī vārtā. Chaturbhuja Dāsa.
Mānak Shāh charitra. Jeshaṅgdāsa Trikamdāsa Paṭel.
Manorañjaka vārtā. Maganrāma Naraharārāma.
Mundrā ane Kulin. Jahāngīrshāh Ardsher Ṭāli'yārkhāṇ.
Nanda batrīṣīnī vārtā. Ṣāmala Bhaṭa.
Padmāvatīnī vārtā. Ṣāmala Bhaṭa.
Parṇelo pīḍāo mare, *etc.* Mañchhārāma Ghelābhāī.
Pativratā strī. Viṭhṭhaladāsa Dhanjībhāī.
Pravīṇasāgara. Merāmaṇajī.
Pṛithirāja chahuāṇ. Ātmārāma Keṣavajī Dvivedī.
Rāṇak Devī. Anantaprasāda Trikamlāla.
Rāṇī Rūpasundarī. Haragovinda Dvārakādāsa Kāṇṭāwālā.
Sadevanta Ṣāvaliṅgānī vārtā. Sadevanta.
——— Ṣāmala Bhaṭa.
Sadharājesaṅgha. Mahīpatrāma Rūparāma Nīlakaṇṭha.
Ṣālibhadra Shāhno rās. Matisārajī.
Saluknī dikrinuṇ jarā kothuṇ to juvo. Māṇekjī Barjorjī Minucheher Homjīnā.
Samarāditya Kevalīno rās. Padmavijaya.
Sāt avatāranī Sadevanta Sāvaliṅgānī vārtā. Lālā Bāroṭ.
Satī Rāṇak Devī. Bhagavānlāla Bāpālāla Saiyadh.
Ṣrīchand Kevalīno rās. Jñānavimala Sūri.
Sudāmacharitra. Premānanda.
Sumati Nāgila charitra. Sumati Nāgila.
Sundara Kāmdārnī vārtā. Sundara Kāmdār.
Sureṣa-charitra. Oṃ, *pseud.*
Tridampati varṇana. Anantaprasāda Trikamlāla.
Udyamakarma saṃvāda. Ṣāmala Bhaṭa.

TALES.—Translations from European Works.

Bāḷamitra. Berquin (A.)
Henrī tathā tehenā chākar. Butt, afterwards Sherwood (M. M.)
Nakliyāt-nāmuṇ. Khurshedjī Nasarvānjī Pestanjī.
Rābinsan Krusonī charitra. Defoe (D.)
Rāsalasnuṇ charitra. Johnson (S.) *LL.D.*
Tārā. Taylor (M.)

TALES.—Translations from Oriental Works.

Anusūyābhyudaya. Ṣaṅkaralāla Maheṣvara.
Badrmunīr Benazīr. Ḥasan, *Mīr.*
Bāgh o Bahār. Khusraū, *Amīr.*
Bhogavatībhāgyodaya. Ṣaṅkaralāla Maheṣvara.
Bhoja subodha ratnamālā. Baladevarāma Kṛishṇarāma Bhaṭṭa.
Daṣakumāra charitra. Daṇḍin.
Dhīrā Mārujīnī vārtā. Harsadrāya Sundaralāla.
Fasānah i 'ajā'ib. Rajab 'Alī Beg, *Mīrzā.*
Ghāṣīrāma koṭwāl. Morobā Kānhobā.
Gul i Bakāwalī. Kṛishṇadāsa.
Gulistan. Sa'dī.
Hātam-nāmuṇ. Ḥātim Ṭā'ī.
Hazār ane ek rāt. Arabian Nights.
Ḥusn-ārā. Naẓīr Aḥmad, *Khān Bahādur.*
Jahāndār Shāh bādshāhnī vārtā. Ṣāmala Bhaṭa.
Kādambarī. Bāṇa.
Kāshṭhanā ghoḍānī vārtā. Ṣāmala Bhaṭa.
Maḍāpachīsīnī vārtā. } Ṣāmala Bhaṭa.
Mādhavānalanī vārtā. }
Menāpopaṭnī vārtā. }
Mirāt al-'arūs. Naẓīr Aḥmad, *Khān Bahādur.*

Pānanābiḍānī vārtā. } Ṣāmala Bhaṭa.
Pañcha daṇḍanī vārtā. }
Pañchatantra. } Pañchatantra.
Pañchopākhyāna. }
Paṅkhinī vārtā. Ṣāmala Bhaṭa.
Singhāsan Battīsī. Vikramāditya, *king of Ujjayinī.*
Suḍābahoterī. Ṣāmala Bhaṭa.
Taubat al Naṣūḥ. Nazīr Aḥmad, *Khān Bahādur.*

TOPOGRAPHY.

Āryānārya deṣajñāpaka charchāpatra. Pannyāsa Ratnavijaya Gaṇi.
Gāyakavāḍī rājyano itihāsa. Paramānandadāsa Bholābhāī Pārekh.
Kachchhnī bhūgoḷavidyā. Dalpatrāma Prāṇajīvana Khakhkhar.
Kāṭhiāvāḍ sarvasaṅgraha. Kathiawar.
Rāṇpurnī mukhtaṣar ḥakīkat. Khīmajī Premajī Mehetā.

TRAVELS.

Greṭ Briṭan bātenī musāpharī. Ḍosabhāī Frāmjī Karākā.
Hindusthānamāṇ musāfirī. Ardsher Frāmjī Mus.
Inglandmāṇ pravāsa. Karsandās Mūljī.
Junāgaḍhno bhomiyo. Junagarh.
Mumbāithī Kashmīr. Jahāngīr Bahrāmjī Marzbān.
——— Yūrop tarafnā pravāsnī nondh patrikā. Frāmjī Dīnshājī Piṭīṭ.
Yūrop ... tarafnī musāfirīnī nondh patrikā. Frāmji Dīnshājī Piṭīṭ.

VOCABULARIES. See DICTIONARIES.

LONDON: PRINTED BY GILBERT & RIVINGTON (LIMITED), ST. JOHN'S HOUSE, CLERKENWELL, E.C.

Lightning Source UK Ltd.
Milton Keynes UK
UKHW031043100720
366327UK00009B/491